Journalism Today

Journalism Today

Fifth Edition

Donald L. Ferguson

Jim Patten

Bradley Wilson

National Textbook Company
a division of NTC/CONTEMPORARY PUBLISHING GROUP
Lincolnwood, Illinois USA

Editorial Consultant

Laura Schaub, Executive Director,
Oklahoma Interscholastic Press Association

Executive Editor: Marisa L. L'Heureux

Editor: Lisa A. De Mol

Cover and interior design: Ellen Pettengell

Cover illustration: Wendy Grossman

Design Manager: Ophelia Chambliss

Production Manager: Margo Goia

Acknowledgments begin on page 495, which is to be considered an extension of this copyright page.

ISBN: 0-8442-5975-6

Published by National Textbook Company,
a division of NTC/Contemporary Publishing Group, Inc.,
4255 West Touhy Avenue,
Lincolnwood (Chicago), Illinois 60646-1975 U.S.A.
© 1998 by NTC/Contemporary Publishing Group, Inc.

Library of Congress Cataloging-in-Publication Data

Ferguson, Donald L.
   Journalism today / Donald L. Ferguson, Jim Patten, Bradley Wilson.
   —5th ed.
      p. cm.
   Includes index.
   Summary: Discusses the history and responsiblities of the media, the gathering, writing and
presentation of news, and the future of journalism as technology changes
      ISBN 0-8442-5975-6
   1. Journalism. 2. Journalism, High School. [1. Journalism.]
   I. Patten, Jim. II. Wilson, Bradley. III. Title.
   PN4776.F47 1997
   070.4—dc21   97-345
                                                    CIP
                                                     AC

   0 QB 098765

Contents

Introduction xv

Section One

Journalism in a Democracy   1

Chapter One

Looking Back: The History of American Media 2

America's First Newspapers 4

Establishment of Freedom of the Press 5

The Birth of the Nation 6

The Penny Press 8

The Effect of the Telegraph 9

Yellow Journalism 9

Muckraking 11

The Development of Minority Media 11

The Advent of Radio 13

The Impact of Television 15

Trends and Issues: Changing Wartime Coverage 16

The Effects of Technology 17

Journalism Today 19

Wrap-up 20

On Assignment 21

Career Profile: Journalism Professor 23

Chapter Two

Meeting Ethical and Legal Responsibilities 24

The Functions of a Journalist 27

Evaluating the Media 30

The Ethics of Journalism 33

Libel Law 40

Limits on Scholastic Journalism 45

Trends and Issues: Responses to Hazelwood 50

Wrap-up 52

On Assignment 53

Career Profile: Media Lawyer 55

Section Two

Gathering News for the School Newspaper 57

Chapter Three

Deciding What Is News 58

News Judgment 61

The "Who Cares?" Method 61

The Elements of News 62

Trends and Issues: Getting On-line 68

Generating News Story Ideas 69

Information from Polls 72

Wrap-up 77

On Assignment 79

Career Profile: Editor 81

Chapter Four

Organizing the Staff to Capture the News 82

The Newspaper Staff 83

News Sources 87

Trends and Issues: One Adviser's Tale of Staff Reorganization 88

Wrap-up 91

On Assignment 94

Career Profile: Executive Editor 95

Chapter Five

Making the Interview Work 96

General Interviewing Guidelines 98

The Formal Interview 101

Writing the Interview Story 106

An Ethical Question 109

Trends and Issues: Protecting Sources 110

Wrap-up 111

On Assignment 111

Career Profile: Columnist 113

Photo Essay: *Putting a Story Together: From the Idea to Final Film* 114

Section Three

Writing and Delivering the News   121

Chapter Six

Writing News Story Leads 122

The Inverted Pyramid 124

The "AP," or Summary, Lead 126

Writing the Lead 128

Good Leads 132

Leads with Problems 135

Trends and Issues: Real Versus Created News 136

Wrap-up 143

Evaluation Checklist: News Story Lead 143

On Assignment 143

Career Profile: Managing Editor 145

Chapter Seven

Writing News Stories 146

Building on the Lead 148

Using Transitions 148

The Body of the Story 151

Organizational Patterns 152

Newspaper Style 156

Trends and Issues: The News On-line 157

Wrap-up 165

Evaluation Checklist: News Story 165

On Assignment 166

Career Profile: Reporter 167

Chapter Eight

Handling Quotes Fairly and Accurately 168

Direct Quotation 170

Paraphrasing 172

Partial Quotation 174

Attribution 175

Speech Stories 178

Trends and Issues: Quoting out of Context 180

Wrap-up 181

Evaluation Checklist: Interview Story 183

Evaluation Checklist: Speech Story 183

On Assignment 183

Career Profile: White House Correspondent 185

Chapter Nine

Doing In-Depth Reporting 186

Stories with Substance 188

The Role of the Scholastic Press 191

Trends and Issues: Invasion of Privacy 192

Finding Space 193

Elements of In-Depth Stories 194

Wrap-up 200

Evaluation Checklist: In-Depth Story 201

On Assignment 201

Career Profile: Investigative Reporters 203

Chapter Ten

Editing, Headline Writing, and Design 204

Copy Editing 205

Writing Headlines 211

Elements of Design 217

Selecting and Using Type 217

Trends and Issues: Hot Fonts 218

Using Graphics 224

Basic Principles of Design 224

Creating Pages 228

Wrap-up 234

Evaluation Checklist: Layout 235

On Assignment 235

Career Profile: Art/Technology Coordinator 239

Photo Essay: *Getting a Newspaper Ready for Distribution* 240

Section Four

Writing Features, Sports, and Editorials   245

Chapter Eleven

Writing Feature Stories 246

Characteristics of Feature Stories 248

Personality Profiles 250

Features and School Papers 251

Trends and Issues: Zines 253

Wrap-up 257

Evaluation Checklist: 257

On Assignment 257

Career Profile: Feature Writer 259

Chapter Twelve

Writing Sports Stories 260

Sportswriting: The Good and the Bad 262

Preparing for Sports Coverage 264

The Pregame Story 265

The Game Story 266

Trends and Issues: Achieving Gender Equity 269

The Postgame Story 270

The Importance of Features 270

Sportswriting Today 272

Wrap-up 272

Evaluation Checklist: Sports Story 273

On Assignment 275

Career Profile: Sports Reporter 277

Chapter Thirteen

Writing for the Editorial Page 278

Functions of Editorials 280

Writing the Editorial 286

Other Elements on the Editorial Page 289

Trends and Issues: Understanding and Recognizing Bias 292

Wrap-up 300

Evaluation Checklist: Editorial 302

Evaluation Checklist: Column 302

Evaluation Checklist: Review 303

On Assignment 303

Career Profile: Editorial Cartoonist 305

Section Five

Other Aspects of Scholastic Journalism   307

Chapter Fourteen

Producing the Yearbook 308

Getting Finances in Order 310

Planning the Yearbook 312

The Yearbook Spread 319

Staff Organization and Responsibilities 329

Working with the Yearbook Company 334

Trends and Issues: Yearbooks on CD and Video 335

Wrap-up 336

Evaluation Checklist: Yearbook Spread 337

On Assignment 337

Career Profile: Graphic Designer 339

Chapter Fifteen

Writing for Radio and Television 340

Writing for Broadcast 342

The School Broadcasting Station 347

Broadcasting Careers 352

Trends and Issues: Does TV Belong in the Courtroom? 353

Wrap-up 354

Evaluation Checklist: 355

On Assignment 355

Career Profile: TV Anchor 357

Chapter Sixteen

Understanding and Using Public Relations 358

Defining Public Relations 360

A Public Relations Model 361

Trends and Issues: Keeping the Truth Foremost 362

Public Relations for Student Journalists 363

Public Relations Careers 368

Wrap-up 370

Evaluation Checklist: Press Release 371

On Assignment 371

Career Profile: Public Relations Executive 373

Chapter Seventeen

Handling Finances: Advertising and Business 374

Staff Organization 375

Getting and Using Advertising Information 376

Preparing Advertising Copy 385

Trends and Issues: The Editorial Ad 390

Newspaper Circulation 392

Keeping Records 394

Wrap-up 396

Evaluation Checklist: Ad 397

On Assignment 397

Career Profile: Advertising Director 399

Section Six

Photography 401

Chapter Eighteen

Taking and Using Effective Photographs 402

Good Photo Composition 404

The Photography Staff 407

Getting and Using the Most Effective Photographs 408

Trends and Issues: Photo Ethics 412

Photo Essays 413

Wrap-up 414

Evaluation Checklist: Photo Composition 415

On Assignment 415

Career Profile: Photo Editor 417

Chapter Nineteen

Understanding Technical Aspects of Photography 418

The Camera 419

Controlling Light and Exposure 420

Trends and Issues: Photos from Cyberspace 427

Working in the Darkroom 428

Art vs. Science 434

Wrap-up 435

Evaluation Checklist: Print 435

On Assignment 435

Career Profile: Newspaper Publisher/Editor 437

Section Seven

Computers and Desktop Publishing 439

Chapter Twenty

Taking Advantage of Technology 440

Desktop Publishing 441

Hardware and What It Can Do 442

Software and What It Can Do 446

Trends and Issues: Computers Are Important, But . . . 450

Digital Photography 451

On-line Services 452

Beyond 2000 454

Wrap-up 455

On Assignment 455

Career Profile: Electronic Journalist 457

Stylebook 458

Newswriting 458

Sports Guidelines and Style 476

Punctuation Marks and How to Use Them 483

Glossary 487

Acknowledgments 495

Index 497

Introduction

Although this section of any book is called the Introduction, it is invariably the last part written. So it is with *Journalism Today, Fifth Edition.* You can even think of this as a retrospective now that the main body of work is finished. What can you expect from this book?

The book you have in your hands reflects deeply held philosophies about both yesterday and tomorrow. A great deal of new material in the book stems from the dawn of the Information Age and the incredible impact of the Internet. Technology continues to boom, and we urge you to get in on the action. Computers, on-line resources, and improving techniques are woven into the discussion throughout the book.

No one, however, should mistake journalism for mere computer keystrokes. The news, as you will read, does not gather itself. There will always be a need for reporters and editors, even though they may not be called that in the next century. The world will always need people who can identify society's information needs and fulfill them. In other words, someone will always have to cover the city council, and it does not matter a great deal whether news of that meeting appears in a newspaper, on a TV news program, on a World Wide Web site, or even beamed directly into the audience's brain by some yet-undiscovered means. That is just the delivery system. The information itself is what counts.

Good journalism necessarily entails good writing. Bad writing, whether in cyberspace, on the air, or on paper, has a damaging effect on your audience. It pays to learn how to write well, and the instruction and exercises in this book are designed to help you develop your newswriting skills.

Contents

Journalism Today, Fifth Edition, has been extensively rewritten and revised. It is practically a brand-new book. The book is divided into seven sections, with new material in virtually every chapter. The first section, "Journalism in a Democracy," covers the rise and responsibilities of American media. Chapter One, "Looking Back: The History of American Media," covers the development of journalism in America. The roles and responsibilities of journalists are covered in Chapter Two, "Meeting Ethical and Legal Responsibilities."

Sections Two, Three, and Four are "how to" chapters, with an emphasis on newspapers. Section Two, "Gathering News for the School Newspaper," focuses on student publications. In Chapter Three, "Deciding What Is News," you will learn what makes a good story. Chapter Four, "Organizing the Staff to Capture the News" covers ways to structure your staff and has been extensively revised since the last edition. How to conduct an interview and then write it up are the focus of Chapter Five, "Making the Interview Work."

Section Three, "Writing and Delivering the News," covers writing good news stories. You will learn how to best capture your audience's attention in Chapter Six, "Writing News Story Leads." The body of the story is the focus of Chapter Seven, "Writing News Stories." In Chapter Eight, "Handling Quotes Fairly and Accurately," you will learn how to use quotes correctly and to your best advantage. Chapter Nine, "Doing In-Depth Reporting," teaches you how to do substantive stories. And Chapter Ten, "Editing, Headline Writing, and Design," shows you how to polish and present your articles.

Section Four, "Writing Features, Sports, and Editorials," focuses on more specialized areas of journalism. Chapter Eleven, "Writing Feature Stories," Chapter Twelve, "Writing Sports Stories," and Chapter Thirteen, "Writing for the Editorial Page" cover the various aspects needed to write well in each of these areas.

Section Five, "Other Aspects of Scholastic Journalism," covers a variety of journalism-related topics. Chapter Fourteen, "Producing the Yearbook," has been significantly updated since the last edition. It covers the elements of producing a yearbook from planning to page layout. Chapter Fifteen, "Writing for Radio and Television," focuses on broadcast journalism. In Chapter Sixteen, "Understanding and Using Public Relations," you will learn about public relations, both what it is and how to use it. The business aspects of journalism, such as budgeting and advertising, are found in Chapter Seventeen, "Handling Finances: Advertising and Business."

Section Six, "Photography," covers both practical and aesthetic aspects of photography. Chapter Eighteen, "Taking and Using Effective Photographs," shows you how to shoot and then use good photographs. In Chapter Nineteen, "Understanding Technical Aspects of Photography," you will learn about the practical side of photography: how cameras work, how to control exposures, and how to work in a darkroom.

Section Seven, "Computers and Desktop Publishing," covers the technological resources available. The final chapter, "Taking Advantage of Technology," offers more advice on using computers, desktop publishing, and on-line resources in journalism.

A variety of other features are included to help you learn about journalism. The "On Display" features show examples from student newspapers and yearbooks from around the country. Seeing samples of what other students are doing can inspire and encourage you. The end-of-chapter material includes summary material and both individual and team activities to help you practice what you have just learned.

In addition, each chapter contains a "Trends and Issues" feature. These present an issue at stake in journalism, from on-line resources to invasion of privacy. The "Career Profiles" at the end of each chapter highlight a well-established journalist discussing his or her career path as well as offering advice for up-and-coming journalists.

Journalism Today and in the Future

The craft of journalism today demands that you maintain a balance between yesterday and tomorrow. As a journalist, you should cherish the traditional values—ethics, concern for the community, hard work, honesty, and the craft of true journalism. The examination of ethical issues will always be critical, from how a criminal case is handled in the press to the way guests on talk shows are treated. This edition contains the latest and best Code of Ethics from the Society of Professional Journalists to demonstrate the ethical standards that journalists are expected to live up to.

As you develop your journalistic skills and techniques, remember to stay flexible about the inevitable stream of change, from how the news is researched to how it is delivered. Journalists and scholars are concerned with a number of issues at the turn of the century. Will the new media kill print media? Is there a future for newspapers? Most believe that newspapers will survive well into the twenty-first century and beyond. On-line distribution may even help newspapers. Generally, new media supplement the current media, rather than replace them. Radio and TV have not driven out newspapers, though they have brought about certain changes. The point is that no one can predict the future.

As the lines between print, TV, cable, cyberspace, and computers blur, journalists need to remain open to new ideas about packaging and delivering information. To resist the wave of technological change would be detrimental to your career. However, good journalists will remain true to the essentials of journalism: to report the news fairly, accurately, and well. As Katherine Fulton advised, "The wisest strategy . . . is to remain committed to high-quality reporting and storytelling—and to invest seriously in understanding new media" (*Columbia Journalism Review,* March/April 1996, 19).

A final word of advice to those who want to become journalists: Start reading. Put down that joystick, turn off the TV and the computer, and grab a book. Read it, then read another one. Read the recipes on the cereal box at breakfast and the signs on the bus. This text will teach you the essential journalistic skills, but you cannot become a journalist solely by reading this book—or any other, for that matter. You learn journalism by doing journalism. The doorway to journalism is closed, however, to all but the truly literate. And that means devouring the written word.

Journalism Today

Journalism in a Democracy

Chapter One

Looking Back: The History of American Media

Chapter Two

Meeting Ethical and Legal Responsibilities

Looking Back: The History of American Media

Key Terms

partisan press

penny press

wire service

yellow journalism

muckraking

shock jock

global village

computer-assisted reporting

Key Concepts

After reading this chapter, you should

- understand how the printed press in America developed

- know how the American concept of freedom of the press came into being

- understand the development and impact of radio and television

- know how the Internet became a tool for gathering and disseminating information

- recognize some of the issues facing journalism going into the twenty-first century

The Information Age has dawned—with a bang.

Millions—soon to be billions—of people around the planet are electronically linked, building virtual communities with little regard for international boundaries.

Fiercely independent, sometimes chaotic, always resistant to government regulation, the Internet appears to have changed communication as much as any development in history. In its impact on the way humans communicate, the Internet ranks with the invention of movable type; the advent of the telegraph, telephone, radio, and television; and the creation of satellite technology.

Or so it seems.

The exact meaning of this development is unknown to anyone. Journalists and communication scholars struggle to glimpse the ultimate outcome of the changes. Some think the world of news and information has changed in some fundamental way. Others think the electronic changes merely represent the delivery system for news, about on the level of having your newspaper delivered on-line instead of being tossed onto your driveway.

While no one can yet guess where we're going with new technology, one thing is certain: We're not going backward. Someone suggested the Internet is to the 1990s what citizens band radio was to the 1970s: just a toy whose novelty will fade. That's highly unlikely.

The amount of information available on-line is staggering. Some of it is excellent—and some of it is junk. And that just about describes information as it has always been. Somebody has to sort it out, to make sense of it, to organize it, to judge it, and to interpret it.

That's what journalists do. The job is being done in the Information Age just about the way it has always been done, whether with quill pens, typewriters, or computers. Journalists scan the environment, picking from thousands of possibilities those that are the most important or that affect the most people. Information about topics is gathered, facts are weighed, pictures taken, graphics designed, decisions made, and stories written, packaged, and delivered.

More and more news is becoming available via the Internet. Careful and conscientious journalists, however, still have to make judgments as to its value.

Journalists need the same skills and talents they have always needed. They need to be broadly educated. They need to know about everything, because that's what they cover: everything. They need people skills and language skills.

Certain fundamentals will always apply for the journalist: good sense, good judgment, good writing, poise under pressure, ethical and moral standards. These fundamentals apply whether information is delivered to the audience on-line or in the traditional fashion. The Internet and the technology that accompanies it have created new and different opportunities for appropriately trained journalists. But the classic standards are unchanged: Be fair. Get it right. And do not expect the technology to do the journalist's work. As former NBC President Bob Mulholland told a 1995 gathering on the future of communication, "The news does not gather itself."

Not that it ever did. Think for a moment about communication and information in "the old days." If you had lived in colonial America—indeed if you had lived only fifty years ago—you would recognize how far the world has come in journalism and in information processing.

The colonists and Native Americans of the seventeenth century were information paupers who rarely saw a newspaper. Communication was by letter and word of mouth. By way of contrast, most people of today have access to books, magazines, radio and television programs, music and information on CD-ROMs, movies to show on home videocassette players, information from databases, and information from commercial on-line services such as Prodigy and CompuServe—not to mention newspapers, which is how it all began.

America's history is inseparable from the history of its journalism. Early newspapers printed essays that stirred the revolutionaries and that chronicled the historic break from England. Today, journalists still help set the agenda. It has been said, in fact, that although journalists don't tell us *what* to think, they do tell us what to think *about*. They help a democratic nation make historic decisions by providing the facts and opinions needed to elect the leaders who decide national policy.

America's First Newspapers

The first American newspapers didn't look like the colorful, thick papers you see today. Often they were only one sheet long and contained little of what you think of as news. Letters, essays, material borrowed from whatever source an editor could find—but little news—made up the journalistic

Numb: 1,

PUBLICK
OCCURRENCES

Both *FORREIGN* and *DOMESTICK*.

Boston, Thurfday *Sept.* 25th. 1690.

IT is defigned, that the Countrey fhall be fur-
nifhed once a moneth (or if any Glut of Occurrences happen, oftener,) with an Account of fuch confiderable things as have arrived unto our Notice.

In order hereunto, the Publifher will take what
pains he can to obtain a Faithful Relation of all
fuch things ; and will particularly make himfelf
beholden to fuch Perfons in Bofton whom he knows

from them, as what is in the Forces lately
gone for *Canada*; made them think it almoft
impoffible for them to get well through the
Affairs of their Husbandry at this time of the
year, yet the feafon has been fo unufually
favourable that they fcarce find any want of
the many hundreds of hands, that are gone
from them ; which is looked upon as a Mer-
ciful Providence

The first newspaper published in the American colonies, *Publick Occurrences* was suppressed by the British after only one issue.

fare. The first American newspaper, *Publick Occurrences*, was published in Boston in 1690 by Benjamin Harris. After only one issue, the British colonial authorities suppressed the paper because they didn't like what Harris printed.

Fourteen years later the colonies had their first continuously published newspaper: *The Boston News-Letter*, started by John Campbell in 1704. It was published "by authority," meaning it had the government's approval. Soon, though, as pioneers moved south and west, more newspapers cropped up. Most carried the "by authority" tag and were closely supervised by the British government.

Establishment of Freedom of the Press

In those days, newspapers that criticized the government were guilty of sedition, the stirring of rebellion. The truth of their statements was no defense. In fact, the principle then was, "The greater the truth, the greater the libel." The government figured that false criticism (which is how libel is defined today) was easier to turn aside than well-founded criticism.

A case in 1735 established truth as a defense against libel charges. In the *New York Weekly Journal,* John Peter Zenger printed articles critical of Governor William Cosby. Zenger did not write most of the articles himself, but as the publisher he was arrested on a charge of seditious libel and thrown into jail.

The case was considered open-and-shut. If Zenger printed attacks on the British Crown, he was guilty of libel, even if his statements were true.

The Boston News-Letter has the distinction of being the first continuously published newspaper in America.

Worth Quoting

"Were it left to me to decide whether we should have a government without newspapers or newspapers without a government, I should not hesitate to prefer the latter."

—THOMAS JEFFERSON

Andrew Hamilton of Philadelphia, considered by many the finest attorney of the period, defended Zenger. Then in his eighties, Hamilton was still brilliant and forceful. He stunned the crowd when he said: "I do confess (for my client) that he both printed and published the two newspapers set forth in the information. I hope in so doing he has committed no crime."

To the court this seemed in effect a guilty plea, since its only concern was to prove that Zenger was responsible for publishing the articles in question. But Hamilton continued, "I hope it is not our bare printing or publishing a paper that will make it a libel. For the words themselves must be libelous—that is, false, malicious, and seditious—or else we are not guilty."

The judge denied Hamilton the right to prove the facts in the papers, so Hamilton appealed to the jury: "Every man who prefers freedom to a life of slavery will bless and honor you as men who have baffled the attempt of tyranny; and by an impartial and uncorrupt verdict, have laid a noble foundation for securing to ourselves, our posterity, and our neighbors, that to which nature and the laws of our country have given us a right—the liberty both of exposing and opposing arbitrary power (in these parts of the world, at least) by speaking and writing—Truth."

The Crown had not counted on the will of people struggling to be free, in this case represented by the jurors. They deliberated only briefly before shouting "not guilty," and the celebrations began.

The Birth of the Nation

The Zenger trial fanned the flames of freedom that were beginning to burn in the colonies. The colonial press of the day played a vital role in the birth of the nation. By 1775, when the Revolution began, thirty-seven newspapers were being published. These newspapers generally allied themselves with the patriots, at least partly because of their anger over the taxes imposed on them by the Stamp Act. They backed the Revolution and printed the cries to battle that rallied the rebels. In fact, some historians believe there would not have been a Revolution without the support of the press.

Newspapers then, and for the next century, lined up deliberately with political parties: This was the era of the partisan press. Readers who supported the fight for independence bought a Whig newspaper; those who were loyal to the British Crown bought a Tory paper. (Most papers today try to report political news objectively, although some ally themselves with a particular party on the editorial page.)

When the war ended and the Constitutional Convention met in Philadelphia, the framers did not, as many people believe, spend much time on the question of freedom of the press. The Constitution made no mention of a free press, because most state constitutions already covered the matter. But the Bill of Rights—the first ten amendments to the Constitution—was ratified in 1791. The First Amendment guarantees a free press with the words, "Congress shall make no law . . . abridging the freedom of speech, or of the press."

After the Revolution, the young nation grew rapidly, and so did the newspaper industry. Hundreds of newspapers opened all over the new land. The first daily, *The Pennsylvania Post*, was founded in 1783. The first student newspaper, *The Students Gazette*, also was founded even earlier in Pennsylvania, in 1777.

Even small towns had papers, put out by printers who had to set the type by hand, one letter at a time. The presses were clumsy, but the Industrial Revolution was at hand, and soon newspapers joined in a race for better technology, a race that continues to this day.

Student newspapers appeared in the new United States remarkably early. The oldest of these, *The Students Gazette,* published its first issue in 1777.

The Penny Press

An important publisher during the penny press era, Horace Greeley established the *New York Tribune* in 1841 and advocated many reform causes in its pages.

The early newspapers carried little actual news. They were filled largely with essays, letters, editorials, and a few advertisements. Then in 1833, Benjamin Day founded the *New York Sun*, filled it with news, and sold it for only a penny. Day's staff covered the police beat, wrote about tragedies and natural disasters, and toned down the opinions. Thus was born the "penny press," probably more truly the forerunner of today's newspapers than either *Publick Occurrences* or the *Boston News-Letter*.

Because it was so inexpensive and distributed by street sales rather than subscription, the penny press achieved a mass audience, made up primarily of the new working class of the Industrial Revolution. For the first time, too, advertising took on a major role. (To this day, it is advertising that pays the cost of producing newspapers and getting newscasts on the air.)

Two years later James Gordon Bennett started the *New York Morning Herald*. Although it sold for two cents, it continued the newsy ways of the *Sun*. Similar papers were soon founded in Boston, Baltimore, Philadelphia, and other cities.

One of the most influential penny presses was the *New York Tribune*, founded in 1841 by Horace Greeley. The *Tribune's* daily circulation never matched that of the *Sun* or the *Herald*, but its weekly edition had 200,000 subscribers—more readers than any other publication of that time.

Women had contributed to the growth and development of American journalism since colonial times, operating newspapers and print shops. As the nation changed, so did the role of women. Cornelia Walter was editor of the *Boston Transcript* in the 1840s, and Jane Grey Swisshelm became the first woman to cover Congress, in 1850, working for Greeley's *Tribune*.

The New York Times, which today is usually considered the best newspaper in the country by professional journalists, was founded in 1851 by Henry Raymond. Until Adolph Ochs bought it in 1896, the paper was always in a precarious financial position. From the beginning, however, it set a standard for fairness and accuracy in reporting, a standard that has been widely imitated but rarely equaled.

In cities like Pittsburgh, Chicago, New Orleans, Atlanta, St. Louis, and Louisville, the penny press grew and prospered. Headlines grew larger and designs better as newspapers competed for street sales. It was not at all unusual for a major city to have eight or nine competing newspapers.

The Effect of the Telegraph

Newswriting and news coverage began to change in 1861, when reporters at Civil War battle sites began to use the telegraph, invented some eighteen years before, to transmit their stories. To get the outcome into the story in case the telegraph broke down, reporters became more concise and began to develop inverted-pyramid writing.

Shortly after the telegraph began to speed the reporting of news, the first news-gathering service was formed. This service, a forerunner of the Associated Press, began selling news to client papers in 1849. Over the next few decades other such wire services, including United Press, sprang up. By 1910 there were 2,600 daily newspapers in the United States; some of them had bureaus in the nation's capital and around the world. The information explosion was beginning.

Newspaper reporter Nellie Bly, working for the New York *World,* was willing to travel anywhere to get—or create—a story.

Yellow Journalism

The late nineteenth century saw an era most journalists would rather forget, the age of "yellow journalism." The term refers to an unethical, irresponsible brand of journalism that involved hoaxes, altered photographs, screaming headlines, "scoops," frauds, and endless promotions of the newspapers themselves. "Yellow journalism" derives from the name of the Yellow Kid, a cartoon character that appeared in the *Sunday World* during the 1890s.

The most notable of the yellow journalists were William Randolph Hearst, publisher of the New York *Journal,* and Joseph Pulitzer, publisher of the New York *World.* Their newspapers attracted huge audiences, and their competition for readers, advertisers, and each others' most talented writers was fierce. Color supplements, more illustrations, cartoon strips, and dramatic coverage of wars and sporting events sent the papers' circulations soaring.

Nellie Bly

The period was perfect for the circulation-building exploits of Nellie Bly, the name used by Elizabeth Cochrane, the most famous of the women journalists beginning to make names for themselves. Bly worked for Pulitzer's *World* and was noted for her "stunts," stories in which she made

Yellow journalism reached its peak during the late 1800s. The headline on this paper exploited the sinking of the battleship *Maine* and whipped up public sentiment to go to war.

the news herself. Once she pretended to be mentally ill and was committed to New York's Blackwell Island Asylum. When she was released after ten days, she wrote a story exposing the asylum's poor conditions. The story sparked reform around the country.

Bly's most famous story was about her trip around the world. A book of that period, Jules Verne's *Around the World in Eighty Days*, was very popular. Bly set out to circle the globe in fewer than eighty days, and as readers everywhere followed her adventures, she did it—in seventy-two days.

Whatever Happened to . . . ?

The Pulitzer name lives on today through the Pulitzer Prizes, awarded for specific areas of journalism, literature, and music, as well as through some association with distinguished newspapers.

The Hearst name is also still connected with newspapers but many fewer than its peak of forty-two dailies. The Hearst Foundation makes a valuable contribution to journalism education through newswriting, broadcasting, and photography contests for college journalism students.

Spanish-American War

During this period, a movement began in Cuba to seek independence from Spain. Beginning in 1895, the *World* and the *Journal* whipped up a war climate in support of the Cuban nationalists and tried to lure the United States into the conflict. One famous story of the time was about a *Journal* artist in Cuba who cabled Hearst that there was no war and he was coming home. Hearst is said to have wired back, "Please remain. You furnish the pictures, and I'll furnish the war."

When the battleship USS *Maine* blew up in Havana harbor in 1898, the Hearst paper featured a huge drawing and the headline: DESTRUCTION OF THE WAR SHIP *MAINE* WAS THE WORK OF AN ENEMY. Congress demanded that Spain leave the island, and war resulted. While the press is not solely to blame for the Spanish-American War, the yellow journalism of the time certainly contributed to an unhealthy atmosphere.

Muckraking

The end of yellow journalism ushered in a period when American newspapers developed a significant social consciousness. Many papers crusaded for child labor laws, promoted hospitals and tuberculosis sanitariums, collected money for the needy, and exposed public graft. Critics of the crusading journalists labeled them muckrakers, which the reformers came to think of as a term of praise.

A new medium came into its own during the late nineteenth and early twentieth centuries: the magazine. Such publications as *McClure's*, *Collier's*, *Munsey's*, and *The Saturday Evening Post* joined the fight for social justice that the newspapers had kicked off. They had circulations in the hundreds of thousands, and they battled corruption in all its forms. Patent medicine companies, child labor, the status of African Americans, and the meat-packing industry all came under scrutiny. The Pure Food and Drugs Act of 1906 grew out of the crusades, as did many other reforms. Ida Tarbell's series on "The History of the Standard Oil Company" in *McClure's* was one of the first attacks on big business. Her investigative reporting put John D. Rockefeller, Standard Oil's president, on the defensive for years to come.

The Development of Minority Media

As the nation progressed, minority groups began taking on important roles in American journalism. *The Chicago Defender*, one of the nation's largest and most influential African-American newspapers, was founded in 1905 by Robert S. Abbott, whose parents had been slaves. *The Defender* took the lead in encouraging Southern blacks to move to the North in

As founder of *The Chicago Defender,* Robert S. Abbott was the first to give African Americans a public forum for addressing civil rights and other issues.

search of better jobs in that region's growing industries. *The Defender* became a daily in 1956 under Abbott's nephew, John H. Sengstacke, who built a large chain of African-American newspapers.

African-American magazines also have prospered. One of the most famous, *Ebony,* celebrated its fiftieth anniversary in 1995. *Essence* and *Black Enterprise,* though newer, exhibit similar staying power. On television, the Black Entertainment Network is making its presence felt: It had the first major post-trial interview with O. J. Simpson.

Hispanic media have also taken their place on the American media scene. Two of the largest Hispanic-American newspapers are *El Diario-La Prensa* in New York City and *Diario Los Americas* in Miami. Hispanic-American papers are also published in Washington, D.C., San Francisco, Dallas, Houston, Los Angeles, Chicago, and many other cities. Today the highest-rated FM station in Los Angeles is Spanish-speaking KLVE; and Hispanic Online, the electronic version of *Hispanic Magazine,* can be found on the Internet.

The first Native-American newspaper was the *Cherokee Phoenix,* which appeared in 1828. It was shut down by the government five years later for publishing ideas seen as antigovernment. Today the independent (from tribal control) *Lakota Times* is perhaps the most prominent Native-American newspaper, and its publisher, Tim Giago, probably the most prominent Native-American journalist. Giago also publishes *Indian Country Today* in Rapid City, South Dakota.

Asian-American interests are covered by such publications as *Sampan* in Boston, *The Filipino Reporter* in New York City, *Pacific Citizen* in Los Angeles, and *Korea Times* in Chicago—as well as through many smaller papers around the nation.

News industry leaders place great emphasis on attracting minorities to news work. The National Association of Hispanic Journalists, Native American Press Association, National Association of Black Journalists, Asian American Journalists Association, and similar groups are active in the cause of diversifying newsrooms. Additionally, many colleges and universities offer special job fairs and scholarships designed to

The Largest Newspapers

The five largest newspapers, in terms of circulation, in the United States today are the following:

The Wall Street Journal

USA Today

The New York Times

Los Angeles Times

The Washington Post

All but *The Washington Post* have daily circulations of over one million.

make young people aware of journalism opportunities. These practices not only open career doors, they improve the sensitivity of news organizations covering stories involving race.

The Advent of Radio

At the turn of the century, a development was looming that would change the nature of the news—and of the world—forever. In 1906, Dr. Lee De Forest made improvements in the vacuum tube that made possible the new medium of radio. Although no one person invented radio, De Forest's vacuum tube was the key breakthrough.

De Forest made the first newscast in 1916 when he broadcast over a limited area the returns of the Wilson-Hughes presidential election. Regular daily programs started in Detroit in 1920, broadcast from experimental station 8MK, which became WWJ the following year. Station KDKA in Pittsburgh, Pennsylvania, broadcast the Harding-Cox presidential election returns of 1920, considered a milestone in radio journalism.

The National Broadcasting Company (NBC) was formed in 1926 and the Columbia Broadcasting System (CBS) in 1927. The Mutual

Radio brought many American families together in the 1930s and '40s through its mix of comedy, sports, and news.

Broadcasting System went on the air in 1934, and when part of NBC's network was sold, it was renamed the American Broadcasting Company (ABC) in 1945.

It soon became clear that the airwaves, which legally belong to the public, had to be regulated. Stations were saturating them and interfering with each others' broadcasts. In 1912, a law was passed that empowered the Department of Commerce to assign wavelengths to license applicants. The Radio Act of 1927 broadened this power and created the Federal Radio Commission. This was the forerunner of today's Federal Communications Commission (FCC), which has jurisdiction—though not censorship power—over both radio and television.

Radio fascinated the American public in the 1920s, '30s, and '40s. Great comedians like Jack Benny, Bob Hope, and Fred Allen drew huge audiences, and sporting events like football and baseball became accessible to everyone. Today, more than 500 million radios are in use, beaming words and music from about five thousand AM stations and nearly an equal number of FM stations around the country.

Radio still occupies an important place among the media. Most stations play music mixed with news, and millions of Americans get their first word of major news events from radio as they drive to or from work or school. In the 1990s, though, radio has taken an unusual turn. So-called "shock jocks" and call-in talk shows have begun to dominate, especially on AM radio. Shock jocks—Howard Stern is the best known, with Don Imus not far behind—make careers out of being insulting and outrageous, saying whatever comes to their minds, apparently in the hope that their comments will offend.

Radio talk shows also have wide appeal—and stir wide controversy. Millions tune in to such conservative hosts as G. Gordon Liddy, convicted Watergate figure, and Rush Limbaugh, whose blasts from the right are echoed enthusiastically by approving "ditto heads." Some people find such personalities' criticism of the president and other high-ranking officials disrespectful and offensive. Others argue that it's in the finest tradition of American irreverence toward its leaders.

It's important to distinguish legitimate journalism from the work of shock jocks and radio talk-show hosts. Journalism is devoted to providing accurate, objective, untainted information that the public can use in their lives and in decision-making, particularly political decision-making. Part of the role of the journalist is to entertain, of course, but that's the *exclusive* aim of the jocks and hosts. They're not journalists; they're entertainers. They stimulate conversation and debate, and that's good. But what they say should be taken with a grain of salt.

The Impact of Television

The first television newscast took place in 1940. By the mid-1960s, sixty million TV sets were in use. Thirty years later, the number exceeded ninety million.

TV dramatically changed radio and newspapers. It took much of the entertainment role away from radio and claimed much of the spot, or breaking, news role traditionally held by newspapers. Today, newspapers put less emphasis on breaking news; it makes no sense for a newspaper to announce breathlessly that an event occurred when most of its readers probably saw an account of it hours earlier on television. Modern newspapers put more emphasis on examining the background of current news events and covering trends and lifestyles in depth.

Early TV pictures were snowy, and transmission facilities were erratic. Today, both color and sound have improved. During a major news event— such as the verdict in the O. J. Simpson criminal trial in 1995—the nation stops to watch television. Some events, such as the Olympic Games, are viewed simultaneously around the world. Communications philosopher Marshall McLuhan called this phenomenon the "global village."

In the 1930s, President Franklin Roosevelt reached the American people through radio with his fireside chats. Today's presidents come to us in color through live news conferences, and presidential candidates debate each other as the voters watch. Press conferences also give the public a close-up look at news reporters in action.

Today, the traditional major TV networks—ABC, CBS, and NBC—have seen their audiences fragmented by the growth of other programming. The new networks include CNN, the around-the-clock news service that usually beats everybody on breaking news; Fox, which scored a coup when it acquired the rights to NFL football telecasts; and C-Span, which provides gavel-to-gavel coverage of many government and related public-affairs meetings, conferences, and other events. Most U.S. cities also receive good programming through PBS stations, though cuts in government support are a threat to that programming. Additionally, the hundreds of cable TV stations provide alternatives to the networks by broadcasting shows that appeal to smaller, more specific audiences. And, of course, the audience also has to be divided among those who prefer to rent movies and watch "television" on their VCRs.

In some ways television, like radio, has reverted in the 1990s to yellow journalism practices of one hundred years ago. Daytime TV talk shows that feature dysfunctional guests with off-the-wall relationships and lifestyles have helped revive the sensational practices of the past. So, too, he relationship between the press, the public, and the government in times of war has long been an issue. By the late 1800s, as you have seen, newspapers such as the New York *Journal* were not above creating stories in order to incite public sentiment and thus help lure the government into conflict. In the twentieth century, however, as the media developed the means to gain more and quicker access to wartime information, the government's reactions to having that information made public seemed to change with the times.

During World Wars I and II, the press and the government enjoyed generally friendly relations. World War II, in particular, regarded by many Americans as "the good war," had widespread support, and war correspondents such as Ernie Pyle became public heroes. The radio came into its own during this war, with President Franklin D. Roosevelt using the medium not only to pass along selected battle information but to exhort the public to cooperation and steadfastness.

In both world wars, information and images transmitted from the battlefield were carefully censored. Most noncombatants remained unaware of the brutality and horror of war.

The widespread availability of television in the 1960s had a great influence on the public perception of war. During the Vietnam War, for the first time correspondents

going into battle areas not only reported their stories but had them conveyed to the public almost immediately. If an ambush occurred, the correspondent could tape and record it. If a bullet flew past, the whole television audience could experience the fear. And if soldiers were carried back from the battlefield bloody and bandaged, or even dead, the public could see that, too. Television brought the horror of war home, often in living color.

Largely because of its effect on public sentiment, Vietnam was the last time the press was allowed unrestricted wartime coverage. In October 1983, when U. S. forces invaded the island of Grenada, government policy kept American journalists well away from the action. No reporters were allowed on the island for two days after the invasion. This was the first time in U. S. history that journalists were not permitted to accompany soldiers into battle zones. But public opinion had changed, too: Many Americans had become suspicious of the press and applauded the restrictions on journalists.

Press restrictions were felt again in 1989 when the U. S. invaded Panama and similarly in 1991 when combined U. S. and U. N. forces went to war with Iraq. During this so-called Gulf War, journalists again felt restricted in their access to combatants and sensed that the information they received from official military sources was less than complete. When the war broke out, journalists from CNN, including Pulitzer Prize winner Peter Arnett, continued to report from behind enemy lines. Some Americans believed their accounts, censored by the Iraqi government, were suspect. But journalists applauded their courage and pointed out that news from official U. S. sources was also censored.

Approaching a new century, it does not seem that government censorship of wartime news will suddenly go away. Yet it is clear that even one strong battlefield image can vastly influence public opinion. Perhaps this tension is what is needed to keep everyone honest.

have some network TV shows that have the look and feel of news documentaries but in fact give emphasis only to the exploits of the rich and famous. Serious news can be hard to find; "if it bleeds it leads" remains the unspoken philosophy of a great many local television news shows, and a careful look reveals that even traditional newspapers and magazines are running more trash news at the expense of serious news these days. One example is the all-out coverage of Britain's royal family and its frequent crises.

However, as the 1990s come to a close, TV executives have installed a new ratings system to monitor sex and violence on television, similar to movie ratings, even as controversy grows over congressional attempts to control obscenity on the Internet.

The Effects of Technology

As mentioned in the introduction, technology is beginning to make vast differences not only in how people receive news, but also in the kinds of information available. The Internet has made the transmission of information both amazingly quick and exceedingly efficient.

The Internet began to be developed in the 1960s as scientists at research institutions all over the world began putting together independent computer networks that could convey information in the event of a nuclear holocaust. The Net came into popular use in the early 1990s when commercial services such as CompuServe, Prodigy, and America Online made access to it available to anyone with a computer and modem. The development of the graphical World Wide Web browser allowed users to access the Internet by categorizing much of the information on it, and accessing programs like *Mosaic, Microsoft Internet Explorer*, and *Netscape* made surfing the Net not only popular but downright easy.

An Internet user can send a message virtually instantaneously to thousands of people all over the world by using mailing lists or chat via modem in real time with people everywhere. Material can be read and downloaded from worldwide sites at the stroke of a key.

News on the Net

The news is "up there," too. The development of hypertext links, or easy ways to make connections from one article to another, allows access to newspapers, magazines, government reports, census data, texts of presidential speeches—literally millions and millions of words, pictures, and

Many newspapers, such as the *Chicago Tribune,* have on-line versions. Besides their interactive capacity—readers can move around the issue easily and send e-mail to columnists—such publications may also increase the public's interest in the news.

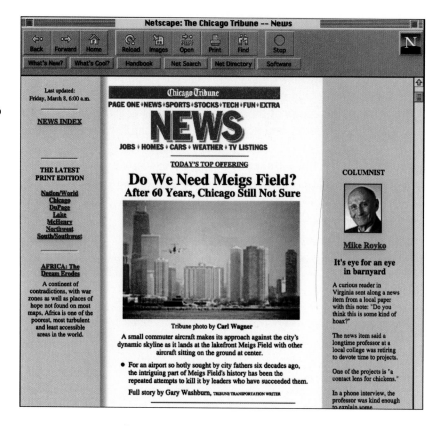

sounds about everything under the sun. Not surprisingly, this vast array of information even includes high school and college publications, including some designed specifically for the Internet.

The Internet has changed the ways news is presented and read. For example, it has freed print journalists from the constraint of space. In traditional newswriting, stories have to be brief because space is limited. But there's no shortage of space in cyberspace, so sometimes stories get too long, and some are worthless. News stories used to be simply linear—that is, read from beginning to end. Today, readers may continue until they find a link that interests them, at which point they leave the original story and go surfing for related information. A click of a key returns them to the original document.

In addition to traditional news, on-line publications offer links to restaurant reviews, travel tips, e-mail addresses of columnists and editorial writers so readers can provide instant feedback, and even community forums where readers can debate and discuss ideas—just like the old days of town meetings.

Computer-Assisted Reporting

Computers have led to another change in journalism. It's called *computer-assisted reporting*, and it's a valuable new tool for digging out complicated information in a hurry.

It works this way. Suppose a reporter wants to check police performance in responding to calls for help. Maybe the hunch is that police respond more quickly to calls from affluent neighborhoods than those "on the wrong side of the tracks." The reporter could pore over hundreds of pieces of paper and dig out this information. But he or she could also access the police database and probably find the answer in minutes.

Databases all over the world are accessible to wired journalists, provided by private sources and governments. Government agencies make information available on crops, educational trends, health threats, crime, and a host of other issues. Bulletin boards on various topics convey not only information, but also a sense of how users feel about it. Listservs bring people together who are interested in the same subject, including many high school and college journalists. The trick with all the information available is, of course, making sure it's true.

Though a great deal of information can be accessed on-line, it's not clear whether newspapers' future lies in providing information in this way.

Newspapers on-line are having difficulty turning a profit. And one thing is certain: It's not sufficient just to dump the newspaper into cyberspace. While that has a satisfying and modern feeling to it, it's difficult to see how readers are served any better than in the old, traditional way (though trees are saved, and that's important, too). No, the on-line publication is just a start.

Journalism Today

Only a little more than a generation ago, it was common for families to subscribe to two newspapers a day, one in the morning and one in the evening. (Today, many cities do not even have two newspapers.) Whole families spent large parts of their day reading newspapers. People today, however, do not buy and read newspapers in the same numbers as their parents did, a development that has leaders in journalism alarmed. To interest younger readers in particular, they are responding with special youth pages; a program called "Newspaper in Education," in which many newspapers provide copies to schools at special rates and offer other special services to journalism educators; and more stories and features that appeal to a younger audience.

The reporters of tomorrow are being trained in high school and college journalism classes today.

The efforts are paying off. The number of young people reading newspapers and watching TV newscasts is rising steadily. More than 90 percent of so-called Generation Xers, those in the sixteen- to twenty-nine-year-old bracket, read newspapers. Forty percent read a paper daily, and nearly two-thirds read both a weekday and Sunday paper.

Some studies have suggested that the current generation is less informed about world and national events than any generation in more than half a century. This appears to be changing, however. Among eighteen- to twenty-four-year-olds, 52 percent read a daily newspaper and 62 percent read a Sunday paper. About sixty million newspapers are sold every day—and 2.29 people read each paper. Newspapers continue to lure more advertising dollars than any other medium, and they lead all media in providing on-line services.

It is important that the audience keep up with the news, for adding a less-informed electorate to a media trend away from reporting on government and toward less serious news creates an alarming combination. Good citizens should keep abreast of the news . . . and journalism students *must* do so.

Today, students are flocking in record numbers to the schools and departments of journalism on college and university campuses. Some of the very best minds are being educated for journalism careers. The job market is crowded but not impossible, and journalism educators remain confident that jobs will always be there for students who are well-educated and enthusiastic. The future of American journalism, in fact, rests in the hands of people like you.

Wrap-up

The dawn of the Information Age has changed the world and journalism dramatically. Millions of people are connected to each other via the Internet. Information on virtually every topic is readily available. Journalism will be affected, but the basic skills and attitudes journalists need to do their jobs will not change.

The Internet is the latest in a series of important changes in communication. Over the past fifty years, the processing of information has speeded up to the point that important events are known around the world within minutes of their happening. By comparison, the people who lived in colonial America were information paupers.

The history of journalism in America cannot be separated from the history of the country. The first American newspaper, *Publick Occurrences*, was suppressed after only a single issue in 1690 because the British authorities disapproved of it. In 1735, the authorities tried to suppress John Peter Zenger's *New York Weekly Journal* because of its criticism of the government. A jury acquitted Zenger, finding that truth, not government approval, was the standard for publication.

The press was instrumental in the colonial drive for independence from England, and the First Amendment to the Constitution of the new country guaranteed freedom of the press.

In the 1800s newspapers began to devote more space to events and less to opinion and, because they cost only a penny each, newspapers became immensely popular.

Technology, in the form of the telegraph, accelerated the transmission of news during the Civil War and led eventually to the establishment of news wire services like the Associated Press.

The close of the nineteenth century saw the era of "yellow journalism," sensational stories and screaming headlines aimed at boosting circulation. Joseph Pulitzer's New York *World* and William Randolph Hearst's New York *Journal* helped incite the Spanish-American War and prompt the U. S. invasion of Cuba.

Gradually, sensationalism gave way to reform. Magazines like *Collier's* and *The Saturday Evening Post* tried, often successfully, to better society and its institutions.

The improvement of the vacuum tube in 1906 led to the development of radio, the founding of the networks, and the creation of an instant news source for the American public. Television added pictures to sound, and a new medium was born.

Because of television, newspapers figure less prominently in the lives of students than they once did. However, this appears to be changing for the better. Young people are returning to the printed page, and this encourages journalistic leaders. They know that the responsibilities of citizenship, of keeping fully informed, require a deeper understanding than TV alone can provide.

The Internet is a rich new source of information. Growing very rapidly, the Net has become easier to navigate with the proliferation of commercial on-line services and easy-to-use software. Hundreds of newspapers are on-line, along with every other type of information, all available at a keystroke. Reporters using databases for their research have created a whole new category of reporting, computer-assisted reporting, a major late-twentieth-century development in news gathering.

On Assignment

Individual Activities

1. Write a brief definition of each of the following terms:

computer-assisted reporting	global village
muckraking	partisan press
penny press	shock jock
wire service	yellow journalism

2. From this list of the journalists most closely associated with the development of early newspapers in America, select two. Write brief biographies of each and discuss his or her role.

Benjamin Harris	John Campbell
Andrew Hamilton	Benjamin Franklin
Cornelia Walter	Benjamin Day

Robert S. Abbott	Anna Catherine Zenger
Nellie Bly	Jane Grey Swisshelm

3. From this list of twentieth-century journalists, select three. Write brief biographies of each and discuss his or her role.

Ben Bagdikian	Bryant Gumbel
Carl Bernstein	Christine Craft
David Brinkley	Edward R. Murrow
Gloria Steinem	Helen Thomas
John Quiñones	Katharine Graham
Margaret Bourke-White	Marshall McLuhan
Molly Ivins	Newton Minnow
Walter Winchell	

4. Research the history of your local newspaper. Find out who founded the paper and when. Was it ever affiliated with a political party? Who owns the paper? Write a summary of your findings.

5. Research the history of a radio or television station in your town. Use the same questions as in activity 4 above. Write a summary of what you find out.

6. The following newspapers have interesting histories. Choose one of the papers and do some research into its background. Write a brief report on what makes it interesting.

   The *Philadelphia Inquirer*

   The *Des Moines Register*

   The *Chicago Defender*

   The *Milwaukee Journal-Sentinel*

   The Alton (Ill.) *Observer*

   The *Lakota Times*

   The Tombstone (Ariz.) *Epitaph*

   The *Berkeley Barb*

   USA Today

   The *Wall Street Journal*

7. Find out about the development of cartoon strips in American newspapers. Who produced the first one? Which newspaper carried it? Write an account of what you find out.

8. Test your critical thinking. Take either side of the following question and write an essay: Should the American press be restricted by the government? Consider the following questions:

   a. If so, who would decide what the restrictions would be?

   b. What would the penalty be for violating the restrictions?

   c. Would such restrictions change the nature of American life? How?

   d. Is that good or bad?

   e. TV is to some extent a controlled industry. Is that good or bad?

Team Activity

9. Work with a team of three or four classmates. Each of you is to interview two or three students in your school to get answers to the following questions. Choose students from all different grade levels.

   a. What newspapers, if any, do you read? Which newspapers do members of your family read?

   b. Which news programs, including specials, have you watched recently?

   c. From where do you get your information about world and local events?

   d. Do you use the Internet? If so, what do you use it for primarily?

   e. How well-informed about what's going on in the world would you say you are?

   Compile the information from all team members and summarize it in a report. If you wish, use graphs to clarify points. Compare your results with those of other teams in a class discussion.

Ben Bagdikian began his newspaper career by chance. A chemistry major in college, he was on his way to a job interview in Springfield, Massachusetts, when he passed the *Springfield Morning Union* newspaper office and noticed a "help wanted" sign on the window.

"I wasn't crazy about chemistry anyway, so I went in and asked about the reporter job," he said. Bagdikian got the job, and this changed the course of his life.

"I loved it right away," he said. "It's a kind of license to look into all parts of society. Reporters are given access to people and circumstances most people never see, from the poor, drunk, and thieves to the governor."

Bagdikian went to work for the *Providence* (R.I.) *Journal and Evening Bulletin*, *The Washington Post*, and the *Columbia Journalism Review* before becoming a journalism professor at the University of California at Berkeley Graduate School of Journalism. He taught from 1977 to 1990 and was dean of the graduate school from 1985 to 1988.

He has been project director for the Mass Media Technology Study by Rand, project director for the Markle Foundation's Newspaper Survival study, and president of the Mallett Fund for a Free and Responsible Press. Bagdikian has also written several books and received numerous honors, including the George Foster Peabody Award, the Sigma Delta Chi National Journalism Award, and a citation of merit from the American Society of Journalism School administrators as "journalism's most perceptive critic."

Bagdikian believes that the media need to do a better job. Most of the media, he said, are aimed at the middle class, depriving at least a third of the population of systematic coverage of the issues that affect their lives.

"The media are the only view that most people have of issues and events that citizens need to decide on," Bagdikian said. "The media have to do a better job to make sure the citizens get all the information they need to make informed decisions."

The media's role is more important today than it's ever been, Bagdikian believes.

"Life was not as complicated fifty years ago as it is now," he said. "People didn't have to make the decisions then that they have to make now. Most people only had to make one career choice and lived in one town their whole life. But the whole world changed after World War II and there is so much going on now that people have to know about. The media are better today than they were fifty years ago, but they still fall short of what the citizens need."

Being a member of the press demands a responsibility for fairness, thoroughness, and accuracy, he said. There is a trust placed on the media by the public that cannot be betrayed.

"Getting the story means getting it right, complete, and fair," he said. "It does not mean getting a sexy quote or a sound bite."

Journalism is not an exotic profession, he said. "If you're looking for a trench coat and a job that's filled with romance, forget it," he said.

Nonetheless, for students considering journalism Bagdikian asks the following question:

"Do you really care about how your communities work? Because if you don't really care, you shouldn't go into journalism."

Chapter Two

Meeting Ethical and Legal Responsibilities

Key Terms

ethics

"composite characters"

slander

right of reply

plagiarism

libel

privileged statements

fair comment

prior restraint

credibility

objectivity

in loco parentis

Forum Theory

Key Concepts

After reading this chapter, you should

- understand the functions the media must fulfill in modern society

- know criteria to evaluate the performance of the various media

- understand the ethical principles of journalism

- recognize some of the major criticisms of the press

- understand libel laws and what defenses journalists have

- be familiar with major court rulings regarding the scholastic press

The *Columbia Journalism Review*, produced at Columbia University in New York, is a highly regarded publication devoted to covering the press—to watching the watchdog. In December 1995, Joan Konner, then publisher of *CJR*, wrote the following:

> One of the most awesome changes of our time is the increase in the power and pervasiveness of the news media. That's why the question of standards is so important. Around the world there is growing public concern about the performance and behavior of the news media. The bottom line is that the public no longer trusts us. And for journalism, that is critical. Trust is our most important product.

Konner is right. Journalists increasingly find themselves under a public microscope, their motives and sometimes even their morals questioned. Poll results vary, but by and large it is true that what used to be a healthy relationship with the audience ("If you see it in the newspaper it must be true") has deteriorated. Trust has been lost.

This is a dangerous situation for the country. Journalists have serious responsibilities to meet. If they're failing to live up to those

Being well-informed about the news is essential to many people. Vast numbers start their day by reading a paper.

responsibilities—or if the public believes they're failing—the good, clear lines of communication a democracy needs may be picking up static. Skepticism about the press can, of course, be healthy. But carried to an extreme, it can lead to negative coverage and further alienation.

Journalists are viewed by many people as rude, arrogant, uncaring people who think only about "getting the story." Increasingly, people object to intrusive behavior by journalists—for example, shoving a microphone into the face of someone whose house has just burned down and demanding, "How do you feel?"

Such behavior probably doesn't happen as often as people believe—but it *does* happen more often than journalists like to talk about. Inaccuracies, preoccupation with the trivial or the bizarre, insensitivity to minority groups or issues . . . the criticism is widespread.

The media are also criticized for their *bigness*, especially the largest newspapers and the major networks. People seem to be suspicious of giant organizations, although they eat at McDonald's and shop at Sears without any problems. The media, however, are seen as pervasive and powerful.

People say the media are inaccurate. The media respond, "There's so much pressure on us, for time and space, it's a wonder there aren't more errors." That's an excuse people wouldn't accept from their dry cleaner—and certainly not from their doctor. And it shouldn't be accepted from the media, either. Sure, it's tough. But that's no excuse.

Then there is the charge of bias. Often, journalists are portrayed as left-leaning people who want to remake the country in their image. The truth is, most journalists are pretty middle-of-the-road, in all ways.

Some criticism is well deserved—and taken seriously by journalists. Some criticism is misplaced. Scandal, crime, economic uncertainty, frightening and rapid social change—this turbulence is the daily fare of consumers of the mass media. Journalists are at the center of these events; they carry the message and often bear the brunt of the frustrations such messages arouse.

The public bears some responsibility, too. By the millions, Americans said they thought the coverage of the O. J. Simpson double-murder trial was excessive. But by the millions, they tuned in, sending the ratings of CNN, which provided minute-by-minute coverage of the trial, soaring.

Similarly, many Americans criticize those elements of the press that demonstrate a disturbing return to old-time sensational journalism—while regularly watching the very shows and buying the very publications they criticize.

This chapter will examine the media from two angles. First, it will describe what you can do to become a more discerning consumer of news. Second, it will look at what the media are doing to ensure that they properly use the power entrusted to them in a free society.

The Functions of a Journalist

There are ways to determine how well journalists do their jobs. Traditionally, journalists are charged with the following responsibilities or functions in a culture that guarantees a free press.

The Political Function

The press (by which we mean radio, television, newspapers, magazines, and all other news-gathering and disseminating agencies) is the watchdog of government. Freedom always carries with it certain responsibilities. The guarantee of a free press carries the obligation of providing the audience with information upon which to base political decisions. Thus, the news organization doing its job properly will cover in detail the activities of government. It will fight attempts by the government to do the public's business behind closed doors. It will watch for scandal and wrongdoing. It will scrutinize budgets and programs to see if the public's tax money is being spent properly. This is the foremost of the press's responsibilities, whether in New York, Washington, and Ottawa or in Des Moines, Sacramento, and Dallas.

Unfortunately, there has been a noticeable decline on the part of major elements of the press in coverage of government. So-called soft news (features, "news you can use") dominates many newscasts and newspapers.

The Economic Function

The public needs information about products, goods, and services in addition to events. Business, industrial, and agriculture news conveys this information, but so, to a large extent, does advertising. (Advertising, it should be noted, although much maligned by consumers, is what pays the bills. Without it, there would be no newspapers or broadcasts as we now know them.)

Advertising often is criticized for being in bad taste, and some of it is. You might, for example, find a commercial for a laxative offensive, but the

In its sentry function, the media's responsibility is to keep the public informed of current and upcoming problems. The rise in homelessness in the 1980s, for example, was brought to many people's attention through the media.

presentation probably is not. The big question about advertising is this: Can advertising techniques be used to sell ideas as well as automobiles? Or, to put it another way, "Can advertising cause people to buy something they don't need or to vote for one candidate rather than another?" There is disagreement, but most people subscribe to the "limited effects" notion of mass media. That is, consumers have psychological defenses by which they resist and mold messages from the mass media, including political advertising and product advertising, to fit their own needs. Consumers are neither children, unable to understand a commercial, nor zombies, powerless to resist. Advertisers seek brand-name recognition, not control over minds.

The Sentry Function

The press watches society's horizons. What is peeking over the horizon to challenge us tomorrow? The growing importance of computers, patterns of change in criminal justice, crime by very young children, and issues of obscenity and censorship on the Internet all became public knowledge because the press brought them to people's attention. In other words, the press must report not only what is happening today but also what is likely to happen tomorrow. When the United States became involved in the social, political, and economic difficulties of Central America in the 1980s, many experts thought the press had failed in its duties as a sentry. They believed that journalists who lacked understanding of the region's culture, history, politics, and economics had not alerted the nation to the true extent of the problems there. On the other hand, the press is doing a good job in the 1990s alerting us to threats to the environment.

The Record-Keeping Function

The mass media should reflect an accurate record of local, national, and world news. Who was elected to the school board? What bills passed Congress? What happened to the price of oil? Who died? Who won and who lost in sports? Who filed for bankruptcy? Who filed to run for public office? This function, too, is basic. The journalism of big headlines and splashy news programs depends on the underpinning of record-keeping. Consumers need to know many basic things, including the data often found tucked away in the back of the paper.

The Entertainment Function

Mass media consumers need diversion as well as information. The comics, entertaining feature stories, and pictures help meet this need. The business of the press is serious, of course, but the audience is made up of people of all ages and interests. Few newscasts or newspapers should be without an entertaining or light element.

The Social Function

In times long past, people got their news from their neighbors on a person-to-person basis. Today, the mass media perform this function. "Did you watch 'The Tonight Show' last night?" is a reflection of the social function. The media substitute for simpler relationships of the past.

The Marketplace Function

The press provides the forum in which all sorts of ideas are presented; it becomes the marketplace of ideas. If the audience is concerned about the environment and conveys this concern through the press, then perhaps something will be done. If citizens don't want their trees to be cut down for a street-widening project, they turn to the forum of the mass media to generate support. Thus, a city's agenda is reviewed: Do we want wider streets for more efficient moving of traffic, or do we want the trees to remain and the automobile's dominance of our lives to be curtailed?

The Agenda-Setting Function

Scholars of the media have added another function to the list, the agenda-setting function. This function is summarized by the comment noted earlier, "While journalists don't tell us what to think, they do tell us what to think about." This new concept suggests that far from dictating our thoughts—a power once believed available to the mass media—the media have the power to determine what we talk about as individuals and address as a nation. If the media place saving the environment on the agenda, then the people will begin to pay more attention to improving the environment.

The media sometimes use their agenda-setting function to place certain issues, such as the need to protect the environment, before the public.

It is almost impossible ever to isolate the effects of the mass media, because certain causes are too complex to trace. Certainly, the media play a role in setting the agenda. In a drought, the media emphasize that responsible citizens conserve water. And water usage drops. But no one knows what exactly is cause and what exactly is effect. And here is a large question: Who sets the agenda for the mass media? Can the government place an item on the media's agenda (the war on drugs, perhaps) and then have the media place it before the public?

Evaluating the media in your city or community can make you aware of how well they perform their various functions.

Evaluating the Media

How well is the press performing its agreed-upon functions? No one can read all the newspapers and magazines; no one can listen to all the radio and television newscasts. But you can monitor your own news agencies. To evaluate the media you use, try this system.

Newspapers

Study your local newspaper. Is it choked with self-seeking publicity releases? Are local issues and problems ignored in favor of Associated Press stories from afar? Is government on the local level covered thoroughly? Does the editorial page contain a lively and readable forum

through a letters-to-the-editor column? Is an occasional longer and
more thoughtful letter published
with special prominence? Do the editorials treat local issues, candidates,
and problems, or do they comment
only on national and international
issues? Do the sportswriters really
cover the sports scene, with probing
stories and questions, or are they
cheerleaders for the athletic programs? Are "minor" sports covered?
Are the same people in the paper
every day, with little coverage of
minority or low-income groups? Does
the paper have in-depth or investigative stories? How much space is
devoted to stories of crime and violence? How much space is devoted to
trivia: bridge columns, advice-to-the-
lovelorn columns, and the like?

Radio

Listen to your local radio station or
stations. Is the news mostly noisy bul-
letins and yesterday's stories culled
from a newspaper? If the city faces a
storm emergency or national disaster,
does the station provide continuous,
up-to-the-minute information? Are
the news reporters disc jockeys who
read wire service reports, or are they
real journalists? Is there an excessive
amount of sports reporting? Are
there special programs centered on
critical *local* issues? Are any in-depth
interviews ever aired? Do all talk
shows represent just one side of the
political spectrum? Is there a forum
for opposing viewpoints?

Who's Number One?

People often ask journalists and journalism educators to name the nation's best newspaper. A common answer is *The New York Times*. Beyond that, however, the best paper for any one critic could be a 10,000 circulation daily in Western Texas or Southern California or Upstate New York or Downstate Illinois. There's no real way to know.

Here are some of the larger papers consistently mentioned as outstanding by journalists:

The Washington Post

The Christian Science Monitor

The Miami Herald

The Philadelphia Inquirer

The Wall Street Journal

The Los Angeles Times

The Chicago Tribune

The Boston Globe

The Des Moines (Iowa) *Register*

The St. Petersburg (Florida) *Times*

Newsday

The Bergen County (New Jersey) *Record*

San Francisco Chronicle

Chicago Sun-Times

Dallas Morning News

Detroit Free Press

Houston Chronicle

Cleveland Plain Dealer

Minneapolis Star-Tribune

San Diego Union-Tribune

The News and Observer in Raleigh, North Carolina, also has acquired a national reputation among smaller papers, as have *The Oregonian* of Portland, Oregon, *The Times* of Seattle, and *The Eagle-Beacon* of Wichita.

The Best Small Papers

The National Newspaper Association honored some of the nation's best community newspapers in a publication called *Community Newspaper Showcase of Excellence*. The list included the following:

The Herald Times (Bloomington, Ind.)

Ledger Dispatch (Antioch, Calif.)

Daily News Record (Harrisonburg, Va.)

Cranberry Journal (Mars, Pa.)

The Riverdale Press (Bronx, N.Y.)

Federal Way News (Federal Way, Wash.)

The Fauquier Citizen (Warrenton, Va.)

Ozaukee Press (Port Washington, Wis.)

Hungry Horse News (Columbia Falls, Mont.)

The Tigard Times (Tigard, Ore.)

Bainbridge Island Review (Bainbridge Island, Wash.)

Hood River News (Hood River, Ore.)

Kiel Tri-County Record (Kiel, Wis.)

Morenci Observer (Morenci, Mich.)

Monticello Times (Monticello, Minn.)

Television

Watch your local television newscasts. How much of a 30-minute newscast is devoted to commercials? How much local news is presented? How much sports? How much weather? Does the station use its newscast to entertain you or to inform you? Do the anchors and reporters devote precious minutes to inane chatter? Are there ever any in-depth or investigative stories? How much time is devoted to such trivia as shopping center promotions, key-to-the-city presentations, and parades? Do the stations save their best—or most preposterous—stories for ratings sweeps periods?

Magazines

The general-interest magazine with a huge circulation is a thing of the past. *Life, Collier's, Redbook, Look*—names out of journalism history—folded or changed so as to be unrecognizable. Except for *Time, Newsweek*, and *U.S. News & World Report*, today's magazine is apt to appeal to a narrow, special interest. There are magazines for every hobby and line of work, from baseball-card collecting to, yes, journalism (*Quill*, for example). Judging their performance requires special expertise, but some observations can be made. For example, is the magazine fair even when it has a preconceived position? A magazine promoting gun control should be fair to opponents of gun control, and vice versa. Are the articles varied in nature—some light, some serious? Are the graphics up-to-date or old-looking? Does the writing fit the overall tone of the publication? As for the three major news magazines, they are prime targets for study. Identify one important issue and read the coverage it receives in each publication. What can you conclude about the magazine from what you read, especially on the question of fairness? Does it seem to have a political bias? What differences in tone can you identify among the three magazines?

Application to Scholastic Journalism

Many of the questions raised in this section apply to school, or scholastic, journalism as well. As you work on your school newspaper, yearbook, news bureau, or broadcast, give some thought to how these questions pertain to you.

The Ethics of Journalism

Fair play is a cherished idea in American life. People expect justice to be blind. They demand honesty from public officials. They require all institutions—schools, churches, courts, Congress, the presidency—to set high standards. Throughout society, value is placed on right over wrong. Journalists are no exception to these expectations, nor should they be. Just as people expect the Sunday afternoon football game to be an honest contest, they also expect honesty from the press.

Many people, however, are alarmed about the state of journalism. More and more, polls indicate the audience is wondering just how fair and honest journalists are.

The 1980s brought an outbreak of unusual violations to journalism. Several reporters were caught making up stories or parts of stories. Janet Cooke of *The Washington Post* had to give back a Pulitzer Prize, journalism's highest honor, when it was discovered that the main character in her prize-winning story, an eight-year-old heroin addict, didn't exist.

Cases of plagiarism came to public attention. There were incidents of "composite characters," fictional characters a journalist had created by using characteristics of several real people. In some cases, quotations were found to be made up. These problems eroded public confidence in the press to the point where some citizens want to pass laws regulating journalists' behavior.

Credibility

Thoughtful journalists are alarmed, too. They know the value to society of a free press. They also know how valuable the credibility of the press—that is, its ability to be believed and trusted—is. To restore that credibility, journalists today are putting more emphasis than ever on their ethical standards. Erring journalists find their colleagues in no mood to tolerate or forgive unprofessional conduct.

Many things govern journalists: time, space, economics, competition, geography, and the law. But it is the journalist's ethics, above all else, that provide the daily working guidelines to decide what gets into print or onto the airwaves. The responsible journalist tries to serve the audience's best interest.

Various codes of ethics, one of which is reprinted in this chapter, have been written and agreed upon by journalists. These codes all suffer from one fact: They are not enforceable by law. The Constitution's First Amendment states: "Congress shall make no law . . . abridging the freedom of speech, or of the press." It would be unconstitutional to jail a journalist who violated the ethical codes. A journalist who violates the *law*, of course, faces the same penalties as any other citizen.

Nor is it possible to require licensing or exams for journalists like those doctors and lawyers must pass. Licensing laws also run afoul of the Constitution. You can stop buying an unethical newspaper or stop watching the unethical newscast, but you can't lock up a journalist for a violation of ethics unless he or she has actually broken the law.

The framers of the Constitution believed a free press, even though occasionally irresponsible, is vastly preferable to a government-controlled press. Does that mean that newspapers, for example, may print anything they please, without regard to consequences? No. The law does play a role. If a newspaper prints libel (false defamation), it may be required to pay money to the libeled person. But note that this penalty comes *after* publication, not before. Prior restraint—the halting or forbidding of publication—is not permitted in the United States except under the rarest of circumstances, usually pertaining to national security in wartime. Government censorship is against the law.

With the protection of the Constitution and our customs supporting the right to publish, what keeps journalists honest? The answer is: ethics—devotion to journalists' cherished idea of fair play.

Accuracy

Ethical journalists subscribe to the previously mentioned codes, enforceable or not. Journalism attracts high-minded people who are devoted to serving their audience. Their principles are many, and the highest of these is accuracy.

To the ethical journalist, *accuracy* has a special meaning. Close doesn't count. Names must be spelled exactly right, down to the middle initial. A journalist cannot say a person lives at 1010 Sycamore Street if the address is really 1010 Sycamore Drive. There is no such thing as a small error. No one lacking a sense of detail should go into journalism. It is not sufficient to bat .300 or even .400, averages that would get a baseball player into the Hall of Fame. For journalists, the batting average must be 1.000. They must be accurate, in every detail, all the time.

How often does the press achieve this super-accuracy? Not often enough, of course. If you have ever been the subject of a news story, you may have observed an error. Maybe your name was misspelled, or your year in school was wrong. What was the effect, for you, the next time you read a story in the newspaper that had spelled your name wrong? Of course, you doubted what you read. Even the smallest mistake reduces credibility. Check. Double-check. Ask the source another question. Never guess about anything. And never forget the importance of fair play.

Objectivity

Another of the journalist's highest principles is objectivity, the state of mind that journalists acquire to make them fair, neutral observers of events and issues. Journalists do not permit their personal feelings, their likes or dislikes, to color news stories. (Opinion, of course, is to be desired in columns and editorials.) You may not like a speaker or what is said, but you report it straight, without any hint of your own feelings. You may think Kiwanians or Ku Klux Klan members or any other group is wrong, but you report what they do and let the audience decide.

Some people say that objectivity is impossible, that it is impossible to have opinions and not let them show. Even if this is true, which we doubt, the journalist still must strive for that ideal.

If you find the idea of objectivity hard to grasp, think in terms of neutrality, fairness, impartiality, balance (that is, telling all sides of a story), and honesty. Whatever you call it, the fact is that journalists must set aside personal feelings. Always seek to provide the audience with unbiased accounts of the news. The journalist who vows to do this has taken a long first step on the road to professionalism.

The article in the "On Display" feature on page 36 demonstrates objectivity in reporting by presenting both sides of a volatile school issue in an evenhanded, nonjudgmental way.

Other Ethical Principles

Accuracy and objectivity are perhaps the two most important ethical principles journalists try to live by. But they are by no means the only ones. Some other important precepts follow.

Seniors Demand Sophomore Disqualification

by Tim Nicholson, from The Tower, *Grosse Pointe South High School, Grosse Pointe Farms, Michigan.*

Stating that the Sophomore Class utilized adult help in the construction of certain Homecoming decorations, the officers of the Senior class have submitted an appeal which has delayed the announcement of Spirit Week winners.

Senior Class officers submitted an official letter of appeal 10:30 a.m. Saturday. Because of the protest, all the Homecoming and Spirit Day awards were given to the Senior Class except for the best banner award, which is involved in the appeal. The announcement that an investigation was pending was made during halftime of the football game.

Specifically, the letter of appeal charges the Sophomore Class with not adhering to the Homecoming by-law stating that "All spirit week projects should be the work of the students." The by-law also states that "Any other (than the students) will result in disqualification."

The Senior Class officers claim that the sophomores hired Kinko's Copy Center to assist in their outside banner production. The seniors also point out that since the sophomore outside banner was produced with the aid of a professional, the inside banner may have also been produced in such a manner.

Members of the Sophomore Class were outraged.

"It really takes the heart out of everyone who put hard work into spirit week," said Sophomore Class President Cheryl MacKechnie.

MacKechnie said that she worked on the outside banner and no outside help of any kind was utilized. According to MacKechnie, the banner was drawn on graph paper and then scaled up until it fit the banner. She does not understand where anybody would get the idea that Kinko's had anything to do with it.

She did say, however, that the devil which adorned both banners and the Sophomore Spirit Day shirts was a non-original tattoo adapted for their purposes.

Eric Shulte '98 said he was in charge of the four artists who designed the inside banner for the sophomores. He also expressed anger.

"I have drawn and done artwork since I was a kid. This is a real insult to me. The seniors just can't handle the fact that sophomores beat them," said Shulte.

Senior Class officers said they are simply asking for an investigation.

"I think it's important that all the classes follow the Homecoming by-laws. I know for a fact that everything the seniors made for Homecoming was made by seniors only. It upsets me that our senior artists worked hard all summer preparing for Homecoming when other classes may not have been in compliance with the by-laws. My hope is that the right and just decision is made in this matter," Senior Class President Gretchen Carter said.

The investigation itself will be led by Assistant Principal Paul Pagel, according to Student Association (SA) Adviser Rod Scott. According to the Homecoming by-laws the SA president, adviser and proper administrator are in charge of any disqualification. Scott said who has the final say on the issue is not clear.

Pagel would not comment on the issue.

Christine Galnore, SA president, said that the SA is not trying to accuse the Sophomores of cheating. She said that "we (the SA) are just trying to be fair to everyone and find out what really happened."

Galnore stressed that a decision cannot be made on hearsay and she, Pagel and Scott will only go with what they positively know is fact.

Scott said that the investigation will most likely take a few days and all parties involved are being met with in order to establish factual information.

Good taste. Avoid sensationalism, and stay away from sexually explicit material. Sex and crime are subjects that require extreme caution in reporting and editing. Seek understatement, not overstatement. Never glorify bad behavior. Do not invade the privacy of others. Avoid profanity.

Simultaneous rebuttal, or right of reply. If you must print or air criticism of someone, permit that person to respond to the criticism *in the same story*. It is not enough to run the criticism this week and the response next week. The response may never catch up with the original criticism.

Fairness to all. Everyone in your audience—regardless of race, color, philosophy, religion, gender, age, or economic status—has an equal right to expect to be treated fairly. Do not apply different standards to different people or groups.

Plagiarism. Do not pass off the work of others as your own. No matter how much you like someone else's lead or phrase or story, you may not publish it as if you had written it. This is an absolute. You may quote from others' work, but you must give credit. In most classrooms, students are failed for this offense; in the newsroom, reporters are fired for it.

Attribution. Identify where the information came from ("the President said today. . . .") so the audience can judge for itself the value of the information. Do not use anonymous sources.

The truth. Never fake anything—your identity as a journalist, a quote, a photograph, a detail. Report only what you know beyond a doubt. Never speculate or guess.

This list is incomplete and is, in some ways, abstract. It is, however, sufficient to make the point: Journalists must play fair.

Before turning to a discussion of legal issues, read the ethical code that follows. It is the code of the Society of Professional Journalists (SPJ), expressing in forceful language what most ethical journalists believe. This society, based in Indiana, is the nation's largest journalistic group, including professional and student chapters all over America.

Society of Professional Journalists' Code of Ethics

Preamble

Members of the Society of Professional Journalists believe that public enlightenment is the forerunner of justice and the foundation of democracy. The duty of the journalist is to further those ends by seeking truth and providing a fair and comprehensive account of events and issues. Conscientious journalists from all media and specialties strive to serve the public with thoroughness and honesty. Professional integrity is the cornerstone of a journalist's credibility.

Members of the Society share a dedication to ethical behavior and adopt this code to declare the Society's principles and standards of practice.

Seek Truth and Report It

Journalists should be honest, fair and courageous in gathering, reporting and interpreting information.

Journalists should:

- Test the accuracy of information from all sources and exercise care to avoid inadvertent error. Deliberate distortion is never permissible.
- Diligently seek out subjects of news stories to give them the opportunity to respond to allegations of wrongdoing.
- Identify sources whenever feasible. The public is entitled to as much information as possible on sources' reliability.
- Always question sources' motives before promising anonymity. Clarify conditions attached to any promise made in exchange for information. Keep promises.
- Make certain that headlines, news teases and promotional material, photos, video, audio, graphics, sound bites and quotations do not misrepresent.

They should not oversimplify or highlight incidents out of context.

- Never distort the content of news photos or video. Image enhancement for technical clarity is always permissible. Label montages and photo illustrations.
- Avoid misleading re-enactments or staged news events. If re-enactment is necessary to tell a story, label it.
- Avoid undercover or other surreptitious methods of gathering information except when traditional open methods will not yield information vital to the public. Use of such methods should be explained as part of the story.
- Never plagiarize.
- Tell the story of the diversity and magnitude of the human experience boldly, even when it is unpopular to do so.
- Examine their own cultural values and avoid imposing those values on others.
- Avoid stereotyping by race, gender, age, religion, ethnicity, geography, sexual orientation, disability, physical appearance or social status.
- Support the open exchange of views, even views they find repugnant.
- Give voice to the voiceless, official and unofficial sources of information can be equally valid.
- Distinguish between advocacy and news reporting. Analysis and commentary should be labeled and not misrepresent fact or context.
- Distinguish news from advertising and shun hybrids that blur the lines between the two.
- Recognize a special obligation to ensure that the public's business is conducted in the open and that government records are open to inspection.

Minimize Harm

Ethical journalists treat sources, subjects and colleagues as human beings deserving of respect.

Journalists should:

- Show compassion for those who may be affected adversely by news coverage. Use special sensitivity when dealing with children and inexperienced sources or subjects.
- Be sensitive when seeking or using interviews or photographs of those affected by tragedy or grief.
- Recognize that gathering and reporting information may cause harm or discomfort. Pursuit of the news is not a license for arrogance.
- Recognize that private people have a greater right to control information about themselves than do public officials and others who seek power, influence or attention. Only an overriding public need can justify intrusion into anyone's privacy.
- Show good taste. Avoid pandering to lurid curiosity.
- Be cautious about identifying juvenile suspects or victims of sex crimes.
- Be judicious about naming criminal suspects before the formal filing of charges.
- Balance a criminal suspect's fair trial rights with the public's right to be informed.

Act Independently

Journalists should be free of obligation to any interest other than the public's right to know.

Journalists should:

- Avoid conflicts of interest, real or perceived.
- Remain free of associations and activities that may compromise integrity or damage credibility.
- Refuse gifts, favors, fees, free travel and special treatment, and shun secondary employment, political involvement, public office and service in community organizations if they compromise journalistic integrity.
- Disclose unavoidable conflicts.
- Be vigilant and courageous about holding those with power accountable.
- Deny favored treatment to advertisers and special interests and resist their pressure to influence news coverage.
- Be wary of sources offering information for favors or money, avoid bidding for news.

Be Accountable

Journalists are accountable to their readers, listeners, viewers and each other.

Journalists should:

- Clarify and explain news coverage and invite dialogue with the public over journalistic conduct.
- Encourage the public to voice grievances against the news media.
- Admit mistakes and correct them promptly.
- Expose unethical practices of journalists and the news media.
- Abide by the same high standards to which they hold others.

Sigma Delta Chi's first Code of Ethics was borrowed from the American Society of Newspaper Editors in 1926. In 1973, Sigma Delta Chi wrote its own code, which was revised in 1984 and 1987. The present version of the Society of Professional Journalists' Code of Ethics was adopted in September 1996.

Libel Law

"If you print that I'll sue you for everything you own!"

Gulp.

Hearing someone threaten to sue you is an unpleasant experience. Stay in journalism long enough, however, and chances are fair that it will happen eventually. And if you go to court, the case will likely involve libel—or at least an accusation of libel.

Libel is printed false defamation of character. (Spoken defamation is slander, which we include under the general heading of libel.) To defame someone is to reduce that person's reputation. For libel to have occurred, you must have written something false.

Should an accusation of libel arise, the journalist needs to be prepared. And that includes the scholastic journalist. The student press is not exempt from libel law.

Libel laws are complex and changeable. Each court ruling provides subtle shifts in the law. One year it seems the press can print almost anything; the next year the law seems very restrictive. Libel laws vary from state to state and often involve whether the person libeled is a private person, a public figure, or an elected official. What follows is a general overview.

First, libel is seldom considered a crime. It is usually a civil action, heard in a civil court. Commit burglary and you go to a criminal court, where the docket says: "State vs. John Smith." Libel cases are actions between citizens; the docket says: "Johnson vs. Jones." The person asserting that libel has occurred, that his or her reputation has been reduced, is the plaintiff. The person accused is the defendant. The penalty involves a money judgment, which can run into millions of dollars, awarded to the plaintiff.

What can reduce a person's reputation? "She cheats on exams." "He is immoral." "She is a liar." "He falsified his academic record." The possibilities are endless. Certainly, the gravest libels occur when one's basic morality, decency, or wholesomeness is questioned. Any publication of information that harms a person requires the greatest of care. In scholastic situations it should be avoided virtually all the time.

Assertions that someone is dishonest, associates with criminals, committed a crime, has a loathsome disease, or has general low character are dangerous. Proceed with special care. Remember that even if you *may* print or air such a story, you may decide *not* to for ethical reasons. Be aware that there is often a distinction between what you can get away with and what is right.

Defenses Against Libel

The best defense against a successful libel suit is good reporting. Check all facts. Get the other side. Let the accused person respond to any charge. Run corrections quickly and prominently.

Other defenses exist should you be sued.

Truth. The courts have made it clear that no publication will be held responsible for libel if the story in question is true.

For example, suppose that you learn that thirty years ago the mayor of your city was convicted of burglary. He spent one year in prison for it. If you decide to run that story, and there is proof (that is, if the story is true in the eyes of the jury), you are almost certainly safe from successful libel action.

But that's only part of the story. You may *not* be safe from an invasion-of-privacy suit. That's a suit in which the plaintiff in the example says, "Yes, that's true about the burglary charge. But since that case I have had no further trouble with the law. In fact, I went to college, earned two degrees, and have been a successful banker and civic leader since then. I have a family and attend church regularly. To dredge up that old case invades my right to be left alone and to live in peace."

You probably would lose a privacy suit.

Legal questions aside, however, be aware that in such cases as these the responsible journalists do the right thing: They serve the audience as a whole and its members as individuals. What good is served by bringing up the old case? If you are fair, honest, and ethical, legal questions usually take care of themselves.

Another possible trap is the misconception that attribution is always a defense in libel cases.

Suppose Eric Sutton accuses Jill Keaton of being a criminal and you report it this way: "Sutton said Keaton had been convicted of burglary." Your sentence is *true*; that is, Sutton *did* say that about Keaton. Since truth is a defense, can you be sued successfully?

The answer is yes, if the charge is false, because you spread the libel. You published it, and the damaged person can recover damages from you. You plead that you did, after all,

Having been advised that they "would be responsible for any libel" contained in their story, CBS in 1995 decided not to let Mike Wallace of *60 Minutes* run a report critical of the tobacco industry.

Worth Quoting

As the free press develops, the paramount point is whether the journalist, like the scientist or scholar, puts the truth in the first place or in the second.

—WALTER LIPPMANN

attribute the information to Sutton. You lose. The principle is, "The one who publishes pays." You cannot duck a libel charge merely by saying that all you did was report accurately what someone else said. Attribution is no defense.

Privilege. There are some exceptions. You may report whatever is said in an *official* legislative or judicial session without fear of a successful libel suit, provided your account is accurate and fair.

What is said on the floor of Congress or the state legislature or in a courtroom is *privileged*, meaning publication of such statements is immune from libel suit. If Eric Sutton accuses Jill Keaton in an open courtroom or on the floor of the state senate, you may print it without fear of a successful libel suit. If one senator says another is a liar, you may print that statement (with attribution, of course). The principle is that the public has a large stake in knowing what goes on in a courtroom or in the legislature. The press, therefore, may report such activities without the chilling effect that the fear of a suit can have.

And that suggests a major point. It may seem to you that the laws are in favor of the journalist. But this country has a deep, fervent commitment to open public debate. Our courts have a general fear of anything that restricts the information needed for that debate to be successful. Remember that a free press is one of the foundations granted in our Constitution. That freedom, properly handled, protects everyone, not just the person who owns the medium.

One last note about truth as a defense: To win a suit, the jury must believe you. What you know to be true may not seem so to the jury. Your witness may not be believed or may refuse to testify. Your documents may not be admitted into evidence. Be careful.

Fair comment. Another defense against successful libel suits is known as fair comment and criticism.

You are free to venture any opinion in reviewing books or records, theatrical events, movies, and the like. This is because a person who, for example, writes a book is thrusting himself or herself onto the stage and virtually asking for comment. If you review this book and say it's bad, the authors won't sue. If you say it's bad because it doesn't have a chapter on the responsibilities of the media, however, the authors may sue. You may express a negative opinion, but the facts you state must be true. For your defense of fair comment to convince a judge, you must explain the facts upon which your opinion is based. If your *facts* are right, your *opinion* is protected. Remember also that you must limit your comment to the public part of a performance or creative work. You cannot claim the defense of fair comment if you say a singer's record album is bad and he is also a thief.

Admission of error. A prompt correction of a published article that has been shown to be false is both a legal and an ethical responsibility. It is only right that you admit it if you're shown to be wrong and run a correction to set the record straight. To do so in a libel case can help if you go to court. In effect, you are saying to the judge, "Yes, there may be libel here but it wasn't malicious. As soon as we found out we were wrong, we ran a correction." This may reduce the money judgment against you. In some states, special statutes make it a more complete defense.

Don't overlook the dangers presented by careless layout. For example, you would be in trouble if you have a photograph of the homecoming queen above a story on drug use or drunken driving. The implications would be read by all. Here, too, if such a mistake slips through, you should run a correction as soon as possible.

Other Points of Libel Law

This general overview cannot touch on all the minute details of the law of libel, which fill whole libraries and have broad constitutional implications. But a few more points need to be made.

The examples mentioned thus far usually refer to newspapers, but the laws and principles apply to broadcasts, yearbooks, magazines, and material on-line as well.

Also, when it comes to libel, some plaintiffs have a tougher time winning their case in court than others. Elected public officials—for example, the President, a U.S. senator, or the mayor—must show a greater degree of *fault* by the press in order to win a libel suit. The senator who thinks he or she has been libeled must not only show the damage (as all plaintiffs must) but must also show that the press either knew it was printing a falsehood or exercised reckless disregard for the truth.

Both of these circumstances are rare, for the press generally does not knowingly print lies or *recklessly* disregard the truth. The idea here is, again, the country's commitment to open debate. The courts have said that for such debate to occur, the man

> **Worth Quoting**
>
> When a man assumes a public trust, he should consider himself as public property.
>
> —THOMAS JEFFERSON

Under the concept of privilege, anything said on the floor of Congress, in the state legislature, or in a court is immune from a libel suit.

or woman who has *sought* office must accept the criticism and attention that come with it.

In addition to the obviously public person, the courts are continuing to define others who must show a high level of fault by the press in order to win libel suits. The police chief is a public figure even if not elected. But what about the beat patrol officer? The custodian in the police station? Such distinctions are difficult and should never be decided without the aid of counsel. The best thing is never to get into libel trouble. The worst is to try to handle it without expert help.

"Successful" Libel Suits

The alert reader may have noticed that virtually every reference to a libel suit has been qualified by calling it a *successful* libel suit. If you have an absolutely airtight defense, you won't lose the suit. But that doesn't mean you won't be sued in the first place. Anyone can sue anyone, and lawsuits are financially and emotionally draining.

Wise editors avoid lawsuits even if they think they can win. Exercise extreme care as reporters, editors, and photographers. (Yes, pictures can be libelous, and they can invade privacy.) Avoiding suits and being ethical are better than counting on legal technicalities. Also, get the other side in the initial story. People who see their side in print seldom sue.

Finally, who can sue? Anyone, as we have said. And who can be sued? The editor? The publisher? The answer is that anyone involved in producing the libelous material may be sued—the reporter who wrote the story, the editor who assigned the story, the editor who drew the layout, even the copy editor who wrote the headline or caption. All these people can be sued—for everything they own.

Limits on Scholastic Journalism

On January 13, 1988, the U. S. Supreme Court handed down a decision involving the censorship of a school publication. The Associated Press covered the case, known as *Hazelwood School District v. Cathy Kuhlmeier.* An excerpt from the AP's report appears below.

> The Supreme Court on Wednesday gave public school officials broad new authority to censor student newspapers and other forms of student expression.
>
> The court, by a 5–3 vote, ruled that a Hazelwood, Mo., high school principal did not violate students' free-speech rights by ordering two pages deleted from an issue of a student-produced, school-sponsored newspaper.
>
> "A school need not tolerate student speech that is inconsistent with its basic educational mission even though the government could not censor similar speech outside the school," Justice Byron R. White wrote for the court.
>
> He said judicial intervention to protect students' free-speech rights is warranted "only when the decision to censor a school-sponsored publication, theatrical production, or other vehicle of student expression has no valid educational purpose."
>
> The dissenting justices accused the court of condoning "thought control," adding, "such unthinking contempt for individual rights is intolerable."

This cool and carefully worded report gave no hint of the debate, heat, and confusion that the court's decision would create in the ensuing years. Generally referred to today as "Hazelwood," the case and the ruling remain at the center of debate over student expression in secondary schools. The arguments on both sides of the issue are fervent and genuinely felt by their partisans.

One side says, "The First Amendment of the Constitution applies to all citizens, including high school students, and therefore school administrators have no right to interfere with what's published in a school newspaper."

The other side says, "The school newspaper is a school-sponsored activity, and the principal is the publisher of the paper, acting on behalf of the citizens of the school district, and therefore has the ultimate, legal control over what's published in the paper."

Before examining in detail the many issues raised by Hazelwood, it is helpful to understand the thinking and legal decisions that predate it.

The Tinker Decision

Until about thirty years ago, most people who thought about it assumed that control of student expression naturally rested with school authorities. The concept of *in loco parentis* seemed to cover the question. Under this legal idea, school authorities acted "in the place of the parent," and assumed a parent's rights, duties, and responsibilities. Some people accepted this idea. Some still do. Some do not.

In 1969, during the uneasy years of the Vietnam War, the U. S. Supreme Court addressed the question of student expression, if not the entire concept of *in loco parentis*, in the case of *Tinker v. Des Moines Independent School District*. Before Hazelwood, the ruling in the case was the court's major statement on student expression.

In the case, three students in a Des Moines, Iowa, school decided to wear black armbands to protest the war. School administrators suspended the students, and the students sued. They lost in district and appeals courts but won when their case reached the U. S. Supreme Court. Said the court:

> **First Amendment rights, applied in light of the special characteristics of the school environment, are available to teachers and students. It can hardly be argued that either students or teachers shed their constitutional rights to freedom of speech or expression at the schoolhouse gate. . . . In our system, state-operated schools may not be enclaves of totalitarianism. School officials do not possess absolute authority over their students. Students in school as well as out of school are 'persons' under our Constitution.**

Later, the court added that students and teachers "are possessed of fundamental rights which the state must respect, just as they themselves must respect their obligations to the State."

Although the Tinker case did not involve student journalists or free press questions, subsequent court rulings made it clear that the principles applied to student journalists. Prior restraint (censorship) of student journalists was held to be illegal unless the material to be censored was libelous, obscene, an invasion of privacy, or "materially and substantially" disruptive of the school.

In his book *Freedom of the High School Press*, Nicholas D. Kristof observed, "In essence, Tinker viewed the school as a public forum where expression must be tolerated. According to forum theory, once the government opens a public forum—be it a park, street, plaza or school—it cannot regulate the debate therein. . . ."

The Tinker ruling meant that student editors had the legal right to decide what would go into the paper, yearbook, or broadcast. But if the students wanted to print obscene material, they could be stopped. Nor were libelous stories or stories that invaded someone's privacy protected. Advisers or administrators spotting this sort of material had the right to overrule the students. This also was true if the students printed material that threatened to disrupt the school environment.

Still, and this is true today, it was not the law that truly governed behavior. Ethics (what is right, not just what is legal), compromise, experimentation, teaching-and-learning tactics—the whole array of elements at work in a school environment came into play. Most principals and advisers and most students worked within a reasonable framework, and legal difficulties were rare.

And that brings us to the Hazelwood decision.

Following the Supreme Court decision in his favor, Hazelwood East High School principal Robert Reynolds speaks to a journalism class.

The Hazelwood Decision

Here are the facts of the case.

In 1983, staff members of *The Spectrum*, the student newspaper of Hazelwood East High School in Missouri, prepared a series of stories about student pregnancy and the effects of divorce on students. The principal, Robert Reynolds, deleted the two pages of the paper on which the stories were to have appeared. Reynolds said he blocked the stories because they invaded the privacy of the students involved, even though they were unnamed. He feared they could be identified anyway.

"He also believed," the Supreme Court said in its ruling, "that the article's references to sexual activity and birth control were inappropriate for some of the younger students at the school."

Reynolds took the position that he was publisher of the newspaper and as such could determine its contents.

The students sued. A federal trial judge ruled in favor of the school district. But the Eighth U. S. Circuit Court of Appeals ruled for the students.

When the U. S. Supreme Court came down on the side of school authorities, it said: "A school may in its capacity as publisher of a school newspaper or producer of a school play 'disassociate itself' not only from speech that would 'substantially interfere with its work . . . or impinge upon the rights of other students' but also from speech that is, for example, ungrammatical, poorly written, inadequately researched, biased or prejudiced, vulgar or profane, or unsuitable for immature audiences." The court said only that censorship must be "reasonably related" to educational goals.

The language was too broad for some people, and reaction came swiftly.

Mark Goodman, executive director of the Washington, D.C.-based Student Press Law Center, an organization that provides legal help to students in censorship cases, said that within hours of the decision, he received two calls from students complaining of censorship where none had existed before. Both cases involved stories about AIDS.

Many, but by no means all, school administrators responded favorably. So did many commercial newspapers, which appeared to favor the argument that the principal of a school has the same power to control content as the publisher of a commercial newspaper. Others argued that this is a bad analogy. They said that what a publisher does is his or her business because the newspaper is part of private enterprise. but, they say, what a principal does is society's business and cannot be capricious or arbitrary, just as police officers and judges cannot be capricious or arbitrary. The difference between a commercial and a student newspaper, this reasoning goes, is that in a school, the publisher is the government—and the United States has never permitted government control of the press.

Arguments for and against. What follows is a look at some of the specific arguments on either side of the Hazelwood dispute.

Some people say school administrators should have the final say about what goes into the newspaper or yearbook because if there is a successful libel suit, the school will have to pay. Others argue that libel is a minuscule problem in a school setting, that lawsuits are extremely rare.

Nevertheless, the other side responds, should a suit occur—rare event or not—it is the school that pays. Student advocates say this: If schools grant students the responsibility for what they print, then the students inherit the responsibility to pay any libel judgments. Naturally, it is pointed out that students do not usually have money to pay such judgments. But nowhere is it written that only the well-to-do have the right to publish. If you sue a poor person for libel and win, you may win only a moral victory—and not any money.

This argument (who has the ultimate legal responsibility?) remains unsettled. It should be pointed out, however, that a principal who watches carefully what his or her students are printing might be doing so out of concern for the school's legal liability.

Another argument is that student journalists are too young and too inexperienced journalistically to make mature judgments about what to print. For some, this is a compelling argument. There are, indeed, risks in permitting student journalists the power of the press. Apart from legal problems, feelings and reputations can be damaged. Mistakes hurt. People in the news are not abstractions; they're humans, and they need to be handled with care.

On the other hand, many student journalists are surprisingly sophisticated and, if they receive proper guidance from well-trained and well-educated advisers, usually can be trusted to do the right thing. Students who embark on irresponsible paths often can be convinced of the error of their ways by their advisers. Many educators believe it is better to teach, to tell why something is wrong and should not be printed, than it is to issue a direct order against publication.

Some people say control of yearbooks and newspapers belongs exclusively to the school because the classes that produce the papers and books are just that: classes. Student activities. Just as the biology teacher controls her class and the history teacher controls his—both guided by the principal—the journalism teacher also exercises control. This is a good argument, all the better in schools where the publications are financed by the school and credit is granted for working on them.

Hazelwood has caused other controversies. How, ask critics of the decision, is it possible to teach First Amendment values in a school where students are censored? What of the educational value of good journalism classes? Aren't they meant to be learning experiences and doesn't Hazelwood undermine them? These questions worry not only journalism advisers and students but school administrators.

Limits on Hazelwood. If a publication is exclusively a class project and used only for training and practice by student journalists, it is difficult to argue for student control. But not even this issue is totally black or white.

The Hazelwood decision brought a great amount of comment on both sides of the issue. Here is a small sample.

"The Hazelwood case . . . involve[s] two separate and very distinct issues. One is a constitutional question, the right of a public school to control its own publication. The other is an educational question, the wisdom of exerting such control in ham-handed fashion."

—*Roanoke* (Va.) *Times & World-News*

"The 5-3 majority is basically correct in upholding the authority of educators over students of this age. But . . . [i]t's a pity that the justices . . . could not find space to admonish school systems to wield their power with wisdom, care, and restraint."

—*The New York Times*

"The real world is different. In a grown-up world, an editor is subject to a publisher. If the publisher says, 'Kill the piece,' that's it, sweetheart, the piece is killed."

—James Kilpatrick, syndicated columnist

"Justice White said the courts may intervene when censorship serves no 'valid educational purpose.' If this decision brings gross abuses, then student journalists will be back in court with justice on their side."

—*Saginaw* (Mich.) *News*

"[W]hat is a student to believe when taught about a free press and the First Amendment in class if the free expression of the school's own journalists is suppressed?"

—Henry Reichman, *Censorship and Selection: Issues and Answers for Schools*

"The reality of newspaper publishing includes making responsible decisions about what to print, in order to avoid unnecessary lawsuits. . . . To assume that these decisions are most appropriately left to the student journalist escapes all reason."

—National School Boards Association/National Association of Secondary School Principals

"As a teacher I don't think I can realistically teach what the First Amendment is and what it means unless I can turn around and practice it. . . ."

—John Bowen, high school journalism adviser

"[I]f we're preparing students . . . to face the real world and to be productive citizens . . . they have to be exposed to as much reality as they can handle."

—Edmund J. Sullivan, Director, Columbia Scholastic Press Association

"[Hazelwood] has caused us to be more careful. It's going to be on our shoulders to prove that we're responsible enough to handle the rights."

—Linda Puntney, Executive Secretary, Journalism Education Association

"[I]f there is no educational, scholastic freedom . . . then all [students] learn is to bow down to whatever particular governmental authority happens to be in charge of the rules at the time."

—Jack Harkrider, high school journalism adviser

"Do we want a generation of potential journalists coming through a system that doesn't encourage freedom of the press? What's going to happen ten years down the road from here?"

—Richard Johns, Executive Director, Quill and Scroll, International Honorary Society for High School Journalists

The Spectrum, the student newspaper at the center of the Hazelwood case, was determined by the Supreme Court not to be an open forum. Had it been ruled a forum, the court's decision might very well have gone the other way. Under Forum Theory, once the government creates a forum, it cannot control the ideas expressed there. A forum is a place where ideas are exchanged. A city park, where people climb on soapboxes and tell what they think, is a forum. Many universities have a mall or a "speaker's corner" where people may speak. These areas are protected by society, and the ideas expressed there are protected as well. If a school newspaper is a forum, Hazelwood probably does not apply.

A school newspaper that has been declared a place where members of the school community exchange ideas—through columns, letters to the editor, guest columns—may be in a different legal position than a pure lab newspaper produced by students for practice and training. This in no way should affect student conduct or judgment, of course. Again, it is not the law that governs student journalists. It is their sense of ethics, of right and wrong.

Some states question Hazelwood itself. The Iowa, Colorado, Arkansas, Kansas, and Massachusetts legislatures have passed bills that, in effect, sidestep Hazelwood. Even before Hazelwood, California had a statute protecting student press rights. Such legislation has been introduced in several other states and is in various stages of the legislative process. Many individual school districts also have made it clear they will stick with the Tinker rules despite the Hazelwood ruling.

How can this be? Isn't federal law the last word? Yes. However, states may grant *more* freedom than the federal government; they just can't grant *less*. So in this case, state and local rules can prevail—if that's what local citizens want.

The research shows without a doubt that there has been a large increase in censorship in high schools since Hazelwood. Some people remain unconvinced, however, about Hazelwood's effect. Although many advisers express dismay over the decision, others say, "This case is no big deal."

One of the most sensible reactions to the decision came from student press scholar Bob Trager. In a Phoenix speech just two months after the Hazelwood decision, Trager urged the following course of action:

> In the majority of schools, where teachers, administrators and students have been uncertain about the place of journalism in the curriculum and the extent to which students should be able to exercise their First Amendment rights, Hazelwood may spur additional discussion and reflection on these matters. And that can be to the good.

Students, the publications adviser and school administrators should exchange views on freedom of expression. Ultimately, maybe they can reach a consensus, one that can be put into a formal, written policy. It should include a recognition of students' freedom to report, write and express their views. Remember, Hazelwood didn't prohibit that—it just said administrators could censor student-written material if they choose to. The goal here is to give them a reason not to.

The policy also should make the adviser's role clear—to teach, guide and be a sounding board for student journalists.

If administrators do review material before publication, they should commit to discussing with the students any concerns they have, so they can be resolved in a timely manner, and so students can learn from the experience. And there should be a means to appeal unfavorable decisions.

Discussions leading to such a policy could begin by focusing on the Hazelwood decision itself.

Wrap-up

Public confidence in the press has fallen. Journalists are often seen as rude and insensitive, at least in part because they are the bearers of unavoidable bad news.

Journalists have many roles assigned to them by society. Their coverage of government fulfills the political function expected of a constitutionally protected free press. Advertising provides information about products and services. As the press surveys the horizon and alerts the public to what's "out there," it fulfills the sentry function. Sports scores, birth announcements, and the like keep society's records. Comics, feature stories, and other light fare entertain people. Information in the mass media provides daily material for conversation and thus enhances people's social lives. And the media help set society's agenda, which can lead to solutions.

Various ways exist to evaluate the media. Interested citizens can compare newspapers, radio, television, and magazines with professional standards.

Journalists try to meet the ethical standards that, more than the law, guide their work. Journalists are expected to be accurate and objective. Their standards emphasize good taste, fairness, care with attribution, and a devotion to truth.

A large problem for journalists is libel. Published material that is both false and damaging to someone's reputation can lead to a lawsuit with heavy financial penalties for erring journalists. Truth is the best defense for journalists. There is no libel without falsity.

The legal situation for scholastic journalists changed greatly in 1988 with the U. S. Supreme Court's ruling in the Hazelwood case. In that case, the court said school officials can legally censor student newspapers and other forms of student expression if the censorship is related to educational needs. The decision tightened up on scholastic journalism freedoms from censorship that seemed to be implied in the 1969 Tinker decision.

Educators and even journalists are divided over whether the Hazelwood decision was good or bad, and there is disagreement over its long-term effects on scholastic journalism.

The decision permits a school principal to assume the role of publisher of the student newspaper. In that position, the principal can control the paper's content. Nothing in the decision requires censorship, and many school districts continue to grant students and advisers final say over the paper. Some states have passed legislation reaffirming this freedom.

School newspapers that are open forums for the exchange of ideas are generally considered exempt from the Hazelwood ruling.

People on both sides of the Hazelwood controversy agree that the responsibility of student journalists is unchanged. The emphasis must remain on accuracy, fairness, objectivity, balance, good taste, good judgment, and good sense.

On Assignment

Individual Activities

1. Write a brief definition or explanation of each of the following terms.

   "composite characters"   credibility
   ethics   fair comment
   Forum Theory   *in loco parentis*
   libel   objectivity
   plagiarism   prior restraint
   privileged statements   right of reply
   slander

2. Test your critical thinking. Have a class discussion about the following news issues. If possible, invite local news executives to class and ask them to comment on these issues:

   a. Is it true that the press is preoccupied with "bad news"? If not, why do so many people have this misconception? What dilemmas do news people face trying to balance news that the audience wants with news it needs?

   b. In what kind of a climate do your local media operate? For example, do the same people who own the radio and TV stations also own a newspaper? Is there only one local newspaper? Are the media locally owned or part of some larger news conglomerate? What do the answers to these questions imply about media independence and competitiveness?

   c. What dilemmas do editors and news executives face because of lack of time and space? Are there any solutions?

   d. Do editors and news executives receive enough feedback from the audience? Do they want more? What would they do with it?

   e. How good is the talent pool from which editors and news executives draw their employees? Are potential employees as skilled in the use of the language as they once were? If not, what does that imply for the news organization and for you, as a consumer?

   f. Whose fault is it when the facts come out wrong in a story? Is it always the newspaper or station's fault? Might it be the fault of the news *source*? Or might the "error" be in the minds of the audience?

   g. How much do reporters use anonymous sources? What ethical questions are involved in using such sources?

   h. If editors and news executives had unlimited money to work with, what would they change? Would the editor buy a new press or hire more good reporters?

3. Write a brief essay on each of the following situations. Be prepared to discuss your position in class.

   a. You're a reporter for your school paper. You're covering a meeting of the board of education. In the middle of the meeting, the president of the board turns to you and says, "I'm sorry, but this part of the meeting is off the record. Please stop taking notes and do not report any of this in the paper." What do you do? Why?

b. You are in the school cafeteria and you overhear two school administrators discussing "the massive number of students who cheat." Do you have a story? How would you proceed? Why?

4. Assume that you are the principal of a high school and you have learned that your school's newspaper intends to publish the following stories. In each case, tell what you would do and why you would do it.

a. A student has created a disturbance in the cafeteria, turning over tables, throwing food, and upsetting an urn of hot coffee. He was subdued and taken to a local hospital for psychiatric observation. The school newspaper wants to run a story about the incident, using the student's name and photographs of the damage.

b. An editorial is planned criticizing the football coach for pressuring the parents of the students he coaches into buying kitchen appliances from him.

c. Newspaper staff members investigating the all-school activities fund, money intended to support all the school's clubs and organizations, have discovered that school administrators have spent the entire fund to support the basketball team. The staffers want to run a story.

d. Members of the student council have circulated a petition in the school to have the council's faculty adviser replaced. The school paper wants to run a story.

5. Assume that you are the editor of the school newspaper for which these articles are planned. In each case, tell what you would do and why.

Team Activities

6. Working in teams, prepare a code of standards for the publications in your school. Compare your code to the First Amendment standards of a free press and to the Code of Ethics of the Society of Professional Journalists reprinted in this chapter. Review the codes prepared by the class teams. Working as a class, prepare a code for your school.

7. Following the steps outlined in activity 6, prepare an editorial policy for your newspaper. Get input from your adviser and school administrator before finalizing the policy.

The calls for legal help come to Jane Kirtley at all hours of the day—and night.

Kirtley, a former reporter turned lawyer, is executive director of the Reporters Committee for Freedom of the Press, a voluntary, unincorporated association of reporters and editors devoted to protecting the First Amendment. The committee is there to assist reporters and media organizations whenever their ability to report the news is threatened by those who would place limits on the First Amendment guarantees of freedom of speech and freedom of the press.

"It's the kind of job that can take over your life," Kirtley said. "But the rewards far outweigh the negatives. It's a perfect job for anybody who loves the First Amendment and journalism."

Kirtley believes the responsibility of the media is to act as watchdog, looking out for the readers' best interests. Any attempt to limit or control the ability of the press to do that must be fought.

"The overriding journalistic ethic is to inform the public," she said. As a journalist, one must "tell the truth as best that you determine it at the time, and trust the public to have the judgment and the sense to take the actions that are necessary to ensure preservation of our democratic system."

Kirtley has overseen the legal defense and publications efforts of the Reporters Committee since 1985. She also edits the group's quarterly newsletter, *The News Media & the Law.*

Before joining the Reporters Committee in 1984, Kirtley was associated with Nixon, Hargrave, Devans & Doyle, a law firm that specialized in media law. She also worked as a reporter for the *Evansville Press*, the *Oak Ridger*, and the *Nashville Banner.* She is a member of the New York, District of Columbia, and Virginia bars.

Kirtley warns of hard times ahead for the media if the public doesn't change its attitude toward the press.

"There is a lack of public understanding of the importance of the media," Kirtley said. "We're on the cusp of radical change. For the last ten to twelve years or so the public has felt it had no stake in press freedom. They felt the media was part of the problem and not the solution."

The public is starting to demand restrictions, she said, that go against the principles of the First Amendment. "If the members of the public don't see a relationship between free speech and free press, then we have a major problem," she said.

Kirtley fears that as new communication technology, such as the Internet, is developed, government officials will find less resistance from the public to attempts to regulate it.

"I do worry that since the new technology vendors are not traditional media, the public won't look at regulation that same way it would if it were CBS News or *The New York Times* being regulated," she said.

Kirtley serves on many advisory boards and committees, including the First Amendment Congress, the Libel Defense Resource Center, the Student Press Law Center, the ABA National Conference of Lawyers and Representatives of the Media, and the editorial board of *Government Quarterly.* In 1993 she received the Distinguished Service Award from the Newspaper Division of the Association for Education in Journalism and Mass Communication, and in 1994, the John Peter and Anne Catherine Zenger Award for Freedom of the Press and the People's Right to Know from the University of Arizona.

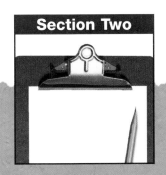

Gathering News for the School Newspaper

Chapter Three

Deciding What Is News

Chapter Four

Organizing the Staff to Capture the News

Chapter Five

Making the News

Deciding What Is News

Key Terms

news judgment

advance

localization

timeliness

proximity

prominence

consequence

human interest story

conflict

brainstorming

random sample

filter question

Key Concepts

After reading this chapter, you should

- understand how definitions of news have changed over time
- recognize the influence of *USA Today* on modern news approaches
- be able to measure news values by audience interest and need
- recognize the classic elements of news: timeliness, proximity, prominence, consequence, human interest, and conflict
- know how to generate ideas by brainstorming
- understand the basics of obtaining information by polls

The three chapters in this section are about gathering the news. And that's a more elusive activity than it once was.

We used to think of news in relatively simple terms. News equaled events. News was automobile accidents, airplane crashes, violent weather, earthquakes, fires, slayings. News was meetings, press conferences, speeches, births, marriages, deaths. Known today as "hard news," its boundaries were not hard to define.

Then life in the twentieth century became more complex, and the nature of news changed. The press moved away from events and concentrated on trends, on in-depth coverage of major issues. News was intricacies of government, damage to the environment, the changing family, population control, educational reform, automobile safety, health care.

At the same time another change started to take place. The news began shifting away from government, social issues, and "where are we going in this society?" Several factors account for this change of direction: declining literacy, loss of young readers, a drop in circulation generally, the mobile society ("Everybody just moved here. They don't care about the city council"), television's need for ratings and the consequent emphasis on

Stories about calamities such as tornadoes or hurricanes are always of interest to readers.

the upbeat or the spectacular, a feeling that people had had enough of "bad news." As someone said, "People are tired of reading about famines in Ethiopia."

USA Today pioneered the new attitude. Colorful, upbeat, optimistic, unconcerned with covering City Hall, *USA Today* was a tremendous hit. Many journalists, eager to find the solutions to the problem of a declining audience, have followed *USA Today*'s lead. These journalists believe readers are bored with government news, with endless stories about squabbles over cable television companies, sewage plants, urban development, and which neighborhoods to zone to accommodate new shopping malls.

Other journalists argue that the press has a role to play and society needs the same kind of news it always did, *with emphasis on government.* Yet many acknowledge that the changes that have taken place are based on economic realities. Perhaps it comes down to a choice like this: a newspaper that compromises its definition of news or no newspaper at all.

So what is news at the end of the twentieth century? It is "all of the above." Events, of course, are still covered. So are trends. But to these add lifestyles of the rich and famous, fashion, health, the arts, leisure, exercise, sex, parenting, recreation, nutrition, film, video, music. The list is endless, because it encompasses all of modern life.

Changes that sweep through society do not go unnoticed by teenagers, of course. Today's school newspapers, yearbooks, broadcasts, literary magazines, and Web home pages reflect the change. What interests teens? Everything from AIDS to grades.

Scholastic journalists wisely have broadened their approaches to the news. News of homecoming dances, international exchange students, new teachers, football games, and the like is still covered by alert scholastic journalists, but today there is much more. It is not uncommon to find student journalists examining school budgets, performance on standardized tests, teacher tenure cases, and lifestyle issues. Teens worry about getting into college, about pregnancy, about how to fit in at school, about abortion—and teen journalists respond with information on such issues.

This change makes some people nervous. They don't like to see stories about the dangers of drug use or sexually transmitted diseases. Yet these are realities for teenagers as the twenty-first century dawns. Once, long ago, the most serious problems in high school classrooms were about on the level of chewing gum or passing notes in class. But times have changed.

The Internet has added a new and as yet undefined element to newsgathering, among both professional and scholastic publications. Now, for good or ill, the world is a few keystrokes away. It can be easier to download a document from a library in South Africa than to get an appointment with a school administrator. Where once student journalists had to scour their exchange papers for story ideas, all they have to do today is conduct a Net search and in no time at all hundreds of documents on any subject are on their screens.

The information superhighway can be like rush hour in Boston—chaotic!—and only Web-wise travelers should venture on. It is easy to find information today. Making sense of it, sorting it out, is the challenge of the twenty-first century. Journalists need to be as skeptical as ever when dealing with the Internet: Just because something is in cyberspace doesn't make it true or accurate.

News Judgment

It is the journalist's job to evaluate what's "out there" and to select what will interest, inform, educate, amuse, or amaze the audience. Decisions have to be made about what's important and what's not, about balancing what the audience wants against what it needs.

How do journalists do this? They use news judgment, their own good sense in determining, for example, which of a dozen items should be included in a story and which should be in the first paragraph or first on the newscast.

No one is born with news judgment; it's something one absorbs through experience, through attending to the mass media (reading newspapers and magazines; watching newscasts; cruising the Internet) and through hard work.

Historically, journalism teachers and texts have gone into some detail about the so-called elements of news or news values. These include such things as timeliness, proximity, and prominence. These elements and others will be examined in detail shortly.

The "Who Cares?" Method

A quick shortcut to news judgment can be found in the "Who Cares?" method. That merely means asking yourself who cares about this story, person, event, or issue. If you can honestly say there is genuine interest, or

An event that directly affects your school, such as the introduction of closed-circuit broadcasting, would pass the "Who cares?" test for inclusion in the school paper.

that the story, person, event, or issue is important for the audience . . . then you have news. If there is neither interest nor need, skip it. Drag it to the trash. Hit the delete key.

Let's try the "Who cares?" method. Here are two simple events; one is news, one is not.

A. The mayor signs a proclamation designating next week as Clean-up, Paint-up, Fix-up Week.
B. The mayor announces an investigation into the disappearance of $75,000 from the city's general fund.

Now, who cares about each event? (This is childishly simple, but it makes a point.) Who cares about Clean-up, Paint-up, Fix-up Week? Practically no one. Politicians constantly issue such proclamations, mostly at the urging of special-interest groups. In this case, the special week is a lure for newspaper advertising from lumberyards, nurseries, seed stores, and paint stores. The media pay scant attention to such weeks.

Who cares about event B? The answer is—nearly everyone in the community. For taxpayers, and that includes practically every citizen, the handling of public money is a critical issue. The conduct of public officials draws intense concern in a democratic society. So, yes, event B is news Obviously, few news decisions in a journalist's life present such a clear-cut choice as those in this example. However, as a starter, think "Who cares?" and you'll be on your way to developing good news judgment.

Not all events are subject to such treatment. If your instructor had a fight with a neighbor, you might get a positive answer to the "Who cares?" question, but you wouldn't have news. Why? Because some things are no one's business. The journalist's duty is to rise above the level of spreading ugly stories that invade the privacy and upset the lives of innocent people. Like so many things in journalism, taste is the issue. One of your jobs as a journalist is to cull items that would offend the audience's taste. This, too, is part of news judgment.

The Elements of News

A warning bell should go off in your head when you come across an item in bad taste. A bell should also ring when an item is legitimate news. This is just another way of saying that news judgment is, to a great extent, intuitive. Seasoned journalists do not need such guidelines as timeliness, proximity, or prominence. Instead, they rely on the bells in their heads.

This is no help, you say, because you do not have bells yet. You have not acquired the intuitive judgment, a sort of sixth sense that allows you to weigh, often in a split second, the news value of an event. This is where the classic elements of news come in.

Depending on which authors you read, there are anywhere from five to twelve elements of news. Here are some of the most generally recognized.

Timeliness

Timeliness relates to the newness of the facts. It is this element that makes a story about football more timely in November than in June. A story lacks timeliness for the school newspaper if the daily newspaper downtown already covered the story at great length two weeks earlier. Instead the school paper might concentrate on advance items, stories about coming events.

Proximity

Proximity refers to the nearness of a given event to your place of publication. Events occurring in your school generally have more news value than those occurring on the other side of the world. People like to read about things they are familiar with, and they are more likely to be familiar with those things closest to home.

A story about the homecoming parade is timely if it is published near the time the parade occurs—not two months later.

This explains the reliance of most journalists on local news, about which a great editor once said, "A tomcat on the steps of City Hall is more important than a crisis in the Balkans." This is no longer true, of course, because today such a crisis has been seen to have far-reaching consequences that may dramatically affect the lives of your audience. What the editor said still makes a good deal of sense, however. To paraphrase him, "A minor dropout problem in our school is more important than a major problem in a school 500 miles away."

Prominence

Prominence refers to the "newsworthiness" of an individual. It is true that names make news, but some names make more news than others. Why? Because they are more prominent. Thus, if the star quarterback flunks a math exam and is ineligible for the big game, his troubles are newsworthy. Suppose you flunk the same exam. Is that news? Not unless there's some other factor involved. The quarterback, like it or not, is more prominent than you, and his failure is more far-reaching. "There goes the ball game," will be the reaction to the news of his failure. When people learn that you flunked, they'll shrug, mutter "How about that?" and go on about their business.

The element of prominence explains a great deal about how news is handled. It explains, at least partly, why the press follows movie stars, why it interviews the governor, and why it runs story after story about well-known persons.

Most newspapers put information most important to their readers on the front page. In the front-page sample in the "On Display" feature on page 65, you can clearly see the issues of significance for this edition of the paper.

Consequence

The element of consequence refers simply to the importance of an event. Let's use our star quarterback again as an example. It is more important to more people that he flunked the math exam than that you flunked it, because of the consequences. The team may lose the big game. Hundreds, maybe thousands, of football fans may be disappointed—or they may be thrilled at the performance of the substitute who gets his big chance and makes good.

The element of consequence, incidentally, offers many opportunities for stories that do not, on the surface at least, seem to have any news value.

EDITORIAL
Reek attack.
Neglected bathrooms
become hazard zones.   PAGE 3

VIEW
DMV with an attitude.
Long lines await students
who pay a visit to DMV.   PAGE 5

FEATURE
A night of starlight and magic...
Students will experience the "Roaring
'20s" during senior prom. It will be held
on June 3 at the Bonaventure Hotel in
Downtown Los Angeles, which is expected to be a dazzling event.
                              PAGES 6-7

SPORTS
Back to the playoffs...
Home runs are what the
baseball players are
thinking of in the first
round match-up against
Fontana High on Friday.
                              PAGE 12

GLENDALE HIGH SCHOOL

EXPLOSION

VOL. LXXVIII, No. 7   1440 E. BROADWAY   GLENDALE, CA 91205   MAY 17, 1995

Photo by Linda Hagopian
THE VOTES ARE IN— Several students turned in their votes on May 10 to elect the new ASB Cabinet for next fall. Out of all the juniors and sophomores, 800 students flocked to the polls to cast their vote.

Students go to the polls

Low turnout for uncontested ASB elections yields easy victory for the majority of next year's officers

* By Saujin Yi
  Asst. News Editor

In preparation for the upcoming school year, ASB elections took place on May 10 as Scott Greenwood came out triumphant as the next president.

With 800 students casting votes, the elections were regarded as a low turn-out considering the fact there was only one person running for each office except for director of publicity.

Along with Greenwood, the winners were the following: David Schmindlel as vice president, Adm Bareeghian as secretary, Kimi Nakazani as treasurer, Jill Stevenson as director of publicity, Melody Nazaryan as director of activities, Tina Yesayan as director of academics, Heather Keaton as director of assemblies, and Annie Joh

as interschool representative.

Greenwood, along with his officers, will focus their efforts on the school budget. They plan to have a written copy of the budget prepared during the summer.

The key to next year's officers is experience. All but one have been involved with ASB at some point.

"I'm looking forward to next year being a great year," Greenwood said.

With drastic changes as a result of the addition of the incoming freshmen, Greenwood hopes to ease the students into the high school atmosphere before school even begins in September. He sees them as the main prospect of yearbook sales and other money making events.

"Next year is going to be an interesting experience because of the two grades coming in," said ASB Adviser Cary Hollingsworth.

Welcome Party lessens worries

Newcomers flock to party

* By Stephanie Loo
  Co-View Editor

The "Welcome Party," an event where new incoming students were welcomed, was held last Friday in the south gym. The event aimed to provide an opportunity for incoming Glendale High students to visit the school.

All eighth and ninth grade students from Wilson and Roosevelt middle schools were invited to experience a high school event through 5th Quarter, the sponsor of the event. Students also had the chance to meet a few of the administrators and teachers.

For a mere $3, it became their passport to all the pizza, music, and dancing they could handle in one night. Many other activities such as a bungee run, a velcro wall, and a slide show were available for students to enjoy, as well as sports tournaments with prizes.

The "Welcome Party" was supervised by GHS staff and administrators, community volunteers, Wilson and Roosevelt middle school staff, and resource officers from the Glendale Police Department.

With a total of more than 1,000 potential freshmen and sophomores, about 500 to 600 students attended the "Welcome Party."

"The Welcome Party' was a success," said Ross Arnold, the Dean of Students at GHS. "It gave a good introduction for [new students] to pave their way next year."

"This was a unique event because the two classes from Roosevelt and Wilson came together for a night of fun, food, and friends," said Cary Hollingsworth, ASB adviser and biology teacher.

Duane Hagen

Former GHS art teacher passes away

* By Alexis Scallon
  News Editor

This evening at 6:30 at Cresse Mortuary in Eagle Rock, memorial services will be held for former art teacher Duane Hagen, who died Sunday after suffering a stroke at the age of 64.

Hagen retired two years ago after teaching at GHS for 30 years as a dedicated and an inspiring teacher in

See HAGEN/Page 2

Barajas family to receive Lilia's class ring

* By Stephanie Hsu
  Asst. Feature Editor

In memory of Lilia Barajas, who was tragically killed after the Homecoming Dance on Nov. 11, Jostens is graciously donating a class ring to her family, which will be presented during the annual PSMA assembly on June 2.

Lilia was struck by a speeding car driving on the wrong side of the road, after departing from the dance at the Castaway restaurant in Burbank.

Barajas suffered major head trauma and was taken to Harbor-UCLA Hospital, where she later passed away November 12. Barajas' death, 16-year-old Gonzalo Espinoza, also sustained a broken arm. Barajas was buried at San Fernando Cemetery in Mission Hills.

Homecoming was Barajas'

Photos courtesy of Stylus
THE RING—A gift from Jostens will be given June 2 to Lilia's family.

first formal dance, and according to friends and family, she was extremely excited to be going. Nov. 11 also marked the day of her 16th birthday.

Three separate parties were being held at The Castaway restau-

rant, and people from each party were questioned. Police failed to capture the hit-and-run driver of the speeding car after weeks of investigation.

An 18-year-old male, who was thought to be the perpetrator, was also questioned about the accident.

He was later released after passing a polygraph test proving his innocence in relation to the accident.

"The [Barajas] family is both very happy as well as very sad to receive the ring," said Jessica Barcena, Lilia's aunt. "The fact that she is not here to receive it saddens

us. But the fact that the ring will be presented in her honor makes us grateful."

A Jostens representative will present the Barajas family with Lilia's class ring.

BELOVED DAUGHTER AND SISTER
LILIA BARAJAS
1978 — 1994
NO MATTER WHERE WE ARE.
NO MATTER WHAT WE DO.
WE'LL ALWAYS BE THINKING OF YOU.

For example, if the state legislature passes a bill providing state financial aid to local school districts, you should recognize that this action, even though it took place in the state capital, has important consequences for your school. Ask school officials how much money will come to your school and what will be done with it.

This is an example of localization, the act of bringing out the local angle in a story. Another example would be the effect on construction plans for a new school in your town if steel or railroad workers went on strike. It is important to keep up with the news outside your school; you never know when an item in a daily newspaper or a periodical will lend itself to localization.

Human Interest

What are you, as a human being, most interested in? Chances are you are most interested in other people and how they behave. Human interest stories cause readers to laugh or cry, to feel emotion. If a little girl is trapped for days in an abandoned well, that's a human interest story. If a dog mourns at his master's grave, that's a human interest story. If that substitute quarterback mentioned on page 64 throws five touchdown passes, that's a human interest story. In other words, human interest stories are unusual. They are about the shortest basketball player, the fastest track runner, the youngest teacher, or the oldest custodian. They tickle the funny bone or evoke feelings of sorrow, pity, or amazement.

Animals or children are usually good topics for human interest stories. Photos can draw readers' attention to the page.

The element of human interest explains why newspapers run a story when a fifteen-year-old genius graduates from college, or when a bride on her way to the wedding gets lost and ends up at the wrong church. The fact that the world has one more college graduate is of no particular significance in itself, nor is the fact that someone got married. But wouldn't you want to read a story about a fifteen-year-old college graduate or a lost bride? Yes, and so would many other people. It's human interest.

> **News Arithmetic**
>
> The idea of "News Arithmetic" comes from *Editing the Day's News* by George Bastian and Leland Case. It may give you some idea of what constitutes news.
>
> 1 ordinary person + 1 ordinary life = 0
>
> 1 ordinary person + 1 extraordinary adventure = NEWS
>
> 1 husband + 1 wife = 0
>
> 1 husband + 3 wives = NEWS
>
> 1 bank cashier + 1 spouse + 7 children = 0
>
> 1 bank cashier - $20,000 = NEWS
>
> 1 person + 1 achievement = NEWS
>
> 1 ordinary person + 1 ordinary life of 79 years = 0
>
> 1 ordinary person + 1 ordinary life of 100 years = NEWS

Conflict

An element of news that enters into many stories is conflict. Why do so many people attend sports events? Conflict. Why are so many people interested in elections? Conflict, at least partly. Why are strikes and labor disputes news? Conflict. Why are wars, to take the most extreme case, news? Conflict. Conflict involves tension, surprise, and suspense. (Who will win the football game? Who will win the election?) People are in an almost constant state of conflict with their environment. Former husbands and wives fight over who will win custody of their children; homeowners fight to keep taverns from opening in their quiet neighborhoods; doctors fight to discover cures for diseases that kill their patients; and countries fight for supremacy in the world arena.

Other Factors

There are many other elements of news, including progress, money, disaster, novelty, oddity, emotions, drama, animals, and children. It would serve little purpose to discuss these at length. Just keep in mind that news judgment rarely involves a simple matching of an event with a list of elements to determine whether the event is news. Professional journalists may not be able to define news, but they know it when they see it. As a student, you just have to develop a system of warning bells. Determining news value is not an exact science. You can't expect to rely on formulas. You're not a physicist; you're a journalist.

Maybe you're one of those people who's on-line every night and could be writing textbooks about it yourself. Then again, maybe you're not. If you're in the second category, the following information about this important trend is for you.

A basic explanation of the Internet is found on page 17. Here are answers to some of the questions that may have arisen as you read through that explanation:

How do I get on the Internet? Besides a computer and a modem, you need some software to connect you. That software can be had through subscribing to a big on-line service such as America Online, CompuServe, Microsoft Network, or several others. The software available from each service connects you to the service; and the service, in turn, gives you access to certain parts of the Internet as well as to material and assistance—for example, an airline reservation system—that only that service has. You can also connect through providers that don't offer other services or help. AT&T, for example, intends to have such a system.

What is the World Wide Web? The Web is a service that hooks up a great number of sites on the Internet and lets the user have easy access to them. The Web sites are pages that may contain text, pictures, sound, and even animation. By clicking on certain links on a page (often words in color) you can connect to other pages that give more information; for example, clicking on the link "Hillary" in a news story about President Clinton will take you to the First Lady's activities that day.

Access to the Web is available through nearly all providers by using a browser, or a program that lets you get to the information on the Web. *Netscape* and *Mosaic* are two commonly used browsers, but there are others.

What do those labels beginning with "http" mean? The labels are really addresses of sites—or home pages of individuals, organizations, or groups—on the Web. For example, just now *USA Today* can be found at

http://www.usatoday.com/. The **http** part stands for the means the browser must use to get to the source; it's short for HyperText Transfer Protocol. The **www**, of course, stands for the Web; and **usatoday** is the host name, the computer where that newspaper (or other resource) physically lives. The **com** at the end lets you know that the computer is run by a company rather than an educational institution (**edu**) or government agency (**gov**).

If there's so much information out there, how do I know where to find what I'm looking for? If you know the exact address of a site, you can, of course, get to it easily. Many people keep their own lists of sites they've been to and want to revisit. But if you're just looking for, say information on the country of Bosnia, you can go to various directories and indexes, sometimes known as search engines. With a search engine like Yahoo!, for example, you can go to the category *Bosnia* and find a list of all Web sites that pertain to it. You may also find subcategories listed under Bosnia that offer material on related topics. Other search engines include *Lycos* and *Webcrawler;* all can be accessed at their own site addresses on the Web (for example, **http://www.yahoo.com**).

Look for news items that will satisfy readers' curiosity, and remember, there are no shortcuts. Telling you that "it isn't news if a dog bites a man, but it is if a man bites a dog" is of little help. If a dog bites the President of the United States, that's news. If a dog with rabies bites a child, that's news. Nor does it help to talk about having a "nose for news." There is no such thing. While it is true that some reporters seem to make a career out of being in the right place at the right time, it's because they have trained themselves to know where the right place is. Their noses have little to do with it.

Generating News Story Ideas

To begin developing interesting, newsworthy stories, your first step is to come up with possible story ideas. One way to generate ideas is for the newspaper staff to hold a brainstorming session. This method allows you to come up with numerous ideas within a short span of time.

It is important that staff time be used as efficiently as possible. Most newspaper and yearbook staffs meet for an hour a day; some meet only once or twice a week. There are stories to write, advertisements to sell, and pages to lay out. There is not a lot of time for discussions that end in long arguments without resolving the problems at hand. So use the brainstorming technique as a fast method of getting a lot of solutions, ideas, or alternatives for action in a very short amount of staff time. You can do it with large groups or you can do it with only two or three participants.

Brainstorming Sessions

Brainstorming, used effectively, will help you move from ideas into action quickly. Here is one proposal for staging a productive session. You can adapt it to your own needs and situations.

First, have the group leader—editor, business manager, or adviser—explain the problem to be considered. (Example: We are planning a special issue of the paper on problems facing today's graduate. What stories should be assigned?)

Give people a few minutes of "think time" in which to consider the problem. They might jot down two or three ideas.

Now have the group leader call on each participant, one at a time, to state a proposal for action in one short and complete sentence. Participants should not need to explain their thoughts or elaborate on them. There should be no discussion or criticism of any idea presented.

Brainstorming is an excellent way to come up with story ideas for the newspaper.

(To continue the example: How does one hunt for a job? What are the additional opportunities for education? Does the government offer various types of employment? How about military opportunities? How does a person establish residency for voting, in-state tuition fees, and other benefits?) Each idea is briefly stated; each can be the basis for a story.

As each idea is given, have it written down by a group recorder. You might want to put the ideas on the chalkboard or an overhead projector transparency.

Go around the group two or three times. Don't let people get by with stating what has already been said. Tell participants always to have more than one idea in mind, and urge them to let their imaginations run wild. Generally, the wilder the ideas the more totally productive the final results. No idea is a bad one unless it is not expressed. Participants can use ideas as springboards for expanding or building on suggestions of others. (Example: The original idea might have been, How does a recent graduate hunt for a job? Follow-up ideas might be, How important is the résumé? How do you arrange for and act during an interview? How do you know if the employer is really interested in you? Should you go to a placement company? Are job placement services available at our school? What references do you need?)

After you seem to have exhausted the input from the group, begin to narrow your list to one of top priorities. Here is where you can lose control, unless you are careful about procedure.

First of all, there is still to be no discussion of the list.

Have the group look over the suggestions. (If meeting time is a problem, have the recorder type the list and make each member a copy.) Have each participant select the five *best* ideas from the list or, if the list is small, the best two or three. Have participants write their choices down on a piece of paper *in order of priority*, with the best idea first. Don't let people try to influence each other; each person must evaluate the list for himself or herself.

Now compile the answers. You will see some common preferences rather quickly. Take the best choices as determined by "secret ballot" and put them into action.

The editors may need a brainstorming session on each of the best ideas to think them through to their final conclusions.

Advantages of Brainstorming

By now the advantages of this system should be obvious. To begin with, participation comes from every staff member on an equal basis. No one person can dominate the discussion; every idea is important and equal for purposes of group evaluation. Furthermore, a large number of ideas can be generated in fewer than five minutes; and the more you use the system, the better you get at it. One brainstorming session came up with 112 ideas in less than one hour on the question of how to restore public confidence in public education. Finally, valuable time, often wasted by lengthy dis-cussion dominated by a few, can be conserved for more vital functions.

Now, for what planning tasks can the brainstorming system be used? Why not brainstorm that question through for a starter? You might begin your list with "topics for editorials," "topics for in-depth stories," "ideas for photo essays." What else could be included?

The brainstorming process is easy, and it keeps getting easier with practice. Naturally, you will modify it to your advantage and to each situation. If meeting time is a real problem, you can even do it all in writing.

> **Brainstorming in a Nutshell**
>
> 1. Announce the topic, problem, or goal for the brainstorming session.
> 2. Allow participants a few minutes to think.
> 3. Each participant in turn offers a brief idea or suggestion.
> 4. No criticism of any idea is allowed.
> 5. A person designated as a recorder writes down all ideas as presented.
> 6. Participants offer additional suggestions, in turn or randomly.
> 7. All participants receive copies of the list of ideas, which they rank in order of importance.
> 8. All rankings are compiled; top ideas are further discussed and/or acted on.

Information from Polls

Some of the most interesting news stories are based on the results of polls. But getting legitimate information from polls can be tricky. Consider the following:

Not long ago, ABC's *Prime Time Live* aired a compelling story about a reporter who hitchhiked across America, from the Pacific to the Atlantic. Video of breathtaking autumn foliage from the reporter's New England beginning to stark desert shots as the trip continued contributed to a lovely video experience. As he journeyed across the country, the reporter made it a point to get close to the people who offered him rides, and he asked them all the same series of questions: Is America a better place or a worse place than when you were growing up? Is America more dangerous now than then? Has America deteriorated, its values shattered?

On the night the show aired, anchor Diane Sawyer looked into the camera with a straight face and announced that 90 percent of the people the reporter interviewed had said yes, the country has gone downhill. That would be scary except for one thing: The reporter's information and the opinions of those he interviewed are practically worthless except as anecdotes. They show nothing of any real value. Why?

For starters, the reporter's sample—the number of people interviewed—was far too small to provide any clue whatsoever about how the population as a whole might feel. He interviewed *thirty-one people!* You don't have to interview a million people to make a good generalization about how the whole population feels, but thirty-one is just not enough.

Furthermore, the reporter's sample was biased. It systematically excluded huge numbers of Americans: those too young or too old to drive, those who do not own motor vehicles, shut-ins, people in hospitals, people in class or at work. And, of course, it excluded all Americans who weren't driving the roads upon which he was hitching.

It's OK to report what thirty-one people said about America. It's bad journalism and bad science to suggest that the opinions of those thirty-one people have broad meaning.

Getting a Fair Sample

A 1991 Gallup Poll found that teenagers are extremely interested in reading polls of student opinion. Even the most casual study of high school publications shows clearly how student journalists are satisfying that interest. Polls are widespread in student publications. But unless done right, they can spread just as much misinformation as good information.

The key is this: *For a poll or survey to have a statistically high chance of representing not just those surveyed but the population at large, every member of the group to be surveyed must have an equal possibility of being included in the survey sample.* A sample so drawn is called a *random* sample, an important concept for would-be pollsters to know.

A properly created sample—one that complies with the definition just provided—will yield results at what is called the 95 percent confidence level; that is, in ninety-five of a hundred cases, the population sampled will respond the same as the total population the group is intended to represent.

This is why polls that, for example, predict the outcome of an election always say the poll can be expected to be accurate plus or minus x number of points. The doubt stems from the .05 percent of the time (in our example) that a random sample will be off.

What this means to the student journalist can be summed up easily: Be careful about leaping to conclusions about polls or surveys. If you go into the hall and stop the first ten people who walk by and ask them a simple yes-no question, that's fine. You may discover that eight of the ten rented a movie last weekend. You can safely report that. You *cannot*, however, say that 80 percent of the student body rented a movie last weekend, because you don't know that. After talking with ten people who just happened to be walking by, you have no information upon which to base a generalization. You need a *random* sample. What you get with people who just

To be accurate, polls must involve a carefully selected sample of participants who are asked thoughtfully constructed questions.

happen to walk by is called an *availability* sample. It's just an accident. Those were the ten strolling the halls when you were there asking about movies.

How many do you need to talk to in order to get a random sample? That's an important question in polls and surveys, but not as important as the one overriding principle that everyone in the group to be studied—often called the "universe"—has an equal chance to be in the sample.

Suppose you want to find out what the seniors in your school are going to do after graduation. Some options might include attending a private college, attending a public university, attending the local community college, entering the military, attending a technical school, and so on. The first thing you need to know is how many seniors there are. If yours is a small school and there are, say, just twenty-five seniors, you have no sampling problem. You don't have to worry about setting up a good random sample: Just ask all of them. And forget 95 percent confidence. You are at 100 percent.

If your school is one or two times larger than the first example, you might still survey all the seniors. A questionnaire distributed in such a way that every senior has an equal chance of receiving one would work.

Caution is in order again, however. You could ask the senior English teachers to distribute the questionnaire. That would catch most of the seniors. But perhaps not *all* of them. Are there seniors who finished English while still juniors? Seniors on occupational tracks and therefore not required to take senior English? And what about those absent that day, or disabled and taking class via TV? They must have an equal chance to be surveyed, too.

Watch not only for bias built in to the process but also your own bias, even if accidental. You want to reach the seniors, so you ask your four favorite teachers, all of whom teach senior classes, to distribute a questionnaire. What's wrong with that approach is apparent: Your favorite teachers may all be in social studies. Therefore, students on auto-mechanic or industrial-arts tracks may be excluded. If your favorite teachers have class late in the school day, you might miss band members or athletes out of school and practicing late in the day.

So what do you do? Go to the school office, get a list of all the seniors, and see to it that each one gets a questionnaire, even if it means sliding one into everyone's locker. An even better idea is to distribute the questionnaires in senior homerooms. Now you're safe.

What if the school has five hundred seniors? Now the question of sample size is truly relevant. Generally, the bigger the sample, the more trustworthy the results (up to a point). How big is big enough might surprise you. A properly drawn sample of one thousand people can accurately represent the opinions of ten million.

Major public opinion pollsters routinely generalize to the entire population of the United States based on interviews with sixteen hundred people. Such a sample must be drawn upon with the population's overall characteristics in mind; that is, if 25 percent of the nation's population is over sixty-five, then 25 percent of the people in the sample must be over sixty-five. If 20 percent are African American, then 20 percent of the sample must be African American as well.

How Many Is Enough?

The chart that follows, from Dr. Philip Meyer's landmark book *Precision Journalism,* shows the sample sizes needed for various population sizes to get a 5 percent error margin at the 95 percent confidence level:

Population	Sample
Infinite	384
500,000	384
100,000	383
50,000	381
5,000	357
3,000	341
2,000	322
1,000	278

However, within that 25 percent of elderly or 20 percent of African Americans people are still selected randomly.

As a scholastic journalist, of course, you have neither the time nor the expertise to define your samples so precisely. Still, you can conduct reliable polls/surveys if you stick to the one main rule: Everyone in the sample has to have an even chance of being questioned.

So what would you do about those five hundred seniors? Assuming that for logistical reasons you cannot break the group down any further (male-female, Protestant-Catholic, parental incomes above or below $50,000 a year), you can still get accurate information.

No sample, random or otherwise, is considered reliable unless it includes at least fifty people. So that's the minimum number.

Asking the Right Questions

Sampling errors are not the only pitfall awaiting a survey-minded student journalist. The questions themselves must be carefully crafted. They must not be ambiguous.

"Do you smoke cigarettes?" is an ambiguous question. Tobacco use among teens, widely believed to be increasing, is a legitimate concern and one a student journalist might want to learn about. But "Do you smoke cigarettes?" won't generate much information. Does it mean the person being questioned smokes them every day—or just on his/her birthday? Does it mean one cigarette a day or two packs a day?

"Do you smoke cigarettes?" can be what is called (no pun intended) a filter question. If you ask that question and the respondent—the person you're interviewing—filters himself out of the survey by saying "no"—then you're finished with him. If the respondent says "yes," *now* you can zero in: Do you smoke more or less than one pack per day? Do your parents know and approve? Are you concerned about the health implications of smoking?

Questions need to be short and simple and should concentrate on only one item. Can you see the problem with a question like "Levi's jeans fit better and last longer. Do you agree or disagree?" A person might agree with the first part but not the second—so how should she answer?

Make sure you ask the right people the right questions, so that the people in your "universe" have a good chance of answering intelligently. For example, don't survey the freshman class on whether teachers in your school should have tenure. It's expecting a great deal of a freshman not only to know what tenure is but to have a reportable response.

Then there's the problem of reporters stacking the deck in the *way* they ask a question: "Are you going to go to college after graduation or just to a technical school?" "Are you going out for football or just joining the choir?"

Respondents can mess things up, too. Think about it: People all like to make themselves as cool, as important, as sophisticated, as well-informed as possible. So if a reporter comes along and asks a certain kind of question, might someone be tempted to stretch things a bit—or even if not, to give the reporter the answer he or she seems to be looking for?

Say that a reporter asks a student, "Did you consume alcohol last weekend?" (Probably a filter question, by the way.) Is it considered cool at your school to drink? Despite the fact that it is a medical certainty that alcohol is bad for people, there are individuals in the world—and probably in your school—who would say "yes" to the question just to seem cool. So report the results with a large grain of salt, or don't ask this sort of question in the first place.

A Few More Cautions

In doing a poll or survey, keep your eye on the calendar. That means watch carefully to see if so much time or so many events have gone by between the time you take your survey and the time you publish it that the results may no longer be valid. Suppose the football team at a major university in your state loses its first six games. A poll asks if the coach should be fired.

A majority says yes. A month goes by, in which the team wins four games. Is the poll still valid? Probably not. Drag it to the trash.

Be careful about conclusions. Just because two events occur together does not mean one *caused* the other. For example, 90 percent of the students randomly surveyed in your school say they rented movies last weekend. At the same time, the school district reports a schoolwide increase in SAT scores. Does that mean watching movies makes you smarter? What do you think?

Remember also that a survey in your school represents only your school. Even a good sample randomly created still represents only the universe studied. Thus, do not report that 90 percent of all students in the world rented a movie last weekend. You didn't survey all the students in the world.

A final word on polls and surveys: Many lend themselves to presentation through charts and graphs. Several software programs easily convert numbers to charts or graphs. This can cut down *the story* about the poll to a more readable size than if the results have to be recounted within the story.

Still, sometimes such charts and graphs can be silly: One school ran a pie chart to give the results of a poll that was split 48 percent to 52 percent. Clearly, a little common sense is in order.

The article in the "On Display" feature on page 78 is based on a poll. In addition to presenting poll results, the article also includes student reaction to the various data compiled in the poll.

Some Statistical Terms

If you really become involved in polling, you will probably use the following terms in analyzing your data:

Mean: *Mean* is another term for *average*. If the basketball team scores 50 points in one game, 75 in the next, and 100 in the next, compute the mean by adding the three scores and dividing by three. The mean score is 75 points a game.

Median: The median is the number "in the middle." That is, in a series of numbers, it's the one with the same number higher as lower. In this series of numbers the median is 10: 3, 4, 5, 6, 7, 8, 9, 10, 11, 12, 13, 14, 15, 16, 17.

Mode: The mode is the most frequent occurrence in a series. Suppose the grades for 200 students divide like this: 25 A's, 50 B's, 100 C's, 15 D's, and 10 F's. The mode is C.

Wrap-up

Once-easy ideas of what constitutes news—mostly events and government—have been revised in view of changes in society and in people's interests. Modern readers, with their busy schedules, appear to want shorter stories, often in list form, more color, and less "bad news." Because of *USA Today* and its colorful and upbeat approach, newspapers are changing. As literacy as well as circulation decline, journalists seek different ways to capture a greater share of an often mobile audience.

Teen Smoking Statistics on the Rise Since 1990

by Michele Kavooras and Palak Shah, The Panther, *Miami Palmetto Senior High School, Miami, Florida*

In the fifth grade when most kids were only studying the dangers of smoking, sophomore Jennifer Klinker was already learning the firsthand effects of nicotine.

"I quit in the sixth and seventh grades and I started again in the eighth grade," Klinker said.

Although most teenage smokers begin smoking later than Klinker, it is estimated by the end of high school 72 percent of high school students will have smoked a cigarette and 32 percent will be labeled as smokers.

Of 183 students surveyed at this school, 19.1 percent said they smoked regularly. However many students feel this statistic is too low.

"I think it is a lot higher than 19 percent. I think at least half the school has tried smoking cigarettes. I think 35 to 40 percent are smokers," junior Alberto Tassenelli said.

According to the survey most smokers began because they were curious or their friends influenced them. Either way, all smokers agree smoking is a method of relieving stress.

"I've tried to quit three times, but I can't because my friends still smoke around me. It is a stress reliever and I am allowed to smoke at home," senior Karli Hansen said.

For some students it took a while for the habit to slowly develop over the course of a few years. Yet for others it seems as if they were addicted virtually overnight.

"When I first started smoking my friends would always ask me why I smoked, then they would ask me for a drag. Then it seemed like overnight they were out buying their own packs. They were hooked really quickly," junior Joy Nicholas said.

Many smokers develop an addiction to nicotine, the most addictive substance in cigarettes, and find it very difficult to stop smoking. There are varying methods experts recommend to stop smoking.

"I've tried a nerve pinch in the ear, the patch, the chewing gum, and smokeless cigarettes. None of these methods worked for me," Assistant Principal Marion Rogers said.

Many times the habit cannot be broken and excessive smoking leads to bodily harm. Cigarettes are a carcinogen and many smokers develop lung cancer. It is predicted that there will be about 13,000 new cases of lung cancer in Florida this year and 153,000 people will die of this type of cancer this year. These statistics have been on the rise since 1990. They will continue to grow each year as long as younger people begin to smoke.

"It is very depressing but it is hard to quit. The only way to really influence someone is to see a parent or someone really close to you die of something like that," senior Ryan Baldwin said.

While eating in a restaurant many people are nauseated when a smoker lights a cigarette.

"I think the right to ban smoking in public places is fair. The people who don't wish to smoke have the right to breathe clean air in public places; however, smokers have the right to have a smoking section," Tassenelli said.

Many people do not want to breathe in secondhand smoke because of the harmful ingredients in cigarettes. Recently cigarette companies released a list of 599 possibly harmful ingredients. Among the ingredients is citronella, which is a type of insect repellent, and urea, an excretion from the human body.

With all of the scientific studies most smokers realize their habit is detrimental to their health but still can not kick the habit.

"I'm not sure why I smoke. I wish that I didn't, but I do," Nicholas said.

These changes concern some people who believe newspapers have a constitutional role to play that mandates coverage of government. But newspapers apparently must decide whether to compromise or fade. Thus, where once newspapers concentrated on government news, they now deliver information on all aspects of modern life, including fashion, health, the arts, leisure, exercise, sex, parenting, recreation, nutrition, film, video, and music.

Despite these changes, students are urged to read newspapers for knowledge of what editors consider news. Serious journalism students certainly need to be users of the news. Reading newspapers is a good way to hone one's news judgment.

Some people decide what is news and what is not by applying the "Who cares?" technique. This means assessing how much reader interest a story has. The more people who care about the information in the story, the greater its news value. Of course, there is reader interest in mere gossip, but ethical journalists avoid tasteless items.

Other journalists rely on more formal elements of news to determine a story's importance. Among many, the most-often cited are timeliness, proximity, prominence, consequence, human interest, and conflict.

Once a journalist is trained and experienced, news judgment becomes a matter of instinct, of course. Professional journalists make judgments without reference to techniques beginners often rely on.

One way to develop ideas for news stories is to make use of the technique of brainstorming, the art of obtaining numerous ideas within a short time. By carefully organizing and controlling brainstorming sessions, the staff can develop new ideas quickly and efficiently.

Many interesting news stories in scholastic publications report the results of polls. Teens like to know what other teens are thinking or doing, so many newspaper staffs conduct surveys of their readers. These can make interesting reading provided the poll is a random one, which means that every person in the group to be surveyed has an equal chance of being in the poll. Surveys in which a reporter grabs the first ten people he or she sees are called availability surveys, and while they sometimes make interesting reading, they are valid only as anecdotes. Scientific surveys must be random.

On Assignment

Individual Activities

1. Write a brief definition or explanation of each of the following terms.

advance	brainstorming
conflict	consequence
filter question	human interest story
localization	news judgment
prominence	proximity
random sample	timeliness

2. Identify three possible school news story ideas for each news element mentioned in this chapter. State the story idea in a single sentence. For example, one idea for timeliness might be, "Grade averages are rising and causing concern over grade inflation." For each idea, identify the news element(s) present. Then identify the audiences to whom the story will appeal.

3. Test your critical thinking. Discuss in class or write an essay on this situation: Assume that a twelve-year-old student has been involved in a serious crime. As a journalist, what do you report? What, if anything, do you leave out about the person? First answer in terms of "Who cares?" Then consider how your code of ethics affects your decision.

4. Brainstorm on these subjects to understand how the brainstorming process works:

   a. What will life be like in the year 2010?

   b. What might your school be like in the year 2010?

   c. To how many uses can you put a jumbo-size paper clip?

d. How many ways can you describe a grapefruit?

e. What are some possible school yearbook themes?

f. How many photo ideas can you develop in five minutes that will illustrate your school's athletic program?

g. How many photo ideas can you develop to illustrate your school's science program?

h. What topics would make interesting editorials for your school newspaper?

i. On what topics could you poll students to develop relevant newspaper articles?

5. Identify one person on the faculty or staff or among the students who would be a good subject for a human interest story. Write one page explaining who and why. How would you approach the story?

6. Look through your local newspaper and identify one story you can localize for your school publication. Write a brief explanation of how you would localize it.

7. Assume you are totally free to identify a topic for a special issue of your school newspaper. Brainstorm a list of topics; then use the complete process to identify the ten best ideas. Remember your audience. For each idea, brainstorm a list of articles you would assign to cover the topic adequately. Narrow that list to the best ten subjects for articles. (Keep these lists for use later.)

8. You want to find out how many juniors in your school have ever cheated on a test. How would you go about learning this with reasonable certainty that your facts are correct? Construct a sample and devise a questionnaire to determine scientifically the number who cheat (or who say they do, which might be different than the number who actually do so).

Team Activities

9. Working in teams, clip all the stories from your most recent local newspaper that contain the news element of conflict. Mount them on sheets of paper, underlining the conflicts.

Next, examine the front page of today's local newspaper and identify all of the news elements in it. Discuss what you have found out about the news judgment of the paper.

10. On separate cards, write a brief summary of each story on the front page you have been studying. Ask 6–8 students to rate the stories in order of importance. Is there a general agreement? Why or why not? What does this represent? How do the elements of news affect the raters' decisions? Write a report on your group's findings. Compare your results with those of the other teams.

11. Brainstorm five purposes for your school newspaper. Under each purpose you identify, brainstorm a list showing

a. how the paper is now meeting each purpose;

b. how the paper can improve its efforts to better meet each purpose.

Compare your lists with those of other groups in your class. Where do you agree? Where do you disagree? Why? Combine all of your lists into one.

12. With a team, find examples of polls written up in local newspapers. Identify the sample used for each one. Decide if the sample was truly random and whether the conclusions drawn are valid. Compare your findings with those of other teams.

The daily newspaper isn't ready to die yet. Most people don't realize how much they need a local newspaper, said Gilbert Bailon, executive editor for metro at the *Dallas Morning News*.

"Newspapers are still the main source for people to find out everything they need to know in their lives," he said. "CNN isn't going to tell them what happened at the local city council meeting or what the schools are serving for lunch that day.

"Newspapers provide a great deal of the sorts of information and entertainment that people need every day in their lives. Providing that kind of information is needed and it's a lot of fun. It's very important."

There is another, equally critical role for the media to play, he said—that of watchdog.

"It's essential to the people that someone be able to communicate to them the information they need while at the same time provide accountability to society's leaders," he said. "I feel like I am doing something that's useful, and not just making money for a company."

Bailon entered journalism because it was an outlet for his creative writing.

"I have always had this love of writing," he said. "A lot of us in this profession like working with words but are shy when it comes to other people. This lets you find ways to express yourself."

After graduating from the University of Arizona in 1981, he was accepted in the Cap Cities Minority Training internship program and worked at the *Fort Worth Star-Telegram* and the *Kansas City Star*. In 1985 he joined the *Dallas Morning News*, where he began taking an active role in promoting organizations that advance journalism education or the promotion of minorities to positions of power.

He was elected president of the National Association of Hispanic Journalists in 1994 and is a 1987 graduate of the University of Missouri's Multicultural Management Program.

At the *Morning News* he has held positions as a reporter, day city editor, assistant metro editor, and executive editor. He has also worked at the *San Diego Union* and *Los Angeles Daily News*.

Bailon heard the talk of how newspapers eventually will be replaced by electronic media but believes there will always be demand for people who can digest facts and write about them.

"It's not as if the medium of the printed word is going away," he said. "There will always be a need for journalists in a greater sense. It may not necessarily be in newspapers—although I don't think newspapers are going to go away—but there will always be a need for someone who can think, digest, and put out information."

Bailon loves what he is doing and believes students will too, if they get the proper training.

"The first thing you must do is master the English language," he said. "Learn how to punctuate, learn grammar, and then practice, practice, practice."

He also advises those interested in a journalism career to join their high school yearbook or student newspaper.

"If you have an opportunity to mess around with photos, graphics, and words, do so," he said.

Organizing the Staff to Capture the News

Key Terms

publisher

managing editor

beat reporter

general assignment reporter

jump

WED

maestro

mainbar

sidebar

future book

Key Concepts

After reading this chapter, you should

- understand both traditional and modern newspaper-staff organization
- understand the role of teamwork in news organizations
- be familiar with ways to break long stories into more palatable pieces
- know some of the basic sources for news

The Newspaper Staff

Change, some would say a revolution, has hit the news industry's organizational styles in the last decade or so.

New ways have been devised to organize and therefore to improve coverage. Traditional beat systems in which each reporter covered a specific area have given way to what one newspaper describes as "topical beat clusters." From the creation of the story idea through the reporting, photo, design, and production phases, teams often work together in an effort to capture not just the superficial day-to-day material, but to get at the heart of readers' information needs. What follows may serve as a guideline.

While staff organization has changed at the newsroom level, the lines of authority and responsibility have remained about the same. The organization of a school newspaper closely parallels that of a commercial newspaper.

At the top is the publisher. In theory, the taxpayers of your school district are the "publisher" of your newspaper and yearbook. In practice, the taxpayers can't perform that function, so they elect a board of education to oversee the school district, including your publications. But not even the board can be publisher and still perform its other duties, so it appoints a superintendent who in turn appoints a principal of your school. And the principal functions as publisher.

Just as the publisher of a commercial newspaper is rarely concerned with the minute-to-minute operations of the paper, neither is the principal in most cases. Instead, the principal, usually working with the journalism adviser and the students, sets certain broad guidelines—general policies within which the newspaper staff, like everyone else associated with the school, must function.

Students who grumble that they are not free to publish or broadcast any story they please should remember that the editor of *The New York Times* has the same problem. Sometimes there's not enough space, sometimes stories are not in the public's best interest, and sometimes stories are about unpalatable subjects. This is a fact of journalistic life. Rarely do publishers issue orders that honest journalists cannot live with. When it does happen, then the journalist—professional or student—has to decide what to do. Take a stand? Fight over every minor transgression? Resign? Or try to compromise here and there for the greater good? Everyone has an ethical line he or she won't cross. For yourself, you need to make sure it's a logical and reasonable line. Don't easily compromise your basic values, but neither should you draw a line in the sand *every time* you lose an argument.

Sometimes caught between conflicting aims of students and administrators is the journalism adviser. This individual serves as liaison to the publisher, the public, the faculty, the students, possibly the printer, and everyone else who wants to talk about the newspaper. The best advisers walk a tightrope and keep all their various publics happy. It is not an easy job.

Next in command in traditional organizations are the heads of the various departments. These include the managing editor, or editor in chief, who has the overall responsibility for the editorial department—that is, the news operation. Other department heads are in charge of advertising, circulation, business, and, depending on how your newspaper is printed, the printing department. (This chapter is concerned primarily with the editorial, or news, department.)

Under the managing editor are various subeditors. Sometimes these are organized by "page," with each subeditor in charge of a page. This is usually unsatisfactory, because the news can seldom be categorized by page. There are some sports stories that rate page-one treatment and some so-called hard news stories that may belong on an inside page. And many stories defy simple classification.

Subeditors carry various titles. The sports editor, obviously, has charge of the newspaper's sports coverage. There may be a news editor, who is, in fact, the chief copy editor and headline writer. There may be an editorial page editor, who works closely with the managing editor and most likely writes the editorials that express the newspaper's opinions.

By whatever names the subeditors go, they form the link between the top person, the managing editor, and the reporters. Under the sports editor, there may be two or three sports reporters, depending on the size of the newspaper. Under the news editor, there is usually a staff of reporters who carry out the assignments that have been determined by the news editor in conference with the managing editor and the publication's adviser.

Traditional Reporter Roles

In a traditional organization, reporters are of two types: beat reporters and general assignment reporters. The beat reporter checks the same news sources for each edition of the paper. If the beat (or run) is the fine

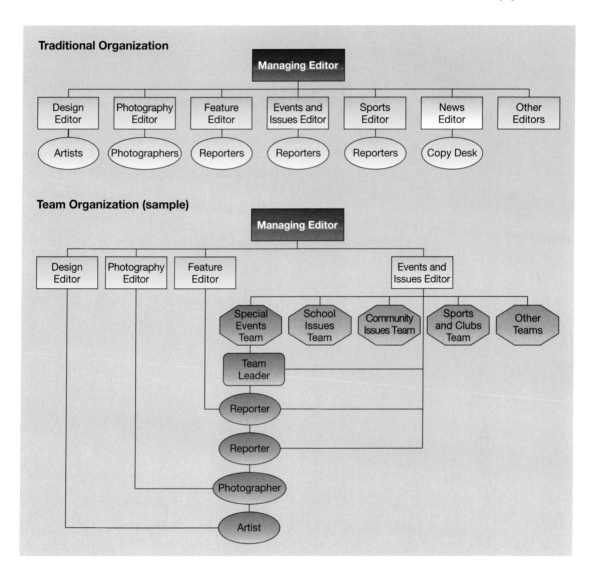

Traditional Organization

Managing Editor

Design Editor — Artists
Photography Editor — Photographers
Feature Editor — Reporters
Events and Issues Editor — Reporters
Sports Editor — Reporters
News Editor — Copy Desk
Other Editors

Team Organization (sample)

Managing Editor

Design Editor
Photography Editor
Feature Editor
Events and Issues Editor

Special Events Team
School Issues Team
Community Issues Team
Sports and Clubs Team
Other Teams

Team Leader
Reporter
Reporter
Photographer
Artist

arts department, the reporter will visit each of the art, music, and speech teachers as often as possible, cover the school plays and concerts, write the story about the soloists being selected for the annual spring music festival, report on the new band uniforms, interview the new speech teacher, and get stories about the debate team preparing for its state competition. Similarly, the beat reporter who covers the school administrators' offices makes a point of seeing his or her news sources as frequently as possible. Beat reporters become specialists; they may not know everything that goes on throughout the school, but they'd better know everything that happens on their beat.

A newspaper staff can be organized in a number of ways. These diagrams show two of the more common ones.

The general assignment reporter, on the other hand, goes wherever necessary. He or she may be covering the convocation speaker today and writing a piece about the lack of parking space tomorrow. Such a reporter is a jack-of-all-trades, doing the work passed out as the news editor sees fit.

Some people would include a third classification of reporter, the "cub." This is the novice, who may be assigned to pick up brief items from fairly regular sources or to check weekly with three or four teachers to see if they have any news to offer. The cub who does this work willingly and well, and who shows enterprise by coming up with an important story on his or her own initiative, will not remain a cub for long.

Repackaging and Redesigning the Staff

Traditional ways of organizing for coverage and presentation of the news worked well enough until a few years ago. Suddenly, journalists looked up and discovered that a great many of their assumptions about readers were wrong. It was OK for journalists to write long-winded stories about oh-so-serious topics when all the audience had to choose from were newspapers, magazines, and the three major television networks.

But they have more choices now: Hundreds of television stations via cable or satellite dish, movies on tape and disk for home viewing, an explosion of niche magazines appealing to small, focused audiences, the Internet generally and the World Wide Web specifically, to name just a few. This explosion of options has forced journalists to take a new look at what they do. With fewer resources available to them—yet more sources available to their readers—editors need to discover ways to reach an audience whose interests and lives are quickly changing.

This audience doesn't read long stories, for the most part. They "scan," jumping from one spot to another on a page. If a story jumps to (is continued on) another page, readers rarely read the jumped part. So long stories are broken into smaller, punchier pieces. Related stories are packaged, not strewn about without a plan. Pullout quotes, charts, boxes all have a more prominent place. Designers strive to provide more points of entry, or spots that attract a reader's eye.

The comment below comes from stellar high school journalism adviser Jack Kennedy, who advises publications at City High School in Iowa City, Iowa, writing in the summer 1994 edition of *C:JET*:

> **The traditional award-winning feature story is a 30-inch monstrosity that mixes together five authoritative sources, seven local students, three paper sources and the quote/transition formula into a tossed salad**

that goes "in-depth" on some teen problem. I have never read one of those stories that couldn't be "factored" into several smaller, more compact pieces.

Newspaper Production in a Nutshell

1. Managing editor or team leader assigns story (or reporter finds story)
2. Team develops mainbar, sidebar, graphics ideas
3. Reporters write stories
4. Photographer takes pictures, provides caption materials
5. Artists do illustrations
6. Reporters pass stories back to editor
7. Copy editor corrects copy, verifies facts, writes headlines
8. Managing editor approves story, photos, art
9. Design editor sizes photos, designs pages
10. Completed page layouts are sent to printer

Smaller. More compact. These are words to plan by.

To produce publications following this new model, many high school publications have replaced top-down planning (Sally, do this story. Juan, get some art. Jim, lay out the page), with all-in-one writing, editing, and design (WED) planning.

It works this way. Teams of editors, reporters, photographers, and designers work together planning stories and graphics before the reporting begins. Some people call this the "maestro" approach to gathering, designing, and packaging news and information. Instead of one writer doing a "30-inch monstrosity," one writes a mainbar (the main story that brings an issue into sharp focus), someone gathers sidebar (related) material for perhaps several short stories, someone else turns some of the sidebar material into charts and graphs for easy reading, and yet another person puts it all together on a page as a complete package. All of the work is done under the direction of a team leader.

The concept requires reporters to think visually, to figure out ways to break long stories into readable chunks, with charts and graphs and other graphic effects. At the same time, it requires designers to understand reporters' problems in telling complete stories: The information is first, how it looks is second. Reporters and photographers must also work together—that is, go out together to get a story. The walls between the newsroom, darkroom, page designer, artists, and production people need to fall, literally and figuratively.

News Sources

Both reporters and editors must know where to go to get the news. They cannot sit back with their feet on their desks waiting for someone to walk in and hand them their stories. They must *go* to the source—and dig, dig, dig, if necessary.

One Adviser's Tale of Staff Reorganization

The trend toward organizing staffs in new ways is sometimes almost a matter of survival. Here, Deanne Heinen Kunz, adviser at Westlake High School in Austin, Texas, tells of her experience.

"We glared, disheartened and forlorn, at the pile of freshly tallied surveys. Discovering that less than 40 percent of our student population read our beloved newspaper caused profound anguish to staff members. Before leaving school that day, we made a pact to pursue more active reader involvement.

"Although the survey results hurt our egos, we gained valuable information. Exposed was the fact that our readers looked at the photos and graphics first, and remembered them longest. Also, our readers tended to skip over lengthy articles in favor of shorter ones. They noted that the topics of the longer ones sounded interesting, but they were unwilling to devote the time to read an in-depth piece spanning two pages of the paper.

"So we took the plunge into uncharted waters. Our primary focus became the "packaging" of stories into palatable pieces that we hoped our audience would devour. Our next step was determining what packaging meant to us and to go about achieving it. Here is our new approach.

"During the initial phase of planning each issue of the paper, writers work with editors to thoroughly think through story ideas, considering items such as the purpose of the story, the audience, the news values, the possible outcomes, the actual story content and its placement in a specific section. Beyond this, they provide ideas for graphic enhancement, as well as introduce ways in which the story presentation might entice readers. They prioritize and break the story ideas down into small pieces, or factor them.

"When packaged into a unit, these factors will provide the reader with multiple entry points into a story, rather than relying on just a headline and photo to grab attention. Entry options include the main story, sidebars, pulled quotes, headline and subhead treatments, tip boxes, quick summaries, checklists, schedules, scoreboards, and infographics, as well as photos and art. Treatment may include objective and subjective views, with staffers determining which of these options are suitable for each particular story idea.

"Because we chose to package news stories, features, and opinions together, it became necessary to rethink the traditional structure of dividing the paper into four or five sections. Our new system of 'Inside,' 'Outside,' and 'Sports' gives the *Featherduster* staff many options.

"The 'Inside' section primarily contains stories and visuals linked with events and activities associated with school: clubs, organizations, students/faculty personality profiles, curriculum changes, etc. 'Outside' contains non-school-related items such as book, restaurant, music, and college reviews; and teen issues such as eating disorders, ethics/religion, alcohol and tobacco use, and so forth. 'Sports' focuses on school programs and athletes as well as recreational sports, activities, and hobbies. (We have since added a separate section, 'Soapbox,' which features staffers' columns on a wide range of topics.)

"Dividing sections in this manner makes packaging the stories into reader-friendly units much easier. Readers can select one part of the package to read or, if we're lucky, might find themselves engrossed in story after story until they have (unknowingly?) read the entire paper.

"And isn't that what they ought to be doing?"

Who are the sources and where are they? Commercial newspapers receive a considerable amount of their news from wire services, organizations such as the Associated Press, United Press International, Reuters, and *The New York Times* News Service. Wire services provide news around the clock from all over the world. No newspaper is fully equipped to cover the world by itself, so newspapers subscribe to services that provide this news for them. Except for these wire services, there is little difference between the types of news sources scholastic journalists use and those the professionals use.

News Tips

Many news stories come in the form of tips. No newspaper staff, no matter how large, can be everywhere at once. Often, someone who is not a member of the staff will inform you of an event you may want to cover. Let it be known that you are on the lookout for tips, and you will be surprised at how many people will volunteer valuable information.

Sometimes material for a school newspaper comes from school administrators, teachers, or students who are not on the newspaper staff. These persons may come to the newspaper with ideas for stories or essays. Sometimes they have already written a story or essay; often these contributions can be valuable additions to the paper.

The Future Book

Another valuable source of news comes with the creation of a future book. A future book is a listing, by date, of events coming up that the newspaper might want to cover. If you hear in December that the board of education is going to consider a school bond issue in May, enter that fact in the future book under "May." The future book is simply a long-range calendar of events and ideas. If the paper runs a story this week that mentions an event that will take place next semester or even next year, someone should clip the story and put it in the future book.

Checking through back issues of periodicals is one way to unearth background information on important news stories.

Public Relations

There is, for instance, the public relations representative, whose job is to provide newspapers—including yours—with news about certain firms or organizations. Perhaps your school system has such a representative; if so, introduce yourself and make sure your newspaper is on the mailing list. Public relations people see that any time the organization they work for makes news, the newspapers are informed of it. Often, the news releases they send will provide the incentive for your newspaper to dig deeper, to

get a more complete story. Never assume that a news release is the whole story; always attempt to find out if something is missing. Remember that public relations people, by definition, are trying to present their employers in the best possible light. They have the welfare of their organization uppermost in their minds. Journalists, by contrast, must consider the welfare of the community they serve. (For more information about public relations, see Chapter Sixteen.)

Reporters and Staff People

Tips, standard reference works, future books, public relations people—all are available. But in the end, how well the news is covered will depend on what the staff knows about the processes of gathering it. In this area, the reporter is the boss. He or she is on the frontlines of journalism, where the action is. No newspaper, radio, or television news department is any better than its reporters.

Reporters are the eyes and ears of the news staff, constantly on the watch for story ideas. But they cannot do the job alone. The entire staff—each person described in this chapter—has an obligation to watch alertly for material. No matter what formal organization is in effect, all must work together if the group is to succeed.

The people at the top of the organization—the editors—have an obligation to maintain good communication with the whole news organization

Even members of a large city newspaper staff need to work together to keep their readers informed.

staff. Editors need to be in constant communication with reporters, photographers, designers, and artists to avoid duplicating assignments and to settle disputes over turf. Memos, bulletin boards, in-house e-mail, and staff mailboxes all provide ways for staff members to keep in touch with what others are doing. Frequent staff meetings are helpful. Such meetings are also one way for editors to publicly praise the work of the staff.

In an efficient news-gathering operation, all members of the group work together creatively and smoothly to produce accurate, high-quality material. In the "On Display" feature on pages 92 and 93, notice the many means by which information about automobile safety has been presented. Different angles on the same general topic can come from many staff members.

Wrap-up

The first requirement for an efficient news-gathering operation is a well-organized staff. In some places, great changes have occurred in news staff organization.

The organization of school publications parallels that of commercial publications. At the top is the publisher. The board of education, elected by the public, appoints a superintendent who in turn appoints a principal of your school. The principal functions as publisher.

The principal, usually working closely with the journalism adviser and the students, sets guidelines—general policies within which the publications staff must function.

Serving as liaison to the publisher, the public, the faculty, the students, and possibly the printer, is the journalism adviser. He or she has a difficult job and is sometimes caught between the conflicting aims of students and administrators.

In the organization of a publication staff, the managing editor is at the top of the pyramid, determining policies and developing story ideas. Subeditors, sometimes organized by the page for which they are responsible, work under the managing editor's direction. Sports editors, chief copy editors, and editorial page editors are in this group. All help supervise reporters.

Many high school publications have replaced traditional organization with the notion of teams—editors, reporters, designers, photographers—all working together to package the news effectively.

Reporters can either cover a beat, returning always to the same sources and subjects, or do general assignment work. General assignment reporters cover whatever is necessary.

Where does the news come from? At commercial publications, the wire services provide a great deal of copy. Student publications have no wire services and have to be staffed by people willing to dig for stories.

Tips from readers and a carefully kept future book help keep the news flowing. Public relations people try to keep publications, including school publications, informed. They are advocates of their employers, however, and the material they generate must be viewed accordingly.

The real eyes and ears of any publication are its reporters. They are on the front lines. How good a publication becomes depends on its reporters and how well they are supported. Helpful editors who maintain good communication are great contributors to any publication. Teamwork is essential to a smooth journalistic operation.

This sample from the Westlake High School *Featherduster* shows how text and graphics can be packaged to create an interesting, inviting spread.

From mild fender-benders to massive pile-ups, assorted accidents eventually plague most drivers

COLLISION COURSE

Time slows to a crawl. A foot pushes, painfully slowly, against the brake. The fender of a Pontiac rushes to meet you. A few loose papers on the seat beside you tumble against the dash and falling, as if in ballet, to the floorboards. Metal groans and rubber squeals as you plow head-on into another driver's car. Most drivers have had their share of close calls. Many have had worse. Whether they result from carelessness or malice, car accidents seem nearly inevitable.

Often, close calls on the road result from hot tempers and irrational judgments.

"About a year ago I was driving down First Street when they were building the new convention center, science teacher Mark Misage said. "And as I turned, there was someone next to me in a big 1971 Buick—just a huge car. As I was coming around the corner, he completely cut me off. My tire hit the curb, and of course I was pretty angry about it. I was honking, yelling and gesturing so they slowed down and almost stopped. As we proceeded on by the river heading to Mopac he tried to stay right next to me. As I came up to the light, I glanced over and there was a chrome-plated .45 leveled right at me. I froze for about three minutes. He was yelling things at me like 'What are you going to do now,' and I just sat there hoping for the best. Then the guy just drove away."

Probably the most dangerous experiences with cars happen in car wrecks. The intensity of wrecks not only causes injuries, but leaves lasting impressions on the lives of the victims involved.

"When I was in seventh grade, we were driving home from school, and it was still drizzling after a hard rain—enough to where the roads were still real wet," senior

Lisa Phipps said. "My mother was driving my friend and me in a Toyota Four Runner. My mom had her seatbelt on, but we didn't. We decided to go home a new way through some winding roads. As we were going around a corner, I looked up and all that I saw was a rock wall rushing towards us. We were totally out of control. My mom slammed on the brakes, but they were locked. We continued towards the rock wall, then for a second were perfectly still. That's when the car began to roll. It rolled onto its top, rocked back and forth a little, and then rolled back upright onto its wheels. The most I remember is being thrown against each side of the car. After realizing what had happened, we got out of the car and another car was there to help us. I had a black eye and a fat lip, and my friend broke her collar bone and her pinky. My mom was okay, but the only thing that saved her life was the seatbelt."

Though injuries are almost inevitable during a wreck, the accidents themselves can often be avoided. Because of the irresponsibility of many drivers, unnecessary wrecks harm innocent people.

"I was riding in my friend's jeep going about 50 mph, and she was showing off," senior Jenny Barrett said. "She took a right into some gravel and swerved back left real fast. I don't remember flipping because I must have flown out first, and I was unconscious. Everyone else was thrown from the car too. My boyfriend jumped out of the car and hurt his foot. Everyone had road burn, and the driver broke her collarbone and a rib. We were all rushed to the hospital and I had to stay the night there, with IVs and staples in my head."

On the other hand, many people fall victim to poor driving on somebody else's

part or something beyond the driver's control. Sometimes in these situations the driver is unfairly responsible for the damages.

"My sister and I were driving in my jeep taking a left into Lost Creek from 360," junior Stephanie Bonner said. "Our light turned green and we started to make our turn, when all of a sudden a car coming in the opposite direction on 360 hit us. I didn't even see him coming because he didn't have his lights on. The driver was drunk and when our cars hit it took off the front end of my car. The wreck was his fault because he ran through a red light. Luckily no one was hurt, but he didn't have insurance so we had to pay for all of the damages. The wreck happened the first of February, and they still haven't been able to repair all of the damage yet."

Other wrecks are no one's fault, but result instead from adverse weather conditions or other uncontrollable factors.

"At 7 o'clock one night, I was rounding a corner on Westlake Drive down by Westlake Beach, and the roads were wet," senior Renick Smith said. "A deer jumped out into the middle of the road and I hit it with the right side of my car. I slammed on my brakes and hydroplaned across the road, hitting a tree with the driver's side of the car. Because I wasn't wearing my seatbelt, I cracked the windshield with my head. Basically the front end of the car was smashed in. I walked home from there. When I went back to get my car, it wasn't there because the cops towed it away, impounded it, and were going to come over to my house and arrest me for leaving my car there. I went to the police station and explained to them what happened, and finally they let me go."

Most of the drivers on the road will at one point in time come face to face with an accident. Though these events are traumatic, many people learn to be more cautious and alert to the drivers around them.

Angie Thompson

DON'T PANIC

How to keep cool if you are involved in an auto accident

Being in a serious car accident, means that there are injuries, a potential fire hazard involved or an obstruction of Austin property. The driver should, according to the Westlake Police Department, do the following:

- First, try to get your car out of the flow of traffic by pulling your car to the side of the road, in accordance with state law.
- Second, call the police. This is an important step because the officer has to take a report, or a blue form. By that time you should know if there are any injuries. If so you can ask for an ambulance.
- Third, make sure you have your driver's license and proof of insurance to show the officer.
- Fourth, if the damage is severe you may need to call a tow truck. It's wise to keep important numbers in your glove compartment, just in case.

If the car wreck is not serious, the police will not come to the scene of the accident.

The Austin Police Department recommends that as long as a person is not in need of medical assistance, they shouldn't call the police. They recommend exchanging names, addresses, telephone numbers and license plate numbers with the people involved in the accident.

In the Travis County area last year, 1,400 to 1,450 car accidents occurred, some involving students. ∎

Valerie Bonner

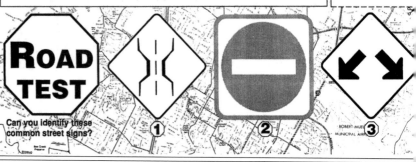

ROAD TEST

Can you identify these common street signs?

1   2   3

Safest cars

This table includes the safest vehicles from each manufacturer, the five most popular cars at Westlake and their safety features. An "s" means standard and an "o" means optional. A "-" indicates that this feature is not available.

Make	Model	Price	Air bags	Std./opt.	ABS	Auto seat belts
Acura	Legend	$29,500	2	s	s	-
Audi	100 series	35,000	2	s	s	-
BMW	740i	54,000	2	s	s	-
Buick	Roadmaster	23,000	1	s	s	-
Chevrolet	Beretta	12,000	1	s	s	-
Chrysler	Concorde*	19,500	2	s	s	o
Ford	Crown Victoria	22,000	2	s * *	s	-
Geo	Prizm	13,000	1	s	s	-
GMC	Sierra pickup	12,900	-	s	s	-
Honda	Accord	17,630	2	s * *	o	-
Hyundai	Excel	8,500	-	s	-	s
Isuzu	Trooper	23,000	-	s	s	-
Jeep	Grand Cherokee	25,000	-	s	s	-
Mazda	929	31,300	1	s	s	-
Mitsubishi	Eclipse	13,000	-	s	-	s
Nissan	Sentra	11,000	1	s	o	s
Pontiac	Bonneville	23,000	2	s	s	-
Saturn	SL1	12,700	1	s	o	s
Subaru	Legacy	17,000	1	s	-	s
Suzuki	Swift	9,500	1	s	-	s
Toyota	Camry	18,885	1	s	o	-
Volkswagen	Passat	17,000	-	s	-	s
Volvo	850	26,000	2	s	s	-

Most popular makes and models

Of 193 students surveyed

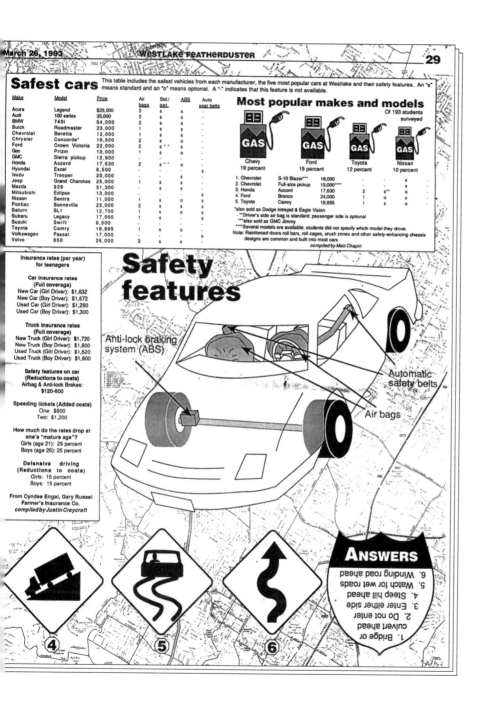

Chevy 19 percent   Ford 15 percent   Toyota 12 percent   Nissan 10 percent

				Air bags	Std./opt.	ABS	Auto seat belts
1. Chevrolet	S-10 Blazer***	18,000		-	-	s	s
2. Chevrolet	Full-size pickup	15,000****		-	-	s	s
3. Honda	Accord	17,630		2	s**	o	-
4. Ford	Bronco	24,000		1	-	o	s
5. Toyota	Camry	18,885		1	s	o	o

*also sold as Dodge Intrepid & Eagle Vision
**Driver's side air bag is standard; passenger side is optional.
***also sold as GMC Jimmy
****Several models are available; students did not specify which model they drove.
Note: Reinforced doors roll bars, roll cages, crush zones and other safety-enhancing chassis designs are common and built into most cars.

compiled by Matt Chapin

Insurance rates (per year) for teenagers

Car insurance rates (Full coverage)
New Car (Girl Driver): $1,632
New Car (Boy Driver): $1,672
Used Car (Girl Driver): $1,280
Used Car (Boy Driver): $1,300

Truck insurance rates (Full coverage)
New Truck (Girl Driver): $1,720
New Truck (Boy Driver): $1,800
Used Truck (Girl Driver): $1,520
Used Truck (Boy Driver): $1,600

Safety features on car (Reductions to costs)
Airbag & Anti-lock Brakes: $120-600

Speeding tickets (Added costs)
One: $800
Two: $1,200

How much do the rates drop at one's "mature age"?
Girls (age 21): 25 percent
Boys (age 25): 25 percent

Defensive driving (Reductions to costs)
Girls: 15 percent
Boys: 15 percent

From Cyndee Engal, Gary Russel Farmer's Insurance Co.
compiled by Justin Craycraft

Safety features

Anti-lock braking system (ABS)

Automatic safety belts

Air bags

ANSWERS

1. Bridge or culvert ahead
2. Do not enter
3. Enter either side
4. Steep hill ahead
5. Watch for wet roads
6. Winding road ahead

4

5

6

93

On Assignment

Individual Activities

1. Write a brief definition or explanation of each of the following terms.

beat reporter	future book
general assignment reporter	jump
maestro	mainbar
managing editor	publisher
sidebar	WED

2. Test your critical thinking. You've learned about traditional staff organization and the newer team organization concepts. Why do you think the team approach has become so popular? What advantages does it have? What possible disadvantages? Which organization do you prefer? Do you think the traditional organization works better in certain circumstances? If so, what circumstances? Discuss your ideas in class.

3. Assume that your editor wants a two-page spread on "what to do on a Saturday night in Yourtown, USA." Using WED/maestro notions of organization, map out who would do what. What will the mainbar be about? How will the stories be broken down so none is a "30-inch monstrosity"? What elements of the assignment can be done with photos? With charts? Graphs? Infographics generally? How about a column or other editorial comment? Summarize your ideas in a short report.

4. Now try the same WED/maestro breakdown of ideas and duties for a story that would be much more difficult to illustrate, to make graphic: the budget of the school district in which your school functions. How do you make figures like $2.3 million mean something to an average reader? What parts of the story lend themselves to charts and graphs? Can the story be told through the eyes of, for example, one small, middle-class family? Write down your ideas and be ready to present them to the class.

5. Research the effects of new technology—computers, modems, e-mail, faxes, satellite feeds, digital photography, page-design software—on the media and media organizational patterns. How are the journalists in your town using the Internet? How advanced are they in the use of computer-assisted reporting to scour information from databases? How do new techniques add to or detract from working in teams? Write a short report on your findings.

6. Interview your journalism adviser or someone on the local newspaper staff to find the steps involved in newspaper production before the advent of the computer. Find out several specific ways in which the computer made production easier—for writing and editing, for layout, and for photographic reproduction. Report your findings to the class.

Team Activities

7. As a class, interview your school newspaper editor to learn the specifics of the paper's organization. Who does what? Do staffers' roles always remain the same? In teams, meet with staff members of other school publications in your town or vicinity, including college and university publications. Ask the questions above about their organization. See if they have ideas you could borrow or adapt to your special needs.

8. Devise new approaches to the organization of your school newspaper. Develop an organization chart. Write short job descriptions for every person on the staff organization chart. What regular beats will you have? What subject-matter teams will you create? Write a summary of the adviser's role.

   Compare your organization plan with that of a local commercial newspaper. How are they alike? How are they different? Why?

   List ten improvements you team would make to your current school newspaper. Explain the reasons for them.

The editors at the *Boulder Daily Camera* were faced with the kind of dilemma editors face every day: whether to run a story on page one or somewhere inside the newspaper.

The story was about a controversial plan to build a large shopping center in a small neighborhood. The editors had put the story on page one when the developers announced the plan. The most recent story was the response from neighborhood groups opposed to the plan.

"We had a long discussion about fairness on that one," said Addie Rimmer, *Daily Camera* executive editor. "I wanted the editors to be aware of what the possible conflicts were if they didn't run the response from the neighborhood on page one."

These kinds of decisions, which must be made several times a day, are what open newspapers to criticism about fairness. Rimmer said that despite what some believe, most papers do not push for certain kinds of stories.

"The news is relative," Rimmer said. "Much of the public doesn't consider what else is competing with certain stories. It may be a day when there are lots of big stories to consider."

Rimmer has been executive editor of the *Daily Camera* since November 1995. She previously was editor of the *Boca Raton* (Fla.) *News* and deputy features editor of the *Long Beach Press-Telegram*. She has held several other editing and reporting positions as well.

She was graduated from City College of New York and the Columbia University Graduate School of Journalism. She is also a graduate of the Editing Program for Minority Journalists and has been a faculty member of the Editing Program since 1983. She is a former assistant professor of journalism at the University of Arizona.

Rimmer meets frequently with city and civic leaders in Boulder to encourage better communication.

"People have to know that you are accessible," she said. "They know you from your name on the newspaper, but they should feel comfortable enough that they can pick up a phone and talk to the person with the name."

The meetings also allow Rimmer to find out what people want to know about.

"It's real important to know what the people who live and work here are thinking," she said. "I don't know that you can find that out if you just get in an office every day and talk to other journalists."

As executive editor, Rimmer is in charge of the paper's daily news coverage. The job includes attending news meetings in which editors decide what stories to cover and how much emphasis to give each.

"We try to anticipate questions readers might have and make sure we've discussed any balance or fairness issues that might be raised," Rimmer said.

The editors also decide at this meeting what stories to put on page one. In the case of the controversial shopping center, the editors decided the neighborhood position had been covered thoroughly in previous stories and that the story did not warrant front-page play.

"That was OK with me," Rimmer said. "I just wanted to make sure we really thought about the issue and made the correct decision."

Chapter Five

Making the Interview Work

Key Terms

formal interview

Q and A

open-ended questions

"est" questions

stock questions

off the record

primary source

Key Concepts

After reading this chapter, you should

- know how to conduct an effective interview, including how to structure the questions as well as the interview itself

- be familiar with issues related to notetaking and the use of tape recorders

- understand the good and the bad with interviews on the Internet

- know how to prepare and to use stock questions

- know what to do if the source wants to go off the record or wants to read your story before it is published

- know the characteristics of an effective interview-based story

It can be terrifying, edifying, gratifying.

You may need a tape recorder, a telephone, e-mail.

And a pleasant smile couldn't hurt.

The subject is interviewing. It's the oldest and still the most common technique journalists use to get information.

It's not a perfect technique. When they published their landmark 1966 study on interviewing, Professors Eugene Webb and Jerry Salancik titled it *The Interview, or the Only Wheel in Town.* The second part of the title referred to how a gambler might view a crooked roulette wheel, and it's an apt comparison with interviewing. The process may be flawed—a gamble sometimes—but journalists have to know how to do it.

On the late-late TV show, the reporter crashes into the police chief's office and threatens, "Either I get the full story—now—or I'll expose you as the incompetent political hack that you are!" The chief pleads for time. "Give me until midnight. If we don't have the killer by then, you can go ahead and print the story."

Reporters rarely threaten news sources during interviews. That old movie scene between the chief and the reporter *is* an interview, however. An interview takes place any time a reporter asks a question. It may be

Even your first experience conducting an interview need not be frightening if you are well prepared and ready to listen.

during a quick telephone call, or it may be in an intimate two-hour chat. The type of interview will be determined by what the reporter wants to know: information, facts, opinions, or personal details.

Interviewers need to be courteous and well-mannered; they need to try to accommodate the demands of their deadlines with concern for the needs of sources; and they need to understand and try to stamp out personal biases that can interfere with their own clear thinking. Above all, however, they have to know that their work has a noble side to it, a public-service side. If a question is appropriate and in the public's interest to be asked, pushing for an answer is appropriate behavior for a journalist.

Conducting one's first interview, especially when it's with an intimidating authority figure or celebrity, can indeed be terrifying. Ask any experienced journalist to recount his or her own first interview and you can expect an anecdote about nervousness, missed follow-up questions—and, often, a kind source who took pity on a neophyte and saved the day.

Journalists vary in their interviewing skills and techniques, of course. Most agree, however, that there are no *great* reporters who are not good at the interview. A tough hide, coupled with an open and friendly demeanor, is essential.

Some people believe the best way to learn how to conduct an interview is to, well, conduct an interview. The notion has merit, and practice interviews in class or lab can be helpful. Still, some things about interviewing are known and can be transmitted to beginners. The sink-or-swim notion of just-go-do-an-interview ignores the fact that some people sink. So this is a swimming lesson.

General Interviewing Guidelines

The first step in getting ready for an interview is knowing what it is you want to find out. The second step is deciding whom to ask. This, of course, means knowing who can be expected to know what. The rule is to go to the primary source of information, the person whose business it is to have the best and most reliable information about what you want to find out. This seems painfully obvious, but it apparently is not. An instructor was startled when two of his students, sent to get information about a power failure, quoted him in their stories. He had said, "I understand it was caused by construction workers who cut a power line." As it turned out, however, that was not the cause—and the stories looked pretty silly. Ask only what someone is likely to know (unless, of course, you simply want an opinion).

Once you know what it is you want to find out and whom to ask about it, you can decide what sort of interview is involved. If you want information about plans for a new building, make an appointment to talk to the appropriate administrator. If you want fifteen opinions about the grading system in your school, ask fifteen instructors or students. Always identify yourself as a reporter before asking questions. (There are exceptions to this on the professional level, but they are not the issue here.) A simple statement such as "I'm _____ of the paper, and I'd like to ask . . . ." will usually suffice.

You must be comfortable with people and be able to meet and talk with them. Reporters run the risk of distracting their subject if they are overly nervous. If you're nervous, try to hide it. Remember that most people enjoy being interviewed. They enjoy talking about themselves and expressing opinions to interested people. This works in your favor.

Asking Questions

Prepare your questions *before* the interview. Know what you're going to ask. Be straightforward. Don't make a speech every time you want to ask a question. Ask clearly and simply. Avoid questions that can be answered with a simple yes or no. When you give subjects that choice, too often they will take it. And "no" is not the liveliest quote in the history of journalism. You want to ask open-ended questions that will get a quotable response. "What do you think about . . .?" is a better way to start a question than "Do you think . . .?" In other words, ask good questions. If your questions are superficial, the answers will be, too. Ask an administrator if the citizens of your community are adequately supporting the school financially. Ask what he or she would do to upgrade the school if unlimited funds were available. Ask about grading policies: Are they fair? Ask if the student government is too powerful or too weak.

Some people object to "est" questions (proudest, saddest, biggest, etc.) because such questions have a tendency to be "high schoolish," and in their simplicity they can distort people's views. Ask a father his proudest moment and he may mention the birth of his son—but that doesn't mean he wasn't proud when his daughter was born. (The son came first, that's all.) Ask the football coach to name the "best college football team in history,"

Chancy Opening Lines

These tongue-in-cheek introductory lines won't get your source to talk unless he or she has a good sense of humor.

1. Hi. Sorry to bother you.
2. I only have one question.
3. This will only take a minute.

and you've forced him to pick just one team, when in fact he might logically list five great teams. In a way, "est" questions are almost like yes and no questions—they can cut off conversation. And that's not usually what a reporter wants to do during an interview.

The questions you ask are your key to the success of any interview story. Student journalists often are advised to avoid asking embarrassing questions. This is bad advice. As a journalist, you *must* ask embarrassing questions. But keep good taste in mind. Then ask what you must ask. Don't pry; don't snoop. Don't ask hostile or leading or loaded questions. But you do have to get the truth if you can; that's almost a definition of journalism. Ask what you have to, as politely as possible. If you don't get an answer, ask again.

Listening to Responses

Pay attention to *how* the question is answered. Does the subject answer calmly and easily, as if the question has been asked a thousand times before? Or does he or she grope a bit? Does the subject, perhaps, pay you the finest compliment: "That's a good question"? Note also what questions the source does *not* answer. Sometimes a "No comment" can be very revealing. Above all, if you don't understand what is said, stop and ask for clarification.

Asking relevant, well-thought-out questions often gets your subject talking freely and naturally.

Don't ever threaten your news source or use coercion. Don't challenge what the source says except for clarification (and then don't fail to do so). Don't argue; listen. That's important. You can't hear if you're talking. So be quiet and listen, even when the source seems to be wandering from the subject. Sometimes the digression is more interesting than what you asked about.

Just before the interview ends, ask if there is anything else you should know. Many a routine story has been turned into a good one simply because the reporter had the good sense to leave time for the source to volunteer information.

> **Stock Questions, Part 1**
>
> When reporters have to interview someone on short notice, some rely on stock questions—all-purpose questions usable in any situation. If you find yourself in this situation, remember the following device, invented by Professor LaRue Gilliland. It will give you enough questions to get started:
>
> **Goals** ("What do you hope to accomplish with this project?")
>
> **Obstacles** ("What obstacles stand in the way of your achieving your goals?")
>
> **Solutions** ("How can you solve this problem? How can you overcome these obstacles?")
>
> **Start** ("How did all this begin? Whose idea was it?")

The Formal Interview

Much of what we have been talking about so far in this chapter applies to all interviews—that is, all the times when you as a reporter ask questions. But there is another kind of interview that involves all of the above and more. This is the formal interview, in which the reporter tries to paint with words the portrait of a human being. Properly done, such a story reveals the subject's personality to your readers. They come to *know* the person through your story.

The formal interview requires more preparation than the informal variety. You must be fully informed about your subject before you even call to make an appointment. Dig through old copies of your newspaper or your city's paper. Talk to the subject's spouse or old friends. Remember, you are trying to portray a complete human being. Know the subject as intimately as possible before you start the interview. There can't be any "dead air" while you think of your next question.

Your choice of language can work in your favor. The very word "interview" can scare off a subject, so perhaps "talk" or "meeting" would be better when you call for that appointment.

You've made the appointment, done your research, and arrived on time at the person's house or office. To start the interview, to get yourself and the subject warmed up to each other, try asking the relatively trivial but necessary questions. Get down the basic data: exact name (including middle initial), age, address, family status (for example, number of children).

Look ahead to the inverted pyramid discussion in Chapter Six. Now imagine a right-side-up pyramid. Why not ask questions in that order? Start with the small, unimportant things first and then, as you and your subject become comfortable and the tension fades, get to the bigger, more important questions. Avoid the mistake of a student whose first question to the instructor was, "Do you think your contract will be renewed next year?" The question was blurted out as a result of nervousness, and it certainly got the interview off to a rocky start.

Observing Actions

In formal interviews, the reporter tries to make the reader "see" the subject. This is best accomplished with a description of the subject's actions and surroundings through his or her own words. Look for the quotes that convey personality to the reader. When the star of a Rose Bowl game of fifty years ago says, "I'm always glad to talk about that game, because it gets better every year," you get a certain insight into his personality.

Actions are important. Does the subject sit on the edge of the chair or pound the desk for emphasis? Does he or she tell a particularly revealing joke? (If so, don't just laugh and go on; put it in the story.)

Being Friendly

How do you get subjects to give you solid information and personal detail? How do you get them to open up to you and to enjoy talking with you? You already know the answers intuitively from your personal life. Nobody likes a grinch. Nobody likes a smart-aleck or a show-off. Nobody likes people who talk too much or seem to know everything.

Successful interviewers let their pleasant personalities come through. Smile. Laugh at your subject's jokes. Notice the children's pictures on the desk and say how attractive they are. You want to establish rapport, to connect as a person.

For most ethnic groups in America, good eye contact is considered a sign of interest. So look your subject in the eye—without staring, zombie-like, at him or her. (Be aware, though, that in some ethnic groups, eye contact is considered rude—so be sensitive to the other person's views. The same can be said of a firm handshake: Remember that a soft handshake is preferred by some, including Native Americans.)

Express interest in the subject and what he or she has to say. You don't have to agree. You *shouldn't* agree. (You're neutral, remember?) Be flexible. Relax. Listen carefully. Listening is often overlooked as a communications tool, and it shouldn't be. Pay close attention to what's being said. (There's a famous story of a journalist who covered a speech and then wrote a story about "youth in Asia" when the speaker really had talked about "euthanasia." Listen!)

Use the person's name in the conversation. Most people like to hear their name, so use it. Be polite. Don't chew gum or—horrors!—smoke during a formal interview. Don't rearrange the desktop so you can plop down a big notebook or tape recorder.

Try to ask interesting questions. Be tolerant toward the source's ideas. Again, you don't have to agree, but neither should you argue. It's the source's ideas, not yours, that matter. Examine and understand your own biases and set them aside. Dress properly. Say "hmmmmm" and "that's interesting" when the subject speaks. Maintain an alert, not slouching, posture.

Try to develop an atmosphere of trust. Yes, there are rare times when a reporter has to be tough, has to get angry, has to let the source know that it's clear he or she is not being straightforward. But being nice works better most of the time.

Taking Notes

How does an interviewer take useful notes? People talk faster than reporters can write, generally. So what journalists do is develop their own systems they can rely on and can translate after the interview. Skill in shorthand can be helpful, for example. Lacking that, you might invent a system of speedwriting. Then you can fill in the details after you've left the interview. If the source agrees, a tape recorder can be valuable in the interview.

Some people freeze up in the face of a tape recorder, but others are reassured by it, knowing the reporter with a tape recorder has made a commitment to accuracy.

There are pros and cons to the use of tape recorders. On the plus side is the fact that they permit you to get exact quotes, quotes that sound precisely the way the source talks. That's also the minus side. People talk

Tape-recording an interview can assure your subject that you have an accurate rendition of what he or she said.

funny. They say "ya know" a lot and they start sentences that they never finish or they switch tenses in the middle of a sentence. You don't want to reproduce all of that (see Chapter Eight, "Handling Quotes Fairly and Accurately"). But you want the exact words when they're important, and that's what you get with a tape recorder.

Another problem is that tape recorders capture every sound, not just the sound you want. Thus you should be careful not to use a tape recorder in a crowded restaurant or on a busy street. The sounds you want may be obscured by sounds you don't want.

If you have a tape recorder running, you should be able to listen more attentively than if you're struggling to listen and to take notes at the same time. But always write down the really important information—names, exact figures, dates—just in case the tape recorder fails. And keep taking notes throughout the interview. If you stop taking notes the source will think you're not interested and may stop talking—which usually is exactly the opposite of what you want.

If you use a tape recorder, get a small one, the kind you can easily hold in one hand. You don't want to go into an interview carrying a boom-box lookalike.

Conducting Internet Interviews

A small but discernible trend toward using the Internet as an interview tool is taking place. If you and your source both have e-mail accounts, your interview can take place over the Net. With modems in so-called "chat" mode, you can conduct the interview in real time.

Be aware, however, that the face-to-face interview is almost always better than one on the telephone or via modem. People send messages in other ways besides words, and you miss the messages sent by smiles, frowns, body language, and gestures if you're not in the same room with your source.

In a sense, you can "interview" thousands of people simultaneously on the Net. It's very common these days for student journalists doing research to post a note in a newsgroup to solicit opinions. For example, let's say you're doing a story about censorship in your school. A common practice would be to post a note in a student journalism group asking other student journalists to relay accounts of their experiences.

This is fine, but remember that not everyone you meet on the Internet is as honest and committed to accuracy as you are. The very fact that so many people on the Internet are anonymous should alert you. Use the Internet, of course. But use it wisely.

Going Off the Record

Sometimes sources suggest providing information to a reporter "off the record." You need to be prepared should that happen.

Stock Questions, Part 2

In lighthearted interviews with willing subjects, stock questions can be intriguing. In his book *The Craft of Interviewing* (Cincinnati: Writer's Digest, 1976), John Brady listed several such questions:

What three books (records, movies, presidents) would you take with you if you were stranded on an island?

If you were fired from your present job, what sort of work would you undertake?

If you could live at any time in history, what age would you choose?

If you could be anyone you wanted to be today, whom would you be, and what would you do?

If someone gave you a million dollars, how would you spend it?

If your house were afire, what would you grab on the way out?

You can invent your own stock questions:

What's the proudest moment of your life? The saddest?

What do you want more than anything else in the world?

Whom do you admire most in the world?

What's your biggest worry?

If you were doing this interview, what would you ask?

Some people object to "est" questions (proudest, saddest, biggest, etc.) and with reason. But remember, the idea here is how to handle an interview for which you have no time to prepare.

The first item to ponder is what is meant by "off the record." Does that mean the reporter can use the information but not give the name of the source? Or does it mean the information cannot be used at all? Before you agree to anything, make sure both parties know the rules.

If you agree to accept off-the-record information, make sure you and the source agree as to when the interview is back on the record.

Remember that no information is off the record unless you agree. If a source tells you "this is off the record," it really isn't unless you agree. No one used to dealing with journalists would ever tell you anything off the record unless you've agreed—but then not all sources know the rules.

One thing is certain: If you accept information off the record, you are honor-bound to stick by the agreement. If "off the record" in the context of your interview means using the information but without giving the name of the source, that's what you have to do.

Writing the Interview Story

When writing up the interview, try to avoid general descriptions of your subject. Don't for example, say that the store owner is short; tell the reader he's 5' 2". Don't say the executive is lively; say she moves about the office during an interview, juggling project after project even as you talk. Don't just say the author is intelligent; point out that he's written six books. Don't say the volleyball coach is athletic; say she has won four championships and displays the trophies in her office. In other words, be specific in your detail.

Using Details

Here are some examples of detail by Gay Talese, a fine American journalist, writer, and researcher. The first describes a man:

> [He was] fifty years old, a lean and well-tailored man with gray hair, alert blue eyes, wrinkles in the right places . . . .
> He had an angular face that suggested no special vitality; wavy gray-black hair combed tightly back from his high forehead, and soft, timidly inquiring eyes behind steel-rimmed glasses. His voice was not strong; it was, in fact, almost high-pitched, wavering and imploring when he spoke normally.

The second describes an office:

Traditional English, thirty-five feet long and eighteen feet wide, trimmed in draperies of a white linen stripe, it is lined with a blue-black tweed rug that conceals the inky footprints of editors who have been up to the composing room. Toward the front of the room is an oval walnut conference table surrounded by eighteen Bank of England chairs. . . . In the rear of the room, a long walk for visitors, is Daniel's big desk and his black leather chair which, according to the decorator, was selected because it produces a minimum of wrinkles in Daniel's suits.

Using Quotes

Use many direct quotes when you write the interview story. Quotes, the person's own words, bring him or her to life. It is through these that your readers come to know the subject best, especially if you've asked the right questions. Probably the single most important question is Why? Others are Who? What? When? Where? How? (That's six questions right there.) As you write, remember to stay out of the story. Don't say, "I asked . . ."; just give the answer.

> **NOT THIS:** When asked how it felt to be the first man on the moon, he replied, "It was exciting and exhilarating."

> **THIS:** He said being the first man on the moon was "exciting and exhilarating."

Q and A Technique

One effective story technique that has won acceptance from readers is what journalists call "Q and A." In this system, the reporter's exact questions are reproduced, followed by the source's exact answers. Instead of a story, in the usual sense, the newspaper presents virtually a verbatim transcript of the interview.

This means, of course, that the journalist has no way of signaling to the reader the most important statements in the interview. But that might not be a bad thing. The Q and A technique allows the reader to determine, without interference, what is or is not important. It's a good technique, approved by many sources. Don't try it without a tape recorder, though.

The article in the "On Display" feature on page 108 is based on an interview with a television reporter in Phoenix. Notice how in this excerpt the writer not only presents details to characterize the interviewee but also, through direct quotes, lets the interviewee do most of the talking.

Professional Profile: Mary Kim Titla

by Kara Ritter, The Phoenix Journalism Monthly,
May/June 96 SPJ, Valley of the Sun Chapter

From the San Carlos reservation in eastern Arizona, the pattern of Mary Kim Titla's life almost has made a full circle.

The Channel 12 reporter and fill-in anchor was born as a member of the San Carlos Apache Tribe and began her life in a large family within a small Indian community.

Although working as a broadcast journalist for 10 years between Tucson and Phoenix, Titla thinks breaking back into that community and culture on the reservation would be a good move for her family.

"The way Native Americans are described is as people who live in two different worlds. It's as if there is a 'mainstream lifestyle' and an 'Indian lifestyle.' Even though I live in the 'city' now, I miss the freedom, the openness, the culture. I want that for my boys."

The 35-year-old mother of three has worked for KPHX-TV Channel 12 for two years, and prior to that, she hosted a public affairs program for KVOA-TV Channel 4 in Tucson. Titla also was an assistant producer for KTVK-TV Channel 3 in Phoenix.

Being one of a dozen Native American broadcasters, Titla considers herself as a role model.

"I'm the only Native American who is a public figure that people see a lot. I take that seriously. they need to hear and see their own people," she said.

During an interview on the Gila River Reservation, Titla covered a story about some of the NFL players visiting the area. Before the camera crews loaded up, she had more children and people ask for her autograph than the players on the Dallas Cowboys and Pittsburgh Steelers.

"They see me on TV, and I think inside it makes them challenge themselves to say, 'Well, maybe I can do that too.'"

But by a glance, it's hard to think Titla started in the Phoenix journalism market as a news station receptionist.

"It was the only opening, and I had to get my foot in the door. I looked at it as a start, and said to them, 'Well then, I will be the very best receptionist I can.'

But they knew I was there because I really wanted to climb the ladder."

The receptionist job was just a small beginning for Titla, who recently was featured in the Super Bowl XXX pre-game show. In a fully beaded buckskin dress, she translated the Star Spangled Banner into American Sign Language as musician Vanessa Williams sang her version.

Although she knows traditional Indian sign language from her past, Titla quickly learned how to interpret American Sign Language, which is a little more complex with its hand signals that represent numbers and letters of the alphabet.

"One of the neat parts about being involved with the production was that the Native American community here nominated me to the pre-game committee. That made me feel pretty good. . . ."

As popular as her name is and as much as people recognize her, Titla originally just wanted to write.

She received a print journalism degree from the University of Oklahoma, where she met her husband John.

"I really liked writing. That's what hooked me into journalism. I always thought about teaching English because that was my strong subject. . . .

"Going to college was something we all knew was the next step. It wasn't ever an option. I grew up in poverty, and it was really important to our parents to break the cycle of alcoholism. My parents wanted their children to be education-minded and be successful at whatever we choose to do."

Titla's family of seven all have their bachelor degrees, including her parents.

"They went back to school after we were grown, and my mother now is a social worker and my father is an art teacher. I think it's great they went back. You hardly ever see a family on a reservation with a few graduating from college—let alone a family of seven including the parents.

"I didn't want to be a negative statistic. I'm glad I went and finished. I did think about leaving in the beginning, but I stuck with it, and I'm glad."

An Ethical Question

What if the person you interview wants to read the story before you print it? At one time, this was considered an open-and-shut case: Tell the source no. It's an intrusion on the journalist's right to print whatever he or she decides. Besides, there's no time. Those are still good arguments and plenty of journalists operate that way. But there is a distinct trend away from this: More and more journalists are reading back stories to their sources. In at least one course in the School of Journalism at the University of Missouri, students are *required* to do so. Many other journalists have decided to abandon the old way. The first rule if you decide to do this, however, is to make clear to the source that you don't *have* to do this and that you don't *have* to accept his or her suggestions about your story. In other words, you have to keep control of the story.

There are reasons a reporter might want to read back a story to a source. First, it's good human relations. It shows the source that you care about accuracy. Second, it helps eliminate mistakes. There's a story about a reporter who asked an official in a telephone interview how many people had been killed by a tornado that struck a town. The source answered, "Three to five." The reporter heard and reported "thirty-five." Major error! Had the reporter read back the story, this error would have been eliminated. (In fairness, of course, reading back a story to a source is probably impossible when working on deadline on a breaking story.) The small errors that irritate sources will be caught in a readback. If the source says he graduated from Arizona State University and you write down University of Arizona, the readback will reveal the mistake.

Finally, it would be very difficult for a source who sues you for libel to prove actual malice if you have read the story to him or her. As you know, for public figures to win a libel suit against a journalist, they must show actual malice—that the story was published with reckless disregard for the truth or with a known falsehood. If you read the story to the source, you certainly cut off libel suits based on actual malice.

Advisers and staff members should discuss this issue and adopt a policy that applies to all staff members. It would not be good for some staffers to read back stories and others not to.

Most news stories are the result of interviews with people who have useful or interesting information to impart. But sometimes the person with the story is willing to tell it only if he or she is not revealed as the source of the information. The question then arises as to when, or in what circumstances, a source should be allowed confidentiality.

Sources request anonymity for various reasons. For example, someone telling an interviewer about shoddy practices in a manufacturing company may very well lose his or her job if revealed as the source of the information. Political workers often "leak" information about the motives, opinions, and decisions of their employers, particularly if they disagree with what's going on. One of the most famous political sources of all time was used by reporters Bob Woodward and Carl Bernstein in breaking the Watergate case in the early 1970s. This source, known only as "Deep Throat," provided extremely sensitive information on the Nixon administration's cover-up activities. Though the quality of the information suggested this source was a high figure in government, his or her exact identity has never been revealed.

Once a source has been promised anonymity, a reporter cannot betray that trust. Besides the moral problem of going back on one's word, there is the very practical consideration of using that source in the future. If a reporter can't be trusted in one instance, why would a source feel confident about giving him or her information in other circumstances? Most reporters do, in fact, take their promises of confidentiality very seriously; more than one has been jailed for protecting sources in court cases.

But are all sources worthy of protection? Are all equally credible? Suppose a reporter states in an article, "According to a highly placed source, President So-and-So had no intention of supporting that legislation." The source's statement may very well be true. However, he or she clearly cannot be tracked down by other newswriters for further questions or clarifications. And terms like "highly placed" (or "well-informed" or "unimpeachable") may mean little or nothing. The source may be an important, knowledgeable official; then again, he or she may be a clerk in the office of such an official. There's no way to know, and thus there's no real way to judge the worth of the statement.

Newspapers have sometimes found themselves in the situation where a reporter has promised anonymity to a source whose motives were suspect. An example might be a source who has information about some youthful indiscretion of a middle-aged political candidate. On later investigation, however, it is found that the source is a financial supporter of the candidate's opponent. As protection from embarrassing situations like this, many newspapers have developed strict guidelines about promising anonymity. They include such things as not letting a reporter be the sole determiner of whether anonymity is appropriate, not allowing anonymity to be used for personal attacks, and only permitting its use if there is no way the material can be obtained on the record. Furthermore, papers may decline to publish a story if they feel a reporter granted anonymity to an unworthy source, and most will reveal a source's identity if it turns out that he or she has lied. These common-sense practices help ensure that anonymous sources are in fact used appropriately.

Wrap-up

Interviewing is an essential journalistic skill. Good techniques can be learned and should be understood before students begin interviewing. The first rule of good interviewing is to go to the primary source. Good reporters select their sources carefully and prepare well for each interview, making up a list of questions and deciding in what order those questions will be asked. They also listen. They realize they cannot learn anything while doing the talking themselves.

Good questions are clear and understandable, short and to the point. Open-ended questions ("What do you think about . . .?") usually are better than yes-no questions ("Do you think . . . ?") because quotable responses are needed. Journalists sometimes have to ask difficult or embarrassing questions to do their jobs well, but this should always be done with care and concern. So-called "est" questions ("Who is your greatest hero?") are generally simplistic and not appreciated by some interviewees.

Formal interviews require preparation. Reporters need to research the subject in advance and set up an appointment in a comfortable place to talk. The opening minutes of the interview should permit the source and the reporter to warm up to one another. The reporter should use this time to determine basic data (exact name, age, and so forth).

Reporters should try to establish rapport with the interviewee. It helps to dress properly—that is, not too casually. Reporters should try to look directly at the subject and to rely on a tape recorder or a shorthand system of notetaking to make it seem like they are really conversing with the person. Reporters who are friendly and relaxed with their sources often do better than those who are nervous or artificially tough. It does not hurt to smile or to laugh at a source's jokes.

It is also important to leave the door open for another talk. Even with the most careful preparation, a reporter may forget to ask an important question.

Good quotes and concrete detail are emphasized in stories based on formal interviews. Descriptions of people and their surroundings help bring those people to life. The quotes should illustrate the source's personality.

One effective story technique, called the "Q and A," reproduces in question-and-answer form the reporter's exact questions and the source's exact answers. It is a transcript of an interview, rather than a story. The Q and A technique allows readers to determine what is important.

Journalists typically do not permit their sources to read stories before publication, but this practice is changing. Prepublication checking now takes place more frequently, but only if the journalist wants it to and only if the journalist maintains control of the story. Prepublication checking can eliminate inaccurate names, dates, and figures.

Scholastic journalists need to be prepared if a source suggests providing information off the record. Be sure you know what is meant: Can the information be used at all, or used only without the source's name? No information is off the record unless the reporter and source both agree. One thing is certain: If a reporter accepts information off the record, it must stay that way.

On Assignment

Individual Activities

1. Write a short definition or explanation of each of the following terms.

"est" questions	formal interview
off the record	open-ended questions
primary source	Q and A
stock questions	

2. Test your critical thinking. You have been assigned to interview a person who, in past interviews, has answered basic background questions in several different ways—in other words, the person seems not always to tell the truth. What additional responsibilities, if any, does this put on you as an interviewer? How would you go about interviewing this person?

3. Select one of the following historical figures to interview. Do some research into the person's life and times; then develop the questions you would want to ask him or her. If the class agrees, you may decide to role-play this interview with another student.

   Dolley Madison

   Chiang Kai-shek

   Golda Meir

   George Gordon, Lord Byron

   Peter the Great

   Homer

   Joan of Arc

   Paul Robeson

   John D. Rockefeller

   Sitting Bull

   Nellie Bly

   Mary, Queen of Scots

4. Watch one of the Sunday-morning news-interview shows and write a critique. What research went into the reporters' questions? How did the journalists react to vague answers from the guests? Did they follow up? Did they follow up on each others' questions? See if you can find a newspaper account of the interview the next day. Does the story reflect what you saw happening? Why or why not? How would you have handled the interview? How would you have written the story? Compare your perceptions with those of classmates who saw the same program.

5. Prepare all the questions you want to ask of a high-ranking school official or local official, in the order you want to ask them. Exchange your list with another student and critique each other's approach. What was missed? Did you include follow-up questions? Keep your refined list handy for writing an interview story later.

6. Record an interview with a classmate, taking notes as you interview. Using only your notes, write a story of the interview, with plenty of quotes. Then listen to the tape of the interview. Are your quotes accurate? If not, what do you think is wrong with your note-taking techniques?

7. As a class, listen to and analyze a recorded radio or television interview. Were the questions soft or hard? Were the answers predictable? Do newspaper reporters tend to be tougher interviewers than broadcast journalists? How could the interviewers have done a better job?

8. Discuss this question: Do the reporters on *60 Minutes* have an advantage over local reporters? What is the difference between the techniques available to a network reporter who comes to town for one story and those available to a local reporter, who must deal with the same sources over and over? Write a short essay on your thoughts.

9. Conduct a telephone interview with a classmate in or out of the journalism class. Observe how your note-taking changes when there is no need for eye contact. Also note how you use your voice to compensate for not being able to nod or smile. Write a short report on your observations.

Team Activities

10. Devise ten questions you would like to ask the President of the United States. What news elements did you include? Will each question be of interest to your student readers? Teams should compare their lists. What accounts for your agreements and disagreements?

11. As a team, brainstorm to develop a list of stock questions. Review your list and select the 8–10 best questions. Compare your list with other teams' lists. Compile the best questions from each list into a class resource book.

Dinah Eng is the first Asian-American columnist whose commentary is available nationwide. Her weekly column, BRIDGES, moves on the Gannett News Service wire.

Eng's column runs the gamut from personal relationships to politics. At the heart of every topic she examines how to create bridges in society—whether the conflict is within the family, at the office, or between ethnic groups. She has written about Asian-American concerns, spiritual values, and women's issues.

"The satisfaction I get from other people is what keeps me in this business," she said. "Because of this business I connect every day with people I might never meet in person."

Eng uses her column to work for better understanding between people.

"It's a vehicle," she said. "By writing I'm working with other people to promote understanding."

Finding something to write about is not hard, according to Eng.

"The subject matter always varies," she said. "Each week I try to look at something different. I ask myself what issue in the news most affected me that week. Then I try to take my personal reaction to whatever that issue was and turn it into a broader issues-oriented column that I can use to try to bring people together.

"By sharing my reactions with others we can find a connection that pulls us together."

Eng serves as national president of the Asian-American Journalists Association and was founding president of the Multicultural Journalists Association. She has written for the *Houston Chronicle*, *National Observer*, and the *Detroit News* and received several writing awards. At Gannett she is special sections editor.

Eng started her newspaper career as editor of her junior high school newspaper "because I knew how to run the mimeograph machine" and later was editor of her high school paper.

"One of the biggest reasons I became a journalist is because I had a great teacher in high school," Eng said. "He was a former reporter and taught the class like it was a newspaper. As a result, I was really interested in making it a career."

Eng was graduated from Syracuse University in 1975 with a degree in journalism and English literature. She earned a master's degree in journalism from Columbia University in 1977 and went to work covering education and county government for the *Montgomery County Sentinel*. Three years later she joined the *Detroit News*, where she worked covering general assignments, courts, special projects, and as a reporter on the national desk. She has been special sections editor at Gannett News Service since 1987.

Along the way, she determined she could use a career in journalism to help bring different people together.

"Even though I've stayed in newspapers, my life is not about journalism," she said. "It is about building bridges between people. I write about what goes on in the world and how it relates to who we are; to what's inside of us."

Eng describes herself as "kind of shy" and says newspapers are a way to go places most people cannot.

"A notebook or a camera is kind of an excuse or way to fit in with other people," she said.

Putting a Story Together: From the Idea to Final Film

▲ Before going out on a story, the reporter discusses the assignment with his editor to get a clear idea of what is wanted.

►Talking with other staff members can help put a story idea into better perspective.

▼ If the reporter is planning a formal interview, setting up an appointment in advance is essential.

▲ Once the groundwork has been laid, it's time to go out and get the story.

▲ Greeting the subject and exchanging pleasantries is the right way to start an interview.

▲ The responses to questions need to be recorded carefully. The reporter uses a tape recorder but takes notes as well.

▶ Good follow-up questions are essential if the reporter is to get the complete story.

116

◀ Back in the office, the writer discusses the interview with his editor prior to writing the story.

▲ After the interview, the reporter reviews his notes to make sure he hasn't missed anything important.

▲ The completed story goes to a copy editor for editing and headline writing.

▼ At some newspapers, a layout editor positions the final story on the page by hand.

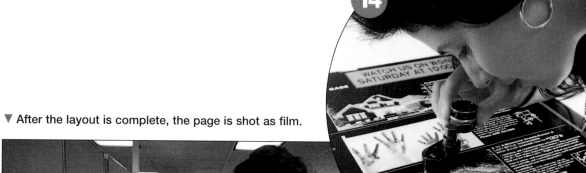

▼ After the layout is complete, the page is shot as film.

▲ The film must be checked carefully for imperfections before it goes for actual printing.

◀ Other newspapers do page layout electronically.

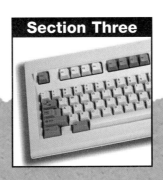

Writing and Delivering the News

Chapter Six

Writing News Story Leads

Chapter Seven

Writing News Stories

Chapter Eight

Handling Quotes Fairly and Accurately

Chapter Nine

Doing In-Depth Reporting

Chapter Ten

Editing, Headline Writing, and Design

Writing News Story Leads

Key Terms

lead

summary lead

inverted pyramid

tease

five W's and the H

quote lead

question lead

Key Concepts

After reading this chapter, you should

- understand the elements of lead writing

- understand the inverted pyramid structure

- know how to write the traditional AP, or summary, lead

- feel comfortable writing inventive, colorful leads for all kinds of stories

- recognize good and bad story leads

- know which lead techniques to avoid

Walk into any beginning journalism classroom in the first week of the term and you'll hear approximately this from the instructor:

> The lead is the most important paragraph in the story. It has to get the reader's attention. It has to inform the reader quickly. It has to be honest but colorful. It should have lively verbs. It should be brief, concise, and above all accurate.
>
> It shouldn't be cluttered with a lot of unfamiliar names, either of people or organizations. It has to represent the best writing you can muster. Depending on the story, the lead probably ought to be attributed. The lead ought to inform sometimes, tease sometimes. It probably ought to include some—but definitely not all—of the 5 W's and the H.

Sounds easy, but it isn't. Even such a brief overview as the instructor provided can leave beginners gasping. As simple as these ideas might seem to a pro, they're a large bite for a beginner.

> "When exactly does a lead need attribution and when doesn't it?"
>
> "What's a lively verb?"
>
> "What some people think is colorful others think is trite. How do I know the difference?"
>
> "What does *tease* mean? How do I know when to use it?"
>
> "How long is brief?"
>
> "How do I know which names are too unfamiliar to be used in a lead?"
>
> "What on earth are the 5 W's and the H—and how do I know when to use all of them and when to use some of them?"
>
> "Why do you keep saying 'probably'? Can't you give us a rule?"

To begin at the beginning: The lead (rhymes with *seed*, sometimes spelled "lede") most frequently is the first paragraph of the news story. (Some leads, really more like introductions, can run several paragraphs.) It is the do-or-die paragraph, the most important in any story. It is the place where you win or lose the reader. So the lead has to have impact, and it (usually) should come to the point quickly.

Everyone knows the problem. The audience is made up of people of all ages and all education levels. They're in a hurry. TV, the VCR, the computer all compete for their attention. So leads have to grab readers.

The Inverted Pyramid

One device journalists have traditionally used to catch their readers' attention is the inverted (or upside-down) pyramid. The broad part at the top is where the main facts go. That's the lead. As the pyramid narrows, the facts become less significant until, as you reach the pointed bottom, the facts may not be essential. The (rare) story that springs a surprise at the end doesn't follow this pattern. Nor do the increasingly common feature and in-depth stories, for which no quick diagram can be drawn.

Plenty of evidence today suggests the decline of the inverted pyramid as a news-story device. While this is true, it also is a fact that the inverted pyramid will be around forever, or for as long as the printed word exists for people in a hurry.

There are many reasons for using the inverted-pyramid style in newswriting. First of all, it's a natural way to tell a story. If you want to tell a friend about a football game, you begin by telling who won; you don't start with the kickoff. The final score, then, goes into the broad part at the top.

Second, the inverted-pyramid style enables a reader in a hurry to get the essential information without reading the entire story. Suppose the lead says:

Central High defeated Tech High last night, 23–0.

Readers who have time to read only the first paragraph may not know who scored the touchdowns, or how or when, but they know the essential fact. They know who won.

Third, the inverted pyramid is an aid for the headline writer. Most headlines are based on information contained in the first paragraph, so *the most important facts should be in the first paragraph.* Finally, the inverted pyramid makes it easy to trim a story that won't fit into its allotted space. A properly organized inverted-pyramid story can usually be cut from the bottom up without too much damage.

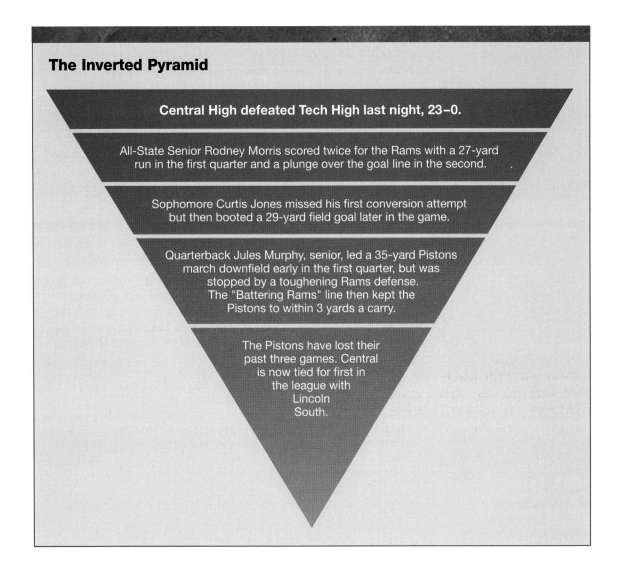

The Inverted Pyramid

Central High defeated Tech High last night, 23–0.

All-State Senior Rodney Morris scored twice for the Rams with a 27-yard run in the first quarter and a plunge over the goal line in the second.

Sophomore Curtis Jones missed his first conversion attempt but then booted a 29-yard field goal later in the game.

Quarterback Jules Murphy, senior, led a 35-yard Pistons march downfield early in the first quarter, but was stopped by a toughening Rams defense. The "Battering Rams" line then kept the Pistons to within 3 yards a carry.

The Pistons have lost their past three games. Central is now tied for first in the league with Lincoln South.

Sounds easy, doesn't it? Just arrange the facts in descending order of importance and write them down. A computer could do it. And what's worse, there's nothing creative about it.

But how do you decide which facts go first? This decision is made on the basis of your news judgment, and by now you know how sticky that can get. After you've written the lead, how do you make it flow into the second paragraph, and the second into the third, and so on? Writers using inverted-pyramid style juxtapose *related* facts in descending order. They

The inverted pyramid is a traditional yet effective way to organize a news story. The most important facts come at the top, in the lead.

must make judgments. They must decide when to weave in some background, when to break the steady flow of the story with some colorful or explanatory material. All this requires practice—and creativity.

The "AP," or Summary, Lead

The Associated Press—or AP—is famous among journalists for its straightforward, no-nonsense writing. AP prefers plain vanilla writing for the most part. AP's leads usually are short, to the point, and filled with information.

Good newswriters can bang out AP leads almost while thinking of something else. These leads are not very creative—but they work because they convey information quickly. They work particularly well on traditional inverted-pyramid stories. Here are some AP leads, also widely known as summary leads because they summarize the main facts:

> A three-alarm fire Friday destroyed several fuel storage tanks just outside Centerville, injuring three firefighters and causing an estimated $1 million in damage.

> The City Council voted unanimously Monday to begin planning for a major study of the city's traffic patterns.

> NASA launched a spacecraft yesterday on a three-year voyage to an asteroid that may contain clues to the birth of the solar system.

"A three-alarm fire Friday destroyed several fuel storage tanks just outside Centerville, injuring three firefighters and causing an estimated $1 million in damage."

> Seniors Jaime Garcie and Mary Jo Shanahan were named Nov. 12 as King and Queen of Homecoming.

> An airplane bound for New York City skidded off the Centerville Airport runway Tuesday, injuring three passengers slightly.

The AP or summary lead, the straightforward inverted-pyramid lead, is something of a formula. And that formula is extremely valuable, especially for plain-vanilla stories that you have to write in a hurry. As a place to start for a beginning journalist, the formula is fine. Just plug the facts into a structure: Start quickly with the news ("Traffic is smothering the city") and follow it with attribution ("an urban-affairs specialist"), give the verb (usually "said"; sometimes a word like "told" or "reported") and the time element (Tuesday), and the lead is done:

> Traffic is smothering the city, an urban-affairs specialist told Optimist Club members Tuesday.

The news, thus, comes to the point in a hurry—which is, of course, the point. If a story is about a fire, the first word probably ought to be "fire." As someone said, if you're doing a story about a bear, *bring on the bear.* In this sort of approach, it is not enough that the news is in the lead; it ought to be in the first few words of the lead.

Here are three strong summary leads—packed with clear, solid information—from an edition of *Tiger Tales*, the school paper of Joliet (Ill.) Township High School, West Campus:

> With a key win against Lockport, the varsity girls' team snapped a three-way tie for the SCIA title two weeks ago, then claimed sole possession of it when Romeoville defeated Joliet Central last week.

> With an undefeated 3–0 record, the Scholastic Bowl Team is heading toward another flawless season, following last year's 9–0 record and SCIA championship.

> Promoted as the last dance before the Prom, the girls-ask-guys Valentine's Dance will be held February 17 from 8–11 P.M. in the cafeteria.

Summary leads can be bright and attractive, but they can also be a crutch for the lazy journalist because they are relatively easy to write.

As newspapers shift their emphasis from hard news to soft news and as TV continues to beat newspapers to the punch on breaking stories, the inverted-pyramid and summary lead are waning in importance. Still, every journalist should be able to construct a quick, clean lead under deadline pressure. Everything else builds on that skill.

Writing the Lead

If you want to write truly effective leads, try picturing a reader over your shoulder. You know what you want that reader to know. And you're aware the reader has choices. He or she can turn on TV or cruise the Net. So don't bore your reader with a lead he or she has seen a thousand times before. Unless the AP/inverted formula is called for, don't just fill in the blanks. *Write.*

Getting Inspired

Ah, you say. That's easier said than done. Someone put it this way: "Writing is easy. All you do is stare at the paper until blood appears on your forehead."

How true. Occasionally the words flow easily. Occasionally your fingers fly and you're blessed with talent you can almost feel leaping from them. In those precious moments, your stomach quivers a little and perhaps you smile inwardly at the pleasure writing gives you. More often, however, you stare until the blood appears. Or until an editor or adviser yells at you.

Every journalist—indeed, every writer—has the same problem: How do I get started? Columnist James Kilpatrick once passed along these observations:

> **All of us have those mornings. The sluggard mind cannot be moved. One studies the ceiling. Nothing there. Silently one prays for inspiration. The muses are out to lunch. The clock moves on. A deadline approaches. What to do? This usually works: Grind out one short sentence. Then grind out a second. . . .**

Other techniques include taking a deep breath, taking a walk, pretending you're writing a letter ("Dear Mom: I'm in journalism class and can't get started on this story. . . ."). You might also note how others start not only stories but all other types of writing.

Herman Melville coined a famous opening for *Moby Dick* when he wrote, "Call me Ishmael." Leo Tolstoy began *Anna Karenina* with what has become a permanent "saying" in books of quotations:

Using the Writing Process in Journalism

No doubt you have been using the writing process in your English classes for quite a while now. Should you use it for newspaper writing, too? Well, since you have to plan, draft, and then rewrite and strengthen newspaper articles just as you would most other pieces of writing, it certainly makes sense to follow the writing process steps. In fact, it may even be more important in journalistic writing because you're always writing for a real audience, not just your instructor. Here is how the writing process steps can be applied to newspaper writing.

Prewriting involves the gathering and organizing of information preparatory to writing the piece. For newspaper writing, this means finding out the who, what, when, where, why, and how of the story. It means talking to the right people and following up with information they give you. It means having good questions prepared for an interview and getting good, usable quotes. It means making sure you get the facts about all sides of the story.

Before you begin writing, you need to analyze the information you have and see how best to present it. What are the most important details, the ones that should go in your lead? What order should the rest of the material come in, and where should quotes be inserted? For many news articles, you can use the inverted pyramid as a planning device, jotting down and then rearranging details in descending order of importance.

When you begin **writing**, follow the plan and order you worked out earlier and write an article that's as long as or slightly longer than you need. Spend some time on the lead and the transition to the body, but do not labor over any one part of the piece. Concentrate on getting the entire story written; then go back and smooth out the rough parts.

In the **revising/editing** stage, spend some time looking at both what you've said and how you've said it. Strengthen your lead if it could be clearer or more interestingly stated. Make sure all key facts and quotes are accurate and properly attributed. Work on transitions so your ideas flow smoothly. Eliminate any pieces of information that don't have a direct bearing on your story. Take a careful look at your sentence structure (it should be clear and direct), your language (it should be simple, appropriate, and unpretentious), and your organization (it should go from most to least important).

When you are happy with how your story reads, do a quick check on grammar, spelling, and capitalization, keeping your stylebook handy. A copy editor will probably review your work as well, but there is no reason why you can't hand him or her a story that is as correct and accurate as you can make it.

Happy families are all alike; every unhappy family is unhappy in its own way.

Charles Dickens' "lead" to *A Tale of Two Cities* is also well known:

It was the best of times, it was the worst of times, it was the age of wisdom, it was the age of foolishness, it was the epic of belief, it was the epic of incredulity, it was the season of light, it was the season of darkness, it was the spring of hope, it was the winter of despair.

Then there's the story of the grade-school boy who began his essay this way:

"Damn," said the Duchess as she lit her cigar.

Could you resist a story that began that way? No, and that's a pretty fair definition of a good lead: It makes you want to read the rest of the story. Leads are hooks. They're flashlights shining down into the story.

Be Creative

Suppose your assignment is to write about the appointment of a new drama coach at your school. You could write this:

Arthur Learned, 42, has been named drama coach at Central High School.

That lead comes to the point quickly and certainly conveys the essential information to the reader. But let's face it—it's dull. It's a formula lead, and it lacks luster. Suppose you dig into Mr. Learned's biography—you might be able to write a lead like this:

An Air Force flier with a closetful of medals is the new drama coach at Central High School.

Better? Sure, but the objection could be raised that the second lead used more interesting information than the first. Exactly! The best material goes into the lead, provided it doesn't distort the story or emphasize the wrong angle.

Be Objective

Here is another example. The citizens of your town vote to build a new high school. You know that this is big news and you want to write a good story. You sharpen your imagination and write:

At long last, the citizens of Smithville opened their pocketbooks in recognition of the value of education. Yesterday they demonstrated their faith in the youth of America by approving a $5-million bond issue for a new high school.

Your news editor tosses the story back at you with a curt order: "Rewrite it." Puzzled? Here's the point: The lead is full of clichés ("at long last," "value of education," "demonstrated their faith," "youth of America"), and it's full of opinion. *Your opinion has no place in a news story*, in the lead or anywhere else. The reporter must be *objective*. Clearly, the example shows the writer's own feelings of elation over the new high school.

Here's one way the story could be handled:

> **Smiling and relaxed after hearing that a $5-million bond issue for a new high school has been approved, Principal María Ortega today commended Smithville citizens for what she called their progressive attitude toward education.**

All the facts are there, and instead of the reporter's opinion the reader learns the principal's viewpoint.

Some journalism texts teach leads by category; that is, the student is told there are summary leads, staccato leads, parody leads, punch leads, cartridge leads, astonisher leads, and so on. Or they say there is a type of lead for each of the parts of speech, and six more for the five W's and the H (Who, What, Where, When, Why, and How). Perhaps these methods serve a purpose. If they encourage students to use imagination and creativity, then they are worthwhile. But such categories may only cloud the issue. Can you imagine a reporter for *The New York Times* hurrying back from a meeting of the United Nations Security Council thinking, "Should I write a summary lead or a cartridge lead? Or maybe I ought to try an astonisher." It doesn't work that way. What the *Times* reporter is thinking is, "I need a lead that will pull my reader into the story. It must be smooth, concise, readable, and interesting." Before the reporter gets back to the office to write the story, he or she may have mentally constructed and discarded a dozen leads before deciding on the one to use. Not once do the categories come to mind.

The Five W's and the H

WHAT?	Second Place in the National Secondary School Drama Festival
WHO?	Taneesha Fields and Wendel Chang
WHERE?	The Barrington Center for the Performing Arts, New York City
WHEN?	May 17
WHY?	Best Duet Acting
HOW?	Competed against students at the regional, state and national levels

Seniors Taneesha Fields and Wendel Chang won second place at the National Secondary School Drama Festival held at New York City's Barrington Center for the Performing Arts on May 17. The two competed in the Best Duet Acting category against high school students in regional, state, and national run-offs.

The bottom line is that you need to make the lead work for you. Write it as well as you possibly can and then rewrite it. Writing, someone once said, is *re*-writing; this is particularly true of leads. Seldom is the first lead that pops into your head the best one.

The five W's and the H are elements that properly belong in nearly every story. There was a time when editors felt all six belonged in the lead, but this is no longer true. The best lead is the one that tells the story best.

Good Leads

Here are some examples of good leads that appeared in *The New York Times*. Why are they good? For one simple reason: They make the reader want to read the rest of the story.

> A monument that attempts to encompass the unspeakable in granite was dedicated today in the former death camp of Birkenau.

> Angelo Rafael Luna returns to his Puerto Rican birthplace next week, seven years after leaving, seven months after his Army induction and one week after his death.

> They wave one finger, two fingers, a frantic hand; they use a shrill whistle and even a shapely leg. But New Yorkers are finding it as hard as ever to get a taxi, despite reports and studies and public complaints.

> An antipoverty program has gotten happily out of hand here.

In the hot, inhospitable lowland
In the north of Rhodesia, from
The Nafungabusi plateau
Down through dusty river beds to the
Great, roaring Zambesi River.
A party
Of infiltrating
    Black
        African guerrillas
Has disappeared—
Dead
Or in
    Jail or
Lost in the thick, unending bush.

> Ever hear a band play "Happy Days Are Here Again" with a question mark at the end?

Pay particular attention to the lead beginning, "In the hot, inhospitable lowlands. . . . " It is virtually poetry. It is evidence that the journalist can be creative, and that the writer who wants to may attempt any device, as long as it works. There's no rule against writing a news story in iambic pentameter, *if it works*. Don't be afraid to try, though be prepared to work far harder than you would have to for a more conventional lead.

These inventive leads moved over the wires of United Press International:

> CAPE TOWN, SOUTH AFRICA—A dead woman's heart pumped life Monday through the body of a 55-year-old grocer who gambled on medical history's first human heart transplant even though he is a diabetic.

> LONDON—Psst . . .wanna buy London Bridge?

> Hattie Finkleday, 77, says she'd rather die than give up her dog.

The Associated Press, mentioned earlier as a wire service with a penchant for no-nonsense leads, can be creative, too. Here are some fine AP leads, beginning with an oldie by Paul Recer on a story about an early space shot:

> A black silhouette that is the earth chokes off the sun. As the light dies, it bursts into space with blues and red and pinks and pure white rimming the earth. It is a sight never seen before by man—an eclipse of the sun by the earth. . . .

> Since April Fools' Day is [Sunday] there won't be as many calls for Mrs. Shark and Ms. Perch at the Aquarium, and the switchboard at the Botanical Gardens may not be besieged with inquiries for Theresa Greene.

> Never fully awake; never soundly asleep. Never unbearably uncomfortable; never at ease.
> The world of the American prisoner of war . . . is a twilight world in which he does not live, but vegetates.

> People go to him when they want to get something on their chests.

This last one began a story about a tattoo artist. The one just before it was about American prisoners of war in Vietnam.

Some leads are so good they become famous, like this one by H. Allen Smith on a weather forecast story in the now-defunct *New York World-Telegram*:

> Snow, followed by small boys on sleds.

After a visit to Oxford University in England, President Clinton took it on the chin in this lead from *The New York Times*:

> President Clinton returned today from a sentimental journey to the university where he didn't inhale, didn't get drafted and didn't get a degree.

Here are some good leads collected by Brian Cooper, executive editor of the *Dubuque* (Iowa) *Telegraph Herald* and published in *The American Editor*, magazine of the American Society of Newspaper Editors:

> Last year the Arizona Cardinals had a great defense and an awful offense. Coach Buddy Ryan vowed that he would equal things out this year. Now both units are lousy.
> —Lee Lewis, *Waterbury* (Conn.) *Republican-American*

> Consider Sid Greer the Maytag repairman of Vero Beach's reserve police force.
> "I'm the only one left," said Greer with an air of loneliness in his voice. "Right now, I'm a coordinator of one."
> —Adam Chrzan, *Vero Beach* (Fla.) *Press Journal*, on the lack of volunteers.

> The largest airplane in the world is sitting on the tarmac at Houston Intercontinental Airport.
> How large is the Antonov 124-100?
> If it did a wheelie in the Astrodome, its nose would stick 18 feet through the roof.
> If a Houston Oiler returned a kickoff from the 20-yard line to score a touchdown, he'd run the width of the airplane from wing to wing.
> The Antonov's gas tank holds the fuel of 5,419 Honda Accords.
> —Dan Feldstein of the *Houston Chronicle*

> Behind a chain-link fence topped with barbed wire, past a handwritten warning that "trespassers will be shot," down a long dirt driveway, beyond two security system signs and two Rottweilers, a man and a woman were found dead early Tuesday.
> —Nancy Lawson, *Tampa* (Fla.) *Tribune*, on the deaths of two 26-year-olds.

> It's a hot dog eat hot dog world out there.
> —Barbara Chavez, *Albuquerque* (N.M.) *Journal*, on a story about heated competition between rival licensed hot dog carts.

> When Princess the miniature schnauzer started rolling over and playing dead without being asked, her owners got worried.
>
> —Carla Crowder, *Albuquerque* (N.M.) *Journal*, on a story about a pacemaker being implanted into a 7-year-old dog.

> Maxine Quinn should wear a cape. She can leap eight stories in a single bound and make jaws drop with two words:
>   Going up?
>
> —Cliff Radel, *Cincinnati Enquirer*, on a story about an elevator operator.

> A horse led itself to water, but someone else had to pull it from the drink.
>
> —Marshall Wilson, *San Mateo* (Calif.) *Times*, on a story about a horse that fell into a well.

The leads in the "On Display" feature on pages 138 to 139 all come from student newspapers. Some are tease leads—that is, they coax the reader into the story by making him or her want to know what the lead is referring to. Notice that some of the leads are two or more paragraphs long. A good lead can be any length, as long as it works.

Leads with Problems

Now here are some bad leads.

> At a meeting at City Hall Monday evening, which was attended by several residents of the community in addition to the Village Board of Trustees, the council passed an ordinance forbidding the sale of alcoholic beverages within the corporate limits of the village of Cornstock on Sunday.

The news here is the board's action about alcohol on Sunday, and that should have been in the opening words. Instead, readers were told where the meeting was, when the meeting was, what the attendance was, and the name of the body taking action—all before the key words "alcohol on Sunday."

Some writers try to use a chronological approach, much like taking the minutes of a meeting. Unless there are extraordinary reasons to do so—

Once upon a time, people thought that they could make fairly clear distinctions between public occurrences and news stories. Elements of the public made news, and the media reported what had gone on. But a time came when people began to realize that they could use the media to help them create news. Today, many would argue that the lines between straight reporting and media manipulation seem to have blurred. And an ethical question arises: Are the media allowing themselves to be taken advantage of?

One of the first times this issue arose was in the 1960s, during the era of various kinds of protests. Though many occurrences were spontaneous and genuine, a certain number were staged. A small number of protesters would gather and then call in the media to report on their event. Television cameras tended to make the number of protesters look larger than it was, and the public could be led to think that a cause was supported by a large number of people, whether it was or not. Thus a group could use the media to promote its cause.

As time went on, the practice of feeding selective information to the media became fairly commonplace. Current-day presidential election campaigns, for example, are almost totally engineered in this way. Advisers will plan what topic the candidate will address on a given day and then try to permit media questions and discussion only on that topic. Is the topic newsworthy? Very often it is. Is it

necessarily the only issue the candidate should be addressing that day? That really depends on the circumstances. And, to be fair, the technique doesn't always work: It is pretty hard, for example, for a candidate to stick only to welfare issues on a day when a huge airplane has crashed.

Some critics see a problem only when the media seem to allow outside forces to manipulate them uncritically. Before the alleged Unabomber was captured, he promised to stop his wave of mail-bomb terror if *The New York Times* and *The Washington Post* published his lengthy manifesto on the evils of technology. Both papers had a hard time agreeing to be used for such a cause, but finally published the piece in the hope that it would lead to the bomber's capture. Here an individual was clearly using the media for his own purposes, but this had to be weighed against the destruction he was causing.

Some events staged for the media can become tragic. In 1996 a seven-year-old girl, together with her father and a flight instructor, attempted to be the youngest person to fly across the United States. The media were notified before the event began, and each refueling stop was carefully publicized so that reporters could be there to report on the flight's progress. Unfortunately, the plane crashed at the first refueling stop while attempting to take off in a severe rainstorm, and the parents faced a barrage of criticism. Though every large news source in the country had publicized the planned expedition, virtually none had questioned the appropriateness of letting a child attempt such a dangerous feat.

In this incident, as in other similar cases, the media were quick to analyze their coverage and pinpoint their shortcomings. But the problem of being taken advantage of will continue to hound the media. Vigilance, and an ability to learn from past mistakes, will be the only defenses.

some dramatic turn, perhaps—straight news stories should never unfold chronologically. Don't do this:

> The Skiler City Council met July 15 with a light agenda. First order of business was a communication to the city clerk from William Pulsey of Pulsey Corp.

Length

Most effective leads use short sentences. The following lead is too long:

> Seniors would be given the last Friday of May for final examinations, the school colors would be changed from red and blue to crimson and blue, retiring teachers would be given plaques of appreciation from the student body, and the editor of the school newspaper would be elected from the student body under bills introduced in the regular weekly meeting of the Central High School Student Council Friday.

Short leads catch people's attention because they are easier to read. Furthermore, long paragraphs, both in the lead and in the body of the story, are unacceptable for typographical reasons. Since most newspaper columns are narrow—just over two inches wide—paragraphs must be kept short, usually about three or four typewritten lines. Even a paragraph that appears short on the screen will seem long when it is squeezed into a narrow printed column. Here is one way the preceding lead could be rewritten:

> Bills introduced at the Friday meeting of the Student Council would do the following:
>
> - Give seniors the last Friday in May for final examinations.
> - Change the school colors from red and blue to crimson and blue.
> - Provide for plaques to be given by the students to retiring teachers.
> - Provide for election of the editor of the school paper by vote of the student body.

This is a common way of dealing with stories that have more than one "main fact."

Here is how the *College Clamor* at Mott Community College in Flint, Michigan, handled a similar problem.

> The MCC Board of Trustees voted Jan. 26 to
>
> - pink-slip the entire faculty and staff, with the exception of President Charles N. Pappas.
> - approve a budget of $11,905,009 for this year.
> - transfer $208,500 from auxiliary enterprise income and student fees to an emergency operating fund.
> - change the rules on registration and tuition payment for next fall.

People stopped talking and slowly turned to face the blackboard as Assistant Superintendent Dr. Robert Jericho wound his way toward the front of the board auditorium.

—*The Lakewood* (Ohio) *Times*,
reporting on election returns in a school-financing issue.

The ferocious winter storm that dropped over a foot of water on parts of the state and sent Bay Area rivers pouring over their banks held a surprise for Saratoga students arriving at school Jan. 10: the heavy winds and rain had forced classes to be canceled for the day.

—*The Saratoga* (Calif.) *Falcon*

We know her as the quiet, patient librarian who is there to organize books and help keep peace and tranquility in the library at all hours of the day, but Nellie Sanders has a wild side.

—*The Chronicle*, Harvard-Westlake School, North Hollywood, California, referring to the librarian's intense interest in ballroom dancing.

The houselights dim, and before long, your favorite teachers are dying left and right.

—*The Echoes*, Abraham Lincoln High School, Council Bluffs, Iowa, referring to teachers at the school staging a murder mystery.

Hunched over a table, concentrating on the artwork before him, Senior Kevin Box guides his pencil across the paper in careful but loose strokes. Each line is a part of the image in his mind that he brings to life through his hands.

—*The Fourth Estate*, Bartlesville (Okla.) High School

It may be chicken feed to some, but for the Schreiber family of Carol, Ken and Pat, it's a serious business. Part of a prizewinning clan of chicken raisers, they've accumulated two grand champions and one reserve champion.

—*Bugle Call*, R. E. Lee High School, San Antonio, Texas

On the day after Thanksgiving, the entire world was Christmas shopping in Houston.

—*The Bear Facts*, Hastings High School, Alief, Texas

Sue's hands were sweating and she "felt funny." Pulling her car quickly off the St. Paul street, she told her friend, "Something's happening to my twin sister Sheri in Chicago."

Then it came to her. Sheri, who was about seven months pregnant, was having her baby prematurely. She drove home, called Chicago and confirmed her "awareness." Sheri had indeed just had a baby.

—*Blue Jay Free Flyer*, Worthington (Minn.) Community College

I heard loneliness today and I heard courage. I talked to Bill Biggs.

After his Dec. 30 auto accident Bill was in the hospital for three months. Then for three months he was at the Gonzales Rehabilitation Center. Now he's home, learning to cope with paralyzed legs and damaged eyesight.

—*Big Stick*, Roosevelt High School, San Antonio, Texas

Mrs. Lillian McCutcheon was sitting in the housemother's room on the tenth floor with her feet up on the air conditioner giving herself a manicure.

—*The All-Stater*, University of Nebraska Journalism Workshop

The sun creeps up over Stone Avenue Railroad Station. Briefcased urban cowboys cluster around chipping green radiators and iron-grilled ticket windows. There they wait, in the sweet-stale aroma of years past, for their silver stallion.

—*The Lion*, Lyons (Ill.) Township High School

Norman Williams gets paid to do unto others what he would not want others to do unto him.

—*Teen Perspective*, publication of the Marquette University
Summer Journalism workshop

While dressed in protective white suits with respirators that looked like something out of a science fiction novel, four trained professionals from ALAMO Incorporated spent the summer removing asbestos from West's pipework.

—*Tiger Tales*, Joliet (Ill.) Township High School, West Campus

Under an almost full Friday the 13th moon, the Red Devils suffered an 18–13 defeat to the second-place York Dukes as York scored the game-winning touchdown with 30 seconds remaining on the clock.

—*The Devils' Advocate*, Hinsdale (Ill.) Central High School

What was once a flourishing, green, spider plant of Kathy McKown, business teacher, in room 222 is now a mere stub in the soil, on the edge of its death bed.

—*The Rustler*, Fremont (Neb.) Senior High School

As he inched his way around the corner of the mountain, he found himself suddenly staring up at a huge expanse of rock directly in front of him. Looking over his shoulder, he could see the tiny dotted trees of the Colorado landscape thousands of feet below him; the river had become nothing more than a thin, blue line.

—*The Arlingtonian*, Upper Arlington (Ohio) High School

Jim is 16 years old. He is a straight "A" student who rarely gets in trouble and never breaks the law. However, when Jim gets his driver's license, his father's insurance will nearly double.

—*X-Ray*, St. Charles (Ill.) High School

Grammar and Content

Can you see what the problem is with this lead?

Your Student Council is considering several new projects.

The trouble is that it doesn't say enough. What projects are being referred to? The lead must provide information. Another problem is the use of "your," which should be reserved for direct quotes and editorials, because it puts the writer into the story. The word "the" should be substituted.

Here is another problem lead:

A reminder to those who enjoy new recordings. The library has 22 new compact discs that it is willing to loan out! All students are invited to come and look them over!

In the first place, the opening sentence isn't even a sentence. There are times when sentence fragments are acceptable, if you use them effectively, but that first sentence isn't one of them. Furthermore, is it news that the library is willing to "loan out" its materials? That's what libraries are for. (The word "out" is unnecessary. And "loan" is an adjective or noun, not a verb. "Lend" would be correct here.) Inviting students to the library, or anywhere else, is not the function of the newspaper. Quote someone as saying that students are invited, if that is appropriate information. Also, exclamation points should be avoided in newswriting; they are seldom necessary. Here is a better way to express the thoughts in this lead:

Twenty-two new compact discs have been placed in the school's lending library, the head librarian announced.

Consider the grammar of this lead:

Alumni and friends of Iowa State University in the northern California and Nevada area will meet for their annual dinner meeting Friday in Las Vegas, Nev.

The problem here is the misplaced modifier. Where is Iowa State University, in Iowa or spread over northern California and Nevada? It is the alumni, obviously, who are in California and Nevada, but that's not what the lead says. The solution is simple. Keep modifiers and what they modify close together in the sentence. Careful rereading of your stories will eliminate many such problems.

Remember to keep the time element clear:

Working on a computer makes it easy to revise a lead until it is clear and grammatically correct.

> The lawyer for three persons convicted of contributing to the delinquency of a minor today remained certain that he would win their freedom from jail terms.

When did the three contribute to the delinquency of a minor? Today? That's what the lead says, but common sense tells us otherwise. This lead illustrates the general need to *keep the principal verb and the time element together.* The following is much clearer:

> The lawyer for three persons convicted today of contributing to the delinquency of a minor remained certain that he would win their freedom from jail terms.

Be sure your lead contains meaningful information:

> Principal María Ortega discussed some of the problems of our school at the Science Club meeting Monday afternoon.

Why not tell your readers which problems were discussed and what was said about them? In stories about speeches, panel discussions, and the like, the emphasis should not be on the fact that someone spoke or that a panel discussion was held. Instead, the lead should emphasize *what* was said. This lead could have been written *before* Dr. Ortega spoke to the Science Club, in contrast to a successful lead, which provides fresh, real information.

The Quote Lead and the Question Lead

Some approaches to lead writing are to be used most sparingly. These are the quote lead and the question lead. This is a quote lead:

> I promise the people of this city that we are going to solve our parking problem next year.

That's not writing or reporting; it's recording. It's lazy and, unfortunately, used too frequently. Rare, indeed, is the story that can be summarized, its essence distilled, in one direct quote. The lead above should be something like this:

> Mayor Smith promised today that he will solve Centerville's parking problem this year.

Here is another poor quote lead:

America must solve its problems in this decade or face the loss of world leadership.

A clearer version would read like this:

The U.S. faces loss of world leadership unless it solves its problems, Sen. Wright said today.

Quote leads can lead to distortion. The reporter pulls one quote out of a speech or interview, slaps it at the top of the story, and the headline is based on that quote. Unless the quote is exactly right, the exact heart of what the person was trying to say, readers will see a lead and a head based on a fraction of an entire event.

The term "quote lead" refers to this construction: "Word word word word word word word"—in other words, just a quote without context or information about who spoke. The next example is different—and acceptable (occasionally):

"You've got to send me to a hospital," insisted the eight-year-old boy, "because I'm going to kill myself."

That's compelling and interesting and tells a reader, at least to some extent, what the story is about. Here is another example of an almost-quote lead that works:

"She told us to pray," he recalled softly. "The nun told us to pray, and it would all go away."

The second paragraph quickly wipes out the one weakness of this lead, which is that readers do not know what "it" is. It's a fire.

Question leads also are to be used rarely. A question lead is one that asks a question:

Where is Centerville headed in the 21st Century?

The trouble with such a lead is that it contains no information. If a reporter has some information about where Centerville is headed, he or she should provide it.

TV journalists are addicted to question leads, typified by this one heard almost nightly:

What kind of weather will we have tomorrow in the (valley, city, metropolis, three-county region, borderland, southland, foothills, front range—whatever)? Dave will tell us when we return.

This style is OK for a TV teaser, but not a good idea in print.

Wrap-up

Getting started specifically in newswriting means working on leads, or first paragraphs. If the lead fails, no reader will read on. So leads should grab readers' attention quickly and in few words.

Many news stories are written in inverted pyramid style. The main facts go at the top of the pyramid. As the pyramid gets smaller toward the bottom, the facts become less important.

The inverted pyramid style is fading somewhat in the face of changing news values—more soft news, less hard news—and because television almost always has fast-breaking hard news before newspapers. The inverted pyramid is used because it gets to the point quickly and is a natural way to tell a story. The pyramid also makes it easy to trim a story from the bottom up if it's too long for its allotted space.

Leads need to get the reader's attention honestly and quickly. They should be creative and interesting and make use of the best material the writer has.

The lead should be objective and not convey the writer's attitudes or beliefs.

One kind of lead often used is the AP, or summary, lead, which conveys the basic information in a simple, straightforward manner. Leads need to be smooth, concise, readable, and interesting—no matter what label they carry.

All stories should include the five W's and the H (who, what, where, when, why, and how) but not in the lead. The best lead summarizes the entire story but uses the best elements—not all of them.

Good leads are creative and make use of various techniques but share one characteristic: They make readers want to continue. Bad leads are slow getting to the point, are too long or contain too many peripheral points (unnecessary times and places, for example), express the writer's opinion, or confuse readers through misplacement of the time element. Other leads that generally should be avoided are direct quotes presented with no context (quote leads) and question leads.

Evaluation Checklist: *News Story Lead*

✓ Does the lead summarize the main facts of the story in one or two sentences?

✓ Is it written in a succinct and direct, yet interesting, way?

✓ Does the lead avoid expressing the writer's opinion?

✓ Has the writer avoided beginning with a question or a quote?

✓ Is the lead correctly punctuated and free from capitalization and spelling errors?

On Assignment

Individual Activities

1. Write a brief definition or explanation of each of the following terms.

five W's and the H	inverted pyramid
lead	question lead
quote lead	summary lead
tease	

2. Secure copies of two different newspapers and study their accounts of the same news event. What are the news elements? How do the papers differ in their selection of lead elements? Why? Which approach is more effective? How could either have done a better job? Rewrite the leads to demonstrate your ideas. Write a two-page essay on your findings, and attach the articles.

3. Test your critical thinking. Compare the leads on radio and television accounts of news with those in a newspaper. How do they differ? Do the needs of their different audiences call for a different kinds of leads? Why or why not? Discuss your ideas in class. Use specific examples to back up your ideas.

4. Do the writers of short stories or novels have problems with leads? Read the first five paragraphs of a successful book and see if you find any similarities between newspaper leads and book leads. Write a short essay on your findings. In your essay, use a lead based on the beginning of the book.

5. Ask the city council, board of education, or zoning commission to provide you with the minutes of its last meeting and the agenda for the next meeting. Write a lead based on the minutes. Then write a lead based on the agenda.

6. Write a lead based on the following information.
   - The new phone book for your town has been published.
   - It contains 18,573 names of individuals and 675 names of business organizations.
   - It contains 453 white pages and 87 yellow pages.
   - It includes listings of 654 federal, state, county, and city governmental offices.
   - Last year's book had 432 white pages and 54 yellow pages.
   - Last year's book had 16,342 names of individuals and 534 names of business organizations.
   - Last year's government listings added up to 578.
   - The first individual listed in the book is George L. Aardvarque. The last is Shirley P. Zgbniewski.
   - The first business is Aaaaacme Motors, Inc. The last is Zart's Bicycle Co.
   - In a press release, the telephone company (United Phones of Anytown) announces, "This is the most complete, most thorough, most accurate telephone book in Anytown history. We are extremely proud of it."
   - You reach Mr. Aardvarque and ask him about being first. He says, "Who cares? My phone bill is out of sight no matter where I'm listed."
   - Ms. Zgbniewski says, "I'm always last. It was even that way in grade school. Always last to recess, last in the lunch line. I guess I'm just destined to be last, no matter what I do."

7. Find the questions you developed in Chapter Five for interviewing a ranking school official or other local official. Now plan and conduct the interview. Write three different styles of leads, and attach your questions. In the next chapter you will complete the story.

Team Activities

8. Working in teams, visit the library and examine old newspapers. Copy the leads of several stories for each of the eras mentioned in Chapter One: the partisan press era, the yellow journalism era, and the Civil War era. Also look at old magazines. What changes have been made in lead style? Make a short presentation on your findings to your class. Include examples.

9. At the library or local newsstand, find copies of English-language newspapers published outside the United States. Contrast them to U. S. papers. How do the writing styles differ? Do foreign newspapers seem to look at the news differently? Why or why not? Prepare a presentation on your findings for your class.

Fernando Dovalina, an assistant managing editor at the *Houston Chronicle*, has been committed to good writing, good editing, and diversity in the nation's newsrooms most of his professional life.

At 53—which he considers young—he is one of the highest ranked Hispanics in the newsrooms of the Texas major daily newspapers.

Dovalina is responsible for the daily operations of the news desk, wire desk, copy desk, and the *Chronicle*'s bureau in Mexico City. He also supervises most of the *Chronicle*'s international coverage.

He was born and grew up in Laredo, Texas, the son of an immigrant mother and father whose roots in Texas predate Davy Crockett's. His first language was Spanish, which he admits embarrassedly he has lost proficiency in over the years. Since he has a reputation as a good editor and has won writing awards, he says that proves that having spoken Spanish or any other language before learning English is no barrier to a successful career in the English-language media.

His parents' emphasis on education was a central theme in his and his two brothers' lives.

"My parents always had reading material in the house," he said. "I was always writing things—fiction, poetry, song lyrics. I just like to play with words."

It was sports and his father's baseball talent that drew him to newspapers.

"My father had been a semi-pro, minor league baseball player," Dovalina said. "Baseball has always been a part of my family. I paid a lot of attention to baseball in the sports sections. I probably got into newspapers that way."

He was graduated from the University of Texas in 1963 and worked at the *Beaumont Enterprise* and *Fort Worth Star Telegram* before joining the *Chronicle* in 1968. He has been a police and general assignments reporter, a pop-rock music columnist, copy editor, makeup editor, assistant city editor, wire editor, and news editor.

In 1991, he supervised a project for the *Houston Chronicle* that was named a Pulitzer finalist in international reporting. Since then, other projects he has supervised have won other awards. In 1990 and 1991 he was a Pulitzer Prize juror and was invited to rejoin the juries in 1996.

As an editor, Dovalina frequently spots a common mistake made by reporters.

"Reporters get a lot of information but don't know how to organize their story," he said. "The first thing a reporter should do is ask 'What's the story I'm trying to tell?'"

"If it's a news story the reporter should ask how to tell a coherent story. If it's a feature, the reporter should ask, 'How do I hook the reader with the first paragraph and then tell the story in an interesting and compelling way?'"

Dovalina believes the emergence of new information sources for readers to choose from makes good writing more important.

"There's too much out there competing for our readers' attention," Dovalina said. "If we can't write an interesting tale we probably ought not be in the business."

Dovalina is one of several *Chronicle* staff members who teach a high school journalism class in the summer. He advises aspiring journalists to read every day.

145

Chapter Seven

Writing News Stories

back-up quote

transition

tieback

chronological style

sexist language

jargon

stylebook

redundancy

cliché

After reading this chapter, you should

- know how to use a back-up quote
- be able to construct a news story held together with appropriate transitions
- understand news story structures beyond the inverted pyramid
- know the importance of newspaper style
- be alert to sexist and otherwise inappropriate language
- know the importance of conciseness and of avoiding jargon, clichés, and redundancies

The proper study of journalism begins not in the journalism class but in the English class. This is because there is one skill so basic to journalism that anyone who doesn't have it, or the willingness to work to acquire it, might as well look elsewhere for a career.

That skill is writing. You've seen how important it is to write clear, well-crafted leads. As you go on to write a news story, an editorial, a column, or even a headline, you must continue to hone your writing abilities. This doesn't mean you have to be an Ernest Hemingway or a Virginia Woolf. But it does mean that you must be comfortable with words, that you can grasp the fundamentals of spelling, grammar, and punctuation, that you know a good sentence from a bad sentence. It implies that you read a lot, and not just newspapers, either. All writers are readers.

Writing is not, as many people believe, an inherent talent that some have and some don't. Writing *can* be taught, or be *self*-taught through trial and error. By writing, and by having your writing criticized, you learn to avoid certain errors. There is nothing quite so educating as real criticism. But again, the burden is the student's. Your instructor can help by preparing you and making you write and rewrite. But the writing is up to you.

A story about the President signing legislation might identify the bill in the lead, then repeat the President's name as a transition into the next paragraph telling where and when the bill was signed.

There is nothing awesome about writing news stories. Your basic writing skills and some specialized information—because, after all, journalistic writing is specialized writing—are all you need.

Building on the Lead

Let's say you've written a good lead and you have readers interested in your story. You have them on the hook; now you want to reel them in. If the lead paragraph or paragraphs are the most important in the story, what immediately follows is next. You don't want your reader losing interest, not after all the effort you put into writing the lead.

One way to hold interest is to use a quote—the sound of a human voice—immediately. Quotes add a personal touch to a story.

Here's a lead:

> **The library will remain open two hours longer than usual as students prepare for final exams, guidance counselor Elizabeth Anderson announced Friday.**

Now here's what some people call a back-up quote, one designed to support the lead:

> **"We need to make it as easy as possible for students to study," Dr. Anderson said. "It's one way we can help to ensure better test results."**

What you're doing is linking the lead to the second paragraph, making your story unfold logically and coherently. You're using transitions.

Transitions are one of the indispensable tricks in a writer's repertoire. They are words, phrases, even whole paragraphs that hold a story together. Transitions take your readers from subject to subject, fact to fact, time to time, and place to place without losing or confusing them along the way. News stories without adequate transitions fall apart.

Using Transitions

Transitions come in many forms. For instance, are you able to recognize the transition between these two paragraphs?

> **President Clinton today signed into law a new tax reform bill, expected to raise an additional $10 billion a year for the federal treasury.**
> **Clinton signed the bill in a White House ceremony and then handed out two dozen souvenir pens to the Democratic senators who steered the bill to passage.**

The transition there is the repetition of the word "Clinton." Because the word appears in both paragraphs, the reader knows the subject hasn't changed. It is still President Clinton we're talking about; our reader has not been lost.

Here is another, more subtle example from the body of a story.

Useful Transitional Words		
for example	then	therefore
besides	later	meanwhile
consequently	and	thus
however	but	in addition
likewise	or	finally
nevertheless	also	in general

> "There is no reason why the people in this country have to worry constantly about losing their jobs," Jones said. Companies need to consider more than just the impact on stock prices when they downsize.
>
> "Of course, there still are unnecessary jobs in some companies," he added.

In this example, the quotation marks at the beginning of each paragraph serve as a signal that the person who was speaking in the first paragraph is still speaking in the second.

Generally speaking, the transition should be unobtrusive. That is, it shouldn't stick out; it should accomplish its job with a minimum of attention. While this is desirable, it is not always possible. The first duty is to the readers, and if it takes an obvious, blatant transition to help guide them through the story, so be it.

Read the excerpt below and note the transition, set in italics. The transition is necessary because the author is signaling a complete change of subject.

> . . . The battle eventually led to the establishment of the Interstate Commerce Commission for regulation of rates.
>
> *But that was later. A discussion of the Populist Revolt, a fascinating chapter in the state's history, now seems in order.*

The entire paragraph is a transition; there's nothing subtle about it. See if you can spot the problem in these two paragraphs:

> A Democrat, Smith was more important in the inner workings of the administration of former Gov. John P. Jones than his administrative title indicated.
>
> A native of Central City and holder of business administration and law degrees from State University, Anderson is a jet pilot veteran of the U.S. Air Force and presently is a captain in the Air National Guard.

If the story is more complex—that is, if it has more than one main fact—your job is harder. You must summarize, giving all three or four main facts in the lead, if possible. In the next section of the story, give the most important detail of each main fact; after that, provide additional but decreasingly important information on each fact.

Organizational Patterns

Not all stories can be written in inverted-pyramid style. As you have seen, fewer and fewer are being written that way because of the influence of the nonprint media. It makes little sense for a newspaper to announce something that everyone saw on television ten hours earlier. So newswriters have modified the inverted pyramid. Newspaper writing reads more and more like magazine writing.

Surprise Ending

There are still traditional story types that do not lend themselves to inverted-pyramid style. For instance, there is the story with the surprise ending, a rare story these days. Compare these two treatments of the same facts:

INVERTED PYRAMID

The 18-month-old son of East High School janitor Mark O'Rourke was unhurt Friday when he crawled into his father's car, pulled it out of gear, and rode it down a hill where it struck another car.

O'Rourke said he had put the boy, Gerald, in the car and was trying to get in himself when the boy pulled the gearshift.

The car, parked in front of the O'Rourke home at 222 S. 12th St., rolled backward about 50 feet and struck a parked car.

SURPRISE ENDING

Police Friday decided not to book a young "driver" involved in an accident on 12th Street.

The youngster was behind the wheel of a car that careened backward down a hill and struck a parked car.

The driver was Gerald O'Rourke, son of East High janitor Mark O'Rourke.

The car was parked in front of the O'Rourke home at 222 S. 12th St. when Gerald, who had been put in the car by his father, pulled it out of gear.

Gerald is 18 months old.

The story also illustrates one way an event can be given reader appeal through novel treatment. Such treatment often means the difference between a story that appears on page one with a box around it and a story that ends up on page 27, buried near the want ads. Never be afraid to try an unusual approach.

Personality Interview

The personality interview, in which the writer sketches with words the portrait of one individual, is another type of story that cannot be handled with the inverted pyramid. (See the sample on page 155.) Here the writer may back into the story, perhaps with an anecdote from the subject's life. On rare occasions, writers may use a quote from the person as the lead, but only if it's a great quote!

Action Stories

Still another type of story that requires a different approach is the action story. This is most effectively handled by a chronological unfolding. For instance, if a dog wanders into your school, your story will be more

An action story can always be enhanced with a photo, if your photographer happens to be in the right place at the right time.

interesting if you don't simply state the facts that the dog appeared, sniffed around for a while, and was finally chased out. You may want to begin with the dog entering the building, then give an account of the activities that followed, telling how the dog stopped first in the journalism classroom and was chased from there to the chemistry lab, where it upset some test tubes, and so on. The last paragraph might be about the dog scurrying out the door and heading home.

Combination Style

An increasingly popular way of writing news stories combines the summary lead and the chronological style. The writer summarizes in the first paragraph and then tells the rest of the story in the order in which it occurred. Thus, the story of the dog might begin:

> **A dog with a cold nose for news Thursday strolled into the journalism class, saw that his help wasn't needed, and then took the grand tour of the building, upsetting test tubes, disrupting gym classes, and disturbing study halls before being expelled.**

After that summary, the next paragraph would start the chronological unfolding of the story:

> **The dog's presence became known during fifth period when he stuck his nose in the offices of the** *Oracle.* **. . .**

As you read the news story in the "On Display" feature on page 155, note the clear lead, excellent transitions, good use of quotes throughout, and heavy inclusion of specific facts. Note also the well-organized ending.

Sidebars. The sidebar, a story related to but kept separate from another on the same subject, requires some approach other than the inverted-pyramid style. In the case of a major storm, the main story (mainbar) tells about the number of deaths and amount of damage. A sidebar might be the eyewitness account of a survivor or an interview with an official of the National Weather Service describing how the storm developed. A sidebar supplements the main story, providing extra detail or "color." Often, sidebar

Local Woman Gives Children Chance to Live

by Tiffany Anderson,
Stratford High School, Nashville, Tennessee

When Judy Schwank walks into the village hospital, hundreds of dying children will be there to meet her. Word has spread that she is coming, and as many as 125 homeless, limbless, or sightless children will be waiting for help and waiting to die.

Schwank is trying to help those who can't help themselves. She's on a mission to protect Central and South American children from unnecessary death.

It may sound like a fairy tale, but it's real and happening in Bowling Green.

Schwank has made 35 trips to Guatemala to get sick children and bring them to Bowling Green to heal, and she plans to return in July. She and her husband, William, who is from Guatemala, have kept more than 100 children in their home.

"Most (children) only stay two to three months," Mrs. Schwank said.

The children—ages three weeks to 19 years—come from the poverty-stricken countries of Guatemala, Ecuador, Brazil, Haiti and Honduras.

Four out of 10 Guatemalan children have a disease that can be cured, and it is these children who will gain a chance for life. Families will be left behind, but a new one in America will be made while they heal.

After surgery and bones mend, most of the children will be sent back to live happier lives.

"In these countries poor people are treated just as blacks were treated during slavery," Schwank said. "Everyone in Guatemala isn't poor."

Children rummage through junkyards searching for food.

"One out of three children are severely malnourished," said Schwank, who is also a nurse in Bowling Green. And "babies die because their countries don't have ventilator machines."

All heart machines are unplugged because there is no money to support them. And it isn't uncommon for children to be killed on nearby railroad tracks.

With the assistance of Pam Goff, president of the Kentucky/Tennessee chapter of Heal the Children, Schwank has placed children in 40 homes across Kentucky and Tennessee. Heal the Children is a volunteer organization designed to help sick children in countries around the world.

"Fifty-five to 60 kids stay in Kentucky. They are in Liberty, Lexington, Louisville and Bowling Green. There are also some in Nashville," Schwank said.

About 200 children are on a waiting list to come to homes in Kentucky and Tennessee. Most of the children chosen to participate have polio.

The children's surgeries are paid for as a donation by hospitals, a cost of $2.5 million in the last two years.

Schwank donates more than her time. She said it's not unusual for her to spend $15,000 of her own family income each year.

Besides her own four children, Schwank has four others living with her.

"Most of the children do not have problems" adjusting to life in America, Schwank said, but ironically, the younger children are afraid of Schwank unless they live with her.

Most of the young children burst into tears when they see her.

That's because Schwank is the one that takes them from their village to the doctor for painful medical treatment.

However, most problems occur with the teenagers. They may run away because—once they've lived in the United States—they don't want to go home.

"One child could not cope," she said. "Her treatment was stopped, and she went home and will die."

Schwank said she's drained emotionally, physically and financially, but plans to "pass on the torch" to her children. Schwank feels that if out of 200 kids she can reach 10 and in turn those 10 kids each help 200 kids, Heal the Children could help 2,000 children.

"Everything is worth it just to see that one moment when they go home to their families."

material can be handled in a chart or graph or other infographic. All elements must be packaged together in readable chunks for busy readers.

Newspaper Style

No matter what sort of story you are writing, you must follow newspaper style for capitalization, abbreviation, spelling, and the like. Behind this style, which is set forth in the individual newspaper's stylebook, is the necessity for a newspaper to be consistent. It doesn't make sense for one reporter to spell "basketball" as two words while another spells it as one, or for one reporter to write "Mr. Lee" and another "Lee." (Of course, full names are always used in the first reference to someone in a story.) Consistency counts. If a newspaper is sloppy on details of style, readers will believe that it probably is sloppy on more important things, such as accuracy. So learn your stylebook and follow it.

Appropriate Word Choice

Journalism students, whose stories are widely distributed and closely read, owe it to their audience to be sensitive to the feelings of others. For lack of a better term, student journalists need to be "politically correct."

The term "politically correct" almost contradicts itself. It's almost as if the term itself isn't politically correct anymore. That's because so much stuff is clumped together under "PC." Originally a well-intentioned effort to rid the language of hurtful expressions, political correctness now ruffles some people's feathers for going too far.

It's one thing, critics say, to ban racial stereotypes and the ugly words that accompany them. It's another to insist that your dog isn't your dog but your "nonhuman companion" instead, as if Fido gives a hoot.

Journalism students don't need to carry political correctness to nonsensical extremes—but they do need to be careful. Words hurt. They do not exist in a vacuum. They have overtones that can be painful.

We've come a long way, actually. Watch a 1930s or 1940s movie on late-night TV and be prepared to endure stereotyping of people by race, age, and gender—at least. Women stayed home and cleaned; men wore suits and hats and were breadwinners. African Americans were portrayed as childlike and shiftless. The elderly existed only for long deathbed scenes.

Advertisements from the same period also were offensive. One showed a woman looking with despair at a flat tire on her car; the caption said, "There's never a man around when you need one." Women didn't seem to care about much except soap and lipstick.

If you are an Internet user, you already know some of the things it can do. With it, you can communicate directly with people all over the world. You can find advertisements for, and purchase, a wide variety of products and services. For a journalism student, however, the most interesting and relevant service the Net provides is the capacity to find—and provide—news.

In late 1996 *Editor & Publisher*, magazine of the newspaper industry, said that 819 newspapers from around the world were on-line. That means that many newspapers of varing sizes have versions of themselves in cyberspace. If you want, for example, to get a firsthand account of a work stoppage in Kuala Lumpur, you can probably find an English-language Malaysian newspaper that will give you detailed, up-to-the minute information. If you want to get a sense of how an important presidential address was received in various parts of the country, you can read accounts of it in newspapers from several regions. On a more down-to-earth level, if you are a Cubs fan vacationing in Kansas City, you should be able to find reports of last night's game simply by connecting with the *Chicago Tribune* on-line.

For a while, newspapers on-line tended to cost the viewer nothing—and, of course, sometimes the news presented

was rather sketchy. The *San Jose Mercury News*, which became known for its late-breaking news coverage on-line, was the first to charge for access. Now a good number of newspapers present only the first paragraph or two of a story in their free version. To get the whole story, you have to be a subscriber. You also generally have to pay to get access to news wire services such as Knight-Ridder and Reuters, as you do with the Clarinet news service, a Net-originated news service with over a million subscribers.

Some news on the Net emanates from the considerable number of news groups on Usenet, a large on-line bulletin board. Though these nonprofessional sources have been known to break stories earlier than the traditional news media, their accuracy can sometimes be suspect.

The broadcast media also disseminate news on the Internet. Although CNN has had a library of significant video news clips available for some time, up-to-the-minute coverage by the big networks has been done mainly by audio or through short video clips that mostly promoted their stations. A recent collaboration between NBC and Microsoft, however, has resulted in an all-news cable channel/Internet service, to be available twenty-four hours a day. The kinks and the quality of coverage in this venture still need to be worked out so that there are clearly some advantages to using the service rather than turning on an all-news station on your television.

Student publications can take advantage of the Internet both to circulate their own products and to obtain information. Any number of school newspapers can be found on-line, some created expressly for that medium, and many others can be requested by contacting an adviser or other involved party. Additionally, many papers use the Internet as a source of information. Some see this as one of the biggest potential changes in student newspapers. As reporters are able to access more publications from around the country, their stories about student lifestyles and concerns, as well as issues in general, will widen in scope.

The stereotypical American family of the 1940s no longer exists—if it ever did. So people should not be stereotyped in newswriting either.

So, yes, the hurt was real. And while there are certainly abuses associated with the PC movement, it's a small price to pay for reducing the hurt.

Offensive terms describing anyone's racial or ethnic background are absolutely forbidden unless in a direct quote that is—truly and without doubt—essential to the understanding of a story. For example, if the president of the college or university in your town uses a racial slur and is fired over the incident, journalists will have to use the word in their stories about the case. This would be a rare exception.

The whole class of pejorative words that ignorant people sometimes use to describe another person's religious faith or ethnic group also is banned from ordinary use, as are stereotypical images in general. Stereotyped references to Native Americans, for example, have offended many Americans recently. Drums, tomahawks, and warpaint thus join our earlier array of offenses against groups: the Irish drink, Asians are inscrutable, fat people are jolly, the elderly can't remember, professors are absent-minded, women are obsessed with shopping, men are obsessed with sports. This list doesn't even touch on the truly egregious words the races apply all too often to each other.

As a journalist you should watch carefully for bias—deliberate or accidental—regarding race, age, gender, sexual orientation, or philosophy of life. An environmentalist is an environmentalist, not a tree-hugger. Your grandfather isn't a geezer. Women aren't chicks, babes, or dolls. Men aren't hunks. A woman can be a doctor. A man can be a nurse. A woman can be an airline pilot. A man can be a cabin attendant. People with disabilities aren't crippled. The elderly can make love. Pictures are meant to illustrate the news, not to titillate. Sneaking words with double meanings into print or on the air doesn't impress many intelligent people.

Eliminate sexist language. Do not write as if every person on the earth is a man; on the other hand, writing as if every person were a woman does not solve anything either. Notice these examples:

> SEXIST: For a student to pass the course, he must pass the final exam. (No girls in the class?)
>
> SEXIST: For a student to pass the course, she must pass the final exam. (No boys in the class?)

You could do *both,* of course:

> BETTER: For a student to pass the course, he or she must pass the final exam.

The best solution, whenever possible, is to make the noun plural and avoid the problem:

> BETTER: For students to receive credit for the course, they must pass the final exam.

Below are some sexist traps and expressions you can use to avoid them.

mankind	*use* humanity
man-made	*use* manufactured, synthetic
mailman	*use* letter carrier
businessman	*use* business executive, merchant
fireman	*use* firefighter
policeman	*use* police officer
chairman	*use* chair
actor/actress	*use* actor

Follow this rule: Don't describe a woman's physical appearance or give her age if you would not in the same circumstance describe a man's appearance and give his age. If Bill and Hillary Clinton come to your town today, don't write stories about his magnificent speech and her new hairdo.

Courtesy titles (Mr., Ms., Miss, etc.) are optional and governed by local style. However, staff members should make sure that their style isn't dictated by gender. It's not "Jones" if a man, "Ms. Jones" if a woman. That's sexist.

Clarity

Because as a newspaper writer, you are never certain who will read your stories or under what circumstances, you must select words with the utmost care in order to eliminate as much confusion as possible. Develop a clear, simple, concise way of expressing yourself. *This does not mean that you should write for someone with a sixth-grade mentality.* This is a myth that has been repeated so often that a lot of people believe it. With public education free and required by law, where would all these sixth-grade minds come from? The answer is that these minds are in the sixth grade.

The important thing, to repeat, is to develop a clear, concise, simple writing style. Cull all excess wordage from every sentence:

> DON'T WRITE: "The Association of the Bar of the City of New York."
> WRITE: "The New York City Bar Association."
> DON'T WRITE: "He was wearing a shirt that was made of cotton and that had been borrowed from a friend of his."
> WRITE: "He was wearing a borrowed cotton shirt."

Go over every sentence you write looking for words to cut. Don't expect the copy editor to do this for you; the editing process begins with the reporter.

> He was wearing a shirt that was made of cotton and that had been borrowed from a friend of his.

Sentence Style

The good newswriter uses short words and sentences as well as short paragraphs, not because the audience is ignorant but because such elements are easier to read. Writing in short sentences doesn't mean adopting a "Dick-and-Jane" style. (The flag is red. It is white. It is blue.) But it does mean writing most of the time in *simple, declarative sentences* rather than complex ones. It means avoiding the semicolon (except in lists) and relying on the period. In this way you not only limit the length of the sentence (and make it more readable) but also reduce the amount of information the reader has to swallow in one gulp.

Don't get the idea that all good writing comes in short words and short sentences; there is no ideal sentence length. Certainly writers who decide never to write a sentence of more than, say, fifteen words are in trouble. Not only will they have a series of choppy, jerky sentences, but they will never finish a single story because they'll be too busy counting words.

Big Words

As a journalist, you need to remember that the reason you write is to communicate, not to show off your vocabulary. Here are some examples of pretentious words, with shorter, clearer synonyms in parentheses:

assuage (ease)	fallacious (wrong)
corpulent (fat)	endeavor (try)
circuitous (roundabout)	indisposed (ill)
appellation (name)	purchase (buy)
identical (same)	proceed (go)
erudite (learned)	inebriated (drunk)
conflagration (fire)	terminate (end)
inundated (flooded)	constituency (voters)
edifice (building)	demeanor (behavior)
precipitation (rain, snow)	location (site)

A writer who typically uses words such as these may feel stifled at first, but he or she should recognize that journalism is "controlled creativity." Because journalists must, above all, communicate, they are not free to sling words around with abandon. They have to watch their language. Besides, it's as easy to be creative with small words as it is with big ones. Can you translate the following?

> **Objective consideration of contemporary phenomena compels the conclusion that success or failure in competitive activities exhibits no tendency to be commensurate with innate capacity, but that a considerable element of the unpredictable must invariably be taken into account.**

You might recognize this paragraph if we restore it to its original, simplified form—the way it appeared in Ecclesiastes:

> **I returned, and saw under the sun, that the race is not to the swift, nor the battle to the strong, neither yet bread to the wise, nor yet riches to men of understanding, nor yet favor to men of skill; but time and chance happeneth to them all.**

You may know the football tactic where everyone rushes the passer as a "blitz," but don't use the term in newswriting if your audience isn't familiar with it.

Jargon

Jargon is the inside language of groups. Generally, journalists should avoid such language, translating it instead into the common tongue.

Players of various sports use jargon. Football players say "blitz" when they mean more players than usual go directly after the passer. Baseball players say "around the horn" when they mean around the bases. Police officers overuse "vehicle" instead of saying car, truck, or bicycle. People in the military go to "chow" instead of to dinner.

Journalists are no different. The say "spike that story," which means "kill that story," which means "do not publish that story." They play fast and loose with the term "art," using it to mean any illustration when the rest of the world uses the word in a loftier sense. Journalists often get their art out of the "morgue," which the rest of the world calls the library. Sometimes they need art from the morgue to do an obit for the bulldog—which means finding a photo for use with a death notice for the first edition. When they're in a real hurry, they send things out HTK, which means "head to come." They write "wild lines," which are captions for photos unaccompanied by stories.

The problem with jargon is that it can be so "inside" that people on the outside can't understand what's being expressed. Translate it. If the invitation says "continental breakfast," let your readers know that means juice, a roll, and coffee.

Redundancy

Still another trap is redundancy. Such expressions as "2 A.M. in the morning" and "the globe is spherical in shape" are redundant. You may write "2

A.M." or "2 in the morning," but there's no sense saying it twice. And it is sufficient to say the globe is spherical. "In shape" isn't needed because the word "spherical" contains the concept of shape. Similarly, do not write "surrounded on all sides," for that's what it means to be surrounded.

Clichés

Beginning writers can get into trouble with clichés, too. The cliché is an overworked, overused, old, and trite expression such as "free as a bird" or "since the dawn of time." Clichés reveal to the alert reader that the writer is too lazy to invent bright new figures of speech. A good guideline is: *Never use a figure of speech that you're used to seeing in print*. Journalism instructors usually take great delight in spotting clichés in their students' stories. Write "high noon" in a story and you may get a sarcastic note asking, "When is low noon?"

Common Clichés

acid test	in the limelight
at long last	in-your-face
avoid like the plague	kicked off the event
beat around the bush	Lady Luck
Been there. Done that.	last but not least
bite the bullet	light as a feather
blunt instrument	little white lie
calm before the storm	milk of human kindness
dead as a doornail	raining cats and dogs
dull thud	sadder but wiser
get down to brass tacks	selling like hotcakes
hands across the sea	smart as a whip
heated argument	take off the gloves
hit the nail on the head	white as a sheet
Hope springs eternal.	with bated breath

Fear of Repetition

A master of the English language, Theodore Bernstein of *The New York Times*, coined a word to describe the next writing hazard. The word is *monologophobia*, and it means, roughly, the fear of repeating a word. As Bernstein points out, the ailment leads to such paragraphs as "Sugar Ray flattened Bobo in twelve rounds in 1950, outpointed him in fifteen sessions in 1952, and knocked him out in two heats last December 9." This leaves the reader wondering if a round, a session, and a heat are the same thing (they are). Have no fear of repeating a word, because if you do you may end up with such silly synonyms as "yellow metal" for "gold," "grapplers" for "wrestlers," and "thinclads" for "members of the track team."

The article in the "On Display" feature on page 164 elegantly sums up all these points about newspaper style.

Four Bananas Aren't Three Bananas and One Elongated Yellow Fruit

by James L. Kilpatrick

HOLLINS COLLEGE, VA.—The student editors had come from a dozen Southeastern colleges to swap suggestions and receive awards; and now we were assembled on a white veranda, with a spring rain drenching the boxwoods, and the talk turned easily to shop talk.

All of the young writers had read E. B. White's *Elements of Style*, and most of them had browsed in Fowler's *Modern English Usage*. They had profited from Ernest Gowers and Ivor Brown and from courses redundantly styled "creative writing." They put the question to me, as a visiting newspaperman. Would I give them my own set of rules with a few random examples thrown in, for writing newspaper copy? It was a temptation not to be resisted.

I pass these rules along here, for whatever value they may have to fellow workers in the carpentry of words. Every editor in the land could add some admonitions of his own.

1. *Be clear.* This is the first and greatest commandment. In a large sense, nothing else matters. For clarity embraceth all things, the clear thought to begin with; the right words for conveying that thought; the orderly arrangement of the words. It is a fine thing, now and then, to be colorful, to be vivid, to be bold. First be clear.

2. *Love words*, and treat them with respect. For words are the edged tools of your trade; you must keep them honed. Do not *infer* when you mean to *imply*, do not write *fewer than*, when you mean *less than*. Do not use *among*, when you mean *between*. Observe that *continually* and *continuously* have different meanings. Do not write *alternately* when you mean *alternatively*. Tints are light, shades are dark. The blob on the gallery wall is not an abstract. Beware the use of *literally*, *virtually*, *fulsome*, *replica*, *many-faceted*, and *the lion's share*. Pinch-hitters are something more than substitutes. Learn the rules of *that* and *which*. When you fall into the pit of "and which," climb out of your swampy sentence and begin anew.

3. As a general proposition, *use familiar words*. Be precise; but first be understood. Search for the solid nouns that bear the weight of thought. Use active verbs that hit an object and do not glance off. When you find an especially gaudy word, possessed of a gorgeous rhinestone glitter, lock it firmly away. Such words are costume jewels. They are sham.

4. *Edit your copy*; then edit it again; then edit it once more. This is the hand-rubbing process. No rough sandpapering can replace it.

5. *Strike the redundant word.* Emergencies are inherently acute; crises are grave; consideration is serious. When you exhort your readers to get down to basic fundamentals, you are dog-paddling about in a pool of ideas and do not know where to touch bottom. Beware the little qualifying words: *rather*, *somewhat*, *pretty*, *very*. As White says, these are the leeches that suck the meaning out of language. Pluck them from your copy.

6. *Have no fear of repetition.* It is better to repeat a word than to send an orphaned antecedent in its place. Do not write *horsehide*, *white pellet*, or *the old apple* when you mean *baseball*. Members of City Council are not solons; they are members of City Council. If you must write banana four times, then write banana four times, nothing is gained by three bananas and one elongated yellow fruit.

7. If you cannot be obviously profound, *try not to be profoundly obvious*. Therefore, do not inform your reader that something remains to be seen. The thought will have occurred to him already.

8. *Strive for a reasoned perspective.* True crises come infrequently; few actions are outrageous; cities and economies are seldom paralyzed for long. A two-alarm fire is not a holocaust. Not much is imperative or urgent; still less is vital. To get at the size of a crowd, divide the cops' estimate by 3.1416.

9. *Style depends in part upon the cadence of your prose.* Therefore listen to your copy with a fine-tuned ear. In the prose that truly pleases, you will find that every sentence has an unobtrusive rhythm that propels it on its way. With a little re-arranging, you can keep the rhythm going. . . .

10. *Beware of long sentences*; they spread roots that tend to trip the reader up. The period key lies nicely on the bottom row of your machine, down toward the right-hand end. Use it. Use it often.

Wrap-up

If the lead paragraph is the most important in the story, what immediately follows it certainly is next in interest. One way to hold the interest built up in the lead is to follow with a quotation, the sound of a human voice, immediately. Some people call this a back-up quote, one designed to support the lead. Such a quote links the lead to the second paragraph, helping the story unfold logically and coherently. This is one type of transition.

Transitions can be entire sentences but usually they are one word: *but, also, therefore, however.* To aid the reader, sentences and paragraphs should be tied together logically.

After the lead and back-up, the story—told in skeletal fashion in the lead—is then simply retold in greater detail.

The preceding describes the inverted-pyramid style of writing. Many other techniques are used, including the rare surprise ending.

One increasingly popular style uses a summary lead followed by a chronological account. This is especially effective in describing action.

Details of style should be kept in mind. A publication needs to be consistent, always spelling words the same way ("adviser," not "advisor"). The publication's stylebook dictates these decisions and everyone should follow it.

Modern writers avoid sexist language and avoid using the pronoun "he" to describe the entire human race. Words that are inappropriately male ("mailman") should be eliminated (use "letter carrier" instead). The whole array of issues surrounding so-called political correctness is appropriate for a journalism student to ponder.

Short words ("rich," not "opulent"; "marriage," not "matrimony") and short sentences aid busy readers. So does tight writing. Eliminate such usages as "Easter Sunday" and "Jewish rabbi." Redundancy is an enemy of clarity. It is 2 in the morning or 2 A.M. but never 2 A.M. in the morning. There is no need to say it twice.

Jargon also can interfere with communication. Don't use "precipitation event" when you really mean "rain." Clichés also should be avoided. Do not use such worn-out expressions as "in-your-face," "last but not least," "dead as a doornail," or "avoid like the plague." Use of clichés exposes lazy, uninventive writers.

Fear of repeating a word ("monologophobia") can lead to inelegant expressions, such as "elongated yellow fruit" for "banana." Have no fear of repeating words.

Evaluation Checklist: *News Story*

✓ Does the story begin with a succinct and direct, yet interesting, lead?

✓ Does a back-up quote or other transition connect the lead with the next paragraph?

✓ Is the style used to develop the story—inverted pyramid, chronological, or a combination—appropriate to the content?

✓ Are the majority of the sentences simple declarative ones?

✓ Has the writer avoided sexist language and other offensive terms, big words, clichés, and jargon?

✓ Does the story follow the publication's and general AP style?

✓ Is the story free from errors in sentence structure, capitalization and punctuation, and spelling?

On Assignment

Individual Activities

1. Write a definition or brief explanation of each of the following terms.

   back-up quote   chronological style
   cliché   jargon
   redundancy   sexist language
   stylebook   tieback
   transition

2. Test your critical thinking. Recall several newsworthy events that have recently occurred in your community or school and evaluate possible approaches to handling them. Which could best be treated in an inverted-pyramid story? Of these stories, which would be simplest to write? Why? Which would be hardest to write? Why? Which stories could best be handled through some other approach? Discuss your ideas in class.

3. Rewrite the following news story based on what you've learned about style in this chapter.

   • Meeting at 3:45 P.M. in the afternoon, the Centerville High School Student council got down to brass tacks at long last and decided this year's Senior Prom will be Friday, May 11.

   • Tickets to the event began selling like hotcakes. Students rushed to purchase tickets, and florist shops were inundated with corsage orders.

   • The location for the prom was not known, but the council promised to hire extra policemen to be on duty in case anyone becomes inebriated. Businessmen also were to be approached and asked to support the prom with donations.

   • Also wanted by the council was a way to utilize student input in ascertaining which school personnel would attend as chaperones. Approximately five teachers are presently needed.

   • Future plans made by the council call for the prom queen to receive a bouquet of flowers exactly at the hour of midnight.

   • After a heated argument in the council meeting, members exhibited the milk of human kindness by pronouncing the dispute dead as a doornail.

   • On the level of basic fundamentals, council members set aside a large number of issues to be merged together at the next meeting. Qualified experts will be called in as consultants and past records studied carefully for the purpose of finding important essentials.

   • Council members voted unanimously 14–0 to ask a Jewish rabbi to say the invocation.

   • "I'm glad this issue is settled," sighed President Sally Smith.

   • "Me, too," stated the vice president, Chang Lee.

   • "You can say that again," laughed a new freshman whose appellation was unknown.

4. Complete the stories for which you wrote leads in the exercises in Chapter Six.

5. Complete your interview story from Chapter Five.

Team Activities

6. Working in teams, scour the sports and news pages of your local newspaper to find examples of the clichés and other overworked figures of speech mentioned in this chapter. Clip the articles and compare what you find with the other teams' articles. Rewrite what you find.

7. Develop a stylebook for your school publications. You may want to use the *AP Stylebook* as a guide, but also include the sorts of things that stylebook does not cover. How will you, for example, refer to women on the second reference in a story? To instructors on second reference? Does the word *the* in the name of your paper take a capital T? Compare your stylebook to those created by other teams and the one being used by your newspaper. As a class, select one official stylebook to use in future assignments.

Like many successful journalists, Katti Gray started small. Now a reporter for *Newsday* in Long Island, New York, she began her professional journey in Wichita Falls, Texas.

Armed with a journalism degree and internships at the *Dallas Times Herald* and the *Fort Worth Star-Telegram*'s Washington bureau, Gray set out for her first job as a reporter for the *Wichita Falls Record News*.

Gray graduated from Texas Christian University with majors in journalism and political science, an education she feels is a good combination for a journalist. Like many new journalism graduates, she took a job at a midsized daily in a midsized town, hoping to get practical experience reporting a variety of stories.

Covering the social services beat, she learned how to establish and maintain rapport with her contacts on a day-to-day basis, as well as how to dig out underlying issues from daily news.

While at Wichita Falls, she completed a series on the impact of desegregation on minority students and one on alternative schools for troubled and/or disabled students.

Through her more general assignments, she said, she has learned how to be enterprising.

"I learned quickly that you can't come back from an assignment and tell the editor there was no story," she said.

With some professional experience under her belt, Gray left the *Record News* and in June 1985 joined the *Fort Worth Star-Telegram*, where she covered suburban education, social services, and government. Four years later she moved to *Newsday* to cover town government. Today she covers education across Long Island. She has also done work for the national, features, and travel desks, and for a now-defunct Sunday magazine.

"This is one job where you feel you really can make a difference," Gray said. "The stories you do can change someone's life forever or right what's wrong."

Big city journalism has also taught her to be "a whole lot more sensitive to how the media exploit people's tragedies."

"We do not respect people's privacy," she said. "There are times when I want to jump up and say I don't want to do this."

Being in New York hasn't changed Gray.

"I'm still very much the same person," she said. "I still believe the media have the potential to make a difference in people's lives."

But newspapers have a long way to go to give voice to people who have none.

"We need to make the media a fairer craft," she said.

Her New York City bosses, she said, would benefit from visiting smaller newspapers to see the brilliance there. "Good journalism goes on all over the country."

"Kids need to realize that to be important you don't have to be a *New York Times*, *Washington Post*, *Chicago Tribune*, or *Newsday* reporter," she said.

College fueled her idealism, pointing out the great power and potential of the media, but she also had to learn to deal with practical realities.

"Not everyone can win a Pulitzer. Every story you write will not liberate or emancipate somebody. You sometimes do things you are intellectually opposed to."

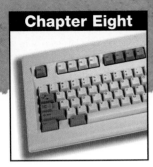

Chapter Eight

Handling Quotes Fairly and Accurately

Key Terms

direct quotation

paraphrase

partial quote

attribution

Key Concepts

After reading this chapter, you should

- understand the need for precision in quotes

- know the appropriate uses of direct quotes, partial quotes, and paraphrasing

- know the issues associated with taping interviews

- know how to handle attribution

- understand techniques for reporting on speeches

A couple of years ago, football teams representing the University of Florida and the University of Nebraska met in the Fiesta Bowl in Tempe, Arizona, to determine the national football championship. After the game, coaches and players spoke to the many journalists who covered the game. Here are some of the ways Nebraska coach Tom Osborne's remarks were quoted in various newspapers:

> **"It wasn't a ho-hum thing, but our players were confident they'd win tonight."**

> **"I think the players expected to win. It wasn't ho-hum. But it was matter-of fact."**

> **"I certainly did not think it would be a blowout."**

> **"I didn't think it would be a blowout."**

> **"I guess there's still a place in college football for a running quarterback. The option still has a place in football."**

> **"This does point out the fact that there is still a place in college football for a running quarterback. We believe there is still a place for the option."**

Obviously, at least one of the papers had to be wrong on each quote, for the coach could not have said *both* things attributed to him.

Does it matter? Do direct quotes—this is what a person said, in his or her own words—have to be word-for-word accurate? Is there no margin for error?

The changes made in what the coach said or didn't say were quite harmless. There really is not much difference between "I certainly did not think it would be a blowout" and "I didn't think it would be a blowout." Still, it's bothersome. The world doesn't turn on the exact phrasing of the words of a football coach in the midst of a noisy press conference. But it can turn on the exact phrasing by a president, a secretary of state, or a foreign leader. So, as always, 100 percent accuracy is a goal, a place to start.

One journalism instructor frequently asks students if they have had their names in the paper in the past year or two. Typically, one hundred hands go into the air. Then he asks, "Were the stories completely, totally accurate?" Virtually all the hands go down. Upon discussion, it turns out

Nebraska football coach Tom Osborne gives press conferences after many important games. Though the exact wording of his remarks is perhaps not of vital importance, reporters should still try to quote him accurately.

that the students feel they were misquoted or their words distorted. In fairness, of course, sometimes—frequently—it is a case of, "Boy, I wish I hadn't said that!" But too often words are misquoted or twisted.

Direct Quotation

As a beginning journalist, you should pay a great deal of attention to the skills involved in handling quoted material.

Ideally, when you enclose a sentence or part of a sentence in quotation marks (quotes), you are telling your readers that the quoted material is *exactly* what the speaker said. You're not saying it's close or almost. You're saying, "These are the exact words." Anyone who's ever spent any time reporting, however, knows that this ideal is seldom, if ever, reached.

How is it possible to reproduce exactly what people say? People start sentences they never finish; they back up and start again; they say "ya know," "like I said," "ummmm," "ahhhh," and so on. We expect precision and logic in written communications or in a prepared spoken presentation. But extemporaneous human speech doesn't work that way. People think out loud, expressing half-formed thoughts and working out what they want to say as they go. It is virtually impossible to reproduce this speech exactly, and *why would you want to?* The job is to convey information . . . and there's no information in "ya know."

A Question of Exactness

There's a Lesson Here Somewhere . . .

". . . you should say what you mean," the March Hare went on.

"I do," Alice hastily replied: "at least—at least I mean what I say—that's the same thing, you know."

"Not the same thing a bit!" said the Hatter. "Why, you might just as well say that 'I see what I eat' is the same thing as 'I eat what I see.'"

—LEWIS CARROLL, *ALICE'S ADVENTURES IN WONDERLAND*

The journalistic ideal of reproducing speech *exactly* as it was uttered needs to be reexamined with an eye toward slight and very careful change. Studies indicate sources care about this issue a great deal less than do journalists. Sources want their thoughts and ideas conveyed accurately to the public. They care less about their exact words. So does this mean journalists can just come close, be almost perfect? Of course not. Regardless of everything that's been written here, most quotes must be 100

On the momentous occasion of the first moon landing in 1969, the media considered it vital to record astronaut Neil Armstrong's exact words.

percent, absolutely word-for-word perfect. These would include important remarks by politicians (What *exactly* did the president say about the nation's economy?), remarks certain to touch off controversy (a business executive's remarks that could be interpreted as racist), or historic words. In 1969, for example, there was discussion by journalists over what Neil Armstrong said as he took the first steps on the moon. Was it "one small step for man . . ." or "one small step for *a* man . . .?" No one was inclined that day to just come close.

You can invent your own scenarios in which the exact language is crucial. Most of the time, journalists simply take out the "ya knows" and the "hmmms" and no harm is done. Faced with a tangled, unclear sentence, most journalists decide not to use a direct quote but to try and convey the source's ideas in clearer words. No one (at least no one with a commitment to ethics) alters quotes a great deal. A bit of sanitizing goes on, of course. But that's about the extent of it.

Use a Tape Recorder

Tape recorders can be a great aid to a reporter for any assignment in which capturing someone's exact words is important. Buy a small recorder, since some people are intimidated by large ones. If the source agrees, turn on the recorder at the beginning, set it aside, and just let it run. Never, however, tape-record someone without permission, either in person or on the telephone. You can use a tape recorder during speeches and meetings, too. In some cities at school board or city council meetings, the area near the speaker's podium is a forest of recorders placed there by print and broadcast journalists.

Remember always to take good notes even if you're using a tape recorder. Sometimes the batteries go dead or the tape breaks or gets twisted in the mechanism. Don't rely completely on a tape recorder.

If you're not using a tape recorder and are still concerned about exact quotes, take very careful notes, in shorthand or speedwriting if you know how, and flesh them out from memory as soon as possible. You will be surprised at how well your memory works. In most cases, no one expects you to reproduce every single word, every "ah-hem," but your goal is to come as close as possible.

When Not to Qoute

There are exceptions to using exact quotes. What if, during a speech or interview, the subject uses a profane four-letter word? What do you do? The easy answer (and frequently the right one) is to simply take it out, ignore it. But there are times—rare times, to be sure—when profanity is exactly right, when it conveys the point in the best possible way. If that is the case, then quote it. But don't ever sprinkle in four-letter words just to prove your sophistication or your freedom.

Another exception occurs when the subject uses poor grammar. There's no need to reproduce bad grammar exactly as it was spoken, especially if there is no reason to expect the speaker to be a grammarian. For example, if you are interviewing your elderly custodian who has only a few years' formal education, don't make him seem illiterate. On the other hand, it would be foolish for you to take a colorful character who uses a lot of quaint phrases and make her sound like an English professor.

Paraphrasing

Often, paraphrasing is helpful. It is perfectly proper, often even desirable, for a reporter to paraphrase a person's words: to put the speaker's ideas into the reporter's own words. Thus, if a direct quote is long or rambling or poorly stated, the writer may revise it, knock off the quote marks, and simply add "he said" or "she said" at the end of the sentence.

Suppose the speaker says the following:

> **"We are doing everything in our power at police headquarters to see to it that there is a parking place for everyone who drives to school. We hope everyone involved will be patient. We'll work it out, I promise."**

There's little doubt that a journalist could say that more concisely by paraphrasing, in which case it could read like this:

> **Chief Jones said police are trying to find parking space for everyone at school. He urged patience and promised to find a solution for the crowded lots.**

There is one hazard to paraphrasing: Certain words must be adjusted. For instance, if the direct quote is, "We decided to go to a movie," the paraphrase has to read: "They decided to go to the movies, he said." Notice the shift in pronouns. "We" is a word reserved for direct quotes and editorials; so are "us" and "our." It is *the* country, *the* school, *the* town, not our country, our school, our town. Writing in the first person injects the reporter into the story; it amounts to an editorial position.

Paraphrase for Facts

Quotes should not be used to convey facts. Quotes make a story lively, give it a human touch, let readers begin to understand what a source is like. Capture good quotes and use lots of them. But paraphrase when you're simply conveying facts.

Here's the explanation. Let's say you interview the school librarian and he says the following:

> **"We have 3,543 books in Room 101 and 4,589 in Room 209, and 400 movies and 250 CD's in the annex—and if we don't pass the bond issue so we can get more room I'm going to resign."**

Whatever you do, don't make a quote out of the first part of the statement. Paraphrase it:

> **Mr. Taylor, the school librarian, said the library houses more than 3,500 books in Room 101 and more than 4,500 in Room 209, plus some 400 movies and 250 CD's in the annex. He said he plans to resign as librarian if voters reject a bond issue to expand the library.**

If the head of the Red Cross says, "We are going to deliver a planeload of food and supplies to the disaster area. The plane takes off from Municipal Airport at 8:15 A.M.," don't use that as a direct quote.

Paraphrase it:

> The head of the local Red Cross said the Red Cross will airlift food and supplies to the disaster area. The plane takes off at 8:15 A.M. from Municipal Airport.

The direct quote is for color, for impact—not for conveying merely factual information.

Avoid Repetition

Do not present the same information as both a paraphrase and a direct quote. Copy editors the world over regard this as a bane of their existence. Here's an example:

> The mayor promised today he would never embezzle money from the city again.
> "I will never embezzle money from the city again," the mayor said.

The exact same information is presented in each sentence. It makes copy editors want to tear out their hair. Here's another example:

> The coach said his team could win if it eliminates turnovers, penalties, and mental errors.
> "We have to eliminate turnovers, penalties, and mental errors to win," the coach said.

Hit the delete key!

Partial Quotation

One method to avoid the overuse of both paraphrased material and long blocks of quoted material is the partial quote. A writer is free to directly quote part of a sentence while paraphrasing the rest. For example:

> The school needs a dress code, the principal said, because students are becoming "sloppy in dress and sloppy in thought."
> Jones said he was "ready to do cartwheels" after scoring the winning touchdown.

The material enclosed in quotes in the preceding sentences constitutes partial quotes.

Beware, however, that you do not carry this practice to absurd extremes. For example:

> **Jones said he was "happy" after scoring the touchdown.**
>
> **She was in "critical" condition, the hospital spokesperson said.**

What purpose do the quotation marks serve in these examples? None at all.

Here are some other instances where quotes are unnecessary:

> **After three defeats, it appears the season is "down the drain."**
>
> **The course is "a piece of cake."**
>
> **The music is "hot."**

You get the point. If a slang word or phrase is exactly right, use it and skip the quotes; they will add nothing except confusion. The reader will either understand the slang or not. The quotation marks will not make any difference.

Attribution

Beginning writers often have trouble with attribution. What is meant by attribution is this: Since it is often not possible to really know what people mean or feel or believe, report what they *say* they mean or feel or believe. Report what the person said and make a point of saying who said it. Attribution amounts to giving the reader the name of the source. For example:

> **The superintendent *said* she will resign.**
>
> **The police chief *said* Jones had confessed.**
>
> **Taxes will go down, the governor *promised*.**
>
> **Police *said* the accident occurred because of slick streets.**
>
> **There is no way Tech can win, the coach *said*.**

The verb you use to indicate your source is important: *stated, declared, noted, pointed out*, and so on. The best of all such words is *said*. It is a neutral word that contains no editorial overtones; it is unobtrusive and rarely becomes tiresome no matter how often it appears in a story.

Words to Use

Be very careful which word you select when you depart from *said. Stated* is very formal. *Pointed out* should be reserved for absolute facts (The sun

When reporting on a controversial event such as a car accident, statements made by witnesses as well as participants must be correctly attributed.

rose, he pointed out). *Charge, demand, shout,* and the like have editorial connotations. Whatever you do, stay away from this kind of construction:

> "I could care less," he frowned.
>
> "It's no problem of mine," she shrugged.
>
> "How bad is this," he grimaced.
>
> "Wonderful idea," she smiled.

You can frown, shrug, grimace, or smile all you want, but no words will come out. The verb you use must indicate speech formations by lips, mouth, and tongue.

Here is an excerpt from "The Gambler, the Nun, the Radio," a short story by Ernest Hemingway. Notice it did not bother him to keep repeating "said," nor does it get monotonous. (Italics were added for emphasis.)

> They wheeled him in, thin, his skin transparent, his hair black and needing to be cut, his eyes very laughing, his teeth bad when he smiled.
>
> "Hola, amigo! Que tal?"
>
> "As you see," *said* Mr. Frazer. "And thou?"
>
> "Alive and with the leg paralyzed."
>
> "Bad," Mr. Frazer *said*. "But the nerve can regenerate and be as good as new."
>
> "So they tell me."
>
> "What about the pain?"
>
> "Not now. For a while I was crazy with it in the belly. I thought the pain alone would kill me."
>
> Sister Cecilia was observing them happily.
>
> "She tells me you never made a sound," Mr. Frazer *said*.
>
> "So many people in the ward," the Mexican *said* deprecatingly.
> "What class of pain do you have?"

"Big enough. Clearly not as bad as yours. When the nurse goes out I cry an hour, two hours. It rests me. My nerves are bad now."

"You have the radio. If I had a private room and a radio I would be crying and yelling all night long."

"I doubt it."

"Hombre, si. It's very healthy. But you cannot do it with so many people."

"At least," Mr. Frazer *said*, "the hands are still good. They tell me you make your living with the hands."

"And the head," he *said*, tapping his forehead. "But the head isn't worth as much."

Said Whom?

Is it "Smith said" or "said Smith"? That little wrinkle in the ways of attribution gives people trouble. Here's the solution. If all the writer wants to do is tell who said what, then the construction is "Smith said." For example:

"I love journalism class," Smith said.

If, however, the writer wants to tell a bit about Smith besides his or her name, it goes this way:

"I love journalism class," said Smith, whose mother is the journalism teacher.

Need for Attribution

When should you attribute? The need for attribution is in direct proportion to the amount of controversy attached to the statement. Thus, a story about a robbery and the arrest of two suspects would need heavy attribution. But a story saying a downtown street has been closed for repairs would need little attribution, because it is common knowledge and non-controversial. The best approach is—when in doubt, attribute.

The next question is where to attribute, where to place the "he saids" and "she pointed outs." In general, attribution works best at the end or in the middle of a sentence. Give the quote first and the source of the quote second. In a long quote, attribution should come at the first logical point in the first sentence. Try this lead:

Professor Pat Braintower on Thursday told a group of law students that America's poor need free legal advice or they will lose their rights.

This version is easier to read and comes to the point more quickly:

America's poor need free legal advice or they will lose their rights, Professor Pat Braintower told a group of law students Thursday.

It is also perfectly acceptable to interrupt a quotation in the middle for attribution. For example:

"Our students are mature," Kuzinski told teachers Tuesday, "but they do not always act like it."

On the other hand, this interruption for attribution is awkward:

> **"Our students," Kuzinski told teachers Tuesday, "are mature, but they do not always act like it."**

It is especially helpful to interrupt in the middle if the quote is long and unwieldy; then the interruption serves as a breath pause for your reader.

Perhaps the most important point concerning attribution is this: Always make it absolutely clear *whose* opinion is being expressed. Given a choice, the reader may conclude that the opinion is the reporter's—and this is *not* the impression you want to leave. So don't let quotes float free of their source. This construction, for instance, is wrong:

> **Schwartz was elated. "It was my first touchdown ever."**

And so is this, because the reader has to wait too long to find out who is talking:

> **"It was my best day. I got the ball on a dead run. It was a perfect pass, and I just outran the secondary. One guy dived at me near the goal, but he missed," Schwartz said.**

In the latter example, the writer should have identified Schwartz as the speaker right after "It was my best day."

The article in the "On Display" feature on page 179 reports what a number of people said about a new school policy allowing students to buy food all day. As you read it, look for paraphrasing, direct quotes, and the positioning of various attributions.

Lest anyone doubt the importance of attribution, consider the embarrassment on the part of the press and the confusion on the part of the audience when media across the country reported that prisoners, during a New York prison riot, had slashed the throats of their hostages. Almost without exception the press failed to attribute this "fact" to its source, and when it became evident later that no throats had been slashed, the press looked pretty bad. And the public must have wondered how many other statements in the story were false.

Speech Stories

A fruitful source of news is the speech. Speeches given by newsworthy individuals are almost always covered by the press, because journalists know that public pronouncements of great importance are often made in speech format.

Food for Thought

by Holly Wolfe, Abraham Lincoln High School, Council Bluffs, Iowa

Hungry students will soon have access to nutritious snacks throughout the day.

Vending machines offering juice and non-candy snacks will be located in the science, social studies, English, and business wings as well as the commons area.

Principal James Lake said these machines, along with the pop and candy machines, will be on all day, giving students a chance to purchase snacks and juice between classes. He said passing periods will be lengthened to eight or nine minutes to accommodate student use of the machines.

Lake and teachers stressed that student cooperation is necessary to do this.

"Students have been pretty good this semester and deserve something," Lake said. "They must be respectful and organized and realize that this is a privilege. As soon as there are wrappers or trash around the campus, the machines will be turned off."

Lake said the decision to permit food in the classroom is entirely up to each teacher. Several teachers already allow food in class.

"I think a lot of kids rush around in the morning and don't have time to eat," said Linda Patton, Spanish instructor. "After it hits them, they just don't function as well. That's why I decided to allow kids to eat in class."

Many students agree with Patton.

"It's easy to be distracted when you're hungry," Sarah McLean '96, said. "If you have a break with food, you're able to stay on track longer."

Teachers are hopeful that students will perform better after a snack.

"I'd be willing to give it a try," said Alynn Jaeger, English instructor. "If it really does improve students' academic performances or attention spans, I guess it's a good idea."

Some students feel this might even be an incentive for staying in class.

"I think it's a great idea," Sally Christensen '95, said. "It might even help with the problem of skipping because a lot of kids leave school to go get a pop or food."

Teachers were recently asked to consider the idea of a set time during the day where the entire school would get a nutrition break, but they voted down the idea. Many believed it would be impossible to have nearly 1300 students in the halls or cafeteria at one time.

"I'll try this to see how it goes," said Dennis DeVault, American History instructor, "but they're going to have to earn the privilege of having food in my classroom."

Covering a speech or any oral presentation is, in a sense, one of the easiest of all assignments. On the surface, at least, it consists of one person speaking—and that is quite simple. But dangers are present. The reporter must be careful to get down exactly what the speaker says. Then the reporter must try to select the speaker's main points for inclusion in the story. There probably has never been a speech story that could have been written in the order the speech was given. The lead, the speaker's main point or points, often comes late in the speech, and the writer must tell the reader immediately what the main point was.

Having direct quotes from a source can be the ground on which interesting, informative news stories are built. But a number of situations can arise involving direct quotes that can make their use controversial and, in worst-case scenarios, even the source of lawsuits.

One issue is quoting out of context. Most newswriters are responsible and take pains to explain the situation in which a statement was made. But often enough the quoted person complains afterward that the spirit of his or her statement was completely different from the way it was presented in the news story. For example, a statement like "When I get this angry, I just don't worry about the consequences" can be taken out of context to characterize the speaker as irresponsible or perhaps even violent. But what if the speaker was talking about how angry he felt as he loudly criticized a neighbor woman for kicking her pet dog? The "consequences" referred to in the quote may simply have been having a public argument with his neighbor, something the speaker ordinarily wouldn't do. Using the quote out of context has taken a probably justifiable act and made it seem like the response of a dangerous person.

Quotes taken from movie reviews are frequently used in ads. "An appallingly bad script that even Gugliamo's beautifully staged scenes can't begin to overcome" can be quoted out of context as simply "beautifully staged

scenes." In cases like this, not only is the quote taken out of context, but it is truncated to totally change its intended meaning.

Occasionally a situation will arise when a person finds his or her remarks in a news article without having any previous indication that they will end up there. This seems to happen more often to people who aren't used to being interviewed or quoted. A case that made headlines in the last few years was one in which reporter Connie Chung interviewed the mother of then-Speaker of the House Newt Gingrich. An elderly woman, Mrs. Gingrich was unused to the media spotlight, and somewhere in the interview mentioned that her son Newt not only disliked First Lady Hillary Clinton but also had a name that he usually called her. Chung cajoled the woman into repeating the name, suggesting strongly that it would be kept just between the two of them, but then turned around and quoted her on a news show. Not surprisingly, media as well as public criticism came quickly and strongly. There was no question that what Chung did was less than proper.

Sometimes a journalist's alleged distortion of quotations can bring about a lawsuit. One famous example is the so-called "Malcolm case," in which reporter Janet Malcolm, in a long article on psychiatrist Jeffrey M. Masson, attributed direct quotes to him that there was no record of him ever having said. (The interview was recorded, but Malcolm had additional notes in which she claimed to have recorded the quotes in question.) Masson sued Malcolm, as well as her employer, saying that she fabricated quotes that made him look unscholarly, dishonest, and vain.

Interestingly, the courts in this case sided with Malcolm, saying that her characterization on Masson was not a distortion of the overall impression his interview responses had created. But it might be argued that Malcolm was quite lucky to get off. A safer and ultimately more ethical way to handle quotes is to present them accurately and to fully establish their context.

The best speech story is a well-designed mixture of direct quotes, paraphrasings, and partial quotes. The lead distills the essence of what the speaker said; it summarizes and explains. The lead gets to the point. It does not waste the reader's time with needless detail, such as where the speech took place. Save that for later, unless there are special circumstances. The lead emphasizes *what* was said, not the simple fact that a speech was made.

When you cover a speech, pay close attention to the audience. How many people were there? How many times was the speaker interrupted by applause? Which lines calculated to get applause stirred no one? Were there hecklers or protesters present? How many? What was the speaker's reaction?

Watch for the obvious omission, for what the speaker does *not* say. (She did *not* announce the new budget, she did *not* announce her candidacy, she did *not* say who would pay for the new programs she proposed, she did *not* say who would draw up the new policy or who would approve it.) And realize that the phrase "he [or she] concluded" can be used only once in a speech story.

The article in the "On Display" feature on page 182 reports on a speech—really a eulogy, or speech praising a dead person—given by the granddaughter of Yitzhak Rabin, assassinated Israeli prime minister, at his funeral. Because the speech was brief and beautifully worded, the writer quotes from it in some detail.

News stories about the speech Noa Ben-Artzi gave at the funeral of her slain grandfather, Israeli prime minister Yitzhak Rabin, tended to quote her at length.

Wrap-up

Reproducing accurately what people say is a basic journalistic function. Sometimes sources claim they were misquoted when they really were not, but journalists still need to emphasize accuracy in quoted material.

Too often, there are great differences between what is said and what is published or aired. Words can be misquoted or twisted.

Beginning journalists should pay a great deal of attention to the skills involved in handling quoted material. When journalists enclose a sentence or part of a sentence in quotation marks, they are telling readers that this is *exactly* what the speaker said. They are not saying it is close to or almost what was said.

It is difficult to reproduce exactly what people say. People start sentences they never finish, they back up and start again, they say "ya know," "like I said," "ummmm," "ahhh," and so on.

The journalistic ideal of reproducing speech *exactly* as it was uttered needs to be reexamined with an eye toward slight and careful change. Studies indicate sources care about this issue a great deal less than do journalists. Sources want their thoughts and ideas conveyed accurately to the public. They care less about their exact words.

Most of the time, journalists take out the "ya knows" and the "hmmmms" and no harm is done. Faced with an unclear sentence, most journalists decide not to use a

The Saddest Farewell

by Tom Hundley, Chicago Tribune

When Yitzhak Rabin's 17-year-old granddaughter spoke, tough old Israeli generals wept.

"You will forgive me, but I do not want to talk about peace today. I want to talk about my grandfather," said Noa Ben-Artzi, delivering the family's eulogy before the slain leader's coffin on the slopes of Mt. Herzl cemetery.

"Grandfather, you were the pillar of fire before the camp, and now we're just a camp left alone in the dark, and we're so cold and sad.

"Very few people knew you truly. They can talk about you. But I feel they know nothing about the depth of the pain, the disaster and, yes, this holocaust," she said, brushing back tears.

"You were so wonderful. . . . You are our hero, lone wolf."

Kings and presidents had come to eulogize the Israeli leader. They spoke of his long and brilliant career as a soldier and statesman, of his determination to make peace with his enemy.

His granddaughter spoke of the private Rabin, a man they could never know. Many at the funeral were weeping during her moving address. Even the translator spoke in a choked voice.

"People greater than I have eulogized you, but none knows the caress that you placed on my shoulder and the warm hug you saved only for us and your half-smile that always told me so much—the same smile that is no more," Ben-Artzi said.

"I harbor no feelings of revenge because the pain is too great.

"Grandpa, you were our hero. I want you to know that everything I did, I always saw you before me.

"Your appreciation and your love escorted us through every way and road. You never abandoned us, and here you are, my eternal hero, cold and alone, and there's nothing I can do to save you," she said, her voice strong, but her shoulders shaking.

"We love you grandfather, forever." Tears streamed down her cheeks as she left the podium.

---

direct quote but to try to convey the source's ideas in the journalist's words.

Tape recorders can aid a reporter. Small, unobtrusive ones are best. Good notes are important, however, even when a tape recorder is used. Sometimes batteries die or the tape breaks. Journalists should never tape-record someone without permission, either in person or on the telephone.

Generally speaking and depending on circumstances, most journalists clean up profanity and bad grammar. Often they simply paraphrase the source's words—that is, they express the source's words in their own way and take off the quotation marks.

Quotes should be used to present interesting or noteworthy statements by speakers. The use of quotes to present facts, such as the number of people attending a school, should be avoided. Also to be avoided is copy that both paraphrases and quotes the same statement.

Journalists carefully attribute quotes. It is important that readers know at all times where the information they are looking at came from. The verb most favored for attribution is *said* because it has no overtones.

Various rules and suggestions apply to handling quotes, including where to interrupt a sentence to insert attribution.

Stories about speeches, panel discussion, and similar events that are basically about what someone says should be written with a mixture of direct quotes, paraphrased material, and partial quotes. Always remember to write about what was said, not about the simple fact that someone spoke.

Evaluation Checklist: *Interview Story*

✓ Is the person being interviewed identified at the beginning of the story?
✓ Is the story a mix of text and interesting, relevant direct quotations?
✓ Are paraphrases used in place of rambling speeches and lists of facts?
✓ Are all important, controversial, or opinion-based statements clearly attributed?
✓ Is the story free from grammatical errors and in accordance with the publication and AP stylebook?

Evaluation Checklist: *Speech Story*

✓ Are the time, place, and speaker made clear at the beginning of the story?
✓ Are the most important points from the speech reported in the lead?
✓ Does the rest of the story summarize the speech and quote significant statements directly?
✓ Are noteworthy facts about the audience response included?
✓ Is the story free from grammatical errors and in accordance with the publication and AP stylebook?

On Assignment

Individual Activities

1. Write a brief definition or explanation of each of the following terms.

   attribution   direct quotation
   paraphrase   partial quote

2. Ask each member of the class to write a 10-minute speech, using complete sentences. Select someone to deliver the speech and ask others to write about it. Then compare the stories with the speaker's text to see if the quotes are accurate. Now test your critical thinking. Ponder: What's more important, getting the speaker's words right or getting his/her thoughts right? Why? Have a class discussion about the issue.

3. Clip all the stories from your last newspaper or magazine that quoted someone. Send the stories to the persons quoted to find out whether they were quoted

accurately. Conduct interviews—either in person or by phone—with one or more of these people. Write a brief report summarizing your findings.

4. Tape-record an interview; then write a story from it. Is it possible to quote every person verbatim every time? What do you do about the "ya knows" and the incomplete sentences? The bad grammar? The profanity? Discuss your ideas in class.

5. Interview someone who is quoted frequently by the press, perhaps the mayor or one of the coaches. Does he/she want to be quoted exactly? Or is meaning more important? Report your findings to the class.

6. Write a story based on a presidential news conference or televised speech. Compare your story with that of a classmate. Did he or she choose to emphasize the same or different topics? Why?

7. Ask ten students you do not know well for their opinions on a school issue. Write a story suitable for publication, quoting them correctly.

8. Find a story on a speech covered by a daily newspaper. Underline the verbs. Is "said" used most? What other words appear frequently? Study the use of attribution by professionals. Begin a log of verbs and keep it in your notebook. Which ones seem to be used most often? Which are rare?

Team Activities

9. Invite members of a speech class to give speeches to teams of journalism students. Each team should hold a question-and-answer session with the speaker. Now write a news story covering the speech given to your team. Compare your story to those of others on your team. Analyze the differences. Have the speech students review the stories and compare the writers' coverage with the original text. Each speaker should note where he or she was misquoted or quoted out of context.

10. As you noted in the story excerpt on pages 176-177, the attribution used by Hemingway is simple and short. This practice is recommended for journalists; it helps keep the focus on the quote. To reinforce this point and have some fun at the same time, you might try writing some Tom Swifties.

Tom Swift was the hero of a series of children's adventure books who never simply "said" anything. Today, a Tom Swiftie is a humorous exaggeration of an elaborate method of attribution, often with a pun or an allusion thrown in. Here are some Tom Swifties:

- "I'll have a hot dog," said Tom frankly.
- "Let's dig into it," said Tom gravely.
- "We need a fielder who can hit sixty home runs," he said ruthlessly.
- "I don't care for fairy tales," she said grimly.

Working in teams of three or four, try building an extended dialogue of Tom Swifties. Compare your team's dialogue with those of the other teams.

Like a lot of would-be movie stars, Helen Thomas started her career working in a restaurant.

Graduating from Wayne State University during World War II, she moved to Washington, D.C., to be near the center of power. She waited tables for a year before she got her break—as a $17.50-a-week copy clerk at the *Washington Daily News*.

"I've always wanted to be a reporter," said Thomas, who today is the senior member of the White House press corps and has been named one of the twenty-five most influential women in America. "I got hooked in high school."

Thomas covered several federal agencies and departments until 1960, when she was assigned to cover President-elect John Kennedy. She followed him into the White House in January 1961 and has been there questioning presidents ever since. It is the only job she wants.

"This is the seat of power in the world," she said. "There is such an infinite variety of stories."

For nearly three decades Thomas wielded a different kind of power. Presidential news conferences used to be limited to thirty minutes, and it was Thomas's job as senior correspondent to end the press conferences at the appointed time—or to keep presidents talking until time was up. The tradition of the thirty-minute press conference lasted until George Bush took office and began to decide himself when to end the questioning.

Covering presidents and the federal government is not easy. Government officials, even presidents, often try to keep information from reporters. A presidential press conference is the only opportunity to ask a president questions and demand answers.

Thomas quotes Thomas Jefferson when asked about the need for a news media to question government. Jefferson noted 200 years ago that a nation ignorant will never be a democracy.

Other founding fathers were also mindful of the role a free press should have in a democracy and wrote into the First Amendment to the Constitution provisions guaranteeing freedom of the press.

It is an adversarial relationship. Thomas said no president has ever liked the press and that it doesn't matter whether the press likes the president.

"It is our job to get the facts," she said. "People will never, never know how difficult it is to get information. We're constantly trying to break down the barriers. That means constant questioning, healthy skepticism, and never giving up. We can't give up because we are the watchdogs for the truth."

Journalists, particularly high-profile ones who cover presidents, are becoming less and less popular with the public, but Thomas is unfazed.

"We didn't get into this business to be loved," she said. "It's our job to keep the government from doing things in secret. We have an important role to play in this country. We can hold our heads high because we seek the truth."

Thomas has had many honors during her career. She was the only print journalist to accompany President Nixon on his historic trip to China in 1972. She is the first woman officer of the White House Correspondents Association and was the first woman officer of the National Press Club. She has received several honorary degrees from colleges and universities across the country.

Chapter Nine

Doing In-Depth Reporting

in-depth reporting

Watergate

news-brief format

nut graph

After reading this chapter, you should

- be familiar with the issues teenagers say they care about most, issues that deserve in-depth treatment by journalists

- understand trends in professional and scholastic journalism leading to new emphasis by students on in-depth reporting

- know how to condense certain items in a newspaper or magazine to find room for in-depth stories

- understand the difference between the lead on a routine news story and the introduction of an in-depth story

- be able to construct in-depth stories by using an introduction, a nut graph, and an ending

Tremendous change has come to high school journalism. Once monuments to trivia, most high school publications today are tributes to serious journalism, produced by talented students committed to their task of serving a modern audience. Even the most casual inspection of the best of today's scholastic publications quickly reveals the extent of the change. If Rip Van Winkle had started his famous nap in the 1970s and awakened in the 1990s, he would be stunned. Where homecoming queens once reigned and editorials went no further than urging school spirit, scholastic publications today are on top of the news. And the coverage is complete and detailed.

Despite forces in society to the contrary, most notably *USA Today* and its imitators, high school journalists are producing thoughtful, in-depth pieces on a wide range of important subjects. Bucking the trend toward short, superficial stories, while adopting some of the contemporary media's best innovations (notably in graphics), are the nation's scholastic journalists.

Modern scholastic publications, often making creative use of desktop publishing tools, consistently produce high-quality stories—even whole sections—on topics once considered out of bounds for students. These days, you're apt to see in-depth treatment by scholastic journalists on everything from school budgets to the environment; from censorship to family

What's Important?

The 1995 TRU Teenage Marketing & Lifestyle Study was conducted to provide concrete information about teenagers' top three interests. The resulting list—which, depending on their point of view, educators find either depressing, heartening, or unlikely*—is a virtual litany of society's problems. Anyone looking for topics for in-depth reporting can get a good start by scanning this list.

Here are the issues, with the percentage of teens listing each issue in his or her top three:

AIDS	44	Economy	14
Education	40	Unplanned pregnancy	14
Child abuse	28	Homelessness	13
Race relations	28	Women's rights	10
Violence	28	War	11
Drinking and driving	24	Suicide	9
Abortion	22	Threat of nuclear war	8
Drug abuse	18	Health care	7
Environment	18	Divorce	6
Animal rights	15		

*Asked to comment on the list, one prominent journalism educator said he doubted the findings. In his view, the number one issue among students is the same as it was fifty years ago: fitting in with peers.

crises; from animal rights to standardized tests, teen stress, teen insurance rates, school security, and student rights.

And much more. The list is long. It represents the catalog of interests young people have today. It also represents, in many ways, a catalog of subjects that teens need to know about.

What these and similar subjects have in common is the need for sensitive, objective, *in-depth* treatment. Subjects such as these do not lend themselves to superficial treatment.

A frequent criticism of the professional press is that it is superficial. Critics argue that the lack of space or time forces the press to hit only the highlights—and too often the sensational highlights—of public issues and events. These critics claim that issues laced with subtleties cannot be explored properly under the constraints of speed and brevity.

The critics have a point. Not *all* stories need in-depth treatment, but many do. Unfortunately, too many journalists operate superficially even when covering the stories that need deeper treatment. This chapter explores the need for such treatment.

Stories with Substance

In too many newsrooms, the reporter who suggests an in-depth story that may require weeks of research and writing is told that there is no time for such a project and no space to run it. But it doesn't have to be that way. Here are some examples of in-depth reporting. Watergate is the most famous example, but stories with substance don't have to uncover wrongdoing. They may present information on important economic or social issues. Such stories can benefit readers' lives in many ways.

Development of the Boeing 757

At age 28, Peter Rinearson was a reporter for the *Seattle Times*, newly assigned as the paper's aerospace writer. Searching for an interesting, in-depth project that would help him get a grip on his new beat, Rinearson hit upon the idea of preparing "a special report on the conception, design, manufacture, marketing, and delivery of a new jetliner—the Boeing 757."

"I discovered," Rinearson remarked later, "that just as I didn't really understand what Boeing does, the community didn't really understand. Even a lot of people at Boeing didn't know much beyond their direct area of responsibility."

So he went to work. For six months, Rinearson did little but work on the Boeing 757 story. He compiled about 1,200 single-spaced typewritten pages of interviews. He talked with fifty to sixty people. His project occupied almost every waking hour. "If I wasn't eating or sleeping, I was reporting or reading in libraries, involved with the story at one level or another," he said.

The *Seattle Times* ran his stories as a series spanning eight days. It was 25,000 words long, and when reprinted in a special package later, it occupied 16 full-size newspaper pages. And for his efforts Rinearson was awarded the Pulitzer Prize for feature writing.

Some people call the type of stories Rinearson did in-depth reporting. Others argue that such reporting is investigative by nature, and in some quarters investigative reporting is unpopular. Was Rinearson's story investigative? He says no.

"I don't know what that is. Investigative reporting sort of suggests uncovering wrongdoing, and I have done some of that. It pleased me that I was able to win the prize with something other than an account of wrongdoing. Since Watergate and beyond, if you want to win a Pulitzer Prize, it seems you have to go out and topple a president, or find something wrong."

Watergate

If ever there was an investigative story, it was the story of Watergate, the name applied to an array of deeds and events in the early 1970s that led to the resignation of President Richard Nixon.

The Watergate story began with a phone call to Bob Woodward of the *Washington Post*. Five men had been caught inside the offices of the Democratic Party at the Watergate apartment complex. The young reporter, later teamed with Carl Bernstein, was launched on one of the biggest stories of the century—the story that did, indeed, help topple a president.

It did a lot more, too. It stirred a wave of infatuation with investigative reporting on the part of the media.

Two schools of thought exist on such reporting. One says the media have no greater duty than to sniff out and expose wrongdoing and that it is impossible to overdo it. The other says the media definitely *are* overdoing it, that they are seeking evil rather than seeking news, and sniffing prizes rather than sniffing wrongdoing.

There is probably truth on both sides. Done right—repeat, done right—thorough, in-depth stories represent journalism at its finest. Sometimes there *is* wrongdoing.

Other Examples

There are many examples of investigative reporting that bring out legitimate problems readers need to know about.

Consider Ken Herman. Barely out of college, he was a reporter for the *News*, a small paper in Lufkin, Texas. Covering a story about the death in training camp of a local Marine, Herman was dissatisfied with the official answers to his questions. He discovered that the victim, a young man of limited intellectual ability, had been beaten to death during recruit training. The entire investigation was done on the telephone. The *News* won the Pulitzer Prize for the story.

Pat Stith and Jody Warrick of *The News & Observer* in Charlotte, North Carolina, demonstrated through investigative reporting how high-tech hog farms pollute North Carolina's air and water. Investigative Reporters and Editors, Inc. (IRE), a group that devotes its time, energy, and resources to helping investigative reporters, said, "Reporters revealed how the powerful hog industry convinced the government to go easy on environmental controls for the sake of profit. Some of the most powerful writing of the year."

Investigative stories on mass murders in Bosnia won David Rohde of the *Christian Science Monitor* commendations from the Investigative Reporters and Editors group.

Ignoring personal danger, David Rohde of the *Christian Science Monitor* exposed a massacre in Bosnia. He discovered mass graves and also interviewed survivors in what IRE called "outstanding investigative and foreign reporting in one package." His stories exposed those at fault.

> **Worth Quoting**
>
> The power of the press is very great, but not so great as the power of suppress.
>
> —LORD NORTHCLIFFE

In each of these cases and many more, one theme stands out: Reporters must dig and dig and dig. They must ask and ask and ask. Stories with substance do not come easily.

The Role of the Scholastic Press

So what does all this have to do with the scholastic press? You're not "Woodstein," as the two Watergate reporters came to be known, and chances are you could sniff around your school forever and not find scandal. But you can decide that superficiality and sensationalism are the enemy. You might not be able to undertake massive investigations (though lots of school papers have), but you certainly don't have to settle for shallow stories that contribute nothing to public understanding.

Rather than produce gossip columns, frothy features about the "in" crowd, and other trivial stories, you can explore the news in depth, dig beneath the surface, and report stories that really count. You can concentrate on causes as well as effects; you can ask, "Why?" *Why* do so many students drop out of school? *Why* are so many students killed in traffic accidents? *Why* do some students cheat? *Why* do some of the best teachers leave the profession? *Why* do the media bombard us with violence? *Why* is there so much homelessness in our community? You must, in other words, be ready to tackle any subject.

Emphasizing in-depth reporting, or backgrounding, or complete reporting (or whatever you decide to call it), implies several things to the scholastic journalist. First, of course, it means better reporting. No longer can a student grab a couple of quick quotes from a school official, dash off six or seven paragraphs, and call it a good news story. On one assignment one reporter—or a team of reporters—may speak with the same sources four or five times, interview a dozen faculty members, attend city council and board of education meetings, and talk to scores of students. Reporters are

Student reporters doing in-depth stories on school-related issues must be willing to interview and reinterview sources.

One of the basic rights that Americans treasure most is the right to privacy—that is, not to have their lives or their affairs unduly pried into. Prying of this sort can be done by government, and it can also be done by the media.

Interestingly, there is no specific wording in the Constitution that guarantees the right to privacy. Louis Brandeis, later to be on the Supreme Court, wrote a famous essay defining the concept in 1890, and many judicial scholars have found a legal basis for it in the Bill of Rights. Still, the right to privacy is neither absolute nor perfectly defined, and for the media, there is a constantly shifting boundary between the right to privacy and the so-called public's right to know.

The courts have generally found, for example, that public officials, by the very nature of their work, cannot use the right of privacy to protect themselves. Yet up until the last twenty years or so, what politicians did in their private lives was, by unspoken agreement of the press, allowed to remain private. Exceptions were made only when the politician's private actions had become widely known anyway—for example, when a congressman's private alcohol problem had descended into frequent public drunkenness.

Today, however, it seems that any element of a public figure's life is fair game for media exposure. Candidates for high office especially are scrutinized for the smallest failures—not only in their present lives but often stretching back twenty or thirty years to their college days. As a result, many potentially good candidates have declined to run for office rather than allow themselves and their families to be put through such scrutiny.

There is no doubt that the public does need to know certain things about a candidate. Certainly it would be newsworthy if he or she had been jailed for embezzlement. But it is questionable whether smaller failures, particularly those in the past, always need to be publicized.

In the case of semipublic figures, the line between privacy and the public's rights can be a very delicate one. For example, the 1996 suicide of a high Navy official was blamed by some on the media's continued probing into his affairs. He did, in fact, kill himself as he waited to be questioned by two *Newsweek* reporters about medals he wore but hadn't earned. But here it is hard to see how the media are responsible. There were legitimate questions to be asked, and his subordinates, as well as others, had the right to know the answers.

For private citizens who feel that the media have invaded their privacy, a common response is to initiate a lawsuit. Such suits are often the result of a writer reexamining an already well-covered issue: In other words, the public already knows about this—need they know even more? Thus a West Virginia woman whose husband's death in a bridge collapse had been covered five years earlier sued when a reporter came back and wrote about the family's subsequent poverty. Thus an Illinois man who had won the right to take back his natural son from an adoptive family sued when a columnist continued for months to write stories critical of the natural family.

There are no easy definitions of when the public's right to know crosses over into invasion of privacy. Two possible criteria might be whether the public actually benefits from having the information and whether the reporter would feel violated if it were his or her life being held up to similar scrutiny.

becoming dedicated to the proposition that their publication can inform its readers about what they are most interested in—their school—better than any other newspaper in the world. And even with non-school-related subjects of interest, student reporters can still do an excellent job of in-depth reporting.

Finding Space

Many (though by no means all) in-depth stories are quite long. Where are you going to get the space to run such stories? It is too scarce already. The first thing to do (if you haven't already) is eliminate trivia.

Many of the small stories you run can be condensed into one "bulletin board" type of column. Instead of publishing three paragraphs on the coming meeting of the Spanish Club, three on the Science Club, and four or five on the class play that you've already devoted half a dozen stories to, combine them into a bulletin board or calendar. Here is an example:

Thursday
Spanish Club, room 407, 3:45 P.M.
Science Club, physics lab, 3:50 P.M.
Repertory Theatre rehearsal, campus center, 6:30 P.M.

Friday
Pep rally, auditorium, 3:45 P.M.
Dress rehearsal, senior class play, auditorium, 8 P.M.

Instead of running five stories, which taken together might eat up an entire column of space, you have included all the information in just a couple of inches.

Another way to save space for in-depth stories is condensation of usually lengthy stories into a "news brief" format. Thus, a four-paragraph story about band tryouts can be condensed into just one paragraph:

BEFORE: Do you like music, travel, flashy clothes?
          Students who can answer yes to these questions should contact John P. Jones, band director.
          Jones is seeking new talent to fill out the 100-piece organization that plays at all home games.
          Tryouts are scheduled for Sept. 1 at 3 P.M. in the music room.

AFTER: Band tryouts will be held Sept. 1 at 3 P.M. in the music room, Director John P. Jones announced.

Also consider breaking up that one long story into one medium story, two small stories, and a chart (for example).

A Pro's Opinion

Professional observers of scholastic journalism have noted that the upgrading of subject matter and writing go hand in hand: As the student journalist tackles more difficult subjects, he or she tries harder and as a result writes better.

—SAUL J. WALDMAN, AMERICAN NEWSPAPER PUBLISHERS ASSOCIATION

Go through the story and decide exactly what it's about. Extract from it a mainbar, or main story, one that gives the pertinent facts that set up other stories. Called sidebars, the other stories are related to the mainbar but elaborate on it, illuminate it. If the story has a lot of numbers making it hard to read, consider pulling the numbers out of the mainbar and translating them into a chart or a graph for the "scanners," people who don't actually *read* newspapers but *scan* them, looking here and there for bits of information.

For example, if the mainbar is about drug use, it might give information about drug dangers, recent arrests, and so on. One sidebar might be on interviews; the other might be a chart summarizing important facts and statistics about drug use. This sort of in-depth treatment might be produced by a team of students, including writers, researchers, an interviewer, a photographer, and people responsible for graphics.

Finally, teams of writers could independently write several mid-length articles, all on aspects of the same topic. On a topic like cleaning up a local dumping site, one reporter could deal with current clean-up efforts, another could trace the earlier uses of the site, another could write about legislation involving use of public land, and someone else might attempt to interview the worst dumping culprits. Charts and other graphics could be added as needed.

Even fairly long articles on non-"glamorous" topics can be made to hold readers' attention if divided into enough different facets, as the sample page from Naperville Central High School in Naperville, Illinois, shows. The articles in the "On Display" feature on page 195 are part of a series on money issues that won a National Scholastic Press Association Story of the Year competition.

Elements of In-Depth Stories

Serious, in-depth stories cannot unfold the same way a story about the sophomore class election might.

When writing longer pieces—in-depth stories—you need to stop thinking of leads and start thinking of *introductions*. That just acknowledges the fact that stories of 20, 30, or 40 inches can rarely be summed up in one quick sentence—the traditional lead—the way the class election can be.

The packaging of an in-depth story into smaller, more visual pieces can increase readers' understanding even of complicated issues, as this sample from the Naperville Central High School *Central Times* shows.

The ◆Central Times

Vol. 5 No. 6   Naperville Central High School 440 W. Aurora Ave. Naperville, Illinois 60540

Funding cuts threaten science program

District 203 plans to cut the purchase of educational equipment and supplies by 75 percent next year. Teachers, administrators and students anticipate effects of the cut on an already strained Science Department.

Fifth priority on the District 203 Budget Reduction Option List, "a 75 percent reduction in acquiring educational equipment" will save the district $450,000. "Right now, I think there is a substantial possibility that this option will...pass," School Board member Marcia Aspinall said.

THE 'BUDGET CRUNCH'

Already, teachers have felt the "budget crunch" as insufficient funding has resulted in a lack of high-tech equipment and up-to-date materials. But, according to Aspinall, the problem isn't poor allocation of resources but simply a lack of funds. "The budget is very lean. Very little, if any, money is wasted. But, we just don't have enough money to both meet our needs and balance the budget," she said.

This lack of funds has hampered the Science Department's ability to purchase new equipment. "There have been [tax] cuts at the state level, and this has led to cuts at the local level," Science Department Coordinator Bill West said. "Taxpayers [must] support technology and its costs."

In the meantime, the Science Department's need for new equipment has been met through a number of fund-raising and cost-reducing methods. The Science Department has been allotted $5 per student for instructional supplies, such as chemicals and glassware. Because this figure has never been adjusted for inflation, the department has had to economize in order to buy the most basic equipment.

"We [can] make ends meet because our enrollment increased, and we've instituted lab fees to raise additional revenue," science teacher Sherry Yarema said.

While this additional revenue has been sufficient to purchase basic supplies, more expensive equipment (over $25) is covered by the capital outlay budget of the educational fund — the same budget that the school board is planning to cut.

This budget has been inadequate to keep science equipment up-to-date. "I know that we haven't been able to keep up technologically, especially in the area of computers, but the only feasible solution is to raise the tax rate," Aspinall, a former NCHS science teacher, said.

UNORTHODOX FUNDRAISING

Teachers have resorted to unorthodox methods in order to obtain educational supplies. Some science fields such as genetics have grown rapidly and require up-to-date equipment. "Our knowledge of genetics is expanding at a rapid rate," Advanced Biology teacher Gary Slaybaugh said. "We need updated equipment to run labs that utilize this knowledge."

Advanced Biology, along with Advanced Placement Biology, requires specialized equipment to run complex experiments. "The A.P. and advanced science classes are college-level courses with college-level labs. We need updated equipment in order to run them effectively," A.P. Biology teacher Yarema said.

When Slaybaugh realized that he didn't have enough up-to-date genetic engineering equipment for his students to use, he sought outside assistance. "I've done everything I possibly could to obtain up-to-date equipment. I've enrolled in a class at the University of Illinois because the Howard Hughes Foundation grants free use of equipment to class members," he said.

This equipment is still insufficient for the department's needs. "Even though we have this free equipment, we still need much more. That's why I've been trying to get more teachers, and student teachers, to take this course," Slaybaugh said.

THE TECHNOLOGY GAP

Biology isn't the only area of the department affected by lack of funding. One thing lacking throughout the entire department is computers and computerized equipment such as temperature probes and software. "We want to have computers in all of the science classes with the hardware and software we need — state-of-the-art equipment, not hand-me-downs," physics teacher Allan Etzbach said.

While the administration has outlined a technology plan, little visible effects are seen in the science classrooms, which need new technology. "The District has sent us to workshops that have shown us how to implement computers and other high-tech devices in the classroom," chemistry teacher Sharon Vetter said. "Unfortunately, this equipment is unavailable."

This new equipment would allow teachers to run improved labs. "We've wanted to have a computer at each lab station for quite some time," chemistry teacher Patti Kenton said. "That would allow us to use accurate instruments such as temperature probes to find and record data."

The administration recognizes the need for technological innovation in the classroom. Principal Tom Paulsen said, "We need to keep up with technology because 10-year-old...equipment doesn't help...the students, who will be farther behind students from other schools because of it."

But lack of funds forces the district to sacrifice technology for fiscal responsibility. "Delaying the acquisition of hardware and software" is a higher priority item on the District 203 Budget Reduction Option List than the 75 percent Capital Outlay cut. According to Aspinall, this option has a very good chance of being implemented.

POSSIBLE SOLUTIONS

Science teachers are trying to find a solution to this lack of funding. The administration should have a liaison to contact local science-based firms like Nalco, Amoco or Bell Labs to get used equipment at little or no charge, Vetter said.

While concerned teachers can help solve the problem, they are not the complete solution. "Teachers receive computers through workshops or donations," West said, "but there is only one source for funding — the public; we're a public school."

That's why the administration is considering a tax increase to raise funding. "We have the highest IGAP scores in the state of Illinois at the lowest cost," Aspinall said. "Hinsdale has lower scores than us but spends twice as much as we do. We have great teachers, but we haven't had a tax increase since 1976. We need to [give] our teachers the funding they deserve."

Genetic Engineering

Central Times Investigative Report
Investigative Team
Director: Renata Horvath
Writer: Renata Horvath
Researchers: Derek Woo, Nicole Dominak
Interviewers: Asad Shaikh, Saif Patel

The Human Genome Project is a $3 billion experiment which will attempt to isolate and create quantity identify almost all of the 100,000 genes in the average human being's chromosomes. This will facilitate scientists in the field in their attempts to read the blueprint (DNA) making up the human organism. With this information, more accurate and helpful diagnoses and treatment of many different diseases will be possible.

Research in other areas of genetics will provide information aiding in the development of plant species with the capability to help the environment. Also, fruits and vegetables can be grown, including more prolific vitamins and a much longer shelf life with resistance to disease.

Genetics is one of the last scientific frontiers not fully explored today. New, high-tech equipment makes these types of experiments possible. But at NCHS, the teachers do not have access to this necessary equipment because of funding problems. Science Department Coordinator Bill West said, "Lab fees in the biology classes account for about $2,000. But with the lead pig dissection card, we're talking about $1,500. Thus, in the area of genetics, for larger expenditures are needed.

DISSECTION OF SCIENCE FUNDING
HOW MUCH DO THEY GET?
(as of June 25, 1993)

Total expense per pupil (in thousands of dollars)

District	
Hinsdale	
Fenton	
Glenbard	
Naperville	

Source: Finance Section of Illinois State Board of Education

WHAT DO THEY NEED?

Computers

"I know that we haven't been able to keep up...especially in the area of computers."
—Board Member Aspinall

"We want...computers in all of the science classrooms with the hardware and software we need." —Physics teacher Etzbach

Textbooks

Since textbooks need to advance with the technology, "there is a science committee next fall which will request possible replacements. We've used the current ones for six years, and we're on a seven-year replacement curriculum. It used to be a five-year replacement." —Science Department Chairperson West

HOW DOES THIS AFFECT EDUCATION?

• "We are not able to keep up technologically." —Board Member Aspinall

• "The students will be...farther behind students from other schools." —Principal Paulsen

WHAT DOES THE FUTURE HOLD?
75% Cut:

"A 75 percent reduction in acquiring educational equipment [has a] substantial possibility [of being] passed by the board." —Board Member Aspinall

Possible Solutions:

• Referendum: "We want a referendum [to increase taxes] to deal with the future."

• Higher Lab Fees: "We could increase funding by increasing user fees, too, but then [we would be hitting people] twice, and this would turn them off." —Principal Paulsen

Pencil & Paper Labs

Because of the tight budget, sometimes, necessary equipment is not available to perform experiments in science classes. In these situations, pencil-and-paper labs, simulating a real lab with real data collection, are substituted. Although these experiments are viable for learning, they do not allow for "hands-on" activity.

PERSPECTIVES: How different people view Science Department funding

BY SAIF PATEL

School Board Member — Marcia Aspinall

Aspinall, a former NCHS science teacher, has first-hand experience with the NCHS Science Department and feels that there will not be many immediate effects of funding cuts.

But in the long run, as increased funding becomes necessary for better technology, Aspinall said, "We should be allowed to keep up the cutting edge."

Aspinall feels that the board does not "waste a lot of money." But if more money becomes necessary, she says, "people [will become] concerned about their taxes."

Her outlook, though, is that people will benefit, since their "houses will [gain value] because of good schools."

Principal — Tom Paulsen

Paulsen feels that the public is the main source for the school to turn to. "In the long run, higher tax rates [for the people] are necessary," he said.

Paulsen also feels that the "community would support a higher rate to maintain the levels of funding and even to move forward [with technology]."

Although he feels a referendum to increase taxes is necessary, he says, "only the Board of Education can ask for a referendum," and it has made "no official decision yet."

He is optimistic the referendum will pass.

Biology Teacher — Sherry Yarema

"We have a first-rate Science Department," Yarema said. "[It] tries to be very up-to-date with emphasis on problem-solving and critical thinking...we [also] believe in hands-on."

But Yarema feels that in the past, although "$5 per student...has been the budget for instructional supplies," this had "no accounting for inflation."

So the only reason "we have been able to survive," according to Yarema, is "because of increasing enrollment [which also increases the money from per-student fees]."

In the future, though, Yarema sees the science program troubled. "[Since] AP classes are college-level courses with college-level labs," she said, "equipment should be like students will use in college...[this is] expensive."

Longer pieces need to be *set up*. They generally should begin with a scene or an anecdote.

For example, if you're writing an in-depth story about the state champion free-throw shooter, you might have something like this at the top:

> **Carmen Ruiz first touched a basketball when she was 3. She didn't dribble the ball. She dribbled *on it.***
>
> **When she was 9, she joined a neighborhood team that beat the boys' team every day one winter.**
>
> **In high school, she led Centerville to the state finals, recording a record 27 points per game average. She was named to the All-State team the same day she was elected senior class president.**
>
> **Last week she learned that in a little-known competition held in conjunction with the state tournament, she had won the state free-throw shooting title. She credited the title to years of practice, practice that began in her backyard at age 4 and continued until . . . well, today.**

The first three paragraphs function together as a "lead." They're more of an introduction, more of a setup to the rest of the story, which presumably is an exploration of how one becomes a free throw champion.

If the in-depth story is about, for example, anorexia, it might begin with the story of one victim, detailing how she fought in unhealthy ways against imagined weight gain, eating wrong, exercising fanatically, hiding the secret from friends and family—even from herself.

After several paragraphs—the introduction—the writer would introduce the story's real theme: how the disease affects its victims, how it's treated, what the future holds. The paragraph in which the rest of the story is foreshadowed—an internal lead, really—is often called the "nut graph." It's the paragraph that says to the reader: I hooked you with my intro, now here's what the story's about; here's where we're going together.

In the "On Display" features on page 197, the first four paragraphs of both stories follow this pattern—introduction, nut graph, elaboration on the nut graph.

In-depth stories present another structural challenge not usually encountered in shorter, routine stories. In-depth stories need *endings*. The sophomore election story can just end. It's probably an inverted-pyramid story, and when the writer is finished, he or she hits the period key and quits. If the last paragraph gets trimmed in production, it's probably OK.

Not so with the in-depth story. It has to be wrapped up; it can't just fade into nothingness the way an inverted-pyramid story can. Before journalists came along and invented their particular way of telling stories, stories had beginnings, middles, and endings. And so it is with in-depth stories.

Consider the mythical free-throw champion. The ending on her story might be something like:

A Pirate's Loot

by Alex Ellis and Ben Schnoor, Little Hawk, *City High School, Iowa City, Iowa*

"I'm not answering any questions about bootlegs," a record store employee states bluntly, looking uncomfortable as customers survey the store's bootleg-infested shelves.

At another store an employee was a little more informative: "Asking a record store if they sell bootlegs is like asking a dope dealer if he sells dope."

Secrecy, questionable activity, and big profits—so begins the journey into the illegal world of bootleg recordings.

Bootlegs, unauthorized recordings of an artist's work, have been around since the late '60s, when they were produced on vinyl, packaged in plain white sleeves and plagued with extremely poor sound quality. In the early '80s, cassette tapes became the most common medium for bootlegs, due to the relatively cheap cost of duplicating equipment. However, it was the introduction of the compact disc in the mid-'80s that helped production of bootlegs progress from a trivial activity into a multi-million dollar underground industry.

Dating Equity: Students Say Times Have Changed

by Angela Hwang, Arlingtonian, *Upper Arlington High School, Columbus, Ohio*

Before: *she* sits by the phone waiting to find out if she's going to have a date for Friday night. *He* struggles to gather up enough nerve in time to call her for a date, assuming he is able to scrape up enough money for a quick dinner and movie for two.

Now: *she* no longer has to wait for an invitation to go out with the guy she likes. *He* can still go on dates even if he is exceptionally shy and short of cash.

Dating in the '90s has moved toward equality between men and women, where either the man or the woman may be expected to ask someone out and pay for the bill.

Some students said they have observed this movement among teenagers in high school.

Ruiz has long since stopped dribbling on basketballs. These days, it's eager college recruiters doing the drooling.

An ending that returns to the notion of the lead fulfills the human urge for closure. The story comes full circle. Often the first place to look for an ending to an in-depth story is in the story's introduction.

The story above about bootlegged music did just that, returning to a quote by a record-store representative:

For better of worse, bootlegs will be available as long as people are willing to buy them. "It's really no big deal. They've always been out

there," Trent said. "We just sell what's available, whatever people want."

In-depth stories often lend themselves to unusual treatment in other respects, too. In the first story in the "On Display" feature on page 199, the reporter sought insights into the life of the American trucker. Her technique was to ride a couple thousand miles across country with a trucker, soaking up the feeling of life on the road. She decided on a first-person approach. The introduction to her story is shown; in the remainder of her article she will examine in detail each of the issues this introduction raises.

An in-depth story on the increasing number of bootleg recordings at music stores may require a several-paragraph introduction prior to the nut graph.

The second "On Display" feature on page 199 introduces a story in which a reporter decided to trace her family's roots in a small town in South Dakota. She begins by describing the setting.

The final "On Display" feature, on page 200, is about the little town in Kansas where four killings led to Truman Capote's book *In Cold Blood* (itself a gripping example of in-depth reporting). Author Jim Pratt, then a student at the University of Nebraska, set out years after the killings to see what effect the book and a movie had on the town.

Pratt's dramatic, prize-winning story follows the introduction–nut graph–elaboration on the nut graph pattern exactly. First the reader is taken to the scene, where wind and dust mix with the picture of horses shaking their manes and a dog loping down a deserted street—all in all, a compelling opening. From there, the author flashes back to the day of the slayings and captures the mood of the town then: police, ambulances, the curious. Finally, in the tenth paragraph (the one beginning "For a while. . . ."), comes the nut graph.

Research, organization, time for reflection on what your research uncovers, and writing–these are the elements of in-depth reporting. If you're looking for further examples in the professional press, read the *Washington Post*, the *Philadelphia Inquirer*, the *Los Angeles Times*, the *Wall Street Journal*, the *Des Moines Register*, the *Miami Herald*, *The New York Times*, and similar newspapers. For top examples of writing, see *Sports Illustrated* and *Rolling Stone*, among other magazines.

On the Road: A Reporter's Account

by Nancy Kehrli

If a reporter wants to learn about truckers—as I did—she climbs into a 16-ton truck loaded with 38,300 pounds of beef in Spencer, Iowa, and heads for Elizabeth, N.J.

She becomes a trucker for 2,659 miles through Iowa, Illinois, Indiana, Ohio, Pennsylvania and into New Jersey and back again.

During three days and seven hours of trucking, she talks to dozens of truckers. She learns to sleep for two or three hours at a time and to be wide awake and jostling down the Interstate before sunrise.

She learns to be ready to hop down from the truck when it stops so she can interview drivers while the truck is fueled.

Recently, I rode with Darrell and Jan Smidt of Milford, Iowa, who truck for J. & L. Trucking, Inc.

From Iowa to New Jersey and back, this is what the truckers talked about:

Truckers have problems. The speed limit's too low; fuel prices too high. Because of this, they say, their revenue is suffering. The government has done little since the last two shutdowns to alleviate their situation, truckers say. Consequently a May 13 truck shutdown is being planned.

Many drivers have Citizen Band (CB) radios they rely on to communicate with each other on the road. However, some states want stricter regulations on CBs, and some would like to see them taken out of trucks. The truckers say "no way."

What they call high prices and poor service at truck stops also anger the truckers. . . .

Vitame Vas

by Lynn Silhasek

"Vitame Vas" reads one store window along the snow-packed main street in Tabor, S.D. The Czech greeting means "we welcome you."

The townspeople are Czech, too. A Petrik owns the Pheasant Bar. The name Cimpl is painted on the town's grain elevator. Vyborny owns the machine works and Koupal has the construction company.

The names peer at me from the storefronts, like old folks staring at a newcomer in town. They haunt me as I drive through town until I remember the distant cousins who go with them. And they offer their own "we welcome you."

For me, it's a welcome back. Back to my own first generation whose story begins in several southeastern South Dakota communities west of Yankton. Back to a time when the names on the shops, the stores and the bars were intertwined with those of Kocer and Base, the names of my mother's parents.

A Kansas Town Remembers

by Jim Pratt

HOLCOMB, KAN.—A harsh north wind whips dust through Holcomb, battering a few worn-down stucco dwellings before losing itself in the western Kansas plains. Ponies tied to fence posts shake their manes in the wind and a dog lopes down a deserted dirt street.

Holcomb is a quiet town. Discounting the Mobil gas station (3.2 beer, soda pop, a few groceries), the only gathering place with refreshments is El Rancho Cafe, and in an adjacent room, a bar named Something Else.

Holcomb's few streets, mostly unpaved, are often empty.

Thirteen years ago today, however, the streets were jammed with cars belonging to law enforcement people, ambulance attendants and the curious. For Holcomb had just been stunned by four murders.

Subsequent reverberations would make the town known to millions.

It was early Sunday morning, Nov. 15, 1959, when Herb Clutter, 48, his wife, Bonnie, 45, and their two youngest children, Nancy, 16, and Kenyon, 15, were blasted point-blank with a shotgun by two ex-convicts with no previous records of violence. The motive was robbery.

The murders shocked the town. Herb Clutter was a prominent farmer, and he and his family were well liked. But the murders probably would have been forgotten had author Truman Capote not read a *New York Times* story about the killings and decided to use them as a vehicle for his book *In Cold Blood*.

Capote went to Holcomb shortly after the slayings. He spent nearly a year and a half in the area doing research. He followed the hunt, capture, trial, and imprisonment of the two killers, Richard Hickock and Perry Smith, until they were executed April 14, 1965.

The book inspired a movie, also named *In Cold Blood*, which was filmed in the town.

For a while after the killings, Holcomb was gripped by fear, gossip, and controversy. But 13 years has allowed the town to relax and to grow, relatively unscarred by the experience. The population is up 25 percent, from about 270 at the time of the slayings to 340 today. The school has a new addition. There are new homes, a new water tower, a new post office.

Curiosity seekers still stop to view the house near town where the Clutters were slain. Once a showcase, the house now seems weatherbeaten.

Townspeople no longer discuss the murders or the aftermath. They would like to forget it.

"It was such a long time ago that it almost seems like it never happened," one woman said.

Wrap-up

Most high school publications today are tributes to serious journalism, affected deeply by change in the last decade. Where homecoming queens once reigned and editorials merely urged school spirit, scholastic publications today are on top of the news and reporting it in depth.

Despite the forces of superficiality in the commercial press, high school journalists are producing long, well-thought-out pieces on important subjects. Often using desktop publishing tools, high school journalists produce high-quality stories and sections on topics that were once considered out of bounds for students. The list of stories now done by high school students represents the wide range of interests of young people. These subjects need sensitive, objective, thorough treatment.

In-depth stories, stories with substance, can present important information that affects people's lives. Some in-depth stories are investigative—rare but not unheard of in high school newspapers. Perhaps the best-known such work was done by Bob Woodward and Carl Bernstein, *Washington Post* reporters widely credited with exposing the Watergate scandal during the Nixon presidency.

Whether stories are called investigative or in-depth, one theme stands out: Reporters dig. They decide that superficiality is the enemy. The changing high school press is putting more emphasis on the *why* of the five W's and the H.

In-depth stories often run longer than routine stories. This can create a space problem. Handling routine club notices and meetings in a list format can help solve this. Space saved this way can be used for in-depth stories. Furthermore, long articles themselves can be broken up into pieces—a mainbar, two sidebars, and a chart, for example.

Generally, the quality of writing for in-depth stories has to be better than the usual newspaper fare. Readers of long stories must be nursed through them by careful writing and organization. In-depth stories require introductions, not just leads. Scenes, anecdotes, a first-person approach—all can produce a high-quality introduction.

The elements of thorough reporting are research, organization, time, and good writing. Modern high school newspapers are broadening their horizons, looking wherever the news takes them for information that affects students.

Examples of excellent in-depth reporting in the commercial press can be found in many current newspapers and magazines.

Essential to the organization of longer in-depth pieces is the notion of the "nut graph," the paragraph that functions virtually as an internal lead, the paragraph that follows an introduction and that outlines the story's main themes.

In-depth stories need endings, too. The best place to look for an ending is in the introduction. If that works, the story comes full circle and gives the reader a feeling of closure.

Evaluation Checklist: *In-Depth Story*

✔ Is the topic of the story worth in-depth treatment because of its seriousness or relevance?
✔ If the story is one long piece, does it have a full-fledged introduction leading to an internal lead, or nut graph?
✔ Are scenes, anecdotes, and other strong examples used to involve the reader in the story?
✔ If the story is broken into several pieces, does each piece deal with a different aspect of the story?
✔ Are charts and other infographics used appropriately and effectively?
✔ Is the story free from grammatical errors and in accordance with the publication and AP stylebooks?

On Assignment

Individual Activities

1. Write a brief definition or explanation of each of the following terms.
   in-depth reporting   news-brief format
   nut graph   Watergate

2. Test your critical thinking. Newspapers like *USA Today* are known for relatively short, one-time articles rather than in-depth reports. Why do you think they have chosen to take such an approach? Evaluate their audience, the places the paper is sold, and any

other factors that you think might account for the kind of stories they do. Write a brief summary of your ideas.

3. Here is a list of topics known to be of interest to teens. Select one for in-depth treatment. How would you go about approaching this topic? How would the one big story be divided into smaller chunks? What opportunities are there for good graphics, charts, and graphs? Write up your ideas. If you wish, include a rough layout.

AIDS	Smoking
Drug abuse	School violence
The environment	Animal rights
Children's rights	Censorship
Political correctness	Alcohol abuse

4. Evaluate this introduction to an in-depth story in terms of its originality and level of interest. Where is the nut graph? Where do you think the story will go from here? Give a grade to the introduction and then write a brief justification of your opinion.

Testing, Testing
by Lynn Roberts

The following questions will test your knowledge of today's college-bound students and tests they take to measure their reasoning abilities.

For some questions there is no single correct answer. Select the answer that best fits the question and proceed to the next question. Begin when you are told and continue until you finish or are told to stop.

Go.

1. College-bound students today are: (a) smarter than students five years ago; (b) the same as students five years ago: (c) dumber than students five years ago; (d) none of the above.

Recent declines in scores on the Scholastic Aptitude Test (SAT) and the American College Test (ACT) might indicate (c) as the correct answer, but these scores alone probably do not show the complete picture.

5. Go through your local newspaper. Find at least three stories treated superficially that should be expanded and treated in-depth. Interview editors and/or reporters on the paper. Do they agree? Why or why not? Write an interview story on your findings.

6. Identify a thorough story in any newspaper. Compare it to a magazine article on a similar topic. What similarities and differences appear? Which style do you like better? Why? Write an essay on your findings. Attach the story.

7. Go through several issues of your school paper. Where will you find the space for a thorough story? What can be eliminated? What can be condensed? What can be put in a bulletin board column? Could you find a full page of space? Mark your ideas on the issues.

8. Invite to class a local professional reporter who does in-depth or investigative reporting. Ask him or her to explain the techniques. Discuss the pros and cons of this type of reporting. Write a story summarizing the class discussion.

9. Test your critical thinking. Watch a local evening television newscast. Is the station news staff doing any in-depth work? If so, how does their coverage and choice of topics compare with that of newspapers? Discuss the differences, and possible reasons for the differences, in class.

Team Activity

10. Brainstorm with your team for current ideas for an in-depth story for your student readers (or use the list in activity 3 above). Select three. Do the same for related sidebar stories for each of the three ideas. Brainstorm sources, coverage angles, and questions for each story. Then choose your best story topic. Select a project editor (who will write also), and assign stories to team members. Research and write the stories. Edit carefully. Keep all finished stories for use in later assignments.

Sometimes it takes a lot of digging to thoroughly cover a story.

That's the way it was for Marjie Lundstrom in 1990, when she and Rochelle Sharpe disclosed in a four-part series that hundreds of child abuse deaths go undetected each year because of errors by medical examiners and coroners. The series won Lundstrom and Sharpe a Pulitzer Prize in national reporting.

Lundstrom's husband, Sam Stanton, earned his reputation in Arizona. His investigative digging led to the indictment and impeachment of Governor Evan Mecham in 1987 and resulted in Stanton being named a Pulitzer Prize finalist.

Today, Stanton and Lundstrom work at the *Sacramento Bee*, where Lundstrom is an assistant managing editor and Stanton a senior writer.

Lundstrom is proudest of her first effort at investigative reporting, a series of articles that exposed the fact that government officials in Denver, Colorado, had squandered money entrusted to the city by an orphanage.

"I was driving past this really rundown campus one day and just decided to see how it ever wound up in that shape," she said in describing how she got started on that series. "I chipped away at it for months and months."

The series forced city officials to change policies and begin paying back the money.

Stanton made his mark by accepting an assignment that no one else wanted. He was working at the *Arizona Republic* and volunteered to cover political long-shot Evan Mecham's run for governor. Mecham was elected on his fourth try and Stanton found himself covering the governor's office.

It didn't take long for Stanton to begin breaking stories. His digging eventually led to the disclosure that Mecham had accepted an illegal campaign contribution.

"The basis for all that was a reporting affairs class I took in college," Stanton said. "It showed me where to go to look for public records and what kinds of information you can find. Without that, I don't know if most people can figure out where to find information."

Stanton and Lundstrom both took unlikely paths to their careers. Lundstrom turned to journalism when she decided she didn't want to specialize in one field.

"I had a whole variety of interests," she said. "But what I really was was a generalist. So I enrolled in journalism out of desperation and it fit. It was obvious that this is what I love."

Stanton wound up in journalism by getting in the wrong registration line at the University of Arizona. He decided to try journalism anyway.

"I loved it," he said. "That was it. I just fell in love with it and never looked back. It is the most fun you can have and get paid for it. You meet the most interesting people on the planet and witness history at the same time."

Lundstrom was graduated from the University of Nebraska in 1978. After various other jobs she became a reporter at the *Sacramento Bee* in 1989. In 1990 she worked for Gannett News Service, where she did the child abuse series. She rejoined the *Bee* in 1991 and has been an assistant managing editor since 1995.

Stanton began his career in 1982 when he accepted a three-month internship at the *Arizona Republic* and was hired after six weeks of work. He joined the *Sacramento Bee* in 1991.

Chapter Ten

Editing, Headline Writing, and Design

Key Terms

copy editing

kicker

wicket

hammer

font

leading

justified

ragged

dominant element

gutter

eyeline

grid format

pica

point

double-truck

bleed

Key Concepts

After reading this chapter, you should

- understand the role of copy editors in a publication
- understand which skills copy editors need to succeed
- understand the various types of headlines and how to write them
- understand basic typographical principles
- understand the elements of modern newspaper and yearbook design

A publication's goal of getting information to its readers is only partly achieved when all the reporters have turned in their copy. One job remaining is the copy editing process, an often unglamorous but extremely important side of news work. It is the copy editor's responsibility to prepare the copy for publication. The copy editor edits the story (usually on a computer screen), codes the copy, and writes the headline. This job is vital, because if an error has crept into the reporter's copy, it almost certainly will get into the paper unless the copy editor catches it. The copy editor is the last line of defense against inaccuracies.

The other remaining job is the actual layout and design of the issue. As with copy editing, this work is often done on computer these days. Regardless of the method used, however, visual communication is now one of the hottest areas of journalism, and in recent years graphic design has become one of the most important aspects of the overall journalism curriculum. Learning to design copy in a format that attracts readers and makes a strong verbal-visual connection for them is a challenging and interesting task. Today's audiences expect strong visual graphics and stories packaged to attract and hold their attention. Student-produced publications such as newspapers, magazines, and yearbooks must be designed with the visual reading audience in mind. Publications that choose to use the older, more traditional approach to design, featuring numerous small photos and headlines, may lose many of their readers. Today's publications must feature strong, story-telling photos, informational graphics, and carefully selected type to draw in the audience.

Copy editing is one of the oldest, most precise jobs in journalism, and creating strong visual layouts is one of the newest. Yet both are essential for a professional-looking publication.

Copy Editing

The copy editor must be a master of the publication's stylebook. (Is a man referred to as Mr. Jones or just Jones, after the first reference? Is *re-election* hyphenated?) Reporters certainly should know the style rules, too, but

Copy editing requires a thorough knowledge of grammar and an attention to details.

their primary job is to get the facts. The copy editor's job is to polish. Copy editors have to know the rules of grammar, spelling, and punctuation. They need to know whether the history instructor's name is Anderson or Andersen. Every scrap of information, no matter how trivial, that the copy editor can jam into his or her head may come in handy at some point. Copy editors must have a good memory and must know how to locate information—in standard reference books or on the Internet, for example.

In addition to making the reporter's copy agree with the stylebook in terms of punctuation, capitalization, abbreviations, spelling, and the use of titles, the copy editor must also catch repetition, dangling modifiers, misplaced pronouns, subject-verb agreement errors, and a whole list of other grammar and sentence structure problems. Very important, too, are matters of organization. The copy editor may change the order of elements in a story to create a more logical style and to make the story read more smoothly.

Copy editing is vastly different from reporting; the copy editor has to be content with processing the creative work of others. This is not to say that editing isn't creative. It is, very definitely, but in a much less obvious way than a great lead by a reporter. Copy editors are usually anonymous; they rarely get credit.

Copy editors also need excellent judgment and the ability to make fine distinctions in taste and word usage. They must have an ear for rhythm and an understanding of reporting and writing too, because a copy editor should never change anything in a story except to improve it. Slavish adherence to rules—any rules, whether of style or of structure—can lead to editing that harms the copy rather than helps it. If a reporter writes a story in unconventional fashion, selects sentence fragments for impact, injects acceptable humor—and can defend doing so—the copy editor should not tinker with it.

Copy Editing Symbols

Most school publications now use desktop publishing systems that have greatly simplified the mechanical—though not the intellectual—problems of copy editing. Some school publications, however, still find themselves preparing copy with pencil and paper and then handing over the material to a commercial printer. This brief section will be helpful to anyone who needs to mark and correct copy on paper.

On page 207 are the symbols copy editors use as they work—the signals, if you will, that they put on the copy that tell typesetters and printers, or whoever is handling the strictly mechanical phase of publication, what to do.

Indent for paragraph	∟ or ¶
Insert a letter	. . . she told the crod . . .
Lower case	. . . he Ran with the ball . . .
Capitalize	. . . the student council also . . .
Delete	. . . he ran with the ~~the~~ ball . . .
Delete and close up	. . . the studdent council also . . .
Delete and close up	. . . Tech won it's ninth title . . .
Abbreviate	. . . occurred at 9 No. 10th (Street) . . .
Spell out	. . . ⑦ persons were arrested . . .
Insert dash	. . . 17 persons all under 21 wore . . .
Set in numerals	. . . (thirty-seven) fled the scene . . .
Spell out	. . . the (gov.) Tuesday told . . .
Transpose letters	. . . the footabll coach said . . .
Insert a hyphen	. . . a well dressed person will . . .
Transpose words	. . . was also chosen . . .
Insert a word	. . . something was *left* out . . .
Separate words	. . . they arrived on Tuesday. . .
Insert period	. . . he said But Jones . . .
Insert comma	. . . never again she said . . .
Let it stand: ignore copy mark	. . . this is ~~wrong~~ (stet) . . .
Center	] Copyright 1992 [
Set flush right	By the Associated Press]
Set flush left	[By the Associated Press
No paragraph	(no¶) . .but not until then. (Later, however, she said . . .
Insert quotation marks	. . . Get out, he said . . .
Insert apostrophe	. . . its always like this . . .

These copy editing symbols are used in all kinds of publishing.
It is a good idea to become familiar with them.

And here is how a piece of copy looks after it has been edited:

A torrential downpour friday forced the forty-seven members of mrs. Smith's Geology class to call off their fieldtrip. the group has asembled in the North parking lot at dawn but could not make it across the pools of water that had been formed by the tremendous rainfall.

We'll have to hold it next week," said Mrs. Smith. She added the reason for the trip was to locate fossils in an old riverbed sixteen miles from Town.

Senior Tom Johnson received a brake from the rain He overslpt and would have missed the bus anyway.

Checking for Accuracy

If all of the millions of words written about the art of copy editing had to be condensed into one short sentence, that sentence would be *Make sure it's accurate.* Copy editors do many things, but their most essential function is to watch for mistakes. To the reader involved, the smallest mistake may appear enormous.

Good copy editors must know how to spell. For checking spelling, as all computer-wise people know, spell-checking programs are a blessing. But they're dangerous, too. Spell checkers won't alert you to a word that is just wrong. For example, if you want to refer to *guerrilla warfare* and instead write "gorilla warfare," your spell checker will sail right past it. Humans, not spell checkers, have to catch those kinds of mistakes.

Copy editors must also check facts—and know which facts to check. A relatively harmless error, like identifying someone as a freshman instead of a sophomore, casts doubt, for that sophomore, on every other fact in the paper. Obviously there is not time to check every detail in every story. So copy editors develop a sense, a suspicion, about certain kinds of things.

For instance, they pay special attention to stories with numbers. Does the lead say six students won scholarships, but the story lists only five names? Does the story mention four federal grants to the school totaling $3,600 and then provide figures that add up to only $3,000? Does the story say teacher salaries are going up 3 percent and then name a teacher getting a 15 percent pay increase? In all these cases something is wrong, and it is up to the copy editor to find out what it is and to correct it.

Accuracy also involves special attention to names. Copy editors should not assume that the usual spelling is the correct one. They must check: Is it Patti or Patty? Smith or Smyth? Hansen or Hanson? Curtis or Kurtis? The same is true of titles. Is a person assistant superintendent or associate superintendent? Counselor or chief counselor? It is never safe to guess.

Special attention also must be given to stories involving police activity and morals. If you incorrectly involve someone in a crime or in any way suggest that his or her moral standards are less than they should be, you will be in deep trouble very fast. High school newspapers do not frequently deal with stories of this nature, but they might. The copy editors who work (process) these stories must be extra careful.

Editing

Copy editors have other jobs besides catching inaccuracies. They must make sure the story conforms to newspaper style. It makes no sense to spell out a word in one story and abbreviate it in the next. Although style is arbitrary, consistency is everything. The whole staff must observe house style.

The copy editor also watches for loose writing and tightens it by eliminating excess words and by substituting single words for phrases. For example, a sentence like "The field of journalism offers many challenges" should be changed to "Journalism is challenging." "At the present time" becomes "now," and "he continued by saying" is changed to "he added." Trivia is edited out.

The copy editor smoothes rough passages in the copy, often by cutting long sentences into short, simple ones. For example, this sentence is badly in need of repair:

> Appointments are now being made for students wishing to interview for the positions of managing editor, news editor, sports editor, feature editor, and editorial writer now open on the staff of the *Banner*, according to Mr. Jones, journalism adviser.

Spelling Demons

Here are the correct spellings of some of the most frequently misspelled words in the English language:

a lot	extension	Pittsburgh, Pa.
accordion	fiery	plagiarism
Albuquerque	fluorescent	questionnaire
auxiliary	fulfill	receive
buoy	governor	recommend
calendar	guerrilla	rescind
category	harass	resistance
cemetery	hemorrhage	restaurant
committee	homicide	seize
computer	judgment	separate
consensus	lieutenant	sergeant
defendant	missile	sherbet
definite	misspell	sheriff
dependent	mustache	siege
develop	nickel	silhouette
dormitory	niece	subpoena
dilemma	ninety	suppress
embarrass	occurred	weird
embarrassed	paraphernalia	wield
existence	pavilion	yield

That's certainly too much for one bite. So the copy editor makes the repairs:

> **Students wishing to work on the *Banner*, Central High School's student newspaper, are being asked to make interview appointments, said Abdul Jones, journalism adviser. Positions open are those of managing editor, news editor, sports editor, feature editor, and editorial writer.**

Now the reader can say it and breathe at the same time.

Copy editors also check for careless things, such as this common error:

> **The committee voted to turn over their profits to the council.**

Their profits? "Committee" is singular and "their" is plural, so the sentence is not grammatical; "their" should be "its." An alert copy editor will not let such mistakes get by.

Almost all sentences in a story should be in the active, not passive, voice. If a sentence says, "Suggestions are wanted by the student council," the copy editor changes it to "The student council wants suggestions."

Organization should also be checked in the editing process. Is the best material at the end of the story instead of near the top, where it belongs? Is something referred to in the lead but not mentioned again until the twelfth paragraph? Does the next-to-last paragraph belong somewhere else? In these situations the copy editor makes the changes.

Attribution

Attribution, providing the source of the facts in the story, is another area that often needs to be checked. Many reporters provide attribution in the lead and then never mention the source again, leaving the reader to believe that the opinions are the writer's—which should not be the case. In such circumstances the copy editor goes through the story and puts in all the necessary "he saids," "she saids," "he addeds," "she pointed outs," and so on. The reader must know at all times whose opinion is being expressed or where the information came from.

When all the corrections have been made, the copy editor goes over the story one more time, reading it for sense, for total effect rather than for mechanical problems. The editor takes the role of the reader and asks, "Are all the questions answered? Is it clear? Easy to read?" If the answer in each case is yes, then this phase of the work is finished. It is now time to write the headline.

Writing Headlines

Headline writers face what seems a nearly impossible task. From perhaps five hundred words of copy in a story, they must select three or four or five that tell the entire story. And they must do it according to a rather strict set of rules.

The headline's job is to lure the reader into the story. But it must do it honestly; the headline can't promise something that isn't in the story. The headline should be lively and interesting, with sparkling verbs. It must cram as much information into those words as possible, since readers tend to scan headlines looking for something of interest. When they do, they should be able to pick up some information they would not have otherwise.

Headline Size

Glance at a newspaper and the first thing you are apt to notice about head-lines is that they vary widely in size. Headlines, or heads, are measured by *points*. A point is 1/72 inch high. Thus, a 72-point headline is 1 inch high, a 36-point head is 1/2 inch high, an 18-point head is 1/4 inch high. This measurement system is transferable to any newspaper anywhere.

The smallest headline usually is 12 points high. From there it goes in specified gradations: 14, 18, 24, 30, 36, 42, 48, 54, 60, 72, 84, 96, and on into the really large type saved for truly fantastic events.

Composing headlines on a computer makes it easier to determine what will fit into the allotted space.

Headlines vary in width and number of lines as well as in type size. A headline may be anywhere from one to six columns wide if you have a six-column paper. Most headlines are one, two, or three lines long. Occasionally they may be four or five lines long, but only for special effect.

Editors have a definite system of referring to these dimensions. A busy editor cannot constantly be telling copy editors to write, for example, a 3-column, 36-point, 2-line head. Instead the editor uses shorthand and asks for a 3-36-2. The first digit specifies the width (3 columns), the second the size (36 point), and the third the number of lines (2). Thus, a 6-84-1 would call for a very large, six-column streamer, or banner, all in one line.

Headline Style

Headlines are typeset in various ways. Some are centered.

This Is a Centered Head

A few are "stepped," or given a kind of stairstep effect.

This Head
    Is Shaped
      That Way

A flush-left headline rests squarely against the left-hand side of the column.

This Represents
Flush Left

Many other varieties of headlines exist, some coming into use through the relative ease of desktop publishing. Once columns were rigid and type was made of lead. Not so anymore, and that has led to refreshing new styles of headlines.

For example, there is the hammer head. Usually the top line is twice as large as the bottom line. One line should be italic—sort of leaning to the right, as is the bottom line here—and the other should be Roman—or straight up and down. The hammer is used for important stories where the primary head receives the most attention.

Hammer Head
Big on top, small on bottom

Another style is the kicker. Featuring one secondary headline over one or more lines of primary, the kicker headline can be used when the writer wishes to feature a single word or phrase as the main title and add more specific information in the secondary headline.

This is a kicker, or overline
The main head is indented

In the headline style known as a wicket, several lines of type, up to about six lines, are used as a sort of super-lead or introduction. Then a one-line head set in contrasting Roman or italics follows, serving more as a magazine-type title than a headline.

After 26 years at Centerville High School, English department chair Joan Bowes is stepping down, retiring, she says, to "spend more time with my grandchildren" and with her hobbies of writing poetry and riding horseback. For this month's The Student Voice
Bowes Reminisces

Headline styles have become quite informal. The following represents a style called a read-out head.

Get their attention here
And then you can expand on that in a longer deck, using just about as many words as you need to get a reader really interested. Some publications actually use the lead as a sort of deck, placed like this.

The next example is called a read-in head.

From the state basketball tournament, a story of
Champions!

And one more word about headline style:

AVOID ALL-CAP HEADS

All-cap headlines should be avoided because they are difficult to read. People read not only the letters in words but the words' shapes, which are lost when the letters are all capitalized.

Unit Count System

Letter	Count
Capital I	1
Capital M, W, O	2
All other capitals	1 1/2
Lowercase j, l, f, t, and i	1/2
Lowercase w and m	1 1/2
All other lowercase letters	1
Spaces	1/2
Numerals	1
The numeral 1	1/2
Question mark, dash	1
All other punctuation	1/2

Making It Fit

No matter how cleverly a headline is styled, it still has to fit. A headline cannot go beyond its allotted space. On most systems, the process is simple. The editor writes a headline and then taps a button that commands the computer to decide if the headline fits. If it doesn't, the offending line may break apart on the screen, or the part that is too long may change color. Either way, the editor knows and can start over.

On a computer, you do have the option of *slightly altering* the size of the type. Depending on the system you're using, if your 36-point head won't fit, you can make it 35.9 or 35.8. Some commercial newspapers permit individual editors to make a decision to squeeze the type. At others, that decision has to be made by a desk chief. And no one permits anyone to squeeze a head more than two points. That 36-point head can't go below 34 points because large changes in point sizes done by editors can spoil the careful work of page designers.

At newspapers with less sophisticated equipment, a system once used at virtually every newspaper in the land is still in effect. Journalists have assigned a numerical value to each letter of the alphabet, based on the letter's width. Notice how much fatter a capital M is than a small i; or how much fatter a capital W is than a small t. These variations in width complicate headline writing. Two words, both with, say, five letters, can vary a great deal in width: the word "mommy" is a great deal wider than the word "title." To compensate for these variations, headline writers use the numerical system called the unit count system.

Suppose you have been asked to write a 2-36-2, with a maximum count of 16. First you write:

**Fifteen Seniors Win
University Scholarships**

Under the unit count system, the top line counts 17-1/2 and the bottom line 21—too long. So you try something else:

University Cites
15 AHS Seniors

The top line is 14, the bottom 14—and that is close enough. You may not violate the maximum count, of course, and you should be no more than two counts short.

Writing Do's and Don'ts

Those are the mechanics. Now let's turn to the writing itself.

First of all, headlines are written in a telegraphic style. All extra words are trimmed. The articles *a*, *an*, and *the* usually are left out.

School Wins High State Rating

Headlines are also written in present tense to give readers a feeling of immediacy.

Tigers Defeat Tech, 7–0

Occasionally a story about something historic will crop up, and then the past tense is acceptable; for example: **Volcano Erupted 50 Years Ago Today**. Headlines about future events are written with infinitives to indicate future tense: **360 Seniors to Graduate Sunday**.

Punctuation in headlines usually involves just three marks: the comma, the quote sign, and the semicolon. Whenever part of a headline is enclosed in quotes, to save space a single quote (') is used, not a double quote ("). The semicolon is used whenever a period seems appropriate:

Clinton Announces Freeze;
Congress to Discuss It

A comma is used in place of the word "and"; **Smith, Jones Win Scholarships**. The period is never used except in abbreviations, such as U. S. Exclamation points are used rarely, and then only for good reason; their value is debased if they are used often.

There are other considerations. Most newspapers prefer not to use headlines that split infinitives or names. It is also not acceptable for a line to end with a preposition. Each line should be a coherent unit by itself.

Wrong: Smith to
            Go Abroad

WRONG: Jim Williams, Jane
North Win Elections

WRONG: Smith Critical of
America's Journalists

Parts of the verb "to be" also are to be avoided generally: **15 Seniors Chosen**; not, "15 Seniors Are Chosen." Lively, active verbs attract more attention than the dull "are."

Headline writers should avoid repeating a word in a headline. Avoid this, for example:

WRONG: Student Council to Discuss Student Rights

As for capitalization, most newspapers use "down style." That is, all letters except proper nouns and the first letter of the first word are lowercase, or down. Such a headline looks like this:

Library offers amnesty on all overdue books

If you decide to use a style with capital letters, you may either capitalize prepositions and articles or leave them uncapitalized. Both ways are acceptable, though the latter style is preferable.

Aside from all these considerations, the headline writer must cultivate a special vocabulary of short words, such as "panel" for "committee," "kin" for "relative," "blast" for "explosion," "cuts" for "reductions," "quits" for "resigns," and "named" for "selected."

The headline writer should also cultivate a sense of humor. Puns are considered particularly appropriate. The play on words often is a handy way to tell a story:

Phone Users Have No Hang-ups

New Spray Bugs Farmers

Three Booked in Library Dispute

Use alliteration sparingly. A little of this—*Tigers Tame Tech Team; Teachers' Tests Trigger Trauma;*

Heads to Remember

Sometimes significant stories result in memorable headlines. Here is a sample.

Th-Th-Tha-Tha-That's All Folks!
Dodgers Miss
—IN THE *Los Angeles Times*, AFTER THE DODGERS LOST THE DIVISION CHAMPIONSHIP

Stix Nix Hix Pix
—IN *Variety*, WHEN RURAL AMERICANS STOPPED ATTENDING MOVIES ABOUT COUNTRY LIVING

Up on the Housetop
Slick, Slick, Slick
—IN *The Omaha World-Herald*'S CHRISTMAS STORM STORY

Ford to City:
Drop Dead
—IN *The New York Daily News*, AFTER PRESIDENT FORD REJECTED THE CITY'S APPEAL FOR FEDERAL HELP

Wall Street Lays an Egg
—in *Variety*, after the stock market crash in 1929

Bartered Books Bring Big Bundle—goes a long way. The same is true of verse. Unless it's really good, toss it out.

Elements of Design

Once the copy has been read and edited, the main articles and sidebars, together with any photographs, are ready to be transferred over to the designer. Now the designer needs to turn all these pieces into a well-conceived final product.

In producing any type of student publication, a designer must fully understand the content of the publication. In other words, he or she must know how many stories and visuals are available and what types of secondary pieces, such as sidebar stories, informational graphics, quote boxes, or timelines, need to be included. The designer needs always to remember that the content dictates the design.

Selecting and Using Type

From a design standpoint, the basic component of any article is type. There are many typefaces to select from, with new faces constantly being developed and made available for computer use. The designer's choice of type will determine if and to what extent an article will be read by the audience.

When choosing typefaces for particular projects, you as a designer should always keep the target audience in mind. For example, young readers, such as early elementary students, and older readers, such as senior citizens, require larger type with extra leading, or white space, used between the lines. Teenage audiences may not require large type, but may prefer type set a bit larger in certain instances in order to attract and hold their attention.

They Can't All Be Winners

Sometimes, if we nod off at the wrong moment or just get careless, headlines can come out . . . strange. Here are a few:

State pupils below average in raeding

Cold wave linked to temperatures

War dims hope for peace

Grandmother of eight makes hole in one

Man is fatally slain

Iraqi head seeks arms

Milk drinkers turning to powder

If you're a person with any interest in design whatsoever, chances are you're also interested in fonts. The rise of desktop publishing has given the page designer, and even the copy writer, access to many more fonts than even existed in the pre-desktop world. Companies like Adobe, URW, and ITC, to name a few, can make available to you, at relatively low cost, literally hundreds of different fonts. And these as well as many smaller companies tend to turn out more new fonts every month or so.

In a heated-up climate such as this, fonts appear, take the marketplace by storm, are used on every possible kind of printed material, become tiresome from overuse, and then seem to disappear almost as quickly as they surfaced. Ten or fifteen years ago, for example, a lovely-looking font called Souvenir made its appearance this way; today it is not often seen. More recently Tekton also grabbed the marketplace by storm. Its influence also is now waning.

At the risk of their also becoming quickly dated, here are some current trends with fonts.

Grunge fonts. Grunge fonts are novelty fonts that look, well, unplanned. Random rather than consistent in shape and appearance, they often seem to have no baseline; one, named Harding, looks like a bad typewriter ribbon. Type companies like House Industries and Emigre turn out grunge fonts, and although they can be quite hard to read, certain magazines and alternative publications use them because they bring excitement to a page. They are also beginning to be seen in headlines in yearbooks. Remedy, House Paint, and Amoeba Rain are a few more examples of grunge fonts.

Handwriting fonts. Only a few years ago it was difficult to create and digitize a font that looked like cursive handwriting. Then a company streamlined the technology. Soon they were offering to take your very own handwriting and create a personalized font of it. As long as you had a computer available, you might never have to take pen in hand again.

Handwriting fonts have become the latest trend in the marketplace—and it doesn't have to be your own chicken-scratchy-type writing. Now you can go out and buy a beautiful font created out of someone else's well-formed script and, if you want, use it entirely in place of your own. One reason for the popularity of such fonts may be a need on some people's part to convey a softer image, to backtrack from the regularized world of serif type. Or it may simply be that too many of us have illegible handwriting.

Clearly, it's impossible to predict either how long these two font trends will last or what the next trend will be. The only certainty is that, given the technological advances in developing typefaces, the next trend is just around the corner.

Type Categories

Type can be categorized in many ways. A number of experts classify type in seven groups.

Oldstyle Roman. This kind of type is characterized by its roughly hewn serifs, or tiny cross-strokes projecting from the primary part of each letter, and by the slight difference between the thin and thick parts of the letters. It is good for headlines, captions, or body copy, as it is considered easy to read by most experts. Because the rough serifs cause each letter to look significantly different from other letters in the same font, the reader's eye can flow smoothly across a line of type. For that reason, Oldstyle Roman is the easiest type group to read.

Bookman and Caslon are two common examples of Oldstyle Roman typeface.

Bookman
Caslon

Modern Roman. Characterized by thin, precisely attached serifs and dramatic differences between the thin and thick portions of the letters, Modern Roman type is excellent for nameplates, headlines, logos, and display lines in advertisements. Its readability factor diminishes as the type is set smaller. Therefore, it should not be used for small-type areas, such as body copy or captions. It is rarely used in sizes smaller than 14 point.

Bodoni and Modern are two examples of a Modern Roman typeface.

Bodoni
Modern

Text. Also referred to as Black Letter, Text type was based on the "pointed gothic" handwriting style popular in the days of Johannes Gutenberg, the developer of movable type. Text type is ornate and very difficult to read. It reflects a feeling of formality and is often used for formal communication, such as wedding or graduation announcements. In student publications, it might be used as a primary headline for a spread on a Medieval Fair, for example, but not throughout a section. Because of the beauty and ornate structure of the letters, it should never be used in all capital letters, as it is much too difficult to read.

Old English and Linotext are two common examples of Text typeface.

Old English
Linotext

Square serif. Square serif type is characterized by "block-type" serifs. It is good for serious messages and conveys a "steadfast and true" or "staunch, stern and unwavering" feeling. Historically, square serif types were used on wanted posters in the Old West. Square serif types are good for certain nameplates, logos, or display lines, but they are rarely used for headlines unless the designer is trying to convey a particular message. A square serif type probably should not be used for body copy or captions because of its lower readability.

Courier and Rockwell are two examples of square serif typeface.

Courier
Rockwell

Sans serif. The word *sans* means "without" in French; thus, a sans serif type has no serifs. Its smooth, clean appearance works well in headlines, logos, nameplates, and advertisements but makes it difficult to read when set in blocks of smaller type, such as body copy. Sometimes, when set bold, sans serif works well for captions. When set regular, it can work well for short copy areas, such as sidebars or other types of secondary coverage.

Helvetica and Futura are two common examples of sans serif typeface.

Helvetica
Futura

Scripts and cursives. Both scripts and cursives resemble handwriting. Scripts usually seem to be "connected" while cursives do not. These types should be used like spices in food—very sparingly. Because of low readability, they should never be used for body copy or captions, although they could be used for small headlines or subheadlines over or within these areas. They also should never be set in all caps.

Linoscript and Brush Script, respectively, are examples of script and cursive typefaces.

Linoscript
Brush Script

Novelty. Novelty types are numerous and can look like smoke, neon signs, "down-home country," computer type, or a variety of other objects or ideas. Novelty types should be used with care and only to convey or reinforce a message to the reader. They should never be used in all caps or in small-type areas, such as body copy or captions.

Here are some examples of novelty types.

Addled
Paisley

Working with typefaces. Some designers choose to use only one family of type to create a printed piece, changing the styles from regular to bold, italic, outline, or a combination of these. This is called family harmony. Other designers choose to use blending harmony, selecting one family of type from three of the seven type groups. If you as a designer decide to use this method, be sure to choose only one family from each of the three groups rather than two from the same group. Using more than one family from one particular type group causes reader confusion. It also makes the printed piece appear to be unplanned.

Rules of Typography

Typography experts agree that designers should follow a basic set of rules when selecting types for printed publications. Their suggestions are as follows:

Set body copy in 9-, 10-, or 11-point type. Choose an Oldstyle Roman typeface for body copy, as it is the most readable of all type groups. Use 8-point type for captions, and generally use bold type for headlines to provide better contrast for the reader.

For primary headlines, secondary headlines, and subheadlines, select the type style most appropriate for the document. Display lines and subheadlines are often set in types that convey the "personality" of the printed piece. Some designers choose to mix two type groups together in one headline design, one for the primary headline and one for the secondary headline. The contrast in size, weight, and style produces an eye-catching, readable headline design reflecting the document's personality.

Type Talk

Here are some basic terms used when talking about type.

Roman—letters that are straight up and down.

Italic—letters slanted to the right.

Light—a thin version of a regular typeface (e.g., Helvetica Light).

Bold—a heavy, dark version of a regular typeface (e.g., Helvetica Bold).

Condensed—letters squeezed together from each side, causing them to have a tall, thin appearance.

Extended—letters that appear to be flattened to a shorter, fatter appearance than those in normal widths.

Ligature—two or more letters joined as a set.

Point—a small unit of measurement to describe the size of type. There are 72 points in one inch.

Pica—a unit of measurement in design. There are 12 points in a pica and 6 picas in one inch.

Baseline—imaginary line on which type rests.

Descenders—parts of letters that extend below the baseline (as in g, j, p, q, and y).

Ascenders—parts of letters that rise above the baseline (b, d, d, f, h, k, l, t).

Type Talk (continued)

x-height—the actual height of the lowercase *x*; may vary from face to face.

Type measurement—done from the highest point of the ascender to the lowest point of the descender; 72-point type is approximately one inch high from the top of an *h* to the bottom of a *p*.

Font—traditionally, all characters in one size of one particular typeface (e.g., 24-point Palatino Regular). Often used now as a synonym for typeface (e.g., Palatino is a font).

Small caps—complete alphabet of capital letters that are the same size as the x-height of the lowercase letters.

Leading—the white space inserted between the lines. It is normally set two points larger than the type itself. A 10-point type set on a 12-point leading would be referred to as set "10 on 12."

Justified—type set even on both sides of a column.

Ragged—type that is set uneven. Often type will be justified on the left and ragged on the right ("ragged right").

Centered—type centered within a given horizontal area.

Set body copy at a "readable" width. Setting 10-point copy wider than 22 picas or narrower than 10 picas causes difficulty for most readers. Try to follow a specific column format and use consistent copy and caption widths to maintain unity in the printed piece. In narrow column widths, consider setting the type ragged right rather than justifying it in order to keep large "rivers" of white space from forming between words or letters within words. Type justified left with consistent word spacing is easier to read than type that is justified and variably spaced.

Be sure to set the leading at a readable level. Though the use of two points of white space between lines in body copy is usually standard, in special cases such as theme copy in yearbooks or sidebars in other publications, extra leading will sometimes attract readers or enhance readability.

Keep type within the external margin framework of the page. Captions or copy that creep into the external margin look more like mistakes than "planned copy" areas. External margins give the reader room to "breathe" and allow the eye to rest periodically.

When placing boxes around type areas or lines between columns, place the copy one pica from the rule lines. If type is allowed to run into a box or rule line, reader interference occurs.

Use boxes and lines to "package" copy and headlines together as one unit. Avoid boxing each column of type separately. Also, try to avoid breaking the reader's eye flow from headline to body copy by inserting lines between the two elements.

When mixing types, look for faces that have strong contrast in characteristics. Mixing an Oldstyle Roman with a sans serif, for example, would

work well. Adding a third type, perhaps a script or cursive, would add
even greater contrast. Make certain
that the types look good together or, if
you're not sure that they do, stick to a
single face. You can still get variation
by changing type size, case, weight,
width, or style within that face.

Remember that the use of all capital letters often lowers readability.
Lowercase letters, especially those in
the Oldstyle Roman group, are distinctive and allow the reader to see

> **Standard Type Sizes**
>
> 6-point (used for indexes and photo bylines)
>
> 8-point (used for captions)
>
> 9-, 10-, 11-, or 12-point (used for body copy)
>
> 14-, 18-, and 24-point (used for large initial letters, headlines, and overlines on captions)
>
> 30-, 36-, 42-, 48-, 60-, and 70-point type (used for headlines and display lines in ads).

each letter quickly. Lines set in all caps are harder to read because the capital letters have similar characteristics. Furthermore, they tire the reader's
eye. Therefore, if you use all caps, use them for no more than two or three
short lines, and use only Oldstyle Roman or Modern Roman faces, which
are the easiest to read.

When designing copy-heavy areas, try to help the reader through the
materials by using subheads, large initial letters, inset photos, pulled
quotes, or other graphic devices to break up the gray space. "Rails" of
white space strategically placed can also help pull the reader into the copy.

Avoid running large blocks of type in color. High contrast between the
type and its background is essential for improved readability. Reversed
type on a dark background can work well for headlines and secondary
coverage, but it should be limited to areas of impact rather than used in
large, copy-heavy places. For specific effects, color in display type or other
emphasis areas can create an interesting, eye-catching effect.

Avoid overprinting or reversing type on photos, patterned screens, or
"busy" backgrounds. Always place type in a spot where it can be easily
read. Similarly, avoid placing type diagonally or vertically.

In designing logos and primary headlines, try to make a connection
between the verbal and visual elements. For example, if you were creating
a logo for the concept "Sticking Together," you might select and place the
type in such a way that it actually "stuck" together.

Don't be afraid to try something new and different, even if it stretches
or breaks a rule. After designing the typographic element, take a step back
and look at it from the reader's point of view. Also, ask impartial sources
for their opinions to make sure the design is readable and attractive.

Using Graphics

Once you as a designer have a basic understanding of type and how to use it effectively, you can add graphics, such as lines, boxes, art, photos, spot color, and other devices, to enhance the design and to draw the reader into the page.

It is important to remember that graphics must have a specific reason or purpose when used in a printed piece. In general, graphics serve three purposes.

To Unify Elements

Boxes and rule lines can be used to pull related elements together on a page. For example, if you were planning to use a series of quotes and photos of the individuals quoted, you might choose to run them vertically, grouped together in a box or aligned beside a rule. If you were planning to show a sequence of events in a "timeline" fashion, you might use boxes, rules, or a combination of those to pull the events together as a unit.

To Separate Elements

Rules and boxes also function to separate elements from other elements. In addition, they serve as "barriers" for the reader, causing the reader's eye to stop at one point and pick up copy at a different point. When used effectively, lines and rules can help guide and direct a reader's eye around a page. When used ineffectively, they can inhibit the reader's ability to fully understand the message.

To Call Attention to Elements

Screens, boxes, borders, large type or photographs, areas of spot color, and distinctive art allow the designer to attract the reader's eye to specific areas on a page. When placed in key positions, these graphics can enhance the design of the page and will guide and direct the reader's eye to specific areas of interest.

Basic Principles of Design

Keeping the rules of effective uses of typography and graphics in mind, you must also consider the principles of design when creating a printed piece.

Dominance

Every single page and every double-page spread should have one dominant element that is at least two-and-one-half times as large as any other element on the spread. The dominant element serves as a point of visual entry for the reader—in other words, a place where the reader can actually enter the page. If no dominant element exists, the reader's eye will either bounce around the page, or the reader will skip that page and go on to the next.

The dominant element is usually a large, well-composed photo that is representative of the story it illustrates. The content of the photo should also tie to the message expressed in the primary headline.

Unity

One way to unify a page or spread is by using consistent internal and external margins. Most designers use one pica between all elements as internal margins. External margins on single pages are usually three to four picas at the top of the page, four to five picas on each side of the page, and five to six picas at the bottom of the page. For double-page spreads the only difference is a one-pica margin on either side of the gutter (the dividing space between two pages that falls in the fold).

On double-page spreads the placement of the dominant photo can also create unity. Running the photo across the gutter ties the two pages together, making them appear to be one connected page. Another technique is to use an eyeline, one pica of horizontal white space that goes across the spread. An eyeline should run at least six picas above or below the horizontal center of the spread.

Unity is also achieved through the entire design or "personality" of the publication. The "On Display" feature on page 226 shows an effective use of graphics to tie together as well as to separate elements. Notice also the strong dominant element and the consistent headline style.

Screens and other visual devices can call the reader's attention to certain areas on a page. Many kinds of screens are available on computer design programs.

Contrast

One of the most important aspects of design is contrast—that is, the use of opposites in size, shape, and weight. For example, a design should feature one dominant photo contrasted by several smaller photos, and horizontal as well as vertical photos. The use of different typefaces also creates contrast.

The design of this page, from the Yukon High School *The Miller Insight*, is unified by the strong, dominant photo, the consistent headline treatment, and the use of graphics.

Hispanic culture has large influence in society

National Hispanic Week focuses on language, culture, fun

FIESTA•Celebrations of the Hispanic culture fill halls

*mindy*JOHNSON
reporter

One week before the long awaited break from book reports and research papers is National Hispanic Week. The high school and mid-high Spanish classes are celebrating March 11-15 in a unique way. Every day this week, the high school holds something different.

Monday•Decorating the halls
Tuesday•Volleyball games
Wednesday•Playing a Spanish game called Loteria
Thursday•Spanish commercials and/or speaker
Friday•Teachers luncheon

All week long there are luncheons that students may attend. The mid-high is having a speaker from the State Arts Council of Oklahoma.

The United States is surrounded by the influence of the Hispanic culture. Even the school has been affected by it. A couple of years ago eighth graders were given the opportunity to take Spanish 1 and receive high school credit for it. With this opportunity, students are able to graduate with 5 years of the Spanish language.

"It has enhanced them to master the language. Students don't learn a language in only a few years, but just the basics. With this program they have more experience and can go on to obtain fluency, if they so choose to draw," Mrs. Wilhite, Spanish teacher said.

In the job force, students need to have some knowledge of a language. If one is not fluent, it does help to have a little background in a language.

"Because of the global society, people need a foreign language to function in the job area. The school's language department is something in which to be proud of," Wilhite said.

Puerto Ricans, Mexicans, Cubans, Chicanos, Latin Americans and some Spaniards make up the second largest group of minorities in the United States. Anyone who has cable television has seen the Spanish channel. Oklahoma is not the only state that airs these channels, but all over America Spanish TV can be seen and heard. The Spanish culture has even effected and become some of the favorite foods of students.

Taco Bell with its famous phrase "Run For the Border" made a smashing hit all across America with its Tex/Mex fast food. Though one might not call it authentic Mexican food, one can see how it was inspired by the Mexican influence. When students are in a hurry they run by Taco Bell and maybe just may be get a glimpse of fine Mexican dining.

---

the miller
INSIGHT

Vol. 4 No. 7   Saturday, March 16, 1996   8 pages

Mock trial argues way to third straight state title

CHAMPS•Team beats Woodward; eyes national championship

*ashi*KINSEY
editorial board

Standing in astonishment, the Yukon Mock Trial team waited for the presentation of the first place trophy. The team defeated Woodward on March 5 to win state for the third year in a row. This is the first time, in Oklahoma, a team has won three consecutive state titles.

The team will travel to Pittsburgh in May to compete in the National competition.

In '94, the team placed 6th. The following year the team made the top 3. This year, they have their eye on first.

"I think we have a great chance of placing at Nationals because we work so well together. The fact that almost all of us received outstanding attorney and witness awards shows we don't have a weak link," Stacie Herron, senior said.

At the state finals, Amanda Herrman, junior, was named outstanding attorney. John Graham, sophomore, was named outstanding witness. Herron received a book scholarship.

"My teammates really pumped me up and made me proud of my achievement," Herman said. The team had finished a brochure and mailed letters to law firms and local businesses asking for donations. Parents are also planning fund-raisers.

The team has about a month before receiving the national award and beginning practice at night again. However, the team agrees that is worth all the hard work.

"I highly suggest Mock Trial to all of my peers who don't have a fear of commitment. It takes a lot of hard work but everything pays off in the end," Mandee Chapman, junior said.

The team gives a lot of the credit for their success to their coaches.

"It amazes me how much time and energy Mrs. Corn and Mr. Seglar put into this program," Herron said.

Sophomores learn lesson about wearing seatbelts

WRECK•Sophomores learn hard way about speeding on gravel roads

The speed limit sign read 30 miles per hour, but apparently four Yukon students chose to test fate and pushed the speedometer up over 70 miles an hour. Whether in a hurry to get somewhere or lost and constructing a car-jesst, these students learned a lesson about speeding, the hard way.

On Friday February 23 at the 6100 block of Morgan road, sophomores Michael Yetter, Dallas Edwards, Bob Cassidy and Ashish Masih were involved in a near-fatal car accident.

Traveling north on Morgan road, better known as the road that leads to "live mile," Cassidy, the driver, lost control of his three-month-old '96 Pontiac Sunbird. The car slid sideways on the left side of the road, collided with the ditch and began flipping end over end. The left rear of then car then collided with a ditch and constructed flipping. When the right rear end of the car collided with the ditch it rolled onto its top and slid 19 feet, where it finally came to a stop.

Cassidy was wearing his seat belt, his driver's air bag deployed and he sustained minor injuries. Yetter, sitting in the back seat of the car also had on a seatbelt, but sustained more intense injuries. Yetter was treated in the ER and released.

Edwards, sitting in the front passenger seat was not wearing a seat belt and though the air bag deployed, Edwards was thrown through the windshield and ejected from the car. Edwards remained in the hospital for five days. Masih , also in the back seat, was not wearing a seat belt and was ejected from the car. Yetter and Cassidy are the only two who have returned to school. At press time, Masih still remains in Pediatric Intensive care at Integris Baptist Medical Center in critical condition.

Though the police report stated that Cassidy was in apparently normal condition (not intoxicated), he was cited for reckless driving and speeding. The report also stated that the road was severely washboarded. The damage to the car at the time of the wreck was estimated at $12,000.

See **RELATED EDITORIAL** Pg. 4.

Vocal earns top honors at UCO

TUNED IN•Choir sings way to scores of 1+

*mindy*JOHNSON
reporter

Singing a cappella in front of three judges while the choir is trying not to go flat or sharp every nerve-racking, but the chamber choir, also known as Yukon Rapella singers, came over those nerves to win the best of the 5-A class.

On Friday February 16, at the University of Central Oklahoma (UCO) the chamber choir competed against several different choir in the class 5-A district. The songs they sang were Music's empire and Witness. In March, the chamber choir will compete in state competition.

"The state competition will be more difficult than the UCO, but we can handle it, we will do good," Natalie Mingard, junior said.

Members said the choir the road to success was a lot of hard work, but it paid off when each of the judges gave them the top score of 1+. It has required work since the beginning of the year with before and after school practices.

"We have been working on the music since the beginning of school and have been practicing before and after classes," Christy Lynch, senior said.

"There was a lot of individual work included. Mrs. Renek has good ability in dynamics. She helped us on when we should get louder and when to back off," Mingard, said.

On Saturday, Lynch and Renek went to see the posted list of the winning choir.

"I was elated when I saw the list, since it was just me and Mrs. Renek I got the tell everyone the news," Lynch said.

Pom returns at No. 15

Waiting with nerves fluttering and emotions running high, the squad anxiously awaited to be called to perform. The goal was to out-do the 20th rank from last year. The squad came back with the mission accomplished.

After the many hours of relentless practice, numerous fundraisers and several costume fittings, the squad was thrilled to make it to the finals. They came home late Feb. 25 being ranked 15th in the finals.

"We worked so hard and when we made finals we were so excited, and that was our goal. We knew our practice had paid off," Shelley Stirg, junior said.

Also receiving individual honors was Rayna Falen, senior, placed 9th in the lyrical dance category.

AREA CHAMPS•Members of the varsity boys basketball team celebrate with their fans after the 57-55 over the favored Putnam City Pirates on March 1 at Norman High. The team earned Yukon's first berth to the state tournament since 1983, when the Millers lost first round to Tulsa Washington. The Millers, unranked during the regular season, finished the year ranked in the state's number 10 teams. The Millers drew Tulsa Memorial first round. See related story and photos page 8.

---

miller MINUTES

$1,000 scholarship deadline March 31

This spring one '96 graduate of YHS will receive a $1,000 scholarship from the Shelter Insurance Foundation. The award will be sponsored and partially funded by local Shelter agent Roger Karns, who has participated in the scholarship program for 12 years.

The recipient of the $1,000 award will be chosen by a committee of local high school officials and community leaders. The committee will consider each applicant's scholastic achievement, educational goals, citizenship, moral character and participation and leadership in school and community activities. The scholarship will be given without regard to race, creed, religion, national origin, sex or employment status of applicant's and their relatives. The name of the scholarship winner will be announced at the close of the school year.

The scholarship may be applied toward tuition, fees, room and board for course of study beginning the fall after the recipient's high school graduation and lending to an academic degree at any accredited college or university. Payment will be made directly to the school the winner selects.

Applications and additional information about the Shelter Foundation Scholarship will be available in early March and should be completed and returned to the school official on the committee by March 31. For more information, interested seniors should contact the high school counselor, principal or Karns.

The Shelter Insurance Foundation is a not-for-profit corporation for charitable, educational and scientific purposes.

Tryouts coming soon

Cheer clinic is April 1-4 with tryouts on the 5th. Pom clinic is April 8-11 with tryouts on the 12th. Contact Mrs. Anderson at the high school for cheerleading details.

226

One area where contrast frequently comes into play is in headline design. Each story should feature a headline with both primary and secondary components. The primary headline should be at least twice as large in point size as the secondary headline. In other words, if the primary headline is 72 points high, the secondary should be no larger than 36 points high. Usually, the primary headline is set in bold type and the secondary headline is set in a regular or lighter face. For special newspaper features, magazine layouts, and yearbook spreads, you may want to choose a special type such as a novelty, script, or cursive for the primary headline and then set up a contrast by using a sans serif or an Oldstyle Roman face for the secondary headline. In standard newspaper design, however, stick with one type family, using bold for primary headlines and regular for secondary headlines throughout the newspaper.

Rhythm

Repetition, or rhythm, involves the use of a repeated color, graphic, or typographic element to hold a design together. For example, the designer of a yearbook or magazine spread may choose to use a specific headline design and then repeat it in a smaller, modified version as the design of all the captions on the spread. This pattern would then be used on each spread throughout a particular section of the book, such as the sports or student life section, to create unity and consistency within the section. The designer of a newspaper spread might repeat a color pulled from a photograph as the background for a secondary coverage box or as a part of a headline design to instill unity on the page or spread.

Balance

By using the design principles mentioned above, the designer can create a page or spread that features formal or informal balance. Pages that are balanced formally can be folded in half vertically, with each half mirroring the other half of the page. Informally balanced pages feature weight distributed diagonally. Bigger, bolder elements are moved toward the center and white space, copy, headlines, and captions are pushed to the outside so that pages do not "weigh heavy" to one side or the other. Most designers use informal balance to create variety and improve interest in the page.

Consistency

Certain elements of a publication should remain unchanged. For example, the staff should establish a byline style, folio (or page number) style, and standing headline design and keep these consistent in size, font, weight, and style throughout the publication. These elements should also be consistent from issue to issue.

In yearbooks, consistency is established by using the same design elements, typography, and graphics throughout the theme pages, on the cover, and on the front and back endsheets. Consistency within each section is established by using the same column format, headline design, caption design, and secondary coverage design throughout the entire section. These elements provide unity within the section for the reader and allow him or her to recognize when a new section begins.

Creating Pages

Newspaper designers basically work with four elements: copy (stories), art (photos or artwork), headlines, and white space. Using basic design principles, the designer selects the elements he or she plans to use on the page and creates the visual "personality" of the newspaper.

When you as the designer establish the basic format of the paper, it is a good idea to make a blueprint or a dummy of it, mock it up in paste-up fashion, and then design it on the computer. When the design is finalized, mark it with type sizes and faces and place examples of the design on the wall in the journalism room for future reference. Also, if possible, include the information in the stylebook.

Before designing a particular issue, meet with editors, reporters, artists, and photographers about the content of the issue so that you can plan the design of each page effectively. Work with your photographers in order to obtain the types of photos that will best illustrate the stories in the publication.

To begin a design, draw rough sketches first, usually on miniature layout sheets, and then transfer them to dummy sheets. On the dummies, indicate where photos, copy, captions, and headlines will be placed, being sure to keep consistent internal margins of one pica. When you are finished, either typeset and paste the copy on grid sheets or lay out the publication on the computer with a design program. If you are working on a computer, you can print your completed layout on a laser printer and paste it on grid sheets, or, if your publication's printer has the capability, you can send the copy straight to the page negative department on a disk or through a modem or other delivery system.

Designing the Front Page

When coming up with the basic design for the front page, create a nameplate that reflects the "personality" of the paper. The nameplate should be distinctive but not overly decorative. It should include the name of the publication, date, school's name, address, volume, and issue number. Above the nameplate, on the side, or at the bottom of the page, some staffs choose to place a "menu" or several "teasers" to entice the reader into looking inside the publication.

The rest of the front page is usually devoted to one, two, or three major news stories. In newspaper design, it is acceptable to use a varied column format on the same page in order to emphasize the difference between the stories on the page. For a letter-sized paper (8 1/2" x 11"), you will probably have a three-column format. Tabloid-size papers usually feature a four- or five-column format, and broadsheets may feature five, six, or seven columns across the page. The front page shown in the "On Display" feature on page 230 has a nameplate with an interesting design as well as a menu of contents. Notice also the varied column widths.

When placing stories on the page, follow a modular format, packaging stories, headlines, and accompanying graphic elements into neat rectangular shapes. You might drop your dominant photo in the center three columns, wrap the copy around it, and place a headline over the entire package. At other times, you might place a photo to illustrate the story to the right or left of it. The headline will usually extend across the copy and photo, thereby creating a solid rectangular block, or "module," for the reader.

Designing Inside Pages

The same basic principles used for the front page also apply to inside pages. For example, when planning the editorial page, the staff may wish to use an editorial cartoon as the primary optical area. An accompanying editorial should be "packaged" with the editorial cartoon.

A masthead, listing newspaper staff members and headed with a miniature version of the nameplate, should be placed at the bottom of the editorial page. It should be small and inconspicuous, but also readable. Remember that it is inappropriate to run ads on the editorial/opinion page(s) and on the front page as well. (See page 298 for a sample editorial page layout.)

Other inside pages are designed in a similar fashion, with one dominant photo, several smaller photos, stories, and headlines; however, most of the inside pages contain advertising. Ads are usually placed across the bottom of the page with one pica of white space between them and so that the tops of the ads are even across the page.

In addition to a varied column width, this front page sample from the James Bowie High School *The Lone Star Dispatch* contains an interesting nameplate and table of contents design.

Next Week	Feature	Feature	Next Month
■ Christian students plan prayer meeting Sept. 21 ■ Students reap benefits of new staffing formula	Teen parents struggle to keep commitments, finish high school careers **4**	Principal Kent Ewing celebrates TASSP's announcement as Texas High School Principal of the Year **5**	The victim of a gunshot wound, former student Mike Clark copes with paralysis

the lone star dispatch

Volume 7, No. 1   James Bowie High School ★ 4103 W. Slaughter Lane ★ Austin, Texas 78749-6914   Thursday, September 8, 1994

A Redbook Magazine School of Excellence & A United States Department of Education   Blue Ribbon School

Board admits to funding errors

By Holly Hughes
Dispatch Reporter

Juggling an almost $300 million budget, the Austin Independent School District Board of Trustees "lost" all proposed high school newspaper funding.

In what administrators are calling a mistake in budget preparations, the Board voted Aug. 24 on a budget which excluded a $56,000 free newspaper fund, a subsidy established about 25 years ago, according to Thom Prentice, Austin High newspaper adviser. The funding that was cut allowed students free access to publications, regardless of economic situations, Prentice said.

"From what I understand, the $56,000 was never proposed to [the School Board]. It had inadvertently been left out," said Michael Hydak, instructional coordinator for journalism curriculum. "The Board acted in good faith. They weren't trying to cut the program."

District 7 representative Melissa Knippa called the loss of funding an unfortunate mistake.

"It was clearly a mistake from the beginning," Knippa said. "When you're working with a big budget, unfortunately some things fall through the cracks."

According to Hydak, the "crack" in this case occurred somewhere between himself and the Board. Hydak says he prepared a journalism budget. He says the free newspaper fund made up about 94 percent of his original budget. He also included $84,000 for new technology.

"The budget that got to the Board, however, did not include the newspaper funds," Hydak said. "We don't send things directly to the Board. It goes through a ... number of people [at central administration.] In that process, the $56,000 amount was inadvertently taken out. I don't think the Board even got to see that."

Trustee Liz Hartman went on record Aug. 24 in the *Austin-American Statesman*, saying the Board's had no intention to cut the funding.

Hydak said that principals were told that the free newspaper fund had been cut and, in turn, they told the newspaper advisers.

"The Board directed the administration to put the money back, and that's what we're going to do for the newspapers. The technology is still up in the air."

the price is right

$299,083,732 budget requires cuts, additions, refocusing of priorities

■ Reduced class size: High school teachers will teach 5-6 periods with 28 students per core academic class

■ Higher teacher salaries: An average 1.5% of midpoint raise

■ Improved professional development: Funding priority will be given to open a Professional Development Academy

Dispatch graphic by Holly Hughes

... *and the winner is*

■ PTSA yearbook cover raffle nets $725, picks 162 winners

Members of numerous clubs and organizations drew 162 winners in the yearbook cover raffle last Friday from 4:20 to 5 p.m. in the courtyard.

Winners will have professional portraits taken tomorrow. Photos will appear on the front and back covers, endsheets, theme and portrait pages of the 1995 yearbook.

Courtney Hopkin, yearbook co-editor-in-chief, says the yearbook staff raised $725, what she called a "disappointment. We expected to raise between $5,000 and $10,000."

Yearbook editors and John McCartney, yearbook adviser, decided at the end of the 1994 school year to develop a yearbook theme that would appeal to students and create an unusual, but productive, fundraiser. The editors chose "The Fine Line" as the book's theme.

"The theme has a two-fold purpose," McCartney said. "We hoped it would be a creative way to raise money. It also gives students a sense of ownership of the book."

The first order of business was to find a 501(3c) organization to sponsor a raffle. McCartney spent six weeks of the summer researching 501(3c)'s, and discovered that the PTSA could hold a raffle.

McCartney and yearbook editors Kevin Campion, Hopkin and Linda Hsieh presented a written proposal to the PTSA Executive Board Aug. 1. The general PTSA approved the raffle Aug. 9.

Reported by Melissa Shepard

SPEAK UP
PTSA President Melanie Naumann presents the faculty with the PTSA Executive Board. Margaret McQuiston, Sherry Thompson and Vicki Hebert enjoy the PTSA back-to-school booklet.

Ewing to travel to D.C. for national recognition

By Joel Odom
Editor-in-chief

Principal Kent Ewing will represent Texas as he travels to Washington, D.C., Oct. 1-4, to begin competition for the honor of National High School Principal of the Year.

The Texas Association of Secondary School Principals named Ewing Texas High School Principal of the Year in front of 1700 principals at its Summer Conference June 9-10 at the Hyatt Regency Hotel in Austin.

"When I found out he won, I thought, 'Finally, people have recognized what we already know,' " said Mary Walker, science department chairman. "I felt the honor was long overdue."

First Reaction

When Ewing heard the news, he says he couldn't believe it.

"My first thoughts were, 'Is this for real? Am I dreaming this? Did it really happen?' " Ewing said. "I felt very humble, considering the quality of principals across the state.

"I was excited for the honor it brought Southwest Austin, the honor it brought Austin Independent School District, and, most importantly, the honor it brought Bowie."

Staff Support

The Bowie community joined former Asst. Supt. Toni Turk in nominating Ewing for the award last February.

"He is the best principal around," said Elaine Hopkins, Ewing's secretary. "Nominating him was a way for the people who work with him to let him know how much we appreciate him."

After narrowing down the field of applicants to nine finalists in May, a six-member TASSP panel interviewed the finalists June 7. Julkar Shaddik, TASSP executive director, says although he did not sit on the panel which selected Ewing, he has an idea of what the selection committee saw in Ewing.

"Kent is willing to stand up for what he thinks is good for

Principal Kent Ewing

kids, even if it makes him unpopular," Shaddik said. "And it does. I know there are some people in the Bowie community who are not happy with Kent because he is willing to stick his neck out if it's in the best interest of students. That's the thing I'm most impressed with."

The Whole Picture

Ewing refuses to take full credit for the award. He says he is just a representative of Bowie High School, doing his best to serve its students.

"Bowie's had a lot of attention," Ewing said. "I'm smart enough to know it's not just because of me, but because of everyone working together. No one person can make that much of a difference. I live by the idea that 'We're a whole lot smarter than I am.' "

The three-month selection process for National High School Principal of the Year will begin Oct. 1-4 at the 1995 Educational Leaders Symposium in Washington, D.C. The National Association of Secondary School Principals sponsors the award, along with Metropolitan Life and the United States Department of Education.

An NASSP/MetLife panel will meet Jan. 4, 1995, to decide the national winner.

The 1995 National High School Principal of the Year will travel to Washington, D.C. Jan. 16-20, and will be recognized by NASSP in San Antonio Feb. 3-7.

■ Please see related story, Page 5

TAAS scores fall short of goals, decrease 1%

By Amanda Boesen
Dispatch Reporter

Although Bowie sophomores met both Austin Independent School District and state standards, student scores on the sophomore exit-level Texas Assessment of Academic Skills test remain below the Campus Leadership Team's goals.

The overall results of the March, 1994, exit-level TAAS scores were one percent lower than the 1995 sophomore exit-level scores.

Principal Kent Ewing says Bowie's TAAS passing rates were much lower than he expected.

Although percentiles have not decreased significantly in relation to state and district expectations, Ewing says Bowie's math scores remain a weak point.

Math scores decreased from 69 percent to 68 percent. Writing scores also decreased from 86 percent to 85 percent.

However, Ewing says he is pleased with the scores in the reading portion of the test, in which 88 percent of Bowie students passed on their first attempt, a four percent increase over last year.

■ Look forward to an in-depth analysis of Bowie's TAAS statistics, state and district goals in next week's issue of The Lone Star Dispatch.

On the Inside

Buildings and Hot dogs	3
Cover raffle winners	3
Cross country	12
Curlew	2
Editorials	8
Football	11
Golf	11
Hawaii	5
Live music review	7
Music review	7
Metallica review	6
Silver Stars review	6
Swimming	13
Tennis	12
Traffic accidents	2
Volleyball	11

For a more open appearance, some papers use the "grid" format, a format based upon a series of narrow or "mini" columns used to create areas of planned white space. In this format, a page that normally features five columns is divided into ten columns. Specific numbers of grids are combined to create a standard copy width for a particular story. One grid is generally used as a "framing device" to surround the main story package and to make the package resemble a "poster." The grid width is repeated somewhere on the page to make the "planned" rails of white space appear as such. The use of the grid in newspaper pages allows the designer to package the story with "air" or "breathing room" for the reader. The white framing space draws the reader's attention to the story quickly.

Design a Double-Truck

Sometimes staff members like to plan an inside double-truck (double-page spread) focused on a specific idea. Because the designer crosses the gutter with copy and art on a double-truck, it is important to remember that the double-truck pages must fall exactly in the middle pages of the paper. In other words, if the paper is eight pages, the double-truck would fall on pages four and five. The double-truck presents the designer with a unique challenge to create an interesting design through the use of related material. It also allows the designer more freedom in working with the space available. In addition, the double-truck helps the designer fit more information into the paper because the gutter can be used in placing copy or artwork.

When designing a spread, use a specific column format. Draw the columns from the inside of the spread and move toward the outside.

Place the dominant photo near the center of the spread. Try to position it so that it crosses the gutter, but avoid placing people's faces in the gutter. Then establish the horizontal eyeline, in either the upper third or lower third of the spread.

After placing the dominant photo and establishing the eyeline, place all other photos on the spread. Each will be either a one-, two-, three-, or four-column photo with all vertical lines of the photo falling on the predetermined column guidelines. It is a good idea to contrast the shape of the dominant photo with that of the smaller photos.

Place captions in one-column widths as close as possible to the photos they represent. By keeping captions one column wide, you will be following the rules for consistency and unity on the spread. Place captions to the outside corners of the layout and, with the exception of related groups of photos, do not put them between photos.

Now add the copy, setting it in one-column widths and placing the columns of type side by side in a solid rectangular block. Finally, put in the headlines, trying to use the primary-secondary style discussed earlier. The double-truck shown in the "On Display" feature on page 233 uses an illustration and text combination as its dominant element in the center of the spread.

Yearbook and Magazine Design

Most of the rules of good design mentioned earlier apply to yearbooks and magazines as well as to newspapers. Here are a few more to keep in mind for these types of publications. (For additional discussion of yearbook design, see Chapter Fourteen.)

- By crossing the gutter with the dominant photo and clustering the other photos around it, you can create a "photo pinwheel" for the reader. The reader's eye will strike the dominant photo first and travel in a clockwise or counterclockwise direction around the page. Thus the reader's eye won't bounce around the page.
- When using a specific-column format design style (as opposed to a grid style), set all captions and copy in one-column widths in order to maintain consistency on the spread.
- Keep copy and captions, as well as white space, to the outside of the page. This prevents large areas of unplanned white space from appearing on the spread. By working from the inside and progressing to the outside corners of the design, unplanned white space will be pushed to the outside of the design.
- Remember to place copy and headlines on the spread as a unit. The headline should be placed directly over the copy or on the side of the copy so that it leads the reader into the story.
- Try to use the eyeline to lead the reader's eye across the page. It is acceptable to break the eyeline; however, the element that breaks it must go at least eight picas above and eight picas below the eyeline to make a formal break.
- Plan to have one high point near the center of the spread and place other elements below that point. This will cause the dominant element to become the high point at the top of the page, creating a graphic curve where all elements on either side of the dominant progress downward from the top of the page. Create the same kind of curve at the bottom of the page by placing another dominant photo near the bottom center and allowing other elements to progress either at the same point straight across the bottom or to move upward from that point.

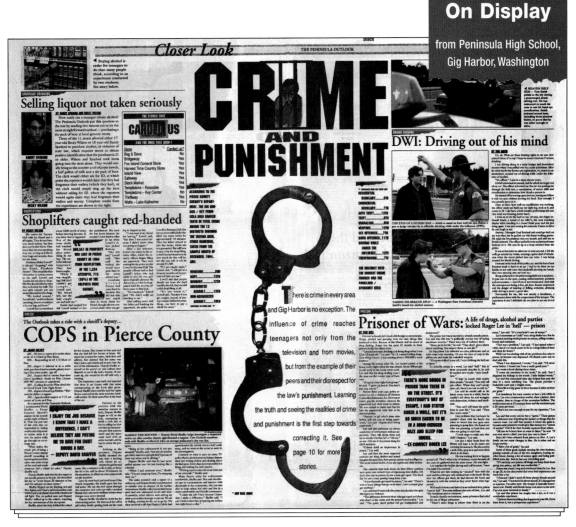

A double-truck should be laid out from the inside to the outside of the spread. Notice the placement of illustration/text dominant element in the center of this sample double-truck, from the Peninsula High School *The Peninsula Outlook.*

- If you choose to bleed a photo—that is, to let it run off the edge of the page—be sure to do so for emphasis only. And do no more than one bleed per side of the spread.
- When selecting a photo for the dominant position, choose the photo with the best quality, most news value, and greatest contrast. In addition, ask the photographer to enlarge the photo to at least an 8" x 10" before sending it to the printer. This will improve the reproduction quality of the photo.

- Make sure that all subjects in the photos face the center of the spread. If subjects seem to look off the page, the reader's eye flow can be interrupted.
- When including graphics (screens, copy starters, boxes, rules, spot color, etc.), always make sure you have a reason and purpose. Avoid the use of "clip art," mascot art, sports art, and other fillers for unplanned white space.
- Avoid the use of decorative or heavy borders or lines, using a one-point border instead.
- Use the same column or grid format throughout a section, but change formats from section to section. Change also the shape and placement of the dominant photo and other design elements from spread to spread. For example, if you have used a vertical dominant on one spread, use a horizontal dominant on the next.
- In the people section, it is recommended that you use one design style for seniors, another for underclassmen, and yet another for faculty. The variation could feature the use of a different headline design—perhaps using the same type in a varied manner—or a more noticeable change. Creating these distinctions will add variety to the section and will create a unique "personality" for each group featured. Additionally, place a thin hairline of space between rows of portraits and place names to the outside. Avoid using one full pica of space between portraits and placing names under individual pictures, as this is considered difficult to read.

The spread shown in the "On Display" feature on pages 236 and 237 shows good positioning of portraits and adds other photos to increase student interest in the spread.

Wrap-up

The editing process at a newspaper is unglamorous but extremely important. Copy editors prepare the copy for the typesetter or edit it on-screen, doing the coding and headlining before placing the story on a page. An error in a reporter's copy will almost certainly get into the paper unless the copy editor catches it.

Copy editors must master the stylebook and check stories for proper punctuation, capitalization, abbreviations, and spelling. They need good news judgment and must make fine distinctions in taste and word usage.

Copy editors use traditional editing symbols whenever they need to edit on paper.

The biggest responsibility facing copy editors is watching for mistakes. There is no such thing as a small mistake; all mistakes undermine the credibility of the publication.

Stories are trimmed, attribution smoothed, grammar repaired. Then editors write headlines. Some schools continue to use the traditional headline unit count system, although most headline writing today is on-screen. In either system, headlines have to fit their allotted space and writing them can be difficult.

Headline style is changing as a result of desktop publishing. New styles such as the hammer, the wicket, and the kicker are now frequently used.

Good design, a vital part of contemporary publications, often begins with type selection. Designers may choose typefaces from seven categories—Oldstyle Roman, Modern Roman, square serif, sans serif, Text, script/cursive, and novelty—although faces from the first four of these are most often used. Designers need to know appropriate sizes of type to use for different situations, as well as ways to package, position, and mix type appropriately.

Graphics such as lines, boxes, art, and photos should only be used for specific purposes, such as to unify, separate, or call attention to elements on a page. Designers should also understand and adhere to the basic design principles of dominance, unity, contrast, rhythm, balance, and consistency.

When creating actual page designs, a designer should do an overall plan at the beginning of the year and post samples of it for the staff's benefit. Specific page design begins by placing the dominant element, usually a photo, and then positioning other photos and copy around it. Double-trucks, designs that go across a spread, follow the same general procedure but must be handled carefully. Columns may be the same width throughout a page or spread or follow a grid format, which varies their width according to specific design principles.

Though the same basic design principles apply to all publications, yearbooks are designed mostly in spreads and need to be especially concerned with a spread's overall unity.

Evaluation Checklist: *Layout*

✓ Are headline and body typefaces sized appropriately and chosen to complement each other?

✓ Is the dominant photo or cartoon strong and well-positioned?

✓ Are copy and other photos placed on the page according to some sort of modular format?

✓ Are boxes, rules, and screens well used but not overused?

✓ Are internal and external margins consistent and not violated by type?

On Assignment

Individual Activities

1. Write a brief definition or explanation for each of the following terms.

bleed	copy editing
dominant element	double-truck
eyeline	font
grid format	gutter
hammer	justified
kicker	leading
pica	point
ragged	wicket

2. Test your critical thinking. Find five headlines, of different styles, in your school or local newspaper. Clip them out, along with the articles, and then evaluate them. Do the heads fairly represent the articles? Are the heads well worded? Is the style used the most effective for the article? Write a brief evaluation of each headline and then clip it to the head and article.

3. Brainstorm this question. If you had no concept of what a newspaper was, and someone told you to design one, how would you go about it?

4. The purpose of this assignment is to make you more aware of graphics and their use in guiding and

This sample from the Putnam City High School *Treasure Chest* combines well-laid-out portraits together with other student photos to create an interesting people-section spread.

Brent Riley
Amy Rinker
Roslyn Robbins
Darryl Roberts
Tim Roberts

Dustin Rocke
Maria Rodriguez
Melissa Rucker
Aley Ruelas
Shameka Ruffin

  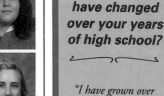

Tobie Russell
Kerri Ryden
Emily Sabala
Windell Salter
Jason Sapp

OUT OF THE CROWD

How do you think that you have changed over your years of high school?

"I have grown over the years of high school from a quiet wildcat to an outgoing pirate. Being involved in school has allowed me to get to know all sorts of people and although it kept me very busy, I would go back and do it again. My high school career has not changed me, but through the external changes it has allowed me to internally discover myself."

–Lance Schmidt–

Lance Schmidt
Shila Scott
Sandeep Shah
Craig Shaw
Todd Sheldon

Amy Sherrer
Tanshanika Shirley
A.J. Slaven
Christy Sloan
Antwan Smith

Jean Smith
Jeremiah Smith
Michele Smith
Misty Smith
Ryan Smith

Wes Spencer
Beth Stewart
Jennifer Stone
Shawna Stone
Eric Stratton

CHANGING TIMES

Change.

It might be the coins returned at MacDonalds.

It could be the green hair Monday that was purple last Friday.

Or it could be the minor changes that arise in four years of high school. People change drastically in high school, some for the worse, some for the better.

"Everyone has matured a lot since we were fresh-men," Danielle Rainbow admitted.

People's outlooks on life sometimes alter dramatically while in high school.

"High school changed my outlook on life," Matt Will said.

Three years of school can certainly change a person's life. These changes may creep up on a person, but in time friends and relatives begin to notice. These changes are also much more drastic in some students than they are in others.

Often the changes are in the school itself.

"High school hasn't really changed much, except for the freshmen coming up here this year," Terri Britton said

Once in high school people feel they have more responsibilities, possibly to their families or friends they make at school.

"I have more responsibilities because I'm looked up to by the underclassmen," Antwan Smith said

"High school has certainly changed my life. I have really opened my eyes to face my responsibilities," Arlen Bourland said.

From the leftovers of a dollar bill to the constant variations in fashions and styles, change left its mark.

EVERY WHICH WAY

While at the bonfire, Tara Barnes and Marisa Richmond watch the events and festivities cheerfully. From the days of red and white pep club uniforms to the high school bonfires, school spirit has taken on many different forms. (Amy Thompson)

MEMORIES

At College night, Shawna Stone is being directed towards another college table from a student at North. Seniors attended college night to get information to help aid for their selection process. (Amy Thompson)

directing the reader's eye in printed materials. Locate and clip one example of each of the following:

- Interesting headline design
- Type shadowed in an unusual manner
- Interesting caption design or design that could be converted to caption design
- Creative use of spot color with black ink
- Textures and patterns used effectively as graphics
- Eye-catching use of borders/rules
- Pulled quote box
- Copy set in an unusual manner
- Use of art or photos in conjunction with headlines
- Informational graphics
- Creative use of white space

Paste the examples in a notebook. Keep them in the order listed above. In addition, create a cover for the notebook that reflects your personality.

5. Edit the unnecessary words from the following expressions:

- assembled crowd of people
- brown colored cloth
- set a new record
- hot water heater
- soothing balm
- personal friendship
- in the city of Chicago
- the present incumbent
- an actual fact
- spoke on the topic of football
- for a period of three weeks
- every single year
- was completely decapitated
- during the winter months
- was completely destroyed
- played a small, cameo role
- a small-sized child
- made advance reservations

- was of circular shape
- his future plans
- her future prospects
- told his listeners
- unsolved problem
- specific example
- official government document
- past history

Team Activities

6. Sketch a "dummy" design for the front page of a newspaper. Include an original nameplate designed specifically for your target audience. Use a column format in preparing your sketch. Be sure to include a dominant element. Keep your headlines over your copy so that they lead the reader directly into the story. In addition, avoid "bumping" unrelated headlines next to each other.

   After sketching your design, paste up a mock-up of the design, using copy and photos from magazines or newspapers. Then, create the page on computer, following your sketch and mock-up.

7. Design an inside double-truck spread for your newspaper. Use the entire spread to cover one particular subject in-depth. You may use photos with captions, one main story with a large headline, and one or more areas of secondary coverage. You may also include a "logo" indicating the subject of the spread in an artistic design, as well as pulled quotes, informational graphics, sidebar features, lists, quote boxes or timelines. In addition, use a consistent caption design style for all the photos on the spread.

   Include folios and folio tabs. Try to design these as continuous elements in a style reflecting that of the nameplate on your newspaper.

Bryan Monroe is a storyteller who doesn't rely on words. Photographs, headlines, graphics, art, and design are some of the tools he uses in conjunction with words.

"I'm a firm believer that readers don't just read text by itself," said Monroe, assistant managing editor of the *San Jose Mercury News*. "Every mark you make on a page means something. If you don't give it meaning the reader will."

Monroe is in charge of the photo, art, design, and systems departments at the *Mercury News*. He is also the newsroom coordinator for technology, color, and pagination issues. In 1992 he engineered a major redesign of the paper, the third newspaper redesign he has worked on.

Monroe is a regular visiting lecturer at the Poynter Institute for Media Studies in St. Petersburg, Florida. He was a founder of and is on the executive board of the National Association of Black Journalists Visual Journalism Task Force. He is also chairman of the Society of Newspaper Design Diversity Committee.

Before coming to San Jose he was assistant project director for Knight-Ridder Inc.'s 25/43 Project—a newspaper research and development project targeting readers age 25 to 43. Monroe and other editors worked out of the Knight-Ridder paper in Boca Raton, Florida, redesigning it into a daily living laboratory for experimentation into the future of newspapers.

Monroe has been a speaker at various universities and organizations, including the Detroit Design Council on Minorities and the Asian American Journalist Association.

As graphics editor and director of photography at the *Myrtle Beach* (S.C.) *Sun News*, Monroe helped engineer a redesign in 1988 and was responsible for the overall look and visual content of the paper.

"Creating a new newspaper from scratch for most people is a once in a career thing," Monroe said. "I've been fortunate enough to be able to do it three times already."

Monroe got his start as a photographer for the *Seattle Times* but soon was named graphics editor of the *Myrtle Beach Sun News*. It was there that he first got the opportunity to use what he calls his toolbox.

"It was my first chance to learn about growing; to learn about integrating visuals into journalism. We started using visual elements that tell stories.

"We give readers information, ideas, and emotion. Words are just one tool in your toolbox.

"In the old days newspapers did a great job of getting the information you need and putting it on a page. But it's not good enough anymore to get it to the page. You've got to get it from the page to the reader's head.

"Photos, graphics, headlines, and everything else you can do are more tools for your toolbox. My background and desire is storytelling and I've gravitated to certain tools. I had to learn how to write."

Don't be afraid to experiment is the message Monroe leaves with page designers.

"Go out to the edge of the tree limb and jump up and down. If the limb doesn't break go out farther and jump up and down some more. Keep doing that until the limb breaks and then step back one step."

Getting the Newspaper Ready for Distribution

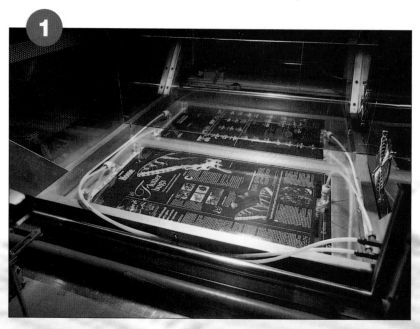

▲ The manufacturing process begins by making negatives of the pages that will be used to make metal plates to go on the printing presses.

► The metal plates are hand-positioned on the presses.

▲ As printed paper goes throughout the press, it is formed and cut into newspapers.

◀ Sections of the paper are stacked as they come off the conveyor.

▲ The whole process can be monitored from the packaging control room.

▲ Preprinted sections await the inserting of advertising supplements.

7

◀ The assembled papers, now wrapped and bundled, are ready to be loaded onto delivery trucks.

8

▶ A worker loads the papers onto delivery trucks.

9

◀ The delivery trucks set out on their daily runs.

Writing Features, Sports, and Editorials

Chapter Eleven

Writing Feature Stories

Chapter Twelve

Writing Sports Stories

Chapter Thirteen

Writing for the Editorial Page

Writing Feature Stories

Key Terms

Key Terms

hard news

feature story

soft news

"evergreen"

news-feature

news peg

personality profile

Key Concepts

After reading this chapter, you should

- understand the difference between a feature story and a straight news story

- recognize the kinds of topics often covered in feature stories

- know the characteristics of the personality profile

- understand the increased, but limited, latitude feature writers have compared to straight-news writers

To some people, feature stories are journalistic dessert: tasty to consume, but really not necessary. Hard news—speeches, elections, budgets, meetings, and so on—is the meat and potatoes for hungry readers, and if they still have room, well, dessert is OK, these folks concede.

But eating—and reading—habits change. Dessert no longer, feature stories have become a staple to print journalists. Forever the runner-up to radio and TV for breaking news, newspapers and magazines turn to well-written, readable features to keep their audience.

The trick, for pros and students alike, is striking a good balance. A newspaper or magazine with *only* features wouldn't lure many serious readers. Readers still want the important stuff—like what the government is doing today—covered. They don't want a steady diet of either features or hard news, however.

Traditional perspectives still have merit. If a school newspaper or magazine suddenly lost all its advertisers and had to reduce its pages from, say, eight to two, what would be cut? Probably most of the feature stories. Not all of them, though: Many times in scholastic settings a feature approach is used to spruce up what really is hard—but old—news. Thus a two-week-old story about the election of a new school board, which has already been covered extensively in the local press, is featurized into a story about the youngest—or oldest—member of that board. Student journalists often are forced into such approaches because they cannot compete with daily publications or newscasts.

Features, which may be considered soft news, thus should be of increased interest to the scholastic journalist. While banging out quick and readable inverted pyramid stories remains an essential journalistic skill, crafting artful features is just as critical. It takes a real artist to write a clear, concise, balanced 12-inch inverted-pyramid story. Still, let's face it: Features are more fun.

Holidays and anniversaries are natural feature topics. One talented young feature writer, assigned to do a Christmas feature—and with no more guidance than that—took a chance. Mindful of the seasonally popular movie *Miracle on 34th Street*, she walked up and down 34th Street in her town, knocking on doors and asking people if they had experienced any "miracles." Lots of people

A story about a school-board meeting that happened several weeks ago is more appropriately handled in the school paper as a feature than as a straight-news story.

laughed at her and shut the door in her face—but several talked to her about spiritual or unexplained events in their lives. Her feature was a delight to read.

The same young reporter, assigned to do a *post*-Christmas feature, produced a winning story without saying a word. With permission, she positioned herself at the returns counter of a popular department store the day after Christmas, listened, and wrote down the excuses people used to return Yule gifts they didn't want. The story provided a good laugh to combat the after-Christmas letdown (Hmmm, there's a feature story idea right there).

Then there's the famous—because it has been recounted for years in *Journalism Today*—story of the news editor who needed a fresh angle for a St. Patrick's Day feature. On deadline at his paper in the Midwest, he picked up the phone and called the lord mayor of Dublin, Ireland—where it was the middle of the night. The editor didn't get through to the lord mayor, but he did get an aide on the line. A humorous story about the difficulties of transatlantic telephone hookups made a fine March 17 tale. The article was a feature story—and so good that management didn't even complain about the telephone bill.

On another night at the same paper, an enterprising young reporter was assigned to do a Halloween story. Not one to take the easy way out, he walked through a cemetery—at midnight—alone. His feature story made chilling reading.

Then there's the story of the young sportswriter at a daily newspaper who did something to make the sports editor angry. In retaliation the sports editor made the following assignment: "Get a feature story. I don't care what it's about or where you get it, but I want it on my desk before you go home tonight." Panicking, the reporter set out to find a feature story. He ended up going water-skiing, even though he had never tried it before and couldn't swim. Pictures taken from the shore clearly showed his fright.

The feature story he wrote about the experience was given special treatment in the Sunday edition of the paper and drew many favorable comments (as well as restoring him to the good graces of the sports editor).

Characteristics of Feature Stories

Just what is a feature story? Would it help to note that a feature story is usually lighter, more human, possibly funnier than a regular news story? That most feature stories are not related to any current news event? That a feature story is usually not written in inverted-pyramid style and that it may be about anything or anybody?

That description may give you an idea. By now you have guessed that, like news, a feature story is tough to define. Some people say there is no such thing; by that they mean that *all* stories should be readable (and a feature story that isn't easy to read isn't worth the effort). They fear that the only time a reporter will "write bright" is when the assignment specifies a feature story.

Timelessness

Some properties of the feature story can be isolated. The main characteristic of most features is that they are "evergreen." That is, they are just as acceptable for publication in next week's paper as in this week's. There is no time element involved. But even this is not always true. The news-feature, for example, is pegged to a specific item of news and is usually published the same day as the news story, or at least as soon as possible afterward. When your school wins the state science fair competition, for example, the feature story about the student whose exhibit took first place is a news-feature, a feature closely tied to the main news story. And a feature on how band members feel about the possible elimination of the band is a news-feature related to a news story about a school budget cut. Such stories as these are said to have a news peg, a reason for existence on their own.

Creative Style

Feature stories provide latitude but not license. While feature writers are a trifle more free with regard to the use of the language, they certainly are *not* free to throw away the rule book entirely. Opinion and speculation are not allowed. The same ethical standards that apply to the straight news story apply to the feature story. But the good feature writer soon recognizes that such stories sometimes provide a better chance than straight news for literary ingenuity. It's hard to write a truly clever, bright story about the student council meeting, particularly if nothing out of the ordinary happens.

Truly clever or bright stories can be hazardous, too. The danger is that writers, especially (but not exclusively) beginners, will become carried

> ### Pulitzers for Feature Stories
>
> What kind of feature stories win Pulitzer Prizes? As you might expect, the subject matter runs the gamut of human experience. Since 1990, some of the prize-winning topics have been floods in the Midwest; an investigation of the writer's daughter's murder; a fond remembrance of a writer's childhood housekeeper; a mother who abandoned her newborn baby; and a series of stories on contemporary life in America.

away by the sound of their own words. They will try to be funny, or cute, or even overly somber. Such stories are difficult to pull off, and will be miserable if they fail. The delightful thing about feature stories is that often the subject matter itself is funny or cute or somber. If the writer doesn't intrude too much, these elements will come through on their own. Sometimes a writer can kill a good story by being too expressive.

Unlimited Subject Possibilities

Another characteristic of the feature story is that it is not limited in subject matter. It may be historical, throwing new light on an old subject or simply reviewing some events of years past. It may be about a remote place or an obscure person. It may be about someone's unusual hobby, or someone's interesting relative. It may be written in the first person (as the water-skiing feature was). It may provide background to a developing or continuing news story. It may summarize or wrap up a story that has been told in small pieces over a long span of time. It may rely heavily on the use of anecdotes.

In many cases, a feature story concentrates on the mood of an event and therefore may be more accurate than the straight news story. (This is also true of some sports stories.)

Above all, the feature story is about what people are interested in. That is close to the definition of the human interest story, and trying to separate the two is difficult. Is an interview with the fifteen-year-old genius who graduated from college a feature story or a human interest story or both? The fact is that it doesn't make any difference how you label it as long as you are able to recognize and gather such stories. One of the problems of journalism is overlabeling. For example, these are some of the labels given to feature story leads: news summary, distinctive incident, quotation, question, analogy, picture. Many people believe that having a label for every lead and every story makes it easy for students, but it probably confuses them. Journalism students should be concentrating on reporting techniques and sentence structure—on *writing*—not on memorizing lists of labels.

Personality Profiles

Many feature stories deal with individuals, and this makes sense. In fact, it's fair to state that every person on earth is worth a personality profile, or feature story about that person. Somewhere in the background of every human being there is an incident, an idea, a problem, a thought, a relative, an opinion, a hobby, a hope that will make interesting reading. A journalism instructor once decided to prove this notion to his students. On the first day of class he picked a name at random from the roster and called a student to the front of the class. The instructor didn't know her; in fact, he had never seen her until that day. As the class watched, he interviewed her. The next time the class met, the students were amazed at the personality profile he had written. Some even thought the whole thing was rigged. But the fact is, the result would have been about the same no matter which student had been chosen. Today, the student the professor chose is a feature writer for *Newsday* in New York.

All human beings are possible subjects for a personality profile. Some people make better stories than others, however. Perhaps your school newspaper publishes many stories quoting the president of the student body, but has never gotten around to doing a personality profile about him or her. While all the students know the student body president's name, they probably don't really know anything about the person. This is a subject ripe for a personality profile. When you do a personality profile, try to answer the question "Who is this person, anyway? What does he or she do on weekends? What are his or her opinions on politics? The environment? Sports? What are his or her goals for your school?" If you ask enough questions, you're bound to get an answer that will lead you down the road to a personality profile. In this kind of feature, as in everything else in journalism, there is no substitute for the hard work of digging for the facts. While actually writing the story, however, the feature writer usually has a chance to exercise more imagination than the straight news writer.

Notice how the personality profile in the "On Display" feature on page 252 uses a combination of details and direct quotes to give the reader a sense of really knowing the person being featured.

A personality profile of a student who won a science-fair award would try to reveal interesting facts that made the student a unique individual.

Features and School Papers

Feature stories play a particularly important role in the scholastic press. Because most such newspapers come out only once a week or every two weeks or even once a month, they should rely heavily on features. The straight news has already been covered by the daily newspaper downtown; as a scholastic journalist, you should be on the watch for feature stories and should featurize even straight news stories. You might also pay special attention and devote more

---

Good Features Need Good Headlines

Feature stories need feature headlines. If the story is light, bright, and colorful, the headline should be, too. If the story is creative and fun, the head should be, too. Here's a famous one. The story reported on a woman who gave birth to quadruplets, all boys. Said the head: **Boy oh boy oh boy oh boy!**

Artist for Hire

by Ruvane Kurland, **The Echoes,** *Abraham Lincoln High School, Council Bluffs, Iowa*

The hope and dream of every artist is to be discovered. For Andrew Johnson '98, the dream became a reality.

Johnson's mother noticed his talent in third grade when he won Henry Doorley Zoo's poster contest for "Catch Jungle Fever."

In sixth grade, Johnson entered a contest entitled "Written and Illustrated By," a contest in which he had to write and illustrate 28 pages. Johnson placed in the top 100 in the national contest.

Art instructor Randi Kennedy began to guide Johnson's talent when he was still in elementary school.

"I began giving Andy private art lessons when he was in sixth grade," she said. "Andy is one of the most accomplished artists for his age that I have ever taught. He has been involved in many contests and exhibits in the past as well as designing and executing a 40 foot mural at Kirn."

The mural depicts the Kirn Eagle doing various activities such as sports, music and fine arts. After volunteering to paint the mural, Johnson took three months to design it, then the rest of the school year to paint it.

"I procrastinate. That's why it took me so long," Johnson said. "I'd stay after school for a couple hours; then I'd go home, eat dinner, and come back. My mom helped me a little with painting it, but the biggest thing she did was take me back and forth to the school." Like any other artist, Johnson soon faced some complications.

"Some people drew graffiti on it, but for the most part they left it alone," Johnson said. "What we couldn't erase, my mom went over with white paint."

Some may think spending that much time on a mural wouldn't be worth the time. But Johnson said it all paid off in the end when he was paid $200 for the job.

"I wasn't expecting any money, it wasn't talked about in the beginning. I thought it was pretty cool to get out of classes to paint the mural," he said. "Even though it got to be a hassle spending time on it, I think it was worth it because I was happy at what I received. It's nice having the recognition and the money."

With this experience under his belt, Johnson found other offers coming in.

Principal Joy Stein at Lewis and Clark is also interested in his artwork, and wants him to paint a mural at his old elementary school. Johnson said he probably would request $200 for the time consuming job.

"Right now, I want to go into feature animation when I get older, hopefully to work for Disney or Warner Brothers," he said. "But until then I'll stick to drawing cartoon characters."

space to events that are going to happen rather than to those that have already taken place (and been covered by commercial competition).

Examples of good features are easy to come by in the scholastic press The article in the "On Display" feature on page 254 was the lead story on a full page about left-handedness.

In the story in the "On Display" feature on page 255, information about rock climbing is presented through interviews with three students who frequently participate in the activity.

Want to create your own publication and circulate it to hundreds, maybe thousands of readers? Join the ranks of creators of zines.

Zines, or e-zines, are magazines on-line, and they fall into two general groups. There are print publications such as *People* or *Rolling Stone* that have their own zine versions, and then there are zines created especially for cyberspace. Into this second category go many publications created by individuals or small groups rather than giant corporations. Zines can be about any topic under the sun, but many, especially the ones found only in cyberspace, are fairly specialized.

Quill Magazine reported that more than 830 new zines were born in 1994 alone (67 were about sports). Other sources put the total number now in existence at over 10,000. Trying to keep a count is futile, of course, because like all other elements on the Net, zines are growing by the minute.

Specialty zines can cover a wide range of topics—games, hobbies, science fiction, geographical regions, government, films and film stars, various types of music, bridge playing, cooking, thrift shopping, and on and on. There is more than one zine devoted to the intricacies of skiing. There are many devoted to the wishes and problems of girls and young women. There are others that focus on political positions or causes. The audiences for these zines may be in the tens, hundreds, or thousands, and, of course, as new zines are created others fade away. The publication *Factsheet 5* is one useful directory of the various zines out there.

What makes zines special, and different from traditional media, is that they are interactive. That zine on skiing, for example, may let you call up information on snow conditions in various ski areas near you. A so-called girlzine might give you a chance to respond directly to an article on anorexia or direct you to where you can find more information about the topic.

The zines put on-line by professional publications try to offer different materials than in their print versions. For example, the print form of a magazine may offer an interview with a rock group. Its zine counterpart may go one step further and, taking advantage of its interactive capabilities, make the star of the group available on-line to answer questions directly. Or it might provide a clip from the group's most recent performance. Since most zines also have screens that function as tables of contents, one click of a button will take you directly to the article you're interested in .

How are zines in cyberspace able to stay in business? The ones related to print publications have an easier time of it, for one reason because the two media more or less feed on each other. If you see the clip of that rock group's concert on-line, you may well go out and buy the magazine to get the in-depth interview with them. For independently produced zines, even those with ad revenues, the future may be a bit dicier. *Web Review*, for example, was one of the most popular zines on the Web till it stopped publication in early 1996. Its founder cited the public's general unwillingness to pay for zine access as one reason why well-written, midsized products such as his may flounder.

So—how about you? Do you have a topic you know well and/or feel passionately about? Are you willing to write articles and share your information with the vast cyberspace public for little or no financial reward? If your answer is yes, get going on your own zine!

Lefties Do It Right

by Steph Brewer, The Stinger, *Emmaus High School, Emmaus, Pennsylvania*

It isn't often that junior Bea Polanco is put in the same category as Pablo Picasso, Babe Ruth, Marilyn Monroe, Billy the Kid and Queen Victoria.

One might wonder what a high school student, a painter, a baseball player, a movie star, an outlaw and a queen could possibly have in common.

Truthfully, they don't have much in common except for one unusual trait; they are all left-handed.

Fifteen to 20 percent of Americans are left-handed, according to Carol Riddle, marketing and public relations director of Topeka, KS, based Lefthanders International.

The number of lefties has gone up in recent years, Riddle said, because children are usually not encouraged by teachers to use their right hand instead of their left.

Throughout history, left-handedness has been regarded as a nasty habit and social inconvenience, according to *The Lefthander Syndrome* by Stanley Coren. It has been associated with traits such as artistic ability, rebellion, creativity, criminality, bed wetting and sports proficiency.

Polanco does not agree with these typical theories.

"I really don't think it makes any difference whether you're left- or right-handed," she said.

Health teacher and lefty George Gibbs attributes the theories of creativity to the number of great left-handed artisans. He said he could not think of a reason why the theory involving criminality was developed. He did however offer one explanation.

"I guess being a criminal you would have to be creative," he said.

Although many modern-day lefties don't think anything of their oddity, the lefties of the past were painfully aware of the difference between them and their right-handed counterparts.

In the 1600s, left-handedness was considered a sign of witchcraft, according to Coren. In Morocco, lefties are called *s'ga's*, which means "devil" or "cursed person." In the Eskimo culture, lefties are thought of as potential sorcerers.

Because of the negative connotations associated with left-handedness, many left-handers have been forced to use their right hands.

Senior Stacey Nagle does many things with her left hand but was forced by her father to write with her right hand when she was young.

"My dad would always switch things, like my fork, to my right hand," she said.

Senior Beth Demers said her left-handed uncle went to parochial school and was hit on the knuckles every time he used his left hand. Eventually, he just learned to write with his right hand.

Left-handed people are more intuitive and creative because they are right brained, according to Riddle.

However, sociology teacher Robert Braun said he would like to see statistics before he believes the theories about lefties.

Area psychologist Dr. Richard Weiss agreed with Braun.

"In my opinion, there isn't enough research to say left-handers are more creative," he said. "It still remains theoretical." Aside from the problem of being stereotyped, lefties also face many other problems, the main one being they live in a right-hand world.

Lefties must use special scissors; they can't use some desks or spiral notebooks; and they have problems writing in pen.

"We live in a right-handed world but we operate from the left side," Gibbs said.

The goal of Lefthanders International is to make the world easier for left-handed people, Riddle said. They even publish a magazine full of products for left-handed people.

So while Polanco, Picasso, Babe Ruth, Marilyn Monroe, Billy the Kid and Queen Victoria may not have a lot in common, they all faced, or are still facing, the trials and tribulations of being a lefty.

Rocks are No Obstacles

by Nelly Khidekel, Arlingtonian, *Upper Arlington High School, Columbus, Ohio*

Imagine the feeling of being pressed against an endless wall of rock while suspended 1000 feet over the ground by a rope only one inch thick.

Seniors Jim Hauswirth, Jeff Reaser and Ben Nelson don't need to imagine it; they've experienced it. The three rock climbing enthusiasts (who have been climbing for one, one and a half, and two years respectively), said rock climbing is an activity that is uniquely exciting.

"It gives you an incredible rush," Nelson said. "It's fun and different, and it helps to build self-esteem."

Nelson, who has built a climbing box in his basement as a part of his senior thesis, said he climbs most often indoors at Vertical Adventures in Columbus.

Hauswirth said rock climbing in Ohio is "easy to do" because the Ohio area provides many areas for indoor as well as outdoor rock climbing.

"It is a terrific workout, especially outdoors, but it can cut up your hands pretty badly," he said.

Hauswirth said he climbs "once or twice" a month indoors, but he said he prefers climbing outside.

"When you're indoors you do the same thing over and over again," he said. "Outside you have varying terrain and can go multiple pitch climbing [climbing to different levels of the mountain], as well as climb to a mountain peak."

Hauswirth said he once got the opportunity to climb to an elevation of "about 8000 feet" while backpacking in Washington State.

"The thrill when you're up that high is just incredible," he said.

Reaser said he climbs three to seven days a week, and six to seven days a week in the summer.

"I love climbing," he said. "It's perfect because I enjoy the exercise and I like being outdoors."

Reaser said along with being so enjoyable, rock climbing also provides many physical benefits.

"It helps you build strength, body control and flexibility," he said.

Both Nelson and Reaser said climbing is not as difficult or frightening as many people assume.

"After the first couple of times," Nelson said, "you aren't really scared anymore. The rush comes from the original fear."

Reaser agreed with Nelson.

"If you climb smart by not doing reckless things," he said, "there really isn't all that much risk. If you keep your gear in good shape, and you know your limits, it can be a safe sport."

Hauswirth said although climbing is physically demanding, it is an activity in which most people can partake.

"Some people climb using primarily their upper body, some climb with their lower body," he said. "There are lots of different ways to climb, so you can make it as easy or as difficult as you want it to be."

Reaser said the one obvious drawback to rock climbing is the cost.

Nelson said prices vary, but good equipment is not cheap. He said a harness is $50, the rope is $100, and the shoes may be up to $120.

Reaser said he has had one bad experience with rock climbing because of his disregard for safety.

"I used to climb the walls of a ravine that a friend had in his back yard," he said. "I fell down the ravine and had to get stitches in my forehead, then I realized the importance of climbing safely."

Hauswirth said he once had an experience he called "nerve-wracking."

"I was climbing in Washington once and got tangled in the rope," he said. "I crashed against the wall of rock, but I was okay because I was wearing a helmet."

Besides the obvious physical benefits, Nelson, Hauswirth, and Reaser encourage students to rock climb for other reasons.

"It's very challenging," Nelson said, "it makes me feel good about myself, and when I'm done I have a sense that I really accomplished something great."

Teacher's Pet

by Natalie Hansen, Beak 'n Eye, *West High School, Davenport, Iowa*

He's West's best teacher's pet. Going from class to class, listening in on the lessons for the day, he loves school so much that he would rather stay in school and chat with faculty members and students than leave the school grounds.

Yes, it's Rocky the squirrel.

Faculty on the first floor call the squirrel Bucky, but faculty on the second floor call it Rocky. So there is no confusion, we'll call him Rocky since newspaper is on the second floor.

Since September Rocky has been living in the main courtyard. The teachers decided that Rocky probably couldn't get out, so Gene Soehl, science, caught Rocky in a live trap and then released it outside the building. In three or four weeks Rocky came back.

Rocky seems to be unable to get out of the courtyard, but head counselor Roger Begthol says if he really wanted out he would find a way. "One thing you should never do is sell a squirrel short," he said.

Faculty and students enjoy feeding Rocky. There are at least four places outside of teachers' windows where food is available for him.

Rocky climbs up to the second floor at least once a day to visit Dave Wessel's history class and then get some of his favorite food, nuts.

Wessel leaves nuts outside of the social studies office for Rocky, and he says that life here is good for Rocky. "He's smart, it's a good retirement in here."

Begthol, who seems to be Rocky's favorite faculty member, even feeds Rocky out of his hand. "You just have to be patient, let them grow accustomed to you," says Begthol.

There are no plans to trap Rocky again, but once school is out something will have to be done with him. Or maybe he will just stay for summer school.

The feature story elevates routine news to page-one news. For instance, consider the article in the "On Display" feature above (or is it human interest?) about a squirrel in a school courtyard. What makes the story worth a feature is the way teachers and students have taken to the squirrel—and vice versa.

The feature story must be objective, just as the news story is. But do you detect a note of sympathy in the tone of the squirrel story? This is part of the latitude allowed in feature writing. You may not come right out and express your opinions, but you may, through careful choice of words, write a story whose tone is emotional. The total effect of the story may appeal to the reader's emotions, but you are on thin ice if personal opinion is openly expressed.

Wrap-up

Feature stories have taken on greater importance in journalism. Though they will never completely replace the inverted-pyramid story, they are essential to good journalism.

Feature stories are generally lighter in tone than regular news stories. They usually are timeless, or "evergreen," unless they are news-features and are related to a specific timely news story. Features permit writers to exercise more creativity in language than do regular news stories, but the rules about objectivity and opinion still apply. Writers have latitude but not license.

Features permit creativity in story ideas, too. Topics range from historical events to interesting people and everything between. Features occasionally are written in first person. They may rely on anecdotes.

All people are possible subjects for a personality profile, a feature story that answers the question "Who is this person, anyway?" Personality profiles are thorough, in-depth stories about one person.

Many routine stories have been elevated to page-one status through feature treatment. This treatment does not permit opinion, but it allows a different tone, a different total effect.

Features are important for scholastic publications. Often, the news available to a school paper has already been covered by the commercial press. So school newspapers frequently have to rely on features to hold the interest of their audience.

Evaluation Checklist: *Feature Story*

✓ Is the story on a topic of interest for its intended audience?

✓ Do the style and tone make it clear from the beginning that this is not a hard news story?

✓ Does the story use anecdotes and other interesting examples to make its points?

✓ If the story is a personality profile, does it focus on interesting or unusual aspects of the person's life?

✓ Is the story free from grammatical errors and in accordance with the publication and AP stylebooks?

On Assignment

Individual Activities

1. Write a brief definition or explanation of each of the following terms.

   "evergreen"   feature story
   hard news   news-feature
   news peg   personality profile
   soft news

2. Test your critical thinking. Go through editions of your local newspaper to find three to five feature stories. After reading each one, evaluate the author's purpose in writing it. Who was the intended audience? In what specific ways did the writer try to reach that audience? How might the article have been improved? Write up your response to each feature and clip it to a copy of the feature.

3. Choose one of the individuals below for a personality profile. Interview the person; then plan and write the story.
   a. a disk jockey on an oldies radio station
   b. a faculty member married to another faculty member
   c. a person born on February 29
   d. a student with the same name as a famous person
   e. the groundskeeper at a pet cemetery
   f. a member of the state champion basketball team from ten years ago
   g. a department store Santa Claus
   h. the clerk at the card counter on Valentine's Day
   i. a member of the first graduating class from your high school
   j. a student who has never missed a day of school

4. Choose one of the topics below for a feature story. Research, plan, and write the story.
   a. what your second-grade classroom looks like now
   b. how your school's mascot and colors were chosen
   c. the ten most unusual sites on the Internet
   d. the most dangerous intersections in your town for motorists
   e. unusual pets owned by students at your school
   f. the earliest libraries in your city or county
   g. Olympic sports little known in the United States
   h. careers in the outdoors
   i. names movie stars were born with and why they changed them
   j. what people's color preferences tell about them

5. Develop your own idea for a personality profile or feature story. Get it approved by your instructor; then outline how you would present the story. Your instructor may have you actually do the research and write the story.

6. Write a feature story based on this information.
   - A poet gives a speech.
   - His name is Rasputin Roundy.
   - He says he cuts dictionaries apart and randomly pastes the words on paper. He says this is poetry.
   - "Because I am a poet, everything I do is poetry by definition," he says.
   - He is dressed in a three-piece light-green suit and wears socks that do not match.
   - He is from Princeton, New Jersey.
   - The speech, first in a local university's series, was given Monday.
   - After the speech, no one applauds and Roundy leaves the stage angrily.

Team Activity

7. With a team, stage an argument, play, skit, or other three-minute activity. Other class members should watch your production, taking notes as needed. When all productions have been performed, discuss them as a class. Then, with your team, write a feature story about all the productions.

Milwaukee Journal Sentinel food editor Nancy Stohs wants readers to have fun with her section. On a recent day readers were given a story detailing the pros and cons of Jell-O.

"We don't just print recipes or teach people how to cook," she said. "We try to have fun and teach people how to grasp the basics at the same time."

Stohs has worked in a features department since 1979. She has also worked on a city desk, so she knows the differences in operating styles. Working in features, she said, is a way to do what she loves, and get paid for it.

"My story is pretty typical," she said. "I like writing, and journalism was a way to make a living and write."

Prior to becoming food editor of the *Milwaukee Journal Sentinel*, she held positions as suburban reporter, education reporter, features reporter, health columnist, features copy editor, and food reporter.

Generally curious by nature, Stohs feels journalism gives her the opportunity to find out more about what goes on around her.

"Being in newspapers gives you free rein to ask questions," she said. "No other job lets you ask so many questions and get away with it. It's a fun way to do research and do things you wouldn't get the chance to do in other jobs."

It's also a way to communicate information to readers in a lighter vein.

"We're always trying to be creative," she said. "We're always trying to give readers something fun."

At the same time, however, Stohs believes features reporters are considered in a different light by their counterparts on the city desk.

"The traditional division between the newsroom and features has been very slow to change," she said.

Stohs has won awards for packages of stories on illiteracy and for general reporting on nutrition issues.

She graduated from the University of Nebraska in 1976 and joined the *Lakeland* (Fla.) *Ledger* in 1977 as an education reporter. She joined the *Milwaukee Journal* in 1979 and in 1994 was named food editor, a position she held when the *Journal* and the *Milwaukee Sentinel* merged into the *Milwaukee Journal Sentinel*.

Stohs opted for a career in features to get away from the pressure of daily deadlines.

"With no daily deadlines there's more time to give more thought to your stories, to make sure everything in the package goes together," she said. "It's more fun. You can have more freedom with your writing style. You can get into people's personality.

"Our goal is to serve the reader in the best possible way; to make sure the photographs tell a story, the headlines go with the story, and all the other elements mesh. Everything has to fit together."

Stohs advises students who are interested in a career in journalism to read a newspaper every day and to ask questions.

"Keep your eyes open," she said. "Look at people differently."

259

Chapter Twelve

Writing Sports Stories

Key Terms

pregame story

game story

postgame story

featurize

"slanguage"

Key Concepts

After reading this chapter, you should

- recognize and learn to avoid the use of trite expressions in sportswriting

- understand how important it is for sportswriters to be experts in the sports they cover

- understand the difference between being partisan and being a cheerleader for your team

- know how to write clear and lively pregame, game, and postgame stories

- be familiar with the role of featurized sports coverage in scholastic publications

> Outlined against a blue-gray October sky, the Four Horsemen rode again. In dramatic lore they are known as Famine, Pestilence, Destruction and Death. These are only aliases. Their real names are Stuhldreher, Miller, Crowley, and Layden. They formed the crest of the South Bend Cyclone before which another fighting Army football team was swept over the precipice at the Polo Grounds yesterday afternoon as 55,000 spectators peered down on the bewildering panorama spread on the green plain below.

What you have just read is perhaps the most famous lead ever written for a sports story. It was written by Grantland Rice, one of the best-known sportswriters of all time. Such a lead would never get past the copy desk on today's streamlined newspaper. Heartless copy editors, trained that a lead should come to the point immediately and concisely, probably would rewrite it to read as follows:

> NEW YORK—Led by an all-star backfield, Notre Dame yesterday defeated Army at the Polo Grounds before 55,000 fans, . . .

The blank is for the score. Did you notice that Rice did not include the score in his first paragraph? He can be forgiven because he was writing in a different time and for an audience that had not seen the game on television. That audience had time to read on to the second paragraph—or the third or fourth—to get the score. Today's audience does not.

In fact, today's audience generally doesn't care much at all about the score as such in their newspapers. By the millions, Americans watch TV—and even record games they're keenly interested in. So when they pick up a newspaper a day after the game, the last thing they want is a simple announcement of who won and who lost.

But Rice's lead still has a good deal of appeal, despite the fact that it is outmoded today. It is colorful, and full of action. If all sports leads had these qualities, there would not be such a split in the attitudes toward sportswriting. But as it is, there are two schools of thought. One holds that sportswriting is the *worst* writing in American journalism today. The other holds that sportswriting is the *best* writing in American journalism today.

When sportswriting is bad, it's awful. But when it's good, it can be truly excellent.

Sportswriting: The Good and the Bad

For the moment, take the view that sportswriting is some of the best writing there is and try to decide why. One reason is that sportswriters, while they must be objective, are allowed more freedom to be partisan. They're for the hometown team, and everyone knows it. Thus they are able to do a bit more than simply describe an event. They can—indeed, they must—interpret it. If the coach rants and raves on the sidelines, or if the spectators boo the officials, sportswriters are free to pick words more descriptive than "angry" (the word most likely to be used by a reporter telling the mayor's reaction to some city council action). Sportswriters are expected to convey a word picture of exactly what happened, and this inevitably leads to colorful language.

Further, sportswriters are aware that the events they describe have been witnessed by hundreds, perhaps thousands (or even millions, if televised) of people. These people do not turn to the sports page to read a play-by-play rehash. They want to know how the coaches and players reacted, what kind of pitch Ryne Sandberg hit for the winning home run, or what all the quarreling was about in the third quarter when the officials handed out a fifteen-yard penalty. Long before the rest of America's journalists had recognized the need for interpretive reporting, sportswriters were forced into it. This led them to be more aware of reporting (they had to have *something* to offer fans who had seen the game) and of writing.

The action and excitement of a sports event such as this soccer game can be captured in a colorfully written story.

Sports fans want the stories they read to reflect the tension, the color, the excitement, the joy, or the sorrow of the game. The audience, in other words, demands colorful, lively writing; it is preconditioned to it, for most fans tend to believe that they are just as knowledgeable as sportswriters. Let the city council reporter question the mayor's wisdom in vetoing the new city budget and readers will object that opinion belongs on the editorial page. But if the football coach decides to go for it on fourth down deep in the team's own territory and the strategy backfires, eager fans expect to find the writer's opinions about the coach's unwise decision in his or her coverage. (Just ask Dallas Cowboys coach Barry Switzer, who did exactly that in a losing game en route to a Super Bowl championship year!)

Now here's the argument for why sportswriting is often bad. One of the reasons is that sports reporters tend to be the worst overusers of trite expressions. This apparently stems from two things: the fact that sports has developed some perfectly acceptable semi-slang of its own and the fact that games are action events. The former tends to make writers believe that if some slang expressions are permissible (knockout, blitz, bomb), then so are others. The trouble, however, is distinguishing between the vivid language of sports and the trite language of mediocre sportswriters. The second fact causes many sportswriters to believe that, because sports

---

There Must Be a Better Way

List after list of the trite phrases and terms used by lazy sportswriters has been drawn up. Here are some that wise sportswriters avoid:

burn the nets	odds-on favorite
capped the drive	two and 0 on the night
snagged the aerial	circuit clout (for home run)
crushed the opposition	play one game at a time
forms the nucleus	freshman phenomenon
knights of the maples	paydirt (for end zone)
under the arcs	hoopsters (for members of the basketball team)
scoreless deadlock	
tally	thinclads (for members of the track team)
canto	
stanza	sank the shot from three-point land
hot corner	tanksters (for members of the swim team)
banged the apple	
booted the pigskin	cagers (for members of the basketball team)
triple threat	
run roughshod	threw a Hail Mary pass
pellet	snagged the aerial (for caught the pass)
pilfered sacks	
raised the curtain on the season	fans had barely settled into their seats
	grapplers (for members of the wrestling team)
rang down the curtain on the season	
	slammed a homer (for hit a home run)
functioned like a well-oiled machine	
	counter (for period)
local gridiron	on the heels of controversy
the tide shifted	welcome additions to the lineup
the oval	
fought an uphill battle	brilliant in defeat
nailed the three	

is so full of action, they must adopt a special kind of English to capture it. The truth is that action will be evident in the story if it is inherent in the event; special language, such as "toed the ball," "split the uprights," or "whacked a four-bagger" merely disguises the action.

Many sportswriters defend such language on the grounds that it is colorful. They call it sports "slanguage" and say there is nothing wrong with it. What they are doing is confusing legitimate sports terminology (birdie, eagle, etc.) with the tired clichés of a past era. There is no reason for sportswriters to be any less conscious of good English than straight news reporters. Readers of the sports page appreciate plain English and lively verbs as much as anyone else. Sportswriters need figures of speech, but these should be bright and inventive. For instance this is how columnist Jim Murray once described the University of Southern California football team: "The USC varsity hits the field like a broken ketchup bottle. They're not a team; they're a horde. You can't beat them; you must dismember them."

Preparing for Sports Coverage

In addition to feature stories that may or may not be directly related to a game, scholastic sportswriters write three types of stories: pregame, game, and postgame. Before writing any of these, you must know as much about the game as possible: all the rules, all the various strategies, and all

To write compelling sports stories, reporters need to get across the feelings and motivations of players and coaches.

the reasons behind them. You must get to know the coaches and players, the sources of information and interviews that brighten the coverage. Bare facts of the contest are seldom enough for the curious fans. They want to know how the coaches and players feel, what they think of their opposition, and how they view the big game. You need to read the sports pages thoroughly, watch sports events on television, perhaps participate in sports. You should immerse yourself in the subject matter. This means watching practice sessions as well as games, to become as familiar as possible with how the players perform and how the coaches think, and traveling with the teams. Once you thoroughly understand what you are going to write about, you can plan your coverage.

The Pregame Story

Because your account of the game itself will be old news by the time it gets into print, you need to pay special attention to pregame, or advance, stories. This may be the only way you can give readers any information they can't read in the local daily newspaper.

In order to get information for that crucial pregame story, the sports staff will have to organize early, perhaps even before school starts, for such sports as football.

The problem is not in getting information about your own team, but in finding out about the other team. Letters sent to the coaches of your school's opposing teams asking *specific questions* almost always will produce usable material. The opposing coach usually is glad to tell you how many returning letterholders there are; which of them were all-state or all-city last year; how many starters were lost from last year's team; the size, weight, position, and year in school of everyone on the team; last year's record; and similar information. The coach will likely cooperate if you ask for an assessment of the team's strengths and weaknesses, although this information will probably be of a general nature. More specific information may come from the sports editor of the school whose team your school is going to play. The coach may be a bit close-lipped about the team's chances; the sports editor probably will level with you.

Armed with information about the opposing team, you can then turn to your own team to gather material for the pregame story. This story should contain the following information:

- The score of last year's game(s) between the two schools
- The team's physical condition (any injuries)
- the starting lineups

- Comparisons between the two teams' records so far this season, including how they came out against common opponents
- Comments on the styles of play (Does one team emphasize offense, the other defense?)
- Significance of the game (Will the winning team be the conference champion?)
- Analysis of individual players (Does each team have a player competing for all-state recognition?)
- Historical background of the rivalry (Who leads in the series of games between the two schools?)

It will help the present staff and future staffs if you compile a complete record of your school's sports history. Old yearbooks and microfilmed copies of the local newspaper on file in the city library should provide the information. Fans will be interested to learn that since the rivalry began, Central High School has won 34 games, lost 22, and tied 4 against Tech.

Pregame coverage should not overlook related spirit activities. The sports page is the proper place for stories about the band's plans for a half-time show, new cheerleaders, pep rallies, and the like. The conscientious sports editor does not ignore the so-called minor sports, such as volleyball, soccer, tennis, and golf, either. There is reader interest in these sports, just as there is in reserve or junior varsity teams. These are the varsity players of the future, and how they fare is highly important not only to the teams but to the fans. And certainly, sports activities by both sexes should be covered.

The article in the "On Display" feature on page 267 was run at the beginning of girls' basketball season. After discussing the players' closeness and winning attitude, the article went on to explain the strengths of each returning senior in detail.

The Game Story

Covering the game is one of the true tests of sportswriters. As a game reporter, you must keep detailed, accurate notes of an event that is happening too fast for the untrained observer to follow. You have more comfortable surroundings—the press box—than the fans, and must make good use of this working space. A note-taking system, a method of keeping a play-by-play record, and some system for recording statistics may be of your own invention, but should be simple and easy to read. Nothing is more frustrating than searching after the game for some missing fact that

Seven Seniors Jam on Court

by Julie Hsu, Charles Wright Academy,
Tacoma, Washington

After three years together, seven senior women begin their final basketball season, and their final chance to win the state title with an undefeated record.

The women's varsity basketball team consists of 11 players, seven of whom are seniors: Molly Wilcox, Heather Meyer, Clara Peck, Laura Lee, Heather Tapp, Sarah Tommervik, and Heather Turner. The majority of the team has played over 90 games together in the last three years.

"After playing with each other for so long, we've learned to play to each other's strengths and avoid our weaknesses," said team member Molly Wilcox.

"Since we all are really motivated and have high expectations for our individual selves, it brings a feeling of unity among the team," said team member Sarah Tommervik.

The team's ultimate goal is to win the state tournament. . . .

"As seniors we've been playing with this team for three years and we all know this is our last chance to meet the goals that have been set," said team member Heather Turner.

The unity and closeness of the team has been formed throughout the years of athletics and friendships that have grown among them. The team believes that this unity is the strongest factor that has aided them through their three years of playing together.

"They love playing basketball with each other, and they do extremely well," said varsity coach Larry Berg.

The players strongly believe in each other's ability, which is apparent in their positive outlook on their teammates. . . .

you should have written down when it happened. You must watch for turning points in the game: the fumble that sets up the winning touchdown (and who recovered the fumble); the substitute who comes off the bench and leads the team to victory; the shift from zone to man-to-man defense that bottles up the opponent's top scorer.

As a sports reporter, you are free to analyze the game. If it was a case of your school's offense overpowering the opponent's defense, say so (if you're sure). If the wet field or the wind played a part, say so. Reiterate the consequences. Tell the fans once more that the winner is the conference champion.

It should be obvious from all this that you will be busy during the game. You must watch the game, the sidelines, the spectators, and the officials, all the while keeping careful, detailed notes. Therefore, *you cannot be a cheerleader*; you can be partisan, but you can't let this interfere with the job of reporting. About the second time a student sports reporter jumps up, shouting "Kill the referee!" and spilling the professional reporter's coffee, he or she will no longer be welcome in the press box.

Student reporters have every right to cover the games and should resist any attempts by professionals to eject them from the press box. The student will find little support, however, from a professional whose notes are soggy from spilled coffee.

If sports editors are to function effectively within limited space, they need to limit details on game stories, since these are old news anyway. Brief accounts, crediting those who scored or who played well, will suffice most of the time. If the sports editor decides to run a complete game story even though the local daily newspaper has already done so, then a new angle must be found, perhaps combining the advance on tonight's game with accounts of past games. The editor must be able to offer something the daily newspaper did not. If he or she can't do that, then by all means the game story should be featurized, as there is little point in a lead announcing a game winner two weeks after the game has been played. If you are the reporter assigned to write such a feature, remember not to make the same "mistake" Grantland Rice did. Include the score, somewhere, and if needed for clarity, tell the name of the game and make it clear whether it was the boys' team or the girls'.

A personal interview with a star athlete can add an interesting perspective to a story about a sports event.

There is no question, in this day and age, about the need for fair coverage of men's and women's sports activities. Attendance at and interest in events such as girls' basketball games is skyrocketing. The recent Olympic competitions brought sports such as women's gymnastics, swimming, and track back into the public eye. No scholastic sports page can afford to overlook the trend, for it is no longer a simple matter of trying to be fair to both genders. These days, fan interest truly drives the coverage.

How much coverage is appropriate can be something of a dilemma, however. Consider the situation in a big-time college football town such as South Bend, Austin, Lincoln, Tallahassee, College Station, or Columbus. Should every other sports event at a Notre Dame or Nebraska or Ohio State take a back seat to what the football team is doing? Fans of women's sports in such towns often complain about being shunted aside, but should a journalist devote as much coverage to women's soccer, played before 50 people, as to football, played before 75,000? Your answer here really depends on your own idea of priorities.

Sometimes the situation is reversed. In a state like Iowa, there has always been intense interest in girls' basketball. The springtime statewide tournament for girls' teams often generates much more interest—and thus more press coverage—than the boys' tournament. So here it might be argued that the boys are getting the short end of the stick. The same situation holds true in Tucson, Arizona, where women's softball often draws larger audiences than men's baseball: The news coverage reflects that fact.

Some would say that the rise in coverage of women's sports really began with the Olympics and the star system that Olympic coverage tends to create. Up until 1972, for example, very little attention was paid to women's gymnastics. In that year, however, a tiny seventeen-year-old Russian named Olga Korbut dazzled audiences with her prowess. Coverage of her sport on television increased dramatically, and she herself became the inspiration for the gymnasts who followed her. The popularity of athletes such as Nadia Comaneci and Mary Lou Retton not only kept women's gymnastics in the limelight in which it basks today, but opened the door for popular interest in other female athletes and athletic events.

Is it fair that women's gymnastics during the Olympics—or the Iowa girls' basketball tournament—gets such extensive coverage? This is really just the other side of the football coverage question raised earlier. If audience interest in an event is there, then sports reporters will write stories about it, regardless of how one-sided this coverage might seem.

A high school newspaper, of course, is not a commercial enterprise. For a school journalist, the basic goal should be to treat all athletes and all sports equally. Don't automatically cover football more than, for example, girls' basketball—or more than any minor sport, girls' or boys'. Be guided by fairness, not merely by attendance. Yet recognize that there will be times when your coverage will be skewed. If a girls' team is winning championships and a boys' team is 5–11, your coverage will have to reflect the situation. "Fair" or not, there's really not much else you can do. A winning team will always be news.

269

The Postgame Story

The postgame story could just as easily be called a sports feature, sideline story, background story, sports interview, or locker-room story. Postgame stories include, among others, interviews with the players after the game, descriptions of the spectators' actions during the game, historical features on a sport or rivalry, wrap-ups (or reviews) of the season after the last game, and discussions of rule changes.

The lead and the tone of such stories are usually somewhat different from those of game and pregame stories. The latter are usually written with standard techniques, probably including a summary lead. (The exception would be a game story published two weeks after the game, when a feature angle would be needed.) Sports feature stories, on the other hand, follow the same general pattern as feature stories; they should be vivid and colorful, but not overdone.

The postgame story provides an opportunity to untangle confusing events that occurred during a game—by talking with the official who made the controversial ruling, for instance. It also gives you as the reporter a chance to update readers on scoring records and individual statistics that you didn't have time to compile immediately after the game—for example, the new team scoring standings in basketball or the number of yards per carry of the backs in football.

A word of caution, however: Don't carry partisanship to extremes. A sports columnist who invariably predicts his or her team will win, for instance, eventually loses all credibility.

The Importance of Features

Because few scholastic publications can compete in timeliness with daily newspapers or radio and TV broadcasts, most sports coverage should be featurized. Coverage of games and matches should take a featurized, anecdotal approach—because the outcomes are already known. Even regular coverage should emphasize features rather than game accounts.

The story in the "On Display" feature on page 271 is a good example of featurized event coverage. The outcome of the event is reported, but in a featurized and interesting way rather than in straightforward who-won-and-who-lost fashion; that information was probably reported by the daily newspapers.

Men in Tights

by Jeremy Schnitker, The Echoes, *Abraham Lincoln High School, Council Bluffs, Iowa*

After splitting his head open during a second round match at the Harlan Invitational last Saturday, Andy Meyers '96, walked off the mat with blood running down his face. He wondered if he would wrestle again that day.

Before the injury he had won his first round match by pin over Josh Kritenbrink from Tee Jay, who had qualified for State last year. Meyers ended up finishing his second round match, but he lost 7–4 before he was taken to the hospital. He was forced to forfeit the rest of his matches for the day.

Although the rest of the Lynx didn't split their heads open, their day went much like Meyers'. They started off in the first round winning all but two of their matches, but they went on to lose all but two second round matches.

"I thought we did pretty good in the first round, but I could tell that we were all having early season jitters, and we all were nervous, and it showed in the second round," Dennis Sigafoose '97, said. "But it's nothing that we can't work out towards the end of the season."

As a team, the Lynx placed fifth out of the nine teams in the tournament, but they had to forfeit two weight classes, which hurt their standings.

The grapplers also placed six individuals in the top four: seniors Mike Porter, Aaron Jerome, and Dan Mohatt took first, second and third. Zach Beam '96, Nolan Respeliers '97, and Jeremy Schnitker '97, all took fourth.

The fifth place finish was not an accurate reflection of how hard the wrestlers and their coach work.

As basketball players huddle around Coach Dave Brown each day, they strain to hear the explanation of a new play over the screams and yells of wrestling coach Clark Allen.

"It gets us pumped up when Coach Allen gets excited at practice," Beam said. "He does it a lot because he gets excited when he wrestles us. He's not screaming because he's mad at us; he does it to get us into practice so we work harder."

Wrestlers start off practice doing calisthenics, which consist of 100 push-ups and sit-ups. After that, they do normal stretching and then start their first of five 6-minute matches. Following their matches, they do calisthenics again and run.

"The toughest part of practice is having to wrestle the big guys who weigh 20 to 30 more pounds than you; then when you're dead tired, you have to do calisthenics and run," Beam said. "It's very tiring."

But wrestlers' vigorous practice routine goes even beyond the hour and a half practice after school.

"I usually run extra laps after practice or come up in the gym before school and run laps if I have to lose some weight the day of a match," Jerome said. "On top of all that, I can hardly eat anything or I'll be overweight."

Allen's grueling practices have always paid off. He has compiled a 141-20-1 record and led the Lynx to three consecutive first place finishes in the Metro. He has also been honored as Southeast Iowa Head Coach of the Year five times in his 17-year career. Wrestlers believe they will produce similar results this season.

"We should be pretty good this year," Sigafoose said. "We have a good shot at beating Lewis Central and going undefeated in dual meets, and we expect to place in the top three at the Metro tournament."

An effective story about a wrestling tournament may combine straight reporting about the matches with featurized information about players and coaches.

The story in the "On Display" feature on page 273 represents what the scholastic journalist should generally strive for: a feature not pegged to any specific game or match. Such stories go a long way toward solving the problem most scholastic journalists have: how to provide new information when daily newspapers and radio and TV have already covered specific events.

Sportswriting Today

Sportswriting is fun, but it isn't easy. The sports reporter must be a keen observer and a good interviewer—and as good a writer as anyone on the staff. The article in the "On Display" feature on page 274 points out some of the pleasures and hazards involved in sportswriting.

Wrap-up

Two schools of thought exist about sportswriting. One says sportswriting is the best writing in journalism. The other says it is the worst. It can be both. When it is bad, it is awful. When it is good, it is excellent.

Some sportswriters overuse trite expressions like "tally" for points and "cagers" for basketball players. The language of sports has color built into it so there is no need for clichés.

Sports stories often need interpretation, and occasionally judgments can be made by writers to provide this interpretation. Readers want sports stories to reflect the tension, color, excitement, joy, or sorrow of the contests.

Careful planning is needed for effective sports coverage. Often schools exchange information from coaches or writers. Good records need to be kept to aid future staff members.

Scholastic journalist follow professional rules and do not cheer in the press box. They keep busy tracking the game, looking for key plays or turning points.

Scholastic journalists often are at a disadvantage in getting their stories printed because the commercial press publishes first. This means student journalists need to develop different angles and approaches, often emphasizing advance stories of contests.

Because few scholastic publications can compete in timeliness with daily newspapers or radio and TV broadcasts, most sports coverage should be featurized. Coverage of games and matches should take a featurized, anecdotal approach—because who won or lost is already known.

Sports stories should be vivid and colorful but not overdone. Open partisanship for one team can damage credibility.

Sportswriting has been called "the most pleasant way of making a living that man has yet devised." Without sportswriters, there would be no record of the grand achievements of athletes. But the work can be difficult and demanding, requiring odd work hours and a great deal of travel. Coaches and players are not always cooperative with the press, particularly after defeats.

Sportuguese Baffles Fans

by Jocelyn Porzei, The Central Times, *Naperville Central High School, Naperville, Illinois*

Belly back, trap, pinch, dormie, yachtsman, chippy, wing, alley, dink, hook . . .
Baby talk? Senile mumblings?

No, simply the jargon used by athletes to describe plays and positions. Fluency in "sportuguese" is a necessary part of communication on and off the field. Senior Brad Mandeville, Varsity football player, said, "It's an easy way of [communicating] without the opposite team knowing what you're doing."

According to the book *The Language of Sport* by Tim Considine, football uses a lot more different play names compared to other sports.

Soccer player junior Scott Vallow agreed but also talked about how the constant communication on the field helps everyone know what's going on. "Being the goalkeeper, you can see who's being marked or remind defenders to mark up so you keep constant communication with the players during the games," Vallow commented.

Along with football and soccer, volleyball uses a lot of plays and formations in its games, but numbers and letters are used to code them.

"It's easy to use one-syllable plays such as colors, letters and numbers because then you have time to call them so the setter knows where to put the ball and who's open," said Varsity volleyball member junior Jayla Ryan.

Although specific language is necessary in games and on the field, it is also helpful off the field during practices. Flag team member junior Mary Kapellen pointed out that "using names for moves and telling the [others] what the timing is for the move help every one do it faster and quicker and takes up less practice time."

Coaches are primarily responsible for the special jargon. They're the ones who personalize the terms used by athletes. "From high school to college and pro, the techniques are the same, but the names change," explained Varsity football player senior Kyle Buss. "If you've been with a [sport] for a while, you know that year-by-year, the names aren't going to change because you have the same coach. There are some universal terms, but most of it is personal to your team."

Kapellen and Mandeville both added that the coaches will usually name the play after some aspect of the play.

Poms member junior Erin O'Neal summarized that "after the first week, everyone understands everything. It's between the poms, and everybody listens and follows the instructions. All you have to say is leap, jump, and turn!"

Evaluation Checklist: *Sports Story*

✓ Does the content of the story reflect support for the local team without being excessively partisan?

✓ If the story is pregame, does it give specific information about the opposition as well as the home team?

✓ For game and postgame stories, has the writer taken essentially a featurized approach?

✓ Is the language fresh and original, with "slanguage" kept to a minimum?

✓ Is the story free from grammatical errors and in accordance with the publication and AP stylebooks?

The Best Seat in the House

by C. Bickford Lucas

Once upon a time, sportswriters wrote about athletic heroes and heroines and their exploits in grandiose style with the emphasis on adjectives, clichés, and adoration.

Managing editors took a dim view of sports departments, frequently calling them toy shops peopled by undisciplined, unprofessional, beer-guzzling, poker-playing, illiterate journalistic misfits.

The sportswriters took pride in being mavericks, but that's about all they took pride in. Many were unabashed supporters for the schools, teams, or sports they covered. They were often flattered, frequently pampered, and sometimes paid by sports promoters.

And they were envied. Sportswriters were paid to watch events other folks paid to see, and the writers usually had the best seats in the house.

It was exciting and fun.

It still is and probably always will be, even though the business has changed dramatically. Standards for sports departments are as high as or higher than the standards on the city and news desks of most newspapers, particularly the better newspapers.

The excitement of covering a Super Bowl or World Series has to be experienced to be appreciated. For the most part, you are dealing with interesting people doing interesting things. And your audience is virtually guaranteed.

Sometimes the sports reporter must be the bearer of bad tidings. If a writer's team is doing something it shouldn't, the writer must cover—not cover up—the story. The writer's responsibility is to the reader, not the team he or she is covering.

A homer means two things to a sportswriter. One is a four-base hit in baseball. That's okay. The other is a writer who believes in "my team right or wrong." That's not okay, even at the scholastic level. Among responsible journalists there is no reason for hometown bias and boosterism.

That's not to say a writer can or must be totally impersonal. Writers are not made of plastic. It's difficult not to have feelings about teams or individuals you deal with on a regular basis.

A sportswriter without emotions will write colorless, dull stories. But the writer's feelings should not be apparent to the reader. Cheering in the press box is unacceptable.

The positives of being a sportswriter far outweigh the negatives, but students considering this line of work should be aware of the pitfalls.

It is hard work, and the hours can be devastating. Forget weekends—that's when many sports events take place. Forget nights—even baseball usually is played at night these days.

It puts a strain on family life, primarily because of the hours and travel time. Some sportswriters on larger newspapers spend almost as much time on the road as they spend at home. It's a nice way to see the country or the world (with your employer paying the way), but it can create havoc with your family or social life.

An increasing number of athletes are refusing interviews. Some coaches and players verbally, and sometimes physically, abuse writers.

In spite of the recognition and visibility, many sportswriters lead lonely lives. There are lots of parties and press conferences, and hobnobbing with celebrities can be fun, but it's tough to socialize with athletes who may earn more in a week than you earn in a year.

But there is camaraderie in the profession, and the majority of the athletes, coaches, and owners are decent, friendly people. The problem is getting too close. It is difficult to write a story that might cost a friend a job or cause embarrassment. But sometimes it must be done if the writer is to retain credibility.

To be successful, a writer must be enthusiastic, dedicated, devoted, tireless, ethical, imaginative, resourceful, inquisitive, stubborn, flexible, fair-minded, thick-skinned, knowledgeable and, above all, accurate. Lazy people looking for an easy way into the stadium need not apply.

Mr. Lucas was sports editor of the Denver Post *for fourteen years.*

On Assignment

Individual Activities

1. Write a brief definition or explanation of each of the following terms.

   featurize   game story

   postgame story   pregame story

   "slanguage"

2. Rewrite the following cliché-filled football story to eliminate trite expressions. *Note:* Not all of the sports expressions are incorrect. Some are legitimate colorful language of the sport.

   > The Centerville High School Tigers clawed their way to the Intercity League football championship Friday with a 14–0 shellacking of the Anytown Cougars—who played more like kittens.
   >
   > Playing under the arcs at the local gridiron, the Tigers broke a scoreless deadlock late in the second stanza when quarterback Tommie James threw a Hail Mary pass to wide receiver Corey Campbell, who snagged the aerial for 65 yards and a waltz into paydirt for the tally. Kicker Carlos Sanchez split the uprights. The Tigers took a 7–0 lead into the clubhouse at the intermission.
   >
   > In the second half, the Cougars mounted an aerial attack but it was thwarted by the Tigers' D. Playing out of a 3–4 alignment, the Centerville defenders tagged Cougar mailcarriers for 46 negative yards in the third canto alone.
   >
   > Meanwhile, James nixed the Tigers' pro set offense with plays out of the I to take Centerville into the red zone three times in the second half. Tiger gridders were able to punch the pigskin into paydirt only once, but that was enough.
   >
   > Triple threat I-back Dave Williams brought down the curtain on the season with a six-yard scamper into the promised land on a counter play as time ran out in the fourth chapter. Sanchez kicked the extra point.

   > Williams and James return for their senior season next year, thus forming the nucleus of what should be another well-oiled Tiger machine.

3. Watch a college or professional game on television. Make notes of the turning points of the game, the major strategies, the major errors, the star players. Clip an article about the event from the local paper. Compare your list of key elements to those that appear in the newspaper. Are they the same or different? Why? Who do you think is "right"? Why? Write an essay on the findings.

4. Test your critical thinking. Did you know that sports commentators on radio and television often are paid, at least in part, by the teams they cover? What does that suggest? Can such commentators be objective? Do team officials want them to be? What if they criticize the team's performance? How do your school coaches feel about this? How do you feel? Write an essay on the subject.

5. Assume you know that a member of your school team is ineligible, perhaps for academic reasons or because he or she is too old. The player is a star whose loss would be critical to the team. Should you run a story? Ask the coaches what they think. Write an essay on your position. Does your code of ethics affect your position?

6. Attend your school's major sports event this week and write a feature story about all that happens at the game: the cheerleaders, the band the crowd, the weather, the excitement, the halftime show, and so on. Do not write about the game itself.

7. Write a pregame, game, and postgame story of a major athletic event in your school this week. Attach comparable stories from the local paper and compare them to your stories. Are the news elements different? Try to account for any differences.

8. Write a story about a school sport with which you are unfamiliar. Choose an upcoming event for your article; then, in order to become more knowledgeable about the sport, interview the coach and players, observe a practice, and watch an actual game. Read others' stories covering the sport. Write your story and check it with the coach or one of the players for accuracy.

9. Exchange sports stories with another student. Your task is to edit the other's writing to make it more lively, exciting, and immediate. Try to make readers feel they were in the stands participating in the event.

Team Activities

10. Make a list of so-called minor sports. Each team should select one of the minor sports, and each member of the team should identify and write at least one story about that sport. Make sure the stories explain key parts of the game: scoring, rules, terminology. Interview the coaches and players. After the stories have been critiqued and evaluated, keep them for use in a later chapter.

11. Have each team member survey ten students on the importance of sports in a scholastic setting. How many students attend games? What reasons are given by those who don't? Are sports overemphasized? Do they cost too much? Do athletes' grades suffer because of the time spent at practice and traveling to games? Are boys' and girls' sports financed equally? How do the students feel about minor sports? About the sport your journalism team is covering? Compile all the answers into one in-depth story to go along with the package of stories developed on your minor sport.

Gender and ethnic changes in newsrooms across the country may be best reflected by the increasing number of women moving into the traditionally all-male bastion of sports news.

"More and more African Americans and females are in the business," says Valerie Lister. "We're always going to be challenged. Women aren't supposed to know anything about sports. And racism is a part of society."

Lister joined the staff of *USA Today* in January 1988. She feels that today, when the number of papers is on the decline, the sooner a young person gets started the better. "If you want to go into this business, if you are serious about it, start now," Lister said. "Read and write as much as you can and find a mentor who will help you."

Although she is not trying to discourage people, Lister is realistic. At *USA Today*, minority representation has fallen second to making a profit. Affirmative action issues are taking a back seat to survival. She encourages students who are serious to apply for any and all scholarships and internships they can find.

For Lister, journalism wasn't always her goal. She originally studied civil engineering at the University of Texas at El Paso.

"I flunked pre-calculus. That's when I realized I wasn't going to be an engineer," she said.

She began looking into public relations as a career until a professor read some of her work and convinced her to go into print journalism.

With no high school newspaper experience and only one semester on her college paper, Lister had to work extra hard.

"Most of what you need to know you learn on the job. You have to expect to start small and work your way up."

Her chance to join *USA Today* came while she was at the *Pensacola* (Fla.) *News Journal*. Both publications belong to the Gannett Newspapers group, which brings up journalists from its local publications for four-month training programs with *USA Today*. Lister was one of those brought up.

Coming from a small paper and being an African American female sportswriter, Lister says she thought she would be "pigeonholed into doing little things."

"It was not as bad as I thought it would be. I was just surprised at how much freedom I was given," she says.

Talking to other writers and reading the newspaper helped her learn more about *USA Today's* terse writing style.

"I can see now a lot of excess stuff you really don't need. You can be informative in a short space. It's a challenge."

She also has been challenged by the competition and by the needling she sometimes faces as a female sportswriter.

Her interest in sports started when she was a child. Because her father didn't get his first son for several years, she says, she became his "surrogate son." She remembers going to many Atlanta Braves games with him.

Even though that changed after her brother was born, the love of sports was ingrained in her.

"Don't give up," Lister advises women aspiring to be sportswriters. "Hang with it. This is not an easy profession."

Chapter Thirteen

Writing for the Editorial Page

Key Terms

editorial

editorial page

subjective writing

masthead

editorial column

point-counterpoint

mini-torial

editorial policy

Key Concepts

After reading this chapter, you should

- understand the opinion function of a newspaper and the various ways in which it is expressed

- know how to write effective editorials for a variety of purposes

- understand the various types of editorial columns

- be able to write reviews of products and productions

- understand the functions of other elements on the editorial page

The newspaper editorial is often referred to as "the voice of the paper." It is up to the staff to make sure this description is accurate. It is not a simple task. The editorial page is the only part of the paper that focuses completely on subjective writing—that is, writing that is not necessarily impartial but instead expresses a point of view.

Everyone has opinions. The newspaper, when it expresses its opinions—or the radio or television station that offers opinion features and editorial voices—amplifies its voice by the number of its readers or listeners. Therefore, when an editorialist speaks or writes, the responsibility weighing on his or her expression is extremely heavy. Editorials have the ability to make or break a project or program, to affect the amount of acceptance given to a new policy, or to lead to changes in existing policy. Such a degree of influence cannot be taken lightly.

In the past, student newspapers found little to editorialize about other than school spirit or the food in the cafeteria. Student editors were often told they should not editorialize on curriculum, athletics, administrative policy, school board decisions, or such issues outside the school as politics (local, state, or national), the environment, social issues, or the economy.

Today, however, student journalists write about almost any issue of interest to their readers. And, realistically, what issue would not be of importance to a student? The very word *student* implies the role of a seeker of knowledge, and that knowledge is certainly not limited to the walls of the classroom, or to the activity or sports program. The list of topics on page 187, suggested as possible subjects for in-depth articles, could certainly also be considered as possible editorial topics.

Research is the first essential step in writing a good editorial. Rushing to the computer to write a couple hundred words on a burning issue, then discovering that the inferno was really only a lighted match that quickly went out when the truth was known, is not the way to write responsible editorials.

Some of the research done by editorial writers may include direct interviews with people knowledgeable about the issue. Using these people's quotes as part of the editorial adds depth and credibility, as well as providing alternative opinions. Other research information may come from surveys and opinion studies that can be conducted in the school, or may even have been done by research firms. Some of these national studies are available through on-line databases. Other on-line services—newspapers, general and specialty publications, zines, encyclopedias, and government information files, to name a few—are also available to aid in the search for background information on editorial subjects.

As an editorial writer, the journalist should first become saturated with all of the available information on the subject to be discussed. Only when a position has been reached, and the research completed to support it, should the editorial be written. Most editorials average 200–500 words, seldom longer. Once you have written the editorial, let it sit overnight if you can. Take a look at it the next day—you may see the need to start over, or find that some critical information has been left out.

Functions of Editorials

Editorials serve a variety of functions. For example, there are editorials that explain, persuade, answer criticism or a question, express a warning or caution, criticize, praise, entertain, or provide leadership on a subject. A brief discussion of each of these functions follows. But an editorial can also be a blend of types. For example, the editorial could praise the board of education for developing new guidelines for graduation, but criticize how they are being implemented, while offering constructive solutions to the implementation problems.

Explain

A new policy on graduation requirements may have been issued over the summer. Your staff feels the system deserves clarification and an expression of support. Naturally, you probably will cover the policy in a news story. But that writer is reporting the news, not commenting on it. An editorial is the place to do that.

The editorial in the "On Display" feature on page 281 explains some of the problems physically disabled students face in a school, as well as the costs of renovations.

An editorial about the need for better handicapped access in a school may involve explanation as well as persuasion.

Persuade

There are many issues within and outside the student world that require persuasive, responsible voices in order to help readers reach valid resolutions. Maybe your school has just been forced to close the student lounge

Building Needs Modifications

Arlingtonian, *Upper Arlington High School, Columbus, Ohio*

In this school, physically disabled students and faculty face challenges most people overlook. Although school officials say the high school attempts to accommodate people with special physical needs, it does not exceed the minimum standards, as would be the Arlington norm.

Whether struggling to open a heavy door, trying to tear a paper towel from a dispenser too high on the wall, or attending a school event without a convenient place to sit, some students and teachers have noticed that high school does not always meet the needs of the physically disabled.

School officials claim not enough money is allotted in each annual budget to fix all of the problems physically disabled people face. If the district would grant the high school enough money, however, some changes could be made to greatly improve the quality of school life for the physically disabled.

To begin the renovations, the high school should lower paper towel dispensers in the restrooms. This will benefit not only the physically disabled, but other students and faculty who cannot easily reach the dispensers. According to the *Upper Arlington Accessibility Study Handbook*, compiled in May 1994, the district would need to pay approximately $100 for this change.

Unfortunately, other corrections are more expensive, and officials say the high school does not have ready access to large amounts of money.

Providing both gymnasiums, the stadium, the Little Theater and the auditorium with specific wheelchair areas for the physically disabled is one example of costly change. The Accessibility Handbook states this cost at an estimated $5000. This expense could be achieved, though, by renovating the areas over a selected number of years.

Other needed changes in accessibility for the physically disabled included adding "accessible drinking fountains ($1800), modifications of one female and one male second floor restroom for the handicapped ($2400) and volume control for the high school's public telephones ($1000)."

The physically disabled students and faculty deserve a school which offers them the conveniences most others already take for granted. The district needs to create an annual budget which allows for specific amounts of money to be set aside for these changes, which will enable the physically disabled to learn in an environment of freedom and opportunity.

---

area because of the mess continually left by students using it. Your job might be to persuade the student council to appeal to the administration for a second chance, or to persuade the students to change their attitude toward the lounge if they want to keep it. Your editorial might try to persuade the school to reopen the lounge by spelling out guidelines for supervising what goes on there through student service clubs.

The persuasive editorial in the "On Display" feature on page 282 gives several specific reasons to make its case in favor of a standard academic policy.

Academic Policy Should Be Adopted by the State

Beak 'n Eye, *West High School,*
Davenport, Iowa

The academic policy set for Davenport athletes requiring them to maintain a "C" average and fail no classes has been a successful one, and should become a statewide policy.

The current statewide policy, which requires students to pass four classes the semester before they are to compete, is not strict enough. The State Board of Education is considering raising the standard to a 2.0 grade point average. Not only does the Davenport policy enforce good study habits and self-discipline, but making Davenport schools the only schools under the policy is unfair to Davenport athletes.

This policy enforces good study habits and self-discipline, as well as giving the athletes a little extra motivation to do well academically. Making them put their studies above their extra-curricular activities is a lesson athletes will need to learn as they leave high school and fend for themselves in the real world. Without this policy, many athletes would never learn the self-discipline it takes to become successful off the field.

The whole state would surely benefit from such a policy, and a statewide policy would also ensure equality to all schools competing against each other. Under the present system, however, Davenport athletes are held to higher academic standards than their competition. Someone may be competing against them that would not be eligible under their requirements. We obviously need to establish a level playing field at least in the MAC conference, if not statewide.

Some people fear that such a policy would cause some students to drop out of school or their sports altogether. However, no student has dropped out of school in Davenport as a result of the policy, and there have been many cases of students raising their grades to comply with the policy.

Making athletes keep their grades up before they can participate in interscholastic competition is a good idea because it makes student athletes have their priorities in the right order. The policy adopted by the Davenport school district has been successful, and a similar policy should be adopted statewide to ensure fairness to all competitors.

Answer

Suppose that there has been criticism about your student delegation's conduct at a recent convention. Your job may be to answer that criticism in the form of a defense. Or, if the situations described are true, you may choose to answer the criticism with facts and admissions, along with an apology if appropriate.

Warn

An alert staff can see problems that lie ahead. (An early warning, for example, might have kept that student lounge mentioned earlier open.) Your reporters should know what is going on around the school or in the community and issue warnings when appropriate. The warning might be a strong one, or a mild one, more like a yellow light of caution.

Criticize

There are times when editorials that criticize the actions of others may be appropriate. But writers of critical editorials must remember that, since the editorial is the voice of the newspaper, they have a special responsibility to be constructive. If editors are not able to offer solutions to the actions they criticize, the newspaper will soon lose the respect of its readers. If, for example, the school calendar being considered by the board of education is considered faulty, the writer should offer constructive solutions to remedy the problem. But before rushing to write, he or she should be sure to fully understand the reasoning behind the proposed changes. Such an understanding could make the criticism invalid. Additionally, editorials of criticism should focus on the issue at hand, not on the personalities involved.

Editorialists have a journalistic responsibility to balance criticism with suggested solutions or alternative courses of action. Notice how the editorial in the "On Display" on page 284 criticizes both teachers' and students' handling of a new advisory period, but at the same time offers ways that the situation can be remedied.

As the voice of the newspaper, an editorial can have considerable influence on its audience. Thus even critical editorials should also propose constructive solutions.

Advisory Periods: Success Depends on the Changing of Attitudes

The Cavalcade, *W. T. Woodson High School, Fairfax, Virginia*

1994 seems to be the year for confusion, since students are being hit with new changes before they have the chance to adjust to the last ones. While most of these changes have gone smoothly, the new advisory period in particular is presenting problems.

In theory, the advisory period is supposed to be a forum for students to connect with their teachers and peers and discuss issues, but that's in theory only. Teachers lecture from a tightly scripted schedule handed down to them, and students either skip the period or fall asleep in class. Something needs to be done about this.

To begin with, the class as a whole should be less structured. As it stands, teachers have a set agenda they can't deviate from, and students have no input. A looser period along the lines of the hugely successful racism seminar last spring would stir more student interest/participation. That activity was popular because of its meaty subject. This year we get to fill out time charts and name different parts of the school. No comparison.

The attitudes of some of the teachers involved need work also. Students are complaining that their teachers are distant or uninterested. These teachers should remember that for this one special period they are more counselor-mediators than teachers. Teachers who don't have an active interest in communicating with their students shouldn't take part in the advisory activity, since students will return indifference with indifference.

We students aren't saints either. Most of us tend to dismiss the period out of hand, which diminishes the class atmosphere. We should be more open to the period and try to make constructive changes instead of griping, and parents shouldn't encourage us by excusing us for skipping, either.

As a concept, the advisory period is fresh and has the potential to revitalize Woodson's student-teacher relations, but that's not going to happen unless we try.

Praise

Don't forget that you can issue words of praise and congratulations through editorials. When a person or group does something worthy of praise, pass it on. The editorial in the "On Display" on page 285 commends an entire school district's combined recycling program.

Entertain

Some issues are just not worth handling with heavy comment or criticism. Then a useful approach might be to create a little humor through an entertaining editorial. Perhaps there was a humorous incident relating to a computer foul-up when your grade reports were issued; fifty student identification numbers got jumbled and a lot of failures appeared where there should have been pass grades or even A's. You can reconstruct the untangling, report other people's reactions, and comment lightly on the computer age.

Recycling Revamped

*Black and White, Walt Whitman High School,
Bethesda, Maryland*

By taking the steps necessary to establish an effective and well-organized recycling program in county schools, MCPS has made overwhelming improvements over the volunteer and experimental recycling programs formerly done on an individual school basis.

The addition of nine recyclable items and the increased reliability of MCPS' maintenance are significant advances in the county recycling program.

Under a new county mandate, beginning Nov. 1, schools will be required to recycle aluminum cans, newspapers, both white and mixed-color paper, steel cans, glass bottles and jars, corrugated cardboard, plastic containers, polystyrene and grass trimmings. This is an enormous advancement from recycling only white paper and grass, as Whitman has done in past years.

Whitman's former recycling program, sponsored by the SGA, was not maintained on a frequent basis. Paper was taken out for recycling only once a week, a responsibility left to the students, many of whom used it as an opportunity to miss class. Under the new county program, however, the material to be recycled will be picked up two to three times a week by a private recycling company, ensuring that the program will be well-maintained.

Additionally, a new recycling curriculum will be introduced in elementary schools in January, teaching younger students to think of recycling as an effective and necessary measure in preserving the environment. Students in kindergarten through fifth grade will be taught that recycling is something to be taken seriously, and teaching them to recycle early on will ensure that they continue the practice in the future.

MCPS has set a precedent in its efforts to organize and maintain an effective recycling program in county schools. Its attempts to expand and sustain productive recycling programs in all schools, and its foresight in educating a younger generation on the benefits and practicality of recycling should be used as a model for other area school systems.

Entertaining editorials are not easy to write, but they are rewarding. You might find some good topics in fads and fashions, the weather at the last football game, or the mountain of forms needed to change classes or sections. Some entertaining editorials have clear morals and make a point more effectively than taking off the gloves and slugging away.

Lead

Since a newspaper can magnify its voice and opinion greatly, it can become a force for change; it can provide community leadership. Many community newspapers have started the wheels turning to build freeways, recall local politicians, establish commissions or study committees, get schools built or streets beautified. And school newspapers can have a similar effect within their own communities. Remember, though, that not much is accomplished through constructive criticism

Giving praise for a job well done, such as the development of an effective recycling program, is a legitimate editorial function.

The Power of a Number

Ever wonder about the reason why -30- is typically placed at the end of editorials, news copy, and news releases? No one is really sure, but here are three possible theories:

-30- was the sign-off used by telegraphers in the days of Morse code. So journalists, especially when they began sending stories by wire, began signing their stories in the same way.

The first news communication actually sent by telegraph—during the Civil War—contained thirty words. So the number -30-, along with the word "goodnight" and the operator's name, was placed at the end of the message.

At the time when news stories were written out by hand, "X" marked the end of a sentence, "XX" marked the end of a paragraph, and "XXX" marked the end of a story. And XXX is the Roman numeral for 30.

alone. Seek improvement and development. Granted, there may be obstacles, such as budget limitations. But student bodies have furnished their own lounges, built their own student centers, provided funds to build Peace Corps schools, landscaped their school properties, established minority or special scholarship funds, initiated or changed laws, and done many other things on their own. Many newspapers have brought together boards, parents, students, and community members to achieve goals. A newspaper that fulfills the leadership role wisely through its editorials will find itself widely respected.

Briefly Comment

Finally, there are a number of situations about which opinion might be limited but in need of expression. Many editors will write an occasional potpourri editorial in which they comment briefly on a wide variety of subjects. They might commend the freshmen for their excellent clean-up project, the volleyball team for its sportsmanship, the school board or trustees for the new school calendar or science facilities, and a scholarship winner for his or her academic achievements.

Writing the Editorial

An editorial is only slightly different from a news story as far as the writing goes. Research your topic; then write a clear, concise, simply worded editorial. The idea is to reach your readers quickly, to grab their attention about an important issue. After getting readers' attention, you want to carry them with you—smoothly, logically, and consistently—so they begin to think seriously about the issue you are presenting.

Generally you can divide an editorial into three or four parts. Though other organizations are possible, the following usually works well:

- **Introduction:** Give a brief statement of background concerning the editorial topic. Don't assume your readers already know the basis for your comment.
- **Reaction:** Explain the position of the editorial and your newspaper.
- **Details:** Provide support for the position you are taking.
- **Conclusion:** Comment on recommended solutions, alternatives, and direction, and restate the paper's position.

Introduction

In the introduction, state, as briefly as possible, the background needed for the editorial:

> Last week the student council voted unanimously to close the student lounge because the students were not keeping it clean. Trash left from lunches or cleaned-out notebooks were found on tables, benches, floors, and in the hallways. Council members had placed warning signs and signs urging cleanliness throughout the lounge for the past few weeks to no avail.

This introduction gives a brief history leading to an action. You and your readers are starting off together.

Reaction

Next comes the reaction. You set the reader up to receive your opinion. Continuing the example above:

> The council action was justified and necessary. Not only does the lounge require costly time to clean, it reflects on the school and the students' pride in it. A "who cares?" attitude toward maintaining the school's clean appearance could translate into a "who cares?" attitude toward scholastics, sports, and other activities that are sources of school pride.

Effective Editorials

Writers who fulfill the following criteria will generally produce successful editorials.
1. Be fair.
2. Be brief.
3. Do your research.
4. Come to the point quickly.
5. Base opinions on fact.
6. Be sincere.
7. Don't take yourself too seriously.
8. Avoid gossip and hearsay.
9. Admit errors when you have been wrong.
10. Don't preach; persuade.

Details

The reader knows your opinion, but you aren't finished. You now go into details that support your reaction and lead to a conclusion. Here, especially if there are strong opinions on the topic, you should acknowledge these and demonstrate why your idea is preferable:

> The situation became evident several weeks ago when council member Stephen Smith urged the council to establish clean-up patrols to keep the lounge areas presentable and usable. The council responded by appealing to the students' sense of pride, especially those who use the lounge. Signs were posted throughout the school in an effort to capitalize on this "spirit."
>
> Last month, Dr. Jane Roberson, student activities adviser, appeared before the council and made an appeal at the honors convocation for students to clean up their mess in the lounge.
>
> All of these efforts and appeals evidently fell on deaf ears. The lounge is an eyesore. We cannot take pride in such a situation. A picture appearing with a story on the lounge closing on page one of this issue gives the reader a view of the problem. We are sure you will agree—it is a mess.

Conclusion

You have established some background, expanding and repeating in some cases what you briefly mentioned in the introduction. Now conclude your editorial. You could end by saying, "Shame on you," or by applauding the council's decision to take strong action. You could make an effort to lead, compromise, or appeal for a second chance. You may want to offer several alternatives and leave the options up to the council or the student body:

> The council should conduct an open forum next week concerning the problem and seek student suggestions on how the lounge might be reopened and kept clean. Among the issues students and council members might consider are student clean-up patrols, as recommended several weeks ago by council member Steve Smith. It might be possible for several organizations to volunteer for a week of clean-up duty, spreading the job around and making more people aware of the need for cleanliness.
>
> The decision to close the lounge was right. But now it's time for the council, the administration and students to seek solutions for reopening the lounge as soon as possible.

In writing editorials you will find that not all subjects fit into this formula. You will generally have all four basic elements, but they may be in a different order or have a different emphasis. After the introduction in the

"On Display" feature on page 290, the writer uses much of the editorial to explain a policy and reacts only at the end. The editorial is still effectively constructed, however.

Points to Remember

In selecting editorial subjects, choose those important to your readers. Readers are not as likely to care about ecology in Australia and how monetary policy is plaguing Europe as about significant changes in graduation requirements or pollutants recently dumped into the local river. Just as in a news story, proximity and the other elements of news play an important role in determining editorial subjects. If there is not enough time to do a good job of writing an editorial, wait until the next issue or don't write one.

If you select controversial subjects, don't write until you have done the necessary research; and don't be afraid to ask for outside opinions or criticism on the editorial before it is published. Your letters-to-the-editor column will offer the opposition a chance to reply to your editorial. Be sure your editorial can withstand such arguments without the need for a battle of "can you top this?" with counter-letters and editorials. An editorial should be strong enough to be judged on its merits and the criticism it might get in light of those merits.

When you are finished writing, ask yourself if you can summarize the entire point of your editorial in one or two sentences. If not, you had better start over or forget it, because you have missed the point—and your readers will miss it, too. Ask another staff member to read the editorial and write a one-sentence summary. Limit yourself to making just that one essential point.

Remember, too, that editorials are not written in the first-person singular; never say "I." But do use "we" and "you." Develop an informal approach. An editorial should be read as a conversation between two people, the writer and the reader.

Other Elements on the Editorial Page

In addition to the editorial, there are a number of other components that may appear on the editorial page. These include editorial columns, cartoons, letters to the editor, reviews, and opinion features.

Editorial pages also carry the newspaper's masthead. It lists the paper's staff adviser and sometimes the principal, the school address, phone, electronic mail address, fax number, and the names and positions of staff

New Out-of-School Policy More Effective for Students

The Hi-Lite, *Carmel High School, Carmel, Indiana*

Out-of-school suspension. It used to be that we all thought of suspension as a way to punish us in the future (college admissions, semester grades) while giving us a holiday in the present (eat lunch at Taco Bell and play Nintendo).

No longer is this the case. The Carmel Clay school system, in conjunction with the Hamilton County prosecutor's office, has come up with a new plan to end the latter part of our perception of a suspension. The new rule states that the number of days a student is suspended can be spent in a juvenile correctional facility. The aim of the new policy is to target those who see little punishment in getting a day off from school. This new and innovative idea is just one more step toward renewing students' respect of the current disciplinary policies.

The former policy of suspension was inclusive to all kinds of delinquent behavior. Whether caught forging a pass or possessing a firearm, a student would be given an out-of-school suspension.

The new policy, although more strict and severe in its methods, will allow the lesser "criminals" to have a second chance, while giving those seen as committing some kind of "anti-social behavior" a true punishment. An actual punishment of this kind has been anticipated for several years here.

As is evident from the reports of the 11 other schools in which the system has been implemented, the new policy will be an effective deterrent for would-be offenders. While we would like to say that the new policy is cruel and injust, the facts and realities point toward the effectiveness of and the need for this newly implemented disciplinary punishment.

members. In addition, some newspapers print their editorial policy and their policy on letters to the editor.

Editorial Columns

An editorial page frequently will carry a number of columns written by students—some serious, some amusing. Unlike editorials, which are the voice of the newspaper, these editorial columns, or commentaries, express the personal viewpoints of individual, identified student writers. A column requires the same amount of hard work and research before writing it that an editorial does, and columnists must be fair and accurate in the information they use. Editorial columns can express a diversity of opinions and often are written in an informal, personal style. In some cases, columns may be written by one or more journalists on the same topic, but from different points of view.

While columnists in major newspapers express their own opinions, few papers run columns by writers with whom they disagree philosophically. For example, a newspaper known for writing editorials that support conservative causes and issues is not too likely to run the editorial views of a nonconservative. This is usually not the case in the student media, where diverse viewpoints are important. Furthermore, student journalists have broader options for developing editorial columns than their counterparts on the local newspaper. While people like Art Buchwald, William Safire, Ellen Goodman, Carl Rowan, and Clarence Page are confined to editorial columns that usually deal with politics and government, the school columnist has an array of subjects available. Because of the limited space in a student paper, columnists should be selected carefully and with variety in mind.

One important reminder: Gossip columns, reporting all the latest rumors and who had the "wild" party last Saturday, are not responsible subjects for the school press. They are examples of the kind of writing that has been a major source of problems. In many schools, they alone have been the reason for the paper's coming under tight supervision and limitations by the school's administration or journalism sponsor. The student media are not immune to libel suits. Newspaper columns should be in good taste and in keeping with the canons of responsible journalism.

Common Types of Columns

There are as many types of columns as there are prospective writers. There also is no requirement that the same type of column has to appear in each issue.

Regardless of type, editorial columns express the writer's personal opinions, make personal interpretations, and often suggest the writer's conclusions for the reader. Columns generally are clearly indicated as opinion and identify the author with a byline. They usually appear on the editorial pages, but may appear elsewhere if topical. For example, a sports column is usually in the sports section. Examples of some types of columns are:

Profile columns. A profile column centers on an outstanding individual—a student, instructor, or person in the community. The writer discusses the individual's views on current topics and weaves into the column little bits about him or her: likes and dislikes, plans after finishing school,

True or False: An editorial, or editorial commentary, is the only place in a newspaper or TV news show where the writer doesn't have to be impartial—in other words, where bias can show. Your answers to a question like this depend not only on how you define *bias* but also on how you view news writers and reporters.

Bias is generally defined as presenting information in such a way as to lead readers or listeners to the conclusion that the presenter wants them to reach. One way bias can be created is by communicating only those pieces of information that support the presenter's opinion. For example, in a biased portrayal of a politician as anti-environment, a reporter would mention only a politician's statements against an environmental policy when he or she actually also made statements in favor of the policy. Bias can also be conveyed by word choice—for example, by using loaded words such as "misguided" or "Big Government influenced" in describing a candidate's stance on a tax issue.

So, does *The New York Times* present biased stories in its news columns? Does *CBS News* deliberately slant the facts to force viewers to see events only one way? Some people think so. They point to media studies that show, for example, that the majority of reporters are Democrats and pro-choice. They then use the results as evidence that these are the positions these media figures also try to push in their news stories.

While it would be irresponsible to suggest that bias never occurs in news reporting, certain facts should also be considered. First of all, even if it is true that reporters tend to be liberal in their outlook, owners and managers of news media tend generally to be conservative. So a balancing effect occurs. Secondly, just because a reporter holds one political view doesn't mean that he or she cannot give objective coverage to a different point of view. (People whose idea-processing was so one-sided wouldn't last long in any business!) And finally, an individual program or publication can't be judged fairly on the basis of one or two selected stories. To be fair and unbiased in your own evaluation of news, you really have to take a look at the way a source handles it over a period of time, not just in single, isolated reports.

News programs on radio and TV seem particularly susceptible to the bias label. Here, it helps to be aware that different news programs have different purposes. A national "Nightly News" program is expected to exhibit nonbiased reporting in its hard news stories, but bias, in the form of reporters' opinions, is certainly allowed to creep into some of its features. News commentary programs are a different species altogether. These shows often try to feature a mixture of reporters from across the political spectrum who, like columnists in a newspaper, are not expected to be impartial. You can only determine if these shows lean toward one side or the other by watching them over a period of time, to see if their coverage ultimately balances out. And you should not confuse even these commentary shows with individual talk show hosts on radio, who really have to be considered more as personalities than as serious news reporters.

When you read or listen to the news, it is wise to be alert for bias. You may not find much, and what you do find may be unintentional or only in commentary-type situations. But the important thing is that you do not let it stop you from thinking about both sides of an issue as you form your opinions.

activities, and community contributions. The column writer can take liberties in drawing conclusions or using phrases that would not appear in a news story or feature (such as "an outstanding sports record," "an unsung hero," or "a genuine concern for people").

There are some problems with this type of column, and you should have solutions to them. What criteria will be used to select the students you write about? In a large school, the number of candidates for such an honor is considerable. You will get a lot of criticism unless you have firm standards. Do not use popularity alone.

Unfortunately, many profile columns resort to such trivia as the subject's favorite food, where he or she likes to go on dates, and whether he or she wears designer jeans. Rather, write about the subject's views on student activities, the value of being in sports, plans for the future, issues facing youth, why he or she has made a particular career choice, or how a teacher contributed to his or her success.

Satirical columns. These are one of the more common types of columns in the student paper. They take a lot of work to be effective and should not run unless there is a valid reason for writing the column. Like an editorial, a satirical column must be able to make its point to the reader. If you write one, be careful to verify any facts you use.

Fashion and fad columns. It is difficult and probably unnecessary to write a column on the changing world of styles very often during the year. An occasional fashion column might be refreshing if it is done with flair and some study of fashion trends. Some publications run columns like this in special issues containing several fashion-related news features and special advertising.

A clubs column is a good way to briefly cover the activities of various groups or organizations.

In-the-clubs columns. A good way to give credit to clubs or student groups may be a "club" column. In it you write briefly about the activities of various clubs or organizations, urging attendance at groups' dances or other activities and briefly commenting on each. An occasional column of this nature might eliminate a lot of small stories that may be weeks old. An important note, however: Don't ignore clubs that have only a few members or that you aren't personally interested in. It may be easy to write

Student Freedom of Expression Vital to Future
by Adrian Rogers, Midland High School, Midland, Michigan

When I was in ninth grade, I was allowed to serve as editor for a yearbook and a newspaper, attend Junior Achievement meetings that I could not stand (squeegees and resin owl nite-lites, it turned out, were not for me), produce a district-wide literary magazine, earn straight A's and attend leadership seminars. Other kids with divorced parents and I were allowed to do things like choose between parents, take responsibility for little brothers and sisters and, in some cases, testify in court. And during school, my classmates and I were allowed to listen to AIDS presentations (in graphic detail), view cartoon filmstrips on Mr. Sperm and Ms. Egg (in graphic detail) and hear about each others' sometimes unfortunate weekend adventures (in graphic, gory detail). In ninth grade, we dealt with stuff.

My ninth grade was also the year House Bill 4565, the bill that would restore freedom of the press to high school students, died in the capital, apparently because students weren't mature enough to handle constitutional rights.

The bill was needed because in 1988 freedom of the press for high school newspapers was lost in a Supreme Court case. The Supreme Court ruled that administrators could remove anything from a school publication that they think contradicts the mission of the school. This is called prior review: the principal reviews the stories before the paper is sent to press, and can pull any story.

This made me angry when I was in ninth grade. But it makes me even angrier now, after I have received a top-notch education about a Constitution that barely applies to me at this point. It makes me worried, too, now that I will enter college with the multitudes of other members of the class of 1995 throughout the state, and very few of us will have practical experience with the rights guaranteed in the Bill of Rights to citizens.

Because the Midland High School administration does not practice prior review, the editorial content of our student newspaper is determined by the editorial board. We are lucky. But education in the Constitution is distant theory to most students because they are denied any practical application. Our editorial board has faced and succeeded in the challenge of foreseeing consequences of the articles we print and the value and necessity to the entire community of fair reporting and balance of sources. We have learned the importance of the truth, painful and controversial as the truth often is.

That's why it's so disappointing to me when, during journalism conferences and workshops, I hear students from other schools explain that there is no way they could cover the issues being discussed, simply because their administrations would not allow it. Coverage of topics from date rape to ineffective classes is not even considered by many Michigan high school newspaper staffs. This is not because students are incapable of making decisions or taking responsibility for what is printed. The lack of coverage is due to the fact that many school administrators are incapable of "allowing" the Constitutional rights that are preached in classrooms.

about the Letter Club but perhaps it takes more work to come up with comments about the Reptile Lovers' Club.

Names in the news column. Another way to wrap up awards and pass out congratulations to officers, groups, or people in or outside of your school or the student community is a column about people. Be sure this doesn't become a gossip column. Never make obscure comments; every reader should be able to understand who and what you're talking about.

Question-and-answer columns. You are familiar with the Ann Landers and Dear Abby columns. A question-line column can address student concerns on a number of subjects such as career- or community-related topics like "How do I enroll in a study skills program?"

Other ideas for columns. Look at other student and community newspapers for more ideas, such as hobby columns, sports columns (there is no requirement that they have to be on the sports page), humorous columns, anecdotal or historical columns, or guest editorial columns—by famous people, other students, alumni, faculty, administrators, or parents.

Use the same approach toward writing any type of column—research, develop your position, write, think, rewrite if necessary, and then publish.

Reviews

In recent years, student newspapers have started to review not only movies and theater performances, but also new CDs, favorite watering holes and coffee shops, and even computer software and games. When writing reviews, it is important to look at comparisons. For example, if you have two new coffee shops, the focus of the review may be on the quality, flavor, and aroma of their espresso. How do the products differ, if they do? How is the atmosphere of the shops similar or different? How about the appearance and attitude of the staffs? The other menu items?

If you are writing about a new computer game, it may not be necessary to directly compare it with another game. Instead, you might evaluate it on the basis of the excitement in the action it produces, the level of difficulty and challenges it poses, the skill and knowledge needed to play. The evaluation should be based on characteristics that will have meaning to the reader.

Should I Care How You Feel?

How much of yourself should you put into a film review? William Javitz, author of *Understanding Mass Media*, has this to say:

"When attempting film criticism, especially to an audience that does not know you, making statements about yourself is of limited value. If I tell you that a certain film is 'sickening,' that does not mean that you will find it 'sickening'; you might enjoy the film . . . . A common error is to confuse statements about the film with statements about oneself."

296 Chapter Thirteen   Writing for the Editorial Page

A CD review can do a number of things. It should probably talk about the good and not-so-good tracks on the recording, giving the reviewer's reasons for his or her opinions of each track mentioned. In addition, a comprehensive review will also evaluate a CD in terms of the artist's entire body of work, and perhaps compare the CD with similar recordings made by other artists or groups.

A review of a film, television production, or play has to tell what the story is about, but without giving the whole plot away. In addition, such a review may also deal with the following elements:

- **Acting:** Did the actors play their parts in a believable manner? Were they able to express the emotions that the role required?
- **Settings:** Were the settings appropriate to the period in which the production is set? Did they look realistic? In a stage production using understated settings, how did the settings convey something of the mood, atmosphere, or period of the production?
- **Dialogue:** Did the dialogue sound realistic for the time and place of the action? Did the lines sound like things people would actually say to each other?
- **Lighting:** Did the lighting help establish a mood? For a film or television production, were any striking lighting techniques used to convey ideas about characters or situations?
- **Sound:** Could you hear the lines clearly? If there was background music, how did it add to or detract from the production?
- **Direction:** Did all the parts of the production work well together? Was the tone consistent? Was it clear that the director knew the story he or she wanted to tell and how most effectively to tell it?

In addition, in film reviews you may want to discuss such elements as editing, camera techniques, and special effects. The review in the "On Display" on page 297 focuses mainly on theme—that is, the underlying idea or message of the film—comparing it with other, similar films.

Letters to the Editor

The editorial page should always contain a place where readers can react to editorial opinions or comment on subjects that concern them. A letter to the editor must be responsible, based on fact, and signed by the writer. The newspaper has an obligation to verify that the person whose name is on a letter actually wrote it. While newspapers allow the use of pen names

War Is Hell: *King of Hearts* Proves There Is More to War than Violence

by Zack Jemison, Featherduster, *Westlake High School, Austin, Texas*

Might makes right. Or so we are led to believe. The movies, television shows and books of today are filled with bulked-out men fighting people smaller than themselves and coming up, to no big surprise, the victors. But we still haven't found a film that can be identified as the best war movie. Some contenders might be *Apocalypse Now*, *Full Metal Jacket* or *Platoon*. However, the most eligible film for this title is also probably the least known about. I'm talking about the French film, *King of Hearts*.

The movie takes place in France during World War One. A German regiment, complete with a young and eager Adolf Hitler, wires a small town to blow up at midnight. All of the villagers evacuate the town, leaving the inhabitants of the local insane asylum to fend for themselves. Charles Plumpick, a Scottish bird expert, is sent in to disarm the explosives and save the town. When he arrives at the scene, the crazies have taken up the various jobs around town where the townspeople left off.

Through his interaction with the then-lunatics, now-villagers, Plumpick discovers the true depth and nature of war. The killing done in wars is senseless as well as useless. There are no winners in these senseless slaughters, only losers.

I think the most powerful scene of the movie is the one in which the lunatics lock themselves into their asylum, subsequently locking all the danger out. We, like the lunatics, sometimes view locked doors as barriers keeping us in or out, depending upon our location. For the lunatics, the door works as a two-way barrier: as their protection from the outside world, as well as the outside world's protection from them.

This cult film examines the extremely touchy subject of war. Along with the film adaptations of the classic anti-war novels *All Quiet on the Western Front* and *Johnny Got His Gun*, I believe that *King of Hearts* should be recognized as a classic by moviegoers. Though similar to these other works in many ways, it differs in a very important vein. The other two plots primarily deal with the effect the war had on the soldier before, during and after the war. *King of Hearts* examines the war from the standpoint of a spectator. The lead characters, instead of going out and actually fighting the war themselves, witness what has happened to the so-called survivors of the war. I especially liked the way that the soldier, in this case Charles Plumpick, was portrayed as the minority.

I wholeheartedly recommend this amazingly touching war movie to anyone. Although it was made in 1966, the ideas presented remain tried and true. While the movie uses subtitles, they don't make this film more difficult to watch. The ideas expressed are visibly liberal, but hey. Don't refrain from seeing it just because you're a conservative. Diversity builds character.

or initials, all letters should be kept on file for several weeks, whether they are printed or not. If a letter is in bad taste or libelous, you are correct in turning it down. If several letters are received on the same topic, in order to save space, you may select one that is representative and add a note: "We have received several similar letters from . . . ."

Editorial Cartoons

Just as a picture is worth a thousand words, one good editorial cartoon may be worth a thousand editorials. An editorial cartoon is usually simple in design, centered on one topic, well drawn, and timely. Usually it relates to a subject or event familiar to readers in their everyday lives. It may stand alone or tie in with a news article elsewhere in the paper or with the lead editorial. In any event, an editorial cartoon is valuable journalism.

The cartoon in the "On Display" on page 299 appeared in conjunction with the editorial on page 290.

The editorial page can contain a number of elements besides editorials and the paper's masthead. This sample page, from the Brentwood School *Flyer,* also includes an editorial cartoon, a letter from the editor, and a correction from an earlier edition.

Random Opinion Features

Sometimes a paper will want to show various people's opinions on a subject—people not associated with the newspaper. The subject can be anything of general interest; often it is the same subject treated elsewhere on the editorial page. A typical way to handle this information is to use a roving reporter, who asks the same question—for example, "What do you think about seniors' rights to choose their own graduation speaker?"—of five or six people at random. The views of the people interviewed are presented without further comment.

Point-Counterpoint

If you study the editorial pages of leading newspapers, you will see a variety of editorial page elements. Many newspapers are adopting ways to broaden viewpoints beyond those of the staff and editorial writers. A popular technique is to use a point-counterpoint approach, inviting individuals with opposing views on a topic to express them in side-by-side opinion articles. Then, going a step further, the paper may ask four or five people to give a one-paragraph opinion on the same issue, thus ensuring that a variety of viewpoints have been expressed. Most often, the lead editorial of the newspaper—the newspaper's point of view—addresses the same topic. The reader is served through the variety of opinions expressed, and encouraged to look at more than one side of the issue.

Editorial cartoons, such as this one from the Carmel High School *The Hi-Lite,* may either stand alone or be related to an editorial or article elsewhere in the paper.

Mini-torials

A mini-torial is a very, very brief editorial, usually one or two sentences. Like the editorial cartoon, it gets its point across quickly. It usually is written in a humorous manner but conveys a serious message. Readership is quite high, and several mini-torials in each issue accomplish much. It is also something to which all staff members can contribute on an equal basis.

Here is a series of mini-torials from *The Contact Lens*, a student workshop publication at the University of Nebraska:

Awakening Love

How do I love thee, All-State activities. Let me count the ways—one, two, threeee . . . . zzzzzzzzzzz.

—Judy Thompson

Terse Verse

In all the world there's nothing worse
Than editorials set to verse.

—Michelle Grady

Oh Bring Back

To solve the poverty problem, the Federal funds must be brought back from outer space and used in the inner cities.

—Marcia French

Running, Running

There's one thing wrong with the idea of people who jog. They are usually the ones who drive two blocks rather than walk them any other time.

—Joe Hermsen

Open Up

There is a serious problem confronting the world. Why do people lock up their minds and refuse to stimulate themselves with the ideas of others?

—Debbie Rosenwinkel

Statement of Editorial Policy

Most journalists think of themselves as editorialists. But they need to constantly keep in mind the tremendous degree of responsibility that goes with the right to express editorial viewpoints. Most student publications have responsible editorial pages. A statement of editorial policy, such as the one in the "On Display" feature on page 301, can set the tone of an editorial page with the reader.

Wrap-up

Editorials play an important role in today's media. Along with the opportunity journalists have to express opinions comes the obligation to do the needed research. You must understand the diverse points of view and background on an issue before presenting the paper's opinion.

Editorials serve a variety of functions. They may *explain* an issue; try to *persuade* others to support a viewpoint; *respond* to statements or positions of others; *warn* or caution readers, viewers, or listeners about events ahead; *entertain*; *provide leadership* by initiating or encouraging action; or offer *brief comments* on an action or event.

Editorial Policy Named

Hi-Spot, *Waverly High School,*
Waverly, Nebraska

Hi-Spot members will, at all times, be working under the code of ethics that has been set down as journalistic standards. Freedom of the press, honesty, accuracy, impartiality, decency, and equality will be used to benefit reporter and story subjects. Never will a statement be considered true just because an accusation is made.

All editorials will reflect views that are backed by research and fact. Questions on story content, editorial policy and controversial issues will be interpreted by the executive board which will consist of the editor, managing editor, photography editor, page editors, business manager, advertising manager, and adviser.

Hi-Spot editorials will never be by-lined because they represent the ideas of a part of the staff with whom others may disagree. The **Hi-Spot** will protect the rights of any person submitting editorials. The executive board will decide when editorials are suitable for publication.

All letters to the editor will require a signature (or signatures) of those who submitted them. The names may not be published but pen names will be substituted upon request of the writer. Again, signatures are required on the original for the protection of the **Hi-Spot**.

Speak-outs and letters to the editor are encouraged from staff and non-staff members alike. All let-ters must be signed and turned in to the mailbox provided in the journalism room (room 18S) or to a **Hi-Spot** staff member. The **Hi-Spot** reserves the right to edit all letters, with regard to libel, without changing the substance of the letter. The **Hi-Spot** also reserves the right not to publish any letter for incriminating reasons or that person will be given a chance to respond in the same issue. The **Hi-Spot** will not publish obscene or libelous material; rulings will be made by the executive board.

Money for the publication of the **Hi-Spot** will come from advertising sales. No ads are to appear on the cover page nor the editorial page.

In accordance with Nebraska law, staff reporters may not be required to show a completed story to the source for the source's approval. If a question comes up about a story, the source will be contacted to verify information and direct quotes.

The **Hi-Spot** will not reveal a minor's name in a story (a Nebraska minor being any person under the age of 19 years old) who attends Waverly High School and is involved in a felony crime. But the **Hi-Spot** may include the name of students involved in misdemeanors serious enough to stimulate permanent expulsion from Waverly High School.

One good way to organize an editorial is to begin with an *introduction* to ensure your audience understands the background of your subject. Then, clearly state the *position* you are taking. Following that, provide clear and concise *detail* or background materials that strongly support your position, and address directly or indirectly the possible positions of others. *Conclude* your editorial by restating your position and indicating your recommendations or solutions.

Newspaper editorial pages may consist of a number of elements in addition to editorials: editorial columns, editorial cartoons, reviews, other types of guest columns, opinion features, and point-counterpoint features expressing diverse views on a specific subject. Mini-torials, short one- or two-sentence commentaries stating a strong position on a well-known topic, are useful editorial elements in many publications, as are brief opinion sections that use photos of several individuals giving their opinions on an issue of the day. Elements like these, along with letters to the editor and guest editorials, help open the opinion pages of the newspaper to the readers.

Student publications should develop and communicate their editorial policies to their readers, and should provide ways for those with differing positions to respond to editorials and other opinion features. The editorial pages should stimulate thought and discussion and help resolve important issues facing your readership.

To ensure that they serve the important functions for which they were intended, editorials require as much homework and research as news, sports, or any other form of journalism.

Evaluation Checklist: *Editorial*

✓ Is the topic a suitable one to take a stand on?

✓ Are there enough specific points to make about that topic?

✓ Does the editorial have a clear purpose, and is that purpose established early in the piece?

✓ Does the editorial follow the introduction/reaction/details/conclusion organization or some other reasonable format?

✓ Is the editorial free from grammatical errors and in accordance with the publication and AP stylebooks?

Evaluation Checklist: *Column*

✓ Does the topic lend itself well to a column?

✓ Does the column have a tone—light, serious, humorous, angry—that is appropriate to the subject matter?

✓ Are anecdotes or other specific examples included when appropriate to make points?

✓ Have all facts—names, dates, and the like—been checked for accuracy?

✓ Is the column free from grammatical errors and in accordance with the publication and AP stylebooks?

Evaluation Checklist: *Review*

✓ Does the review deal with a film, TV show, place, or item that the writer is clearly familiar with?

✓ Does the review explain the basics of the thing being reviewed, such as the plot of a movie or the rules for a game?

✓ Does the review discuss some of the item's specific strengths and weaknesses, such as good and bad songs on a CD or strong and weak characters in a book?

✓ Does the review make recommendations based on the audience's interests as well as the writer's feelings?

✓ Is the story free from grammatical errors and in accordance with the publication and AP stylebooks?

On Assignment

Individual Activities

1. Write a short definition or explanation of each of the following terms.

   editorial   editorial column
   editorial page   editorial policy
   masthead   mini-torial
   point-counterpoint   subjective writing

2. To test your critical thinking, write an editorial or column on one of these questions:

   a. How appropriate is it for a school publication that is partially financed by public funds to endorse candidates for public office? To endorse candidates for the board of education?

   b. Should all editorials express the position of the newspaper, or only of the writer? Should they be signed?

3. Research the most recent elections in your community. Many people feel that the candidates who receive editorial endorsements from the media have an edge over their opponents. Find out who was endorsed by the newspaper. Find out who, if anyone, was endorsed by your local radio or television stations. Did those individuals win? Interview the candidates who won, the candidates who lost, and the editorial writers to determine how important they believe the endorsement was. Now use the research to write an editorial that expresses your opinion on this subject.

4. Look at the editorials and/or columns in an issue of your school newspaper. Now, examine the news content of the same issue.

   a. Are there background stories to provide information on the topics covered in the editorials and/or timely columns? If so, clip and mount them.

   b. What evidence do you find that the writers of the editorials or columns did their homework before writing? Write a paragraph to explain your evidence.

   c. Does the editorial explain, lead, entertain, answer, persuade, warn, criticize, praise, or briefly comment? Write a paragraph explaining your answer and a one-sentence summary of the key position taken.

   d. Rewrite one of the editorials or columns, taking a different approach and an opposite position. Write a one-sentence summary of your position at the end of the editorial or column.

5. Invite the local newspaper editor to visit your class and explain how editorial decisions are made. Discuss the following: Does the newspaper use an editorial board? What is the reporter's role in editorial decisions? Does the paper have a written editorial policy? What is the role of the publisher or owner? Who actually writes the editorials? What kind of research does the editorial writer usually do?

6. Write an essay comparing the editorial pages of your local newspaper, your school newspaper, *The Wall Street Journal*, and *USA Today*. What are the differences in the elements used? Is more than one page used? What types of columns appear? First make a chart showing the contents of each one. Analyze the differences you find. Why do they exist? Clip the editorial pages to your essay.

7. Using the last issue of your school newspaper, clip five news, sports, and/or feature articles and mount them on separate sheets of paper. Now, write one or more mini-torials for each story.

8. Make a list of editorial summary sentences on which you would like to write. Submit the ideas to your instructor, who will select one of the topics. Write the editorial. Mark each key editorial section on your copy. At the top of the page, identify the type of editorial you wrote. Attach a summary of the research done before writing.

9. Assume you have total freedom to select a type of editorial column you want to write for the school paper. Prepare a list of five topics that fit the category you have selected (for example, opinion, fashion, profile, entertainment). Your instructor will select one for you to write.

10. Write a review of a current movie or television show that you have recently seen. Then find one or more reviews of the same film or show in a local newspaper. How does your review compare with the professional ones? Are there points either you or the professional writers should have covered but didn't? Make copies of all of the reviews and discuss their merits in class.

11. Working in pairs, select a controversial topic of current interest to other students. Each of you should take an opposing point of view. Write editorials expressing your views. Then ask six non-journalism students to write a one-paragraph summary opinion on the same issue without telling them your positions. Discuss in class how these viewpoints differ, the pros and cons of stimulating discussion through this technique, and how the views of the students compare to those of the editorial writers. Would you change your editorial positions after hearing the discussion? Why or why not?

Team Activities

12. Your team is to be an editorial board setting editorial policy. After careful discussion, write out an editorial policy for your school newspaper on a major issue, such as raising or lowering the legal age for drinking alcoholic beverages; endorsing political candidates in the next election; requiring that no student activities, such as pep rallies or athletic events, be allowed to interrupt the academic schedule. Be sure you include the reasons for your decision. Compare your policy to those of other teams. Discuss and resolve differences on similar topics. Now research and write an editorial that expresses the position of your editorial board.

13. Working as a team, develop a new look for the editorial page of your school newspaper. Prepare a mock-up, cutting similar elements from various newspapers to show the desired visual image. Write a brief essay on your team's approach, explaining why you chose your design.

When Ed Fischer sits down to draw an editorial cartoon each evening, he doesn't stare at a sheet of clean paper and wait for inspiration to strike.

"It's something that's intuitive," said the syndicated editorial cartoonist, based at the *Rochester* (Minn.) *Post-Bulletin*. "I don't think anybody can explain how you come up with ideas."

But the ideas come to Fischer because he prepares carefully for his daily two-hour stint when an idea is transformed into words and pictures. Fisher wouldn't last long at his job if he didn't prepare carefully, since there are only about two hundred jobs for full-time editorial cartoonists at U. S. dailies.

Fischer browses through newspapers, reading national and local news stories. By late in the day, he has picked the general topic he feels is the day's most important news event. Then he watches the evening news shows on television. By that time he is ready to put his wit and artistic talent to work.

"I think every cartoonist has the urge to sit down and put his or her fantasies in graphic form. But an editorial cartoonist has to make a point," Fischer said.

Although he never earned a degree, Fischer attended classes at three colleges. "I always took things that were related to art and journalism, and that's what cartooning is—a combination of both," he said.

With so few cartooning jobs available, Fischer began his career in advertising, a field he saw as "kind of related." He made drawings to "get through to the common person." All the while, though, he pursued a cartooning job.

Persistence paid off. The *Minneapolis Star* began to buy cartoons from him after the paper's cartoonist took an interest in Fischer's work. Soon Fischer was selling the paper three cartoons a week.

"The big things I can offer a paper," he said, "are things that are area-wide, state-wide, or city-wide.

Those are my best cartoons. Everybody can relate to them. There is a lot happening in your own area.

"There are some great cartoonists who are not syndicated," said Fischer, who is himself syndicated to 80 newspapers. "I believe there are many good jobs held by people who are paying attention to what's happening locally."

With so few jobs on daily newspapers, Fischer admits prospects aren't all that bright. "It's very difficult to get into this profession, but it's not impossible," he said.

Fischer believes that sometimes just being able to poke fun at someone is its own reward. "Even if high school and college cartoonists don't go on to become professional editorial cartoonists, they can have a lot of fun with it," he said.

Even though he likes to make a point in his work, Fischer also wants to make people laugh. So he doesn't always try for biting satire. Once or twice a week, he'll do something a little softer.

Fischer has also produced a number of books on different, less topical subjects: *You're No Spring Chicken* is about getting older, and *Minnesota: A Cold Love Affair* is about what makes his home state unique. Both demonstrate Fischer's unique cartooning voice.

Other Aspects of Scholastic Journalism

Chapter Fourteen

Producing the Yearbook

Chapter Fifteen

Writing for Radio and Television

Chapter Sixteen

Understanding and Using Public Relations

Chapter Seventeen

Handling Finances: Advertising and Business

Producing the Yearbook

Key Terms

ladder diagram

theme copy

caption

modular design

Key Concepts

After you reading this chapter, you should

- understand the roles a yearbook serves

- know how to set up a system for financing the yearbook

- know how to plan sections and spreads in a yearbook

- be able to recognize and write strong yearbook copy

- know the basics of yearbook spread design

- understand the roles of the various yearbook staff members

The cost of the average yearbook today is between $30 and $50, but its real value will be measured in years to come when you want to relive high school memories. In recent years sales of yearbooks have been declining as fewer students see the benefit of buying a book. However, schools are constantly getting calls from people who graduated twenty or thirty years ago. "I didn't buy a yearbook before I graduated, but I'd really like to get one now," they tell the principal's secretary. The fact is that books more than a few years old are rarely available.

As you take on the responsibility of producing a yearbook, remember that you're producing a book with a value that may not be realized for a long time. You have to anticipate what will make the book valuable for all students—seeing themselves in the book—and then you have to work hard to convince them of that value. Along the way, you have to realize that the yearbook is more than just a few photos and words thrown on a page. The yearbook serves as a historical record, a picture book, a public relations tool, and an educational experience.

As a historical document, no other publication in the history of the school will record the activities of students like the yearbook. In fact, in years to come, if it's not covered in the yearbook, it won't be remembered. Like the *Guinness Book of World Records* and the *World Almanac*, the yearbook serves to document the facts, scores, figures, and dates of the school year. Since these facts won't be recorded anywhere else for general use, the yearbook will serve as a reference book.

The yearbook is also a picture book. No other source, including the community or school newspaper, has as thorough coverage of the year through photos. For most events, it's the photos that tell the story. And the people who are in the photos are the people who will use the yearbook most. The copy serves to supplement those photos and explain in detail what the photos can't.

Another function of the yearbook is as a public relations tool. Administrators and businesses love to have copies of the yearbook in their offices as a sign of their support for a school. These businesses are potential financial supporters of the yearbook, and somewhere along the line you will probably need their help.

Finally, the yearbook provides an educational experience for those who work on it. Few other classes offer the real-world experience of producing a tangible product that will be remembered for decades to come. Experiences in writing, editing, photography, design, production, desktop publishing, team work, leadership, and attention to deadlines make the yearbook class a unique experience.

As a yearbook staff member, you will be influencing the way this school year will be remembered in years to come. It's a serious responsibility and one that you shouldn't take lightly.

Getting Finances in Order

Even though it may not be all that creative, the first task any yearbook staff has to take on is figuring out how to finance their product. While costs will change for this year's book depending on printing cost increases and changes in the format of the book, using the cost of last year's book will give you a starting point for budgeting. Then you have to plan on how to raise enough money to finance the book, including printing and production as well as photo and computer supplies.

Funding of the Yearbook

The following sources are the usual methods of funding the school yearbook. Your adviser will guide the search for funds.

School funds. The first place to start looking for funds is within the school district's budget. Some schools allocate funds to be used for the production of the yearbook or for photo and computer supplies. Besides these directly budgeted funds, districts may also use funds from sources such as school portraits as a way to offset costs. Use of these discretionary funds is strictly up to the campus administration.

Although using school budget or discretionary funds can be a dependable source of money, few schools entirely finance a yearbook this way. Most schools use book sales, advertising, and other fund-raisers as well.

Yearbook sales. The most obvious source of funding is through the sale of the book itself. Students will pay over $100 for a pair of shoes, but you'll have to do market research to find out what they will pay for a yearbook. At the beginning of the year, after last year's book has been delivered, survey students. Will they buy a yearbook this year? If so, how much are they willing to pay? Using last year's cost is always a start and all cost increases must be justified.

To give students incentive to buy books early—and thus get earlier access to monies—many staffs begin selling around the beginning of the year. They offer the yearbook at a discount during the first week of sales; the cost of the book then goes up as the delivery date approaches. For example, you might sell the yearbook for $30 during the first week of sales to encourage people to buy. After that week and until the end of the first semester, the cost might be $35. After the first semester and until the end of the year, the book might cost $45. When the books are delivered, you can sell any extra copies for $50. Selling individual copies will often come close to paying for the printing of the book.

Typical Yearbook Budget

Expenses

Printing...	$15,000
256 pages (16 pages of four-color)	
One color cover + foil	
Photo supplies.......................................	$3,000
Computer/production supplies..........................	$1,000
Total estimated cost	**$19,000**

Revenue

Book sales

Opening week $30/copy..............................	$1,500
First semester $35/copy..............................	$8,750
Remainder year $45/copy	$2,250
Delivery $50/copy	$1,000
Ad sales..	$7,000
Total estimated revenue...............................	**$20,500**

As you're planning for yearbook sales, don't forget to market your product. Put up posters around the school with samples of the pages that will appear in the book. Send out press releases to the local newspapers and radio and television stations. Get on the school announcements and marquee. Do the same when the book is delivered. In short, make the yearbook a school event in which everyone wants to participate. Some schools have had great success selling and then later delivering the book at a school dance or schoolwide party.

Advertising. Selling ads is an additional source of revenue for many schools. The amount of income that can be raised selling ads varies greatly depending on the aggressiveness of the staff and the willingness of the community to support school activities. Schools that are well organized and that believe the yearbook is a way for businesses to generate revenue can raise several thousand dollars in advertising sales. The key to success is having a professional, organized approach and making the purchase of a yearbook ad different from other fund-raising activities. After all, businesses who advertise in the yearbook will have their business remembered for years to come. (For more tips on selling ads, see Chapter Seventeen.)

Selling ads early in the year is one way to ensure having enough money to produce a quality yearbook.

Senior ads and personal ads are another way for the yearbook staff to generate revenue and for individuals to purchase space in the yearbook without jeopardizing unbiased coverage of school events. For example, a graduating senior's parents could purchase a quarter-page ad as a tribute to their daughter. Such ads can be colorful and include pictures of the individual that wouldn't fit anywhere else in the book. By expanding coverage through this sort of ad, you can ensure that more people will buy a yearbook.

Fund-raisers. One final source of monies can be various kinds of fund-raisers. You might choose to make holiday greeting cards, using production skills you've learned working on the yearbook. You can sell candy. You could produce programs for the football team, the drama department, or the band. You might sell subscriptions to magazines. Fund-raisers of this type can be distracting to staff members who are trying to produce a yearbook, so they need to be very well organized. Encourage your fellow staff members to participate and help them understand the importance of raising money to adequately fund the yearbook. The more money you have, the more options you have, such as expanding coverage, increasing your page count, adding color, and so on.

Planning the Yearbook

With the financing plan taken care of, you can get on with thinking about the yearbook itself. Your underlying goal must be to ensure that as many students as possible are included. After all, the more students included, the more likely they are to purchase a book and to support the program.

As you begin to plan how the yearbook will be organized, start with, but don't be limited to, last year's book. The number of pages in the book, the number of pages in each section, and even the number and type of sections can be exactly the same as last year or radically different.

Determining the Sections

The most popular way to divide a yearbook is into sections that ensure balanced coverage of school events, students, and faculty/staff. While some staffs organize their book chronologically, most divide their book into some combination of the following sections: student life, academics, clubs/organizations, sports, and people.

Student life. The student life section, usually the first section in the book, includes coverage of people and activities not included in other sections. Events such as homecoming, topics such as pep rallies and people working, and even things such as favorite pets or favorite vacations might be found in the student life section. This section also gives you a chance to cover people who aren't directly involved in school activities and who might otherwise not be covered in the yearbook, such as the owner of the corner drugstore where students wait for buses.

Academics. Coverage of academics—the real reason you're at school— should go beyond the obvious. Look for those teachers who do unique activities or students who stand out, but don't forget that many other people have interesting stories, too. Include the biology teacher who's been teaching for thirty-five years or the person who missed being in the top 10 percent of the class by one person. The biggest challenge to academics coverage is taking pictures that are more than just students sitting behind desks or teachers working at blackboards. Getting unique coverage means having photographers always on the lookout for picture opportunities, even to the extent of carrying their cameras to class regularly. Keep your eyes open for teachers hosting special activities such as a Hawaiian luau or a class full of computer science students trying to work wearing the "clean room suit" garb of computer chip makers.

Organizations and teams. The clubs/organizations and sports sections are the easiest to complete because coverage is dictated by the activities of the various groups. However, you still have to work closely with them to get good, action photographs of things that are going on. Learning of an event after the fact means you have missed an opportunity to cover something that can never be re-created.

Provide coverage of these groups that is different from anything done in past years. Look for things that make this year unique. After all, people aren't paying $35 to read the same stories they read in last year's book or to see the same photos. If your cheerleaders got new uniforms, find out why. If your band used an electric guitar during football halftime shows for the first time, find out why. Explore why the student council went to a local nursing home to work with senior citizens.

Be sure to leave space when planning this section for the group shots that ensure coverage of a significant number of students. Or make plans to include the group shots in another area of the book such as the index.

When planning the people section, consider going beyond portrait shots to include interesting personality profiles.

People. The people section, which includes portrait shots of everyone in the school, including faculty and staff, doesn't stop with the portrait shots. It's another opportunity for you to expand coverage by including, for example, personality profiles of the all-state violin player, a student who traveled to the Great Wall of China, or a student who placed first in a Special Olympics event.

Don't stop your coverage with personality profiles. Consider including the results of polls and surveys. Poll students about their favorite vacation spot, fast-food restaurant, television show, computer game, teacher, and class. Work with your student artists to turn this information into interesting art (infographics) to supplement photos and stories.

Also use this section to include stories and photos that don't fit neatly in other sections or to cover topics that don't warrant a full spread of coverage. Some schools choose not to include anything but portraits in their people section and that may be adequate, but by including stories and action photos, you get people to look at pages they otherwise wouldn't ever see.

Assigning pages to sections. To figure out how many pages to devote to each section, use the following formula. Take the total number of pages minus:

- number of theme development pages: title page (page one; also includes the volume number of the book, the name of the school, the school's address and phone number and the number of students attending the school); opening and closing pages (the pages that introduce and conclude the book; division pages (the pages or spreads between each section)

- number of advertising pages you plan to sell
- number of pages in index

Equals:

- total number of pages available for sections

Once you know the number of section pages available, use the following percentages to figure out how many pages to devote to each section.

Student life	25–30%
Academics	10–15%
Clubs/Organizations	15–20%
Sports	15–20%
People	15–35%

When you plot out exact page counts, you'll find that you have the most flexibility in the student life and academics sections. The number and type of groups can dictate, to some degree, the number of pages in the sports and clubs/organizations sections, and the number of portraits can dictate the number of pages in the people section. However, don't be totally constrained by those limitations. You can make the mug shots smaller or larger to increase or decrease the number of pages required for the people section. You can combine the groups in different ways or run the group shots as part of the index to have more flexibility with the sports and clubs/organizations sections.

Using a Ladder Diagram

Planning how many pages you intend to include in the book and how many pages each section should have is only the beginning of organizing coverage. After you've mapped out the overall organization for each section, start planning what is going to be on each individual spread, since facing pages in a yearbook are always related. Decide what the overall topic for the spread will be—what will be its unifying theme. For example, if your yearbook is to include 48 pages of student life coverage beginning on page 10 in the book, decide what's going to go on pages 10–11, 12–13, and so on until you have a plan for each spread in the book.

To decide what's going on each spread, again begin by looking at last year's book. Undoubtedly, there are things you covered last year that you'll want to cover this year. But don't stop there. Look at older yearbooks. Look at yearbooks from other schools. Poll students and find out what they would like to see in this year's book that they didn't see in last year's book.

Signature #1

1 title page — black + white — 1st deadline	
2 opening spread—4-color photo (bio) and intro copy	**3** — 1st deadline
4 student life division page—4-color photos + copy	**5** — 1st deadline
6 student life: Places to go —black + white + copy	**7** — 1st deadline
8 student life: People to know	**9** — 1st deadline

Natural double-page spread

10 student life: ??	**11**
12 student life: The best part of the day— 4-color & copy	**13**
14 student life: Learning to drive—black + white w/copy	**15**
16 student life: ??	

A ladder diagram is a useful aid in outlining and organizing the contents of a yearbook.

Figure out ways to expand coverage and to include more students in the book.

As you begin mapping out a plan, write it down on a ladder diagram, a "map" of the yearbook provided by your yearbook publisher or one you make yourself. First, write in all the fixed pages, including the title page, opening, division pages, closing, and other pages that have fixed content such as ads and index. Then write down the topic for each spread on the ladder diagram and whether it will be in black and white or color; post it for everyone to see. It's also helpful to code the spreads by deadline. For example, you might color-code the first deadline with red ink. That way, everyone will know that pages listed on the ladder in red must be turned in on the first deadline.

Choosing and Developing a Theme

Along with developing a map for the yearbook early in the year, you need also to develop a theme, a unifying concept that gives the book a unique personality. As with any good novel, the theme is a common thread that reappears throughout the entire book to provide continuity for the reader.

When selecting a theme, realize that it will set a tone for the entire book. It can be built around a word, a phrase, a color, or a graphic element. It should not be gimmicky or cute but should be applicable to the year. It also should be easily developed and easily understood by the reader without jeopardizing coverage.

Coming up with a theme is rarely easy. Since the theme sets the tone for the entire book—subtle, sophisticated, fun, spirited, or even serious—it requires creativity and brainstorming to decide on a good one. Once you have an idea, play with it. Try using a dictionary of idioms or phrases to help you find phrases that fit the concept you're trying to convey. Look around the school for what will make this year unique. Look at other year-books to see how they have handled themes.

Sometimes themes are obvious. For example, if your school is adding one hundred new classrooms and dozens of new teachers, the phrase "Growing Pains" may serve as a theme. Or you might choose to use a pile of bricks as a graphic device. While themes that are stated with a catch-phrase such as "Look Who's Talking," "Try This On for Size," or "Let the Spirit Move You" are the most common, there is no rule saying that year-books must have catchphrase themes. Themes can be developed strictly with graphics or with concepts.

Once you've narrowed the theme concept down to a couple of ideas, begin exploring how you can develop each of them. Translate your ideas into copy, photographs, and page designs. Pick the theme you like best and try writing some theme copy for it. Think of photos that will support it. Sketch out some graphic elements that will accent the theme without dis-tracting from it.

All the theme pages in the book should stand out as separate from the rest of the book with a bold design that grabs the reader's attention. Through graphic development and copy, the theme should appear on

- the cover
- the endsheets (which appear inside the front and back covers)
- the title page
- the opening section (the first section to fully develop the theme through copy, graphics and photos)
- the division pages between the different sections
- the closing.

Possible Yearbook Themes

It Must Mean Something	Ever Been . . .
Where Do You Fit In?	No Boundaries
Outstanding in Our Field	Got It Made
Rock On	Stay Tuned
Welcome to the Real World	People Are Talking
Eye of the Beholder	In a Different Light
Still Waters Run Deep	Just Out of Curiosity
Some Like It Hot	It All Adds Up
It's a Matter of Perspective	Life Is How You Change It

Also consider writing theme spin-offs for each section in the book. Although not required, spin-offs are an easy way to carry the theme throughout the book creatively. For example, if your theme is "Stealing the Spotlight," you could use "In the Light" as the theme spin-off for the student life section; "Sharing the Spotlight" for the people section; "Sore Spot" for the sports section; and "On the Spot" for the clubs section. A dictionary of idioms and a thesaurus can be very helpful in coming up with spin-offs.

While you'll spend a great deal of time developing the theme, it does not appear on every page in the book directly. That is, there is no need to explicitly state or graphically depict the theme on every page. However, in the folio at the bottom of the page, which contains the page number and other information such as the section name, page topic, or page designer, you may choose to carry through part of your theme with graphics. For example, if you use a dotted rule line on the cover in your theme logo, you can use a similar dotted rule line in your folio.

Inevitably, as you explore development of your top theme ideas, one idea will stand out as the most popular or the most applicable to the school year. That will be the theme you decide to work with.

Theme copy. Theme copy is unlike any other copy in the yearbook. It serves solely to develop the theme and help readers understand how the theme applies to the school year. It may or may not include direct or indirect quotes from sources. It may even read more like advertising copy, with phrases rather than complete sentences. It should be easy and enjoyable to read and should clearly explain how the theme fits the year.

For example, if your school has had a surprising and unusual year in many respects and you choose "Just Imagine" as your theme, your opening copy may read like the following from the Winston Churchill High School, Potomac, Maryland, yearbook, *Finest Hours.*

Just Imagine

Starting school at 7:25 A.M. with each class ending a minute earlier.

Coming to school late and finding a parking space up close, thanks to the new policy.

Studying countless vocabulary words and then finding out a new SAT with no antonym section was developed by the Educational Testing Service.

Having undefeated varsity football, boys' soccer, wrestling, and girls' tennis teams in the regular season.

Seeing your teachers dressed up as anything from a lobster to a jack-in-the-box and being interrupted during class singing "Jack-O-Lantern."

Imagine all this and more!

Theme copy, however, doesn't stop, or really even start, with large copy blocks such as this. The headline and captions on the theme pages should also reflect the theme, and the theme should appear in the copy block on every division page. The division page shown in the "On Display" feature on pages 320 and 321 has as its headline a spin-off from the overall yearbook theme, "It's Your Move."

The theme: A few final words. As the book begins to take shape, periodically do a check to make sure you're covering the essentials of theme development.

- Does the theme reflect the school year?
- Is the theme copy interesting? Does it explain how the theme fits the year?
- Are the photographs on the theme pages some of the best in the book?
- Is the design of the theme pages unique, yet unified?
- Is the theme depicted graphically on the cover, endsheets, title page, opening, division pages, and closing?

The Yearbook Spread

Just about every spread in the yearbook will contain several photos and photo captions as well as a certain amount of copy. These elements then need to be drawn together into a layout. If all the parts are done well, the end result is an effective yearbook spread.

On Display

from Hialeah High School, Hialeah, Florida

This division page, from the Hialeah High School *Hiways,* carries a headline based on the overall book theme, "It's Your Move."

Organizations

Section Editor:
Anita Palomino

B rightening an elderly man's day is sophomore Yuvonnie Scott on behalf of the Sorrota club.

130

It's your move!

-*Moving the community*-

With the vast amount of clubs that existed in the school, practically all interests were represented in one club or another. Clubs established their goals and were formed as soon as the year began. Some organizations focused on community service, while the purpose of others was to inform students, make changes, or provide a place where people of common interests could gather.

The reestablishment of the Interclub Council Association allowed club presidents to join and work on major projects, such as the effort to replant the school's patio that was destroyed by Hurricane Andrew.

The extent to which a student was active in the community was the extent to which that student made his move.

Clubs took advantage of Club Fair Day to recruit members. President senior Antonio Delgado and junior Irene Lui help senior Rebecca Valle and junior Victor Puyada sign up for Key Club.

Senior Yetlanezi Mato can not escape senior Gaby Rodriguez from tapping her to make her membership in A.T.C. official.

131

Organizations

Copy

Writing yearbook copy is much like writing feature stories for the news-paper. Yearbook stories should be lively and full of colorful verbs and nouns and descriptive adjectives. The copy should help readers relive the year each time they read the copy.

Inevitably, as you start writing copy, the question will come up as to why the yearbook can't just be full of pictures. "Who ever reads the copy anyway?" staff members may ask. The truth is that few students do read the copy when they pick up their yearbooks. They look at the pictures and read the captions. But yearbook copy isn't written for the present; it's writ-ten to help fulfill the yearbook's role as a historical record of the school year. If the book uses good reporting, good interview style and research, and good editing, one day the stories will become as valuable, if not more valuable, than the pictures.

The most common fault staffs have when assigning yearbook stories is that the assignments are not specific enough. It's easy to look at a ladder diagram showing that the story on pep rallies is on page 14 and then request that someone write a story on pep rallies. Inevitably, a writer with such an assignment will go out and get quotes like, "The pep rallies were a great way to show school spirit," or "They were a lot of fun." Of course quotes like these tell nothing about the pep rallies, why the school had pep rallies, how many people attended, what the goal of the pep rallies was, and so on.

Reporters should strive to know why things were the way they were. A staff discussion prior to the reporter going out to get the story can give a better focus to the kind of information wanted. Instead of asking, "Did you like the pep rallies?" which inevitably results in a useless one-word answer such as "Yes," the reporter could ask, "Why did you attend the pep rallies?" (Or "Why didn't you attend the pep rallies?") The response to this and other open-ended questions will elicit responses that give more infor-mation about what went on in the pep rallies and help form a verbal description of those rallies. Answers to such questions will also help the writer develop a story that will aid the reader in remembering what the year was like.

Good leads and good writing are as important in the yearbook as in any other publication. For example, in the student life section of the yearbook, you might have a story about what hairstyles students were exploring dur-ing the year. A story about getting a new hairstyle could begin with a lead such as the following.

> The blades came closer and closer to her neck. She tried to remain calm, but her voice began to quiver.

Such verbal descriptions will entice readers into the copy, entertaining them while they relive the school year.

But contemporary yearbook copy is more than just a collection of feature stories. In fact, some yearbooks are not using conventional copy at all in one or two sections of the yearbook. Instead, they're using long photo captions that do significantly more than just tell what's going on in the photo. They answer the how and why questions that would traditionally have been answered in a story. Such captions, along with sidebars such as top ten lists, bulleted quotes from a number of students, or survey results, tell the story. Together these elements give details that help paint a picture of what the year was like.

Headlines. Copy blocks and sidebars don't tell the entire story. The headline is important because it serves to tell part of the story while grabbing the reader's attention. Even if students read nothing but the headline, they should end up knowing something about the topic and what happened during the school year.

Many headlines are just one line:

> Unexpected Events Lead to Record-Breaking Year

Some, however, contain a main headline and a secondary headline:

> Students Developed Their Own Style
> Artistic expression was provided by a variety of clubs

Photos

Without good photos, a yearbook can be average at best. It is the photos that give the yearbook life. But most yearbook photography is pretty poor. While staffs are willing to write, edit, and rewrite a story a dozen times, rarely, if ever, do they reshoot or reprint photos, something that should become an accepted part of yearbook routine.

A good yearbook photograph is one of someone doing something unusual. It must be high in technical quality—that is, in focus, not too dark or light, and so on. It must show people, and those people should be doing something besides staring at the camera. The more action the better, and the more people the better. People want to see pictures of themselves and their friends.

Good photographic coverage should be included with the initial planning of the book. In fact, some entire spreads may be dictated by events that lend themselves to good photographic coverage, such as the football season or a drama production.

Some staffs design spreads and then find photos to fit. While this does save time, it also sometimes forces page designers to put horizontal photos in vertical spots and vice versa or to use inferior photos in the dominant spot on the spread, two things that inevitably generate poor-quality spreads. It is better to select the photos and then design the spread; however, in terms of getting all the pages completed on time, this may not be realistic. As a compromise, some staffs will come up with 8–12 designs for each section, using a variety of photo shapes and sizes. After they've selected the photos, all they have to do is pick the layout in which they work best. The spread in the "On Display" on pages 326 and 327 is from the student life section of a yearbook. It uses a simple design and a strong vertical, dominant photo for its effectiveness. The sidebar also adds interest.

Photo Captions

Many people read the photo captions on a spread and nothing else. So every photo caption should fulfill these two goals: to explain what is going on in the photo and to add information.

The first sentence in the caption, the one that explains the activity in the photo, should be written in present tense. As part of this first bit of information, include the names of all easily recognizable people, but don't begin every caption with a name. Other sentences that add information should be written in past tense. This additional information can take the form of statistical information or could be a direct quote from someone involved in the action.

This caption accompanied a photo of two runners:

> **Joining in with the daily practice, Coach Napoli and senior Elizabeth Dominguez begin a two mile run. The Cross Country team practiced five days a week.**

And this one told about a photo of a long line of uncomfortable-looking students:

> **On a warm August evening, freshmen stand in line waiting patiently to receive their schedules. Over 1,131 freshmen registered for the new school year.**

Remember that the photo caption is important. It is one more place where you can increase coverage and get more people in the yearbook.

Layout and Design

You will find a complete discussion of layout and design principles and procedures in Chapter Ten. But the following rules are some basic points to keep in mind:

The first rule of yearbook design is that the content of the page dictates how the page should be designed. The content must be the principal element on the page.

To design a yearbook spread using basic modular design, which keeps stories and photos in rectangular, easy-to-visualize blocks, begin by establishing a column structure. Dividing the spread into between 6 and 24 columns automatically gives you a framework within which to work. Once the columns are established, every element on the page should fall within—not between—them.

Then begin placing the photos on the spread, starting with the dominant photo. This photo should be dominant not only in size (at least 2–2 1/2 times as large as any other photo on the page) but also in content: It should be the highest-quality and most relevant photo on the page. The dominant photo can be placed across the gutter, but be careful to crop photos so that no one's face falls in the gutter. With the dominant photo in position, place a subordinate photo of contrasting size and shape. For example, if your dominant photo was large and vertical, the next photo you place should be small and horizontal. This maintains visual variety.

With two photos on the page, you should have begun to form one of the unifying elements of a yearbook spread—the *eyeline,* one pica of horizontal white space that goes across the spread. If the dominant photo is horizontal, the top of it will begin the formation of the eyeline. If it's vertical, the first subordinate photo placed in relation to it will begin the formation of the eyeline. The eyeline should fall either above or below the halfway mark on the spread and can be broken by the vertical dominant or other vertical element on the page. However, do not break the eyeline by only one or two picas. If you're going to break it, really break it—by at least eight picas.

Continue placing the photos on the page in a clockwise or counter-clockwise direction until the spread contains five to seven good photos, each either above or below the eyeline. Remember to save space for each photo to have a caption on the outside of the spread, touching the photo it represents. It's better to leave too much space for a caption than not enough. A caption is at least five picas tall and about twenty picas wide although longer and skinnier captions will work effectively as well when carefully integrated into the design of the page. Also save space for the copy block, if you have one, and the headline. Remember that all captions,

The clear and simple design of this spread from the student life section of West Henderson High School *Westwind* is built around two strong verticals—the dominant photo and the sidebar quote.

■ ■ ■
POST IT
Advertising for the homecoming dance, Student Council members Emily Shelton and Karen Coachman put up a poster outside the cafeteria. The dance drew a large crowd.

■ ■ ■
SQUEAKY CLEAN
To raise money for the Vocational-Industrial Clubs of America, junior Jeremy Stepp and sophomore Matt Blumm wash cars after school. VICA also sponsored a spaghetti dinner.

■ ■ ■
ANTE UP
Outside the cafeteria at lunch, freshmen Chris Thickett, Craig Mummert, Ben Newsom and Kurtis Backs enjoy a game of cards. The students sometimes resumed their games after school.

14 ▪ Student Life/After Hours ▪

DOWN –TO– DETAILS

"All of a sudden, I fell, or thought I did, and then it happened. One person jumped on me and then four more. The way band members pile on is simple. They slam you on the ground, and then they jump on you. Seniors especially pile on to initiate you."

— Aden Guthrie

photos, and copy blocks must fall within the column structure. Avoid placing captions between photos or overprinting captions on top of photos—inevitably, they are hard to read.

After you have the copy, headline, photos, and captions in place, add the graphics touches you've chosen earlier to give the whole section a sense of

Working Overtime

When the bell rang at the end of the day, it did not always mean the day was over. For many students it was just another beginning.

From practicing sports to club meetings to working part-time jobs, students participated in a number of activities after the school day was over.

Students participated in after-school activities for a number of reasons. Junior Reserve Officers' Training Corps members learned skills for the future. "Every day after school I practiced for color guard or honor guard. This is an excellent way to get ready for the military," senior James Smith said.

Students also used their talents after hours. Senior Shane Drake said, "After school I went to band practice and practiced playing the drums. I feel that playing in marching band was challenging and needed a lot of practice so that I could perform well on Friday nights at the games and also in competitions."

Practicing with sports teams was another reason to stay after school.

"Being a part of the volleyball team really gave me and the other girls on the team a chance to get to know one another," Courtney Skillman said. "The time we spent together at practices and games after school proved to be beneficial when we beat our rival North Henderson and won the conference."

BY CORI CROYLE

Finding time to get everything done means some students must stay after school

■ ■ ■

unity. Unity comes with your choice of fonts, column structure, story placement, and headlines design as well, but a little graphic touch such as an initial letter, inset quote, gray screen, spot color, or rule line can serve as an additional unifier. Graphic embellishments, if they are chosen to help tell a story and not just fill space, will enhance the page design rather

Here are a number of layout possibilities for yearbook spreads. In these sample layouts, blue areas indicate photos; lined areas are for copy; blank areas are white space. A mix of such layouts can add variety to a yearbook.

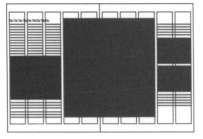

Modular—10 columns per spread

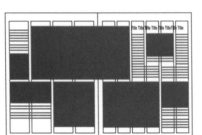

Modular—10 columns per spread

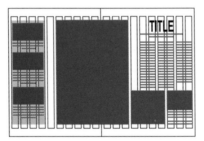

Grid—20 columns per spread

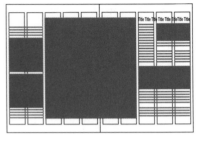

Modular—10 columns per spread

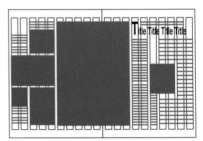

Grid—20 columns per spread

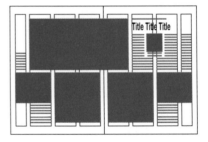

Plus—full and half-size columns

than detract from it. Notice the strong eyeline and horizontal dominant on the spread on the "On Display" feature on pages 330 and 331. The sidebar area may seem complicated, but it is the result of a template that was prepared once and then used on either the right or the left side of many spreads.

Staff Organization and Responsibilities

As you can see, planning a yearbook requires an organized staff willing to complete all the tasks they are assigned. As critical to the organization of the book itself is the organization of the staff, from the editor down to the first-year staff members who have never written a caption in their lives.

The school administration, like the board of directors of an organization, has a role in the yearbook without playing a direct part in it. That role is to work in an oversight capacity, but not in day-to-day oversight. Administrators should get involved as needed with the adviser and staff to see that the yearbook is a public forum for student expression and a true reflection of the school year.

Beyond the administration, there are many people who play key roles in the yearbook.

The Adviser

Integral to any staff and really at the top of the organizational ladder is the adviser. Some yearbook advisers have journalism degrees and have been advising for years. Others are fresh out of college and never thought they would be advising the yearbook. Then there's every situation in between. Nevertheless, the role of the adviser is to facilitate the production of a high-quality book on time. Of course, along the way, the adviser has to motivate the staff, give out grades, supervise and teach five or six other classes, organize school portraits, and perhaps do a thousand other things only remotely related to producing a yearbook.

The Yearbook Editor

The student in the highest role on the staff is the yearbook editor. In addition to making story, photo, and layout assignments, the yearbook editor is responsible for the content of the book and for the motivation of the staff. In fact, in recent years, the courts have held that the yearbook editor can be held responsible for the material in the yearbook.

The chief goal of the yearbook editor should be to get a high-quality book out on time. Secondary goals should include supervising the completion of the ladder diagram and deadline schedule; expanding coverage to include as many students as possible; working with staff members to ensure the on-time completion of high-quality stories, headlines, captions, photos, and layouts; motivating the staff; serving as a liaison between the adviser and the staff; and representing the yearbook staff to the rest of the student body. A good editor will lead by example, volunteering to assist any staff members when needed.

This sports spread from the Independence High School *The American* uses a template that was repeated on many right- and left-hand pages. The template design allows for many photos and an interesting mix of type and graphics.

Cooling Down
Exhausted after just finishing a 2.2 mile run, Alexandra Balagso, 9, pauses a moment to catch her breath. "I joined cross country because it helped me condition for track," said Balagso.

All Together Now
Heading towards the finish line, the runners push themselves every step of the way. "Endurance, strength, determination and the desire to make it through was what made cross country a tough and competitive sport, " said Tamika Bush, 12.

A Step Ahead
Heavily focusing on the race, Ken Stachnik, 9, challenges himself to improve his time. "In order to be the best I pushed myself to improve my time every time I ran," said Stachnik.

The Year Sports

78 Sports

Section Editors

Each section should have one person responsible for the overall look and feel of that section. These section editors have the same responsibilities for their section as the overall editor has for the entire publication: work-

330

Stretching Out
Before the race, Marcelo Caldas, 12, eyes his competition at Alum Rock Park; the last meet of the season. Cross country was a sport which involved rigorous, long-distance running.

Moving Along
After returning from a leg injury, Jenny Do, 12, runs at a constant speed as she makes her way to the finish line. "I was glad I was able to compete for the last time this year, " said Do.

The runners learned that it all started with a steady pace

On The Go

& the Scores

Girls	
James Lick	21-37
Overfelt	28-25
Leland	46-17
Santa Teresa	43-19
Presentation	39-21
Mitty	42-19
Silver Creek	40-20
Mt. Pleasant	29-26
Boys	
James Lick	25-38
Leland	48-15
Mt. Pleasant	48-15
Santa Teresa	25-38
Silver Creek	48-15
Overfelt	39-20

Kris Ajel, 10 Being on the team was a way for me to meet new people, get in shape and apply myself to something I liked. I look forward to a stronger, faster and an injury-free season next year.

Nicole Resendez, 9 The sport really challenged me to make it through the entire course. At one point, Cross Country became really disappointing but it pushed me to do my best.

Edward Chen, 9 Before every race I got butterflies in my stomach. To calm myself I would walk around the park and concentrate on the race. Practice helped to improve the speed and quality of my run.

& You Played It

Duke Nguyen, 11

I had been in Cross Country for three years now, and I didn't think that there was ever a point where I got tired of running. What I liked best about it was the teamwork. We always tried to stay with each other during the race. Everyone encouraged each other to do their best. I knew it was very beneficial to me because I was able to improve my times at the courses and get through the race. I was proud of everyone who ran this year. They really worked hard and had a positive attitude which kept our spirits high.

Copy By: Nathan Panganiban, Annamay Rodriguez & Evangeline Toleza

Composed mostly of young, inexperienced newcomers, runners searched for stamina and stability to make it through the courses. Running long distances required a tremendous amount of dedication. Coaches, Wendell Bradley and Victor Castillo, always made sure they emphasized the team's accomplishments to keep the runners motivated. The coaches focused on teaching the young team that goals would only be accomplished if they applied themselves. The young team was composed mainly of freshman and yet they still were able to overcome the challenges they faced.

Cross Country **Front Row:** Maria Chunn, Veronica Garcia, Ajene Enriquez. **2nd Row:** Nicole Resendez, Edward Chen, Ngan Nguyen, Duke Nguyen, Lorraine Sanchez, Phuong Nguyen, Anna Almejo, Assistant Coach Kolvira Cheng. **3rd Row:** Coach Wendell Bradley, Marie Madeires, Chin Chi, Casimero Agustin, Tamika Bush, Irene Villanueva, Alexandra Balagso, Ken Stachnik. **Back Row:** Mike Meighan, Barry Chen, Ken Powers, Kris Ajel, Franky Toledo, Ajith Satya, Marcelo Caldas, Harninder Meht, Bac Dang.

Cross Country **79**

g with other staff members to get the section completed. The section editor is primarily responsible for dictating the topics that will be covered in the section and for e design of the section. On most staffs, section editors make specific assignments the reporters and photographers working under them.

The Production Editor

In addition to, or in lieu of, section editors, some staffs have a production editor and production staff who are responsible for the actual design and layout of the yearbook pages. These jobs become even more critical as staffs utilize desktop publishing. The chief responsibility of the production editor is to ensure design consistency for each of the sections. It's the production editor who sets up the templates that will be used as the basis for all other pages at the beginning of the year and who worries about design specifics. Often, the production editor helps to maintain the computer equipment as well, assisting with software and hardware problems as needed.

Photography Editor

The role of the photography staff, whether a separate staff or part of the yearbook staff, is to complete photo assignments in a timely fashion. This means taking pictures, developing film, and making prints needed by other staff members and supervising the use of those photos. All photography staff members have a responsibility to ensure that the best photos are used in the dominant positions and that only high-quality pictures are used throughout the book.

Business Manager

The business manager fulfills another important role on the staff: supervising the finances of the publication, including all fund-raising activities, ad sales, and book sales. He or she may work with the editorial as well as the business staff members to raise money to produce the book. Business staff members' other jobs include keeping track of all yearbook receipts and coordinating the delivery of the book on delivery day. They also contact potential advertisers and help make the rate card that gives advertisers all the information they need to advertise in the yearbook. In some schools the business staff may work with both the newspaper and yearbook staffs.

Staff Manual

Vital to the smooth running of any yearbook staff is the staff manual. In addition to specific job descriptions for the various positions, a thorough yearbook staff manual will include a general statement of philosophy for the yearbook staff; a statement regarding the inclusion of individual portraits in the yearbook; the advertising policy, including types of ads that

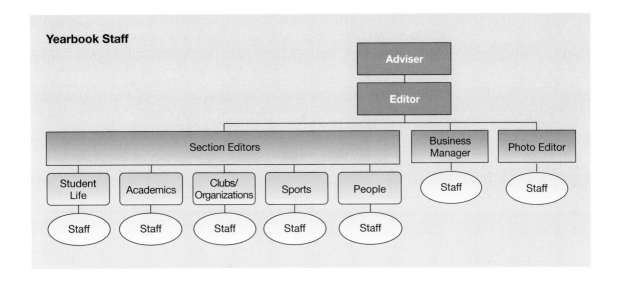

Yearbook Staff

can be rejected according to school board policy; and any other policy clarification that might prevent confrontation in the future.

The general statement of philosophy, written and approved by the campus and district administration, should include a policy on prior review. Policies on prior review by campus administrators or others vary greatly, and having the policy in writing will avoid potential legal hassles during the year.

A general statement of philosophy could be something like the following. Notice how specifically it spells out content and responsibility issues.

This diagram shows a common organizational structure for a yearbook. Other organizational structures and the inclusion of other positions, such as a themes editor and staff, are also possible.

The yearbook is a staff-produced publication, a product of a co-curricular publication class and extracurricular involvement. In general, the yearbook will provide memories, a record of historical events, data regarding the year, and educational opportunities for the staff, including a chance for staff members to plan, to write, to take pictures, and to design the yearbook.

As a public forum for student expression, the yearbook attempts to inform and entertain its audience in a broad, fair, and accurate manner on subjects that affect readers. The entire student body constitutes the primary audience for the book, with secondary audiences including faculty, staff, administrators, parents, and other members of the community.

The content of the book will focus on covering the school year, meeting the needs of the majority of the students. While the staff allows and encourages constructive criticism of any part of the book before and after publication, final authority for the content of the book rests in the hands of the yearbook adviser and student editorial board. Any controversial decisions will be made by the editor, staff, and the adviser. Despite the court ruling in *Hazelwood v. Kuhlmeier,* administrators rely on the adviser and staff to make content decisions.

Students working on the publication will strive to produce a publication based upon professional standards of accuracy, objectivity, and fair play. They will check all facts and verify the accuracy of all quotations. They will not publish or distribute any material that is construed to be obscene, in accordance with state law. They will not publish any libelous material or any material which could cause a material and substantial disruption of school activities. Material that stimulates heated discussion or debate does not constitute the type of disruption prohibited.

The school assumes no liability for the content of the yearbook.

You may wish to elaborate on some of these paragraphs, particularly those that are influenced by school district policy, local procedures, or state laws. The Student Press Law Center and Journalism Education Association can provide further information on writing statements of philosophy. After you've written the policy statement and had it approved by the administration, you may wish to include it with the general statement of philosophy in the student handbook for all students and parents to read.

Working with the Yearbook Company

Obviously, a lot goes into putting together a yearbook. But help is available. While some yearbooks are printed locally, five national yearbook companies print most yearbooks. These companies can give practical assistance to the yearbook adviser and staff for, in addition to printing, each company provides a variety of tools to help with yearbook planning and production.

In some schools, the yearbook company is the same year after year; some advisers just find no reason to consider switching companies. In other schools, the company is selected through a formal process each year, during which each company is asked to bid on the printing of the yearbook. The administration, adviser, and/or staff then consider the cost and other factors in selecting a company. Still other schools use a less formal bidding process or some other combination of factors.

Advisers consistently cite the cost of the book and the quality of the printing as the top two reasons for choosing a yearbook company. However, the type and quality of the supplemental materials provided by the company and a familiarity with the company's field representative, who is the liaison between the staff and the company and who helps the

Trends and Issues

Yearbooks on CD and Video

In these days of multimedia, it may be challenging to convince some students that the hard-copy yearbook is something they need or want. But in some schools, especially where a good number of students have access to VCRs and computers with CD-playing capability, the yearbook can be supplemented by a video and/or CD addition that piques the interest of students.

The CD is not just an electronic version of the yearbook. Instead, it goes beyond the printed book, using the CD's capacities for text, audio, photo stills, and video to augment the printed book. For example, a CD may show video of the homecoming game, school play, prom, and various other group events. Instead of only one story on some of these activities, it may have two or three, presented from different angles. The CD, often including interactive sections, may include not only photos of the graduating seniors, but also audio accompaniments, in the students' own voices, describing their feelings about graduation and their plans for the future. The possibilities are limited only by the staff's imagination and, ultimately, budget.

CD yearbook supplements can be produced in a number of ways. Currently, nearly all schools go to outside producers, as the software used to assemble such multimedia presentations is expensive and complicated to use. Some schools send all their materials—photos, stories, videos, and audiotapes—to an electronic service bureau and let that company handle all stages of production.

Others lower the cost a bit by doing the electronic pre-press—scanning and digitizing images—themselves. And a few staffs actually produce the master CD themselves, an endeavor that requires extensive experience and expensive equipment.

Like a well-conceived CD, an effective video is more than just a collection of video clips. It's another way to tell the story of the year. Video yearbook production companies shoot footage and assemble it into a moving series of snapshots of the year. The mix of sound and video helps bring back the memories. Some schools that have their own broadcast journalism department and video-editing equipment choose to shoot and edit their own video, saving all the expense except duplication of the tapes, but increasing the time commitment involved.

The primary incentive for schools to produce either a CD or video supplement to the printed book is to increase sales. A CD or video will add to the cost of the book, but it often appeals to a broader audience than just the printed book. If marketed correctly and aggressively, the CD or video supplement can result in dramatically increased sales of the yearbook package.

Will the CD or video yearbook someday replace the printed yearbook? Not likely. Even in the technology age, a book, like a printed newspaper, is a more permanent record than a piece of software. And besides, you can't get autographs on a CD or video.

staff with all facets of book production, are also important considerations for many advisers.

After the yearbook company has been selected, the representative will educate the adviser and staff on how to use its tools in preparing the yearbook. All of the companies provide their schools with a production kit that contains everything from layout sheets to picture-cropping tools to marketing materials that will help in selling more yearbooks. These kits contain valuable information that often goes overlooked by the staff.

Look through your production kit when you receive it. Then, on a regular basis throughout the year—not just at deadline time—schedule visits with your representative. Have the rep look over what the staff is doing to make sure production will flow smoothly at the plant. There's nothing worse than submitting one hundred pages on time only to find that they were prepared inaccurately. Pages that are submitted correctly can cause a delay in the printing, and therefore delivery, of the book.

In addition to meeting deadlines with correctly prepared pages, another thing your rep will stress is properly labeling everything you submit. Each of the yearbook companies produces thousands of books every year. If one plant, for example, produces 500 books all due for delivery around May 15, and each of those books contains 128 pages, the company has to produce 64,000 pages, some submitted within just a few weeks of the delivery date. If each of those pages contains an average of 5 photos (an average of 10 photos per spread), that means the plant has to process 320,000 photos. With those numbers, you can see why it's critical that you label every single item with your customer number, including every photo, every envelope, and every layout. Use the stickers or rubber stamps the yearbook company provides to facilitate this labeling. And never send one-of-a-kind materials to your printing company.

Keep in close contact with your yearbook company representative and your in-plant representative. Keep them informed and request that they keep you informed. Remember, the yearbook company works for you to print the quality of book your students and staff demand.

Wrap-up

The yearbook is an important record of what happened during a school year, but it will become even more important as years pass and people want to remember their school years. Therefore, you should seek to include as many students as possible in the yearbook. Besides providing a historical record, a yearbook also functions as a picture book and a public relations tool, and is an educational experience for those who work on it.

The first step in planning a yearbook is to make sure there is enough money to finance it. Though schools may provide some funds, staffs often have to raise additional monies through selling advertising space and fund-raising. When selling the yearbook itself, you can give discounts to students who pay early in the year, thereby bringing in needed cash at that point.

Planning the content of the yearbook begins with planning the sections—usually student life, academics, clubs/organizations, sports, and people. Once you have decided how many pages to allot to each section, you can use a ladder diagram to figure out what will go on each spread. You can also go ahead and develop theme ideas, discussing and testing them until you come up with one that will work for the whole book.

Good yearbook copy should be insightful and interesting. It needs the same kind of good leads and good writing as newspaper copy. Headlines and captions are also important, because sometimes these are all that students read.

High-quality, high-interest photos are a must for any yearbook. Include as many people and as many action shots as possible. Good photographic coverage should be considered in the initial planning of the book.

Page design begins with a consideration of content. Photos should be placed on the page beginning with the dominant photo. An eyeline should be created, and seven to ten photos, as well as captions, a headline, and perhaps other copy, should go on each spread.

Once you begin work on the book, designate a staff member to serve as the coordinator for each section. These section editors, together with the production editor, photography editor, and business manager, must work together and with the staff adviser to ensure consistency and quality within each section. Staffs should also get to know the representative from their yearbook company and follow the procedures and deadlines the company sets up.

Evaluation Checklist: *Yearbook Spread*

✓ Is there a strong, well-positioned dominant photo?

✓ Are four or five other people-oriented photos arranged appropriately around the dominant?

✓ Has a clear eyeline been established?

✓ Are captions accurate, with as many names as possible, and are they correctly positioned on the spread?

✓ Does the copy contain interesting facts presented in sidebars as well as regular copy blocks?

✓ Does the headline summarize the content of the page?

On Assignment

Individual Activities

1. Write a brief definition or explanation of each of the following terms.

   caption   ladder diagram
   modular design   theme copy

2. Test your critical thinking. Look at the themes for the last five yearbooks your school had, and evaluate how well each of them related to the school. Can you see why staffs chose the themes they did? Now choose one of the yearbooks and examine it more closely. How well was the theme executed? In what ways was the treatment good? In what ways could it have been improved? (If your school's yearbooks did not have themes, find five books that did and follow the same procedure.)

3. Design, produce, and distribute a marketing survey that will give the yearbook staff input to help improve this year's book. Include such questions as "What was your favorite/least favorite spread in last year's yearbook and why?" and "If you could have one thing in this year's book, what would it be?" Also be sure to find out if respondents purchased a book last year and, if they didn't, what could be done to entice them to purchase one this year. A good survey will consist of only 10–20 questions and will be distributed to as many students as possible. Compile

and analyze the results when you have them, and use them to create a strategy to expand coverage and to sell more books.

4. As an exercise in reporting, assign each person in the class a different population to interview regarding the purpose of the yearbook and what they like/dislike about it. For example, one person might be assigned to interview parents, another to administrators, another to student leaders, another to students who speak English as a second language, and yet another to students who are attending the school for the first time. Pass all this information along to members of the publication's business staff who can use it when developing a marketing plan for the yearbook.

5. Using the information you obtained in the marketing survey or in the reporting exercise, design a poster that will target one specific population and encourage them to buy a yearbook. Include an idea for a photo or piece of art and write all copy for the poster. For example, if you interviewed a parent who said, "My yearbook has helped me remember the happiest times of my life. I don't know what I would do without it," you might put that quotation and a picture from that person's yearbook on a poster. Then include a selling message and all other necessary information: "Don't you forget either. Buy your yearbook today in the cafeteria. Only $25 this week."

6. Pick any spread in the student life section of any yearbook. Using a rough-draft layout sheet, sketch the page, using boxes for photos and lines for text. Write in the words for headlines. Be neat. Then, in a different color, label the following elements if present: headline, subhead, caption, kicker, eyeline, dominant photo, vertical photo (not dominant), horizontal photo (not dominant), sidebar, white space, folio, rule line, gray screen, initial letter, and art. How many columns did the designer use? On the back of the rough draft, write a brief evaluation of the effectiveness of the design. What did the designer do well? Poorly? Was the design effective? Why or why not?

Team Activities

7. Working in groups of two or three people, identify 25 things that make your school unique. You can include factual things, perceptions others have about your school, and anything new or different about this year. After you've identified these things, brainstorm ideas for five phrases (no longer than six words) or words that summarize your school this year. Then get back together with everyone in the class and share the phrases. Write them up on the board. After a brief discussion of how each one fits the year, have the class vote on which one is their favorite. Pick the top three and erase the others.

8. Divide the class into three groups. Each will be assigned one of the three remaining phrases from the preceding activity and will fully develop it. Each team will do the following:
   a. explain how the phrase fits the year;
   b. explain how the phrase is unique;
   c. write one story for the opening and one story for the closing section of the yearbook based on the theme;
   d. sketch a design for the cover, endsheet, title page, opening spread, and division pages, including as much detail related to choice of photos and typography as practical;
   e. using your sketch as a guideline, produce a "theme packet" consisting of an actual mock-up of the cover, endsheet, title page, opening spread and division pages using pictures, art, and type cut out of magazines and neatly pasted onto layout sheets.

A picture may be worth a thousand words, but the tone of a story or power of an idea also can be expressed in choices of color, typography, logos, and the other visual vocabulary of a graphic designer like Mike Quon.

Self-described as "a graphic designer who illustrates," Quon has influenced modes of visual communication throughout the world since founding Mike Quon Design Office in New York City in 1972.

Quon has created thousands of designs and illustrations for magazines, newspapers, books, advertisements, posters, packaging and record album covers. Among his work for corporate, institutional and non-profit clients are the logo for the New York State Lottery; television commercial graphics for Xerox, HBO, Dristan, and IBM; and banners for the 1994 World Cup Soccer tournament.

His work, ranging from pen and ink and pencil drawings to collage to watercolor to acrylic paintings, is represented in the permanent collections of major museums in the United States and abroad. He also has designed, illustrated and/or co-edited more than a dozen books, many of them for children.

Quon's father, working as an animator for Disney films, discouraged Quon's study of art and graphic design, pushing his son towards science or medicine. Although he took only one art course in high school, Quon found time to draw after his studies, and he won second place in an art contest sponsored by *Surfer Magazine* when he was sixteen.

Quon worked as an art director and designer at agencies in Los Angeles and New York before founding his own studio. He also began visiting Europe regularly, filling up sketchbooks with drawings and watercolors.

"Daily sketching keeps me sane," he said. His client base—and his sketchbooks—reflect subsequent trips to Egypt, Mexico, Hong Kong, Japan, China, South America, Africa, and Australia.

But having a design firm is not just drawing. It's growing a business, solving problems—of clients, staff, and the business—and mastering new technology.

"Who would have thought that teenage computer nerds working in their garages would come up with stuff so highly sought after by today's corporate designers?" he said.

Much of what Quon has to wrestle with is still finding the creative solution. "It's hard to tell where your inspiration comes from," he admitted. "Everywhere I look there is feedback and information. Part of the job is to be inspired with the right inspiration at the right time."

Graphic designers must reach into the "vast library" of their minds, of everything they've encountered in their lifetime, Quon said. "Watch movies. Go to animation festivals. Read lots of books, such as Philip Megg's *History of Graphic Design* and *Graphic Arts*, a compilation of award-winning designs."

"Students should not become discouraged, however competitive the field becomes," Quon advised. "And don't compare yourself with someone who's been in the business for years. Things that seem impossible now come in due time. You just get better each year."

339

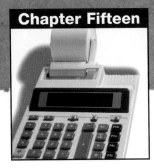

Chapter Fifteen

Writing for Radio and Television

Chapter Fifteen

Key Terms	Key Concepts
broadcast journalism	After reading this chapter, you should
nugget	• know possible ways to experience broadcast journalism in your school
flair	
station manager	• know some of the characteristics of good broadcast writing
program director	• be familiar with patterns of organization for broadcast news stories
technical director	• understand how to prepare news copy for radio or television
	• understand how student broadcasting stations are typically organized

Radio is everywhere—at home, in the car, on street corners, strapped onto joggers' waists, coming from our computers, and as background in elevators, stores, and offices. Television sets are in nearly every home as well as in airplanes, cars, boats, campers, on desks, at the beach, and even in backpacks.

Broadcasting plays an important role in all our lives. Millions of people can watch the Olympic Games, the president's State of the Union speech, the O. J. Simpson trial, a state dinner for the British prime minister, a national political convention, or the coverage of a natural disaster or an assassination. From anywhere in the world, viewers can see or hear instantaneous reports from the site of breaking news. Broadcasting takes the immediacy out of newspaper reporting.

Many schools have television cameras and the means to broadcast programs into every classroom. Sometimes this equipment comes through *Channel One*, which allows schools that broadcast its news programs to use the TV monitors it provides for other educational purposes throughout the day. Other schools take advantage of local access cable television and broadcast to a small, rather specific audience outside the school. But even if such opportunities are not available to you, there are other ways to get practice with the basics of broadcast journalism.

Some schools use the intercom system as a broadcast laboratory. Instead of the traditional bulletin listing school events, usually read by a student or school staff member, student journalists compile the news

Getting practice with the basics of broadcast journalism can be as simple as reading news and feature stories over the school intercom system.

based on the bulletin and bring it to life with good reporting and additional stories. They add interviews with students involved in the activities being announced and prepare radio-style commercials to promote upcoming events. In some schools, arrangements are made to get wire copy of the top news events of the day faxed from a local radio station. Then that copy is summarized to help students keep abreast of current events. Today's online news databases also provide a source for current news.

When the news is ready and edited, it is taped daily for broadcast over the intercom system. Not only is the quality of the basic bulletin enhanced, but students have a practical broadcasting laboratory with real deadline experience. The equipment needed is minimal—a tape recorder, tape splicer, a cassette or disk player (for musical introductions and advertising sound effects), a few sound-effect records, and an adapter to play into the intercom.

In addition to in-house broadcasting, journalism students can prepare news and broadcast features about school events and send them to local radio and/or television stations for use in their programs.

Even if opportunities like these are not available, students can still learn and use broadcasting journalism techniques in the classroom. Reporters can prepare stories in broadcast style, interview students involved in them, and prepare newscasts that can be recorded and played for others in the class to critique.

Writing for Broadcast

You don't hear things the same way you read them. When writing broadcast copy you have to keep your listeners and viewers in mind. Remember that they will hear your words only once. While a reader can go back over and reread a printed news story, there is no opportunity for a listener to go back over a story narrated into a microphone.

So how do you proceed? Begin by applying the principles of good reporting. Dig into the news. Seek to find a "nugget"—a fact or bit of information that will stick in the listener's mind and make your story stand out. Next, organize the information in a way that makes it easy for listeners to understand it. The goal is to create a visual picture in the listener's mind. Pictures in a television story can help you do that, but the words you write and speak are equally powerful in creating a mental picture. This is particularly important in radio broadcasting.

To organize a story you will first have to understand it. Ask yourself some questions. What elements of news make this story important to my listeners? How does the information affect people? The answers to these questions can help you tell a good story. Additionally, there are some basic story patterns that can help you organize your information.

Cause-Effect Organization

In this organization the cause is your main point. It is followed up by one or more effects.

CAUSE: Another heavy snowstorm has brought our city to a standstill.

EFFECT: Schools will remain closed for a second straight week. Superintendent William Onoda says students will have to make up the lost time at year's end.

Problem-Solution-Results Organization

After stating the problem, use this organization to explain the solution offered. Then tell whether that solution was acted on, or whether another, different result took place.

PROBLEM: The Centerville School District is facing serious money troubles.

SOLUTION: President Jimmy Langham and two other school board members say the only way around the problem is to cut school programs. But at least one board member disagrees.

RESULTS: Betty Pendleton says, since last year's spending cuts didn't help avert this year's budget crisis, the only real alternative is to raise taxes.

Comparison Organization

Use this organization to show similarities and differences between two people, plans, or proposals.

COMPARISON: The two leading candidates for Student Council president have similar backgrounds. Barry Miller and Julia Alegría are both honor students. Both want to make Martin Luther King High a center for student social activities after school hours. But on that issue they have different ideas. Miller wants to open a student canteen where students can gather and talk. Alegría wants to double the number of school-sponsored dances. There's money in the student activity fund, but not enough to finance both a canteen and extra dances. Students will decide which idea they prefer when voting next Tuesday.

A creative writing style with strong verbs and specific details can make a good hurricane story into a great one. Here store owners prepare for an oncoming storm.

One of these story organization patterns will almost always work for any story you are writing. Experiment with each. Also remember, as in all newswriting, broadcast stories have a beginning, a middle, and an end. Each should reinforce important facts in the story. You set up the story in the beginning, provide additional details in the middle, and tell what happens in the end.

Writing with Flair

You've already seen that one good way to make your story stand out is to dig hard as a reporter to find a "nugget"—a fact or bit of information that makes your story stick in your listener's mind. Writing creative copy is another way to help listeners better visualize and understand your story. This is one of the most enjoyable parts of broadcast newswriting, but being creative doesn't mean being cute. It just means saying something in an interesting way. Notice the difference between these two samples:

GOOD: Tropical storm Allison is now a full-fledged hurricane. The National Weather Service upgraded the Florida Gulf Coast storm when its winds topped 75-miles per hour. The Florida coast—from Tampa north to Pensacola—is now under a hurricane warning. The storm is expected to hit tomorrow. Ten inches of rain are likely. Residents are being warned to take precautions—which include possible evacuation.

BETTER: Tropical storm Allison is now hurricane Allison. She's whipping the Florida Gulf Coast with 75-mile-per-hour winds. Allison is expected to hit tomorrow, with ten inches of rain likely. A hurricane warning is in effect from Tampa north to Pensacola. Storm experts are warning residents to get ready and to prepare for possible evacuation.

During his career at CBS News, Charles Kuralt set the standard for broadcast-writing creativity. It's called writing with "flair." Kuralt's story about the Wabash Cannonball provides a good example. It's about the last days of a passenger train that had rolled through the Midwest countryside every day since 1884. The flair with which Kuralt wrote is well illustrated in the last few lines of his story:

Set your watch by the Cannonball while you may. Pause at the crossroads to let her pass. Take one last look. Tomorrow, the Wabash Cannonball won't be a train at all, only a banjo tune.

Kuralt's writing and storytelling skills made his reports stand out. But you can find many other excellent reporters. They're all around you. Just listen to the radio and watch TV news. Pick out some stories you like. Use a tape recorder; record and transcribe them. That way you can study how the stories were organized and written.

Preparing Copy for Broadcast

Generally speaking, writing for broadcast is similar to writing for newspapers. All the basic principles of good reporting discussed earlier in this book apply. The goal is to write well, clearly, and concisely. Here are some other basic tips. Gather your information conscientiously; be accurate and objective in writing about it; edit your work carefully.

Style. Be concise. Write short, simple sentences. Use a subject-verb-object pattern. Write one thought to a sentence and activate your sentences by writing in active voice. Active voice helps make news copy more current, interesting, and easier to understand.

PASSIVE VOICE: It has been found by school librarians that student interest in reading is on the rise.

ACTIVE VOICE: School librarians say that student interest in reading is on the rise.

Use present tense if possible. Keep in mind that dates generally are not needed. Broadcast news is immediate; you are there as the news happens.

Eliminate the word "today" almost entirely, and never start a story with the word "yesterday." If it happened yesterday it's old news. Find a "today" reason to report the story or select one.

Eliminate unnecessary words from sentences. Use adverbs, adjectives, and descriptive phrases sparingly. Remember that words are time. The clock is your enemy since it tells you when you must quit. You can only cram about 180 words into a minute of broadcast news. Depending on your delivery rate, that figure could go up or down—probably down. If

Broadcast Writing in a Nutshell

1. Be simple and to the point.
2. Use the present tense.
3. Remember your time limits.
4. If you must use numbers, round them off.
5. Use active voice.
6. Attribute before the statement.
7. Use phonetic spelling for difficult names and terms.
8. Use caps and lower case.
9. Double- or triple-space copy.
10. Write television copy to roughly correspond to the pictures.
11. Put directions on the left, script on the right.
12. Always read copy aloud before broadcasting it.

you use music or sound effects, you have less time to present stories. In television, you have to account for the use of videotapes, film, live reports from the field, or electronic graphics as well.

Minimize the use of numbers. It's hard for listeners to comprehend numbers in a broadcast story. If a number is important, by all means use it. Spell it out in written copy. Round numbers off.

> BAD: The student charity dance raised $4,263.50 for the Cohen Homeless Shelter.
>
> BETTER: The student charity dance raised over four thousand dollars for the Cohen Homeless Shelter.

An attribution, as you recall, is who said something or where important information came from. In broadcast writing, the attribution always precedes the statement of information. Your copy should help the listener understand who is saying what.

> School board president Susan Wong says she's running for re-election.

The same approach holds true for important information that you need to broadcast quickly, but can't personally confirm.

> The Associated Press says that shots have been fired at the President's motorcade.

Mechanics. Prepare your copy in capital and lowercase letters, the same as for newspapers. Many people think they should write broadcast copy in all caps. But all-cap writing is harder to read.

Double- or triple-space your news copy. Keep it free of errors and too many edits. Messy copy should be retyped to make it easy to read.

Use phonetic spellings of confusing words or names. ("McNerny" becomes "Mac-*ner*-nee"; "DeFloria" becomes "Dah-*Floor*-e-uh"). Place the

---

Camera Terms

If you're using a television camera or a camcorder to prepare a program, the following terms will come in handy.

close-up: a portrait-like shot showing a person's head and neckline

dolly: move the camera toward or away from the subject

establishing shot: a camera shot that shows the subject as well as its position and relation to its entire surroundings; a variation of a long shot

long shot: a camera shot that shows the main visual subject in its surroundings

medium long shot: a camera shot in which an entire subject appears, with a little space above and below

medium shot: the body of the person being shot is cut off just below the waist

pan: move the camera head left to right to capture horizontal motion

tilt: move the camera head up or down to create a vertical image

track: capture horizontal movement by moving the entire camera left to right

zoom: manipulate the lens of the camera to create the appearance of moving closer or farther away from the subject

A main goal in writing for broadcast is to make the copy as clear and easy to read as possible.

emphasis clearly in your copy so that you can quickly and easily read it. Verify identifications.

Without fail, always read your copy out loud before going on the air. If it doesn't read easily, it needs to be rewritten.

Write television copy to correspond to the pictures, but not too closely. The pictures should illustrate the subject of the copy. The copy should add what is not said by the pictures alone. Strive for the goal suggested by this sentence: "I saw it on the radio."

When writing television scripts, divide the page down the middle. Always type the story copy on the right-hand half of the page. Use the lefthand half for instructions to the director or the story videotape editor so that he or she knows what studio shots are called for, or what pictures, video, or graphics go with the copy you have written. See the "On Display" feature on page 348 for an example.

Broadcast newswriting is the art of good storytelling. Be creative, but also be clear and relevant. Those who master the art will stand out in a very competitive career field.

The School Broadcasting Station

School broadcasting stations can vary greatly in size and scope. Many involve only a handful of staff members; others employ many more. Some schools, like KIOS-FM at Omaha Central High School, in Omaha, Nebraska, even secure licenses for limited broadcasting from the Federal Communications Commission. The chart on page 349 shows a typical organizational structure for an educational broadcasting station.

Anchor, Abdul Muller:	The two leading candidates for Student Council president have similar backgrounds. Barry Miller and Julia Alegría are both honor students. Both want to make Martin Luther King High a center for student social activities after hours.
(Visual shows April Payne inside proposed student canteen with Miller)	But MLKTV News reporter April Payne tells us that they have different ideas on that issue.
Reporter April Payne:	Barry Miller thinks students here at Martin Luther King should open a new canteen where they can gather and talk about the things that are important to them and the school.
Barry Miller, close-up video	". . . there are a lot of important issues for kids today, and we have nowhere except the street corners to talk them through. I think a student center, open before and after school, will provide an important social outlet for us all."
April Payne: (Video of Alegría with group of students)	But Miller's competition for Student Council president, Julia Alegría, wants to double the number of school-sponsored dances instead.
Medium close-up of Alegría	"We need to find things for kids to do on weekend nights. We know that school dances are a great success in providing a social event for students, and that they offer a safe, enjoyable way to get together over the weekends.
April Payne, standing in front of MLKHS	But there is one problem. There is money in the activity fund, but only enough for one of the two choices. Students here will decide if it's conversation or dancing when they vote tomorrow, starting at 8 A.M. April Payne, reporting from King High.

At the top is the board of trustees, board of education, or similar entity; if the station is licensed, it is licensed under the name of this group. This board is ultimately responsible for the station's operations and programming. In practical terms, day-to-day operations and programming supervision are delegated to a faculty adviser, often someone in communications, journalism, or a related academic department. The adviser may also be a staff member, such as the director of student activities. The adviser oversees the station and serves as liaison between the licensee board and the station itself.

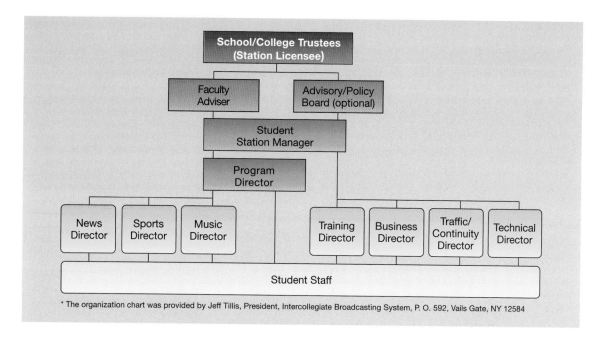

* The organization chart was provided by Jeff Tillis, President, Intercollegiate Broadcasting System, P. O. 592, Vails Gate, NY 12584

An optional advisory/policy board may consist of representatives from various groups within the school, including students, faculty, and administrators. It may also include representatives of the community served by the station. Its role is generally to act in an advisory capacity or to help set overall policy.

From this point, the remainder of the positions shown are normally held by students. Most serve on a voluntary basis, but some might receive a stipend, academic credit, scholarship, or other appropriate recognition of the enormous amounts of time required of them by the station.

An educational broadcasting station is often organized into a structure similar to the one shown here.

Station Manager

The student station manager is the highest-ranking student on the staff. The station manager supervises the department directors and the student staff while also serving as principal liaison with the faculty adviser and advisory/policy board. It is the station manager who balances the individual department interests for the common good.

Program Director

The program director is in charge of all on-air programming. This includes the design of the program schedule, music format, the selection and assignment of announcers, and the mixture of news, sports, and

Broadcast Standards for On-the-Air Personalities, Narrators, Color Commentators & Others Appearing Before the Microphone

The purpose of this station is to provide information in the broadest sense. The channel exists to serve the students, staff, and community as a medium of communication. Additionally, the channel provides a learning experience in all facets of video production for students.

In producing programs for this station, technical crews and on-the-air persons should strive for the highest degree of professionalism possible. Commentators should abide by the following standards:

1. No person is to be slandered through on-the-air commentary or libeled by on-the-air signs or character generated text.
2. Basic conversational good taste should be adhered to at all times. Vulgarities; sexual innuendos; obscenities; racial, sexist or ethnic slurs; or language in poor taste are not permitted.
3. Nothing should be broadcast that is disruptive to the school routine or purpose.
4. In unstructured programs ("freewheeling interviews," sporting events, etc.), commentary should be restricted to the subject, game, or meet. Conversation or dialogue unrelated to the event or subject is not permitted and is unprofessional. Remember, the program may be "freewheeling," but that does not mean that anything goes.

5. News reporters, interviewers, and sports commentators should be prepared to discuss the subject, game, or meet prior to going on the air (i.e., have team rosters and player statistics at hand).
6. Stage directions and conversation between crew and commentators should not become part of the taped program as it is amateurish and unprofessional.
7. Balance, accuracy, and fairness should be the aim of every reporter/commentator.
8. In covering events or activities involving this school and other schools, commentators should strive to show no partiality to their home school.
9. Personal viewpoints that are not expressed in a forum for sharing opinion or presented as analysis, should be kept to a minimum in sports reporting and should not be part of news reporting.
10. "On-the-air" persons shall not use this station as a personal instrument to aggrandize themselves or to control, intimidate, or unduly influence others.

Failure to adhere to these standards may result in a suspension or restriction of programming privileges.

music to be presented by the station. Working closely with the program director will be one or more production directors, who manage all production and editing for broadcast programs.

News Director

The news director works with the program director to select and schedule news programming, news announcers, reporters, writers, and editors. The news director will set the format to be followed for newscasts and other news and public affairs programming. This includes story selection, assignment of reporters, writing style, and integration of audio. He or she also selects (within the realistic limitations of the station's budget) equipment and news services to be used by the news department.

Sports Director

The sports director works with the program director to select and schedule sports programming and sports announcers. He or she helps set the sportscast format and helps decide which sports events the station will broadcast play-by-play. The sports director selects (within budget limitations) portable and remote equipment to be used by the sports department.

A student program director monitors a television program from the control room.

Music Director

The music director assists announcers with music selection within the format(s) decided upon by the program director. The music director is responsible for the acquisition of records for the station and for maintaining continuing contact with record companies. Such contact may take the form of periodic playlists to let the companies (and the station's listeners) know what the station is playing. The music director may also be responsible for cataloging new records received by the station, unless there is a record librarian handling that duty. Even in such cases, the record librarian is usually supervised by the music director.

Training Director

The training director is responsible for recruiting and training new station personnel as well as ongoing training for existing staff.

Business Director

The business director keeps the station's records of income and expenditures, works with appropriate financial authorities within the school, prepares annual operating and capital budgets, and works with the station manager to keep the station's spending within its approved budgetary limits.

Careers in broadcasting range from nightly news anchors to such behind-the-scenes jobs as writers, producers, and camera people.

Traffic/Continuity Director

The traffic/continuity director prepares and schedules all public service announcements and program promotional announcements. He or she also prepares and oversees correction of station logs, including the scheduling of all programs and special programs.

Technical Director

The technical director (sometimes called chief engineer) is responsible for the installation, operation, maintenance, and repair of all studio and transmitting equipment, compliance with all FCC technical requirements, and the recommendation of new studio and transmitting equipment.

Station Promotion

In addition to managing the broadcasting and business functions of a station, it is important to build support for its programming. This support usually comes from two areas: contributions and, naturally, listeners or viewers.

Staffs will usually have a development director, whose job is to seek program underwriting grants and contributions from businesses, foundations, individuals, and other sources. For closed-circuit stations, this position may be called sales director, in which case it involves the sale of advertising time.

A public relations director often will be named to handle promoting the station to its potential listeners or viewers. He or she will write news releases and place them in appropriate media to attract program interest, prepare spot announcements for use on air to promote upcoming programs, and develop special events, such as contests, to attract an audience.

Broadcasting Careers

Opportunities in radio and television continue to grow. The number of specialty networks and cable channels, for example, is increasing constantly. More all-news networks are coming into existence, and more

The question of TV coverage of courtroom trials isn't a new issue. People have wondered about its appropriateness almost since the time on-the-spot TV reporting became possible.

In 1965, the U. S. Supreme Court refused to allow television coverage of federal cases, but let each state decide whether to cover other trials. California was the first state to allow TV coverage in courtrooms; today over forty states permit it.

People in favor of televising court procedures have pointed out the educational value of such programming. When Court TV, the first station devoted entirely to broadcasting trials, came along in the early 1990s, many viewers reported a greater understanding of what goes on in a courtroom. Arguments against televising have had to do with changing the basic nature of the judicial process. Are judges, lawyers, and juries even subtly influenced by the presence of cameras? Is the public being taught that trials are merely another form of entertainment? These are some of the same issues the Supreme Court raised.

Trials of well-known people proved to be the real test of TV courtroom coverage. The 1991 rape trial of William Kennedy Smith, nephew of Senator Edward Kennedy, probably brought much more attention to the case than if it had been covered only by print media. Nightly newscasts breathlessly reported who was in the courtroom, what various defendants wore, even the look on Smith's face as certain statements were made. Smith was acquitted, but virtually everyone in the country had an opinion on the trial based on what they had seen on television.

The question that can be raised here, of course, is, "So what?" So what if people second-guessed Smith's motives and responses? So what if some disagreed with the verdict? The jury was shielded from outsiders' opinions during their deliberations, so Smith's right to a fair trial was not interfered with.

But then there was the notorious O. J. Simpson murder trial. If Smith's name was known to some because of his Kennedy heritage, *everyone* knew about O. J. This trial truly became a media circus, dragging out for months as judge and attorneys jockeyed for position in front of the camera and as the public tuned in nightly to catch the story.

Here again, the question of "So what?" can be asked. But here perhaps a difference can be noted. The jury in this case, after almost a year-long trial, took less than four hours to reach a verdict. Had the length of the trial, dragged out by excessive TV posturing, simply worn the jurors out? No one knows for sure, of course, but many people have thought it might have been a factor.

By the end of this trial, most of the serious-minded public—not to mention judges—had had enough. Trials were not staged for the benefit of the TV-watching public; they were serious affairs that needed to be conducted with dignity and restraint. Not long after the Simpson acquittal, the retrial of the Menendez brothers, whose first trials for killing their parents had resulted in hung juries, began. This time no TV cameras were allowed in the courtroom, and various other strictures were put in place. The Menendez brothers were found guilty in a restrained, regulated, unbroadcast trial. It is certainly not fair to suggest that a guilty or innocent verdict depends on whether or not a trial is broadcast. It does seem fair, however, to say that the public's belief in the appropriateness of witnessing every nuance of a trial seems to be decreasing. People are realizing that courtroom situations are not, or should not be, entertainment.

all-news-and-talk radio stations—representing a wide range of views—are available at the local level. Direct satellite transmission of radio signals and television channels is also growing.

While few people will ever anchor the nightly news on a major network, or even locally, there are many skills needed to keep newscasts on the air—jobs for people who gather the news, write, edit, film or tape, or produce the program. There are places for librarians, secretaries, advertising sales personnel, and even pilots.

It is unlikely that television and radio will ever replace newspapers, magazines, or other printed materials. But they are important vehicles for communications. Many well-trained journalists find it easy to move horizontally from one medium to another.

Wrap-up

Radio and television play an important role in our everyday lives; there are few places you can go that you aren't near a radio or TV set. Even portable radios and TVs find their way into what was once a peaceful retreat into the mountains for a family vacation.

There are many ways that students can have an experience in broadcasting and learn how to do broadcast writing. Depending on resources available, students can, for example, prepare stories in broadcast format, using a tape recorder or video camera, to play in class for other students to critique. They might also use the school intercom system to broadcast the day's news and announcements. In some cases students will be able to operate a complete radio or television station (licensed or closed circuit); or prepare news reports for use by the local radio or television stations.

People hear things differently from how they read them. A story on the radio can't be "reread" if someone didn't hear it correctly. So broadcast writing has to be clear, concise, and to the point.

Writing for broadcasting starts with the same principles of good journalism as writing for print. You do your homework and dig into the story. Focus on what makes it interesting and how to create a visual image for the listener or viewer. Even on television, the words used to complement the pictures are equally important.

There are basic story patterns that many broadcast journalists use, such as cause and effect, problem-solution-results, and comparison.

When writing copy, find the "nugget"—that bit of information that stands out. This doesn't mean to write cute; it means to be interesting and unique. And write in active voice. Radio and television provide immediacy. The listener is "there"—at the trial; next to the damage caused by the hurricane; with you at the football game; at the scene of the accident; on the floor of the student council meeting. The listener is hearing the words of people making the news as part of your newscast.

There are many staff jobs, such as program director, sports director, and technical director, at scholastic broadcasting stations. Some of these jobs may well lead to careers in the ever-expanding field of broadcast journalism.

Evaluation Checklist: *Broadcast Script*

✓ Have the standard organizational patterns been used to present stories?

✓ Are stories told in an interesting way, built around nuggets whenever possible?

✓ Is the copy made easy to read through phonetic spellings, caps and lowercase letters, and double- or triple-spacing?

✓ Are active voice, present tense, and clear, simple writing used?

✓ If the script is for television, is it set up in standard format, with instructions on the left and copy on the right?

On Assignment

Individual Activities

1. Write a brief definition or explanation of each of the following terms.

   broadcast journalism flair

   nugget program director

   station manager technical director

2. Tape-record a radio or television news story that you think has been reported with flair. Play the story in class and defend its strong points. What made the story good? Was it only word choice, or also the ideas and sequencing of events? Discuss your ideas with others in the class.

3. Clip three news stories from your school newspaper and rewrite them into broadcast style, using the three organizational methods you have learned. Then adjust the stories for television, indicating what visuals you would use to illustrate them. Attach the original stories to your work.

4. Test your critical thinking. Watch the local television news tonight. List the stories in the order presented. How many minutes were allocated to each? Note the visuals. Then read the local newspaper the next morning. How were those same stories treated? Write a news story comparing and contrasting the way news is treated by different media on the same day.

Evaluate the reasons for the similarities and differences. Are some stories more effectively handled in one medium than in the other? Explain your ideas.

5. Write and record a five-minute newscast on the activities in your school for a single day. Plan two commercials to promote school events (the next sports event, play, or dance). Compare your choice of topics to those of other students.

6. Record a brief interview on a specific topic with a teacher, a student leader, or someone in the community. Before the interview, arrange your questions in logical sequence. Be sure your direction is clear (to the interview subject and to a listener who may not know anything about the subject). Be prepared for quick thinking, changes in direction, or following up on new leads as the interview evolves. Have three non-journalism students critique your interview. Were the questions good? Did you follow up? What angles did you miss that would have interested them? Now, ask two classmates to critique your interview. Write a self-critique—what would you change, if you could do it over?

7. Over the past few years, local news programs have expanded their coverage to include national news. Advances in technology and the ease of setting up

local correspondents anywhere in the world have almost made national newscasts a thing of the past. There are those who believe that eventually there will be no ABC, NBC, Fox, or CBS national nightly news programs.

Interview local television news people about this trend. Visit the station and see for yourself the vast number of satellite sources available. Learn about video news releases. See how the local station can prepare stories on major scientific advances, making them look local even though the newsmakers are in some other part of the world. Is the trend toward localizing national stories good? What might be the benefits? What might be the negative results? How do the 24-hour news programs—CNN or CNBC—affect local news coverage? As cable expands, will it make the local news change again? Prepare a short editorial on what you learn, and give your perspective on the future of television news.

Team Activity

8. As a class, brainstorm topics for documentaries about some facet of your school. Select the top ideas so that there is one for each team. As a team, determine your approach to the story. Who are your sources? What research is needed? Outline a possible scenario for your stories so that you have some established direction. How can you truly make this story flow and interest your audience? Next, set up and conduct interviews, using your tape recorder or camcorder. Take good notes to guide your use of the tapes, and prepare introductory and follow-up copy. Produce a ten-minute documentary, and play it for your class to critique. How could it have been improved? What were its strong points? Is it of value to the student audience? Ask a local broadcaster to critique it with you.

"The biggest advantage of being a journalist is being a witness to history," says Katherine Adams, Emmy Award-winning journalist and anchor at Detroit's WDIV-TV.

"A journalist is often given a front row seat to events that impact the lives . . . of people," she said.

A journalist, she adds, has a great responsibility. And Adams takes that responsibility seriously. Her interest in broadcasting was sparked when she watched classmates at Kent State University prepare for a television program.

"They were putting together a half-hour talk show," Adams recalled. "I was fascinated by the technology, the immediacy, and the creativity displayed. It was then I decided to major in telecommunications."

Adams began her career at Storer Broadcasting Company, starting out as a copy aide and eventually becoming a production assistant.

This exposure taught her a few things. "I realized how much knowledge, intensity . . . were needed to make headway in this field," Adams said. So she concentrated on developing her skills.

Soon she showed such promise that she was enrolled in a training program to become a reporter.

In 1976, Adams moved to Cleveland to join the staff at WJKW-TV as a weekend anchor and reporter. After a short time, she was promoted to weekday anchor and host of a public affairs program.

She gained five years of experience at WJKW-TV before moving to Detroit to WJBK-TV. Within one year, she became co-anchor of the six and eleven o'clock newscasts. Today she co-anchors *Newsbeat Today*, the first locally produced and consistently most-watched morning news hour in Detroit.

Adams has half a dozen Emmy nominations, including one for commentary. She won her Emmy for the documentary "Bridge over Troubled Water."

The path to her present success was not always easy, but Adams pushed on. "Every experience—whether good or bad—is an experience I've learned from," she said.

Among her many honors, Adams was nominated twice as Outstanding Woman Newscaster by the American Women in Radio and Television in Detroit. The National American Women in Radio and Television recognized Adams and WJBK-TV for excellence in programming and presentation of a positive and realistic portrayal of women.

Adams gives this advice to aspiring journalists.

"Strive for perfection in your writing and delivery. Use your heritage, and do not deny it. Finally, accept the great responsibility of being a role model, and conduct your life . . . in such a way that it will be an inspiration to others, no matter what their race, creed, or color."

Chapter Sixteen

Understanding and Using Public Relations

Key Terms

public relations

publics

target audience

student news bureau

embargo

news release

Key Concepts

After reading this chapter, you should

- understand what public relations is and why "publics" are important

- be able to use the public relations planning model to develop and implement a PR plan

- know the functions of a school news bureau and a school public relations agency

- be able to write a clear news release

- recognize the career opportunities that journalism students have in public relations

Not all journalism students actually start their careers as journalists, and many who do begin as journalists change careers along the way. Public relations is one field in which journalism skills can be very helpful. Public relations professionals use their writing and editing abilities to shape public opinion in corporations and businesses, for organizations and associations, in public relations agencies, or on their own as freelancers.

Public relations also is a good way to combine other interests with journalism. For example, if you consider yourself an environmentalist, you can seek a career with environmental organizations or companies specializing in that area of business. Most colleges and universities, and many school districts, for example, have public relations departments, allowing professionals to link their skills in media and communications with education interests. The list of possibilities is long.

The purpose of this chapter is not to provide an extensive knowledge of public relations or to make you into a public relations expert. It is, however, to give information about one of the major careers that journalists often move into and to show how you can use your journalistic abilities in

Doing public relations projects for the school or community gives student journalists a chance to use their writing and organizational skills.

Who Are Your Publics?

If you look at a school community, its publics would broadly include the following:

- students
- teachers
- administrators—at the school and in central administration
- office personnel
- support personnel—cooks, custodians, bus drivers
- parents of the students
- neighbors (who do not have students in school)
- businesses

Lists of publics can easily be expanded or tightened depending on the specific audiences to be reached. For example, students might be divided by age, grade level, sex, specific courses being taken, club or specific sports team membership, possession of driver's license, and so on.

developing public relations skills. Journalists, for example, are inquisitive and know how to get and interpret information. Getting and interpreting information is important to PR professionals. Journalists know how to use the information they gather to write in a manner that communicates effectively. PR requires effective, easily understood writing that will help an organization communicate its views to target audiences.

PR professionals also have to know what the media needs and how it works. Companies and agencies often organize their public relations departments to include specialists in media relations—people who have the ability to think, write, and work effectively with journalists. They work as part of an account or department team to develop the organization's public relations strategy, then use their special expertise to help implement media-related programs.

There are many ways student journalists can apply journalistic skills in public relations. To get started, it is important to understand what public relations is and how the public relations process works.

Defining Public Relations

There are a lot of definitions for public relations. Edward L. Bernays, who is credited with being one of the founders of this profession in the early 1920s, saw this new field, based on the social sciences, as combining communications and a knowledge of public opinion, human behavior, and motivations to reinforce, modify, or change how a group of people think or act. These groups of people are each considered a "public," and there are many of them.

On a very simple level, then, PR may be defined (as James E. Grunig and Todd Hunt do in their text *Managing Public Relations*) ". . . the management of communication between an organization and its publics."

According to Bernays, a public relations professional was guided by a set of ethics and a sense of social responsibility. He or she was not to be confused with press agents and publicists of the day (or today for that matter) who used the media as a way to get information to the public primarily to promote a cause, person, or event.

Today, a number of public relations professionals and public relations firms refer to what they do as "reputation management." Paul Holmes, editor of *Reputation Management* magazine, defines the profession as

> ". . . a counseling discipline that recognizes the importance of reputation as an organizational asset, and seeks to ensure that management decisions are made in an environment in which reputational implications are fully understood, evaluated and considered, so that an organization's behavior earns it a strategically appropriate reputation with important stakeholder groups [publics]."

Holmes sees reputation management as using reputation as an asset to help the organization achieve its objectives while minimizing the resistance of various publics to those objectives.

A Public Relations Model

Regardless of definition, effective public relations strategies are designed along models such as this one, which was developed by Alfred Geduldig, a leading public relations consultant:

- **Objectives:** Determining what you want to accomplish for the organization.
- **Audiences:** Knowing which publics are the target for your communications, and which groups are important for their ability to influence those target audiences (positively and/or negatively).
- **Desired action:** Defining clearly what you want the audiences to do (support, stay neutral, buy a product, and so on).
- **Research:** Knowing what target audiences or publics currently know, think, and believe about an organization, issue, or subject; their motivation for the opinions they hold; how they get information and who they feel are credible sources (including the media); fact-finding (including database and library research).
- **Risks:** Defining the risks and barriers that may affect the public relations plan.

Public relations is a worthy and long-established profession, but some people appear to mistrust it. They seem to feel that because PR campaigns try to help companies or organizations put their best foot forward, there must be something underhanded or deceptive going on—that the campaign is helping the client hide something.

According to Clifford G. Christians *et al*'s sourcebook *Media Ethics*, public relations workers do fill a rather unique dual function of both informing and persuading, but there is no reason why this cannot be done in an honest and ethical manner. As in other professions, however, situations do arise requiring hard decisions.

A public relations person is trained in his or her business and does the research necessary to give the client the most effective campaign possible. But suppose that, even in the face of overwhelming research, the client still wants to do the campaign in his or her own, less effective, way. Should the PR person simply acquiesce, even though he or she knows that the client's approach will not achieve the desired results? Is the PR job supposed to be approached from doing things the right way, or is keeping the client happy all that matters? Christians argues that taking the latter approach, even though it may be necessary from a business standpoint, causes the PR person to lose something intangible in the process.

A more clearcut case arises when a client wants to disguise itself as the source of a phone questionnaire done to gather information on attitudes toward its product. The client assumes that it can then use the names and address-es of respondents as leads for new sales. In this case the PR person should refuse to go along with the client. Getting information under false pretenses and using it for gain is unethical.

The question of *how much* of the truth needs to be told in a campaign can be a particularly difficult one to deal with. Christians mentions the case of a charitable organization that, while not entirely destitute, would have to probably curtail some services unless more money could be raised. The PR agency decided to institute a campaign that would focus on some of the very needy people that the charity helped, suggesting, but not saying directly, that help for these people might soon be cut off. Some of the charity's backers objected to the approach, which focused on only one aspect of their work and which would make them look a little worse off than they really were. And yet the organization *did* help such needy people as the ad depicted. Running an ad that viewers would respond to emotionally was not such a great distortion of reality.

A similar conclusion might be reached in the case of an overused, under-funded hospital that decided to limit its trauma services on days when it experienced severe overcrowding or went over its quota of emergency-room patients. Since the policy had been instituted as a way to keep the hospital functioning as the only trauma center remaining in the area, the decision to say little in the PR material about the quota aspect seemed justifiable. However, the PR person would do well to run the decision before a disinterested, responsible group to see whether they concurred.

Ethical questions like these are tricky, and the answers can't be generalized. A PR person needs to consider each situation carefully and get help when necessary to make the most honest and moral decision possible in each circumstance.

Christians, Fackler, Rotzoll, *Media Ethics: Cases and Moral Reasoning.* White Plains, NY: Longman, 1995.

- **Themes and messages:** Developing information based on the research that will help you affect the behavior of target audiences.
- **Action plan:** Determining how you will communicate your messages with these audiences—for example, which media will be used (radio, television, newspapers, newsletters, electronic mail, the Internet, direct mail, billboards, posters); timing; meetings, special events, or other non-media techniques.
- **Budget:** Determining how much the plan will cost in terms of financial resources, as well as determining human resource—that is, people—commitments.
- **Assessment:** Setting measures, in advance, that will help evaluate the effectiveness of the strategy that is implemented—that is, ways to measure successes and failures in achieving the objectives with target audiences (messages were received, action was taken).
- **Course correction:** Taking action to change the strategy, messages, and/or techniques when assessment feedback indicates that the plan is not achieving its objectives as well as it should.

Public Relations for Student Journalists

There are a number of ways—on your own time and in school—that you can gain public relations experience. For example, if you are involved in church, cultural, community and civic organizations you can join their PR committees, using your journalism skills to help prepare materials that will further the group's objectives. This could include writing for newsletters, conducting research, drafting news releases, appearing as a spokesperson before groups or the press, writing speeches, organizing special events, taking photographs, or designing brochures. You might also play a role by planning and implementing campaigns, passing election issues, getting measures through city councils, and supporting issues important to young people and the community.

You might also help your school with its public relations. Take a look at all of the things being written about in the school newspaper—musical events, plays, honor days, scholarship announcements, the start of the school year, major athletic events, a student being named top volunteer of the year, fund-raising projects, sports recognition dinners, class reunions, homecoming, famous speakers addressing the student body, mock elections. There are a lot of events taking place—and each of them is of interest not only to students, but also to one or more of the publics outside the school.

Workers in the student news bureau can phone local radio stations to provide school information or even short feeds to incorporate into their broadcasts.

Establish a Student News Bureau

In its simplest form, you can practice the media specialty of a PR firm or department through a student news bureau. A news bureau provides information about the school to its publics. Articles written about students, faculty, activities, and programs for the student media can be released for use in the local daily or weekly newspaper, on radio, and on television. They can be rewritten, condensed, or expanded if needed, and released early on the day the newspaper is distributed. Major stories can be sent the day before with a note that the story is embargoed (not to be published) until a specific day and time, allowing it to appear first in the school newspaper. Depending on the situation, these articles also can be provided to church, company, and area business newsletters.

Another activity of the news bureau could be to provide short broadcast feeds over the phone for local radio stations to incorporate into their newscasts. Stories might also be put on a World Wide Web home page promoted to and designed for nonstudents.

Writing a news release can be somewhat different from writing a newspaper article. Compare the article in the "On Display" feature on page 365 with the news release on page 366. Notice that the news release distills the most important information from the article.

Form a School PR Agency

Some colleges and universities have an interesting, enjoyable, and educational way of teaching journalism students about public relations. They organize student teams to function like a public relations agency or a company PR department. The student teams work with a local nonprofit organization to help develop public relations strategies and then help implement PR programs.

This approach can be adapted for high school use by looking at upcoming events within the school environment, and developing marketing communications programs for them. For example, the next school play will be of interest to more than students. Using the planning model on page 367, you can develop a plan to help market the event to appropriate school and outside publics. In this instance you can use your advertising skills to develop a part of the total communications program.

Develop a Public Relations Campaign

You also can take on an issue and develop a semester-long communications program dealing with it. Take school bus safety as an example. A key purpose of a school bus safety program is to promote safe rider habits

Olson Captures Community Spirit

by Lisa Martin, Green Mountain High School,
Lakewood, Colorado

For her to simply define the word initiative would be cheating. For her to occasionally want to help the community would be lying. Senior Marissa Olson, one of the 1,447 students at Green Mountain High is neither a cheater nor a liar. Her recent effort in implementing the program S.T.A.N.D. has granted her recognition in both the Lakewood community and The Prudential Spirit of Community Awards program.

On February 13, in Washington, D.C., Olson was named one of America's top 104 youth volunteers for the 1995–1996 school year period. All recognitions were made possible by the Prudential Insurance Company of America in alliance with the National Association of Secondary School Principals (NASSP). The program, designed to promote community involvement, chose two students, one middle level and one high school level student from each of the 50 states, the District of Columbia, and Puerto Rico. Managing to capture the judge's eye, Olson and James Smagala, a fifteen year old at Drake Middle School, snagged two of the votes, earning them recognition as the Colorado State Award Nominees.

"Having seen what they have accomplished has really made us feel that there is a place for this program," said executive director of awards Scott Peterson. "We had over 6,000 applicants, which we think is a very good response."

S.T.A.N.D., Students Taking a New Direction, promotes student involvement within the community and is responsible for such activities as Red Ribbon Week and the Neon Drunk Driving Simulator. Though the program was officially launched in January of 1995, Olson spent close to two years in pure preparation.

Since the time of the organization's implementation, Olson managed to reach a membership high of 30 students, sticking yet another feather in both her and GM's cap.

"There used to be a SADD chapter at GM that dwindled because the leadership was very hypocritical. Many of the students who said, 'don't drink,' were going out and getting drunk. I was very scared of losing any of my classmates in car accidents," said Olson.

With three years of hard work under her belt, The Prudential Spirit of Community Award seemed to Olson like a great opportunity and, to those who knew of her service commitment, a definite win. In October of 1995, Olson submitted her application which, following strict guidelines, explained in three paragraphs the preparation, action, and reflection of her involvement with S.T.A.N.D.

On May 4–7, Olson will receive a silver medallion and a $1000 cash award in recognition of her being named a Colorado State Award Nominee.

Though many programs stop awarding students after one recognition, The Prudential Spirit of Community Awards program has selected a panel of national judges to reexamine the original applications for a second award. The five mid-level and five high school level students who are selected from the 104 state nominees will be announced in Washington, D.C., and awarded a gold medallion and an additional $5000.

Olson, having achieved what many students could only hope to, has yet a second chance to prove her determination in both the community and herself. Those who know Olson and are familiar with her work wish her the best of luck this May.

Hopefully, the judges will see what we, the community, see and will realize that because one involved student took it upon herself to make an impact, GM is one step closer to connecting directly with the community.

Principal Liz Treichler, a promoter of S.T.A.N.D. from the beginning, took pride when saying, "My favorite quote from Einstein, my hero, is 'it is every person's objective to leave the earth a little bit better than her or she found it.' I think Marissa embodies that belief. She really works to make things happen."

News from Green Mountain High School

For more information: Journalism Department, 303-555-9500, Weekdays: 8 a.m. to 4 p.m.

Green Mountain Student Named State's Top High School Volunteer

Lakewood (Colo.) Feb. 27—Marissa Olson, a Green Mountain High School senior, was named today as one of the top 104 youth volunteers in America and Colorado's top high school volunteers in the Prudential Spirit of Community Awards program, sponsored in partnership with the National Assn. of Secondary School Principals.

Olson was recognized for her work in establishing S.T.A.N.D., Students Taking a New Direction, an organization promoting student involvement in the community. It has been responsible for such activities as Red Ribbon Week and the Neon Drunk Driving Simulator. Olson spent more than two years planning the program before it was launched in January 1995.

As the state honoree, Olson will receive a silver medallion, $1,000, and an expense-paid trip to Washington, D.C., with one of her parents for national recognition events. At those events, ten of the 104 will be named as the top volunteers in America, and will receive an additional $5,000, a gold medallion, and a trophy.

"There used to be a SADD chapter at GM that dwindled because the leadership was very hypocritical," said Olson. "Many of the students who said, 'don't drink' were going out and getting drunk. I was very scared of losing any of my classmates in car accidents."

Scott Peterson, Prudential executive director of the annual awards program, said, "Having seen what they have accomplished has really made us feel that there is a place for this program. We had over 6,000 applications."

GM Principal Liz Treichler said that Olson "really works to make things better."

among elementary school students. Elementary school children are your primary public. Secondary audiences that are important for a program to succeed include the children's parents, bus drivers, elementary teachers, and residents in and around the school community.

In doing research for your program, the student PR team will want to get safety statistics on bus-related accidents, their causes, when they happen, and how they can be prevented. This may lead you to database research or to contacting the National Transportation Safety Administration, local police departments, or bus manufacturers.

The PR team also can do primary research, interviewing teachers and student riders to test themes and messages. What messages, communications tools, and techniques are effective in promoting safety to children of this age? A survey can be conducted before starting the program to learn how much your audience already knows about bus safety. At the end of the program, you can survey again, seeing how effective the PR program has been.

After the homework and fact-finding are complete, it's time to develop an action plan and timetable. Here are some possible ideas:

- Prepare and distribute cards with the rules for safe riding.
- Write articles for the school's parent newsletter. Interview the head of school transportation, teachers, bus drivers, and kids.
- Design and print safety posters. Better yet, consider a poster contest for elementary students. The best ones can be reproduced and posted in schools. The poster contest and the winning posters allow an opportunity for you to issue news releases to the media, making the area residents aware of what is going on. The posters can be placed in area businesses, such as the grocery store, as another way to reach parents and student audiences.
- Make a video on riding safely, being sure to stress the simple rules the audience needs to follow.
- Work with the school drama or music department to write and produce a short school bus safety skit that can be taken to the elementary schools and used at parent meetings.

> **Tips for PR Campaigns**
>
> Planning a public relations campaign for your school or community? Here are some helpful hints to consider before you start.
>
> 1. Know the issue clearly.
> 2. Know what community organizations are already involved.
> 3. Don't reinvent a program where one already exists.
> 4. Consider taking existing information and bringing it to the public in new ways.
> 5. Think through your publics carefully to determine which are primary and which secondary.
> 6. Define measurable objectives.

A public relations campaign to promote safer bus riding for grade school students may involve parents and teachers as well as the children. Note that the bus's stop sign, an important safety device, is missing in this photo.

The PR team can brainstorm a wide range of program ideas such as these. Then the best ones can be prioritized for implementation. In developing the program, keep in mind what you want the outcome to be and how you want each audience to behave as a result.

Naturally, a project like this will take resources and may need to be supplemented by a fund-raising activity. Or, depending on school policy, sponsors for the project could be found. A possible sponsor could be a local radio or TV station which, as part of its effort, provides public service time for messages that the PR team prepares. This provides an additional element of support for accomplishment of the program objectives.

When the program has been under way for a while, survey a sample of your target audience and/or the secondary audiences. Make the needed changes, if any, and continue to implement the program.

Public Relations Careers

One function of public relations is helping companies to sell their products in more effective ways. A Levi Strauss campaign to encourage more casual dress in the workplace used mock demonstrations at the stock exchanges in New York and ten European cities to tell its story.

Careers in public relations can be very challenging and rewarding. While not all PR people have journalism backgrounds, those who do are able to use their journalistic skills to develop and implement exciting programs designed to motivate target publics. PR people may be generalists, doing a wide range of things, or specialize in areas like media relations. Specific tasks might include writing, designing, and producing company publications for employees, customers, or investors; writing op-ed pieces for the company, cause, or client; organizing and managing special events such as trade fairs, receptions, art shows, and tours; arranging for speaking opportunities that will reach target audiences with important company or organizational messages—then actually writing the speech and the news release about it, and arranging to reprint the speech to mail to other key audiences.

Some public relations people specialize in marketing communications—helping companies sell their products more effectively. These activities (such as campaigns by Levi Strauss to get companies to allow employees to dress more casually in the workplace) supplement paid advertising programs. Advertising and news articles are used and special events are organized to attract audience and media interest, along with employing other communications techniques.

Code of Professional Standards for the Practice of Public Relations

This Code was adopted by the PRSA (Public Relations Society of America) Assembly in 1988. It replaces a Code of Ethics in force since 1950 and revised in 1954, 1959, 1963, 1977, and 1983.

Declaration of Principles

Members of the Public Relations Society of America base their professional principles on the fundamental value and dignity of the individual, holding that the free exercise of human rights, especially freedom of speech, freedom of assembly, and freedom of the press, is essential to the practice of public relations.

In serving the interests of clients and employers, we dedicate ourselves to the goals of better communication, understanding, and cooperation among the diverse individuals, groups, and institutions of society, and of equal opportunity of employment in the public relations profession.

We pledge:

To conduct ourselves professionally, with truth, accuracy, fairness, and responsibility to the public;

To improve our individual competence and advance the knowledge and proficiency of the profession through continuing research and education;

And to adhere to the articles of the Code of Professional Standards for the Practice of Public Relations as adopted by the governing Assembly of the Society.

Code of Professional Standards for the Practice of Public Relations

These articles have been adopted by the Public Relations Society to promote and maintain high standards of public service and ethical conduct among its members.

1. A member shall conduct his or her professional life in accord with the **public interest**.
2. A member shall exemplify high standards of **honesty and integrity** while carrying out dual obligations to a client or employer and to the democratic process.
3. A member shall **deal fairly** with the public, with past or present clients or employers, and with fellow practitioners, giving due respect to the ideal of free inquiry and to the opinions of others.
4. A member shall adhere to the highest standards of **accuracy and truth**, avoiding extravagant claims or unfair comparisons and giving credit for ideas and words borrowed from others.
5. A member shall not knowingly disseminate **false or misleading information** and shall act promptly to correct erroneous communications for which he or she is responsible.
6. A member shall not engage in any practice which has the purpose of **corrupting** the integrity of channels of communications or the processes of government.
7. A member shall be prepared to **identify publicly** the name of the client or employer on whose behalf any public communication is made.
8. A member shall not use any individual or organization professing to serve or represent an announced cause, or professing to be independent or unbiased, but actually serving another or **undisclosed interest**.
9. A member shall not **guarantee the achievement** of specified results beyond the member's direct control.

10. A member shall **not represent conflicting** or competing interests without the express consent of those concerned, given after a full disclosure of the facts.

11. A member shall not place himself or herself in a position where the member's **personal interest is or may be in conflict** with an obligation to an employer or client, or others, without full disclosure of such interests to all involved.

12. A member shall **not accept fees, commissions, gifts or any other consideration** from anyone except clients or employers for whom services are performed without their express consent, given after full disclosure of the facts.

13. A member shall scrupulously safeguard the **confidences and privacy rights** of present, former, and prospective clients or employers.

14. A member shall not intentionally **damage the professional reputation** or practice of another practitioner.

15. If a member has evidence that another member has been guilty of unethical, illegal, or unfair practices, including those in violation of this Code, the member is obligated to present the information promptly to the proper authorities of the Society for action in accordance with the procedure set forth in Article XII of the Bylaws.

16. A member called as a witness in a proceeding for enforcement of this Code is obligated to appear, unless excused for sufficient reason by the judicial panel.

17. A member shall, as soon as possible, sever relations with any organization or individual if such relationship requires conduct contrary to the articles of this Code.

Wrap-up

Public relations and journalism are professions that rely upon each other. PR people work closely with the news media to communicate messages about their organization, issue, business, or clients to the various audiences important to them. At the same time, journalists use public relations people as resources for many of the stories they write. While not all people who enter the PR profession will be journalists or have journalistic skills, many do.

Public relations, a profession that Edward L. Bernays is credited with founding in the early 1920s, is based on blending social sciences with communications. It uses a knowledge of public opinion, human behavior, and motivation to reinforce, modify, or change how a group of people—referred to as "publics"—think or act.

Regardless of the definition, public relations professionals develop programs and events, utilize media, and use a wide range of other communications techniques to get someone to do something as a result of their work. In many ways, PR seeks to accomplish a call-to-action like that of editorials and advertising.

Public relations strategies are often designed following a model. The model begins with setting clear objectives that are to be accomplished by a PR program, identifying the target publics (audiences), and determining what action the target publics are expected to take, such as supporting a certain position on an issue or making a contribution to a cause. It goes on to utilize research to understand how the target audiences now feel about the issue, how they get information, and how they might react to the message; then develops themes and messages, based on the research, that will help achieve the objectives of the program. Finally, it lays out an action plan, summarizes the human and financial resources required to implement that action plan, determines how the plan will be assessed in order to evaluate if it is having the desired effects on target audiences and provides ways for the plan to be revised if needed.

Student journalists can apply their writing and editing skills to public relations. One way is to join the public relations committees of local nonprofit organizations, political campaigns, or other groups. By offering to help plan PR programs, as well as to help write materials needed and to assist in other implementation, students can make useful contributions to a group's PR efforts.

A news bureau is another approach that will allow students to experience the media relations activity that is important to public relations. Students can have news releases prepared based on articles that will appear in the next student newspaper. These can be sent to the local radio or television station and to local newspapers, thus disseminating news about the school to its nonstudent publics.

Another way to get involved in public relations is to form a PR team to work on a special issue of interest to the group. This could range from organizing the PR team to accomplish a specific objective, such as increasing attendance at school plays, to developing a semester-long program on school bus safety.

There are many rewarding public relations careers, and a good number of journalists find their way into them. Opportunities exist in community organizations such as the United Way, in businesses, in schools, hospitals, and government, and in many other organizations. There are also specialty PR jobs, such as being a speechwriter or working as a media spokesperson for a political candidate, an issue, or a cause.

Evaluation Checklist: *Press Release*

✔ Does the release include the most noteworthy features of the news story?

✔ Is the information included in the release chosen for its relevance to a particular public?

✔ Have all names, dates, and facts been double-checked for accuracy?

✔ If an embargo is required, are the time and date clearly indicated?

✔ Is the release free from grammatical errors and in accordance with the publication and AP stylebooks?

On Assignment

Individual Activities

1. Write a brief definition or explanation of each of the following terms.

embargo	news release
public relations	publics
student news bureau	target audience

2. In the last issue of the school newspaper, mark each story that you think would be of interest to one of the nonstudent publics of the school. Indicate who you feel are the top two external audiences for each story you have identified. Then take two of the articles and determine what would need to be done to make them acceptable as news releases to those audiences. Rewrite them as needed.

3. Evaluate the various sample articles in this book for their adaptability into news releases. Choose one that contains information that would be of some value to a defined public. Then rewrite the story as a news release. Be ready to explain why you chose the article you did.

4. Choose one of the following topics as a focus for a public relations campaign in your community. Use the PR planning model on pages 361 and 363 to plot the general actions for the campaign. Then compare notes with others who have chosen the same topic. Discuss the strengths and weaknesses of each plan in class.
   a. securing volunteer readers for a local senior-citizens center
   b. getting young adults registered to vote
   c. bringing a greater variety of summertime activities into the community
   d. educating children about being cautious with strangers
   e. keeping people from cutting down large old trees
   f. a school or community issue of your choice

5. If your school has a public relations or public affairs staff member, invite him or her to meet with your class to discuss how public relations is organized and managed. Determine what model is used to develop a communications plan for your schools, and learn how each aspect of the model discussed in this chapter is included in that plan. Write an interview story based on the presentation. You may also want to write to the National School Public Relations Association for information on school communications.

6. If there is a public relations agency located in your community, or a large company that has a public relations department, arrange to visit them for a briefing on how they approach public relations. Write a news feature on what you learn.

7. Test your critical thinking. Reread the Society of Professional Journalists' Code of Ethics. Compare it with the Public Relations Society of America's Code of Ethics in this chapter. What conflicts, if any, do you see between the two codes? How can an ethical PR person work effectively with working journalists? Invite a local media representative and a public relations professional to your school or arrange a three-way telephone discussion. Have them discuss how each views the other profession and what they see as any ethical issues in their relationships. Write an editorial or column on this subject, taking any viewpoint you want.

Team Activities

8. Organize the class into teams. Each team should select a school event that will occur in the next couple of months. Learn all you can about the event. Meet with its sponsors or program chairs. (They become your client.) Using the PR planning model, develop a PR plan. Review the plan with the other teams. Then make additions and appropriate changes. Present the plan to the client. If your client is willing, implement the plan.

9. Implement the public relations plan you worked out in activity 4. Team up with students who have chosen the same topic you did. Combine everyone's ideas into a workable, written plan. Do the necessary research, including interviewing people and getting approvals as necessary. Then implement the plan.

Though Elizabeth Krupnick's journey to a top corporate communications position has been somewhat circuitous and unorthodox, she said she had the "journalism bug" from an early age.

Krupnick, chief communications officer of The Prudential, grew up in New York. The daughter of a journalist, she attributes much of her early interest in journalism to having "four papers on the breakfast table every day."

She graduated from Colby College in Maine with a B.A. in art history, returning to New York to work for a small ad agency. At 25, she went to the prestigious School of Journalism at the University of Missouri in Columbia, where she earned her master's.

Although Krupnick always dreamed of working for a newspaper, she originally opted for teaching college journalism. Jobs took her from Massachusetts to Maine to Oregon.

She then launched her career in public relations at Aetna Life & Casualty, where she rose to become senior vice president of corporate affairs prior to joining The Prudential.

"In many ways, I got lucky," she says. "I was at the right place at the right time."

Luck may have played a role in her career, but she was clearly prepared each time luck offered an opportunity. Krupnick thinks she was served well by her "academic bent," her development and use of analytical skills, and the knowledge and understanding she gained from traveling at an early age.

Krupnick's responsibilities at The Prudential reflect the diverse role of many of today's communicators. Krupnick manages the company's public relations, advertising, internal communications, speechwriting, creative services, issues management, and research functions.

Because of the many potential directions for a journalism-based career today, she senses that "a liberal arts education is more important than ever before," adding that in many cases high school education has been inadequate.

"What is most missing today is strength in writing, and it drives me crazy," she said, "but bringing intelligence is as important as education."

Krupnick believes that one of the keys to her success and to her ability as a writer was her work on the University of Missouri newspaper.

The newspaper was "run as the town daily" in Columbia, providing a remarkable experience for someone who had "a good nose for sniffing out stuff."

"Covering city government is a great experience for a student. It's mundane, yet something fun is always going on—kind of a potent thing in your twenties. That's good for beginning journalists," she said.

She feels that succeeding in journalism today is tough and the competition is strong.

"I suggest you go to a big journalism school because the networks [of contacts] you make there are so important," she said.

Chapter Seventeen

Handling Finances: Advertising and Business

Key Concepts

After reading this chapter, you should

- understand the role and functions of the business staff

- know how to get information about your student market through surveys and other means

- understand how to procure ads and how they pay for publication expenses

- know how to plan, write, and lay out effective ads

- know the importance of record-keeping in managing circulation and keeping track of expenses

In addition to serving a news and editorial function, a student publication has business responsibilities. A newspaper has to be written and edited, and it must have money to pay its bills.

This section will acquaint you with the activities of the business staffs of student publications. The business side is not a competitor with the editorial side; the two must work together for a successful publication.

Too often student editors feel held back because of a shortage of funds. They need to understand that while they have excellent ideas, these ideas take money. Extra pictures, artwork, color at homecoming and Christmas, and extra pages for special features are not gifts from a printer.

In short, just as the staff must exercise editorial and news responsibility, so must it exercise fiscal responsibility.

Staff Organization

Leading the business staff is the business manager. The business manager's role is to see that the three main functions of this department are carried out: advertising sales and preparation, circulation, and record-keeping. The student business manager must be personable, aggressive, and able to lead a sales staff. He or she must also work closely with the editor to plan the number of pages of the publication, work out special layout needs, and coordinate production with the printer.

Assistant business managers, in addition to selling and preparing advertising, generally are assigned other specific duties. One might be in charge of circulation, another of billing or books and records, another of advertising. The specific breakdown naturally will depend on the size of the staff and the publication; in some schools, for example, reporters also help sell advertising. This is not unlike the way

The organization of a business staff need not be elaborate. This model shows a simple breakdown based on the primary tasks the staff performs.

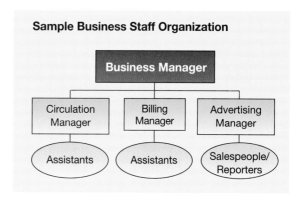

Sample Business Staff Organization

375

some small-town and weekly publications operate. As in any good organization, there must be a spirit of teamwork and a willingness to help one another.

Getting and Using Advertising Information

Advertising generates income for the publication, provides a means of communicating product or sales information from a business to the publication's readers, and assists the reader in selecting that business's products and services. Advertising also stimulates competition and helps keep prices down and the economy active.

Advertising is *not* a contribution to the student publication. You have a real product to sell. School publications are well read by students, who are today one of the largest single segments of purchasing power in this country. Well-prepared advertising aimed at students will bring many returns to the advertiser.

Unfortunately, some student-produced publications do treat advertising as if it were a contribution by the business. A lot of little boxes that merely say Joe's Beanery, Little Theater, and the like aren't doing anyone much good. It takes little effort to get them ready for the printer, but they probably do not sell products. More than likely, they are not even read. The publication that carries this sort of advertising is cheating itself, the reader, and the advertiser.

On the other hand, a publication containing good display advertising that sells products readers like, want, and use regularly is performing a service to all parties concerned. Such advertising also makes student publications more attractive, and good advertising will help attract more good advertising. A successful ad will keep a business using your publication for years to come. In short, you will become a significant vehicle in the communication process between business and consumer.

Who knows better than you what your fellow students do, how they think, and what they want? Or, to hedge on that a bit: Who *should* know better than you?

It's important to know your student market. This does not mean just being friends with a number of your classmates. It means knowing how much money students have to spend, where they spend it, and when. If you have done your research, you will be able to go to your advertisers and

The Advertising Principles of American Business*

Truth

Advertising shall tell the truth, and shall reveal significant facts, the omission of which would mislead the public.

Substantiation

Advertising claims shall be substantiated by evidence in possession of the advertiser and advertising agency, prior to making such claims.

Comparisons

Advertising shall refrain from making false, misleading, or unsubstantiated statements or claims about a competitor or his products or services.

Bait Advertising

Advertising shall not offer products or services for sale unless such offer constitutes a bona fide effort to sell the advertised products or services and is not a device to switch consumers to other goods or services, usually higher priced.

Guarantees and Warranties

Advertising of guarantees and warranties shall be explicit, with sufficient information to apprise consumers of their principal terms and limitations or, when space or time restrictions preclude such disclosures, the advertisement should clearly reveal where the full text of the guarantee or warranty can be examined before purchase.

Price Claims

Advertising shall avoid price claims which are false or misleading, or savings claims which do not offer provable savings.

Testimonials

Advertising containing testimonials shall be limited to those of competent witnesses who are reflecting a real and honest opinion or experience.

Taste and Decency

Advertising shall be free of statements, illustrations or implications which are offensive to good taste or public decency.

*Adopted by the American Advertising Federation Board of Directors, March 2, 1984; reprinted with permission.

tell them what potential for success their ads have. This research is essential as you prepare to sell advertising, and it is relatively simple to do.

Before starting the advertising process, though, you should consider the practical and concise philosophy of advertising that follows. It was written by a veteran expert in the field, a partner in one of the world's leading advertising agencies. Keep these points in mind while doing your market research, preparing ad copy, and selling space. The well-conceived ad, from start to finish, will benefit both your paper and your advertisers.

Market Surveys

A very effective way to get information about the size, needs, and wants of your student market is to prepare and distribute a market survey. If your school offers classes in marketing, members might be willing to help conduct a survey for your staff. Certain computer programs can help process the data you collect. If a computer system is available, talk with knowledgeable personnel *before* you start writing the survey to make sure you prepare it in the proper format and use the proper forms.

One newspaper staff began putting together its marketing study by holding a brainstorming session to determine all the things they and other students might do in a week. Where would they spend money? What types of things would they buy? Where might they go for entertainment? Where might they shop (shopping centers, central business areas)? Related questions were also examined. How much influence do students have over family purchases and deciding, for example, where the family will dine out? How much money do students have to spend each week? Do they have credit cards, savings accounts, checking accounts?

Getting students to participate in surveys of their buying habits and tastes may result in information that will entice local merchants to buy ads in a publication.

The next step was to go to the computer center and determine the alternatives available for processing the information and to learn the format for preparing the survey form. The computer center provided specially overprinted forms for the final survey instrument. Students would use lead pencils to mark the proper response, and the survey forms (similar to many standardized tests) would then be fed directly into the computer.

A task force of staff members prepared the first draft of questions, asking, "Why do we want to know this?" about each question before allowing it to remain in the survey. Then, armed with a draft, each task force member selected five students at random and had them complete the survey (pilot testing). After students had answered the questions, the task force went back over each one and noted anything that was not clear or any other problems they felt students had in completing the survey. Then they went back to the drawing board to revise and finalize the survey for printing.

Next, the survey was administered. In this case, all classes meeting at 9 A.M. took time out to complete the study. Nearly all students participated. (The staff could have prepared a random sample and conducted the study with a smaller group. For more information on random samples, see Chapter Three.) The data were then processed and analyzed, and that analysis provided important marketing information for the advertising sales staff to use in their sales pitch to current and prospective advertisers.

The questionnaire in the "On Display" feature on pages 380 and 381 is adapted from one created by the *Oracle,* East High School, Lincoln, Nebraska.

Other Research Studies

If you are not able to do your own research, you can take advantage of market research conducted by others and reported in the local news media.

For example, Teenage Research Unlimited (TRU), Northbrook, Illinois, probes teen spending habits and buying preferences. In a recent news release, they noted that the more than 29 million teens in the United States spent $109 billion in 1995, a 10 percent (nonadjusted for inflation) increase over the year before. To arrive at this number, the group polled more than 2,000 young people ages 12–19. Of the amount spent, teens indicated that $67 billion came from their own funds (allowance, gifts, jobs), and that they spent family dollars of $41 billion. TRU said that boys and girls spend virtually the same amount each week, $67 for boys, $65 for girls. And the teen market is expected to continue to grow each year through at least 2010.

On Display

from the *Oracle,* East High School, Lincoln, Nebraska

This is a marketing survey to aid the ORACLE in evaluating its advertising efforts. Please answer <u>all</u> questions. Select only <u>one</u> answer for each question.

MARKETING SURVEY

1. Sex

   Male _____   Female _____

2. Age

   under 14_____   15_____

   16 _____   17_____

   18 or over _____

3. Grade

   Freshman _____   Sophomore _____

   Junior _____   Senior _____

4. What section of the ORACLE do you read first?

   page 1 _____   editorial page _____

   sports page _____   inside pages _____

5. Do you take the ORACLE home?

   never _____   always _____

   occasionally _____

6. If you take the ORACLE home, do your parents or caretakers read it?

   yes _____   no _____

7. Do you have a part-time job?

   yes _____   no _____

8. If you answered yes to number 7, how much do you earn weekly?

   under $75 _____ $75–$150 _____

   over $150 _____   over $200 _____

9. Do you have any other regular sources of income, such as an allowance?

   yes _____   no _____

10. If so, how much weekly income do you receive from that source?

    $20 or less _____ $21–$25 _____

    $26–$30 _____   over $31 _____

Which items in questions 11–19 do you pay for with your own money?

11. School lunches

    yes _____   no _____

12. Clothing

    yes _____   no _____

13. Entertainment (movies, dances, etc.)

    yes _____   no _____

14. School supplies

    yes _____   no _____

You can do a computer search or check the *Readers' Guide* for recent stories on the youth market. Translate those results into how much buying power teens have in your community.

If you watch television shows or read publications targeted to the younger audience, you will see ads for nearly every type of product. Companies have become smart. They know students don't buy just sodas, chewing gum, and CDs. They know students influence many decisions at home, and that they often do the shopping for the family. Through market research, companies choose programs and media aimed at teens to tap their buying power and to influence decisions made at home.

This is important information to use in obtaining advertisers for your student publications, too.

15. Gasoline

    yes _____ no _____

16. Cosmetics, toiletries, etc.

    yes _____ no _____

17. Do you own a CD player?

    yes _____ no _____

18. Do you own a VCR?

    yes _____ no _____

19. Do you own your own car?

    yes _____ no _____

20. Do you have a savings account?

    yes _____ no _____

21. About how much money did you (or your parents) spend for clothing at the start of this school year?

    up to $100 _____ $100–$200 _____

    $200–$250 _____ $250–$300 _____

    over $300 _____

22. Where do you do most of your shopping?

    downtown _____ Gateway _____

    other _____

23. Which radio station do you listen to most?

    KFOR _____ KLMS _____

    KLIN _____ KFAB _____

    KOIL _____ others _____

24. What TV network do you prefer to watch?

    ABC _____ NBC_____

    CBS _____ Fox_____

    cable networks _____ other _____

25. About how often do you go to movies each month?

    once _____ 2–3 times _____

    4 or more times _____ none _____

26. About how much do you spend (away from home and school) each week on food items like soft drinks, snacks, etc.?

    less than $5 _____ $5–$10 _____

    $10–$15 _____ over $15 _____

27. Did you order a yearbook this year?

    yes _____ no _____

28. Do you help make decisions about major family purchases?

    yes _____ no _____

29. Do you read ORACLE ads?

    never _____ occasionally _____

    almost always _____

30. If there were a classified ad section in the ORACLE would you utilize it (read and/or place an ad)?

    yes _____ no _____

Advertising Sales

Once you have researched your market and analyzed the results, you are ready to sell advertising. You have the proof of your readers' buying power. You know the market. A business doesn't have to look upon buying advertising in your publication as a charitable contribution.

Now you need a list of prospective advertisers. Ad salespeople should sit down with the business manager and divide the prospects and existing accounts. If a student has a personal interest in a specific type of product, he or she is a natural to sell ads to stores dealing with that product. For example, if you happen to be an avid CD collector, you will do well at selling advertising to music stores. You will know the language and have things to talk about with the stores' advertising managers. Naturally, not all your accounts will be of special interest to you. But every product or service interests some of your readers, so don't overlook any potential advertiser.

Once you get your list of prospects—the advertising beat—contact them on a regular basis. It is always best to show prospects a sample ad to demonstrate your knowledge of the market and their business. You might also prepare a standard pitch on how your publication operates and how this particular advertising idea will benefit the prospect's business.

Let's use the marketing survey as an example. You could go to the local music store and tell the owner that 81 percent of your school's students have their own CD players and 73 percent shop downtown where this store is located, according to the survey of your readers. Use the research to point out that these students spend thousands of dollars each month on entertainment, CDs, and similar items. Then show the prospect an ad featuring artists who are currently popular with your readers, pointing out that an ad like this could bring in business.

Discuss how little it costs to reach each student. For example, if a column inch in your newspaper costs $6, a 20-column-inch ad will cost $120. Divide that cost by the 1,500 students who read your paper, and the ad costs eight cents per reader—a great price for reaching a targeted audience. Be pleasant and answer questions politely. If the answer is no, thank the store owner and leave your name, school phone number, and a rate card if you have one. Visit again when the next issue is being prepared. Don't give up.

Your attitude and appearance will have a direct effect on what you sell. Look neat and clean. It cannot be overemphasized that your appearance and attitiude reflect the image of your school and your publication.

Ad Contracts

Some schools have advertising contracts that they sell before the year starts or that are completed as each issue is prepared. Naturally, contracts are helpful. They provide proof that the advertiser has agreed to the ad you plan to run, obligating his or her company to pay the bills. They also make for a businesslike relationship between the advertiser and your publication. Develop a contract that will best suit your situation, and make sure that completed contracts are signed by all relevant parties.

Some student publications have sliding rates for advertising to encourage advertisers to place more ads of a larger size throughout the school year. It is difficult, however, to keep records on such sales, and a standard rate may be more useful. Remember, you have a product for sale. That product has a value. You sell it for what it's worth. With the buying power of today's student, that value to an advertiser is substantial.

Figuring Out Costs

One question that must be settled before each issue is "How much advertising does it take to pay for the publication?" To answer this, you must consider a number of questions. How many pages will be in this issue? How many photographs will be used? Will the newspaper be printed on newsprint, or a higher-quality offset paper?

For example, assume that your next newspaper will be an eight-page issue. On newsprint, the cost will be about $1,000 for printing 1,800 copies of the issue. Since this is a special homecoming issue, you plan to have four-color photos, each about 3" x 4", for an additional cost of approximately $700. In addition, there will be a number of black-and-white photos that the printer factors into the base printing cost. This means that the newspaper will cost $1,700 to print.

Then you need to factor other costs into the equation. It will cost about $80 for photography. There is an additional $36 for postage to mail copies of the newspaper to other schools and outside subscribers. If you go for full accounting, you will take the yearly estimated cost for computer disks, paper, toner, and other office supplies and factor them into the overall cost per issue. Assume that these miscellaneous costs add up to an additional $75 per issue.

Here, then are your costs:

Printing	$1,000
Color photo, printing cost	$700
Photography	$80
Postage	$36
Supplies	$75
Total:	$1,891

Let's assume that you have $400 per issue in student activity fees as income. This means that the advertising revenue must raise $1,491 to break even.

There are a total of 640 column inches in this issue (eight pages, five columns per page, each column 16 inches). The newspaper policy is that you will sell no more than 40 percent of the space in advertising, or in this case, 256 column inches. (A rule of thumb by most print media is to have a ratio of 60 percent advertising to 40 percent news. But a smaller percentage is not uncommon for school media.) To determine the amount you should charge per column inch, divide $1,491 by 256 inches. The result is $5.82. The amount would be rounded to $5.90 or $6 to provide the advertising rate. If the newspaper sold more or less than 40 percent, the cost per column inch would change.

Advertising contracts such as this one help maintain a businesslike relationship with advertisers and offer a clear explanation of rates and policies of a publication.

The Advertising Contract

Ad rates as listed on the Rate Card are for camera-ready ads or for ads with only a minimal amount of typesetting. All additional art, photography or unusually time-consuming work will be charged at the rate shown on this contract. No ad placement will be guaranteed. However, placement will be granted, if possible, when requested.

Davidson High School
P.O. Box 1808
McDaid, Kansas 66044
913/847-5720

Kenneth Hines
Advertising Director

Debra Keyser
Betty Wilson
Liz Knapp
Steven Declerck
Representatives

Sidney Singer
Adviser

Publications department use only:

☐ Bill
☐ Paid
☐ Placed _____
Rep:

AD SIZE (in col./inches or portion of page)	CHARGE	PUBLICATION	DATE
1.			
2.			
3.			
4.			
5.			

ADDITIONAL CHARGES:

Photography _____

Artwork _____

Unusually difficult work _____

TOTAL CHARGES _____

Firm name _____

Address _____

City _____ State _____ Zip _____

Phone _____

Authorized signature _____

Print name here _____

Date _____

DEADLINES: Yearbook   February 1
Newspaper   Contact your representative.

Naturally, a newspaper would not compute its rate on an issue-by-issue basis. In developing the annual budget, the costs for the above items would be estimated for the total number of issues planned in the year ahead. This would provide an advertising rate.

If you do decide to provide an incentive to advertisers, you could have a discounted rate if the business places an advertisement in every issue for the semester or year, or agrees to purchase a specific number of column inches over the term, or does a combination of the above. For example, the open rate could be set at $8. If a company agreed to place an ad of at least ten inches in each issue for the school term, the advertising cost might be set at $6.25 per inch. If a company agreed to run more than ten inches in each issue, or to run a total of 150 inches or more over the twelve issues each semester, the rate might be set at $6. Though your bookkeeping may be a bit more confusing if you have variable rates like this, you might decide that the prospect of snaring large accounts for extended periods of time is worth the trouble.

There is no hard-and-fast rule for determining advertising costs— beyond staying in the black; your desires as a newspaper staff will determine your goals. Be realistic. Some student papers barely break even from one year to the next. Others earn several hundred dollars each year, which are spent on special issues, darkroom equipment, computers, software, or supplies.

The advertising concepts discussed here also apply to school magazines and yearbooks. After you calculate the subscription or sales income, subtract the costs of production—printing, photography, color, supplies, telephones, and postage. The amount that remains must be made up through advertising revenue or other fund-raising activities.

Preparing Advertising Copy

Writing advertising copy starts with forming the ideas that will sell the products or services of the advertiser. In addition to what you learn from your market research about what appeals to your audience, there are various other techniques and methods to get ideas for copy.

Brainstorming

Remember the brainstorming process? Use it here. Most advertising agencies and internal advertising departments have frequent creative meetings where they brainstorm advertising concepts. Since the most important thing to sell in an advertisement is how the product benefits the student, brainstorm benefits. For example, you don't sell toothpaste: you sell brighter teeth, fresher breath, saving money on dental bills. You don't sell soap: you sell cleaner, fresher-smelling clothes. You don't sell bicycles: you sell transportation. Also brainstorm what students miss by not having the product or service. This can help you characterize the benefits. Look at how students can use the product. What makes this product or service better than what the competition offers?

Personal Experiences and Emotions

If this is a product—or similar to a product—that you use, why do you use it? What has it done for you? How have you felt about it? What makes it a favorite of yours? Your own personal experience and the emotions you have about something can help make your copy writing more vivid with greater impact.

You also can interview customers who now use the product or service and get their personal experiences and feelings. Why did they buy it? How have they benefited from it? Why should others buy? Who knows—maybe a good approach for your copy is to use testimonials from others. Testimonials—or written statements describing the value of something—can be very influential, particularly within your peer market group.

Try the Product; Use the Service

Good advertising copy is particularly effective when it is based on personal experience with the product.

Even if you have done the research, brainstormed attributes, and thought through your own personal experience with this or similar products, you should try the specific product or sample the service you are going to advertise. It's hard to tell readers that this is great pizza if you've never had the pizza. And, by trying it, you can better capture in words how you felt as you tasted the first bite—the rich tomato sauce, the aroma of the sweet Italian sausage and fresh peppers. If you are selling a new, lighter, faster bicycle, experience the ride. If you are promoting snowboards, try them out. If you are selling tuxedo rentals for a prom, try a couple of them on so you can describe the type of service you received, and how the dressy clothes made you feel and look.

Interview the Seller, Manufacturer, or Distributor

Ask the same questions you would in your brainstorming session. Ask why people buy the product; how they use it; how it benefits them; how it benefits others; what are the product attributes; what guarantees come with it; how the price compares with similar products; why this is a better product than the competition offers. Ask for copies of fact sheets from catalogs or product sales literature. Get copies of ads used to sell the product or service to adult or other special audiences. Call the 800 number if there is one, and see how the salespeople describe their product.

Plan and Write the Ad

To start writing, make an outline. Once you have the outline, write a letter to a friend in which you tell him or her about the product or services of your advertiser. This frequently will help you to organize your thoughts and focus on benefits using simple, clear, and descriptive language. Some ad copy writers use this approach to get started and then edit the letters into an advertising format.

The key to successful advertising is the headline. It has to attract the attention of the reader and pull him or her further into the ad. If it does not accomplish that, the ad won't be successful. Don't stop with the first headline you write. Write several. Edit them carefully. And when you have the text written, revisit your headline ideas. Many good headlines come after the copy is complete.

Next, think of how you will start the text. The introduction phrase or sentence continues to build on the headline, bringing the reader further into the ad. The body of the copy stresses benefits, linking the reader's interest with that of your advertiser's products or services. Describe what the reader gets and why it is important to him or her. Then tell your reader where and how to get the product, and urge prompt action. No ad is complete without a call to action.

As you draft an ad, don't worry about whether the copy is long or short. The important thing is what it says and how it is said. You will want to start with a lot more copy than you need, and edit your copy down to what is essential to do the job. Study ads in your local paper and in magazines. Many ads are "heavy" with copy, others very "light," others somewhere in between. Write what you need to sell your product. If you write well, you will draw the reader through your text to the call to action.

Look at the two examples of advertising copy on page 388. Both are approaches to selling insurance to a first-time student car-owner. One talks about the law and why insurance is needed. It notes special rates for, and the importance of, safe driving records. The other approach talks about benefits to the student in terms of money and convenience. Note the tone and language of each, and how the second works more to talk directly to the reader. Also, look at the difference in the call to action.

	Sample A	**Sample B**
Headline	A CAR AND DRIVER'S LICENSE AREN'T ENOUGH—INSURANCE IS THE LAW!	WHAT WOULD YOU DO WITH AN EXTRA $60?
Introduction	State law requires that all cars must be insured. We offer quality, affordable insurance for first-time car owners.	As a new car owner here's our guarantee to you. Special insurance rates put that $60 in your pocket if you've had driver's education. And, if you drive safely, you get an additional $60 or more every time you renew your Super Go insurance policy.
Body	Super Go Insurance provides special rates for young drivers who have had driver's education. And, by being a safe driver without accidents or citations, you will save on your premiums each year.	Our new student-driver insurance is unique. We not only save you money—which you can use for that special date or to help you upgrade the speaker system in your new car—but give you coverage with no red tape.
Call to Action	Come to Donovon Hayes Safe Go Insurance Center today! We will provide a free estimate on your insurance costs and show how being a safe driver with a good record saves money.	Call us now, toll free: 1-800-2SafeGo. We'll take your information and quickly send you a free estimate and all you need to apply. Why wait? We've made it easy for you!

Use Words that Sell

John Caples, for forty years a vice president of a top advertising agency, Batten, Barton, Durstine & Osborn, Inc., made a study of various lists of good headlines. By counting the meaningful words (omitting words like *and, the, this*), he determined the top ten words used by copy writers (the number after each is how many times the word appeared in headlines he studied):

you	31	your	14	how	12
new	10	who	8	money	6
now	4	people	4	want	4
why	4				

Caples goes on to suggest that combining *you* and *your* results in forty-five mentions for that category, and combining *new* and *now* fourteen. He notes his surprise that *free, save, quick,* and *easy* did not appear in the top ten, and that *how* scored so well. (Many direct marketers have found the value in *how* as well. Take note of all the *How To . . .* books and pamphlets you've seen.)

With Caples's list in mind, take another look at the ad copy on page 388. Notice how few of the words on the list appear in the A example, and how frequently they appear in the B sample. The words on the list appeal directly to the reader, helping him or her identify with the sales messages and products or services being sold.

After the audience has seen your ad (or heard it on radio or television),

---

The Most Persuasive Words

Advertising executive and industry leader David Ogilvy has a list of words he classifies as the most persuasive in advertising. In his book, *Confessions of an Advertising Man*, he offers this list of persuasive words.

suddenly	now	announcing
introducing	improvement	amazing
sensational	remarkable	revolutionary
startling	miracle	magic
offer	quick	easy
wanted	challenge	compare
bargain	hurry	

---

you want him or her to take action quickly. Caples suggests copy writers consider phrases like "Act now," "Don't delay," "Get started today," "Be the first," and "While supplies last" to involve the audience. The use of coupons, offering a drawing or special discount on a purchase, are also considered useful to support the call to action in an advertisement.

Create an Effective Layout

There are a number of elements that may be used in preparing the ad for publication. These include the following:

- the headline and any subheads
- body copy
- the call to action
- the company logo (a distinctively designed brand or company name, often called the signature)
- the company address, phone number, store hours
- photographs and photo captions
- art—original drawings, computer or computer-generated art
- price of products advertised
- guarantees, warranties
- testimonials (as part of or separate from the copy)
- coupons
- white space

Can an ad be an editorial? Is there a problem when one looks like the other?

Mobil Oil is credited with pioneering the concept of the Op-Ed ad, or the ad that functions as an opinion column on the editorial page. Companies place the ads, also referred to as advertorials or advocacy ads, in newspapers that reach policy makers or business leaders, such as *The New York Times* or *The Wall Street Journal*, or in leading business magazines. The concept is to write strong advertising style copy on an issue or topic and to seek to educate and motivate readers to support the company's position on that issue. The issue is often something that involves the general well-being of the public, such as protecting the environment or banning assault weapons, rather than something that relates directly to the company's product. Frequently these ads urge readers to write to their senator, today, or to join the membership ranks of an organization that supports the company's cause.

This type of editorial ad can be an effective way for a company to get its information directly to readers. It is easier to pay for the space to present a viewpoint than to try to get a news article written about that viewpoint.

The editorial-ad format is also beginning to be used to sell products or services as well as causes. When used to sell, the ads are placed in local and specialty newspapers as well as in large city publications. Sometimes they appear as testimonials by users of the service or product, and generally their format involves a heavy dose of print and little illustration. In other words, they look like editorials, but they are written with advertising words and phrases to stimulate readers to buy products.

Editorial ads of this sort are also finding their way into student publications. A sports medicine clinic, for example, may place a full-page, print-heavy ad in a yearbook, discussing common types of sports injuries and extolling the strengths of its medical staff in treating them. The ad looks serious and important and tends to draw in readers for that reason. Or an advertiser might sell its product using a column written by a student. For example, for a movie being shown at a local theater, a student might prepare copy giving a summary of the film and citing various positive reviews. The idea is that more students will believe in the ad because it has been written by one of their peers. Or a company may simply want to engender goodwill in the youth market so that students will remember its name later. A real-estate firm, for example, may choose to present a series of outstanding-student profiles in a student publication in hopes of building a future relationship with its readers.

As to the question of whether creating ads that look like editorials creates any ethical problems, nearly all publications require that the editorial ad in some way be set off or identified. Many newspapers, for example, add a line at the top of the ad labeling it as an "Advertisement," some require that the ad be boxed, and others specify that a typeface be used that is different from the newspaper's style. These safeguards are put in place to make it clear that the material is not a story written by a reporter and that it does not represent the opinion of the paper.

The editorial approach adds credibility to the advertiser's cause. As long as it is clearly identified, it is a valid selling approach.

Obviously, no ad will contain all of these elements. In preparing your advertisement, however, you will want to consider how to blend all the elements you do have into a layout that will attract reader attention. Before you start, become a student of other people's ads. You can learn a lot from what others have done.

When laying out your ad, keep in mind two important elements: the optical center of the ad, and white space.

The *optical center* of an ad is not in the middle of the space it occupies, but about two-thirds up from the bottom. This is where most readers will perceive the center to be, and where their eyes are usually attracted first. A photo or illustration filling the top half of an ad will pull readers' eyes into the ad and attract their interest. A strong, appealing headline about one-third down from the top (*What would you do with an extra $60?*); or a strong call to action (*This is your only opportunity!*), will attract readers' attention. Once you have their attention, you have the opportunity to keep it a little longer as they read the copy.

White space is another important element of advertising layout. Just because you have a four column by ten-inch space doesn't mean that it all has to be filled. On the other hand, it doesn't mean that it should not be filled, either. White space is used to help attract attention to that which is important—the headline, an illustration, a price, a unique offer. White space attracts the reader's eye because it is different from the rest of the page.

Most advertisements in student publications are relatively simple. But if they are well presented and laid out, they can still be effective. The samples to the right are examples of simple but effective ads.

Work with the Printer

After you have discussed with your printer how he or she prefers to receive ad copy and layout, you will be ready to prepare ads for publication.

Some printers need only a rough sketch of how the ad is to look when done, accompanied by a copy sheet where you have marked and keyed the style and size of type you want for various elements.

These ads appeared recently in student publications. Though not necessarily sophisticated, they all use techniques to appeal to a student market.

Ads prepared on computer have the advantage of not needing any layout work by the printer before they are processed. Headlines, art, or photos can be inserted and positioned by the student designing the ad.

Other printers welcome camera-ready ads. (You may save money, too.) Camera-ready means the type is already set, the headlines ready, and the art in such a condition that the printer can merely photograph it for printing.

You can submit partially camera-ready copy. For instance, you may prepare the art, set your headline using press-on type (available in bookstores or art-supply stores), and do everything you can to make the ad ready for printing. The printer may then have to prepare the photograph or set some copy blocks before the ad is complete. If you are preparing your ad on computer, you may need only to supply a disk to the printer or even transmit the ad by modem.

Newspaper Circulation

Just getting your publication printed is not enough; you have to have readers. Circulation is another function usually assigned to the business staff.

Some student newspapers and magazines are sold on a subscription basis. The students purchase a subscription card and take it to a circulation point (usually the cafeteria or student lounge), where it is punched in exchange for the newspaper. People without cards can purchase the issue for a single-copy price. The subscription price should make the per-issue cost low enough to serve as an incentive to the buyer. In some cases, the subscription is sold as part of a total activities ticket.

Free Subscriptions

Another circulation method is total or controlled "free" distribution. ("Free" means that students usually helped pay for the issue through either an activity supplement or funds made available from general school revenue.) Under these conditions, the staff publishes sufficient copies for the entire student population. The copies are put in special bins or boxes, placed on counters in the office or in hallways, student lounges, cafeterias, or other student gathering places for free pickup.

In the case of some strong newspapers with no subsidy but sufficient advertising revenue to be self-supporting, the paper often is distributed without cost to students. Both types of controlled circulation give advertisers a known number of readers for each issue. From this, the advertising cost per hundred, a figure generally important to advertisers, can be computed. Many advertisers will also test your circulation by running specials only in your publication or by using a coupon so they can track responses.

You also will have mail subscriptions that need to be processed promptly after each issue is published. Some of these may be mailed to alumni, other student publications, students in other schools, and parents. (In some secondary schools and colleges, every parent is mailed each edition the day it comes out.) And don't forget to deliver copies to advertisers. Subscription lists need to be maintained carefully and purged periodically to make sure you are not mailing to people who have not renewed. Costs also can be kept down by getting second-class mailing permits.

Every publication maintains a list of free subscriptions. These include possible new advertisers, local news media, school board members, key college or school administrators, and leaders in the community. Assuming your product is good, this is effective public relations for your publication and your school.

Furthermore, by mailing to prospective advertisers, you help the advertiser see what the competition is doing and demonstrate the quality of your product. A prospective advertiser who is familiar with your publication may be more receptive when your sales rep makes that important sales call.

Evaluate your circulation system often during the year to ensure that it is the best and most cost-effective method for you to use.

Exchange Papers

Naturally, you'll want to receive copies of publications from other schools. Some student staffs mail several hundred newspapers to other schools and receive copies of hundreds of papers in exchange. This is costly, even if you use second-class mail.

Evaluate the papers you receive and be sure you have a reason for exchanging with a particular school. Papers from schools that are your athletic rivals are very useful, for example. And once you start the exchange process, be sure your staff is taking advantage of the papers you receive by reading them regularly for ideas. It is a waste of money to receive a pile of newspapers and merely hang them on the bulletin board.

Keeping Records

Student-run publications, like small businesses, have to maintain accurate and complete financial records. Some school publications have budgets approaching $100,000, so the need for good record-keeping is clear. Although your adviser is ultimately responsible for maintaining and ensuring the accuracy of records, the student business manager and staff often assist in the managing of day-to-day accounts. Regular monthly financial statements should be typed and distributed to the adviser, the editor, and often to the school business office. All staff members need to understand that you cannot spend money you do not have or that you need for some other purpose.

Records must be kept of all income and expenses, including advertising revenue, fund-raising monies, newspaper and yearbook sales, "entertainment expenses" (such as work-and-pizza nights), and supplies. To stay on budget, publications need authorization slips or purchase order forms for approving expenditures of funds by staff members before money is actually spent.

Maintenance of financial records does not require complex accrual accounting methods. A simple spreadsheet created in *Microsoft Excel* or *ClarisWorks,* an accounting package such as Intuit's *Quicken,* or a paper-and-pencil system based on one of these formats can make record-keeping relatively simple. The benefit of an accounting package is that it makes generating reports and assessing income versus expenditures much simpler.

The samples on page 395 show a typical monthly accounting sheet done using *Excel* and then a summary showing only the transactions from that month. Either type of sheet can also be set up without a computer program.

Every school district has developed procedures for spending and collecting money. Some states have laws that also will affect your activities. Be sure you know the rules.

	B22	▼		September issue					
				newspaper register					
	A		**B**		**C**	**D**	**E**	**F**	
1	**DATE**		**DESCRIPTION**		**SPEND**	**X**	**RECEIVE**	**BALANCE**	
2		Category		Memo	**$**		**$**	**$**	
3	9/1/97	Opening Balance				X			
4		(Activity Fees)					18,500.00	18,500.00	
5	9/5/97	Lajoie Printing							
6		Printing		September issue, 1800 copies	1000.00			17,500.00	
7	9/5/97	Diamond Lithography							
8		Photography/Color separations			700.00			16,800.00	
9	9/5/97	USPS							
10		Postage			36.00			16,764.00	
11	9/6/97	Doctors' Services, Inc.							
12		Advertisement		September issue NP, 2 x 8 ad			96.00	16,860.00	
13	9/6/97	Candlestick Florist							
14		Advertisement		1/2 page ad			360.00	17,220.00	
15	9/10/97	Mac Warehouse							
16		Supplies		Toner cartridge	198.00			17,022.00	
17	9/15/97	Pizzeria Medici							
18		Advertisement		1/2 page ad			360.00	17,382.00	
19	9/15/97	Benjamin's Books							
20		Advertisement		2 x 4 ad			48.00	17,430.00	
21	9/15/97	Newspaper sales							
22		September issue					81.50	17,511.50	
23							**Current Balance:**	17,511.50	

Sheet1 / Sheet2 / Sheet3 / Sheet4 / Sheet5 / Sheet6 /

Ready   NUM

Though budgets can also be handled by low-tech means, a computer spreadsheet is a handy way of keeping track of monies coming in and going out. Notice that the $18,500 opening balance in this sample reflects activity fees, which should be distributed evenly across the year.

Saturday, October 25, 1997
Category Summary Report
9/1/97 through 9/30/97

Income	**Category**	**Amount**
	Activity fees	$18,500.00
	Advertisements	862.00
	Newspaper sales	81.50
Total Income		**$19,445.50**

Expenses	**Category**	**Amount**
	Postage	$ 36.00
	Printing	1,000.00
	Photography/ Color separations	700.00
	Supplies	198.00
Total Expenses		**$1,934.00**
Balance		**$17,511.50**

In the "Category Summary Report" done at the end of each month, income and expense totals can be summarized and analyzed.

Wrap-up

Without money, there would be no media. Advertising and subscription revenues are essential if a publication is to exist. The number of pages in an edition of the school newspaper, for example, is dependent on revenue from such sources as an activity fund, subscription sales, and advertising. Some publications also hold fund-raising events such as a school carnival, or sell book covers or other items to raise money for special features. The more funding a student publication has determines how many color photos, pages, or special features can be added.

Advertising rates are determined on the basis of how many people will read a publication. The more subscribers, for example, the more a publication can charge for advertising space.

The student media are important to local businesses, linking them with a student market that is known to have strong buying power. No other medium can reach this market more efficiently than a school publication. To attract advertisers requires a strong knowledge of the paper's readers. A market research study of the student body will provide important information that can help demonstrate to local businesses the value of advertising to the student market.

Once advertising is sold, it has to be written and designed. Brainstorming techniques can be used to identify the benefits of a product. In preparing copy, writers should also try the product or service in order to describe it effectively to the prospective buyer. And, if a copywriter is familiar with the product or service, writing from personal experience and/or emotions can make the copy stronger. It also is important to interview customers, as well as the seller, manufacturer, or distributor, on product attributes.

When writing advertising copy, start with an outline. Then turn the outline into a letter to a friend telling him or her about the product. Develop several headlines that will bring the reader into the ad; then select the best one. Write the ad copy and edit it several times. Keep pulling readers into the copy as the text talks personally to them, discussing benefits in owning the product or using the service. Then, end the ad with a strong call to action—tell the reader what to do next. Remember to use words that are proven to sell, particularly *you, your, new, now,* and *how.*

When designing the ad, remember that the optical center is about one-third down from the top of the advertising space. That is where most readers will perceive the ad center to be, and where their eyes will be drawn first. This is the place to put a strong headline, or to be sure an interesting photo or art appears. White space also is important. It helps draw attention to key layout elements, such as the headline, art and illustrations, the call to action, and company logo.

Other important business functions are required if the newspaper is to be successful. Once the paper is printed it needs to be circulated and/or sold. Businesses don't buy advertising unless they feel assured that the publication will reach its intended audience. And there is an essential record-keeping function. It is important, for example, that advertisers receive timely invoices for their ad space so that the publication gets the funds needed to pay the printing, photography, or other bills. It is equally important that good books and records are kept on all other income that is received in addition to advertising. A simple accounting system will ensure that each expenditure is carefully entered, that bills are paid on time, and that bills are not paid more than once. Most schools have procedures for making outside purchases, such as the use of a purchase order form. Without a purchase order, bills cannot be paid. Be sure school business procedures are carefully followed.

Evaluation Checklist: *Ad*

✓ Does the headline pull the audience into reading the rest of the ad?

✓ Does the ad copy use words and ideas that make the product or service appealing to the reader?

✓ Does the ad contain a well-worded call to action?

✓ Is the optical center of the ad space used for the headline, a photo, or other attention-getting element?

✓ Does the ad make effective use of white space?

On Assignment

Individual Activities

1. Write a brief definition or explanation of each of the following terms.

   business manager   call to action
   camera-ready copy   market survey
   optical center   testimonial
   white space

2. Test your critical thinking. Write an editorial, column, or opinion feature on one or more of the following statements. Take any position, but provide evidence that you did your homework before writing.

   a. Advertising makes people vote for candidates they should not vote for.

   b. Advertising makes people buy products they don't need.

   c. Advertising has been a leading factor in improving our standard of living.

   d. Advertising should be banned from television.

   e. Without advertising, the economy of our nation would suffer greatly.

3. Develop an advertisement based on the following information.

   • A computer store near your school allows students to rent computers to use at home. The cost is $25 monthly. The computers have built-in modems that can connect to various databases, including games, publications, research libraries, and other records. A printer is also provided.

   • All rental payments will apply to purchase of the computer should the student decide to buy it later.

   • Rental agreements are for three-month intervals.

   • Students who bring in the ad from your paper will be given free software worth $250 that will allow them to access databases for use in doing research.

   • The equipment is easy to use and comes with an instruction manual. A class is held at the store each Saturday for $10.

   • You have a photo of two students in your school using the equipment, and a photo of the store.

   • The store name is ComputeRents & Sales, Ltd.

   • The size is to be 4 columns wide by 12 inches deep.

   Supply any additional information needed to complete the ad.

4. Visit a local advertising agency, or bring in representatives from local agencies and from the advertising sales departments of local media. Discuss how they go about selling ads. Discuss the issues raised in activity 2. What are their positions on those questions? Compare the ad agencies' approaches to those of the media advertising reps.

5. In your library, find articles that discuss research on the buying habits of today's teen and youth markets. In addition to surveys from Teenage Research Unlimited, you might find results from large

polling companies like Roper and Gallup, or useful information in *American Demographics* magazine. Use the information in a sales letter to the businesses currently advertising in your student newspaper. The letter will reinforce their "good judgment" to advertise in your publication. Then write a similar letter to a business that does not use your publication. Make it convincing!

6. Using the research you conducted for activity 5, prepare an article for your school newspaper on the youth market. If possible, contact and do a class interview with one of the researchers. He or she may have even more current information for you.

Team Activity

7. As a team, develop a marketing survey for your school publications. Determine how you would conduct the survey (random sample or all students). Compare your survey plan and questionnaire with those of the other teams. Develop a combined survey instrument.

Invite a local opinion researcher, or someone knowledgeable in testing or evaluation, to class to discuss research techniques and to critique your combined questionnaire and your planned approach to securing student opinion. Meet with the appropriate computer person in your school if you plan to have your results tabulated by computer.

Now, make your final revisions in the instrument and conduct your study. When the results are tabulated, each team should conduct its own analysis of the data. Write a report (four pages at most) on the survey. What are the implications for attracting new advertisers? How can the data be used to keep current advertisers? As a team, prepare a letter to advertising prospects on the benefits of advertising in your publication and to educate them about the student market. Compare your interpretations and marketing report with those of the other teams. Now, write one or two news stories on the study results for your newspaper.

"**P**ractical experience is the lifeline to a position in this industry," says Kent Matlock, president and CEO of Matlock & Associates, Inc., an Atlanta advertising and public relations firm. "I guess it's like the old phrase in politics, which says to vote early and vote often."

Matlock got involved in advertising early. He was a college representative for a major marketing promotion while attending Morehouse College in Atlanta.

That stint in promotion, plus a liberal arts education, helped prepare him to open his own advertising agency. After working for a couple of small agencies, Matlock moved to a FORTUNE 500 company and then formed his own seven-person firm in 1986.

From his college studies, Matlock gained a general idea of advertising and public relations. But he believes that the hard-core realities of the business happen on the job. What is more, he believes that timing is the key to success, whether that means developing expertise about a particular market, winning the business of a client or product that is hot, or landing in a geographical area that is on the upswing. "Pick a growing market, and the opportunities start unfolding professionally and personally," he said.

Matlock said that if you find the right firm, don't worry about starting out at the bottom, because there is enough turnover in most firms to allow you to move up.

Matlock's company is a minority firm and naturally does some specialty work in that area. But he urges recent graduates to begin their careers in larger and more generalized corporate environments. "The smaller the agency," he said, "the more likely you are to acquire bad habits," adding that large firms are good places to learn to manage the pitfalls. "It's important to get a neutral orientation in the business," he noted.

"Learning the fundamentals is of great value long term."

"Working for a larger firm enhances your appreciation for the business," he said. And what you learn there can be applied in a small firm, which, by virtue of its size and the number of diverse tasks to be performed, gives you a broader scope of opportunities.

Besides pursuing paying clients, Matlock believes there is an oasis of fulfillment in *pro bono publico* work—that is, work done free "for the public good."

"My greatest joy is *pro bono* work, perhaps because they [these projects] tend to be the things we do out of kindness," he explained. He added that part of the satisfaction comes from the opportunity to express creativity and not be "policed," as when a client is paying the bill.

Through the years, Matlock has given professional service to the United Way, the American Cancer Society, the Atlanta Chamber of Commerce, the Martin Luther King, Jr. Center, the Southern Christian Leadership Conference, the United Negro College Fund, and his alma mater, Morehouse College. "The community loves the insight, guidance and support," he said, adding that such work often "opens doors" to paying clients. "The most powerful things we cultivate are our relationships," Matlock said.

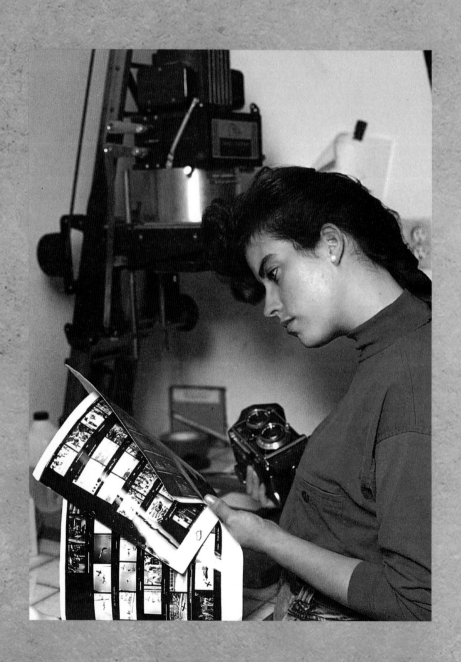

Photography

Chapter Eighteen

Taking and Using Effective Photographs

Chapter Nineteen

Understanding Technical Aspects of Photography

Taking and Using Effective Photographs

Key Terms

"wild art"

rule of thirds

contact sheet

cropping

sizing

halftone

photo essay

Key Concepts

After reading this chapter, you should

- understand the roles of the photograph in a student publication

- know some simple guidelines for composing a photograph

- understand the role of the photo editor and the photography staff

- know how to plan and do a successful photo shoot

- know how to select, crop, and size the best photos for a layout

A good photograph begins in the mind of the photographer—not in the camera, not in the darkroom, and certainly not on the editing table. Photographers begin composing pictures, evaluating lighting, and solving technical problems in their heads long before they put the camera to their eyes.

It's the ability of the photographers to successfully turn what they see in their mind into an image on film that makes for a great publication. For without good photographs, a publication can be, at best, average. Photographs enable readers to see the action as it occurred visually and quickly without having to go into a lot of depth.

In contemporary publications, the most important role of a photograph is to grab the viewer's attention. Photos are the first thing a viewer sees on a page, and poor-quality or uninteresting photos are an immediate turn-off. Even professional daily publications and nightly news broadcasts realize the impact of a high-quality photograph in capturing viewers and increasing sales. Once viewers have been attracted by a single photo, they are more likely to read the caption (also called a cutline), the headline, the associated stories, and the ads. Some publications such as *Life* and *National Geographic* have built an entire reputation on just the quality of their photography.

Good photos can accomplish other goals once they have grabbed the viewer's attention. They may, for example, provide information about a house fire down the street or a flood in a nearby county. In that sense, they serve the same purpose as part of a news story, showing (not telling) who was involved, what they were involved in, and when and where the action occured. A good photograph also shows how a piece of the action took place.

The photo on the left demonstrates several common errors inexperienced photographers make. Notice the window frame growing out of the boy's head, the hand seemingly not attached to a body, and the poor light caused by shooting the subjects in front of a window. The photographer improved the right-hand photo by repositioning the subjects, shooting from a different angle, and making sure that everyone's face could be seen.

Other photographs may just serve to entertain the reader. Editors often select "wild art" (art not associated with a story) simply to provide depth to a page—to appeal to a greater variety of viewers. For example, a news page may have a lead story about the school principal and an associated photograph, but then also include a picture of the choir concert with a long caption. While the story about the principal is timely and has consequences for everyone in the school, the picture of the choir concert may do more to attract readers.

By grabbing the reader's attention, informing, and/or entertaining, photographs accomplish two broader goals for the publication: they give the publication an identity, and they establish a link with the reader.

Some publications use large, dramatic photos to show the story. Others use smaller photos. Some use color. Some are strictly black-and-white. Some use photo essays to tell stories. Others depend on the accurate portrayal of the scene without any manipulation. Each of these approaches gives a publication a look that when combined with type and layout is distinctive and can often be recognized even when the name of the publication isn't known.

The identity that photos establish, their ability to grab attention, and the stories they tell help a publication to form a bond with the reader, a bond that strengthens every time a reader has a successful experience with the publication. As this bond strengthens, readers begin exhibiting loyalty to a publication, one important aspect in its continued success. Readers learn to feel the anger, loneliness, happiness, fear, pain, jubilation, and surprise that the people in the photographs felt. They share experiences and come to feel a part of the action.

Good Photo Composition

While establishing a bond and grabbing a viewer's attention are praiseworthy goals, a poorly composed photograph can seldom accomplish either of them. In fact, a poorly composed photograph can turn off a reader faster than a bad headline or a poorly written lead.

Good composition involves first having good subject matter and the appropriate equipment to shoot it. Photographers should choose their assignments carefully when they're first learning to take pictures, choosing to photograph things that they are familiar with and that they can shoot with their equipment. A photographer who is on the freshman football team may, for example, choose to cover junior varsity football practice for a first assignment. Football practice can easily be covered with a standard 50mm lens under good lighting conditions, such as a football practice field during daylight hours. The photographer's familiarity with what is going on will help him anticipate the action.

It's often helpful for beginning photographers to practice with "point-and-shoot" cameras so they don't have to worry about the technical aspects of photography such as f/stops, ISO, and shutter speeds. This allows them to concentrate solely on composition.

Photographic composition also involves some general guidelines that will help improve any photograph.

Photography Pioneers

Louis Daguerre (1789–1851), generally credited as the inventor of photography. In 1838 he invented the daguerreotype, a single-image photographic process in which a picture was made on a silver surface sensitized with iodine.

William Talbott (1800–1877), invented the first paper-based negative/positive photo process in the 1840s.

Matthew Brady (1823?–1896), one of the first to popularize photography in America, his Civil War pictures were widely reproduced.

George Eastman (1854–1932), in 1888 invented flexible-roll films (replacing the glass plates previously needed) and later, cheap, portable cameras that the average person could use.

Edwin Land (1909–1991), invented the Polaroid Land camera in 1947, using film that could be developed inside the camera in one minute.

Keep It Simple

Good photographs are simple. The best ones involve one, maybe two, centers of visual interest to grab attention. They have nothing distracting in the foreground or the background.

Fill the Frame

When you shoot most photographs, move up close to the subject. Shooting up close will produce photos with the greatest impact. Getting close is the hardest thing for a beginning photographer to do. But good photographs are filled with the subject, not a lot of wasted space.

Avoid Mergers

Objects that seem to merge into the subject or out of the photo, such as telephone poles growing out of heads or feet cut off at the edge of the frame, are distracting to the viewer. These mergers can often be avoided by tight cropping—eliminating unwanted parts of the photo—or by moving around. Avoiding mergers involves paying careful attention to the foreground and the background in addition to the subject.

A photo composed according to the rule of thirds does not have the subject in the exact center. Instead, the frame is broken into thirds vertically and horizontally and significant elements appear at the intersection of those lines.

Use the Rule of Thirds

Subjects should rarely be placed in the center of the frame. Instead, as you shoot, divide the frame into thirds both horizontally and vertically (into a sort of tic-tac-toe board) and place the subject at the intersection of any two lines. By the same token, in wide shots the horizon line should be placed either on the top third or the bottom third of the frame, not in the center.

Work with Patterns and Curves

Repetition, as any artist will tell you, is a powerful composition element. Having a pattern broken by some action (such as a line of dancers with one person out of step) can make for a powerful photo. Similarly, having a subject at the beginning or end of a line or curve (such as a runner at the end of a long path) can draw the reader straight into the action.

Give "Soul" to an Image

A good photograph must do more than just present a subject doing something. It must present a subject doing something in a meaningful way. A good photograph must do more than just record the event—it must give

A shot involving a pattern or repetitive action can sometimes be more effective if something breaks the pattern.

meaning to it. It's the meaning that will turn a good photograph into a great photograph.

The Photography Staff

The photography staff in a school publication can either function as a separate group that takes on assignments for the whole publication or be assigned to work individually with teams of editors and reporters. Regardless of the organization used, there are still basic jobs that the photography staff must fulfill.

The Photo Editor

In general, the photo editor leads the photography staff in taking and developing high-quality pictures. He or she supervises the thorough coverage of all school events. Depending on the staff organization, the photo editor does some or all of the following:

- Works closely with all other staff members to obtain all necessary photos
- Helps staff members maintain a filing system for negatives, contact sheets, and prints
- Distributes photo assignments to the staff
- Keeps all staff members informed of events being covered by recording them on the calendar and by holding regular staff meetings
- Edits photos for quality control, both in the initial negatives and later in the prints
- Maintains the darkroom facilities including mixing chemicals, distributing film, ordering supplies, and keeping the darkroom clean
- Serves as the leader of the photography staff making sure staff members' problems are adequately addressed
- Functions as a photographer when needed.

The Staff Photographer

In general, the photographer takes pictures, processes film and makes prints, and performs all necessary functions to make sure photos required by the publications are taken and processed in a timely fashion. The staff photographer accepts photo assignments from the editors and helps maintain the equipment and darkroom facilities. He or she may also generate photo assignment ideas.

Getting and Using the Most Effective Photographs

You can take good photographs once you understand basic photographic techniques. However, when shooting pictures for a publication, it isn't enough just to take a good photo. The photo must also work with the story it accompanies and fit in with the specific goals of the publication.

Giving Clear Assignments

One way to avoid potential problems with photographs is to make sure that photographers have clear assignments. Photographers need to work closely with photo editors, layout artists, reporters, and others on the staff to make sure everyone is clear about what types of photos are needed.

The best time for a staff or team to discuss photo assignments is at the same time you discuss story assignments and "the budget"—what stories are going to appear where and how much space they're going to be allocated. As you decide which stories require more prominent positioning and more space based on the story's news value, also consider which stories are visually interesting and appeal to the broadest audience.

After the plan for the issue of the newspaper or section of the yearbook is complete, it is time for photographers to get their assignments. Be aware that for you as a photo editor to tell a photographer to shoot "the football game" is to invite disaster. Do you want pictures of the field action? the sideline action? the fans? the band? the drill team? the concession stand? one player? the coaches? One photographer can't cover all the action at a football game adequately. The more specific your assignment the better results you will get.

For example, telling a photographer to shoot pictures of the star quarterback at Friday night's game for a personality profile about the quarterback gives the photographer more to go on. He or she will be able to concentrate on that one player (on the field and off) and is more likely to bring along the proper equipment. A specific assignment also gives the photographer a chance to think about atypical shots, such as a picture of the quarterback studying algebra at home or washing the dishes. The more information that can be given to the photographer, the more likely he or she is to return with pictures that supplement the story and provide the reader with a chance to understand it.

A student photographer should prepare for a shoot by bringing along any equipment that might be needed, including extra film, lenses, batteries, and lighting equipment.

Preparing for a Shoot

When you as a photographer accept assignments, you are doing more than just agreeing to go out and snap a few pictures. You are making a commitment to cover a piece of the school's history. As such, you should take your work seriously.

Plan to arrive early, and then take pictures before, during, and after the event. Be prepared for any problems that may arise. This includes bringing along extra film and batteries, carrying other lenses, having extra lighting equipment on hand, and the like.

Take a lot of pictures. Remember that coverage of a person or event should include different angles, action shots, horizontal and vertical shots, small group shots, shots showing the scene, and other shots that help to tell the whole story. Avoid shots that are posed.

Before going out to cover something, find past publications that have covered similar events. Look for ways to cover the event that haven't been done before.

The Caption. When out on assignment, it is also your responsibility to get caption information—the who, what, when, where, why, and how of the action in the photo. Sometimes caption information may be nothing more than the accurate spelling of the names of the people in the photo, but compiling it is an important responsibility for the photographer.

School photographers often think it's easier to go back and find out who the people are after they've printed the pictures. Indeed, in action-packed events that is sometimes true. However, professional photographers who work on tight deadlines know it's always more efficient to get this information on the scene than to go back later searching for it.

As you work, record details such as the score of the game, the significance of a play, or any other details that may not be apparent in the photo. You may also want to get direct quotations from the people involved to add information to a caption. The first part of the caption explains what is going on in the photo, including the names of all identifiable people, but the second part adds information that may supplement the story. Direct quotations are a great way to add information and to get more people in the publication—if you remember to get the information on the scene.

A final important part of the caption is the photo credit, a credit you earn for taking the picture. The importance of this credit should not be overlooked as a staff motivational device.

Selecting the Best Photos

The first job of the photo editor, usually in conjunction with the photographer and section/page design editor, is to pick the best pictures for a page from a contact sheet (a sheet of photos printed negative size) or a set of proof prints. What "best" means differs from page to page, issue to issue, and topic to topic, but there are some basic principles that always hold true.

To begin with, good photojournalism is about people. So, in general, photos for publications should contain *people*. Rarely do individuals buy a newspaper or yearbook and flip through the pages looking for a picture of an empty hall. They look for pictures of themselves (first and foremost), their friends, their classmates, their acquaintances, and other people with whom they might share common experiences.

When selecting photos for use in a publication, choose as many as possible that involve people doing something—ideally, something unusual.

Secondly, the people should be *doing something*, not staring at the camera. The best photos come when people keep going right on with their lives, totally unaware they are being photographed.

Finally, whenever possible the action should be *unusual*. The more unusual the action, the more likely the photograph is to make the reader stop and look. People are constantly bombarded by visual images. The more unique your image, the more stopping power it has, and the more likely people are to look and say, "Wow."

Working with the Layout

After selecting the best photos, the photo editor also has to make sure they will work on the layout. The best way to do this is to design layouts around the strongest photos. Horizontal photos won't fit in vertical spaces, and it's easier to redesign the page than to reshoot the photo. However, redesigning a page is not always possible. Good layout artists and photo editors will work together to make sure the needs of both groups are met and a pleasing page results.

> **Good, Better, Best**
>
> *An OK photo:* a shot of a chess player rather than of a chess board
>
> *A better photo:* a shot of the chess player concentrating on her next move
>
> *An even better photo:* a shot of the chess player with her hands on her head and a look of bewilderment

The final role of the photo editor is to lobby for the prominent placement of the best photos. Writers want the words to be given top billing. Designers want their design to be what the reader sees first. The photo editor is the lobbyist for the photo. The stronger the photo and the better it fits with the entire story/design/photo package, the harder the editor should lobby. Designers usually realize that a strong photo will attract more readers than any design or text, but they also realize weak photos can destroy a good layout. Photo editors have to help make those decisions.

Cropping. Sometimes photos can be cropped. Cropping a picture means removing unnecessary elements from the photo by reproducing only a portion of it. Cropping can serve two purposes: (1) to improve the composition of the photo; or (2) to make the photo fit a predesigned space. In general, the first purpose is good. Removing unnecessary elements from the photo helps draw attention to the center of visual interest and improves the photo. In that sense, cropping is one of a photo editor's strongest tools.

In general, the second purpose is bad. Rarely are photographs improved by forcing them to fit layouts. This results in the picture of the basketball player going for a basket being crammed into a horizontal hole. Or the picture of the volleyball player lifting weights is packed into a vertical frame. It just doesn't work.

Good photographers will crop their pictures in the camera and when printing the picture. Editors can even indicate cropping instructions on the contact sheet when selecting pictures to be enlarged. If properly cropped in the camera or on the print, all the layout artist has to do is leave a hole in proportion to the picture's shape.

The world we live in has become more and more visually oriented. People read less and depend more on illustrations, particularly photographs, to get information. This reliance on visual images—not only on what they show but also on what they suggest—means that an ethic needs to be in place to ensure that they are used appropriately.

Photos are often used in the professional press that make people look bad, or at least foolish. We have all seen photos of presidents and other public figures with silly looks on their faces. Because hundreds of images of these individuals appear regularly, it is fair to assume that at least some of the pictures will be less than flattering. The reality that is public figures sometimes do look foolish. No lasting harm is done by circulating these photos.

But sometimes unflattering images can have a direct effect on events. When Michael Dukakis was running for president in 1988, a film clip of him riding in circles on a piece of military equipment was widely distributed. The only problem with the clip was that the earguards he wore to keep out excessive noise looked like Mickey Mouse ears. In short, Dukakis looked foolish and the effects reverberated through his election campaign. Many people were also outraged by the photo of O. J. Simpson run on the cover of a popular newsmagazine just before his trial. Apparently artificially darkened, the photo looked like a sinister mug shot. Besides suggesting that he was guilty as charged, the photo also appeared to many to have unwarranted racial implications.

Using photos inappropriately is one issue. Another is the question of just how much a news photograph should show. Usually we do not see the mangled bodies of airplane or car crash fatalities in the mass media. But the results of many other disasters seem to be fair game. There was a time, for example, when the face of a murder victim was never shown in a photograph. It was believed that even a horrific, perhaps public death of this type was at base a private thing—that the person and his or her family were entitled to a certain amount of decorum. Today, things are different. Perhaps we have become more accustomed to violence, both real and movie versions. But it seems, at least in some media coverage, that no moment is too private that it can't be recorded by a photographer. Deaths and loved ones' reactions to deaths, as well as less serious but also hurtful events, are often photographed from extremely close range, so that the subject almost seems to be captured by the camera. The question, and it doesn't always have an easy answer, is how far the public's right to know—and see—really does go.

A photo editor concerned with doing the job ethically will make many decisions about whether to run certain photographs. He or she will also need to be careful about photo positioning. A portrait shot of an innocent individual run next to a headline about a murderer being found will suggest to many casual readers that the person in the photo is the guilty party. Lawsuits have been filed—and won—over this sort of unintentional misrepresentation.

In school publications, photo choice and position also need to be thought through carefully. You may not often deal with life-and-death situations or face potential lawsuits, but you do have people's feelings to consider. Don't unthinkingly operate under the old premise of using a photo "just because we've got it."

Preparing Photos. In real life, photographs rarely come ready to run. A little cropping will improve almost any image. And printing photos the exact size they will run is time-consuming, expensive, and frustrating. Fortunately, it's easy for production staff members to indicate cropping instructions and to resize photographs early on.

Cropping a photo to get rid of unnecessary elements increases its impact. Notice how much more effective the photo on the right is.

Before a photograph can be printed, it must be made into a halftone—converted into a series of black-and-white (or color) dots so it can be printed solely in black ink and still pick up the over two hundred shades of gray in the average photo. At the same time a photo is made into a halftone (now often done by electronically scanning the image), it can be sized and cropped according to instructions marked on the photo, instructions given by the staff or the staff photographer.

While the method of cropping and sizing depends on the type of publication and publisher, it can be accomplished simply by using a calculator to figure out the size wanted and a ruler and a marker such as a grease pencil to draw crop lines. Tools such as proportion wheels and cropping devices make the process easier.

Photo Essays

When a photographer shoots an extended assignment or when a story can be told better through a series of pictures and few words (instead of many words and few pictures), an editor may choose to print a series of photos as a photo essay. The photo essay serves the same purpose as a copy block—to tell an entire story, complete with a beginning, a middle, and an end. Some photo essays may choose to tell one small portion of a much bigger story, such as the story of one person who has to ride the bus to school all the way across town even though she lives only five blocks from another school. The photo essay could show pictures of this girl hanging around with friends in her neighborhood, pictures of waiting alone for the bus, pictures of her riding the bus, and maybe pictures of her at the other school. Through this series of images, the photographer can tell the entire story.

A photo essay need not tell a step-by-step story. It might, for example, show a variety of pictures of Spring Fever Week, not isolating any one event. The essay could include everything from the outfits for Nerd Day to the egg toss to the tug-of-war over the mud pit. Most yearbook spreads use this type of photographic coverage over a span of time to illustrate activities of groups during the year.

A special type of photo essay is the photo series, a group of pictures often taken over a long period of time to illustrate how things change. These photos typically focus on one person or one place and are usually printed side by side. For example, you might show the construction of a new school wing on the day the ground was broken; two weeks later, when the walls were complete; and when the building was ready for occupancy.

Wrap-up

Without good photographs, a publication can be, at best, average. Photographs show the reader what the story tells.

First and foremost, a good photograph grabs a viewer's attention; it entices him or her to take a second look. Photographs also provide information and entertain readers, helping them to form a bond with a publication that will keep them waiting for the next issue to come out. Through the use of high-quality photographs, a publication also establishes an identity with which the reader can feel comfortable.

Learning to compose images that are full of people doing unusual things is the first step to getting pictures that are more than just snapshots. This process starts in the mind of the photographer. After beginning photographers have learned to fill the frame with the subject, some simple composition guidelines apply. They include learning to use the rule of thirds, working with repetition and leading lines and curves, and avoiding mergers. And publishing photos that have a meaning will set some publications above the rest.

The role of the photographer and photo editor goes beyond just taking pictures. It means keeping the photo department organized and the darkroom clean. It means having supplies on hand. It means having working equipment and film. It means knowing how to crop, size, and position photos on a layout. It means communicating with the rest of the staff to ensure thorough coverage of every person and event possible.

Before going out to shoot pictures, photographers must be clear about their assignment. They must know exactly what they are they to shoot. The clearer the assignment, the better the results. Once photographers have accepted an assignment, they have made a commitment to record a piece of history and they should work to cover that piece thoroughly and with as much skill as possible.

Sometimes publications will run photo essays—a series of photos that tell a story or cover various parts of an event. Photo essays work particularly well in situations where the story comes across more effectively through pictures than through words.

Evaluation Checklist: *Photo Composition*

✓ Does the subject of the photo fill up most of the space?
✓ Has the subject been positioned in the photo according to the rule of thirds?
✓ Does the photo show the subject doing something interesting?
✓ Is the photo simple, with only one center of visual interest?
✓ Has any necessary cropping been done?

On Assignment

Individual Activities

1. Write a brief definition or explanation of each of the following terms.

   contact sheet   cropping
   halftone   photo essay
   rule of thirds   sizing
   "wild art"

2. Brainstorm new ways to cover typical school events or classes with photos. For example, how can you illustrate the school play, a concert, or homecoming? How would you cover physics, world history, or vocational or physical education classes? Discuss your ideas in class.

3. Look at the front pages of several daily newspapers published on the same day. Write a critique of the photo usage on each. Were photos used effectively? Was the layout well planned to take advantage of the photos? Were the captions written well? Are national photos used differently in different locations? Why?

How would you have treated stories that have no photos to take advantage of illustrations?

4. Obtain a contact sheet from a photographer, or use your own. Crop two or three photos on the contact sheet. Arrange to have the photos enlarged. (A photocopier can give you a feel for what happens. Enlarge the copies progressively three or four times.) Look at how you cropped them on the contact sheets. Do the photographs still have unnecessary elements at the top, bottom, or sides of the frame? Did you crop them too severely, making them a strange shape? How might they have been cropped more effectively? Attach your answers to your contact prints and enlargements.

5. Test your critical thinking. Clip an effective photo and its caption from a magazine. Also clip one that fails to tell the story. Write a short editorial column critiquing the quality of the photos and comparing them based on what you have learned about the

effective use of photography. Suggest ways to improve the inadequate photo.

6. Find one photograph in newspapers or magazines that fulfills each one of these photojournalistic functions: capturing attention, providing information, providing entertainment, establishing an emotional link, helping establish an identity for the publication. Write a short paragraph on the function(s) each photo performs. Attach the paragraph to the page on which the photo appears.

7. Using the guidelines for good photo composition, go out and take several of your own photographs. Then bring them to class and be prepared to discuss them. Explain what you were trying to do in each photo and whether you feel you accomplished your purposes. Listen to others' critiques of your work and be prepared to analyze their photos in turn.

Team Activity

8. Working in teams, brainstorm topics that would make a good full-page photo essay for your school newspaper. Select one and take the photos. If you are not particularly skilled at photography, use an instant camera. Keep in mind all the guidelines for taking good photos. Select the pictures carefully, crop and size them, mark them for the printer, prepare the layout for a photo page, and write the copy that will accompany the photos (including all captions and appropriate headlines).

If you have access to a photocopier that enlarges and reduces copy, enlarge or reduce the photos and cut them out. Type the copy and do a pasteup of your page if possible.

Exchange your work products with that of other teams. In a class discussion, critique them constructively. How could photos have been used more effectively? Do the captions complement the photos? Does the story work well with the overall photo page? Is the layout exciting?

Some people are writers; some, photographers. A few, like Olga Camacho, are both.

"I could never quite decide. When I was reporting, I wanted to be shooting. When I was a photographer, I wanted to be writing," says the *Honolulu Advertiser* photo editor.

It was Camacho's writing that got her in the door at *The New York Times*. She started in 1986 in the paper's writing program for journalistic newcomers. "I worked as a clerk and a news assistant. You do odds and ends and freelance for the different sections," she said.

After the year-and-a-half program, Camacho left to travel through Europe and Mexico. When she returned, she knew she had to find a job.

"I was trying to figure out what I was going to do. I had decided that I wanted to get into photography again."

Having maintained good relations with the *Times*, Camacho called and asked what was available in photography. "I wanted to know what was—what made—a good photograph. I figured the *Times* was a good place to start," she said. "They sort of invented a position for me." She "bounced around the entire building" for one year, learning picture editing for the paper's various sections. "It was sort of rigorous," she said.

The rigor paid off. Camacho became one of three photo editors at the *Times* and remained there for nearly nine years.

But Camacho knew she wanted experience in other newsrooms. "I didn't want to stay in one place forever," she said. When she was offered the position at the *Honolulu Advertiser* in 1995, Camacho took it because "it was about as different from the *Times* as I could get."

As the photo editor for the *Advertiser*, Camacho manages a staff of six photographers and two electronic picture people. She is responsible for assigning daily photo shoots, editing film, and working with the staff on ongoing projects. In addition to daily assignments, each photographer is always working on a photo essay project (usually a feature) that may take a few weeks to complete. This helps to add variety to the staff's routine.

There are pros and cons to working for a smaller paper, Camacho said. Because the *Advertiser* has a smaller staff, Camacho is more likely to see a project through, perhaps being solely responsible for it. "It's great because you see your work right away. Here, I can come up with a story idea on Tuesday and it may be the main feature in Sunday's paper," she said.

On the down side, Camacho says she misses being able to bounce her ideas off other people. At a large newspaper like the *Times*, there are many more hands involved—new ideas are generated and stories get improved.

Although she attributed much of her success to "confidence, ability, and luck," Camacho gave credit to her journalism education, which began when she was a child.

"It goes so far back I can hardly remember," Camacho said. One day in grade school, she recalled, she went to a teacher and told him the school needed a newspaper. The teacher suggested that Camacho start one.

"It was just a couple of Xerox sheets, but it was neat," she said.

From then on she knew she would pursue a journalism career. After working on her high school paper, Camacho took a double major in photojournalism and journalism at the University of Texas in El Paso.

Students interested in journalism should work on their college newspaper, she said. "That's the best place to make all of your mistakes."

But the key to getting good jobs is making contacts with editors, Camacho said, adding that internships are best for this. "That's how you get jobs," she said. "You call them up and send them clips all the time."

Chapter Nineteen

Understanding Technical Aspects of Photography

Key Terms

lens

aperture

f/stop

depth of field

shutter

ISO

backlighting

flash synchronization
  speed

darkroom

contact sheet

fixer

enlarger

test strip

Key Concepts

After you have completed this chapter, you should

- understand the different kinds of camera lenses

- know the f/stops and their relevance to photography

- know the shutter speeds and their relevance to photography

- understand the process of developing film

- understand the process of making a print

The technical aspects of photography have scared more than one potentially good photographer (not to mention more than one good teacher) away. But it is essential to learn the basic underlying principles that serve as a scientific basis for photography. Photographers who understand why things work the way they do will be better suited to prevent problems and fix them when they do arise.

The ideal way to go through this chapter is not just to sit and read it. You will find it much more helpful to have a camera and film nearby so that you can actually look at elements and experiment with processes as they are discussed.

The Camera

A good photograph begins in the mind of the photographer. Without a camera, however, no one else can view that image. A camera is simply a box that holds the medium on which the image can be recorded. In fact, the earliest cameras were literally nothing more than a light-tight box with a tiny hole in one end and a piece of light-sensitive material in the other. Over the last 150 years, the box has evolved into the modern camera body, the hole into the lens, and the material into the film—but the basic principles are still the same. Light shines through the hole (the lens) and registers on the light-sensitive material (the film).

Kinds of Lenses

Lenses were around long before photography, but without the lens, the high-quality photographs we have come to accept today could not be a reality. Some lenses are fixed lenses—all you have to do is point the camera at the scene. Everything from about six feet to infinity is in focus. Other lenses, such as those on many 35mm single-lens-reflex cameras, can be focused manually. They allow you to zero in on an individual part of the scene.

In recent years camera manufacturers have combined the advantages of both of these types of cameras in the auto-focus camera. This camera combines the simplicity of a fixed focus with the flexibility of a 35mm. You point to the object that you want to have in the sharpest focus and press the shutter release down halfway; the lens focuses on the object. Some photographers find the auto-focus lenses fast enough for average shooting. Others find cameras with manual focus lenses, or cameras that allow the user to override the auto-focus and focus manually, more to their liking.

Lens Sizes and Functions

Many 35mm cameras can accept different sizes of lenses. Interchangeable lenses come in a variety of sizes, ranging from extremely wide angle to long telephoto. The length of the lens is measured in millimeters. Wider lenses, whose focal length is shorter, take in more of the scene.

Kind of lens	Length of lens	Often used for
Fisheye	7.5 or 15mm	Panoramic landscape shots
Wide angle	28 or 35mm	Large group shots
Normal	50mm	Candids
Short telephoto	85, 105, or 135mm	Informal portraits
Long telephoto	200 or 300mm	Spot news
Extremely long telephoto	400mm or longer	Wildlife

Controlling Light and Exposure

The advantage of a manually focused camera is that it allows more flexibility in photo shooting and more precision in controlling lighting and clarity of picture. But to use one effectively, you need to be aware of some of its elements and functions.

F/stops

As the lens evolved and photography advanced, photographers realized they needed more control over the amount of light getting to the film. They began changing the size of the lens opening, or aperture, through which the light would pass before reaching the film. The brighter the light being reflected off the subject, the smaller the aperture a photographer used. If the subject reflected little light (if it was dark), the photographer used a larger aperture. That way, the same amount of light reached the film regardless of the amount of light being reflected.

To quantify the amount of light passing through the lens, photographers developed the f/stop, the position at which the aperture is set. Beginning at f/1 (which appears on very few lenses), each f/stop is a multiple of the square root of two. This mathematical relationship makes it easy to calculate the f/stops without having to memorize them. (Over time, of course, many photographers do end up memorizing f/stops because they use them so much.)

Memorizing the various f/stops, or apertures, is not nearly as critical as knowing the relationship between them. For example, f/1, the widest open lens opening, lets in the most light. As the f/stops get higher, the lens opening gets smaller and less light is admitted. So, knowing that f/4 lets in more light than f/5.6 and that f/8 lets in less light than f/5.6 is very important.

Not only is there a relationship between f/stops and the amount of light reaching the film, there is a direct, quantifiable relationship. That is, f/5.6 lets in exactly twice as much light as f/8 and f/8 lets in exactly half as much light as f/5.6. Consecutive f/stops let in either twice as much light or half as much light as their neighbors.

f/stops

The lens of any given camera will contain most or all of the following f/stops.

1	4	16
1.4	5.6	22
2	8	32
2.8	11	

Depth of field. The lens aperture also controls the amount of the total picture in front of and behind the subject that appears in focus. With smaller apertures such as f/22 or f/16, more of the total picture appears in focus. With larger apertures such as f/2 or f/2.8, less appears in focus. The area in clear focus in front of and behind the specific spot on which the photographer focused is called depth of field. Of the available depth of field, one-third appears in front of the subject and two-thirds behind it.

To illustrate depth of field, hold your hand at arm's length and extend your forefinger like you're using the hand sign for "number one." Focus your eyes on your finger. The background is out of focus—that's low depth of field. Now squint—more of the background is in focus. By decreasing the aperture of your eye, you've increased the depth of field. It's crude, but it works.

The depth of field in this photo is quite narrow, with only one student in clear focus. This was caused by the photographer using a wide aperture, probably to compensate for the lack of light.

Shutter Speeds

The f/stop controls the amount of light reaching the film. But you can also control the length of time the film is exposed to light. You do this by controlling the speed of the shutter, the part of the camera that is released to take the picture.

The shutter speed, the amount of time the shutter stays open, is measured in fractions of a second. Modern cameras have shutter speeds ranging from B ("bulb"), which indicates that the shutter will stay open as long as the photographer has the shutter release depressed, all the way up to 1/4000th of a second. With a few exceptions, the shutter speeds are multiples of two and are expressed without the fraction. For example, 60 indicates 1/60th of a second. Starting with one second and getting ever faster, the shutter speeds are 2, 4, 8, 15, 30, 60, 125, 250, 500, 1000, 2000, and 4000.

Notice that starting with 1/2 second, you can derive the other shutter speeds by multiplying the denominator of the preceding fraction by two. (For example, 1/2 x 2 = 1/4. And 1/4 x 2 = 1/8.) There are two exceptions, between 1/8 and 1/15 and between 1/60 and 1/125. You'll just have to memorize those speeds.

Like the f/stops, each adjacent shutter speed lets in either twice as much light or half as much light as its neighbor. For example, 250 (1/250th of a second) lets in twice as much light as 500 and half as much light as 125.

The outer limits. There are limits to how much you can play with shutter speeds. Due to the motion of the body of the photographer, the slowest shutter speed that can be used with a given lens is approximately the

The action in the left-hand photo is blurred because the shutter speed was too slow. To stop an action such as running, as in the right-hand photo, a shutter speed of 1/500 or faster is needed.

reciprocal of the focal length of that lens (for example, the reciprocal for a 50mm lens is 1/50, approximately the shutter speed of 1/60). Thus with a 50mm lens it is impossible to hold a camera still for longer than 1/60th of a second. For a 200mm telephoto lens, the slowest shutter speed that can be used while hand-holding the lens is 1/250th of a second. Longer shutter speeds require the use of a stabilization device such as a tripod.

On the other hand, to stop action requires fast shutter speeds. A lot of movement can occur in 1/60th of a second: A person running can cover several feet, a car can go several yards, a helicopter blade can make a signification portion of a rotation. To stop most human action, a shutter speed of 1/500th of a second is needed. And all but the fastest action can be stopped with a shutter speed of 2000.

Exposures

Determining the proper exposure for a scene is more than just choosing an f/stop and a shutter speed. The two must work together to provide enough detail in the highlights (the light areas of the picture) and shadows (the dark areas) and to stop the action you want stopped but blur the action you want blurred. A third variable comes into play: the film that you're using and its ISO.

The ISO is a fixed number determined by the type of film you're

Equivalent Exposures

In making exposures, f/stops and shutter speeds are complementary. For example, assuming the same speed film, each of the combinations below would let in the same amount of light.

f/stop	shutter speed
f/1.4	2000
f/2	1000
f/2.8	500
f/4	250
f/5.6	125
f/8	60
f/11	30
f/16	15
f/22	8

using. The higher the ISO, the more sensitive the film is to light. Thus ISO 3200 film is more sensitive than ISO 400 film, which is, in turn, more sensitive than ISO 100 film.

A basic rule of exposure is based on taking pictures in bright sunlight. The f/16 rule states that in bright sunlight at f/16, the shutter speed should be equivalent to the reciprocal of the ISO of the film you're using. To apply the f/16 rule, take note of the ISO of your film and the lighting conditions. For example, if you're using ISO 400 film and taking pictures in bright daylight, the exposure would be f/16 at 1/500th of a second (the closest shutter speed to 1/400).

Exposures are usually written in this fashion: f/16 @ 1/250. This indicates an exposure of f/16 at 1/250th of a second. The ISO of the film is given separately.

With some further information, it's easy to derive a set of basic exposures from the f/16 rule remembering that the shutter speed is equal to 1/ISO.

Bright sun	f/16
Hazy sun	f/11
Weak sun (soft shadows)	f/8
Cloudy (no shadows)	f/5.6
Heavy overcast	f/4
Well-lit interiors	f/1.8

Backlighting. With modern cameras, most of the calculation regarding exposure is automatic. You don't have to give much thought to taking the average picture. However, camera light meters can be tricked into giving false exposure readings.

The most common false meter reading occurs when the subject is backlit—that is, when the light source is coming from behind the subject instead of behind the photographer. The meter, in its attempt to give an exposure that will result in the "average" part of the scene being exposed correctly, will underexpose (make dark) the rest of the scene. The meter tries to make the light part of the scene a neutral gray, causing the rest of the picture to become too dark.

Using the available light, you as a photographer can solve the backlighting problem in one of two ways. You can move yourself, the subject, or the light source; or you can compensate by increasing the overall amount of time the film is exposed to the light. To do this, either use an f/stop that is two stops wider or a shutter speed that is two stops slower. For example, if the original, backlit scene gave a meter reading of f/8 @

1/125, your new exposure could be f/4 @ 1/125. While that will cause the light area of the scene to be overexposed (too light), it will allow more light to reach the film from the dark areas of the scene.

Artificial light. Using available light, although it ends up looking the most natural, is not the only alternative for photographers. Many cameras today, even simple fixed-focus models, come with built-in flashes that create their own, artificial light. Most 35mm single-lens-reflex cameras come with a way to attach a flash to the top of the camera for perfect synchronization with the camera's shutter.

When using a flash, know the fastest shutter speed you can use with that flash to get a properly exposed picture. That speed is called the flash synchronization speed (often 1/60th of a second) and is often marked with a lightning bolt or in red on the camera's shutter speed dial. Some cameras have automatic synchronization with the flash.

While the flash synch speed may seem like an awfully slow shutter speed (and it is), remember that the light for the scene is coming from the flash, which is incredibly fast. As long as there is no other light, a powerful flash can stop the fastest action. If there is ambient light in the scene, such as from lamps or the setting sun, you might, in effect, get two exposures on the scene, one from the flash and one from the ambient light. This can produce interesting but sometimes unpredictable results. It's a common technique when taking pictures in front of a bonfire or sunset, however. The flash lights the subject in the foreground while the bonfire or sunset lights the background.

Another characteristic of artificial light that must be taken into account is its color, since most films are color-balanced for sunlight. Pictures taken

The backlighting in the left-hand photograph obscures and distorts the subject. In the right-hand photo the problem was corrected by shooting the subject from a different direction.

under fluorescent light will turn green. Pictures taken under tungsten light (such as a conventional light bulb) will appear red. Compensating for this color shifting requires either a special film or a color-compensating filter put in front of the lens before taking the picture. Color correction is only a problem with color film, of course.

Alternative Cameras

Most of the discussion to this point has dealt with the manually focused 35mm single-lens-reflex camera. Though these cameras offer great flexibility and relative ease in getting the shots you want, there are alternatives.

The point-and-shoot. In place of the 35mm single-lens-reflex, many newspaper and yearbook staffs are quite successful using automatic point-and-shoot cameras. These cameras, whether the image is viewed through the lens or through a range finder, are usually completely automatic. Some have built-in flash. While they aren't suited for shooting fast action (because the shutter speed is usually 1/60th of a second), they are good for the average candid shot.

To be successful in using a point-and-shoot, remember to fill the frame with the action without getting too close. Keep in mind all the other "rules" of composition (enumerated in Chapter 18) as well. You don't have to worry with f/stops or shutter speeds and can concentrate on taking good pictures. When designing your pages you can edit out the parts of the pictures you don't want.

The digital camera. As technology advances, so do cameras. Appearing on the scene today at affordable prices are cameras with no film—cameras that transmit their images onto a disk for later manipulation and printing from a computer. These digital cameras are primarily in use by newspapers and newsmagazines, but are becoming increasingly popular with individuals who can view the images instantly on a computer or, sometimes, on a television screen.

In general, digital cameras resemble a standard 35mm single-lens-reflex and use the same exposure system. For publications with a short turnaround time, these cameras have two benefits. First, they entirely eliminate the need for a darkroom. Secondly, the images can be transmitted across phone lines, allowing photographers to transmit images taken in one part of the world to another place in seconds. The electronic camera is the future of photography and doesn't mean the end of the artistic aspect of the profession, only a change in the way a photographer paints with light.

Looking for a perfect shot of Mt. Rainier to accompany a travel feature? Can't find a reproduction of a Picasso painting to go with a story about a new show at a nearby museum? Why not turn to the Internet?

The need for a wide choice of accessible images for all types of publications has spurred new cyberspace-based means of obtaining those images. Formerly, when a publication wanted a photograph to reproduce, it had to contact a stock house, a company that holds large collections of images for rental. From the several transparencies that were generally sent back, the publication chose one that best fit its needs. Transparencies had to be treated with care, for if any were lost or damaged, the publication was held responsible. Once a selection was made, the transparency then had to be converted for use in the publication.

Disseminating art and photo reproductions via the computer has made the whole picture selection process much more streamlined. Today, a page designer, photo editor, or even a grade-school student doing a social studies report can visit the Web site of a company that purveys images, click on a photo or painting, and pay a small fee for downloading that image for one-time use.

Creating this easy access to images took a tremendous amount of effort. Museums had to photograph hundreds of paintings. These and hundreds of thousands of other photographs then had to be scanned, digitized, and indexed—all costly and time-consuming processes for image purveyors.

What kinds of images are available? Well, for example, one company has bought the entire Bettman Archive, a sixteen-million image collection that includes some of the most famous photographs of the century, and is in the process of scanning and digitizing it. Painstakingly reproduced, extremely accurate renderings of famous art works from museums all over the world are also available. And, of course, there are the more run-of-the-mill, but very useful, image collections of various stock houses, continually added to and updated.

Here is how a typical transaction of procuring an image could work. An editor looking for a photograph might use a company's search engine to locate what he or she needs, or, if the need is more specific, call the company and describe exactly what's needed. The researcher at the company would send samples to a Web site so that the editor could view them and make a selection. Then, still on the phone, the editor would communicate his or her decision. The image could be sent via the Internet immediately or be put onto a CD-ROM and sent overnight.

Payments for use of images work in two directions. To begin with, photographers or museums that supply the images to companies usually work out flat-rate deals that adequately compensate them no matter how frequently or infrequently their images are used. Publications wishing to use the images also pay. Some supplying companies charge a membership fee as well as a rental fee. Rental fees vary depending on the size and circulation of the publication and the cost and popularity of the image.

The business of procuring photographs and other images over the Internet won't put local photographers out of business. There are still many shots needed of specific events as they occur. But going on-line is a good way to fill specific, and especially unusual, needs quickly.

Working in the Darkroom

Whether it's black-and-white or color, paper or film, most photographic materials are basically the same: an emulsion consisting of silver halide crystals embedded in a gelatin and spread on a plastic or paper surface. Different films and photographic papers can vary. Some films have protective coatings. Some papers use additional thin paper as a backing; some use a plastic resin. But the process is still the same.

The silver halide (most commonly silver bromide or silver iodide) crystals are sensitive to light and change when exposed to light. The crystals that are changed form a latent image that is invisible until developed.

The process of developing film and making prints from it requires some special equipment and skills. Many of the skills are similar to those used in taking pictures with a camera.

Developing Film

Film is extremely sensitive to light. But before it can be developed, it has to be removed from the canister that held it in the camera and put into a tank that will allow the developing agent to reach it. Putting the film on reels and into the tank must be done in complete darkness.

Besides running water, a well-equipped darkroom contains the equipment and chemicals necessary to develop film and make prints. Here, a student checks processed film for spots.

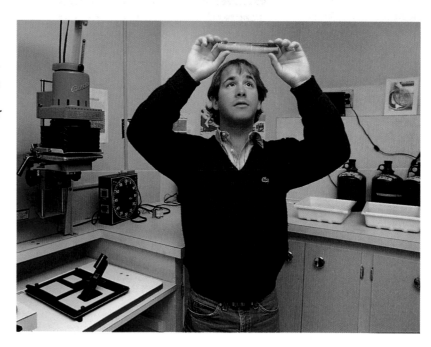

A darkroom can be an old closet, bathroom, kitchen, or some room in the school with close access to running water. A well-equipped darkroom for even a small publication must have running water and good drainage for the chemicals used in development, for these must be considered hazardous waste.

The development process acts first on those crystals that have been changed by light. The developing agent starts a chemical reaction. As long as the developer is removed before the unchanged (unexposed) crystals begin reacting, an image made of silver crystals will appear on the film.

Unless the undeveloped crystals are rendered insensitive to light, they can still be changed by light. So after the development process is complete, the film or paper is fixed through another chemical process. Fixing changes the silver halide crystals so they are no longer sensitive to light.

Other steps in the development of film or prints enhance the process and remove the chemicals used in development or fixing. While color film requires more steps, the basic process is still the same: development, stop development, fix, rinse, and dry.

After the negatives have been dried in a clean environment (so no dust settles on them), they should be cut into strips of five frames per strip and stored in plastic sheets for easy filing and access. A good publications staff will keep all negatives filed for easy access by everyone. And photographers who want to have their prints used in publications will see that the negatives, or contact sheets made from the negatives, are available for the editors to view.

Special developing steps. The following steps would be used in developing Kodak TMax (black-and-white) film, ISO 400. The procedure is similar for all moderate-speed black-and-white film.

- Gather the materials needed, including developing tank, light-tight lid, reels, D-76 developer, rinse water, fixer, wetting agent, and drying cabinet.
- Put film on reels in light-tight room.
- Put reels in tank and cover with light-tight lid.
- Check temperature of developer. D-76 developer is diluted 1:1 for optimum usage. You can use warm or cool water in the dilution process to get the developer to optimum temperature—68°F.
- Put properly diluted developer in tank. Note the start time or set a timer for 12.5 minutes.
- Agitate the film by inverting the canister one time. Hold the lid on the canister securely. To jar loose any bubbles that got on the film during agitation, rap the canister on the edge of the sink gently three times.

- Let the canister sit for thirty seconds. Every half minute, repeat the agitation process, inverting the canister one time and tapping it gently three times. The agitation allows fresh developer to reach the film.
- When the time is up, pour out the developer through the hole in the lid, holding the light-tight lid on the canister securely. Diluted D-76 cannot be reused.
- With light-tight lid still in place, fill the canister with room-temperature water and dump it out three times to remove any residual developer. It is not necessary to use acidic stop bath on film.
- Pour in the fixer (also called hypo) at room temperature. Kodak Rapid Fixer with hardener should be left in the film canister five minutes and inverted for agitation once every minute.
- Pour the fixer back into the designated container. Fixer can be reused several times.
- Now that the silver halides in the film are no longer sensitive to light, the light-tight lid can be removed. Put the film under running water for at least twenty minutes at room temperature. Or, to save time and to conserve water, fill the canister with water and dump it out at least thirty times; then leave the film under running water for five minutes. Some schools use hypo-clearing agent to speed up this process.
- To prevent water spots from forming on the film, apply a wetting agent such as Kodak's Photo-Flo to the film at the recommended dilution. Keep the film immersed for at least thirty seconds.
- Carefully take the film off the reels. Be careful, as the emulsion of the film can be easily damaged at this time, ruining the negatives.
- Put the film in a clean place to dry, hanging by a film clip or a clothespin.
- Clean up the supplies you used, rinsing the canister and reels with copious amounts of water. Dry all your supplies and put lids back on all the chemical containers.

Making a Print

Once you've developed the film, you still need to make prints from it. That process requires subjecting the paper you'll be printing on to a process much like that used in film development. Making prints also requires working in a room with limited light, although complete darkness is not necessary when working with traditional black-and-white papers.

The negative. The first step to making a print is framing the image, using an enlarger that magnifies the negative and projects it onto the photographic paper, where it must then be brought into focus. The negative is an inversed copy of the image. What was light in the scene appears dense; what was dark appears transparent. The photographic paper takes this negative image and makes it positive. In other words, where more light hit the film, more silver crystals were converted causing a dense buildup of silver. The same is true for paper. As more light shines through the negative, the dark areas of the scene (which are more transparent in the negative) pass more light onto the paper. The areas of the paper that are exposed to light turn dark. That's why you should work in a darkroom.

Unlike film, however, which is sensitive to all wave-lengths of light, most common black-and-white photographic papers are highly sensitive only to light on the blue end of the spectrum and are relatively insensitive to red light.

The enlarger and easel. For stable positioning of the negative, put it in the enlarger's negative carrier, emulsion side down (shiny side up). Once it's in position, turn on the enlarger so that light is passing through the negative, through the lens, and onto the baseboard of the enlarger. Using the widest available f/stop, focus the image and fine-tune any cropping. To hold the photo paper securely, use an easel that rests firmly on the enlarger baseboard.

A photo enlarger must be carefully adjusted to make sure the finished print is sharp and clear.

Some easels allow you to make prints that aren't fixed sizes. You can make a 4 1/3" x 5 3/4" print if you want to; you're not limited to standard sizes. These variable easels are handy for publications work and make it easier on the people designing pages, because cropping is left up to the photographer.

Polycontrast filters. To control the contrast of the image, choose a polycontrast filter before choosing the f/stop. The appropriate filter depends on the type of paper you're using and the contrast of the image. Higher numbered filters raise contrast, as do higher grades of single-contrast paper. Lower numbered filters lower contrast. For example, a 5 filter raises contrast, a 1 filter lowers contrast.

The correct exposure. Now, choose an f/stop that appears neither too light nor too dark. This is subjective; you'll get better with experience. An f/stop that is too wide open will result in a test print that's too dark overall. An f/stop that's too narrow will result in a test print that's too light overall. After you've chosen the proper aperture (subjectively) using the same f/stop numbers you memorized on your camera, the only variable left to determine is the "shutter speed," set with a time attached to the enlarger. Exposure times for prints are generally 10 to 30 seconds long rather than fractions of a second. If your exposure ends up being longer than 30 seconds, you've chosen an f/stop that isn't letting out enough light. Try opening the f/stop. Just as on the camera, opening the enlarger's lens one stop lets in twice as much light. To compensate, you have to expose the paper for half as long. For example, if your original exposure was 40 seconds at f/5.6, the equivalent exposure would be 20 seconds at f/4.

Test strips. To determine the exact exposure time without wasting a lot of paper, use a test strip—a series of exposures on one piece of paper. Have each successive exposure (in equal intervals of two to five seconds) expose the paper to more light, making the image darker. Once you've determined the proper exposure time, you can expose an entire sheet of paper cut to the size of the finished print and then develop the paper.

The development process. Just as with film, developing prints involves converting the latent image into a visible image through a chemical process and then rendering the unexposed silver crystals insensitive to light and removing them by fixing the paper. To keep prints for a long period of time, one of the most important parts of the printing process is washing the print to remove all the residual fixer and silver halides.

Failure to remove any of those chemicals will cause the print to turn brown and the image to fade over time.

Prints are fixed and rinsed in trays large enough to hold the largest print you'll be making. It's important to keep fresh chemicals at room temperature in the trays, and it's also extremely important to keep the darkroom clean. Any dust coming from dry chemicals or from book covers or clothes will come to rest on the negative or photo paper, resulting in white spots on the print. In fact, the darkroom should be treated like a chemistry lab. Under no circumstances should food or drink be allowed in the darkroom, and you should arrange for the proper disposal of chemicals, especially fixer, just as chemists do. To ensure correct procedures, Material Safety and Data Sheets (MSDS) sheets should be available for anyone working in the lab.

Specific printing steps. The following steps would be used in making a black-and-white print with Kodak Polycontrast Rapid IIIRC photographic paper.

- Gather all the materials needed, including the enlarger, filters, easel, timer, trays, the properly diluted developer, stop bath, fixer, and rinsing tank.
- Put the negative in the negative carrier, emulsion side down and backwards.
- Turn on the enlarger and open up the lens to the maximum aperture.
- Raise or lower the enlarger to crop the portions of the print you want to use on the easel.
- Carefully focus the image on the easel.
- Based on the contrast of the negative, choose a polycontrast filter (if you're using polycontrast paper). A low-contrast negative (one with little difference between the blackest black and the whitest white) should get a higher-numbered filter. High-contrast negatives should get lower-numbered filters.
- Choose an f/stop that's halfway between too light and too dark. The proper f/stop will result in an exposure of between 10 and 30 seconds.
- Turn off the enlarger.
- Set the timer for five seconds.
- Place a small strip of paper about 1" x 5" on the easel and cover all but one inch of it with an opaque piece of paper, such as cardboard. Expose the paper by clicking on the expose button on the timer. Hold the cardboard still for the entire five-second exposure.

- When the timer goes off, move the cardboard to expose one more inch of paper to the light and repeat the exposure process. Repeat this process until the entire test strip has been exposed.
- Develop this test strip in developer for 60–90 seconds, agitating it constantly.
- Stop the development of the test strip in the middle tray and then place the test strip in the fixer. You can now turn on the room lights to view your test strip.
- Based on the results of the test strip, choose an exposure. The divisions of the test strip should be obvious. The lightest block was exposed for five seconds, the next darker block for ten seconds, etc.
- Set your timer for the desired exposure. Turn off the lights.
- Place another small piece of paper, again about 1" x 5", on the easel. Try to place it over the critical areas of the print, such as the faces of the people. Expose it for the entire exposure time. Develop this test print just as you did the test strip. Consistency is critical.
- View the test print in room light and make any modifications in the filter or exposure time necessary.
- Turn off the lights and place a full-size piece of paper (enough to cover the entire print area plus 1/4" on all sides) in the easel. Expose it to light and develop this print just as you did the test print. Again, consistency is critical.
- The test strips and test prints can be discarded. After the print has been in the fixer for two to three minutes, remove it and rinse it in running water for at least ten minutes. Do not overfix the print, and do not remove it from the rinse water too soon.
- Dry the print in a dust-free environment.
- Put your negatives back in the negative sleeve. Put the filter back in its box. Make sure the enlarger is turned off and raise it up to near the top (so other people don't hit their heads on it). Clean up your area.

Art vs. Science

The process of working in the darkroom is as much an art as a science, but beginning photographers have to concentrate on the science first. Learning how to manipulate the exposure of a print, to keep things clean, to rinse prints for an adequate time, and to use selective contrast filters or paper to manipulate contrast are all skills beginning photographers learn. And learning those skills takes time. If you're interested in photography, concentrate on mastering the basics and then expanding upon those skills to learn the true art of photography.

Wrap-up

Learning the technical aspects of photography can take some time, but having a fundamental understanding of how and why the photographic process works is important. Photography is painting with light: The camera is the brush and the film is the canvas. As a photographer, you control what the brush puts on the canvas by manipulating the f/stop and shutter speed.

The f/stop is the setting on the lens that controls the amount of light that reaches the film. Larger f/stops (such as f/2 and f/1.4) allow more light to reach the film. Smaller f/stops (such as f/16 and f/22) allow less light to reach the film.

The shutter, the part of the camera that is released to take the picture, also controls the amount of light that reaches the film. The shutter remains open for a very specific duration of time; the longer that time, the more light can reach the film. For example, a shutter speed of 1/60th of a second allows twice as much light to reach the film as a speed of 1/125th of a second.

The shutter speed and aperture work together to expose film to light. This principle works both when taking pictures and making prints.

In the darkroom, photographers have to master the chemical processes involved in both developing film and making prints. A developer converts the latent image to a visible image and a fixative agent "fixes" the image to make it permanent. In the darkroom, photographers can control how light or dark an image, or part of an image, appears. They can also crop off unnecessary portions of the picture, leaving the reader with a powerful photo filled with action.

Evaluation Checklist: *Print*

✓ Is the print in focus?
✓ Was enough light used to bring out the details in the photo?
✓ Is the contrast between light and dark areas adequate but not excessive?
✓ Has an appropriate filter been used?
✓ Is the print free from dust spots?

On Assignment

Individual Activities

1. Write a brief definition or explanation of each of the following terms.

aperture	backlighting
contact sheet	darkroom
depth of field	enlarger
f/stop	fixer
flash synchronization speed	ISO
lens	shutter
test strip	

2. Take a series of pictures of the same scene, experimenting with different f/stops and shutter speeds for each shot. Make a note of the settings you used. Then develop the film, or have it developed. Examine the results carefully. What differences were caused by using the different settings? Which exposures turned out better than you expected? Worse than you expected? Write a brief report analyzing the results. Include your photos in the report.

3. Make a list of all the chemicals used in your darkroom. Don't list brand names. Instead, read the packaging and list all the components of, for example, your film developer. Include all chemicals used for both film developing and printing. Then list the chemical compounds common to both processes.

4. If a scene required an exposure of f/16 at 1/500th of a second and you exposed it at f/22 at 1/1000th, would you end up with an underexposed negative or an overexposed negative? Why? Without any further manipulation, would a print from this negative be too dark or too light? Why? Explain your answers in a class discussion.

5. Using five prints supplied by your photography instructor, evaluate them strictly on the basis of technical quality. Was the negative processed correctly? Was the print processed correctly? Is the print free of dust spots? Is the print in focus? Is the print not too high or too low in contrast?

6. Locate the Material Safety and Data Sheet (MSDS) for one of the chemicals used in the darkroom. What hazards does this chemical have? What can you do to avoid any danger?

7. Using only pictures (no text), diagram the process of exposing film to light, developing film, and fixing film. Illustrate the emulsion, silver halide crystals, latent image, unexposed silver halide crystals, and final image.

8. Compare and contrast the process of developing film and making a print. Consider all chemicals and immersion times, temperatures, and agitation rates for all chemicals.

Team Activity

9. With a team, select the best photos each member has taken. Analyze various possible photos before you make your choices, discussing the strengths and weaknesses of each possibility. When you have chosen the photos, have each team member write a critical analysis of his or her photo, describing the f/stop and shutter speed used and the quality of the print. Combine the analyses, along with the photos, into a display book. Compare your book with those of other teams. Discuss your responses in class.

A love of sports sparked Don Flores's interest in journalism and helped him score big in a profession that is trying hard to attract more minorities.

From his first bylines as a young reporter covering Little League in his hometown of Goliad, Texas, to his current position as publisher and editor of *El Paso Times*, in El Paso, Texas, Flores worked his way to the top of the newspaper business.

Although his career has taken him across the country, Flores is happy to be back in his home state of Texas. "I think it's great. I grew up in Texas and I can really blend into the community here. I know its issues," Flores said.

As publisher and editor, Flores says he has the opportunity to see the news process from a different perspective. "Being a publisher, you get to understand the newspaper as a 'total product.' You're able to see how the paper fits the community's needs." If the news product is meaningful and relevant to the community, they will believe in it and continue to support it, Flores added.

That attitude has helped Flores get where he is today.

From writing Little League stories, he graduated to writing for his junior high and high school newspapers. Then, when he entered Southwest Texas State University in San Marcos, Flores joined the student newspaper as its sports editor.

In, 1973, Flores began working for the *Abilene Reporter-News*. He quickly advanced, within three years, to the position of city editor. His career path took him to the *Dallas Times Herald* in 1978 and in 1983 to the *Dallas Morning News*.

During his various moves in the newsrooms of Texas, Flores also was becoming active in organizations and programs designed to bring more minorities into journalism. One program in particular was the summer journalism program for minority high school students that was run by Texas Christian University in Fort Worth.

"That's how we get them [minority journalists] in the newsroom," Flores said. "We track them from high school to college and then snap them up as soon as they are ready."

Flores says he is not a joiner, but his activities contradict that. He regularly attends conventions of both the National Association of Hispanic Journalists, of which he is past president, and the National Association of Black Journalists.

At age 34, Flores left Texas to join media giant Gannett as assistant managing editor of the *Tucson Citizen* in Arizona, a job that allowed him to be directly involved in recruiting. He has also been editor of the *New Mexican*, in Santa Fe; managing editor of the *Times Delta*, in Visalia, California; and president and publisher of the *Press-Citizen* in Iowa City, Iowa. From the *Press-Citizen*, Flores moved back to Texas, where he has been publisher and editor of *El Paso Times* since 1993.

Throughout his career, Flores has clung to his dedication of minority recruiting. Although this position places a greater demand on his time, Flores is determined to continue. "I try to be as involved as I can," Flores said. Although he admits that downsizing in the newspaper industry has hurt minority representation, at least at *El Paso Times*, he is not discouraged. "I will just have to be more aggressive to make it happen," he said.

Reflecting on his early years as a journalist, Flores said, "As hard as it is to imagine, I was the first Hispanic to edit at the *Record* in San Marcos, Texas."

Today minorities are being encouraged more and more to pursue career opportunities in the newsroom. Flores fully acknowledges the importance of his position as a Hispanic journalist in Texas. "I am concerned about being the role model a lot of us didn't have."

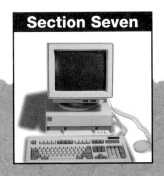

Computers and Desktop Publishing

Taking Advantage of Technology

Taking Advantage of Technology

Key Terms

desktop publishing

CPU

RAM

network

laser printer

word processing

image editing

scanner

Key Concepts

After you have completed this chapter, you should

- understand the various parts of the computer and their functions

- know the types of printers common on the market today and which are best suited for desktop publishing

- understand the role of the various types of software used in desktop publishing

- know the various ways an image can be digitized

- be familiar with the development of the Internet and its influence on journalism

Back in 1988, the American Press Institute hosted a seminar involving some of the top newspaper designers in the United States, surveying them about the newspaper of the future. The institute asked the designers to forecast what they thought the newspaper would be like in the year 2020. About one-third of the designers said they believed the traditional newspaper would be replaced with some interactive media that could be delivered electronically.

They cited statistics regarding the viewing of television versus the reading of newspapers to prove their point. "The newspaper is a product that holds the attention of readers for about 24 minutes a day," John Lees, a Massachusetts graphics designer, said at the API seminar. "Meanwhile, television sets are on in American households seven hours a day, although actual viewing time is only three and a half hours. Newspaper circulation has stalled . . . , penetration has declined substantially, and many publishers insist on producing cumbersome products . . . ."

Since 1988, many remarkable changes in technology have occurred. Some newspapers are, in fact, distributed electronically via the Internet. But these papers haven't replaced the printed version, the fold-up variety that people can stick in their briefcase and pull out to read while waiting for the commuter train. In truth, more changes have occurred in the printed version of the paper, at least in the way it's produced. In 1988 typewriters were just about as common in news offices as computers. Pages were often laid out by hand. Photos were nearly always in black-and-white. The growth of the personal computer, coupled with various other technologically related products, has radically changed the way not only newspapers, but also magazines, yearbooks, and even textbooks are produced. And the change continues as new hardware and software become available.

Thus it is fitting that this course finishes with a look at technology. Change won't stop, and some of the things mentioned in this chapter may be obsolete by the time you read it. But at least you can get a sense of where things have been and, perhaps, where they are heading.

Desktop Publishing

Paul Brainard, then president of the Aldus Corporation, sat around a table in 1985 discussing *PageMaker,* the new software his company was

A page layout program, such as *PageMaker* or *QuarkXPress* (shown here), allows type and art to be positioned and manipulated on a page until the layout is acceptable. Before the advent of desktop publishing, such positioning had to be done by hand.

developing. At that table, Brainard and others coined the phrase "desktop publishing" to summarize what could be done utilizing the recently released Macintosh computer with its user-friendly interface; the laser printer, which would provide "high resolution" output on conventional paper; and their software.

PageMaker wasn't the first pagination software. It was, however, the first software marketed to bring the "power of the press" to the masses. What *PageMaker,* together with the Macintosh and laser printer, did was to revolutionize the printing business. No longer did you need a $15,000 typesetter, chemicals, and developing equipment to output high-quality type. Now, with a $1,500 computer, a $1,000 laser printer, and about $700 worth of software, you could put out your own publication that was virtually indistinguishable from a professionally produced publication. In theory at least, a school newspaper could look just as good as *The New York Times.*

Hardware and What It Can Do

Hardware is, basically, the machinery used in a computer system. This includes the computer itself and various components that may be attached to it, such as a printer.

Computers

In the years since the Macintosh and laser printer hit the market, the user-friendly interface is no longer unique. Now, almost every personal computer on the market utilizes an easy-to-use interface with which you can simply point to something with your mouse, click on it, and go. Here is a brief summary of the various parts of the personal computer and what they do.

The Central Processing Unit (CPU) is the brains of the computer. It controls everything that the computer does. The casing that holds the CPU also holds the power supply, the cooling fan, and slots for things like accessory cards that allow the computer to perform specialized functions.

Using a computer usually involves using two kinds of drives. One is the built-in hard drive. On the hard drive, you can store any software that you need access to, including all of the software for desktop publishing, and the documents you create using that software.

Almost all computers also come with a built-in floppy disk drive. Floppy disks (which are actually hard nowadays) can't hold nearly as much information as the hard drive and often aren't very reliable, but they make information portable. Working on a floppy disk, or transferring work from the hard drive onto one, allows you to easily give documents to another person to view on his or her computer. The floppy is also a place to store files of documents from your hard drive that you no longer need immediate access to.

Because a hard drive might easily contain thousands of files, it is important to keep it organized and clean. Related document files can be put into computer-made folders. Unnecessary files can be discarded —put into the trash. Time should be scheduled each week for maintaining the hard drive and checking the various components.

Efficient maintenance of files becomes even more critical for users on a network, an electronic connection of multiple computers that allows users to share files directly. With the appropriate network software, which comes with most computers today, and a few cables, a system can be set up allowing any user to access any

Humble Beginnings

Apple Computer, the first company to bring simple-to-use desksize computers to homes and small businesses, had its origins in the bedroom and garage of twenty-year-old Steve Jobs. He and his partner, fellow electronics wizard Steve Wozniak, designed and built the Apple I and introduced it in 1976; other computers, including the Macintosh, followed. Both Jobs and Wozniak eventually left Apple Computer, though Jobs later returned.

file from any computer—or restricting access as needed. A network becomes particularly efficient in a publications setting, since editors can edit copy and make it available to the person designing the page without having to switch computers.

Computers also have keyboards and other input devices—that is, tools to use in creating documents. Most computers ship a keyboard and mouse with the CPU, but they may not be the keyboard and mouse best suited to the needs of various staff members. Some artists, for example, prefer drawing tablets, trackballs, or even touch-screens to a desktop mouse.

And, of course, you can't do much with your CPU unless you can see what you're doing. That's where the monitor comes in. Like every other aspect of hardware technology, there are different types of computer monitors. Bigger monitors with higher resolution cost more money, but most users don't need monitors larger than 13" for average use. While some vendors still make black-and-white ones, almost all monitors sold today are color. The only difference is the number of colors a monitor can display and at what resolution, measured in pixels per inch (ppi). The more pixels per inch, the higher the resolution, allowing finer detail to be displayed on the screen.

Some computers run faster than others because their CPU contains a faster central processing chip. Faster processors cost more but allow more operations to be completed in less time. IBM and Macintosh computers (and their respective clones) contain different processors, so a file created, for example, on an IBM clone can't be run on a Macintosh. The PowerPC chip, a joint venture of IBM, Apple, and Motorola, is a processing chip intended to allow complete compatibility between different types of computers, thereby eliminating a frustration of many computer users.

Computers also vary in the amount of memory they contain. The Random Access Memory (RAM) is the memory reserved for the computer to do things. The more RAM your computer has, the more things it can do. Desktop publishing is RAM-intensive. That is, it requires more than the average amount of RAM. While 8 megabytes of RAM may be sufficient to run many software programs, the programs used in desktop publishing might require 24 megabytes of RAM or more. Computers with over 100 megabytes of RAM are common in shops doing very sophisticated desktop publishing and manipulation of images.

Going no further than this, certain advantages of the computer should already be apparent. For one thing, it can hold huge numbers of documents that in the past would all have to have been stored on paper. It can be connected through networks that allow people to work together on different aspects of the same project and to easily see each other's work on the screen. And although it can be used as a writing machine because of its keyboard, it also is capable of being used for other purposes by artists and designers.

Printers

What really made desktop publishing a reality was the capability to print out files created on the computer. Once an individual could quickly produce professional-looking copies of a document rather than having to send manuscript elsewhere for typesetting and printing, whole new worlds of communication possibilities opened up.

There are several types of printers that can be used in desktop publishing, some more efficient than others. Dot-matrix printers use pins that press through a ribbon, much like a typewriter, to form an image on the paper. The more pins the printer has, the higher quality it is. An eight-pin printer is, for example, one-third the quality of a 24-pin printer. Though dot-matrix printers are not that common today, some color printers still use this technology.

Similarly, ink-jet printers squirt ink on the page for a smoother-looking image, but one that is still relatively low in resolution. Color ink-jet printers are particularly popular today because of the smoothness of the image they generate, and many black-and-white ink-jet printers are used in home offices.

When the laser printer came along, the real revolution in desktop printing began. The laser printer actually uses a magnetized drum exactly like a photocopier. The computer gives the printer instructions regarding which portions of the drum to magnetize. As the drum revolves, the magnetized areas pick up toner from the toner cartridge and deposit it on the paper. A heating unit then seals the powdered carbon to the paper. Even the earliest laser printers had a resolution much higher than the highest-quality dot-matrix printer.

The resolution of a laser printer, or any high-end printer for that matter, is measured in dots per inch. A low-end laser printer has a resolution of 300dpi and is more than adequate for material to be photocopied. Midrange laser printers with a 600dpi resolution generate output suitable for offset printing on newsprint, such as most newspapers. High-end laser printers that output to paper have a resolution of 1200dpi or greater.

However, because of the coarseness of paper and imprecision of the paper placement, printing to paper with such high-end printers is less effective than printing to film.

Many schools wanting high resolution printing—for example, for yearbooks—go directly to the publisher or to a commercial service bureau. These suppliers are capable of taking your disk with all your files, graphics, and fonts, putting it in their computer, and printing your file on their imagesetters. The film generated by the imagesetter can be used directly to make the plates that are used to print your pages. Even if all you have at your school is a 300dpi laser printer for proofing, you can get quality rivaling the best in the publishing industry—2540dpi or beyond—by having your files output straight to film. Of course, you pay for quality. The cost of printing a page to film is significantly greater than printing to paper.

Software and What It Can Do

None of the sophisticated things computers and printers can do could be done without the software. It's the software, written by computer programmers, that tells the computer what to do. For example, a software program called *Excel* enables users to create spreadsheets; *PageMaker* facilitates the creation of page layouts; and *FileMaker* makes creating a database simple. While it's expensive to replace and update hardware, updating software is relatively easy and inexpensive.

Operating Systems

Every computer requires some basic software just to tell the computer that it's a computer and not a toaster (or to tell a toaster that it's not a computer). The operating system performs this task, giving the computer its fundamental instructions, such as how to access other programs, how to save files, and how to communicate with other devices, such as printers or monitors.

There are basically two kinds of computer operating systems. One is the Disk Operating System, or DOS, the fundamental operating system for IBM/compatible computers. The other is the Macintosh Operating System, or Mac OS, for Macintosh computers. These systems are often upgraded to provide better performance. The upgrades contain the features of the previous system as well as new ones.

As you learn about your computer, find out about the operating system, what kind it is, how much memory it uses, and what functions it performs. Information about the system software is stored on a computer in the systems folder.

Fonts

Generally, dependable and consistent operation of the operating system software goes without a second thought. There is one exception—fonts, which are the files that define how each individual letter looks on the page. Each font must be properly installed into the system before it can be used in a document.

Early in the development of desktop publishing, PostScript fonts were the standard. PostScript, a high-resolution page description language, gave designers the opportunity to print type—from almost unreadably small to single letters that filled entire pages—that looked like it had been professionally set. Quickly, type foundries began converting their conventional typefaces to PostScript film and selling them as part of a desktop publishing system.

PostScript fonts require two parts, one for screen display and the other for printer output, and so are complicated to install and manage. TrueType fonts simplified things by having only one part for both screen display and printer outputs. Nevertheless, thanks to their higher quality, PostScript fonts are still the accepted standard for desktop publishing.

Today, even the most basic computer comes with eight or ten fonts built into it, and others can be purchased and installed. Companies like Adobe have set the industry standard in font development, but dozens of others developed thousands upon thousands of fonts. Having the capacity to use various fonts in a document, and to change easily from one font to another, is one more technological advantage that could hardly be imagined in pre-desktop publishing days.

Word-Processing Programs

Regardless of what fonts are installed in a computer or what operating system it uses, for most people a word-processing program is the most basic type of software. Word-processing programs like *WordPerfect,* Microsoft *Word,* and Claris *Works* are written to make it easy to type in stories, headlines, and captions, and all have the capacity to perform many other functions as well.

In the pre-desktop publishing days, reporters or editors had to sit down at a typewriter and approximate the length of a story—since they could only work in typewriter type, they had little idea what their finished, type-set document would look like. Errors had to be corrected with correction tape or fluid; spellings had to be checked in a dictionary; style inconsistencies had to be looked for by reading back through completed pages.

Word-processing programs have virtually eliminated the labor associated with these steps. While writing or editing text, you can change the margins and spacing and format the text exactly as you want it to appear in publication. Additional features allow you to spell-check documents and search-and-replace to ensure consistency of style. Styles can even be built in, so that by pressing a key you can automatically change from, say, head-line-size text and typeface to body text. In short, word-processing programs allow you to concentrate on writing and editing without having to be distracted with laborious correction procedures or whether or not the story will fit on the page.

Pagination Programs

A word-processing program makes it easy to work with and manipulate text, but it doesn't help much with putting pages together. Companies like Adobe and Quark have written page-layout (pagination) programs like *PageMaker* and *QuarkXPress* to fill that niche. Although less accepted in the education market, Ventura *Publisher, Ready-Set-Go,* and *FrameMaker* perform similar functions.

Pagination software takes functions that previously had been done by layout people, production people, and designers and allows them to be done in one program. With pagination software, you can not only lay out pages; you can easily introduce boxes, screens, rule lines, graphics, and all sorts of type variations into them. You can set type from 4 to 500 points in size or have rule lines as thin as a hairline or as thick as a headline. You can fill boxes or other shapes with screens from 0–100 percent in 1 percent increments. You can also define almost any color as a spot color or process color mixture and apply it to any element on the page.

Besides providing more flexibility at a cheaper initial cost, the biggest advantage desktop publishing brings to contemporary designers is the ability to have complete control of the design process while ensuring consistency from page to page and issue to issue. Within all pagination software packages, you can eliminate needless duplication of work. For example, instead of remembering that body copy is 10/11 pt. Palatino, justified with a paragraph tab set at one pica, all you have to do is define the style "body copy," select the text, and apply the style. This allows you to concentrate on the overall page design without having to worry about the details.

Illustration Programs

Illustration packages such as Adobe *Illustrator* or Macromedia *FreeHand* allow you to concentrate on drawing, not editing stories or designing pages. Artists use such software to draw everything from the infographics made popular by *USA Today* in the mid-1980s to realistic drawings for the cover of a magazine. In the same way you would with conventional materials, you can change the thickness of lines, shade various areas and apply color to any portion of the graphic. But unlike using conventional materials, if you don't like what you've done, you can simply—and easily—change it until you do like it. Or you can save different versions in case you decide that your first, or third, effort was really the best one.

Image-Editing Programs

While some staffs will work with other types as well, the last major category of software used in most desktop publishing set-ups is image-editing software, led in the market by Adobe *Photoshop*. Anything you can do in the darkroom, you can do with *Photoshop*—and infinitely more.

National Geographic used image-editing programs to move the Great Pyramids closer together to fit better on the cover. *Texas Monthly* used image-editing programs to put the head of the governor on another person's body. But image-editing involves more mundane things as well. Every day, newspapers and magazines use such software to remove dust spots, eliminate annoying objects in the background, or just to bring out the color a little. In any case, the edited image can be saved in Tagged Image File Format (TIFF) or Encapsulated PostScript (EPS) format and placed on the page in the pagination software.

Image-editing software packages require a lot of memory, both RAM and disk space. One four-color snapshot can occupy several megabytes of disk space. In addition to knowing how to manage this software, professional image editors also learn all they can about color correction (how the four basic inks—cyan, magenta, yellow and black—mix together on the press to produce all the colors we see in a typical photo). They learn the difference between dpi (dots per inch; used to specify a printer's

Trends and Issues

Computers Are Important, But . . .

Professor Ann Auman of the University of Hawaii surveyed newspaper editors across the country about which skills they consider important in the people they hire. As these excerpts from her report show, the results tell something interesting about modern-day journalism.

"Newspaper editors often complain that journalism students can't spell or write decent headlines, can't locate Puerto Rico on a map, and don't bother to check even the phone book to make sure a store's name is spelled right. But at the same time, editors say they need people who are computer whizzes. What should an aspiring journalist focus on? . . .

"I asked top-level editors from around the country to tell me what skills entry-level copy editors should have . . . and about the weaknesses they see. About 160 . . . returned the survey . . . .

"Editors ranked grammar, spelling, and punctuation first, followed by accuracy and fact-checking. In third place was editing for wordiness, clarity, and sentence structure. General knowledge was fourth, [followed by] story structure, organization, and content . . . .

"Editors [also] chose traditional editing skills as the top areas in which entry level-copy editors were found to be the most deficient: grammar, spelling, and punctuation;

editing for wording, sentence structure, and clarity; headline writing; and accuracy and fact-checking . . . .

"The top-level editors often mentioned general knowledge as an important skill. 'Copy editors must have good backgrounds in general knowledge (history, science, the arts, prose, and poetry . . . the list is nearly endless) as well as the use of language,' one editor said. 'Copy editors must be able to extract the gem from the story, leaving the rubble behind.'

"Technical skills, such as mechanics of computer editing, pagination, and software for graphics, did not even fall among the top ten . . . . Many wrote that computer literacy was assumed and pagination a must . . . .

"One editor [felt that entry-level editors face big challenges] in the 1990s. 'They're still expected to know the traditional skills of copy editors (headlines, cutlines, editing, managing wires) and also have computer skills to do graphics and paginate pages. They also are often pressed into service as proofreaders and are expected to understand the ethics of [the] craft, stay informed of the world around them, and be underpaid and underappreciated.'

"Anne Glover, assistant managing editor/copy desk (in 1994) for the *St. Petersburg* (Fla.) *Times*, wrote that traditional editing skills are most important even though we must acknowledge the importance of technology . . . . She warned that we shouldn't put technological prowess ahead of journalism, even though 'it's easy to think that the people who know how to work the machines and move the papers will be the people who can get the jobs.' Glover stressed the importance of analytical thinking too—she needs journalists who can 'think about every single piece of information.'

"So where does this leave students? . . . One editor said it all: 'What we need are well-rounded, broadminded individuals who can argue about story play, present an attractive layout to sell their argument, and then write sparkling heads over tight stories. Is that asking too much? Oh yeah—and on deadline!'"

resolution), lpi (lines per inch; used to specify the screen frequency in a printed photo), and ppi (pixels per inch; used to specify the frequency of dots in an electronic image, usually on a screen). They learn how to handle the dozens upon dozens of effects the image-editing software allows them to perform. They also learn about the ethics of the field—when it's inappropriate to edit an image and when the public should be notified that an image has been edited.

Digital Photography

Bringing photos quickly and easily into publications is another advantage of desktop publishing. Once upon a time, a photograph was a separate piece of a page that had to be handled separately. No more, however.

Scanners

Before you can edit an image electronically, you have to get the print or negative converted into an electronic form, or digitized. While this can be done through a number of means, including having it put on a PhotoCD by a local photo store, the most popular means is by scanning the image on a flatbed scanner, a piece of hardware that looks, and acts, something like a small photocopier. Using scanning software, you can bring into your

With a scanner, a photo can be imported directly into a computer document. Until recently, photos were generally not incorporated until the final production stage.

computer black-and-white and color prints. What's more, you can bring them in at resolutions more than adequate for newspaper use.

Negative scanners are also popular. Photographers take the pictures and develop the film. Once developed, the film is scanned with no need for a print. Any manipulation, such as dodging, burning, and cropping, can be done on the computer.

To figure out at what resolution you need to scan an image (in pixels per inch), find out from your printer what line screen (in lines per inch) the image will be printed at and double it. For example, if your printer prints the photos at 150 lpi, which is typical for yearbook reproduction, you need to scan your images at 300 ppi if they're going to be used at actual size. In actuality, you can usually get by with a little less than that, but twice the lpi gives you a little flexibility. Note that the scanning resolution is for the image at actual size. If you're planning to enlarge the image, you need to scan it at a higher resolution. If you're planning to reduce the image, you can scan it at a lower resolution. In any case, work closely with your printer to find the optimum scanning resolution.

Digital Cameras

Another way to digitize images is to shoot them with a digital camera (discussed in Chapter Nineteen). Low-resolution digital cameras are inexpensive and adequate for newsletters and small newspaper photos. Only the more expensive, professional digital cameras, however, have nearly enough resolution to handle output for a magazine or yearbook with photos printed at greater than 85 lpi. The Associated Press and many large newspapers use digital cameras when they shoot assignments close to deadline to avoid having to develop film and then scan the negatives.

On-line Services

The Internet, together with the various services that access it, is one of the most rapidly growing areas of technology in the 1990s. Its development is an interesting story.

As a result of a need to communicate during wartime, the telegraph, radio, television, and satellite communications all in their turn became popular. But in the late 1960s, as government scientists began looking for a way to communicate following a nuclear holocaust, they found no existing system would work. Electromagnetic pulses would disrupt radio signals, eliminating any possibility of communication via the airwaves. Ground blasts and fires would disrupt land lines, inevitably leaving parts of the country separated from defense headquarters. So, over a period of time, scientists at research institutions all around the world began developing thousands of independent computer networks through which messages could flow freely. If one path was blocked, the message would simply take a different route. Thus was born the Internet, named as such in 1982, a network of independent computers that can communicate with any other computer in the world on the Net.

> **The New Entertainment Medium?**
>
> In 1994, for the first time, more computers were sold than television sets. And fifteen-year-olds now spend more time using computers than they do watching TV.
> — *Frontline: High Stakes in Cyberspace*,
> OCTOBER 31, 1995

Initially, this network was clumsy and required special coding and expertise to search out information. Even systems like Gopher and Lynx, which facilitate searching the Internet, didn't make it easy to glean information from the rapidly growing group of interconnected computers. The only people who really got any use out of the system were research scientists, who found that even with complex syntax, they could still get access to information that was inaccessible otherwise.

To pique the average person's interest in the Internet, it took the development of commercial systems such as CompuServe and America Online, whose easier-to-understand user interfaces bypassed any complex coding. People were willing to spend $10 a month to get access to hundreds of businesses that had created forums on CompuServe. America Online successfully formed the graphical user interface to on-line communications that is so popular today.

However, while none of the commercial services were watching, along came the development of the graphical World Wide Web browser. This system allowed users to access a graphical portion of the Internet and the millions of systems that were the backbone of the network. Programs like *Mosaic, Microsoft, Internet Explorer,* and *Netscape* made surfing the Net not only popular but downright easy. Now everyone had access to everyone else for a minimal cost—significantly less than $10 a month in most cases for unlimited use.

Journalists immediately began taking advantage of this access, using the Internet to transmit their stories to and from the field, making newsrooms almost obsolete except for copy editors and allowing writers to spend more time, if not all their time, in the field. It also made transmission of the news to a worldwide audience an instantaneous event. A writer, sitting at his or her computer in France, could transmit a story to millions of users all over the world in seconds. The World Wide Web became the ultimate media with unlimited distribution at a minimal cost.

Many individuals and businesses also take advantage of the World Wide Web, selling everything from cars to flowers to books, as do organizations such as the National Scholastic Press Association and Journalism Education Association.

The easy availability of information inappropriate for children has made many groups, including school districts, install software limiting use of the Internet. Court cases and local policies may further restrict the use of the Web as an information resource, but not without resistance from users.

Only time will tell how the World Wide Web, the Internet, and commercial services will be used. Already, newspapers (including some from high schools) are publishing up-to-the-minute supplements to their printed editions or making supplemental information available to subscribers. Already, television stations are promoting their stations with video clips accessible on the Net. Already, reporters, both scholastic and professional, have found a source for any kind of possible information at their fingertips. The quality of information, the ease of getting to it, and the perceived needs of users, together with constant technological gains, will all help to determine to what extent on-line services will grow and prosper.

Beyond 2000

While no one involved in the journalism industry makes light of the influence of technology on the print media, many still maintain that newspapers and yearbooks in their present form will continue to exist for some time. "I believe that people will still want to handle and read a product that looks like a newspaper rather than computer screens of information," Don DeMaio, an Associated Press graphics designer, said. Marty Petty, executive editor of *The Hartford Courant*, echoed DeMaio's sentiments. "We will still deliver a hard copy of the newspaper to our readers' homes and businesses in 25 years . . . ," she said. Editor after editor and designer after designer, with few exceptions, still believe that the print media will continue to exist, but that each will be supplemented in electronic form.

As you start utilizing the technological media to get information, look for those supplemental sources of news. Surf the Web. Pop a CD in your computer. Do a database search at your local library. Look at what's out there. It's amazing, and it's only the beginning.

Wrap-up

Technology is changing rapidly—so rapidly, in fact, that no textbook could hope to cover it completely. By the time the book is published, the technology will have changed. Nevertheless, computers have and will continue to revolutionize the publishing industry and have made almost instantaneous reporting of the news a reality.

The computer has certain basic parts, such as the CPU, hard and floppy drives, keyboard, mouse, and monitor. The brand is as important as the type of operating system and the amount of random access memory (RAM), for not all computers are compatible with each other. Computers have greatly facilitated information storage and retrieval, among other things.

There are various types of printers, such as dot matrix and ink jet. However, most desktop publications with school-size or larger circulations are printed on laser printers.

While learning about the hardware is important, you need know less about it than about the software. It's the software that allows you to create documents. Software allows you to change fonts easily. Word-processing software gives you the capability to write, edit, and fit copy right on screen. Pagination software, illustration software, and image-editing software allow you to design and lay out pages, create illustrations, and adjust photos.

Photographs can now easily be brought into pages. Scanners allow you to bring a print or a negative right into a computer program. Digital cameras transmit their images onto a disk to be printed directly from a computer.

In the last few years, millions of computers have been connected through the World Wide Web so individuals, organizations, and businesses can share all kinds of information for everything from newspapers to high school research papers.

On Assignment

Individual Activities

1. Write a brief definition or explanation of each of the following terms.

    CPU   desktop publishing
    image editing   laser printer
    network   RAM
    scanner   word processing

2. Pick one of the computers you have access to and find out the following. Write up your findings.
    a. how much RAM it has (for example, 32 megabytes)
    b. what type of central processing chip it uses (Power PC 604, Pentium P6, 68040)
    c. the size of its hard drive (e.g., 250MB)
    d. type and version of system software (Macintosh Operating System 7.5)
    e. number of colors or gray levels the monitor can display (for example, millions)

3. Make a list of all of the software applications on one of your computers—for example, *PageMaker, Word, QuarkXPress*. Then write a short summary of what you like and dislike about the program you're most familiar with.

4. If you have access to the World Wide Web, search and explore a publication from another high school. Write a brief summary on what you learned about this high school, its students, and activities.

5. If you have access to Internet e-mail, get an e-mail address of someone on a publications staff at another school by looking on the other school's home page or even in the staff box of their publication. Send e-mail to that person as an e-mail buddy.

6. Assume you are in charge of purchasing a new computer system for the journalism department. You intend to use this computer for digital image manipulation. Working with the staff of your computer science department, local newspapers and other publications, and a local computer store, write out the specifications for such a system, including details for what types of software, CPU, monitor, input devices, and output devices you would like to have. As you decide on your system, work within a budget set by your instructor.

7. Poll some of your staff photographers, and perhaps the staff photographers of community publications. How do they feel about digital image manipulation? Do they think it will enhance or detract from their photographs?

Team Activity

8. As a team, find at least five computer users in the community who use computers for different purposes—for example, to play games, to run a business. Each team member should interview one or more of these people about their computer use. Do they see what they do on the computer changing? Is there new equipment or software they want/need to buy? What will they want/need from a computer in five years? Take notes on the responses.

   After the interviews are complete, meet to discuss the results. Then prepare a class presentation on "The Computer: Now and in the Future." After all the presentations, discuss the similarities and differences in people's findings.

Before developing the on-line service *StarNet*, Bob Cauthorn made his living as a painter and sculptor. A self-described "free-learner," Cauthorn also enjoys writing.

He enrolled at the University of Arizona in journalism in the late '70s, with an eye toward writing criticism. While working toward his degree, Cauthorn wrote for the school newspaper and eventually became its editor. He was hired by the *Arizona Daily Star* in 1981.

Although hired to write, Cauthorn quickly got sidetracked. On the verge of the rise of the personal computer, Cauthorn jumped in with both feet. He began using the computer to develop database analyses, which helped to support stories.

There was no turning back. He became the *Star*'s computer guru and technology advocate. When the Internet began to take hold commercially, Cauthorn proposed the *Star* develop its own Internet service. He had two goals: to extend the *Star*'s ability to publish and to migrate newspapers back to being community-oriented companies.

"I wanted to use a high-tech means to get back to small-town news values," Cauthorn said.

Today, the small-town camaraderie created by the daily paper is virtually lost, yet Cauthorn said that most dinner conversations are about what people have read in the news.

"If we're responsible for sparking all the dinner conversation, why don't we try hosting one," he thought.

The Internet was a natural place to do this, and *StarNet* was launched May 5, 1995. As a result, the *Arizona Daily Star* became the second daily newspaper to go on-line. Gaining national attention with its approach to cyberspace, *StarNet* combines the daily newspaper, the *Star* library, and the Internet.

As a full Internet service provider, *StarNet* also runs community forums, newsgroups, and e-mail services. Additionally, subscribers have access to Associated Press wires from all fifty states, which are searchable in such areas as national and international news, politics, features, and sports.

Although not the first daily on-line, *StarNet* does have a claim to fame—it is the first profitable one. After less than eight months, *StarNet* turned a profit. Its subscriber base continues to grow by 1 to 2 percent daily and reached approximately 10,000 by August 1996.

For students interested in electronic journalism, Cauthorn says to start now. Many high school newspapers will go on-line, he said. Students should participate in such projects and learn as much as they can. Multimedia skills are very valuable.

"Computer literacy must extend beyond playing video games," he said.

Students must also be good writers and hold high ethical standards. There are lots of enticements to do bad things with computers now, Cauthorn said, especially when it seems so difficult to get caught. Students must rely on their individual strengths and strong moral character when making decisions, he advised.

Most importantly, keep asking "Why?" Too many people think that just by following a curriculum they will get the tools they need to succeed, he said. But Cauthorn disagrees.

"What distinguishes the people who really succeed is their unending curiosity," he said.

457

Stylebook
The Associated Press

Newswriting

A

abbreviations and acronyms A few universally recognized abbreviations are required in some circumstances. Some others are acceptable depending on the context. But in general, avoid alphabet soup. Do not use abbreviations or acronyms that the reader would not quickly recognize.

Some general principles:

BEFORE A NAME: Abbreviate the following titles when used before a full name outside direct quotations: *Dr., Gov., Lt. Gov., Mr., Mrs., Rep., the Rev., Sen.* and certain military designations. Spell out all except *Dr., Mr., Mrs.* and *Ms.* when they are used before a name in direct quotations.

AFTER A NAME: Abbreviate *junior* or *senior* after an individual's name. Abbreviate *company, corporation, incorporated,* and *limited* when used after the name of a corporate entity.

WITH DATES OR NUMERALS: Use the abbreviations *A.D., B.C., a.m., p.m., No.,* and abbreviate certain months when used with the day of the month.

Right: *In 450 B.C.; at 9:30 a.m.; in room No. 6; on Sept. 16.*

Wrong: *Early this a.m. he asked for the No. of your room.* The abbreviations are correct only with figures.

Right: *Early this morning he asked for the number of your room.*

IN NUMBERED ADDRESSES: Abbreviate *avenue, boulevard* and *street* in numbered addresses: *He lives on Pennsylvania Avenue. He lives at 1600 Pennsylvania Ave.*

STATES: The names of certain states and the *United States* are abbreviated with periods in some circumstances.

ACCEPTABLE BUT NOT REQUIRED: Some organizations and government agencies are widely recognized by their initials: *CIA, FBI, GOP.*

If the entry for such an organization notes that an abbreviation is acceptable in all references or on second reference, that does not mean that its use should be automatic. Let the context determine, for example whether to use *Federal Bureau of Investigation* or *FBI.*

AVOID AWKWARD CONSTRUCTIONS: Do not follow an organization's full name with an abbreviation or acronym in parentheses or set off by dashes. If an abbreviation or acronym would not be clear on second reference without this arrangement, do not use it.

Names not commonly before the public should not be reduced to acronyms solely to save a few words.

academic degrees If mention of degrees is necessary to establish someone's credentials, the preferred form is to avoid an abbreviation and use instead a phrase such as: *John Jones, who has a doctorate in psychology.*

Use an apostrophe in *bachelor's degree, a master's,* etc.

Use such abbreviations as *B.A., M.A., LL.D.* and *Ph.D.* only when the need to identify many individuals by degree on first reference would make the preferred form cumbersome. Use these abbreviations only after a full name—never after just a last name.

Do not precede a name with a courtesy title for an academic degree and follow it with the abbreviation for the degree in the same reference:

Wrong: *Dr. Pam Jones, Ph.D.*

Right: *Dr. Pam Jones, a chemist.*

When in doubt about the proper abbreviation, follow the first listing in Webster's New World Dictionary.

academic departments Use lowercase except for words that are proper nouns or adjectives: *the department of history, the history department, the department of English, the English department.*

academic titles Capitalize and spell out formal titles such as *professor, chancellor, chairman,* etc., when they precede a name. Lowercase elsewhere.

Lowercase modifiers such as *history* in *history Professor Oscar Handlin* or *department* in *department Chairman Jerome Wiesner.*

addresses Use the abbreviations *Ave., Blvd.,* and *St.* only with a numbered address: *1600 Pennsylvania Ave.* Spell them out and capitalize when part of a formal street name without a number: *Pennsylvania Avenue.* Lowercase and spell out when used alone or with more than one street name: *Massachusetts and Pennsylvania avenues.*

All similar words (*alley, drive, road, terrace,* etc.) always are spelled out. Capitalize them when part of a formal name without a number; lowercase when used alone or with two or more names.

Always use figures for an address number: *9 Morningside Circle.*

Spell out and capitalize *First* through *Ninth* when used as street names; use figures with two letters for *10th* and above: *7 Fifth Ave., 100 21st St.*

Abbreviate compass points used to indicate directional ends of a street or quadrants of a city in a numbered address: *222 E. 42nd St., 562 W. 43rd St., 600 K St. N.W.* Do not abbreviate if the number is omitted: *East 42nd Street, West 43rd Street, K Street Northwest.*

adviser Not *advisor.*

ages Always use figures. When the context does not require *year* or *years old,* the figure is presumed to be *years.*

Ages expressed as adjectives before a noun or as substitutes for a noun use hyphens.

Examples: *A 5-year-old boy,* but *the boy is 5 years old. The boy, 7, has a sister, 10. The woman, 26, has a daughter 2 months old. The law is 8 years old. The race is for 3-year-olds. The woman is in her 30s* (no apostrophe).

allege The word must be used with great care.

Some guidelines:

—Avoid any suggestion that the writer is making an allegation.

—Specify the source of an allegation. In a criminal case, it should be an arrest record, an indictment or the statement of a public official connected with the case.

—Use *alleged bribe* or similar phrase when necessary to make it clear that an unproved action is not being treated as fact. Be sure that the source of the charge is specified elsewhere in the story.

—Avoid redundant uses of *alleged.* It is proper to say: *The district attorney alleged that she took a bribe.* Or: *The district attorney accused her of taking a bribe.* But not: *The district attorney accused her of allegedly taking a bribe.*

—Do not use *alleged* to describe an event that is known to have occurred, when the dispute is over who participated in it. Do not say: *He attended the alleged meeting* when what you mean is: *He allegedly attended the meeting.*

—Do not use *alleged* as a routine qualifier. Instead, use a word such as *apparent, ostensible,* or *reputed.*

ante- The rules in prefixes apply, but in general, no hyphen. Some examples:

antebellum   antedate

anti- Hyphenate all except the following words, which have specific meanings of their own:

antibiotic	antibody	anticlimax
antidote	antifreeze	antigen
antihistamine	antiknock	antimatter
antimony	antiparticle	antipasto
antiperspirant	antiphon	antiphony
antiseptic	antiserum	antithesis
antitoxin	antitrust	antitussive

*And similar terms in physics such as *antiproton.*

This approach has been adopted in the interests of readability and easily remembered consistency.

Hyphenated words, many of them exceptions to Webster's New World, include:

anti-aircraft	anti-bias	anti-inflation
anti-intellectual	anti-labor	anti-Semitic
anti-social	anti-war	

Arabic numerals The numerical figures *1, 2, 3, 4, 5, 6, 7, 8, 9, 10.*

In general, use Arabic forms unless denoting the sequence of wars or establishing a personal sequence for people or animals.

army Capitalize when referring to U.S. forces: *the U.S. Army, the Army, Army regulations.* Do not use the abbreviation *USA.*

Use lowercase for the forces of other nations: *the French army.*

This approach has been adopted for consistency, because many foreign nations do not use *army* as the proper name.

arrest To avoid any suggestion that someone is being judged before a trial, do not use a phrase such as *arrested for killing.* Instead, use *arrested on a charge of killing.*

average, mean, median, norm *Average* refers to the result obtained by dividing a sum by the number of quantities added together: *The average of 7, 9, 17 is 33 divided by 3, or 11.*

Mean commonly designates a figure intermediate between two extremes: *The mean temperature of the day with a high of 56 and a low of 34 is 45.*

Median is the middle number of points in a series arranged in order of size: *The median grade in the group of 50, 55, 85, 88, 92 is 85. The average is 74.*

Norm implies a standard of average performance for a given group: *The child was below the norm for his age in reading comprehension.*

B

bi- The rules in **prefixes** apply, but in general, no hyphen. Some examples:

bifocal	bilateral	bilingual
bimonthly	bipartisan	

biannual, biennial *Biannual* means twice a year and is a synonym for the word semiannual.

Biennial means every two years.

Bible Capitalize, without quotation marks, when referring to the Scriptures in the Old Testament or the New Testament. Capitalize also related terms such as the *Gospels, Gospel of St. Mark, the Scriptures, the Holy Scriptures.*

Lowercase *biblical* in all uses.

Lowercase *bible* as a non-religious term: *My dictionary is my bible.*

Do not abbreviate individual books of the Bible.

The books of the Old Testament, in order, are: Genesis, Exodus, Leviticus, Numbers, Deuteronomy, Joshua, Judges, Ruth, 1 Samuel, 2 Samuel, 1 Kings, 2 Kings, 1 Chronicles, 2 Chronicles, Ezra, Nehemiah, Esther, Job, Psalms, Proverbs, Ecclesiastes, Song of Solomon, Isaiah, Jeremiah, Lamentations, Ezekiel, Daniel, Hosea, Joel, Amos, Obadiah, Jonah, Micah, Nahum, Habakkuk, Zephaniah, Haggai, Zechariah, Malachi.

The books of the New Testament, in order: Matthew, Mark, Luke, John, Acts, Romans, 1 Corinthians, 2 Corinthians, Galatians, Ephesians, Philippians, Colossians, 1 Thessalonians, 2 Thessalonians, 1 Timothy, 2 Timothy, Titus, Philemon, Hebrews, Epistles of James, 1 Peter, 2 Peter, 1 John, 2 John, 3 John, Jude, Revelation.

Citation listing the number of chapter and verse(s) use this form: *Matthew 3:16, Luke 21:1-13, 1 Peter 2:1.*

bimonthly Means every other month. *Semimonthly* means twice a month.

biweekly Means every other week. *Semiweekly* means twice a week.

C

call letters Use all caps. Use hyphens to separate the type of station from the basic call letters: *WBZ-AM, WBZ-FM, WBZ-TV.*

Until the summer of 1976, the format citizens band operators used was three letters and four figures: *KTE9136.* Licenses issued since then use four letters and four figures: *KTEM1234.*

Shortwave stations, which operate with greater power than citizens band stations and different frequencies, typically mix letters and figures: *K2LRX.*

Canada Montreal, Ottawa, Quebec and Toronto stand alone in datelines. For all other datelines, use the city name and the name of the province or territory spelled out.

The 10 provinces of Canada are Alberta, British Columbia, Manitoba, New Brunswick, Newfoundland (includes Labrador), Nova Scotia, Ontario, Prince Edward Island, Quebec and Saskatchewan.

The two territories are the Yukon and the Northwest Territories.

The provinces have substantial autonomy from the federal government.

The territories are administered by the federal government, although residents of the territories do elect their own legislators and representatives to Parliament.

capital The city where a seat of government is located. Do not capitalize.

When used in a financial sense, *capital* describes money, equipment or property used in a business by a person or corporation.

capitalization In general, avoid unnecessary capitals. Use a capital letter only if you can justify it by one of the principles listed her.

Some basic principles:

PROPER NOUNS: Capitalize nouns that constitute the unique identification for a specific person, place, or thing: *John, Mary, America, Boston, England.*

PROPER NAMES: Capitalize common nouns such as *party, river, street* and *west* when they are an integral part of the full name for a person, place or thing: *Democratic Party, Mississippi River, Fleet Street, West Virginia.*

Lowercase these common nouns when they stand alone in subsequent references: *the party, the river, the street.*

Lowercase the common noun elements of names in all plural uses: *the Democratic and Republican parties, Main and State streets, lakes Erie and Ontario.*

POPULAR NAMES: Some places and events lack officially designated proper names but have popular names that are the effective equivalent: *the Combat Zone* (a section of downtown Boston), *the Main Line* (a group of Philadelphia suburbs), *the South Side* (of Chicago), *the Badlands* (of North Dakota), *the Street* (the financial community in the Wall Street area of New York).

The principle applies also to shortened versions of the proper names of one-of-a-kind events: *the Series* (for the World Series), *the Derby* (for the Kentucky Derby). This practice should not, however, be interpreted as a license to ignore the general practice of lowercasing the common noun elements of a name when they stand alone.

DERIVATIVES: Capitalize words that are derived from a proper noun and still depend on it for their meaning: *American, Christian, Christianity, English, French, Marxism, Shakespearean.*

Lowercase words that are derived from a proper noun but no longer depend on it for their meaning: *french fries, herculean, manhattan cocktail, malapropism, pasteurize, quixotic, venetian blind.*

SENTENCES: Capitalize the first word in a statement that stands as a sentence.

In poetry, capital letters are used for the first words of some phrases that would not be capitalized in prose.

COMPOSITIONS: Capitalize the principal words in the names of books, movies, plays, poems, operas, songs, radio and television programs, works of art, etc. See **composition titles; magazine names;** and **newspaper names.**

TITLES: Capitalize formal titles when used immediately before a name. Lowercase formal titles when used alone or in constructions that set them off from a name by commas.

Use lowercase at all times for terms that are job descriptions rather than formal titles.

ABBREVIATIONS: Capital letters apply in come cases. See the **abbreviations and acronyms** entry.

capitol Capitalize *U.S. Capitol* and *the Capitol* when referring to the building in Washington: *The meeting was held on Capitol Hill in the west wing of the Capitol.*

Follow the same practice when referring to state capitols: *The Virginia Capitol is in Richmond. Thomas Jefferson designed the Capitol of Virginia.*

CD-ROM Acronym for a *compact disc* acting as a *read-only memory* device.

CD-ROM disc is redundant.

Celsius Use this term rather than *centigrade* for the temperature scale that is part of the metric system.

The Celsius scale is named for Anders Celsius, the Swedish astronomer who designed it. In it, zero represents the freezing point of water, and 100 degrees is the boiling point at sea level.

To convert to Fahrenheit, multiply a Celsius temperature by 9, divide by 5 and add 32 (25 x 9 equals 225, divided by 5 equals 45, plus 32 equals 77 degrees Fahrenheit).

When giving a Celsius temperature, use these forms: *40 degrees Celsius* or *40 C* (note the space and no period after the capital C) if degrees and Celsius are clear from the context.

cents Spell out the word *cents* and lowercase, using numerals for amounts less than a dollar: *5 cents, 12 cents.* Use the *$* sign and decimal system for larger amounts: *$1.01, $2.50.*

Numerals alone, with or without a decimal point as appropriate, may be used in tabular matter.

chairman, chairwoman Capitalize as a formal title before a name: *company Chairman Henry Ford, committee Chairwoman Margaret Chase Smith.*

Do not capitalize as a casual, temporary position: *meeting chairman Robert Jones.*

Do not use *chairperson* unless it is an organization's formal title for an office.

See **titles.**

chess In stories, the names and pieces are spelled out, lowercase: *king, queen, bishop, pawn, knight, rook, kingside, queenside, white, black.*

Use the algebraic notation in providing tabular summaries.

In algebraic notation, the "ranks" are the horizontal rows of squares. The ranks take numbers, 1 to 8, beginning on white's side of the board.

The "files" are the vertical rows of squares. They take letters, a through h, beginning on white's left.

Thus, each square vase is identified by its file letter and rank number.

In the starting position, white's queen knight stands on *b1,* the queen on *d1,* the king on *e1;* black's queen knight stands on *b8,* the queen on *d8,* the king on *e8,* and so on.

Other features of the system follow:

—DESIGNATION OF PIECES: The major pieces are shown by a capital letter: *K* for king, *Q* for queen, *R* for rook, *B* for bishop and *N* for knight. No symbol is used for the pawn.

—MOVES BY PIECES: Shown by the letter of the piece (except for the pawn) and the destination square. For instance, *Bb5* means the bishop moves to square b5.

—MOVES BY PAWNS: Pawn moves are designated only by the name of the destination square. Thus, *e4* means the pawn on the e file moves to e4.

—CASTLING: It is written as *0-0* for the kingside and *0-0-0* for the queenside. *Kingside* is the side of the board (right half from white's point of view, let half from black's), on which each player's king starts. The other half is *queenside.*

—CAPTURES BY PIECES: A capture is recorded by using an x after the letter for the capturing piece. For instance, if white's bishop captures the black pawn at the f6 square, it is written *Bxf6*.

—CAPTURES BY PAWNS: When a pawn captures a piece, the players name the file the pawn was on and the square where it made the capture. If white's pawn on a g file captured black's pawn on f6 square, the move would be *gxf6*. If black's pawn on an f file captured white's it would be *fxg5*.

—CHECK: Use plus sign.

—AMBIGUITY: If more than one piece of the same type can move to a square, the rank number or file letter of the origination square is added. Thus, if a rook on d1 were to move to d4, but another rook also could move there, instead of *Rd4* the move would be given as *R1d4*. If there are black knights on c6 and e6, and the one on e6 moves to d4, the move is given as *Ned4*.

The form, taken from a 1993 championship match:

	Short (White)	**Karpov (Black)**
1.	e4	c5
2.	Nf3	d6
3.	d4	cxd4
4.	Nxd4	Nf6
5.	Nc3	a6
6.	Bc4	e6
7.	Bb3	Nbd7

Chinese names Some Chinese have Westernized their names, putting their given names or the initials for them first: *P. Y. Chen, Jack Wang*. In general, follow an individual's preferred spelling.

Normally Chinese women do not take their husbands' surnames. Use the courtesy titles *Mrs., Miss,* or *Ms.* only when specifically requested. Never use *Madame* or *Mme.*

chip An integrated computer circuit.

Christmas, Christmas Day Dec. 25. The federal legal holiday is observed on Friday if Dec. 25 falls on a Saturday, on Monday if it falls on a Sunday.

Never abbreviate *Christmas* to *Xmas* or any other form.

church Capitalize as part of the formal name of a building, a congregation or a denomination; lowercase in other uses: *St. Mary's Church, the Roman Catholic Church, the Catholic and Episcopal churches, a Roman Catholic church, a church.*

Lowercase in phrases where the church is used in an institutional sense: *She believes in the separation of church and state. The pope said the church opposes abortion.*

city council Capitalize when part of a proper name: *the Boston City Council.*

Retain capitalization if the reference is to a specific council but the context does not require the city name:

boston (ap)—The City Council . . .

Lowercase in other uses: *the council, the Boston and New York city councils, a city council.*

Use the proper name if the body is not known as a city council: *the Miami City Commission, the City Commission, the commission; the Louisville Board of Aldermen, the Board of Aldermen, the board.*

Use *city council* in a generic sense for plural references: *The Boston, Louisville and Miami city councils.*

co- Retain the hyphen when forming nouns, adjectives and verbs that indicate occupation or status:

co-author	co-chairman
co-defendant	co-host
co-owner	co-partner
co-pilot	co-respondent (in a divorce suit)
co-signer	co-star
co-worker	

(Several are exceptions to Webster's New World Dictionary in the interests of consistency.)

Use no hyphen in other combinations:

coed	coeducation	coequal
coexist	coexistence	cooperate
cooperative	coordinate	coordination

Cooperate, coordinate and related words are exceptions to the rule that a hyphen is used if a prefix ends in a vowel and the word that follows begins with the same vowel.

collective nouns Nouns that denote a unit take singular verbs and pronouns: *class, committee, crowd, family, group, herd, jury, orchestra, team.*

Some usage examples: *The committee is meeting to set its agenda. The jury reached its verdict. A herd of cattle was sold.*

colloquialisms The word describes the informal use of a language. It is not local or regional in nature, as dialect is.

Webster's New World Dictionary identifies many words as colloquial with the label *Colloq.* The label itself, the dictionary says, "does not indicate substandard or illiterate usage."

Many colloquial words and phrases characteristic of informal writing and conversation are acceptable in some contexts but out of place in others. Examples include *bum, giveaway* and *phone.*

Other colloquial words normally should be avoided because they are substandard. Webster's New World notes, for example, that *ain't* is colloquial and not automatically illiterate or substandard usage. But it also notes that *ain't* is "a dialectical or substandard contraction." Thus it should not be used in news stories unless needed to illustrate substandard speech in writing.

See **dialect**.

congress Capitalize *U.S. Congress* and *Congress* when referring to the U.S. Senate and House of Representatives. Although *Congress* sometimes is used as a substitute for the House, it properly is reserved for reference to both the Senate and House.

Capitalize *Congress* also if referring to a foreign body that uses the term, or its equivalent in a foreign language, as part of its formal name: *the Argentine Congress, the Congress.*

Lowercase when used as a synonym for *convention* or in second reference to an organization that uses the word as part of its formal name: *the Congress of Racial Equality, the congress.*

copyright (n., v. and adj.) *The disclosure was made in a copyright story.*

Use *copyrighted* only as the past tense of the verb: *He copyrighted the article.*

council, councilor, councilman, councilwoman A deliberative body and those who are members of it.

counsel, counseled, counseling, counselor, counselor at law To *counsel* is to advise. A *counselor* is one who advises.

A *counselor at law* (no hyphens for consistency with *attorney at law*) is a lawyer. See **lawyer**.

county Capitalize when an integral part of a proper name: *Dade County, Nassau County, Suffolk County.*

Capitalize the full names of county governmental units: *the Dade County Commission, the Orange County Department of Social Services, the Suffolk County Legislature.*

Retain capitalization for the name of a county body if the proper noun is not needed in the context; lowercase the word *county* if it is used to distinguish an agency from state or federal counterparts: *the Board of Supervisors, the county Board of Supervisors; the Department of Social Services, the county Department of Social Services.* Lowercase *the board, the department,* etc. whenever they stand alone.

Capitalize *county* if it is an integral part of a specific body's name even without the proper noun: *the County Commission, the County Legislature.* Lowercase *the commission, the legislature,* etc. when not preceded by the word *county.*

Capitalize as part of a formal title before a name: *County Manager John Smith.* Lowercase when it is not part of the formal title: *county Health Commissioner Frank Jones.*

Avoid *county of* phrases where possible, but when necessary, always lowercase: *the county of Westchester.*

Lowercase plural combinations: *Westchester and Rockland counties.*

Apply the same rules to similar terms such as *parish.*

See **governmental bodies**.

courtesy titles In general, do not use the courtesy titles *Miss, Mr., Mrs.* or *Ms.* on first and last names of the person: *Betty Ford, Jimmy Carter.*

Do not use *Mr.* in any reference unless it is combined with *Mrs.: Mr. and Mrs. John Smith, Mr. and Mrs. Smith.*

On sports wires, do not use courtesy titles in any reference unless needed to distinguish among people of the same last name.

On news wires, use courtesy titles for women on second reference, following the woman's preference. Use *Ms.* if a preference cannot be determined. If the woman says she does not want a courtesy title, refer to her on second reference by last name only. Some guidelines:

MARRIED WOMEN: The preferred form on first reference is to identify a woman by her own first name and her husband's last name: *Susan Smith.* Use *Mrs.* on the first reference only if a woman requests that her husband's first name be used or her own first name cannot be determined: *Mrs. John Smith.*

On second reference, use *Mrs.* unless a woman initially identified by her own first name prefers *Ms.: Carla Hills, Mrs. Hills, Ms. Hills;* or no title: *Carla Hills, Hills.*

If a married woman is known by her maiden name, precede it by *Miss* on second reference unless she prefers *Ms.: Jane Fonda, Miss Fonda, Ms. Fonda;* or no title, *Jane Fonda, Fonda.*

UNMARRIED WOMEN: For women who have never been married, use *Miss, Ms.* or no title on second reference according to the woman's preference.

For divorced women and widows, the normal practice is to use *Mrs.* or no title, if she prefers, on second reference. But, if a woman returns to the use of her maiden name, use *Miss, Ms.* or no title if she prefers it.

MARITAL STATUS: If a woman prefers *Ms.* or no title, do not include her marital status in a story unless it is clearly pertinent.

court names Capitalize the full proper names of courts at all levels.

Retain capitalization if *U.S.* or a state name is dropped: *the U.S. Supreme Court, the Supreme Court, the state Superior Court, the Superior Court, Superior Court.*

For courts identified by a numeral: *2nd District Court, 8th U.S. Circuit Court of Appeals.*

For additional details on federal courts, see **judicial branch** and separate listings under **U.S.** and the court name.

See **judge** for guidelines on titles before the names of judges.

D

dangling modifiers Avoid modifiers that do not refer clearly and logically to some word in the sentence.

Dangling: *Taking our seats, the game started.* (*Taking* does not refer to the subject, *game,* nor to any other word in the sentence.)

Correct: *Taking our seats, we watched the opening of the game.* (*Taking* refers to *we,* the subject of the sentence.)

dates Always use Arabic figures, without *st, nd, rd* or *th.* See **months** for examples and **punctuation** guidelines.

days of the week Capitalize them. Do not abbreviate, except when needed in a tabular format: *Sun, Mon, Tue, Wed, Thu, Fri, Sat* (three letters, without periods, to facilitate tabular composition).

decimal units Use a period and numerals to indicate decimal amounts. Decimalization should not exceed two places in textual material unless there are special circumstances.

See **fractions**.

dialect The form of language peculiar to a region or a group, usually in matters of pronunciation or syntax. Dialect should be avoided, even in quoted matter, unless it is clearly pertinent to a story.

There are some words and phrases in everyone's vocabulary that are typical of a particular region or group. Quoting dialect, unless used carefully, implies substandard or illiterate usage.

When there is a compelling reason to use dialect, words or phrases are spelled phonetically, and apostrophes show missing letters and sounds: *"Din't ya yoosta live at Toidy-Toid Street and Sekun' Amya? Across from da moom pitchers?"*

dictionaries For spelling, style and usage questions not covered in this stylebook, consult Webster's New World College Dictionary, Third Edition, published by Macmillan, a division of Simon & Schuster, New York.

Use the first spelling listed in Webster's New World unless a specific exception is listed in this book.

If Webster's New World provides different spellings in separate entries (*tee shirt* and *T-shirt*, for example), use the spelling that is followed by a full definition (*T-shirt*).

If Webster's New World provides definitions under two different spellings for the same sense of a word, either use is acceptable. For example, *although* or *though*.

If there is no listing in either this book or Webster's New World, the backup dictionary, with more listings, is Webster's Third New International Dictionary, published by G. & C. Merriam Co. of Springfield, Mass.

Webster's New World is also the first reference for geographic names not covered in this stylebook. See **geographic names**.

directions and regions In general, lowercase *north, south, northeast, northern*, etc., when they indicate compass direction; capitalize these words when they designate regions.

Some examples:

COMPASS DIRECTIONS: *He drove west. The cold front is moving east.*

REGIONS: *A storm system that developed in the Midwest is spreading eastward. It will bring showers to the East Coast by morning and to the entire Northeast by late in the day. High temperatures will prevail throughout the Western states.*

The North was victorious. The South will rise again. Settlers from the East went West in search of new lives. The customs of the East are different from those of the West. The Northeast depends on the Midwest for its food supply.

She has a Southern accent. He is a Northerner. Nations of the Orient are opening doors to Western businessmen. The candidate developed a Southern strategy. She is a Northern liberal.

The storm developed in the South Pacific. European leaders met to talk about supplies of oil from Southeast Asia.

WITH NAMES OF NATIONS: Lowercase unless they are part of a proper name or are used to designate a politically divided nation: *northern France, eastern Canada, the western United States.*

But: *Northern Ireland, South Korea.*

WITH STATES AND CITIES: The preferred form is to lowercase compass points only when they describe a section of a state or city: *western Texas, southern Atlanta.*

But capitalize compass points:

—When part of a proper name: *North Dakota, West Virginia.*

—When used in denoting widely known sections: *Southern California, the South Side of Chicago, the Lower East Side of New York.* If in doubt, use lowercase.

IN FORMING PROPER NAMES: When combining with another common noun to form the name for a region or location: *the North Woods, the South Pole, the Far East, the Middle East, the West Coast* (the entire region, not the coastline itself), *the Eastern Shore, the Western Hemisphere.*

dollars Always lowercase. Use figures and the $ sign in all except casual references or amounts without a figure: *The book cost $4. Dad, please give me a dollar. Dollars are flowing overseas.*

E

earth Generally lowercase; capitalize when used as the proper name of the planet. *She is down to earth. How does the pattern apply to Mars, Jupiter, Earth, the sun and the moon? The astronauts returned to Earth. He hopes to move heaven and earth.*

e-mail Short form of *electronic mail.*

equal An adjective without comparative forms.

When people speak of a *more equal* distribution of wealth, what is meant is *more equitable.*

equal, equaled, equaling

ex- Use no hyphen for words that use *ex-* in the sense of *out of:*

excommunicate   expropriate

Hyphenate when using *ex-* in the sense of *former:*

ex-convict   ex-president

Do not capitalize *ex-* when attached to a formal title before a name: *ex-President Nixon.* The prefix modifies the entire term: *ex-New York Gov. Nelson Rockefeller;* not *New York ex-Gov.*

Usually *former* is better.

F

Fahrenheit The temperature scale commonly used in the United States.

The scale is named for Gabriel Daniel Fahrenheit, the German physicist who designed it. In it, the freezing point of water is 32 degrees and the boiling point is 212 degrees.

To convert to Celsius, subtract 32 from the Fahrenheit figure, multiply by 5 and divide by 9 (77 – 32 = 45, times 5 – 225, divided by 9 = 25 degrees Celsius).

In cases that require mention of the scale, use these forms: *86 degrees Fahrenheit* or *86 F* (note the space and no period after the *f*) if degrees and Fahrenheit are clear from the context.

See **Celsius** and **Kelvin**.

For guidelines on when Celsius temperatures should be used, see **metric system** entry.

TEMPERATURE CONVERSIONS
Following is a temperature conversion table. Celsius temperatures have been rounded to the nearest whole number.

f	c	F	C	F	C
−26	−32	19	−7	64	18
−24	−31	21	−6	66	19
−22	−30	23	−5	68	20
−20	−29	25	−4	70	21
−18	−28	27	−3	72	22
−17	−27	28	−2	73	23
−15	−26	30	−1	75	24
−13	−25	32	0	77	25
−11	−24	34	1	79	26
−9	−23	36	2	81	27
−8	−22	37	3	82	28
−6	−21	39	4	84	29
−4	−20	41	5	86	30
−2	−19	43	6	88	31
0	−18	45	7	90	32
1	−17	46	8	91	33
3	−16	48	9	93	34
5	−15	50	10	95	35
7	−14	52	11	97	36
9	−13	54	12	99	37
10	−12	55	13	100	38
12	−11	57	14	102	39
14	−10	59	15	104	40
16	−9	61	16	106	41
18	8	63	17	108	42

felony, misdemeanor A *felony* is a serious crime. A *misdemeanor* is a minor offense against the law.

A fuller definition of what constitutes a felony or misdemeanor depends on the governmental jurisdiction involved.

At the federal level a *misdemeanor* is a crime that carries a potential penalty of no more than a year in jail. A *felony* is a crime that carries a potential penalty of more than a year in prison. Often, however, a statute gives a judge options such as imposing a fine or probation in addition to or instead of a jail or prison sentence.

A *felon* is a person who has been convicted of a *felony*, regardless of whether the individual actually spends time in confinement or is given probation or a fine instead.

Fourth Estate Capitalize when used as a collective name for journalism and journalists.

The description is attributed to Edmund Burke, who is reported to have called the reporters' gallery in Parliament a "Fourth Estate."

The three estates of early English society were the Lords Spiritual (the clergy), the Lords Temporal (the nobility) and the Commons (the bourgeoisie).

fractions Spell out amounts less than 1 in stories, using hyphens between the words: *two-thirds*, *four-fifths*, *seven-sixteenths*, etc.

Use figures for precise amounts larger than 1, converting to decimals whenever practical.

Fractions are preferred, however, in stories about stocks.

When using fractional characters, remember that most newspaper type fonts can set only 1/8, 1/4, 3/8, 1/2, 5/8, 3/4 and 7/8 as one unit; use *11/2*, *25/8*, etc. with no space between the figure and the fraction. Other fractions require a hyphen and individual figures, with a space between the whole number and the fraction: *1 3-16, 2 1-3, 5 9-10.*

In tabular material, use figures exclusively, converting to decimals if the amounts involve extensive use of fractions that cannot be expressed as a single character.

See **percentages**.

G

geographic names The basic guidelines:

DOMESTIC: The authority for spelling place names in the 50 states and territories is the U.S. Postal Service Directory of Post Offices, with two exceptions:

—Do not use the postal abbreviations for state names. For acceptable abbreviations, see entries in this book under each state's name. See **state names** for rules based on when the abbreviations may be used.

—Abbreviate *Saint* as *St.* (But abbreviate *Sault Sainte Marie* as *Sault Ste. Marie.*)

FOREIGN: The first source for the spelling of all foreign place names is Webster's New World Dictionary as follows:

—Use the first-listed spelling if an entry gives more than one.

—If the dictionary provides different spellings in separate entries, use the spelling that is followed by a full description of the location. There are exceptions:

1. Use *Cameroon,* not *Cameroons* or *Cameroun.*
2. Use *Maldives,* not *Maldive Islands.*
3. Use *Sri Lanka,* not *Ceylon.*

The latter exceptions have been made to conform with the practices of the United Nations and the U.S. Board of Geographic Names. (See the NEW NAMES paragraph below.)

If the dictionary does not have an entry, use the first-listed spelling in the National Geographic Atlas of the World.

NEW NAMES: Follow the styles adopted by the United Nations and the U.S. Board of Geographic Names on new cities, new independent nations and nations that change their names.

CAPITALIZATION: Capitalize common nouns when they form an integral part of a proper name, but lowercase them when they stand alone: *Pennsylvania Avenue, the avenue; the Philippine Islands, the islands; the Mississippi River, the river.*

Lowercase common nouns that are not a part of a specific name: *the Pacific islands, the Swiss mountains, Zhejiang province.*

For additional guidelines, see **addresses; capitalization; the directions** and **regions** entry.

government Always lowercase, never abbreviate: *the federal government, the state government, the U.S. government.*

governmental bodies Follow these guidelines:

FULL NAME: Capitalize the full proper names of governmental agencies, departments, and offices: *The U.S. Department of State, the Georgia Department of Human Resources, the Boston City Council, the Chicago Fire Department.*

WITHOUT JURISDICTION: Retain capitalization in referring to a specific body if the dateline or context makes the name of the nation, state, county, city, etc. unnecessary: *The Department of State* (in a story from Washington), *the Department of Human Resources* or *the state Department of Human Resources* (in a story from Georgia), *the City Council* (in a story from Boston), *the Fire Department* or *the city Fire Department* (in a story from Chicago).

Lowercase further condensations of the name: *the department, the council, etc.*

FLIP-FLOPPED NAMES: Retain capital names for the name of a governmental body if its formal name is flopped to delete the word *of: the State Department, the Human Resources Department.*

GENERIC EQUIVALENTS: If a generic term has become the equivalent of a proper name in popular use, treat it as a proper name: *Walpole State Prison,* for example, even though the proper name is the *Massachusetts Correctional Institute-Walpole.*

PLURALS, NON-SPECIFIED REFERENCES: All words that are capitalized when part of a proper name should be lowercased when they are used in the plural or do not refer to a specific, existing body. Some examples:

All states except Nebraska have a state senate. The town does not have a fire department. The bill requires city councils to provide matching funds. The president will address the lower houses of the New York and New Jersey legislatures.

FOREIGN BODIES: The same principles apply.

H

habeas corpus A writ ordering a person in custody to be brought before a court. It places the burden of proof on those detaining the person to justify the detention.

When *habeas corpus* is used in a story, define it.

Hanukkah The Jewish Festival of Lights, an eight-day commemoration of re-dedication of the Temple by the Maccabees after their victory over the Syrians.

Usually occurs in December but sometimes falls in late November.

heavenly bodies Capitalize the proper names of planets, stars, constellations, etc.: *Mars, Arcturus, the Big Dipper, Aries.*

For comets, capitalize only the proper noun element of the name: *Halley's comet.*

Lowercase sun and moon, but capitalize them if their Greek or Latin names are used: *Helios, Luna.*

Lowercase nouns and adjectives derived from the proper names of planets and other heavenly bodies: *jovian, lunar, martian, solar, venusian.*

his, her Do not presume maleness in constructing a sentence, but use the pronoun *his* when an indefinite antecedent may be male or female: *A reporter attempts to protect his sources.* (Not *his or her* sources, but note the use of the word *reporter* rather than *newsman.*)

Frequently, however, the best choice is a slight revision of the sentence: *Reporters attempt to protect their sources.*

historical periods and events Capitalize the names of widely recognized epochs in anthropology, archaeology, geology and history: *the Bronze Age, the Dark Ages, the Middle Ages, the Pliocene Epoch.*

Capitalize also widely recognized popular names for the periods and events: *the Atomic Age, the Boston Tea Party, the Civil War, the Exodus* (of the Israelites from Egypt), *the Great Depression, Prohibition.*

Lowercase *century: the 18th century.*

Capitalize only the proper nouns or adjectives in general descriptions of a period: *ancient Greece, classical Rome, the Victorian era, the fall of Rome.*

For additional guidance, follow the capitalization in Webster's New World Dictionary, using lowercase if the dictionary lists it as an acceptable form for the sense in which the word is used.

I

inter- The rules in **prefixes** apply, but in general, no hyphen. Some examples:

inter-American   interracial   interstate

intra- The rules in **prefixes** apply, but, in general, no hyphen. Some examples:

intramural   intrastate

IQ Acceptable in all references for **intelligence quotient**.

J

judge Capitalize before a name when it is the formal title for an individual who presides in a court of law. Do not continue to use the title in second reference.

Do not use *court* as part of the title unless confusion would result without it:

—No *court* in the title: *U.S. District Judge John Sirica, District Judge John Sirica, federal Judge John Sirica, Judge John Sirica, U.S. Circuit Judge Homer Thornberry, appellate Judge John Blair.*

—*Court* needed in the title: *Juvenile Court Judge John Jones, Criminal Court Judge John Jones, superior Court Judge Robert Harrison, state Supreme Court Judge William Cushing.*

When the formal title chief judge is relevant, put the court name after the judge's name: *Chief Judge John Sirica of the U.S. District Court in Washington, D.C.; Chief Judge Clement F. Haynsworth Jr. of the 4th U.S. Circuit Court of Appeals.*

Do not pile up long court names before the name of a judge. Make it *Judge John Smith of Allegheny County Common Pleas Court.* Not: *Allegheny County Common Pleas Court Judge John Smith.*

Lowercase *judge* as an occupational designation in phrases such as *beauty contest judge Bert Parks.*

L

lay, lie The action word is *lay.* It takes a direct object. *Laid* is the form for its past tense and its past participle. Its present participle is *laying.*

Lie indicates a state of reclining along a horizontal plane. It does not take a direct object. Its past tense is *lay.* Its past participle is *lain.* Its present participle is *lying.*

When *lie* means to make an untrue statement, the verb forms are *lie, lied, lying.*

Some examples:

PRESENT OR FUTURE TENSES:

Right: *I will lay the book on the table. The prosecutor tried to lay the blame on him.*

Wrong: *He lays on the beach all day. I will lay down.*

Right: *He lies on the beach all day. I will lie down.*

M

magazine names Capitalize the name but do not place it in quotes. Lowercase *magazine* unless it is part of the publication's formal title: *Harper's Magazine, Newsweek Magazine, Time Magazine.*

Check the masthead if in doubt.

majority, plurality *Majority* means more than half of an amount.

Plurality means more than the next highest number.

COMPUTING MAJORITY: To describe how large a majority is, take the figure that is more than half and subtract everything else from it: If 100,000 votes were cast in an election and one candidate received 60,000 while opponents received 40,000, the winner would have a *majority* of 20,000 votes.

COMPUTING PLURALITY: To describe how large a plurality is, take the highest number and subtract from it the next highest number: If, in the election example above, the second-place finisher had 25,000 votes, the winner's *plurality* would be 35,000 votes.

Suppose, however, that no candidate in this example had a majority. If the first-place finisher had 40,000 votes and the second-place finisher had 30,000, for example, the leader's *plurality* would be 10,000 votes.

USAGE: When *majority* and *plurality* are used alone, they take singular verbs and pronouns: *The majority has made its decision.*

If a plural word follows an *of* construction, the decision on whether to use a singular or plural verb depends on the sense of the sentence: *A majority of two votes is not adequate to control the committee. The majority of the houses on the block were destroyed.*

man, mankind Either may be used when both men and women are involved and no other term is convenient. In these cases, do not use duplicate phrases such as *a man* or *a woman* or *mankind* and *womankind.*

Frequently the best choice is a substitute such as *humanity, a person* or *an individual.*

months Capitalize the names of months in all uses. When a month is used with a specific date, abbreviate only *Jan., Feb., Aug., Sept., Oct., Nov.* and *Dec.* Spell out when using alone, or with a year alone.

When a phrase lists only a month and a year, do not separate the year with commas. When a phrase refers to a month, day and year, set off the year with commas.

EXAMPLES: *January 1972 was a cold month. Jan. 2 was the coldest day of the month. His birthday is May 8. Feb. 14, 1987, was the target date.*

In tabular material, use these three-letter forms without a period: *Jan, Feb, Mar, Apr, May, Jun, Jul, Aug, Sep, Oct, Nov, Dec.*

movie ratings The ratings used by the Motion Picture Association of America are:

G — General audiences. All ages admitted.

PG — Parental guidance suggested. Some material may not be suitable for children.

PG-13 — Special *parental guidance* strongly suggested for children under 13. Some material may be inappropriate for young children.

R — Restricted. Under 17 requires accompanying parent or adult guardian.

NC-17 — No one under 17 admitted.

When the ratings are used in news stories or reviews, use these forms as appropriate: *the movie has an R rating, an R-rated movie, the movie is R-rated.*

Mr., Mrs. The plural of *Mr.* is *Messrs.;* the plural of *Mrs.* is *Mmes.*

These abbreviated spellings apply in all uses, including direct quotations.

See **courtesy titles** for guidelines on when to use *Mr.* and *Mrs.*

Ms. This is the spelling and punctuation for all uses of the courtesy title, including direct quotations.

There is no plural. If several women who prefer *Ms.* must be listed in a series, repeat *Ms.* before each name.

N

names In general, people are entitled to be known however they want to be known, as long as their identities are clear.

When an individual elects to change the name by which he has been known, such as Cassius Clay's transition to Muhammad Ali, provide both names in stories until the new name is known by the public. After that, use only the new name unless there is a specific reason for including the earlier identification.

newspaper names Capitalize *the* in a newspaper's name if that is the way the publication prefers to be known.

Lowercase *the* before newspaper names if a story mentions several papers, some of which use *the* as part of the name and some of which do not.

When the location is needed but is not part of the official name, use parentheses: *The Huntsville (Ala.) Times.*

Consult the International Year Book published by *Editor & Publisher* to determine whether a two-name combination is hyphenated.

nicknames A nickname should be used in place of a person's given name in news stories only when it is the way the individual prefers to be known: *Jimmy Carter.*

When a nickname is inserted into the identification of an individual, use quotation marks: *Sen. Henry M. "Scoop" Jackson.* Also: *Jackson is known as "Scoop."*

In sports stories and sports columns, commonly used nicknames may be substituted for a first name without the use of quotation marks: *Woody Hayes, Bear Bryant, Catfish Hunter, Bubba Smith,* etc. But in sports stories where the given name is used, and in all news stories: *Paul "Bear" Bryant.*

Capitalize without quotation marks such terms as *Sunshine State, the Old Dominion, Motown, the Magic City, Old Hickory, Old Glory, Galloping Ghost.*

non- The rules of **prefixes** apply, but in general no hyphen when forming a compound that does not have special meaning and can be understood if *not* is used before the base word. Use a hyphen, however, before proper nouns or in awkward combinations, such as *non-nuclear.* Follow Webster's New World Dictionary.

numerals A numeral is a figure, letter, word or group of words expressing a number.

Roman numerals use the letters *I, V, X, L, C, D* and *M.* Use Roman numerals for wars and to show personal sequence for animals and people: *World War II, Native Dancer II, King George VI, Pope John XXIII.*

Arabic numerals use the figures *1, 2, 3, 4, 5, 6, 7, 8, 9* and *0.* Use Arabic forms unless Roman numerals are specifically required. See **Arabic numerals.**

The figures *1, 2, 10, 101,* etc. and the corresponding words — *one, two, ten , one hundred one,* etc. —are called cardinal numbers The term ordinal number applies to *1st, 2nd, 10th, 101st, first, second, tenth, one hundred first,* etc.

Follow these guidelines in using numerals:

LARGE NUMBERS: When large numbers must be spelled out, use a hyphen to connect a word ending in y to another word; do not use commas between other separate words that are part of one number: *twenty; thirty; twenty-one; thirty-one; one hundred forty-three; one thousand one hundred fifty-five; one million two hundred seventy-six thousand five hundred eighty-seven.*

SENTENCE START: Spell out a numeral at the beginning of a sentence. If necessary, recast the sentence. There is one exception—a numeral that identifies a calendar year.

Wrong: *993 freshmen entered the college last year.*

Right: *Last year 993 freshmen entered the college.*

Right: *1976 was a very good year.*

CASUAL USES: Spell out casual expressions:

A thousand times no! Thanks a million. He walked a quarter of a mile.

PROPER NAMES: Use words or numerals according to an organization's practice: *3M, Twentieth Century Fund, Big Ten.*

FRACTIONS: See the **fractions** entry.

DECIMALS: See the **decimal units** entry.

FIGURES OR WORDS?

For ordinals:

—Spell out *first* through *ninth* when they indicate sequence in time or location: *first base, the First Amendment, he was first in line.* Starting with *10th* use figures.

—Use *1st, 2nd, 3rd, 4th,* etc. when the sequence has been assigned in forming names. The principal examples are geographic, military and political designations such as *1st Ward, 7th Fleet* and *1st Sgt.* See examples in the separate entries listed below.

For cardinal numbers, consult the following separate entries:

act numbers	addresses
ages	aircraft names
amendments to the Constitution	betting odds
century	channel
chapters	congressional districts
course numbers	court decisions
court names	dates
decades	decimal units
district	earthquakes
election returns	fleet
formula	fractions
handicaps	heights
highway designations	latitude and longitude
mile	millions, billions

model numbers
No.
parallels
political divisions
ratios
room numbers
scene numbers
spacecraft designations
telephone numbers
years

monetary units
page numbers
percentages
proportions
recipes
route numbers
sizes
speeds
temperatures

SOME PUNCTUATION AND USAGE EXAMPLES:

—*Act 1, Scene 2*
—*a 5-year-old girl*
—*DC-10* but *747B*
—*a 5-4 court decision*
—*2nd District Court*
—*the 1980s, the '80s*
—*the House voted 230-205.* (Fewer than 1,000 votes.)
—*Jimmy Carter defeated Gerald Ford 40,827,292 to 39,146,157.* (More than 1,000 votes.)
—*Carter defeated Ford 10 votes to 2 votes in Little Junction.* (To avoid confusion with ratio.)
—*05 cents, $1.05, $650,000, $2.45 million*
—*No. 3 choice,* but *Public School 3*
—*0.6 percent, 1 percent, 6.5 percent*
—*a pay increase 12 percent to 15 percent.* Or: *a pay increase of between 12 percent and 15 percent*
Also: *from $12 million to $14 million*
—*a ratio of 2-to-1, a 2-1 ratio*
—*a 4–3 score*
—*(212) 262-4000*
—*minus 10, zero, 60 degrees*

OTHER USES: For uses not covered by these listings: Spell out whole numbers below 10, use figures for 10 and above. Typical examples: *They had three sons and two daughters. They had a fleet of 10 station wagons and two buses.*

IN A SERIES: Apply the appropriate guidelines: *They had 10 dogs, six cats and 97 hamsters. They had four four-room houses, 10 three-room houses and 12 10-room houses.*

O

obscenities, profanities, vulgarities Do not use them in stories unless they are part of direct quotations and there is a compelling reason for them.

olympics Capitalize all references to the international athletic contests held every four years: *the Olympics, the Winter Olympics, the Olympic Games, the Games, an Olympic-sized pool.*

An Olympic-sized pool is 50 meters long by 25 meters wide.

Lowercase other uses: *a beer-drinking olympics.*

organizations and institutions Capitalize the full names of organizations and institutions: *the American Medical Association; First Presbyterian Church; General Motors Corp.; Harvard University, Harvard University Medical School; the Procrastinators Club; the Society of Professional Journalists, Sigma Delta Chi.*

Retain capitalization if *Co., Corp.* or a similar word is deleted from the full proper name: *General Motors.*

SUBSIDIARIES: Capitalize the names of major subdivisions: *the Pontiac Motor Division of General Motors.*

INTERNAL ELEMENTS: Use lowercase for internal elements of an organization when they have names that are widely used generic terms: *the board of directors of General Motors, the board of trustees of Columbia University, the history department of Harvard University, the sports department of the Daily Citizen-Leader.*

Capitalize internal elements of an organization when they have names that are not widely used generic terms: *the General Assembly of the World Council of Churches, the House of Delegates of the American Medical Association, the House of Bishops and House of Deputies of the Episcopal Church.*

FLIP-FLOPPED NAMES: Retain capital letters when commonly accepted practice flops a name to delete the word *of: College of the Holy Cross, Holy Cross College; Harvard School of Dental Medicine, Harvard Dental School.*

Do not, however, flop formal names that are known to the public with the word *of: Massachusetts Institute of Technology,* for example, not *Massachusetts Technology Institute.*

ABBREVIATIONS AND ACRONYMS: Some organizations and institutions are widely recognized by the abbreviations: *Alcoa, GOP, NAACP, NATO.* For guidelines on when such abbreviations may be used, see the individual listings and the entry under **abbreviations and acronyms**.

P

people, persons Use *person* when speaking of an individual: *One person waited for the bus.*

The word *people* is preferred to persons in all plural uses. For example: *Thousands of people attended the fair. What will people say? There were 17 people in the room.*

Persons should be used only when it is in a direct quote or part of a title as in *Bureau of Missing Persons.*

People also is a collective noun that takes a plural verb when used to refer to a single race or nation: *The American people are united.* In this sense, the plural is *peoples: The peoples of Africa speak many languages.*

percent One word. It takes a singular verb when standing alone or when a singular word follows an *of* construction: *The teacher said 60 percent was a failing grade. He said 50 percent of the membership was there.*

It takes a plural verb when a plural word follows an *of* construction: *He said 50 percent of the members were there.*

percentages Use figures: *1 percent, 2.5 percent* (use decimals, not fractions), *10 percent.*

For amounts less than 1 percent, precede the decimal with a zero: *The cost of living rose 0.6 percent.*

Repeat *percent* with each individual figure: *He said 10 percent to 30 percent of the electorate may not vote.*

-persons Do not use coined words such as *chairperson* or *spokesperson* in regular text.

Instead, use *chairman* or *spokesman* if referring to a man or the office in general. Use *chairwoman* or *spokeswoman* if referring to a woman. Or, if applicable, use a neutral word such as *leader* or *representative.*

Use *chairperson* or similar coinage only in direct quotations or when it is the formal description for an office.

planets Capitalize the proper names of planets: *Jupiter, Mars, Mercury, Neptune, Pluto, Saturn, Uranus, Venus.*

Capitalize *earth* when used as the proper name of our planet: *The astronauts returned to Earth.*

Lowercase nouns and adjectives derived from the proper names of planets and other heavenly bodies: *martian, jovian, lunar, solar, venusian.*

plants In general, lowercase the names of plants, but capitalize proper nouns or adjectives that occur in a name.

Some examples: *tree, fir, white fir, Douglas fir; Scotch pine; clover, white clover, white Dutch clover.*

If a botanical name is used, capitalize the first word; lowercase others: *pine tree (Pinus), red cedar (Juniperus virginiana), blue azealea (Callicarpa americana), Kentucky coffee tree (Gymnocladus dioica).*

plurals Follow these guidelines in forming and using plural words:

MOST WORDS: Add *s: boys, girls, ships, villages.*

WORDS ENDING IN CH, S, SH, SS, X AND Z: Add *es: churches, lenses, parishes, glasses, boxes, buzzes.* (*Monarchs* is an exception.)

WORDS ENDING IN IS: Change *is* to *es: oases, parentheses, theses.*

WORDS ENDING IN Y: If *y* is preceded by a consonant or *qu*, change *y* to *i* and add *es: armies, cities, navies, soliloquies.* (See PROPER NAMES below for an exception.)

Otherwise add *s: donkeys, monkeys.*

WORDS ENDING IN O: If *o* is preceded by a consonant, most plurals require *es: buffaloes, dominoes, echoes, heroes, potatoes.* But there are exceptions: *pianos.* See individual entries in this book for many of these exceptions.

WORDS ENDING IN F: In general, change *f* to *v* and add *es: leaves, selves.* (There are exceptions, such as *roofs.*)

LATIN ENDINGS: Latin-root words ending in *us* change *us* to *i: alumnus, alumni.*

Most ending in *a* change to *ae: alumna, alumnae* (*formula, formulas* is an exception).

Most ending in *um* add *s: memorandums, referendums, stadiums.* Among those that still use the Latin ending: *addenda, curricula, media.*

Use the plural that Webster's New World lists as most common for a particular sense of that word.

FORM CHANGE: *man, men; child, children; foot, feet; mouse, mice;* etc.

Caution: When *s* is used with any of these words it indicates possession and must be preceded by an apostrophe: *men's, children's,* etc.

WORDS THE SAME IN SINGULAR AND PLURAL: *corps, chassis, deer, moose, sheep,* etc.

The sense in a particular sentence is conveyed by the use of a singular or plural verb.

WORDS PLURAL IN FORM, SINGULAR IN MEANING: Some take singular verbs: *measles, mumps, news.*

Others take plural verbs: *grits, scissors.*

COMPOUND WORDS: Those written solid add *s* at the end: *cupfuls, handfuls, tablespoonfuls.*

For those that involve separate words or words linked by a hyphen, make the most significant word plural:

—Significant word first: *adjutants general, aides-de-camp, attorneys general, courts-martial, daughters-in-law, passers-by, postmasters general, presidents-elect, secretaries general, sergeants major.*

—Significant word in the middle: *assistant attorneys general, deputy chiefs of staff.*

—Significant word last: *assistant attorneys, assistant corporation counsels, deputy sheriffs, lieutenant colonels, major generals.*

WORDS AS WORDS: Do not use *'s: His speech had too many "ifs," "ands" and "buts."* (Exception to Webster's New World.)

PROPER NAMES: Most ending in *es* or *z* add *es: Charleses, Joneses, Gonzalezes.*

Most ending in *y* add *s* even if preceded by a consonant: *the Duffys, the Kennedys, the two Kansas Citys.* Exceptions include *Alleghenies* and *Rockies.*

For others, add *s: the Carters, the McCoys, the Mondales.*

FIGURES: Add *s: The custom began in the 1920s. The airline has two 727s. Temperatures will be in the low 20s. There were five size 7s.*

(No apostrophes, an exception to Webster's New World guideline under "apostrophe.")

SINGLE LETTERS: Use *'s: Mind your p's and q's. He learned the three R's and brought home a report card with four A's and two B's. The Oakland A's won the pennant.*

MULTIPLE LETTERS: Add *s*: *She knows her ABCs. I gave him five IOUs. Four VIPs were there.*

PROBLEMS, DOUBTS: Separate entries in this book give plurals for troublesome words and guidance on whether certain words should be used with singular or plural verbs and pronouns. See also **collective nouns** and **possessives**.

For questions not covered by this book, use the plural that Webster's New World lists as most common for a particular sense of a word.

Note also the guidelines that the dictionary provides under its "plural" entry.

p.m., a.m. Lowercase, with periods. Avoid the redundant *10 p.m. tonight.*

police department In communities where this is the formal name, capitalize *police department* with or without the name of the community: *the Los Angeles Police Department, the Police Department.*

If a police agency has some other formal name, such as *Division of Police*, use that name if it is the way the department is known to the public. If the story uses *police department* as a generic term for such an agency, put *police department* in lowercase.

If a police agency with an unusual formal name is known to the public as a *police department*, treat *police department* as the name, capitalizing it with or without the name of the community. Use the formal name only if there is a special reason in the story.

If the proper name cannot be determined for some reason, such as the need to write about a police agency from a distance, treat *police department* as the proper name, capitalizing it with or without the name of the community.

Lowercase *police department* in plural uses: *the Los Angeles and San Francisco police departments.*

Lowercase *the department* whenever it stands alone.

political parties and philosophies Capitalize both the name of the party and the word *party* if it is customarily used as part of the organization's proper name: *the Democratic Party, the Republican Party.*

Capitalize *Communist, Conservative, Democrat, Liberal, Republican, Socialist,* etc., when they refer to a specific party or its members. Lowercase these words when they refer to political philosophy (see examples below).

Lowercase the name of a philosophy in noun and adjective forms unless it is the derivative of a proper name: *communism, fascism, fascist.* But: *Marxism, Marxist; Nazism, Nazi.*

EXAMPLES: *John Adams was a Federalist, but a man who subscribed to his philosophy today would be described as a federalist. The liberal Republican senator and his Conservative Party colleague said they believe that democracy and communism are incompatible. The Communist said he is basically a socialist who has reservations about Marxism.*

polls and surveys Stories based on public opinion polls must include the basic information for an intelligent evaluation of the results. Such stories must be carefully worded to avoid exaggerating the meaning of the poll results.

Information that should be in every story based on a poll includes the answers to these questions:

1. Who did the poll? (The place to start is the polling firm, political campaign or other group that conducted the poll.)
2. How many people were interviewed? How were they selected? (Only polls based on a scientific sample of a population can be used as a reliable and accurate measure of that population's opinions. Polls based on interviews on street corners, calling a 900-number or mailing coupons back from magazines may be good entertainment, but such polls have no validity. They should be avoided. In such unscientific pseudo-polls, the opinions come from people who "select themselves" to participate. If such polls are reported for entertainment value, they must never be portrayed as accurately reflecting public opinion and their failings must be highlighted.)
3. Who was interviewed? (A valid poll reflects only the opinions of the population that was sampled. A poll of business executives can only represent the views of business executives, not of all adults. Many political polls are based on interviews only with registered voters, since registration is usually required for voting. Close to the election, polls may be based only on "likely voters." If "likely voters" are used as the base, ask the pollster how that group was identified.)
4. How was the poll conducted—by telephone or in people's homes?
5. When was the poll taken? (Opinions can change quickly, especially in response to events.)
6. Who paid for the poll? (Be wary of polls paid for by candidates or interest groups. The release of poll results is often a campaign tactic or publicity ploy. Any reporting of such polls must highlight the poll's sponsor and the potential for bias from such sponsorship.)
7. What are the sampling error margins for the poll and for sub-groups mentioned in the story? (Sampling error margins should be provided by the polling organization. The error margins vary inversely with the sample size: the fewer people interviewed, the larger the sampling error. If the opinions of a sub-group—women, for example—are important to the story, the sampling error for that sub-group should be included. The sub-group error margins are always larger than the margin for the entire poll.)
8. What questions were asked and in what order? (Small differences in question wording can cause big differences in results. The exact text of the question need not be in every poll story unless it is crucial or controversial.)

When writing and editing poll stories, here are areas for close attention:

—Do not exaggerate the poll results. A difficult situation arises with pre-election polls in deciding when to write that the poll says one candidate is leading another. The rules are: If the margin between the candidates is more than twice the sampling error margin, then the poll says one candidate is leading. If the margin is less than the sampling error margin, the poll says that the race is close, that the candidates are "about even." If the margin is more than the sampling error, but less than twice the sampling error, then one candidate can be said to be "apparently leading" or "slightly ahead" in the race.

—Comparisons with other polls are often newsworthy. Earlier poll results can show changes in public opinion. Be careful comparing polls from different polling organizations. Different poll techniques can cause differing results.

—Sampling error is not the only source of error in a poll, but it is one that can be quantified. Question wording, interviewer skill and computer processing are all sources of error in surveys.

—No matter how good the poll, no matter how wide the margin, the poll does not say one candidate will win an election. Polls can be wrong and the voters can change their minds before they cast their ballots.

possessives Follow these guidelines:

PLURAL NOUNS NOT ENDING IN S: Add *'s: the alumni's contributions, women's rights.*

PLURAL NOUNS ENDING IN S: Add only an apostrophe: *the churches' needs, the girls' toys, the horses' food, the ships' wake, states' rights, the VIPs' entrance.*

NOUNS PLURAL IN FORM, SINGULAR IN MEANING: Add only an apostrophe: *mathematics' rules, measles' effects.* (But see INANIMATE OBJECTS on page 473.)

Apply the same principle when a plural word occurs in the formal name of a singular entity: *General Motors' profits, the United States' wealth.*

NOUNS THE SAME IN SINGULAR AND PLURAL: Treat them the same as plurals, even if the meaning is singular: *one corps' location, the two deer's tracks, the lone moose's antlers.*

SINGULAR NOUNS NOT ENDING IN S: Add *'s: the church's needs, the girl's toys, the horse's food, the ship's route, the VIP's seat.*

Some style guides say that singular nouns ending in s sounds such as *ce, x,* and *z* may take either the apostrophe alone or *'s.* See SPECIAL EXPRESSIONS, but otherwise, for consistency and ease in remembering a rule, always use *'s* if the word does not end in the letter s: *Butz's policies, the fox's den, the justice's verdict, Marx's theories, the prince's life, Xerox's profits.*

SINGULAR COMMON NOUNS ENDING IN S: Add *'s* unless the next word begins with s: *the hostess's invitation, the hostess' seat; the witness's answer, the witness' story.*

SINGULAR PROPER NAMES ENDING IN S: Use only an apostrophe: *Achilles' heel, Agnes' book, Ceres' rites, Descartes' theories, Dickens' novels, Euripides' dramas, Hercules' labors, Jesus' life, Jules' seat, Kansas' schools, Moses' law, Socrates' life, Tennessee Williams' plays, Xerxes' armies.*

SPECIAL EXPRESSIONS: The following exceptions to the general rule for words not ending in s apply to words that end in an s sound and are followed by a word that begins with s: *for appearance' sake, for conscience' sake, for goodness' sake.* Use *'s* otherwise: *the appearance's cost, my conscience's voice.*

PRONOUNS: Personal interrogative and relative pronouns have separate forms for the possessive. None involve an apostrophe: *mine, ours, your, yours, his, hers, its, theirs, whose.*

Caution: If you are using an apostrophe with a pronoun, always double-check to be sure that the meaning calls for a contraction: *you're, it's, there's, who's.*

Follow the rules listed above in forming the possessives of other pronouns: *another's idea, others' plans, someone's guess.*

COMPOUND WORDS: Applying the rules above, add an apostrophe or *'s* to the word closest to the object possessed: *the major general's decision, the major generals' decisions, the attorney general's request, the attorneys general's request.* See the **plurals** entry for guidelines on forming the plurals of these words.

Also: *anyone else's attitude, John Adams Jr.'s father, Benjamin Franklin of Pennsylvania's motion.* Whenever practical, however, recast the phrase to avoid ambiguity: *the motion by Benjamin Franklin of Pennsylvania.*

JOINT POSSESSION, INDIVIDUAL POSSESSION: Use a possessive form after only the last word if ownership is joint: *Fred and Sylvia's apartment, Fred and Sylvia's stocks.*

Use a possessive form after both words if the objects are individually owned: *Fred's and Sylvia's books.*

DESCRIPTIVE PHRASES: Do not add an apostrophe to a word ending in s when it is used primarily in a descriptive sense: *citizens band radio, a Cincinnati Reds infielder, a teachers college, a Teamsters request, a writers guide.*

Memory Aid: The apostrophe usually is not used if *for* or *by* rather than *of* would be appropriate in the longer form: *a radio band for citizens, a college for teachers, a guide for writers, a request by the Teamsters.*

An *'s* is required, however, when a term involves a plural word that does not end in s: *a children's hospital, a people's republic, the Young Men's Christian Association.*

DESCRIPTIVE NAMES: Some governmental, corporate and institutional organizations with a descriptive word in their names use an apostrophe; some do not. Follow the user's practice: *Actors' Equity, Diners Club, the Ladies' Home Journal, the National Governors' Association.* See separate entries for these and similar names frequently in the news.

QUASI POSSESSIVES: Follow the rules above in composing the possessive form of words that occur in such phrases as *a day's pay, two weeks' vacation, three days' work, your money's worth.* Frequently, however, a hyphenated form is clearer: *a two-week vacation, a three-day job.*

DOUBLE POSSESSIVE: Two conditions must apply for a double possessive—*a phrase such as a friend of John's*—to occur: 1. The word after *of* must refer to an inanimate object, and 2. The word before *of* must involve only a portion of the animate object's possessions.

Otherwise, do not use the possessive form of the word after *of*: *The friends of John Adams mourned his death.* (All the friends were involved.) *He is a friend of the college.* (Not *college's,* because college is inanimate.

Memory Aid: This construction occurs most often, and quite naturally, with the possessive forms of personal pronouns: *He is a friend of mine.*

INANIMATE OBJECTS: There is no blanket rule against creating a possessive form for an inanimate object, particularly if the object is treated in a personified sense. See some of the earlier examples, and note these: *death's call, the wind's murmur.*

In general, however, avoid excessive personalization of inanimate objects, and give preference to an *of* construction when it fits the makeup of the sentence. For example, the earlier references to *mathematics' rules* and *measles' effects* would better be phrased: *the rules of mathematics, the effects of measles.*

prefixes See separate listings for commonly used prefixes.

Generally do not hyphenate when using a prefix with a word starting with a consonant.

Three rules are constant, although they yield some exceptions to first-listed spellings in Webster's New World Dictionary:

—Except for *cooperate* and *coordinate,* use a hyphen if the prefix ends in a vowel and the word that follows begins with the same vowel.

—Use a hyphen if the word that follows is capitalized.

—Use a hyphen to join doubled prefixes: *sub-subparagraph.*

principal, principle *Principal* is a noun and adjective meaning someone or something first in rank, authority, importance or degree: *She is the school principal. He was the principal player in the trade. Money is the principal problem.*

Principle is a noun that means a fundamental truth, law, doctrine or motivating force: *They fought for the principle of self-determination.*

prison, jail Do not use the two words interchangeably.

DEFINITIONS: *Prison* is a generic term that may be applied to the maximum security institutions often known as *penitentiaries* and to the medium security facilities often called *correctional institutions* or *reformatories.* All such facilities confine persons serving sentences for felonies.

A *jail* is a facility normally used to confine persons serving sentences for misdemeanors, persons awaiting trial or sentencing on either felony or misdemeanor charges, and persons confined for civil matters such as failure to pay alimony and other types of contempt of court.

See the **felony, misdemeanor** entry.

The guidelines for capitalization:

PRISONS: Many states have given elaborate formal names to their prisons. They should be capitalized when used, but commonly accepted substitutes should also be capitalized as if they were proper names. For example, use either *Massachusetts Correctional Institution-Walpole* or *Walpole State Prison* for the maximum security institution in Massachusetts.

Do not, however, construct a substitute when the formal name is commonly accepted: It is *the Colorado State Penitentiary,* for example, not *Colorado State Prison.*

On second reference, any of the following may be used, all in lowercase: *the state prison, the prison, the state penitentiary, the penitentiary.*

Use lowercase for all plural constructions: *the Colorado and Kansas state penitentiaries.*

JAILS: Capitalize *jail* when linked with the name of the jurisdiction: *Los Angeles County Jail.* Lowercase *county jail, city jail* and *jail* when they stand alone.

FEDERAL INSTITUTIONS: Maximum security institutions are known as *penitentiaries*: *the U.S. Penitentiary at Lewisburg* or *Lewisburg Penitentiary* on first reference; *the federal penitentiary* or *the penitentiary* on second reference.

Medium security institutions include the word *federal* as part of their formal names: *the Federal Correctional Institution at Danbury, Conn.* On second reference: *the correctional institution, the federal prison, the prison.*

Most federal facilities used to house persons awaiting trial or serving sentences of a year or less have the proper name *Federal Detention Center.* the term *Metropolitan Correctional Center* is being adopted for some new installations. On second reference: *the detention center, the correctional center.*

punctuation Think of it as a courtesy to your readers, designed to help them understand a story.

Inevitably, a mandate of this scope involves gray areas. For this reason, the punctuation entries in this book refer to guidelines rather than rules. Guidelines should not be treated casually, however.

pupil, student Use *pupil* for children in kindergarten through eighth grade.

Student or *pupil* is acceptable for grades nine through 12.

Use *student* for college and beyond.

Q

quotations in the news Never alter quotations even to correct minor grammatical errors or word usage. Casual minor tongue slips may be removed by using ellipses but even that should be done with extreme caution. If there is a question about a quote, either don't use it or ask the speaker to clarify.

Do not routinely use abnormal spellings such as *gonna* in attempts to convey regional dialects or mispronunciations. Such spellings are appropriate when relevant or help to convey a desired touch in a feature.

FULL VS. PARTIAL QUOTES: In general, avoid fragmentary quotes. If a speaker's words are clear and concise, favor the full quote. If cumbersome language can be paraphrased fairly, use an indirect construction, reserving quotation marks for sensitive or controversial passages that must be identified specifically as coming from the speaker.

CONTEXT: Remember that you can misquote someone by giving a startling remark without its modifying passage or qualifiers. The manner of delivery sometimes is part of the context. Reporting a smile or a deprecatory gesture may be as important as conveying the words themselves.

R

race Identification by race is pertinent:

—In biographical and announcement stories, particularly when they involve a feat or appointment that has not routinely been associated with members of a particular race.

—When it provides the reader with a substantial insight into conflicting emotions known or likely to be involved in a demonstration or similar event.

In some stories that involve a conflict, it is equally important to specify that an issue cuts across racial lines. If, for example, a demonstration by supporters of busing to achieve racial balance in schools includes a substantial number of whites, that fact should be noted.

Do not use racially derogatory terms unless they are part of a quotation that is essential to the story.

S

satellite communications The following are some generally used technical terms dealing with satellite communications.

—*uplink* The transmission from the ground to the satellite.

—*downlink* The transmission from the satellite to the ground.

—*foot print* The area on the ground in which a transmission from a particular satellite can be received.

—*earth station* Sending or receiving equipment on the ground for a satellite.

—*transponder* The equipment on a satellite which receives from the ground and sends to the ground. A satellite usually has a number of *transponders*.

—*geosynchronous* A satellite orbit in which the satellite appears to always be in the same place in reference to the earth. Most communications satellites are in geosynchronous orbits. Also *geostationary*.

school Capitalize when part of a proper name: *Public School 3, Madison Elementary School, Doherty Junior High School, Crocker High School.*

semi- The rules in **prefixes** apply, but, in general, no hyphen.

semiannual Twice a year, a synonym for *biannual*.

Do not confuse it with *biennial*, which means every two years.

senate Capitalize all specific references to governmental legislative bodies, regardless of whether the name of the nation is used: *the U.S. Senate, the Senate, the Virginia Senate, the state Senate, the Senate.*

Lowercase plural uses: *the Virginia and North Carolina senates.*

The same principles apply to foreign bodies.

Lowercase references to non-governmental bodies: *the student senate at Yale.*

sentences Capitalize the first word of every sentence, including quoted statements and direct questions:

Patrick Henry said, "I know not what course others may take, but as for me, give me liberty or give me death."

Capitalize the first word of a quoted statement if it constitutes a sentence, even if it was part of a larger sentence in the original: *Patrick Henry said, "Give me liberty or give me death."*

In direct questions, even without quotation marks: *The story answers the question, Where does true happiness really lie?*

state Lowercase in all *state of* constructions: *the state of Maine, the states of Maine and Vermont.*

Four states—Kentucky, Massachusetts, Pennsylvania and Virginia—are legally commonwealths rather than states. The distinction is necessary only in formal uses: *The commonwealth of Kentucky filed a suit.* For simple geographic reference: *Tobacco is grown in the state of Kentucky.*

Do not capitalize *state* when used simply as an adjective to specify a level of jurisdiction: *state Rep. William Smith, the state Transportation Department, state funds.*

Apply the same principle to phrases such as *the city of Chicago, the town of Auburn, etc.*

state names Follow these guidelines:

STANDING ALONE: Spell out the names of the 50 U.S. states when they stand alone in textual material. Any state name may be condensed, however, to fit typographic requirements for tabular material.

EIGHT NOT ABBREVIATED: The names of eight states are never abbreviated in datelines or text: *Alaska, Hawaii, Idaho, Iowa, Maine, Ohio, Texas* and *Utah.*

Memory Aid: Spell out the names of the two states that are not part of the contiguous United States and of the continental states that are five letters or fewer.

ABBREVIATIONS REQUIRED: Use the state abbreviations listed at the end of this section:

—In conjunction with the name of a city, town, village or military base in most datelines.

—In conjunction with the name of a city, county, town, village or military base in text.

—In short-form listings of party affiliation: *D-Ala., R-Mont.*

The abbreviations, which also appear in the entries for each state, are:

Ala.	Ariz.	Ark.	Calif.	Colo.	Conn.
Del.	Fla.	Ga.	Ill.	Ind.	Kan.
Ky.	La.	Mass.	Md.	Mich	Minn.
Miss.	Mo.	Mont.	Neb.	Nev.	N.H.
N.J.	N.M.	N.Y.	N.C.	N.D.	Okla.
Ore.	Pa.	R.I.	S.C.	S.D.	Tenn.
Va.	Vt.	Wash.	W.Va.	Wis.	Wyo.

PUNCTUATION: Place one comma between the city and the state name, and another comma after the state name, unless ending a sentence or indicating a dateline: *He was traveling from Nashville, Tenn., to Austin, Texas, en route to his home in Albuquerque, N.M.*

sub- The rules in **prefixes** apply, but in general, no hyphen.

subcommittee Lowercase when used with the name of a legislative body's full committee: *a Ways and Means subcommittee.*

Capitalize when a subcommittee has a proper name of its own: *the Senate Permanent Subcommittee on Investigations.*

T

teen, teen-ager (n.) **teen-age** (adj.) Do not use *teen-aged.*

telecast (n.) **televise** (v.)

temperatures Use figures for all except *zero.* Use a word, not a minus sign, to indicate temperatures below zero.

Right: *The day's low was minus 10.*

Wrong: *The day's low was –10.*

Right: *The temperature rose to zero by noon.*

Also: *5-degree temperatures, temperatures fell 5 degrees, temperatures in the 30s* (no apostrophe).

Temperatures get *higher* or *lower*, but they don't get *warmer* or *cooler.*

titles In general, confine capitalization to formal titles used directly before an individual's name.

LOWERCASE: Lowercase and spell out titles when they are not used with an individual's name: *The president issued a statement. The pope gave his blessing.*

Lowercase and spell out titles in constructions that set them off from a name by commas: *The vice president, Nelson Rockefeller, declined to run again. Paul VI, the current pope, does not plan to retire.*

U

ultra- The rules in **prefixes** apply, but in general, no hyphen. Some examples:

ultramodern ultrasonic
ultraviolet ultranationalism

ultrahigh frequency *uhf* is acceptable in all references.

un- The rules in **prefixes** apply, but in general, no hyphen. Some examples:

un-American unarmed unnecessary unshaven

V

VCR Acceptable in second reference to *videocassette recorder.*

VDT Abbreviation for *video display terminal.* Spell out.

verbs The abbreviation v. is used in this book to identify the spelling of the verb forms of words frequently misspelled.

SPLIT FORMS: In general, avoid awkward constructions that split infinitive forms of a verb (*to leave, to help,* etc.) or compound forms (*had left, are found out,* etc.).

Awkward: *Then she was ordered to immediately leave on an assignment.*

Preferred: *Then she was ordered to leave immediately on an assignment.*

Occasionally, however, a split is not awkward and is necessary to convey the meaning:

He wanted to really help his mother.

The budget was tentatively approved.

vhf Acceptable in all references for *very high frequency.*

vice- Use two words: *vice admiral, vice chairman, vice chancellor, vice consul, vice president, vice principal, vice regent, vice secretary.*

Several are exceptions to Webster's New World. The two-word rule has been adopted for consistency in handling the similar terms.

videotex, teletext Not *videotext. Videotex* is the generic term for two-way interactive data systems that transmit text and sometimes graphics via telephone lines or cable. User can specify desired information and communicate with host computer or other users through terminal keyboard.

Teletext is a one-way system that transmits text material or graphics via a TV or FM broadcast signal or cable TV system. The user can select material desired but cannot communicate with other users.

W

who, whom Use *who* and *whom* for references to human beings and to animals with a name. Use *that* and *which* for inanimate objects and animals without a name.

Who is the word when someone is the subject of a sentence, clause or phrase: *The woman who rented the room left the window open. Who is there?*

Whom is the word when someone is the object of a verb or preposition: *The woman to whom the room was rented left the window open. Whom do you wish to see?*

wide- Usually hyphenated. Some examples:

wide-angle   wide-awake   wide-brimmed
wide-eyed   wide-open

Exception: *widespread.*

-wide No hyphen. Some examples:

citywide   continentwide   countrywide   industrywide
nationwide   statewide   worldwide

-wise No hyphen when it means *in the direction of* or *with regard to.* Some examples:

clockwise   lengthwise   otherwise   slantwise

Avoid contrived combinations such as *moneywise, religion-wise.*

The word *penny-wise* is spelled with a hyphen because it is a compound adjective in which *wise* means *smart,* not an application of the suffix *-wise.* The same for *street-wise* in *the street-wise youth.*

women Women should receive the same treatment as men in all areas of coverage. Physical descriptions, sexist references, demeaning stereotypes and condescending phrases should not be used.

To cite some examples, this means that:

Copy should not assume maleness when both sexes are involved, as in *Jackson told newsmen* or in *the taxpayer . . . he* when it easily can be said *Jackson told reporters* or *taxpayers . . . they.*

Sports Guidelines and Style

A

abbreviations Do not spell out the most common abbreviations: NFL, NBA, CART, USAC, AFC, NFC.

athletic teams Capitalize teams, associations and recognized nicknames: *Red Sox, the Big Ten, the A's, the Colts.*

athletics director Not *athletic.*

B

baseball The spellings for some frequently used words and phrases, some of which are exceptions to Webster's New World:

backstop	ballclub
ballpark	ballplayer
baseline	bullpen
center field	center fielder
designated hitter	doubleheader
double play	fair ball
fastball	first baseman
foul ball line	foul tip
ground-rule double	home plate
home run	left-hander
line drive	line up (v.)
lineup (n.)	major league(s) (n.)
major-league (adj.)	major-leaguer (n.)
outfielder	passed ball
pinch hit (v.)	pinch-hit (n., adj.)
pinch hitter (n.)	pitchout
play off (v.)	playoff (n., adj.)
put out (v.)	putout (n.)
RBI (s.),	RBIs (pl.)
rundown (n.)	sacrifice
sacrifice fly	sacrifice hit
shoestring catch	shortstop
shut out (v.)	shutout (n., adj.)
slugger	squeeze play
strike	strike zone
Texas leaguer	triple play
twi-night double-header	wild pitch

NUMBERS: Some sample uses of numbers: *first inning, seventh-inning stretch, 10th inning; first base, second base, third base; first home run, 10th home run; first place, last place; one RBI, 10 RBIs. The pitcher's record is now 6–5. The final score was 1–0.*

LEAGUES: Use *American League, National League, American League West, National League East,* or *AL West* and *AL East,* etc. On second reference: *the league, the pennant in the West, the league's West Division,* etc.

BOX SCORES: A sample follows.
The visiting team always is listed on the left, the home team on the right.

Only one position, the first he or she played in the game, is listed for any player.

Figures in parentheses are the player's total in that category for the season.

Use the *First Game* line shown here only if the game was the first in a double-header.

One line in this example—*None out when winning run scored*—could not have occurred in this game as played. It is included to show its placement when needed.

First Game

philadelphia					san diego				
	ab	r	h	bi		ab	r	h	bi
Stone lf	4	0	0	0	Flannry 2	3	0	1	0
GGross lf	0	0	0	0	Gwynn rf	4	0	2	0
Schu 3	4	1	0	0	Garvey 1	4	0	0	0
Samuel 2b	4	0	1	2	Schmidt 1	4	0	0	0
Nettles 3b	3	1	1	0	Royster 3	0	0	0	0
Virgil c	4	2	2	3	GWilson rf	4	0	0	0
McRynl cf	4	0	1	1	Kennedy c	4	0	1	0
Maddox c	3	0	0	0	Martinez lf	4	1	1	0
Jeltz ss	2	0	0	0	Templtn ss	4	0	2	1
KGross p	3	0	1	0	Tekulve p	0	0	0	0
Dravcky p	2	0	0	0	Bmbry ph	1	0		
					Lefferts p	0	0	0	0
Totals	**32**	**3**	**4**	**3**		**33**	**2**	**9**	**2**
Philadelphia					010	200	000	- 3	
San Diego					000	200	000	- 2	

None out when winning run scored.

E. Templeton, GWilson. DP — Philadelphia 2. LOB — Philadelphia 3, San Diego 6. 2B — Templeton, Gwynn. HR —Virgil (8).

	IP	H	R	ER	BB	SO
Philadelphia						
KGross W, 4–6	7 1-3	9	2	2	0	3
Tekulve S, 3	1 2–3	0	0	0	1	0
San Diego						
Dravecky L, 4–3	7	4	3	1	1	2
Lefferts	2	0	0	0	0	1

HBP —Flannery by KGross. T — 2:13. A-17, 740.

LINESCORE: When a bare linescore summary is required, use this form:

Philadelphia	010 200 000 — 3 4 1
San Diego	000 200 000 — 2 9 1

K. Gross, Tekulve (8) and Virgil; Dravecky, Lefferts (3) and Kennedy. W - KGross, 4–6, LDravecky, 4-3. Sv - Tekulve (3). HRs - Philadelphia Virgil 2 (8).

LEAGUE STANDINGS:

The form:

All times EDT
national league

East				
	W	L	Pct.	GB
Pittsburgh	92	69	.571	—
Philadelphia	85	75	.531	61/2
etc.				

west				
	w	l	Pct.	GB
Cincinnati	108	54	.667	—
Los Angeles	88	74	.543	20
etc.				

(Night games not included)

Chicago 7, St. Louis 5
Atlanta at New York, rain.

Tuesday's Games

Cincinnati (Gullett 14–2 and Nolan 4–4) at New York (Seaver 12–3 and Matlack 6–1) 2, 6 p.m.

Wednesday's Games

Cincinnati at New York
Chicago at St. Louis, night
Only games scheduled.

In subheads for results and future games, spell out day of the week as: *Tuesday's Games*, instead of *Today's Games*.

basic summary This format for summarizing sports events lists winners in the order of their finish. The figure showing the place finish is followed by an athlete's full name, his affiliation or hometown, and his time, distance, points, or whatever performance factor is applicable to the sport.

If a contest involves several types of events, the paragraph begins with the name of the event.

A typical example:

60-yard dash — 1, Steve Williams, Florida TC, 6.0. 2, Hasley Crawford, Philadelphia Pioneer, 6.1 3, Mike McFarland, Chicago TC, 6.2 4, etc.

100 — 1, Steve Williams, Florida TC, 10.1 2, etc.

Additional examples are provided in the entries for many of the sports that are reported in this format.

Most basic summaries are a single paragraph per event, as shown. In some competitions with large fields, however, the basic summary is supplied under a dateline with each winner listed in a single paragraph.

For international events in which U.S. or Canadian competitors are not among the leaders, add them in a separate paragraph as follows:

Also: 14, Dick Green, New York, 6.8 17, George Bensen Canada, 6.9, 19, etc.

In events where points, rather than time or distance, are recorded as performances, mention the word points on the first usage only:

1. Jim Benson, Springfield, N.J., 150 points. 2. Jerry Green, Canada, 149. 3. etc.

basketball The spellings of some frequently used words and phrases:

backboard	backcourt	backcourtman
baseline	field goal	foul line
foul shot	free throw	free-throw line
frontcourt	full-court press	goaltending
half-court pass	halftime	hook shot
jump ball	jump shot	layup
man-to-man	midcourt	pivotman
play off (v.)	playoff (n., adj.)	zone

NUMBERS: Some sample uses of numbers: *in the first quarter, a second-quarter lead, nine field goals, 10 field goals, the 6-foot-5 forward, the 6-10 center. He is 6 feet 10 inches tall.*

LEAGUE: *National Basketball Association or NBA.*

For subdivisions: *the Atlantic Division of the Eastern Conference, the Pacific Division of the Western Conference,* etc. On second reference: *the NBA East, the division, the conference,* etc.

BOX SCORE: A sample follows. The visiting team always is listed first.

In listing the players, begin with the five starters—two forwards, center, two guards—and follow with all substitutes who played.

Figures after each player's last name denote field goals, free throws, free throws attempted and total points. Example:

los angeles (114)

Worthy 8-19 4-6 20, Rambis 4-6 0-0 8, Abdul-Jabbar 6-11 0-0 12, E. Johnson 8-14 3-4 19, Scott 5-14 0-0 10, Cooper 1-5 2-2 4, McAdoo 6-13 0-0 12, McGee 4-7 4-5 14, Spriggs 4-7 0-2 8, Kupchak 3-3 1-2 7, Totals 49-100 14-21 114.

boston (148)

McHale 10-16 6-9 26, Bird 8-14 2-2 19, Parish 6-11 6-7 18, D. Johnson 6-14 1-1 13, Ainge 9-15 0-0 19, Buckner 3-5 0-0 6, Williams 3-5 0-0 6, Wedman 11-11 0-2 26, Maxwell 1-1 1-2 3, Kite 3-5 1-2 7, Carr 1-3 0-0 3, Clark 1-2 0-0 2. Totals 62-102 17-25 148.

Three-point goals—Wedman 4, McGee 2, Bird, Ainge, Carr. Fouled out—None. Rebounds—Los Angeles 43 (Rambis 9), Boston 63 (McHale 9).

Assists — Los Angeles 28 (E. Johnson 12), Boston 43 (D. Johnson 10). Total fouls —Los Angeles 23, Boston 17. Technicals — Ainge. A — 14,890.

STANDINGS: The format for professional standings:

Eastern Conference
Atlantic Division

	W	L	Pct.	GB
Boston	43	22	.662	—
Philadelphia	40	30	.571	5 1/2
etc.				

In college boxes, the score by periods is omitted because the games are divided only into halves.

ucla (69)

Jackson 1-6 2-2 4, Maloncon 4-7 2-2 10, Wright 4-7 1-5 9, Gaines 4-6 1-2 9, Miguel 5-10 0-0 10, Butler 2-3 6-8 10, Hatcher 3-8 0-0 6, Immel 2-2 1-1 5, Haley 1-1 4-4 6, Miller 0-2 0-0 0, J. Jones 0-3 0-0 0, Dunlap 0-0 0-0 0. Totals 26-55 17-24 69.

st john's (88)

Berry 10-14 3-5 23, Glass 4-5 3-6 11, Wennington 5-9 4-4 14, Moses 5-6 0-0 10, Mullin 6-11 4-6 16, Jackson 1-3 5-5 7, Stewart 0-3 2-2 2, S. Jones 1-2 2-2 4, Bross 0-1 0-0 0, Rowan 0-2 0-0 0, Shurina 0-0 1-2 1, Coregy 0-0 0-0 0. Totals 32-56 24-32 88.

Halftime — St. John's 48, UCLA 35. Fouled out — None. Rebounds —UCLA 25 (Wright 9), St. John's 39 (Mullin 9).

Assists — UCLA 18 (Gaines 5), St. John's 21 (Moses 8).

Total fouls —UCLA 22, St. John's 20.

A-15,256

The format for college conference standings:

	Conference			All Games		
	W	L	Pct.	W	L	Pct.
Missouri	12	2	.857	24	4	.857

C

cross country No hyphen, an exception to Webster's New World based on the practices of U.S. and international governing bodies for the sport.

Scoring for this track event is in minutes, seconds and tenths of a second. Extended to hundredths if available.

National AAU Championship
Cross Country
Frank Shorter, Miami, 5:25.67; 2. Tom Coster, Los Angeles, 5:30.72; 3. etc.

Adapt the basic summary to paragraph form under a dateline for a field of more than 10 competitors.

cycling Use the basic summary format.

D

decathlon Summaries include time or distance performance, points earned in that event and the cumulative total of points earned in previous events.

Contestants are listed in the order of their overall point totals. First name and hometown (or nation) are included only on the first and last events on the first day of competition; on the last day, first names are included only in the first event and in the summary denoting final placings.

Use the basic summary format. Include all entrants in summaries of each of the 10 events.

An example for individual events:

Decathlon
(Group A)

100-meter dash — 1. Fred Dixon, Los Angeles, 10.8 seconds, 854 points. 2. Bruce Jenner, San Jose State, 11:09, 783. 3. etc.

Long jump — 1. Dixon 24-7 (7.34m), 889, 1,743. 2. Jenner, 23-6 (7.17m), 855, 1,638. 3. etc.

Decathlon final — 1. Bruce Jenner, San Jose State, 8,524 points. 2. Fred Dixon, Los Angeles, 8,277. 3. etc.

E

era Acceptable in all references to baseball's *earned run average.*

F

football The spellings of some frequently used words and phrases:

ball carrier	ballclub
blitz (n., v.)	end line
end zone	fair catch

field goal

fullback

goal-line stand

halftime

kick off (v.)

left guard

lineman

out of bounds (adv.)

pitchout (n.)

place-kicker

playoff (n., adj.)

runback (n.)

split end

tight end

touchdown

fourth-and-one (adj.)

goal line

halfback

handoff

kickoff (adj.)

linebacker

line of scrimmage

out-of-bounds (adj.)

place kick

play off (v.)

quarterback

running back

tailback

touchback

wide receiver

NUMBERS: Use figures for yardage: *The 5-yard line, the 10-yard line, a 5-yard pass play, he plunged in from the 2, he ran 6 yards, a 7-yard gain.* But: *a fourth-and-two play.*

Some other uses of numbers: *The final score was 21-14. The team won its fourth game in 10 starts. The team record is 4-5-1.*

LEAGUE: *National Football League,* or *NFL.*

STATISTICS: All football games, whether using the one- or two-point conversion, use the same summary style.

The visiting team always is listed first.

Field goals are measured from the point where the ball was kicked—not the line of scrimmage. The goal posts are 10 yards behind the goal lines. Include that distance.

Abbreviate team names to four letters or less on the scoring and statistical lines as illustrated.

The passing line shows, in order: completions-attempts-had intercepted

A sample agate package:

Birmingham-Houston, Stats

| Birmingham | 7 | 16 | 0 | 7—30 |
| Houston | 14 | 7 | 0 | 6—27 |

First Quarter

Hou — Harrell 23 pass from Dillon (Fritsch kick), 1:00

Bir —Jones 11 run with lateral after Mason, 12 pass from Stoudt (Miller kick), 5:57

Hou — Harrell 6 run (Fritsch kick), 8:07

Second Quarter

Bir — FG Miller, 1:13

Bir — Caruth 6 run (Miller kick) 5:49

Hou – Johnson 36 pass from Dillon (Fritsch kick), 12:12

Bir — FG Miller 43, 14:33

Fourth Quarter

Bir — FG Miller 20, 3:42

Bir — Stoudt 1 run (kick failed), 9:09

Hou — Dillon 8 run (pass failed), 13:58

A —13,202

	Bir	Hou
First downs	21	15
Rushes-yards	46-209	12-70
Passing yards	109	260
Return yards	75	112
Comp-Att	13-24-0	17-33-2
Sacked-Yards Lost	4-23	2-24
Punts	3-38	3-41
Fumbles-lost	1-1	2-0
Penalties-yards	3-25	12-69
Time of Possession	35:57	24:03

individual statistics

RUSHING — Birmingham, Caruth 23-84, Coles 14-59, Stoudt 8-50, Gant 1-5. Houston, Harrell, 4-34, Fowler 5-26, Dillon 3-10.

PASSING — Birmingham, Stoudt 13-24-0 133. Houston, Dillon 17-33-2 283.

RECEIVING — Birmingham, Toler 4-53, Jones 3-15, McFaddon 2-38, Coles 2-12, Mason, 1-12, Caruth 1-4. Houston, Johnson 5-108, McGee 3-59, McNeil 3-36, 2-27, Sanders 3-29, Verdin 1-24.

MISSED FIELD GOALS — Houston, Fritsch 32.

The rushing and receiving paragraph for individual leaders show attempts and yardage gained. The passing paragraph shows completions, attempts, number of attempts intercepted, and total yards gained.

STANDINGS: The form for **professional standings:**

American Conference
East

	W	L	T	Pct.	PF	PA
Baltimore	10	4	0	.714	395	269
New England	9	5	0	.643	387	275
Etc.						

The form for college **conference standings:**

	Conference					All Games				
	w	l	t	Pts.	OP	W	L	T	Pts.	OP
UCLA	6	1	0	215	123	8	2	1	326	233
Etc.										

In college conference standings, limit team names to nine letters or fewer. Abbreviate as necessary.

G

golf Some frequently used terms and some definitions:

Americas Cup No possessive.

birdie, birdies One stroke under par.

bogey, bogeys One stroke over par. The past tense is *bogeyed.*

caddie

eagle Two strokes under par.

fairway

Masters Tournament No possessive. Use *the Masters* on second reference.

tee, tee off

U.S. Open Championship Use *the U.S. Open* or *the Open* on second reference.

NUMBERS: Some sample uses of numbers:

Use figures for handicaps: *He has a 3 handicap*; *a 3-handicap golfer*, *a handicap of 3 strokes*; *a 3-stroke handicap.*

Use figures for par listings: *He had a par 5 to finish 2-up for the round, a par-4 hole*; *a 7-under-par 64, the par-3 seventh hole.*

Use figures for club ratings: *a No. 5 iron, a 5-iron, a 7-iron shot, a 4-wood.*

Miscellaneous: *the first hole, the ninth hole, the 10th hole, the back nine, the final 18, the third round. He won 3 and 2.*

ASSOCIATIONS: *Professional Golfers' Association of America* (note the apostrophe) or *PGA*. Headquarters is in Palm Beach Gardens, Fla. Members teach golf at golf shops and teaching facilities across the country.

The *PGA Tour* is a separate organization made up of competing professional golfers. Use *tour* (lowercase) on second reference.

The PGA conducts the PGA Championship, the PGA Seniors' Championship, and the Ryder Cup matches as well as other golf championships not associated with the PGA Tour.

The *Ladies Professional Golfers Association* (no apostrophe, in keeping with LPGA practice) or *LPGA*.

SUMMARIES—Stroke (Medal) Play: List scores in ascending order. Use a dash before the final figure, hyphens between others.

On the first day, use the player's score for the first nine holes, a hyphen, the player's score for the second nine holes, a dash and the player's total for the day:

First round:

Jack Nicklaus	35-35 — 70
Johnny Miller	36-35 — 71
Etc.	

On subsequent days, give the player's scores for each day, then the total for all rounds completed:

Second round:

Jack Nicklaus	70-70 —140
Johnny Miller	71-70 — 141

Final round, professional tournaments, including prize money:

Jack Nicklaus $30,000	70-70-70-68 — 278
Johnny Miller $17,500	71-70-70-69 — 280

Use hometowns, if ordered, only on national championship amateur tournaments. Use home countries, if ordered, only on major international events such as the British Open. If used, the hometown or country is placed on a second line, indented one space:

Arnold Palmer	70-69-68-70—277
United States	
Tony Jacklin	71-70-70-70 — 281
England	

The form for cards:

Par out	444 343 544-35
Watson out	454 333 435-34
Nicklaus out	434 243 544-33
Par in	434 443 454-35 — 70
Watson in	434 342 443-31 — 65
Nicklaus in	433 443 453-33 — 66

SUMMARIES — Match Play: In the first example that follows, the *and 1* means that the 18th hole was skipped because Nicklaus had a 2-hole lead after 17. In the second, the match went 18 holes. In the third, a 19th hole was played because the golfers were tied after 18.

Jack Nicklaus def. Lee Trevino, 2 and 1
Sam Snead def. Ben Hogan, 2-up.
Arnold Palmer def. Johnny Miller, 1-up (19).

gymnastics Scoring is by points. Identify events by name: *sidehorse, horizontal bars*, etc.

Use a basic summary. Example:

Sidehorse—1. John Leaper, Penn State, 8.8 points. 2. Jo Jumper, Ohio State, 7.9 3. Etc.

H

handball Games are won by the first player to score 21 points or, in the case of a tie breaker, 11 points. Most matches go to the first winner of two games.

Use a match summary. Example:

Bob Richards, Yale, def. Paul Johnson, Dartmouth, 21–18, 21–19.
Tom Brenna, Massachusetts, def. Bill Stevens, Michigan, 21–19, 17–21, 21-20.

hockey The spellings of some frequently used words:

blue line	crease	face off (v.)
faceoff (n., adj.)	goalie	goal line
goal post	goaltender	penalty box
play off (v.)	playoff (n., adj.)	power play
power-play goal	red line	short-handed
slap shot	two-on-one break	

The term *hat trick* applies when a player has scored three goals in a game. Use it sparingly, however.

LEAGUE: *National Hockey League* or *NHL*.

For NHL subdivisions: *the Wales Division of the Campbell Conference, the division, the conference, etc.*

SUMMARIES: The visiting team always is listed first in the score by periods.

Note that each goal is numbered according to its sequence in the game.

The figure after the name of a scoring player shows his total goals for the season.

Names in parentheses are players credited with an assist on a goal.

The final figure in the listing of each goal is the number of minutes elapsed in the period when the goal was scored.

| Philadelphia | 3 0 0 —3 |
| Edmonton | 2 2 1 — 5 |

First period — 1, Philadelphia, Rick Sutter 1 (Ron Sutter, Smith),:46. 2, Edmonton, Coffey 10 (Huddy, Kurri), 4:22 (pp). 3, Philadelphia, Bergen 4 (Zezel, Crossman), 6:38 (pp). 4, Philadelphia, Craven 4 (Smith, Marsh), 11:32 (sh). 5, Edmonton, Huddy 3 (Coffey, Kurri), 18:23 (pp). Penalties — Poulin, Phi (high-sticking), 3:31; Hughes, Edm (high-sticking), 5:17; Messier, Edm (slashing), 5:59; Crossman, Phl, double minor (holding-unsportsmanlike conduct), 8:32; Hospodar, Phl (slashing), 16:38.

Second period — 6, Edmonton, Anderson 10:21. 7, Edmonton, Gretzky 15 (Coffey, Huddy), 12:53 (pp). Penalties —Tocchet, Phil (roughing), :48; Fogolin, Edm (roughing),:48; Paterson, Phil (hooking), 12:11; Allison Phil (slashing), 17:39; Hunter, Edm (roughing), 17:39; Lowe, Edm (holding), 18:02; Crossman, Phil (holding), 19:07; Hunter, Edm (holding), 20:00.

Third Period — 8 Edmonton, Gretzky 16 (Messier, Anderson), 3:42 (pp). Penalties —Hospodar, Phl (hooking), 2:46; Hunter, Edm (kneeing), 7:58.

Shots on goal —Philadelphia 10-6-7 23. Edmonton 10-12-1 —32.

Penalty shots — Ron Sutter, Phl 8:47 1st (missed).

Goalies — Philadelphia, Lindbergh at 8:56 2nd; reentered at start of 3rd, 10–9) Edmonton, Fuhr (23-20). A —17,498. Referee —Kerry Fraser.

STANDINGS: The form:

Wales Conference
Patrick Division

	W	L	T	Pts.	GF	GA
Philadelphia	47	10	14	108	314	184
NY Islanders	45	17	9	99	310	192
Etc.						

M

metric system See the section on newswriting.

S

scores Use figures exclusively, placing a hyphen between the totals of the winning and losing teams: *The Reds defeated the Red Sox 4-3, the Giants scored a 12-6 football victory over the Cardinals, the golfer had a 5 on the first hole but finished with a 2-under-par score.*

Use a comma in this format: *Boston 6, Baltimore 5.*

See individual listings for each sport for further details.

skating, figure Scoring includes both ordinals and points.

Use a basic summary. Examples:
Men
(After 3 compulsory figures)
Sergei Volkov, Russia, 19.5 ordinals, 44.76 points. 2, John Curry, Britain, 21.5, 44.96. 3, Etc.

Women's Final
Dorothy Hamill, Riverside, Conn., 9.0 ordinals, 215 points; 2, Dianne de Leeuw, Netherlands, 20.0, 236; 3, Etc.

skating, speed Scoring is in minutes, seconds and tenths of a second. Extended to hundredths if available.

Use a basic summary.

ski, skis, skier, skied, skiing Also: *ski jump, ski jumping*.

skiing Identify events as: *men's downhill, women's slalom,* etc. In ski jumping, note style where two jumps and points are posted.

Use a basic summary. Example:

90-meter special jumping — 1, Karl Schnabel, Austria, 320 and 318 feet, 234.8 points. 2, Toni Innauer, Austria, 377-299, 232.9. 3, Etc. Also: 27, Bob Smith Hanover N.H. 321-280, 201.29, Etc.

swimming Swimming is in minutes, if appropriate, seconds and tenths of a second. Extend to hundredths if available.

Most events are measured in metric units.

Identify events as *men's 440-meter relay, women's 100-meter backstroke,* etc., on first reference. Condense to *men's 440 relay, women's 100 backstroke* on second reference.

See the **track and field** entry for the style on relay teams and events where a record is broken.

Use a basic summary. Examples, where qualifying heats are required:

Men's 200-meter Backstroke Heats (fastest eight qualify for final Saturday night) heat 1 — 1, John Naber, USC, 2:03.25; 2, Zoltan Verraszio, Hungary, 2:03.50; 3, Etc.

For diving events, adapt the **skating, figure** entry.

T

tennis The scoring units are points, games, sets and matches.

A player wins a point if his opponent fails to return the ball, hits it into the net or hits it out of bounds. A player also wins a point if his opponent is serving and fails to put the ball into play after two attempts (*double faults,* in tennis terms).

A player must win four points to win a game. In tennis scoring, both players begin at *love,* or zero, and advance to 15, 30, 40 and game. (The numbers *15, 30* and *40* have no point value as such—they are simply tennis terminology for *1 point, 2 points* and *3 points.*) The server's score always is called out first. If a game is tied at 40-all, or *deuce,* play continues until one player has a two-point margin.

A set is won if a player wins six games before his opponent has won five. If a set becomes tied at five games apiece, it goes to the first player to win seven games. If two players who were tied at five games apiece also tie at six games apiece, they normally play a tiebreaker—a game that goes to the first player to win seven points. In some cases, however, the rules call for a player to win by two games.

A match may be either a best-of-three contest that goes to the first player or team to win two sets, or a best-of-five contest that goes to the first player or team to win three sets.

Set scores would be reported this way: *Chris Evert Lloyd defeated Sue Barker 6–0, 3-6, 6–4.* Indicate tiebreakers in parentheses after the set score: *7–6, (11–9).*

SUMMARIES: Winners always are listed first in agate summaries. An example:

Men's Singles
First Round

Jimmy Connors, Belleville, Ill., def. Manuel Orantes, Spain, 2–6, 6–3, 6–2, 6–1.

Bjorn Borg, Sweden, def. Jim Green, New York (default).

Arthur Ashe, New York, def. James Peters, Chicago, 6–3, 4–3 (retired).

track and field Scoring is in distance or time, depending on the event.

Most events are measured in metric units. For those meets that include feet, make sure the measurement is clearly stated, as in *men's 100-meter dash, women's 880-yard run,* etc.

For time events, spell out *minutes* and *seconds* on first reference, as in *3 minutes, 26.1 seconds.* Subsequent times in stories and all times in agate require a colon and decimal point: *3:34.4.* For a marathon, it would be *2 hours, 11 minutes, 5:01 seconds* on first reference then the form *2:12:4.06* for later listings.

Do not use a colon before times given only in seconds and tenths of a second. Use progressions such as *6.0 seconds, 9.4, 10.1,* etc. Extend times to hundredths, if available: *9.45.*

In running events, the first event should be spelled out, as in *men's 100-meter dash.* Later references can be condensed to phrases such as *the 200, the 400,* etc.

For hurdle and relay events, the progression can be: *100-meter hurdles, 200 hurdles,* etc.

For field events—those that do not involve running—use these forms: *26 1/2 for 26 feet, one-half inch; 25–10 1/2 for 25 feet, 10 1/2 inches,* etc.

In general, use a basic summary. For the style when a record is broken, note the mile event in the example below. For the style in listing relay teams, note 1,000-meter relay.

60-yard dash — 1, Steve Williams, Florida TC, 6.02 Hasley Crawford, Philadelphia Pioneer, 6.2 3, Mike McFarland, Chicago TC. 6.2. 3, Etc.

100 — 1, Steve Williams, Florida TC 10.1. 2, Etc.

Mile — 1, Filbert Bayli, Tanzania, 3:55.1, meet record; old record 3:59, Jim Beatty, Los Angeles TC. Feb. 27, 1963; 2, Paul Cummings, Beverly Hills TC, 3:56.1; 3, Etc.

Women's 880 — 1, Johanna Forman, Falmouth TC. 2:07.9. 2, Etc.

1,600-meter relay—1, St. John's, Jon Kennedy, Doug Johnson, Gary Gordon, Ordner Emanuel, 3:21.9 2.; Brown, 3:23.5 3, Fordham, 3:24.1. 4. Etc.

Team scoring —Chicago TC 32. Philadelphia Pioneer 29, etc.

Where qualifying heats are required:

Men's 100-meter heats (first two in each heat qualify for Friday's semifinals): Heat 1 — 1, Steve Williams, Florida TC. 10.1 2. Etc.

W

water polo Scoring is by goals. List team scores. Example:

World Water Polo Championship
First Round

United States 7, Canada 1

Britain 5, France 3

Etc.

water skiing Scoring is in points. Use a basic summary. Example:

World Water Skiing Championships
Men

Overall — 1, George Jones, Canada, 1,987 points. 2, Phil Brown, Britain, 1,756. 3, Etc.

Slalom — 1, George Jones, Canada, 73 buoys (two rounds). 2, Etc.

weightlifting Identify events by weight classes. Where both pounds and kilograms are available, use both figures with kilograms in parentheses, as shown in the examples.

Use a basic summary. Example:

Flyweight (114.5 lbs.) — 1, Zygmont Smalcerz, Poland, 744 pounds (337.5 kg). 2, Lajos Szuecs, Hungary, 728 (330 kg). 3, Etc.

wrestling Identify events by weight division.

Punctuation Marks and How to Use Them

ampersand (&) Use the ampersand when it is part of a company's formal name: *Baltimore & Ohio Railroad.*

The *ampersand* should not otherwise be used in place of *and.*

apostrophe (') Follow these guidelines:

PLURAL NOUNS NOT ENDING IN *s*: Add *'s*: *the alumni's contributions.*

PLURAL NOUNS ENDING IN *s*: Add only an apostrophe: *the churches' needs, the VIPs' entrance.*

NOUNS PLURAL IN FORM, SINGULAR IN MEANING: Add only an apostrophe: *mathematics' rules.*

NOUNS THE SAME IN SINGULAR AND PLURAL: Treat them the same as plurals, even if the meaning is singular: *one corps' location, the two deer's tracks.*

SINGULAR NOUNS NOT ENDING IN *s*: dd *'s*: *the churches' needs, the VIP's seat.*

SINGULAR COMMON NOUNS ENDING IN *s*: Add *'s* unless the next word begins with *s*: *the hostess's invitation, the hostess'; seat.*

SINGULAR PROPER NAMES ENDING IN *s*: Use only an apostrophe: *Achilles' heel, Agnes' book, Ceres' rites.*

SPECIAL EXPRESSIONS: The following exceptions to the general rule for words not ending in *s* apply to words that end in an *s* sound and are followed by a word that begins with *s*: *for appearance' sake, for conscience' sake, for goodness' sake.* Us *'s* otherwise: *the appearance's cost, my conscience's voice.*

PRONOUNS: Personal interrogative and relative pronouns have separate forms for the possessive. None involves an apostrophe: *mine, ours, your, yours, his, her, its, theirs, whose.*

Caution: If you are using an apostrophe with a pronoun, always double-check to be sure that the meaning calls for a contraction: *you're, it's, there's, who's.*

Follow the rules listed above in forming the possessives of other pronouns: *another's idea, others' plans, someone's guess.*

COMPOUND WORDS: Applying the rules above, add an apostrophe or *'s* to the word closest to the object possessed: *the major general's decision, the major generals' decisions, the attorney general's request, the attorneys general's request.*

JOINT POSSESSION, INDIVIDUAL POSSESSION: Use a possessive form after only the last word if ownership is joint: *Fred and Sylvia's apartment, Fred's and Sylvia's books.*

Use a possesive form after both words if the objects are individually owned: *Fred and Sylvia's books.*

DESCRIPTIVE PHRASES: Do not add an apostrophe to a word ending in *s* when it is used primarily in a descriptive sense: *a teachers college, writers guide.*

OMITTED LETTERS: *I've, it's, don't, rock 'n' roll, 'tis the season to be jolly. He is a ne'er-do-well.*

OMITTED FIGURES: *The class of '62. The Spirit of '76. The '20s.*

PLURALS OF A SINGLE LETTER: *Mind your p's and q's. He learned the three R's and brought home a report card with four A's and two B's. The Oakland A's won the pennant.*

colon (:) The most frequent use of a colon is at the end of a sentence to introduce lists, tabulations, texts, etc.

Capitalize the first word after a colon only if it is a proper noun or the start of a complete sentence: *He promised this: The company will make good all the losses.* But: *There were three considerations: expense, time and feasibility.*

LISTINGS: Use the colon in such listings as time elapsed *(1:31: 07.2),* time of day *(8:31 p.m.),* biblical and legal citations *(2 Kings 2:14; Missouri code 3:245-260).*

DIALOGUE: Use a colon for dialogue. In coverage of a trial, for example:

> *Bailey: What were you doing the night of the 19th?*
> *Mason: I refuse to answer that.*

Q AND A: The colon is used for question-and-answer interviews:
Q: Did you strike him?
A: Indeed I did.

PLACEMENT WITH QUOTATION MARKS: Colons go outside quotation marks unless they are part of the quotation itself.

MISCELLANEOUS: Do not combine a dash and a colon.

comma (,) The following guidelines treat some of the most frequent questions about the use of commas.

IN A SERIES: Use commas to separate elements in a series, but do not put a comma before the conjunction in a simple series: *The flag is red, white and blue.*

Put a comma before the concluding conjunction in a series, however, if the integral element of the series requires a conjunction: *I had orange juice, toast, and ham and eggs for breakfast.*

Use a comma also before the concluding conjunction in a complex series of phrases: *The main points to consider are whether the athletes are skillful enough to compete, whether they have the stamina to endure the training, and whether they have the proper mental attitude.*

WITH EQUAL ADJECTIVES: Use commas to separate a series of adjectives equal in rank, If the commas could be replaced by the word *and* without changing the sense, the adjectives are equal: *a thoughtful, precise manner; a dark, dangerous street.*

Use no comma when the last adjective before a noun outranks its predecessors because it is an integral component of a noun phrase, which is the equivalent of a single noun: *a cheap fur coat* (the noun phrase is *fur coat*); *the old oaken bucket; a new, blue spring bonnet.*

WITH NONESSENTIAL CLAUSES: A nonessential clause must be set off by commas. An essential clause must not be set off from the rest of the sentence by commas.

WITH NONESSENTIAL PHRASES: A nonessential phrase must be set off by commas. An essential phrase must not be set off from the rest of the sentence by commas.

WITH INTRODUCTORY CLAUSES AND PHRASES: A comma is used to separate an introductory clause or phrase from the main clause: *When he had tired of the mad pace of New York, he moved to Dubuque.*

WITH CONJUNCTIONS: When a conjunction such as *and, but* or *for* links two clauses that could stand alone as separate sentences, use a comma before the conjunction in most cases: *She was glad she had looked, for a man was approaching the house.*

As a rule of thumb, use a comma if the subject of each clause is expressly stated: *We are visiting Washington, and we also plan a side trip to Williamsburg. We visited Washington, and our senator greeted us personally.* But no comma when the subject of the two clauses is the same and is not repeated in the second: *We are visiting Washington and plan to see the White House.*

INTRODUCING DIRECT QUOTES: Use a comma to introduce a complete one-sentence quotation within a paragraph: *Wallace said, "She spent six months in Argentina and came back speaking English with a Spanish accent."* but use a coon to introduce quotations of more than one sentence.

Do not use a comma at the start of an indirect or partial quotation: *He said the victory put him "firmly on the road to a first-ballot nomination."*

BEFORE ATTRIBUTION: Use a comma instead of a period at the end of a quote that is followed by attribution: *"Rub my shoulders," Miss Cawley suggested.*

Do not use a comma, however, if the quoted statement ends with a question mark or exclamation point: *"Why should I?" he asked.*

WITH HOMETOWNS AND AGES: *Mary Richards, Minneapolis, and Maude Findlay, Tuckahoe, N.Y., were there.*

If an individual's age is used, set it off by commas: *Maude Findlay, 48, Tuckahoe, N.Y., was present.*

NAMES OF STATES AND NATIONS USED WITH CITY NAMES: *His journey will take him from Dublin, Ireland, to Fargo, N.D., and back.*

Use parentheses, however, if a state name is inserted within a proper name: *The Huntsville (ala.) Times.*

WITH YES AND NO: *Yes, I will be there.*

IN DIRECT ADDRESS: *Mother, I will be home late.*

SEPARATING SIMILAR WORDS: Use a comma to separate duplicated words that otherwise would be confusing: *What the problem is, is not clear.*

IN LARGE FIGURES: Use a comma for most figures higher than 999. The major exceptions are: street addresses *(1234 Main St.)*, broadcast frequencies *(1460 kilohertz)*, room numbers, serial numbers, telephone numbers, and years (1876).

PLACEMENT WITH QUOTES: Commas always go inside quotation marks.

dash (—) Follow these guidelines:

ABRUPT CHANGE: Use dashes to denote an abrupt change in thought in a sentence or an emphatic pause: *We will fly to Paris in June—if I get a raise. Smith offered a plan—it was unprecedented—to raise revenues.*

SERIES WITHIN A PHRASE: *He listed the qualities—intelligence, humor, conservatism, independence—that he liked in an executive.*

ATTRIBUTION: *"Who steals my purse steals trash."—Shakespeare.*

IN DATELINES:
new york (AP)—The city is broke.

IN LISTS: Dashes should be used to introduce individual sections of a list. Capitalize the first word following the dash. Use periods, not semicolons, at the end of each section. Example: *Jones gave the following reasons:*
   —He never ordered the package.
   —If he did, it didn't come.
   —If it did, he sent it back.

WITH SPACES: Put a space on both sides of a dash in all uses except the start of a paragraph and sports agate summaries.

ellipsis (. . .) In general, treat an ellipsis as a three-letter word, constructed with three periods and two spaces, as shown here.

Use an ellipsis to indicate the deletion of one or more words in condensing quotes, texts, and documents. Be especially careful to avoid deletions that would distort the meaning.

hyphen (-) Hyphens are joiners. Use them to avoid ambiguity or to form a single idea from two or more words.

Some guidelines:

AVOID AMBIGUITY: Use a hyphen whenever ambiguity would result if it were omitted: The president will speak to small-business men. (*Businessmen* normally is one word. But *the president will speak to small businessmen* is unclear.)

COMPOUND MODIFIERS: When a compound modifier—two or more words that express a single concept—precedes a noun, use hyphens to link all the words in the compound except the adverb *very* and all adverbs that end in *-ly*; *a first-quarter touchdown, a bluish-green dress, a full-time job, a well-known man, a very good time, an easily remembered rule.*

TWO-THOUGHT COMPOUNDS: *serio-comic, socio-economic.*

COMPOUND PROPER NOUNS AND ADJECTIVES: Use a hyphen to designate dual heritage: *Italian-American, Mexican-American.*

No hyphen, however, for *French Canadian* or *Latin American.*

AVOID DUPLICATED VOWELS, TRIPLED CONSONANTS: Examples: *anti-intellectual, pre-empt, shell-like.*

SUSPENSIVE HYPHENATION: The form: *He received a 10- to 20-year sentence in prison.*

parentheses ( ) In general, be sparing with them.

Parenthesis are jarring to the reader.

The temptation to use parentheses is a clue that a sentences is becoming contorted. Try to write it another way. If a sentence must contain incidental material, then commas or two dashes are frequently more effective. Use these alternatives whenever possible.

There are occasions, however, when parentheses are the only effective means of inserting necessary background or reference information. When they are necessary, follow these guidelines:

PUNCTUATION: Place a period outside a closing parenthesis if the material inside is not a sentence (*such as this fragment*).

(*An independent parenthetical sentence such as this one takes a period before the closing parenthesis.*)

When a phrase placed in parentheses (*this one is an example*) might normally qualify as a complete sentence but is dependent on the surrounding material, do not capitalize the first word or end with a period.

INSERTIONS IN A PROPER NAME: Use parentheses if a state name or similar information is inserted within a proper name: *The Huntsville (Ala.) Times.* But use commas if no proper name is involved: *The Selma, Ala., group saw the governor.*

NEVER USED: Do not use parentheses to denote a political figure's party affiliation and jurisdiction. Instead, set them off with commas.

periods (.) Follow these guidelines:

END OF DECLARATIVE SENTENCE: *The stylebook is finished.*

END OF A MILDLY IMPERATIVE SENTENCE: *Shut the door.* Use an exclamation point only if greater emphasis is desired: *Be careful!*

END OF SOME RHETORICAL QUESTIONS: A period is preferable if a statement is more a suggestion than a question: *Why don't we go.*

END OF AN INDIRECT QUESTION: *He asked what the score was.*

INITIALS: *John F. Kennedy, T.S. Eliot* (No space between *T.* and *S.,* to prevent them from being placed on two lines in typesetting.)

Abbreviations using only the initials of a name do not take periods: *JFK, LBJ.*

ENUMERATIONS: After numbers or letters in enumerating elements of a summary: *1. Wash the car. 2. Clean the basement.* Or: *A. Punctuate properly. B. Write simply.*

PLACEMENT WITH QUOTATION MARKS: Periods always go inside quotation marks.

question mark (?) Follow these guidelines:

END OF A DIRECT QUESTION: *Who started the riot?*

INTERPOLATED QUESTION: *You told me—Did I hear you correctly? —that you started the riot.*

MULTIPLE QUESTION: Use a single question mark at the end of the full sentence:

Did you hear him say, "What right have you to ask about the riot?"

Or, to cause full stops and throw emphasis on each element, break into separate sentences: *Did he plan the riot? Employ assistants? Give the signal to begin?*

CAUTION: Do not use question marks to indicate the end of indirect questions:

He asked who started. the riot. To ask why the riot started is unnecessary. I want to know what the cause of the riot was. How foolish it is to ask what caused the riot.

QUESTION AND ANSWER FORMAT: Do not use quotation marks. Paragraph each speaker's words:

Q: Where did you keep it?
A: In a little tin box.

PLACEMENT WITH QUOTATION MARKS: Inside or outside, depending on the meaning:

Who wrote "Gone With the Wind"?
He asked, "How long will it take?"
MISCELLANEOUS: The question mark supersedes the comma that normally is used when supplying attribution for a quotation: *"Who is there?" she asked.*

quotation marks (" ") The basic guidelines for open-quote marks (") and close-quote marks ("):

FOR DIRECT QUOTATIONS: To surround the exact words of a speaker or writer when reported in a story:

"I have no intention of staying," he replied.
"I do not object," he said, "to the tenor of the report."
Franklin said, "A penny saved is a penny earned."
A speculator said the practice is "too conservative for inflationary times."

RUNNING QUOTATIONS: If a full paragraph of quoted material is followed by a paragraph that continues the quotation, do not put close-quote marks at the end of the first paragraph. Do, however, put open-quote marks at the start of the second paragraph. Continue in this fashion for any succeeding paragraphs, using close-quote marks only at the end of the quoted material.

If a paragraph does not start with quotation marks but ends with a quotation that is continued in the next paragraph, do not use close-quote marks at the end of the introductory paragraph if the quoted material constitutes a full sentence. Use close-quote marks, however, if the quoted material does not constitute a full sentence. For example:

He said, "I am shocked and horrified by the incident.

"I am so horrified, in fact, that I will ask for the death penalty."

But: *He said he was "shocked and horrified by the incident."*

"I am so horrified, in fact, that I will ask for the death penalty," he said.

DIALOGUE OR CONVERSATION: Each person's words, no mater how brief, are placed in a separate paragraph, with quotation marks at the beginning and the end of each person's speech.

"Will you go?"

"Yes."

"When?"

"Thursday."

NOT IN Q-AND-A: Quotation marks are not required in formats that identify questions and answers by *Q:* and *A:*.

NOT IN TEXTS: Quotation marks are not required in full texts, condensed texts or textual excerpts.

IRONY: Put quotation marks around a word or words used in an ironical sense: *The "debate" turned into a free-for-all.*

UNFAMILIAR TERMS: A word or words being introduced to readers may be placed in quotation marks on first reference:

Broadcast frequencies are measured in "kilohertz."

Do not put subsequent references to *kilohertz* in quotation marks.

AVOID UNNECESSARY FRAGMENTS: Do not use quotation marks to report a few ordinary words that a speaker or writer has used:

Wrong: *The senator said he would "go home to Michigan" if he lost the election.*

Right: *The senator said he would go home to Michigan if he lost the election.*

PARTIAL QUOTES: When a partial quote is used, do not put quotation marks around words that the speaker could not have used.

Suppose the individual said, *"I am horrified at your slovenly manners."*

Wrong: *She said she "was horrified at their slovenly manners."*

Right: *She said she was horrified at their "slovenly manners."*

Better when practical: Use the full quote.

QUOTES WITHIN QUOTES: Alternate between double quotation marks (" or ") and single marks (' or '):

She said, "I quote from his letter, 'I agree with Kipling that "the female of the species is more deadly than the male," but the phenomenon is not an unchangeable law of nature,' a remark he did not explain."

Use three marks together if two quoted elements end at the same time: *She said, "He told me, 'I love you.'"*

PLACEMENT WITH OTHER PUNCTUATION: Follow these long-established printers' rules:

—The period and the comma always go within the quotation marks.

—The dash, the semicolon, the question mark and the exclamation point go within the quotation marks when they apply to the quoted matter only. They go outside when they apply to the whole sentence.

semicolon (;) In general, use the semicolon to indicate a greater separation of thought and information than a comma can convey but less than the separation that a period implies.

The basic guidelines:

TO CLARIFY A SERIES: *He leaves a son, John Smith of Chicago; three daughters, Jane Smith of Wichita, Kan., Mary Smith of Denver, and Susan, wife of William Kingsbury of Boston; and a sister, Martha, wife of Robert Warren of Omaha, Neb.*

Note that the semicolon is used before the final *and* in such a series.

PLACEMENT WITH QUOTES: Place semicolons outside quotation marks.

Glossary

advance: a story about a coming event.

aperture: lens opening. The aperture limits the amount of light that can reach the film.

attribution: telling the reader exactly where or from whom information was obtained.

back-up quote: a quote intended to support the lead in a story.

backlighting: photographic situation when the light source is coming from behind the subject instead of from behind the photographer.

beat reporter: reporter assigned to check the same news source for each issue of the paper (for example, art, music, theater, police administration).

bleed: to let a picture run off the edges of a page.

brainstorming: the art of obtaining many ideas in a short time.

broadcast journalism: journalism produced on radio or television.

business manager: person on the staff of a publication in charge of advertising sales and preparation, circulation, and record keeping.

"by authority": most early American newspapers were published with this statement, which meant they had the government's approval.

byline: the name and often the title of the writer of a story.

call to action: that part of an advertisement urging the reader to take some specific action, such as calling for information or buying the product.

camera-ready copy: copy prepared so that the headlines, body type, and art are already set, positioned, and ready to be photographed.

caption: copy used under or with a photograph. It identifies what or who is in the picture and where it was taken. (Also called **cutline**.)

chronological style: story written in the order in which it occurred.

civil libel: written defamation of an identified individual, group, or corporation.

cliché: overused, overworked, old, and trite expression (for example, busy bees, blushing bride, dull thud).

close-up: a portrait-like camera shot showing a person's head and neckline.

color sidebar: See **sidebar**.

"composite characters": fictional characters a news writer creates by using characteristics of several real people. The creation of composite characters is generally frowned upon by ethical journalists.

computer-assisted reporting: using various news databases and other resources to facilitate the gathering of certain kinds of news information.

conflict: an element of news that involves tension, surprise, and suspense, and arises with any good story topic—sports, war, elections.

consequence: element of news that refers to the importance of an event. The greater the consequence, the greater the news value.

contact sheet: a sheet of photographs, printed negative size, from which photo selection is made.

copy: typed manuscript version of stories, cutlines, and the like, from which type is set.

copy editing: reviewing final copy for errors in mechanics, facts, and style.

CPU: the central processing unit of a computer; it controls everything the computer does.

credibility: ability to be believed and trusted.

criminal libel: defamatory statements that might bring about public anger, revolt, or disturbance of the peace.

cropping: the cutting or marking of a photograph to eliminate unnecessary material and highlight important elements.

cub reporter: a novice reporter assigned to pick up brief items or do weekly checks with sources for news.

darkroom: room with little or no light where film can be developed and prints made.

depth of field: the area in clear focus in front of and behind the subject being photographed.

desktop publishing: using a desktop computer to set and design type, edit, produce graphics, and determine page layout.

direct quotation: the exact words of a speaker. Direct quotes are set off in type with quotation marks.

dolly: to move a television camera toward or away from the subject.

dominant element: the strongest element on a page, usually a large photo, which leads the reader into the page.

double-truck: a double-page spread.

down style: a headline style in which all letters, except the first letter of the first word and proper nouns, are set lowercase.

dummy: a diagram or blueprint for setting up a page for space and placement of copy, headlines, artwork, photos, and other elements.

duotones: photographs printed in two colors. One is almost always black; the other may be any color.

editorial: a relatively short, usually unsigned column offering the opinion of the newspaper on a variety of topics.

editorial column: a column expressing the opinions of the writer, usually signed. An editorial column appears on the editorial page.

editorial page: a section of the newspaper reserved for editorials and various other pieces that contain opinion rather than objective reporting.

editorial page editor: works closely with the managing editor to plan the editorial page. Writes or directs staff to write the editorials that express the newspaper's opinions, the editorial columns, or editorial features.

editorial policy: a statement of the position of the paper on various editorial issues. It includes such things as whose viewpoint the editorials represent, how the newspaper handles letters to the editor, how monies from ads will be handled, etc.

elements of news or news values: the basic elements of news are timeliness, human interest, proximity, prominence, consequence, and conflict. These elements make the information more interesting and useful to the reader or listener.

embargo: request delay of a news story or release until a specified date and time.

end sign: 30 or pound sign #. Either symbol placed at the end of copy signifies "the end" of the copy.

enlarger: a device that allows photographic negatives to be projected at various sizes and then printed.

"est" question: question built around an "-est" word—biggest, proudest, greatest, etc. Most interviewers avoid such questions (e.g., "What was the happiest moment in your life?") because they seem juvenile and often elicit simplistic answers.

establishing shot: a camera shot that shows the subject as well as its position and relation to its entire surroundings; a variation of a long shot.

ethics: a system of moral principles.

evergreen: a term applied to material acceptable for publication at any time. Timeliness is not a factor in the material.

eyeline: one piece of horizontal white space that goes across a spread.

f/stop: a scale for measuring the position at which a lens opening is set.

fair comment and criticism: a complete libel defense protecting a journalist's opinion of public figures or review of books or records, movies, theatrical events, public entertainments, or the public part of a performance or creative art.

feature story: a story that focuses more on entertaining than on simply informing the audience. Feature stories may be written on virtually any topic.

featurize: in sportswriting, making a game story into a feature by injecting anecdotes, background information, and the like.

filter question: a question designed to eliminate people who don't belong to the desired population, posed at the beginning of a survey. "Are you eighteen years old?" would be appropriate filter question in a survey designed to find out about students' voting habits.

five W's and the H: Who, What, When, Where, Why, and How. These elements belong in nearly every newspaper story.

fixer: fixing bath that makes a film image permanent. The film coating not blackened during the development is dissolved away in this solution and the film emulsion is hardened to prevent scratching of the finished negatives.

flair: quality of writing that makes it creative, original, and memorable.

flash synchronization speed: the fastest shutter speed that can be used with a flash to get a properly exposed picture.

flush left: a positioning of copy so that it rests squarely against the left-hand side of the column.

focus: Adjustment of the camera focusing lens closer to or farther from the film so that the subject will appear sharp (in focus) on the developed film.

fold: The imaginary horizontal line across the middle of the page, or where the newspaper could be folded in half.

font: all characters in one size of one particular typeface (e.g., 10-point Palatino) or, more commonly, an entire typeface (Palatino).

formal interview: an interview, set up and planned in advance, in which the reporter's primary purpose is to paint a clear verbal picture of the interviewee.

Forum Theory: the idea that once a forum, or place where ideas are exchanged, is created, the ideas expressed there cannot later be controlled.

future book: a chronological listing of events coming up that you might want to cover. A long-range calendar of events and ideas.

game story: a sports story recounting the play-by-play activities of a game.

general assignment reporter: person who writes articles or does the work on any subject assigned as the editor sees fit.

global village: the concept, so named by Marshall McLuhan, that the world has become a more tightly interrelated community because of simultaneous broadcast of significant events.

grid format: a layout format based upon a series of narrow or "mini" columns used to create areas of planned white space.

gutters: the spaces between columns or between facing pages.

halftone: a screen that prepares a photographic image for reproduction by converting it into a series of very small dots.

hammer: a headline style featuring one or more lines of primary head over one or more lines of secondary head.

hard news: news involving timely, significant events, such as an election, a speech by a public official, or a report on a budget meeting.

headline: a brief description of the contents of a news story printed in larger type, usually above the story.

human interest story: story that causes the reader to feel such emotions as sorrow, pity, or amazement.

image editing: changing, adjusting, or cleaning up photographic images by means of certain computer programs.

in loco parentis: the legal idea that school authorities act "in place of the parent" and assume a parent's rights, duties, and responsibilities.

in-depth reporting: reporting that uses extensive research and interviews to provide a detailed account of a significant story.

inverted pyramid: a style of newswriting in which the main facts go at the top of the article (the lead). The facts become less significant until, toward the bottom, they may be dispensable. This gives the reader the essential facts first and permits expansion or contraction in editing and page layout.

ISO: a standard measure of the speed of film. A film with a higher ISO is more light sensitive than one with a lower ISO. (Formerly called ASA)

jargon: the inside language of specific groups, such as computer users or members of a particular profession. Jargon that is meaningless to the general public should be avoided in student publications.

jump: to continue a story from one page to another.

justified: type set even on both sides of a column.

kicker: a headline style featuring one secondary headline over one or more lines of primary headline.

ladder diagram: a planning device designating what goes on specific pages (as in a yearbook).

laser printer: a printer that uses a laser beam to form characters and graphic images onto paper, similar to a photocopier.

lead: the first paragraph of a news story. It often consists of just one sentence.

leading: the white space between lines of type.

lens: The eye of the camera, designed to control the amount of light admitted. Lenses vary from single pieces of ground and polished glass to complex and expensive groupings of several glass elements.

libel: written defamation; damaging false statements against another person or institution that appear in writing or are spoken (broadcast) from a written script.

"limited effects": the notion that consumers have psychological defenses by which they resist and mold messages from the mass media to fit their own needs.

localization: writing a regional, national, or even international story to bring out the local angle.

logotype: a distinctive treatment of the brand or company name. Also known as the signature, slug, or nameplate. An important layout element in every advertisement.

long shot: a camera shot that shows the main visual subject in its surroundings.

maestro: method of planning pages or sections of publications using writers, editors, photographers, and designers all working together. Also called the team or WED approach.

mainbar: of several stories about a topic on one page of a paper, the main story that brings the issue into sharp focus.

managing editor (editor-in-chief): the person with overall responsibility for the news operation or publication.

market survey: a series of questions designed to get information about specific habits or preferences of a particular audience (market).

masthead: a statement printed in all editions of a newspaper, generally on the editorial page, indicating the publication's name, publisher, editor, staff members, and the like.

medium long shot: a camera shot in which an entire subject appears, with a little space above and below.

medium shot: a camera shot in which the body of the person is cut off just below the waist.

mini-torial: a very brief editorial, usually one or two sentences.

modular design: a design style that uses rectangular, easy-to-visualize blocks.

monologophobia: a term coined by Theodore Bernstein to describe the fear of repeating a word. Also called the "elongated yellow fruit" (rather than "banana") school of writing.

muckraking: journalism that crusades for social justice or to expose wrongdoing.

network: a way for computers to be connected together so that information can be easily passed between them.

news editor: the chief copy editor.

news feature: a feature story related to a breaking or developing news story.

news judgment: the knowledge and instinct a reporter or editor calls on to determine whether an event is news.

news peg: a sentence or paragraph connecting a news-feature story to a specific item of news.

news release: notice sent to the media by a school, business, or organization to alert the public to an important announcement or event.

news-brief format: a condensation of a lengthy story into a sentence or two, usually used to summarize fairly routine stories when space is needed.

newspaper style: guidelines that include standardized forms for capitalization, abbreviation, and spelling. They are set forth in a publication's stylebook and establish consistency for the reader.

nugget: a fact or bit of information that will stick in the audience's minds and make them remember the story.

nut graph: the paragraph within the introduction to an in-depth story that foreshadows the rest of the story; a sort of internal lead.

objectivity: ability to make fair, neutral observations about people and events.

off the record: an agreement reached before an interview begins that the interviewer will not print the information the interviewee provides or will not attribute it to the source if printed.

open-ended question: a question that is structured to allow the interviewee latitude in answering. The structure of an open-ended question does not allow for a simple one-word answer.

optical center: in an advertisement, about two-thirds of the way up from the bottom of the ad. (This is not the physical center of the space.)

pan: to move a television camera head left to right to capture horizontal motion.

paraphrase: to put the speaker's words into the reporter's own words without changing the meaning or inserting opinion. Used to clarify lengthy, fuzzy, or complicated thoughts. Paraphrased material is not enclosed in quotation marks.

partial quote: a quotation using just a few words from a speaker's statement.

partisan press: Early American newspapers that allied themselves with one political party. This was commonplace during the Revolutionary period.

pasteup: pasting type to a grid sheet in preparation for printing. The pasteup shows what the page will look like when printed.

penny press: in the mid-nineteenth century, Benjamin Day founded the *New York Sun* and sold it for a penny. Others soon imitated this new type of paper, which was filled with news, achieved a mass audience, and carried advertising.

personality profile: a thorough, in-depth feature story about one person.

photo essay: a story told in pictures. It often involves three to seven photographs with captions.

photo series: a series of photos that shows how something has changed or developed over time.

pica: a unit of measurement in design. There are 12 points in a pica and 6 picas in one inch.

plagiarism: taking and using as one's own the writings or inventions of another person.

point: a measurement of type sizes. There are 12 points in a pica and 72 points in an inch.

point-counterpoint: a technique in which the opinions of individuals with opposing viewpoints on a topic are run in side-by-side opinion articles.

postgame story: a sports feature written after the event. It may be a sideline story, background story, sports interview, or locker-room story.

pregame story: an advance story on a sports event. It may include background and information on both teams.

press: a word used to refer to the print and electronic news media—radio, television, newspapers, magazines, and all other news-gathering and disseminating agencies.

primary source: a person whose business it is to have the best and most reliable information about the topic. Especially important in interviewing.

prior restraint: censorship banning publication of certain material. This is illegal in the United States except in the rarest of circumstances, usually pertaining to national security in wartime.

privileged statements: statements made on the floor of Congress, the state legislature, or a courtroom that if published are immune from libel suits.

program director: the person in charge of all on-air programming; determines the programming schedule and mix and the choice of announcers.

prominence: an element of news that refers to how well known an individual is in the community, school, or nation.

proximity: an element of news that refers to the geographic nearness of a given event to your place of publication or your readers.

public relations: communication of information between an organization, company, or group and some particular audience to achieve a specific response.

Publick Occurrences: the first newspaper in the American colonies, published in Boston in 1690 by Benjamin Harris. It lasted only one issue before the British authorities stopped it.

publics: various groups or audiences to whom public relations goals and activities may be directed.

publisher: person or body that owns, runs, or controls a publication, setting broad guidelines and general policies.

Q and A: a technique for writing an interview story in which the reporter's exact questions are reported, followed by the source's exact answers.

question lead: a lead that begins with a question. This kind of lead gives little information and is generally to be avoided.

quote lead: a lead that begins with an unattributed quote. This kind of lead is unclear and should usually be avoided.

ragged: type that is set uneven. Often type will be justified on the left and ragged on the right.

RAM: the Random Access Memory in a computer, reserved for information being temporarily put into or taken out of a computer. Desktop publishing requires a high amount of RAM.

random sample: a sample of a population to be surveyed in which every member of the population has an equal possibility of being included in the survey sample.

redundancy: using words or phrases together so that they say the same thing twice (for example, 2 **a.m.** in the morning, a spherical globe).

reporters: the people who carry out the assignments that have been determined by the news editor in conference with the managing editor and the publication's adviser.

right of reply or **simultaneous rebuttal:** Permitting a person criticized in a story to respond to that criticism in the same story.

rule of thirds: method of composing photographs in which the field of vision is divided into thirds horizontally and vertically and the image placed at the intersection of any two lines.

scanner: digitizing equipment that scans and transfers visual material, such as illustration or type, to a computer.

schedule: a list compiled by the editor of everything on each page, including lengths of stories and sizes of pictures.

screens: devices the printer uses when preparing pictures for printing. Halftone screens are used to prepare photos for reproduction, as well as textured screens for special effects.

sexist language: terms and general word choice that suggests that all people are men (or, in rare cases, women)—for example, "mailman," "Everyone . . . her."

shock jock: radio commentator who entertains his or her audience by saying outrageous, often vulgar or offensive, things about people or situations.

shutter: the part of a camera that is released to take a picture. The shutter may be a flap that covers an opening near the lens, or it may be made like a window blind in front of the film in the rear of the camera.

sidebar: a story supplementing, but kept separate from, another story on the same subject in the same issue of the paper.

simultaneous rebuttal: See **right of reply**.

sizing: Reducing or enlarging a cropped photo to exactly fit the space indicated on the layout.

slander: a damaging false statement against another person or institution spoken or broadcast extemporaneously.

slanguage: in sportswriting, trite expressions stemming from the jargon of sports (for example, pigskin for football, grapplers for wrestlers).

slug: brief identifying name (usually one or two words) for a story. Used on copy, page layouts, and the schedule.

soft news: stories that are considered to be not immediately important or significant to a wide audience, such as personality feature stories or "news you can use" columns.

station manager: the highest-ranking student on a broadcast staff; supervises the various department directors and acts as liaison between them and the faculty advisory board.

stepped head: headline set so that each line is indented more than the one above, giving a stairstep effect.

stock question: an all-purpose question usable in any situation—for example, "What are your immediate and long-term goals?"

streamer or **banner:** a headline that stretches across the columns of the page.

student news bureau: an organization set up to provide information about a school to its publics.

stylebook: a book setting forth all the style decisions made for a publication—for example, when to abbreviate, preferred spellings for certain words, etc. The stylebook is to be followed by all writers.

subjective writing: writing that expresses the writer's opinion and viewpoint. Subjective writing in a newspaper belongs on the editorial page.

summary lead: a lead that provides the briefest possible summary of the major facts of a story in the first sentence.

target audience: the particular audience selected to receive a message.

tease: use a lead that coaxes readers into a story by making them read further to see what the lead really means.

technical director: the person in charge of installation and maintenance of all broadcast equipment at a station.

test strip: in photo development, a series of print strips made at different exposures to determine the most appropriate one for the final print.

testimonial: a statement attesting to the value of something.

theme copy: copy in a yearbook that explains and develops the theme chosen for the book.

tiebacks: details that relate a news story to last week's, last month's, or last year's related development.

tilt: to move a television camera head up or down to create a vertical image.

timeliness: an element of news that has to do with how new or current the event is.

tombstoning: placing of headlines of equal or similar size beside each other.

track: capture horizontal movement by moving a television camera left to right.

transition: words, phrases, or even whole paragraphs that hold a story together and smooth the shift from one topic to another.

typeface: the style of type a publication uses.

verbatim transcript: a technique, often called the "Q and A" system, in which the reporter's exact questions are reproduced, followed by the source's exact answers. A verbatim transcript of an interview requires a tape recorder for accuracy. The term can also refer to printing the exact text of a speech or message.

viewfinder: an ordinary sighting frame or a complicated device with lenses that enables the photographer to compose the desired picture before it is taken.

Watergate: the term applied to the whole series of events developing from the break-in at the Democratic Party headquarters at the Watergate apartment complex and leading to the resignation of President Richard M. Nixon.

WED: the concept of planning pages or sections of publications using **w**riters, **e**ditors, and **d**esigners all working together. Also called the team or maestro approach.

white space: the empty space in ads or page design that helps emphasize the message. Used effectively, white space attracts the reader's eye.

wicket: a headline design consisting of two or more lines of secondary head over one or more lines of primary head.

"wild art": art not associated with any particular story. These pictures are usually feature-oriented and are published principally because they are entertaining and catch the reader's attention. They also break up otherwise heavy layouts.

wire services: organizations that provide news from around the world to publications that subscribe for a fee. Some frequently used wire services are the Associated Press, United Press International, Reuters, and The New York Times Service.

word processing: the editing, storage, and reproduction of words by means of certain computer programs.

yellow journalism: a sensational brand of journalism given to hoaxes, altered photographs, screaming headlines, frauds, and endless promotions of the newspaper themselves. The term derives from the name of the Yellow Kid, a cartoon character popular in the late nineteenth century.

zoom: manipulate the lens of a camera to create the appearance of moving closer to or farther away from the subject.

Acknowledgments

The authors thank the following for their generous help in revising this edition of *Journalism Today*.

Reviewers, Advisers, and Instructors

Richard Johns, Executive Director, *Quill and Scroll*
Patricia Kappemeyer, Churchill High School, San Antonio, Texas
Lorraine Liverpool, Cooper City High School, Cooper City, Florida
Carolyn Phipps, Wooddale High School, Memphis, Tennessee
Laura Schaub, Executive Director, Oklahoma Interscholastic Press Association

Student Publications

The All-Stater, University of Nebraska journalism workshop
The American, Independence High School, San Jose, California
Arlingtonian, Upper Arlington High School, Columbus, Ohio
Beak 'n Eye, West High School, Davenport, Iowa
The Bear Facts, Hastings High School, Alief, Texas
Big Stick, Roosevelt High School, San Antonio, Texas
Black & White, Walt Whitman High School, Bethesda, Maryland
Blue Jay Free Flyer, Worthington Community College, Worthington, Minnesota
Bugle Call, R. E. Lee High School, San Antonio, Texas
The Cavalcade, W. T. Woodson High School, Fairfax, Virginia

The Central Times, Naperville Central High School, Naperville, Illinois
The Chronicle, Harvard-Westlake School, North Hollywood, California
College Clamor, Mott Community College, Flint, Michigan
The Contact Lens, University of Nebraska
The Devil's Advocate, Hinsdale Central High School, Hinsdale, Illinois
The Echoes, Abraham Lincoln High School, Council Bluffs, Iowa
The Explosion, Glendale High School, Glendale, California
Featherduster, Westlake High School, Austin, Texas
Finest Hours, Winston Churchill High School, Potomac, Maryland
Flyer, Brentwood School, Los Angeles, California
The Fourth Estate, Bartlesville High School, Bartlesville, Oklahoma
Green Mountain High School, Lakewood, Colorado
The Hi-Lite, Carmel High School, Carmel, Indiana
Hi-Spot, Waverly High School, Waverly, Nebraska
Hiways, Hialeah High School, Hialeah, Florida
The Lakewood Times, Lakewood High School, Lakewood, Ohio
Lincoln East High School, Lincoln, Nebraska
Lincoln High School, Gahanna, Ohio
The Lion, Lyons Township High School, Lyons, Illinois
Little Hawk, City High School, Iowa City, Iowa
The Lone Star Dispatch, James Bowie High School, Austin, Texas
Midland High School, Midland, Michigan

The Miller Insight, Yukon High School, Yukon, Oklahoma

Munster High School Crier, Munster, Indiana

Oracle, East High School, Lincoln, Nebraska

The Panther, Miami Palmetto Senior High School, Miami, Florida

The Peninsula Outlook, Gig Harbor High School, Gig Harbor, Washington

The Rustler, Fremont Senior High School, Fremont, Nebraska

Saratoga Falcon, Saratoga High School, Saratoga, California

The Stinger, Emmaus High School, Emmaus, Pennsylvania

Stratford High School, Nashville, Tennessee

Teen Perspective, Marquette University Summer Journalism Workshop

Tiger Tales, Joliet Township High School, West Campus, Joliet, Illinois

The Tower, Grosse Pointe South High School, Grosse Pointe Farms, Michigan

Treasure Chest, Putnam City High School, Oklahoma City, Oklahoma

Westwind, West Henderson High School, Henderson, North Carolina

Charles Wright Academy, Tacoma, Washington

X-Ray, St. Charles High School, St. Charles, Illinois

Professional Publications and Organizations

American Advertising Federation

American Society of Newspaper Editors

The Associated Press

Chicago Tribune

Dubuque Telegraph Herald

The New York Times

Public Relations Society of America

Society of Professional Journalists

Southfield Public Schools/Kenson Siver

United Press International

Literary Credits

Pp. 176–77: From "The Gambler, the Nun, and the Radio." Excerpted with permission of Scribner, a Division of Simon & Schuster, from WINNER TAKE NOTHING by Ernest Hemingway. Copyright 1933 Charles Scribner's Sons. Copyright renewed © 1961 by Mary Hemingway.

Pp. 458–86: Excerpted from *The Associated Press Stylebook and Libel Manual,* Sixth Trade Edition. Norm Goldstein, ed. Reading, Mass.: Addison-Wesley Publishing Company, Inc., 1996. Reprinted with permission of the Associated Press.

Photographs

The authors wish to thank the students and staff of Larkin High School (Elgin, Illinois), Niles West High School (Skokie, Illinois), and Evanston Township High School (Evanston, Illinois), for their cooperation in the photographic illustration of this text.

Jeff Ellis, photographer, pages 3, 20, 30, 66, 88, 97, 100, 120, 140, 153, 198, 205, 211, 225, 244, 251, 283, 306, 312, 314, 347, 351, 352, 360, 364, 378, 386, 392, 401, 409, 410, 431, 438, 442, 450

Bradley Wilson, photographer, 73, 341, 403, 406, 413, 422, 423

AP/Wide World Photos: 16, 44, 50, 68, 110, 126, 158, 169, 180, 181, 185, 190, 344, 368, 412; Black Star: page 41, John Harrington; page 192, Dennis Brack; Chicago Daily Defender: 12; The Chicago Tribune: 18, 90, 114–19, 240–43; © Corbis: page 427; Corbis-Bettmann: pages 8, 9; Finley Holiday Film/NASA: 171; Gamma Liaison: page 59, Walter Stricklin/Atlanta Journal-Constitution; page 136, Diana Walker; page 147, Brad Markel; page 162, G.B. Rose; page 292, Cynthia Johnson; The Image Works: pages v, xx, 293, 352, Bob Daemmrich; page 30 (t), J. Fossett; Courtesy InterZine Productions, Inc.: 253; PhotoEdit: page 63, Tom Prettyman; pages 104, 353, Michael Newman; page 176, Robert Brenner; pages xiii, 262, 264, 272, 400, Tony Freeman; page 268, Kathy Ferguson; pages 280, 285, David Young-Wolff; St. Louis Post-Dispatch: 47; Stock Boston: pages 62, 191, 269, Bob Daemmrich; page 89, Lalma Druskis; page 247, Ellis Herwig/PNI; page 428, Richard Pasley; The Stock Market: page 28, Thomas Ives; page 151, David Pollack; Tony Stone Images: page 25, J.P. Williams; pages vi, 56, 362, Bob Daemmrich; page 367, Richard Brown; UPI/Corbis-Bettmann: page 13.

Individuals

The authors also thank the following individuals for their important contributions to this text: Terry Anderson; Jody Beck; Jack Botts; Linda Butler; Alfred Geduldig; Dr. Loyal N. Gould; Deanne Kunz; Jimmy Langham; C. Bickford Lucas; Diane McClain; Mike Patten; Susan Bridges Patten; Thomas L. Pendleton; Laura Plachecki; Mary Kay Quinlan; B.C. Rafferty; Barbara R. Sarnataro; Jacqueline Sharkey; Lynn Silhasek; Lynn Smith; Stephen A. Smith; and Holly Spence.

Index

Abbott, Robert S., 11
ABC (American Broadcasting Company), 14, 15
Abilene Reporter-News, 437
Accuracy, 34–35
    checking for, 208–9
    in quoting, 169–70
Action stories, 153–54
Active verbs in headlines, 216
Adams, Katherine, 357
Admission of error as libel defense, 43
Advance news items, 63
Advertising, 27–28, 52
    calculating cost of, 383–85, 396
    checklist for, 393
    contracts for, 382, 384
    developing concepts for, 385–87
    editorial, 390
    to finance yearbook, 311–12
    layout for, 389, 391
    in penny press, 8
    preparation to sell, 377–80
    principles of, 376–77
    in school newspapers, 376–77, 396
    selling, 381–85
    space allotted to, 383
    working with printer of, 391–92
    writing copy for, 387–89, 396
Advertising director, 399

Advertorials, 390
Adviser, yearbook, 329
Advocacy ads, 390
African-American magazines, 12
African-American newspapers, 11–12
Alice's Adventures in Wonderland (Carroll), 170
Allen, Fred, 14
Alliteration in headlines, 216–17
American Broadcasting Company. *See* ABC
America Online, 17, 453. *See also* Internet
Anna Karenina (Tolstoy), 128
Answers as function of editorial, 282
AP lead. *See* Summary lead
Arizona Daily Star, 457
Armstrong, Neil, 171
Arnett, Peter, 16
Artists, 91
Art/technology coordinator, 239
Ascenders, 221
Asian-American Journalists Association, 12
Asian-American newspapers, 12
Associated Press, 9, 21, 89, 133, 452, 454
Attribution
    in broadcast writing, 346
    as defense to libel, 41–42
    editing of, 210

    as ethical principle, 37
    need for, 177–78
    in summary lead, 127
    word choice for, 175–77, 183
Audience analysis, 61–62
Auman, Ann, 450
Availability sample, 74, 79

Backlighting, 424–25
Back-up quote, 148, 165
Bagdikian, Ben, 23
Bailon, Gilbert, 81
Bainbridge Island (Wash.) *Review,* 32
Balance in design, 227
Baseline, 221
Beat reporters, 84
Bennett, James Gordon, 8
Benny, Jack, 14
The Bergen County (N. J.) *Record,* 31
Bernays, Edward L., 360, 370
Bernstein, Carl, 110, 189, 201
Bernstein, Theodore, 163
Bias, 292
Bill of Rights, 7, 192. *See also specific amendment*
Black Enterprise, 12
Black Entertainment Network, 12
Bleed, 233
Bly, Nellie (Elizabeth Cockrane), 9–10

Boca Raton (Fla.) *News,* 95
Boeing 757, 188–89
Bold typeface, 221
Bookkeeping, *See* Record-keeping
The Boston Globe, 31
Boston News-Letter, 5, 8
Boston Transcript, 8
Boulder Daily Camera, 95
Brady, John, 105
Brady, Matthew, 405
Brainard, Paul, 441–42
Brainstorming sessions, 69–71, 79, 385
Brandeis, Louis, 192
British government, regulation of
   American newspapers, 5
Broadcasting, 341
   careers in, 352, 354
   school, 341–42, 347–52, 354
   writing for, 342–47, 354
Broadcast standards, 348
Buchwald, Art, 291
Budget for yearbook, 311
Bulletin board column, 193
Business director, 351
Business manager on yearbook staff, 332
Business staff, 375–76
   duties of, 392–94

Cable News Network. *See* CNN
Call to action, 389, 396
Camacho, Olga, 417
Camera-ready copy, 392
Cameras, 419, 426, 452, 455. *See also*
   Darkroom; Film; Photos/photography
Camera terms, 346
Campbell, John, 5
Capitalization in headlines, 216
Caples, John, 388
Capote, Truman, 198, 200
Captions
   as photographer's responsibility,
     409–10
   for yearbook photos, 324
Career profiles
   advertising director (Kent Matlock),
     399
   art/technology coordinator (Bryan
     Monroe), 239
   columnist (Dinah Eng), 113
   editor (Gilbert Bailon), 81
   editorial cartoonist (Ed Fischer), 305
   electronic journalist (Robert S.
     Cauthron), 457

   executive editor (Addie Rimmer), 95
   feature writer (Nancy Stohs), 259
   graphic designer (Mike Quon), 339
   investigative reporters (Marjie
     Lundstrom and Sam Stanton), 203
   journalism professor (Ben Bagdikian),
     23
   managing editor (Fernando Dovalina),
     145
   media lawyer (Jane Kirtley), 55
   newspaper publisher/editor (Don
     Flores), 437
   photo editor (Olga Camacho), 417
   public relations executive (Elizabeth
     Krupnick), 373
   reporter (Katti Gray), 167
   sports reporter (Valerie Lister), 277
   television anchor (Katherine Adams),
     357
   White House correspondent (Helen
     Thomas), 185
Careers
   in broadcasting, 352, 354
   in public relations, 368, 371
Carroll, Lewis, 170
Cause-effect organization, 343
Cauthorn, Robert S., 457
CBS (Columbia Broadcasting System), 13,
   15, 55
Centered type, 222
Central processing chip, 444
Central Processing Unit. *See* CPU
Chapter One, 341
Charts, 77, 194
Cherokee Phoenix, 12
Chicago Defender, 11–12
Chicago Sun-Times, 31
The Chicago Tribune, 18, 31, 157
Chief engineer, 352
Christians, Clifford G., 362
The Christian Science Monitor, 31, 190,
   191
Chronological style, 153–54
Circulation, 392–94, 396
Civil War, 9, 21
Clarity in writing style, 160
Cleveland Plain Dealer, 31
Clichés, 162–63, 165
Clinton, Bill, 134
Clubs columns, 293–94
CNN (Cable News Network), 15, 16, 26,
   157

Cockrane, Elizabeth (Nellie Bly), 9–10
Collier's, 11, 21, 32
Columbia Broadcasting System. *See* CBS
Columbia Journalism Review, 23, 25
Columnist, 113
Comaneci, Nadia, 269
Combination style of writing news sto-
   ries, 154, 155
Commentary as function of editorial, 286
*Community Newspaper Showcase of
   Excellence,* 32
Comparison organization, 343
Composition, photo, 404–6, 414
CompuServe, 4, 17, 451. *See also* Internet
Computer-assisted reporting, 19, 21
Computers, 443–45, 452
Conclusion in editorials, 288–89, 302
Condensed letters, 221
Cone, Fairfax M., 378
Confidentiality for sources, 110
Conflict as news element, 67, 79
Consequence as news element, 64, 66, 79
Considine, Tim, 272
Consistency, 156, 228
Constitution, 7, 20, 34, 46, 185, 192
Contact sheet, 410
Content in leads, 140–41
Contrast in design, 225, 227
Cooke, Janet, 33
Copy
   advertising, 385–92, 396
   for broadcast, 345–47, 350
   flair in writing, 344–45
   theme, 318–19, 337
   writing yearbook, 322–23, 337
Copy editing, 205–6
   checking for accuracy in, 208–9
   checking for attribution in, 210
   style and grammar in, 209–10
   symbols, 206–8
   writing headlines in, 211–17
Copy editor, 205, 234
Coren, Stanley, 253
Cosby, William, 5
Costs, calculating publication, 383–85
Court TV, 353
CPU, 443, 455
The Craft of Interviewing (Brady), 105
Cranberry Journal (Mars, Pa.), 32
Creative style in feature stories, 249–50
Creativity in writing leads, 130
Credibility, 33–34

Criticism
    as function of editorial, 283
    of the press, 26
Cropping, 411
C-Span television network, 15
Cub reporter, 86

Daguerre, Louis, 405
Daily News Record (Harrisonburg, Va.), 32
Dallas Morning News, 31, 437
Dallas Times Herald, 167, 437
Darkroom. *See also* Cameras; Film;
    Photos/photography
    art *versus* science in, 434
    cleanliness of, 433
    developing film in, 428–30, 435
    making prints in, 430–34
Day, Benjamin, 8
Dear Abby. *See* Van Buren, Abigail
De Forest, Lee, 13
DeMaio, Don, 454
Depth of field, 421
Descenders, 221
Design
    basic principle of, 224–28
    and creating pages, 228–34, 235
    of editorial page, 229
    graphics in, 224, 235
    selecting type for, 217–23
    yearbook, 232–34, 236–37, 325–28,
        337
Designers, 91
Desktop publishing, 441–42, 447–52
The Des Moines (Iowa) *Register,* 31, 198
Details
    in editorials, 288, 302
    in interview story, 106–7
Detroit Free Press, 31
Detroit News, 113
Diario Los Americas, 12
Dickens, Charles, 129
Direct quotations, 169–72
    combining paraphrasing and, 174
Dominant element, 225
DOS (Disk Operating System), 446
Double-truck, 231–32, 235
Dovalina, Fernando, 145
Drake, Sir Francis, 154
Dukakis, Michael, 412

Eagle-Beacon (Wichita, Kans.), 31
Easel, 431–32
Eastman, George, 405
Ebony, 12
Ecclesiastes, 161
Economic function of journalism, 27–28
Editing. *See* Copy editing
Editing the Day's News (Bastian and
    Case), 67
Editor, 90–91
    in chief, 84
    copy, 205, 234
    executive, 95
    letters to, 298
    managing, 81, 84, 91
    news, 84
    photo, 407, 414, 417
    sports, 84
    yearbook, 329–32, 337
Editorial advertisement, 390
Editorial cartoonist, 305
Editorial cartoons, 298, 299
Editorial columns, 290–91, 293–95
Editorial page, 279
    design of, 229
    editorial cartoons on, 298, 299
    editorial columns on, 290–91, 293–95
    letters to the editor on, 296–97
    masthead on, 289–90
    mini-torials on, 299–300
    point-counterpoint on, 298
    random opinion features on, 298
    reviews on, 295–96
Editorial page editor, 84
Editorial policy, 300, 301
Editorials, 279, 301
    criteria for, 287
    functions of, 280–86, 301
    parts of, 287–90, 302
    researching for, 279–80, 302
Editor & Publisher, 157
El Diario-La Prensa, 12
Electronic journalist, 457
El Paso Times, 437
Embargo, 364
Encapsulated PostScript. *See* EPS
Endings, 196–98, 201
Eng, Dinah, 113
Enlarger, 430–32
Entertainment as editorial function, 29,
    52, 284–85
EPS, 449

Essence, 12
Ethics, 52
    in journalism, 33–35, 37, 38–39, 249
    in photography, 412
Evansville Press, 55
Evergreen feature stories, 249, 257
Exchange papers, 393–94
Executive editor, 95
Explanation as function of editorial, 280
Exposures, 423–24, 432
Extended letters, 221
Eyeline, 225, 325, 337
E-zines, 253. *See also* Magazines

Facts, paraphrasing to convey, 173–74
Factsheet 5, 253
Fair comment as libel defense, 42–43
Fairness in journalism, 37
Fair sample, importance of, in polls, 72–75
Family harmony, 221
Fashion and fad columns, 293
Fauquier Citizen (Warrenton, Va.), 32
Feature stories, 247–48
    characteristics of, 248–50
    headlines for, 251
    personality profiles as, 250–51, 252
    in school newspapers, 251–56, 257
    on sports, 270–74
Feature writer, 259
Federal Communications Commission
    (FCC), 14
Federal Radio Commission, 14
Federal Way (Wash.) *News,* 32
Filipino Reporter, 12
Film. *See also* Cameras; Darkroom;
    Photos/photography
    developing, 428–30
    ISO, 423–24
Film reviews, 296
Filter questions, 76
Financing for yearbook, 310–12, 336
First Amendment, 7, 20, 46, 49, 55, 185
Fischer, Ed, 305
Five Ws and the H, 131–32, 143
Flair in writing copy, 344–45
Flash synchronization speed, 425
Floppy disks, 443
Flores, Don, 437
Fonts, 218, 222, 447
Fort Worth Star-Telegram, 167
Forum Theory, 51
Fox television network, 15

Franklin, James, 90
Freedom of the High School Press
    (Kristof), 47
Freedom of the press, 5–7
Free subscriptions, 392–93
Friendliness in interviewing, 102–3
Front page, 229
F/stops, 420–21, 435
Future book as source of news, 89, 91

Gallup Poll, 72
"The Gambler, the Nun, the Radio"
    (Hemingway), 176–77
Gannett News Service, 113
Gathering the news, 72–77, 87–91
Geduldig, Alfred, 361
Gender equity in covering sports, 269
General assignment reporters, 84
Generation X, newspaper reading habits
    of, 20
Giago, Tim, 12
Gingrich, Newt, 180
Global village, 15
Glover, Anne, 450
Goodman, Ellen, 291
Goodman, Mark, 48
Gossip columns, 291
Government, news coverage of, 60
Government Quarterly, 55
Grammar
    in copy editing, 209–10
    in leads, 140–41
    in quotations, 172
Graphic Arts, 339
Graphic designer, 339
Graphics, 224, 235
Graphs, 77, 194, 196, 201
Gray, Katti, 167
Grenada invasion, news coverage of, 16
Grid format, 231
Grunge fonts, 218
Grunig, James E., 360
Guinness Book of World Records, 309
Gulf War, news coverage of, 16
Gutenberg, Johannes, 219
Gutter, 225

Halftone, 413
Hamilton, Andrew, 6
Hammer head headline, 212
Handwriting fonts, 218
Hard drive, 443
Hard news, 59, 247
Hardware, 442–46

Harris, Benjamin, 5
The Hartford Courant, 454
*Hazelwood School District v. Cathy
    Kuhlmeier,* 45–53
Headlines
    in advertisements, 387
    in feature stories, 251
    fitting, 214–15
    rules for writing, 215–17
    sizes of, 211–12
    style of, 212–13
    in yearbook copy, 323
Hearst, William Randolph, 9, 21
Hearst Foundation, 10
Hemingway, Ernest, 176
Herald Times (Bloomington, Ind.), 32
Herman, Ken, 190
Hispanic-American newspapers, 12
Hispanic Magazine, 12
Hispanic Online, 12
History, of American journalism, 4–21
History of Graphic Design (Megg), 339
Holmes, Paul, 361
Honolulu Advertiser, 417
Hood River (Ore.) *News,* 32
Hope, Bob, 14
Houston Chronicle, 31, 113
Human interest, as news element, 66–67,
    79
Hungry Horse News (Columbia Falls,
    Mont.), 32
Hunt, Todd, 360

Illustration programs, 449, 455
Image-editing programs, 449, 451
Imus, Don, 14
In Cold Blood (Capote), 198, 200
In-depth reporting
    finding space for, 193–94
    and role of scholastic press, 191, 193
    of stories with substance, 188–91
    story elements, 194, 196–98, 201
Indian Country Today, 12
Industrial revolution, 7, 8
Information, off-the-record, 105–6, 111
Information Age, 3, 20
Information processing, 4
in loco parentis, 46
Inspiration for writing leads, 128–30
Internet, 17, 21, 55, 86. *See also* World
    Wide Web
    basics of, 68
    conducting interviews on, 104–5

development of, 452–54
    journalism and, 3–4, 20, 453–54
    news gathering on, 60–61
    news on, 17–18
    newspapers on, 157, 457
    as source of photographs, 427
Interviews, 97–98
    formal, 101–6, 111
    general guidelines for, 98–101, 115–16
    on the Internet, 104–5
    personality, 153
    source review of story before publica-
        tion, 109, 111
    writing story from, 106–8, 117
Introductions, 194, 196, 201, 287, 302
Invasion of privacy, 192
Inverted-pyramid writing, 9, 124–26, 143,
    149, 151, 152, 165
Investigative Reporters and Editors, Inc.
    (IRE), 190
Italic letters, 221

Jargon, 162, 165
Javitz, William, 296
Jefferson, Thomas, 6, 43, 185
Jobs, Steve, 443
Journalism. *See also* Scholastic
    journalism
    agenda-setting function of, 29–30, 52
    ethics of, 33–35, 37, 52
    history of American, 4–21
    and the Internet, 3–4
    and technology, 17–19, 441–55
    yellow, 9–10, 21
Journalism adviser, 84, 91
Journalism professor, 23
Journalism Today, 248
Journalists
    electronic, 457
    functions of, 27–30, 52
    fundamentals for, 4
    public relations for student, 363–68
    public trust of, 25–27
    skills of, 450
Justified type, 222

Kennedy, Edward, 353
Kennedy, Jack, 86
Kicker headline, 212–13
Kiel (Wis.) *Tri-County Record,* 32
Kilpatrick, James, 50, 128–30
Kirtley, Jane, 55
Konner, Joan, 25

Korbut, Olga, 269
Korea Times, 12
Kristof, Nicholas D., 47
Krupnick, Elizabeth, 373
Kuhlmeier, Cathy, Hazelwood School District v., 45–53
Kuralt, Charles, 344–45

Ladder diagram, 315–16, 336
Lakeland (Fla.) *Ledger,* 259
Lakota Times, 12
Land, Edwin, 405
Landers, Ann, 295
Language
    sexist, 159–60, 165
    of sportswriting, 263, 274
The Language of Sport (Considine), 272
Laser printers, 445–46, 455
Layout
    advertising, 389, 391
    photographs in, 411, 413
    yearbook spread, 325–28
Leadership as editorial function, 285–86
Leading, 217, 222
Leads, 123–24, 143
    building on, 148
    examples of good, 132–35, 136–37
    in in-depth reporting, 196
    inverted-pyramid style of, 124–26, 143
    length of, 139
    problems with, 135, 139–42
    summary, 126–28, 143
    tease, 135
    writing, 128–32
Ledger Dispatch (Antioch, Calif.), 32
The Lefthander Syndrome (Coren), 253
Lenses, 419–20. *See also* Cameras
Letters to the editor, 296–97
Libel, 5, 34, 40–45, 52
    in scholastic journalism, 48–49
Liddy, G. Gordon, 14
Life, 32, 403
Ligature, 221
Light typeface, 221
Limbaugh, Rush, 14
Lippmann, Walter, 41
Listening in interviewing, 100–1, 103, 111
Lister, Valerie, 277
Listservs, 19
Localization of news, 66
Long Beach Press-Telegram, 95
Look, 32

The Los Angeles Times, 31, 198, 216
Lundstrom, Marjie, 203

Mac OS (Macintosh Operating System), 446–47
Maestro approach to news reporting, 87
Magazines, 11, 21. *See also* Zines
    African-American, 12
    design of, 232–34, 236–37
    evaluating, 32
    Hispanic-American, 12
Mainbar, 87, 154, 193–94
Maine, USS, 11
Malcolm case, 180
Managing editor, 84, 91, 145
Managing Public Relations (Grunig and Hunt), 360
Marketplace function, of journalism, 29
Market surveys, 378–79, 380–81, 382, 396
Masthead, 229, 289–90
Matlock, Kent, 399
McClure's, 11
McLuhan, Marshall, 15
Mean, 77
Media
    development of minority, 11–13
    evaluating, 30–33, 52
    history of American, 4–21
    public perception of, 26
Media lawyer, 55
Median, 77
Megg, Philip, 339
Melville, Herman, 128–30
Menendez brothers, 353
Mergers, 405
The Miami Herald, 31, 198
Microsoft, 157
Milwaukee Journal, 259
Milwaukee Journal Sentinel, 259
Mini-torials, 299–300
Minneapolis Star, 305
Minneapolis Star-Tribune, 31
Minnesota: A Cold Love Affair (Fischer), 305
Minority media, development of, 11–13
Moby Dick (Melville), 128
Mode, 77
Modular design, 325–28
Monologophobia, 163, 165
Monroe, Bryan, 239
Montgomery County Sentinel, 113
Monticello (Minn.) *Times,* 32
Morenci (Mich.) *Observer,* 32

Muckraking, 11
Mulholland, Bob, 4
Munsey's, 11
Murray, Jim, 264
Music director, 351
Mutual Broadcasting System, 13–14
Myrtle Beach (S.C.) *Sun News,* 239

Nameplate, 229
Names in the news columns, 294–95
Nashville Banner, 55
National Association of Black Journalists, 12
National Association of Hispanic Journalists, 12
National Broadcasting Company. *See* NBC
National Geographic, 403, 449
National Observer, 113
National Scholastic Press Association, 194
Native-American newspapers, 12
Native American Press Association, 12
NBC (National Broadcasting Company), 4, 13, 15, 157
Network, computer, 443
New-England Courant, 90
New Mexican (Santa Fe, N. Mex.), 437
News. *See also* News stories
    change in direction of, 59–60, 77
    elements of, 62–69, 79
    evaluating value of, 61–62
    on the Internet, 17–18
    on-line, 157
    real *versus* created, 138
    sources of, 87, 89–91
The News and Observer (Charlotte, N.C.), 190
The News and Observer (Raleigh, N.C.), 31
"News Arithmetic," 67
Newsbeat Today, 357
News brief format, 193
Newsday, 31, 167, 250–51, 252
News director, 350–51
News editor, 84
News-feature, 249
News judgment, 61, 79, 125
News (Lufkin, Tex.), 190
News Media & the Law, 55
"Newspaper in Education," 19
Newspaper publisher/editor, 437

Newspaper(s). *See also* School newspapers
  African-American, 11–12
  Asian-American, 12
  best large, 31
  best small, 32
  changes in, 441–42
  evaluating, 30–31
  future of, 441, 454
  Hispanic-American, 12
  history of American, 4–21
  largest, in United States, 12
  manufacturing process, 118–19,
    240–43
  Native-American, 12
  on-line versions of, 18, 21
  staff organization, 83–87, 91, 375–76
Newspaper style, 156–63, 164. *See also*
  Style; Writing style
News peg, 249
News release, 364, 371
News reporting
  in-depth, 188–201
  maestro approach to, 87
  WED approach to, 87, 92–93
News stories. *See also* News
  beginning, with *the,* 141
  body of, 150, 151–52
  building on the lead for, 148
  generating ideas for, 69–71, 79
  from idea to final, 114–19
  leads, 123–43
  and newspaper style, 156–63
  organization of, 152–56
  rules for writing, 164
  transitions in, 148–51, 165
News tips, 89, 91
Newsweek, 32, 192
The New York Daily News, 216
New York Journal, 9, 10–11, 16, 21
New York Morning Herald, 8
New York Sun, 8
New York Times, 8, 31, 50, 55, 83, 131,
  132, 134, 138, 163, 198, 268, 390, 417,
  442
New York Times News Service, 89
New York Weekly Journal, 5, 20
New York World, 9, 10, 21
Nixon, Richard, 110, 189, 201
Northcliffe, Lord, 191
Note-taking, 103–4, 172
Nugget, 342, 354
Nut graph, 196, 201

Oak Ridger, 55
Objectivity, 35, 130–32
Ochs, Adolph, 8
Off-the-record information, 105–6, 111
The Omaha World-Herald, 216
On-line services, 68, 452–54
Op-Ed ads, 390
Operating systems, 446–47
Opinion columns, 293, 294
Optical center, 391, 396
The Oregonian (Portland, Ore.), 31
Osborne, Tom, 169
Ozaukee Press (Port Washington, Wis.),
  32

Pacific Citizen, 12
Page, Clarence, 291
Pages, 228
  designing, 229, 231
  in yearbooks and magazines, 232–34,
    236–37
Pagination programs, 448–49, 455
Panama invasion, news coverage of, 16
Paraphrasing, 172–74, 181
Partial quotations, 174–75
Partisan press, 6–7
PBS, 15
The Peninsula Outlook (Gig Harbor,
  Wash.), 233
The Pennsylvania Post, 7
Penny press, 8
People, 253
Personality interviews, 153
Personality profiles as feature stories,
  250–51, 252
Persuasion as function of editorial,
  280–81
Petty, Marty, 454
The Philadelphia Inquirer, 31, 198
Photo editor, 407, 414, 417
Photo essays, 413–14, 415
Photo ethics, 412
Photographers, 87, 91
  giving assignments to, 408, 414–15
  preparing for shoot, 409
Photography staff, 407
Photos/photography. *See also* Cameras;
  Darkroom; Film
  bleeding, 233
  composition, 404–6, 414
  digital, 451–52
  Internet as source of, 427
  in layout, 411, 413

light and exposure in, 420–26
  making prints, 430–34
  role of, 403–4, 414
  scanning, 451–52
  selecting best, 410
  yearbook, 323–24
Pica, 221
Plagiarism, 37
Play reviews, 296
Point-counterpoint, 298
Points
  in measuring headlines, 211
  in type size, 221
Political correctness, 156, 158–60, 165
Political function, of journalism, 27
Politics, press coverage of, 6–7, 27, 52
Polls, 72–79
Polycontrast filters, 432
Praise as function of editorial, 284
Pratt, Jim, 198, 200
Precision Journalism (Meyer), 75
Press, public attitude toward, 55
Press-Citizen (Iowa City, Iowa), 437
Primary source of information, 98, 111
Prime Time Live, 72
Printers, 445–46, 455
Prior restraint, 34
Privacy, invasion of, 192
Problem-solution-results organization,
  343
Prodigy, 4, 17. *See also* Internet
Production kit, 335–36
Profanity in quotations, 172
Profile columns, 291–93
Program director, 350
Prominence as news element, 64, 65, 79
Promotion of school broadcasting station,
  352
Providence (R.I.) *Journal and Evening
  Bulletin,* 23
Proximity as news element, 63–64, 79
Public Broadcasting Stations. *See* PBS
Publick Occurrences, 5, 8, 20
Public relations, 359–60, 370
  careers in, 368, 371
  code of professional standards for,
    369–70
  defining, 360–61
  model of, 361, 363
  as source of news, 89–90, 91
  for student journalists, 363–68
  and truth, 362
Public relations campaign, 364, 366–68

Public relations executive, 373
Publics, 360, 370
Publisher, 83
Pulitzer, Joseph, 9, 21
Pulitzer Prize, 10, 33, 249
Punctuation in headlines, 215
Puns in headlines, 216
Pyle, Ernie, 16
Pyramid
    inverted, 9, 124–26, 149, 151, 152, 165
    style of asking questions, 102

Question-and-answer columns, 295
Question leads, 141–42, 143
Questions
    in interviewing, 99–102, 105, 107, 111
    in polls, 75–76
Quill, 32, 253
Quon, Mike, 339
Quotations
    attribution for, 175–78, 183
    direct, 169–72, 181
    exactness in, 170–71
    grammar in, 172
    in interview story, 107, 108, 111
    out of context, 180
    partial, 174–75
    profanity in, 172
    tape recorders for, 171–72, 182
Quote leads, 141–42, 143

Rabin, Yitzhak, 181, 182
Radio, 13–14, 21, 31
Radio Act (1927), 14
Radio talk shows, 14
Ragged type, 222
RAM (Random Access Memory), 444, 455
Random opinion features, 298
Random sample, 73, 79
Raymond, Henry, 8
Reaction in editorials, 287
Reader's Guide, 380
Read-in head, 213
Readout head, 213
Record-keeping
    as function of journalism, 28–29, 52
    for school newspapers, 394–95, 396
Record librarian, 351
Record (San Marcos, Tex.), 437
Redbook, 32
Redundancy, 162–63, 165

Reichman, Henry, 50
Repetition. *See also* Rhythm
    fear of, 163
    in headlines, 216
    in paraphrasing and quotations, 174
Reporters, 84–86, 167
    investigative, 203
    as news sources, 90–91
    sports, 277
    story-writing process, 114–19
Reporter's Committee for Freedom of the
    Press, 55
Reputation Management (Holmes), 361
Research, 87–91
Research for selling advertising, 379–80
Retton, Mary Lou, 269
Reuters, 89
Reviews, 295–96
Revising, 129
Revolution, 6–7
Reynolds, Robert, 47
Rhythm, 227. *See also* Repetition
Rice, Grantland, 261, 268
Right of reply, 37
Rimmer, Addie, 95
Rinearson, Peter, 188–89
Riverdale Press (Bronx, N.Y.), 32
Roanoke (Va.) *Times & World News,* 50
Rochester (Minn.) *Post-Bulletin,* 305
Rockefeller, John D., 11
Rohde, David, 190, 191
Rolling Stone, 198, 253
Roman letters, 221
Roosevelt, Franklin, 15, 16
Rowan, Carl, 291
Rule of thirds, 406

Safire, William, 291
Saginaw (Mich.) *News,* 50
Salancik, Jerry, 97
Sampan, 12
Sampling in conducting polls, 72–75
Sandberg, Ryne, 262
San Diego Union-Tribune, 31
San Francisco Chronicle, 31
San Jose Mercury News, 157, 239
Satirical columns, 293
The Saturday Evening Post, 11, 21
Sawyer, Diane, 72
Scanners, 451–52, 455
Scholastic journalism. *See also*
    Journalism
    evaluating, 33

on the Internet, 18
and libel, 40, 45–52
School newspapers, 33, 45. *See also*
    Newspapers
    advertising in, 376–92, 396
    changes in, 60, 187, 200
    circulation of, 392–94, 396
    feature stories in, 247, 251–56, 257
    gossip columns in, 291
    in-depth reporting in, 194, 195
    record-keeping, 394–95, 396
    role of, 191, 193
    sources of news for, 89–91
    sports stories in, 264–74
    staff organization, 83–87, 88–91
School public relations agency, 364
Search engine, 68
Sengstacke, John H., 12
Sentence style, 160–61
Sentry function of journalism, 28, 52
Sexist language, 159–60, 165
Shock jocks, 14
Shutter speed, 422–23, 435
Sidebar, 87, 154, 194
Simpson, O. J., 12, 15, 26, 341, 353, 412
Simultaneous rebuttal, 37
Sizing, 413
Slander, 40
Slanguage, 264
Small caps, 222
Smith, Red, 268
Smith, William Kennedy, 353
Social function of journalism, 29, 52
Society of Professional Journalists
    (SPJ), 37
    code of ethics of, 38–39
Software, 446–49, 451, 455
Sources
    of news, 87, 89–91
    of photographs, 427
    protecting, 110
Spanish-American War, 10–11, 21
Spectrum, 47, 51
Speeches, reporting on, 178–79, 181, 183
Spelling demons, 209
Spin-offs, 318
Sports director, 351
Sports editor, 84, 268
Sports Illustrated, 198
Sports reporter, 277
Sports stories
    change in style of, 261
    covering the game, 266–68
    featurized, 270–74

good and bad in, 262–64
language of, 263, 274
postgame, 270
pregame, 265–66, 267
preparing for, 264–65
Sportswriters, 273, 274
Spreads, yearbook, 319–28
The St. Petersburg (Fla.) *Times,* 31, 450
Staff
cooperation among, 87, 90–91
management, 83–84
as news source, 90–91
organization of, 83–84, 85, 91
photography, 407
redesign of, 86–87, 88
reorganization of, 88
reporters, 84–86
yearbook, 329–34
Staff manual, 332–34
Staff photographer, 407, 414
Stamp Act, 6
Stanton, Sam, 203
StarNet, 457
Station manager, 349
Statistical terms, 77
Stern, Howard, 14
Stith, Pat, 190
Stohs, Nancy, 259
Student news bureau, 364, 371
Student newspapers, 7
Student Press Law Center, 48
The Students Gazette, 7
Style. *See also* Newspaper style; Writing
style
in copy editing, 209–10
feature story, 249–50
of headlines, 212–13
sports story, 261
Stylebook, 156, 165, 206, 228, 234
Subjective writing, 279
Subject possibilities in feature stories, 250
Subscriptions, free, 392–93
Summary lead, 126–28, 143
Sunday World, 9
Surprise ending, 152–53
Surveys. *See* Polls
Swisshelm, Jane Grey, 8
Switzer, Barry, 263

Talbott, William, 405
Tale of Two Cities, A (Dickens), 129
Talese, Gay, 106–7

Talk shows, radio, 14
Tape recorders, 103–4, 171–72, 182
Tarbell, Ida, 11
Taste, need for good, 37
Tease lead, 135
Technical director, 352
Technology, 17–19, 441–55
Teenagers
buying power of, 379–80
interests of, 187
Telegraph, 9, 21
Television, 15, 17, 21
in courtrooms, 353
evaluating news on, 32
reviews of, 296
sales of computers *versus,* 452
writing copy for, 347, 350
Television anchor, 357
Testimonials, 386
Test strips, 432
Texas Monthly, 449
Theme copy, 318–19, 337
Thomas, Helen, 185
Tiebacks, 151
TIFF (Tagged Image File Format), 449
The Tigard (Ore.) *Times,* 32
Time, 32
Timelessness of feature stories, 249
Timeliness as news element, 63, 79
Times Delta (Visalia, Calif.), 437
The Times (Seattle, Wash.), 31, 188–89,
239
Tinker v. *Des Moines Independent School
District,* 46–47, 51, 52
Titla, Mary Kim, 108
Tolstoy, Leo, 128
Traffic/Continuity Director, 352
Trager, Bob, 51
Training director, 351
Transitions in news stories, 148–51, 165
Trust, public, of journalists, 25–27
Truth
as ethical principle, 37
as libel defense, 41
and public relations, 362
in research information, 19, 61
Tucson Citizen, 437
Type
categories of, 218–21, 235
sizes of, 223
terms, 221–22
Typefaces, working with, 221
Type measurement, 222

Typography, rules of, 221–23

Unabomber, 138
Understanding Mass Media (Javitz), 295
Unit count system, 214
United Press International, 9, 89, 133
Unity in design, 225
U.S. News & World Report, 32
USA Today, 60, 68, 77, 187

Van Buren, Abigail (Dear Abby), 295
Variety, 216
Verne, Jules, 10
Vietnam War, 16, 46

Waldman, Saul J., 194
Wallace, Mike, 41
The Wall Street Journal, 31, 198, 390
Walter, Cornelia, 8
Warning as editorial function, 282–83
Warrick, Jody, 190
Wartime news coverage, 9, 10–11, 16, 21
Washington Daily News, 185
The Washington Post, 23, 31, 33, 138, 189,
198, 201
Watergate, 110, 189–90, 201
Webb, Eugene, 97
Web Review, 253
WED approach to news reporting, 87,
92–93
White House correspondent, 185
White space, 391, 396
"Who Cares?" method of measuring news
value, 61–62, 79
Wichita Falls Record News, 167
Wicket headline, 213
"Wild art," 404
Wire services, 9, 89, 157
Women in development of American
journalism, 8
Woodward, Bob, 110, 189, 201
Word-processing programs, 447–48, 455
Words
for advertising, 388–89
appropriate, 156, 158–60
for attribution, 175–77
big, 161
short, for headlines, 216
World Almanac, 309
World War I, news coverage of, 16

World War II, 23
  news coverage of, 16
World Wide Web, 17, 68, 86, 364, 453–54,
  455. *See also* Internet
Wozniak, Steve, 443
Writing
  advertising copy, 387–89, 396
  editorials, 278–305
  feature stories, 246–59
  of leads, 128–32
  news stories, 147–65
  for radio and television broadcast,
    342–47, 354
  sports stories, 260–77
Writing process, 129
Writing style, 165. *See also* Newspaper
  style; Style
  and appropriate word choice, 156,
    158–60

  big words in, 161
  chronological, 153–54
  clarity in, 160
  clichés in, 162–63, 165
  combination, 154, 155
  and fear of repetition, 163
  in feature stories, 249–50
  inverted pyramid, 124–26, 143
  jargon in, 162, 165
  redundancy in, 162–63, 165
  in sentences, 160–61

X-height, 222

Yearbook(s)
  budget, 311
  on CD and video, 335
  design of, 228, 232–34, 236–37

  finances, 310–12, 336
  functions of, 309–10, 336
  ladder diagram for planning, 315–16,
    336
  layout and design of, 325–28
  photo captions in, 324
  photos in, 323–24
  sections in, 312–15
  staff organization, 329–34
  theme for, 317–19
  working with printer of, 334–36, 337
  writing copy for, 322–23, 337
Yellow journalism, 9–10, 21
Yellow Kid, 9
You're No Spring Chicken (Fischer), 305

Zenger, John Peter, 5, 6, 20
Zines, 253